Clinical and Experimental Hypnosis:

In Medicine, Dentistry and Psychology

Clinical and Experimental Hypnosis

In Medicine, Dentistry and Psychology

WILLIAM S. KROGER, M.D.

Director, Institute for Comprehensive Medicine, Beverly Hills, California; Executive Vice-President and founder, Comprehensive Medical Society; Past President, Academy of Psychosomatic Medicine; Past Vice-President and co-founder, American Society of Clinical Hypnosis; co-founder, Society of Clinical and Experimental Hypnosis; Advisory Editor, International Journal of Clinical and Experimental Hypnosis, Journal of Existential Psychiatry, Journal of Sex Research; Attending Psychiatrist, Brea Neuropsychiatric Hospital; Consultant in Hypnosis, City of Hope; Formerly Associate Professor, Chicago Medical School; Visiting Guest lecturer in Hypnosis, Seton Hall School of Medicine; Board of Directors, Morton Prince Hypnotherapy Institute, New York

J. B. LIPPINCOTT COMPANY

Philadelphia and Toronto

ISBN-0-397-50096-3

Library of Congress Catalog Card No. 62-21273

Printed in the United States of America

9   8   7

To Jimmy, Carol, Debbie, Lisa and Billy
who exert their own special kind of
hypnosis on the author

Psychiatric Foreword

There are a variety of books on hypnosis available to the professions of medicine, psychology and dentistry. A few have been pioneer attempts by innovators to establish fundamental principles and new practices. There are, also, the efforts of clinically motivated practitioners, and, more recently, there have appeared a number of books by psychodynamically oriented psychiatrists, psychologists and dentists.

Dr. Kroger has been practicing the art and science of hypnosis for over 30 years and is one of the outstanding medical hypnotists and teachers of our time. His comprehensive text contains not only a complete description of almost every hypnotic technic and clinical entity but a wealth of case studies as well. It also elucidates the relationship between general semantics, neurophysiology, cybernetics and hypnotic theory and practice. Therefore, this book represents a major attempt to fit hypnosis into the framework of the behavioral sciences, where it belongs.

With the advent of the Freudian Era, at the turn of the century, the dynamic unconscious soon became the acceptable, theoretic concept. Within several decades it was discovered that when a patient finally uncovered an unconscious motive after an expenditure of much time, sweat, tears and money, it did not follow that he spontaneously was "cured" merely because he knew the "reason" why he behaved in a certain manner. This clinical fact, now accepted by every experienced psychotherapist, has led to the surrender of the previous, obsessive and futile search for traumatic infantile memories. Nevertheless, certain psychotherapists *always* report that their patients vividly experience sex relations, become involved in bizarre acting out of symptoms, and express earlier hostilities and conflicts by sobbing and screaming. It has been my experience that these patients were "pleasing" their psychotherapists, who had repeatedly indicated to them that this was the *only* way to get well.

Repeated clinical observation has corroborated Dr. Kroger's thesis that symptom-removal by the sophisticated and permissive technics described in this book is an effective method of treating many patients—*especially those who can endure living without neurotic defenses.* The author properly points out that the dangers of hypnosis have been greatly exaggerated. Most experts agree with Dr. Kroger that *neither one nor many hypnotic sessions can precipitate a psychosis unless a psychotic process already is present.* I agree with Dr. Kroger that the removal of a symptom by appropriate hypnotic technics does not produce a substitute symptom except in *very* disturbed individuals who need their neurotic encumbrances.

The author stresses that hypnosis is a particular kind of interpersonal relationship in which the patient permits increasing restrictions on his sensory intake and excludes all extraneous stimuli except those that the therapist brings to his attention. What is important is not the depth of the "trance" but the degree of rapport and emotional participation by the patient in the therapeutic relationship. Dr. Kroger repeatedly indicates that the therapist only "sets the stage," but that ultimately it is the patient who permits the hypnotic relationship to develop by selective attention.

The history of hypnosis contains descriptions of many patients who have improved and recovered without any psychodynamic 'insight." What may be just as significant as "insight" is the patient's expectation in regard to the type of therapeutic procedure to which he can and would like to respond. The basic ingredients are the trust of the patient in the therapist and the conviction of both that the therapeutic modality elected is the best possible one for this particular patient. This helps to explain why a "therapy" can be effective in one era and a failure in another when both patient and doctor no longer believe in the efficacy of the procedure. A patient is not hypnotized by merely concentrating and staring at a spot or at a revolving disk, unless he *expects* this effect and complies mentally as well as physically. This was Braid's opinion in his later years, and it is also Dr. Kroger's conclusion.

I am in complete agreement with the author that "cures" have been reported without searching for "causes." The common factor in these "transference" cures is the fostering of personal initiative and self-esteem (personal value) which is achieved by effective collaboration in the therapeutic situation.

Clinical and Experimental Hypnosis is a *tour de force* in the field of hypnosis, the best possible guide to the practice and the theory of modern hypnosis. The reader is taught from the very beginning that the "conviction of hypnosis leads to hypnosis," and that the important factors are motivation, belief, expectation, imagination and the subsequent restructuring of the patient's reality percepts. This was also Bernheim's belief, and the author has transmitted the clinical wisdom of the past to a new generation of students of hypnosis.

The reader is fortunate to have available such an excellent text, and Dr. Kroger is to be congratulated for bringing to the attention of the medical, the dental and the psychological professions the results of his many years of critical study and extensive clinical practice.

JACOB H. CONN, M.D.
Assistant Professor of Psychiatry,
Johns Hopkins University Medical
School
President, American Board of
Medical Hypnosis
Past President, Society for Clinical
and Experimental Hypnosis (1960-61)

Foreword

Writing a foreword for this new volume on hypnosis by Dr. William S. Kroger is a difficult task indeed, for he has probed deeply into every scientific discipline that could conceivably shed any light on the still unexplained physiologic or psychological processes that result in hypnotic phenomena. This extensive research has resulted in the most monumental contribution to the literature of hypnosis ever made by a single author or collaboration of authors. I am frankly amazed at the scope of this book, and even more amazed at the collation of reference material that has been brought to bear on each of the topics discussed—or perhaps dissected would be a better word.

Dr. Kroger has made no attempt to avoid controversial theoretical formulations or to confine himself to the theories that have gained most general acceptance. Rather, he has used his encyclopedic knowledge of the physical and the biologic sciences, regardless of whether these have heretofore been considered pertinent or even peripheral to hypnosis, to provide future investigators with as many avenues for exploration as possible. It is his feeling that it is time that we know *how* hypnosis works as well as the indisputable fact that it does.

Although Dr. Kroger has provided future researchers with enough signposts to lead to a dozen or more volumes which would be germane to understanding the nature of hypnosis, he has not forgotten that his main theme is to provide a cogent dissertation on how hypnosis may be employed in the healing arts of medicine, dentistry and psychology. The neophyte in hypnosis will find a wealth of material to aid him in his clinical work, including Dr. Kroger's own tested induction technics as well as those of other pioneers in the field. The clinical applica-tions of hypnosis to the medical specialties are covered adequately, the checkered history of hypnosis and medical healing is presented absorbingly, and the so-called dangers of hypnosis are investigated rationally in order to allay the fears of eligible potential practitioners who have been unduly frightened by widespread tactics designed to intimate that only psychiatrists have the necessary background needed to utilize this valuable modality in their own areas of competence. Dr. Kroger has explained and dispelled many of the myths surrounding direct symptom removal which have been erected as roadblocks in the past several years to discourage the use of hypnosis by therapists who are not deeply oriented in the lengthy uncovering technics of psychiatry. However, in dispelling these myths, Dr. Kroger does not derogate the importance of psychiatry. He is quick to admit that many types of patients should be referred to psychiatrists for treatment, with or without hypnosis, but is forceful in stating that the general practitioner and others could handle competently the bulk of psychosomatic complaints now being referred to specialists who are already in short supply.

Of particular interest to theoreticians is Dr. Kroger's contention that electronic engineers, notably those in the field of cybernetics, can contribute a great deal to the life sciences through an understanding of how the bodily processes are controlled automatically at both hypnotic and non-hypnotic levels. He further contends that the electronic computer can be made to simulate the living system by means of mathematical models, providing new insights into the operation of many biologic systems. However, whether this will help to shed light on hypnosis is still open to question. Also, he anticipates the wedding of the medical scientist with the biomedically oriented engineer. I believe he is prophetic in this projection of things to come.

All in all, I am sure that any serious student in the field of psychology, medicine or dentistry will find this volume vitally necessary. The style is clear and easily readable. I can only commend him for the vast work which he has brought to successful fruition.

Roy M. Dorcus, ph.d.
Professor of Psychology,
University of California, Los Angeles
Past President, Society for
Clinical and Experimental Hypnosis

Preface

The past decade has seen an intense renewal of interest in the clinical applications of hypnotherapy in all branches of medicine and its ancillary disciplines. This resulted from the many investigations that were made by reputable scientists during the preceding half century. Much of this work has been summarized in this book to give the student of hypnosis as broad a picture as possible of the more important advances.

My objective is to present to the beginner, as well as to the advanced practitioner, the most sophisticated and useful hypnotic technics for the induction and the management of the various problems that are encountered in the practice of medicine and dentistry. The principles of suggestion, the phenomena of hypnosis and the various factors that influence hypnotizability are discussed, as well as the indications, the limitations and the precautions for the clinical applications of hypnotherapy in medicine and dentistry. Emphasis has been on the nature of abnormal mental functioning and the importance of making diagnoses of these various psychopathologic conditions.

Hypnotherapy is directed to the patient's needs and is a methodology to tap the "forgotten assets" or the hidden potentials of behavior and response that so often lead to new learnings and understandings. Hence, considerable emphasis has been placed on man's unique ability to manipulate verbal stimuli as symbolic communication to evoke simple and complex physiologic reactions. Thus, the meaning of words (semantic input) effectively influences the state and the activity of cortical and subcortical structures to provoke emotional activities that can be either harmful or beneficial to the organism. This, as adduced by Pavlov, is especially meaningful for interpreting the basis for hypnotic responses.

Because the author is convinced that they will play an ever-increasing role in medical education, he has included in this volume experimental psychology, the psychophysiology of emotional behavior, the development and the psychology of the adaptive functions, and the general principles which govern perception, thinking, memory, learning theory and cybernetics.

An attempt has been made to condense this highly technical material and the huge amount of data, some of which is controversial, that are provided by these disciplines. Thus, the reader can obtain at least an introduction to a unified approach to the study of hypnotic behavior both at adaptive and maladaptive levels. At the same time, the humanistic element in psychotherapy has not been overlooked. This undoubtedly is the chief factor in healing in all methods of psychotherapy, including hypnosis.

The phenomenology of hypnosis has been incorporated into a psychophysiologic frame of reference. It is apparent now that the basic underlying principles of empiric hypnotherapy were never fully understood until the basic principles of faith and the psychology of belief and conviction were integrated with this new frame of reference. In this light, the phenomena of hypnosis are only an extension of the mechanisms involved in normal thought, as all hypnotic phenomena can occur at nonhypnotic levels. Hence, with this new approach, hypnosis can be taken from the realm of the esoteric and placed in the cognitive. This means that hypnosis can now be related to the principles of everyday behavior dynamics, rather than to the "mystique" of psychoanalysis which unfortunately has retarded its clinical acceptance for more than 50 years.

There is an increasing awareness that all schools of psychotherapy, including hypnotherapy, yield approximately the same results; therefore, it appears to be likely or plausible that a placebo effect is present. Hence, as is emphasized repeatedly in this book, the basis for successful psychotherapy depends more on the rapport or the strength of the interpersonal relationship than it does on the methodology, and suggestion at many different levels of awareness is wittingly or unwittingly utilized in this relationship. Since no one knows where suggestion ends and hypnosis begins, the real basis for psychotherapy must be "hypnosis in slow motion."

If one admits that suggestion plays an important role in psychotherapy, it should be easy to take the final step and utilize the acme of applied suggestion-therapy. This is not to imply that hypnotherapy helps more patients than other forms of psychotherapy. It does not, but it is more rapid and less cumbersome and can be used effectively for the "port-of-last-call" patient. It can be employed by the nonpsychiatrist who is capable of assessing its indications and contraindications for various medical conditions, despite the continual keening about the theoretic but remote dangers that are associated with hypnotherapy.

Most of the clinical entities described herein were treated by patient-centered hypnotherapy at the symptomatic level instead of by a physician-directed approach. Specialized hypnotic technics, together with autohypnosis and sensory-imagery conditioning, are vastly different from the older, dramatic and authoritarian types of hypnotic symptom removal. Also, "depth psychology" was directed to the present and the future instead of dredging the past to search for "causative" factors.

The old concept of cause-and-effect to explain emotional illness has been replaced by allowing the patient to develop a healthy understanding of the *needs that he has* for a symptom. Hypnotherapy is directed not only to eliciting these problems but also to enabling the individual to face his difficul-ties in a more mature and realistic manner. An individual is *not* treated by hypnosis, but rather *in hypnosis!* The greater relaxation, concentration, receptivity and self-objectivity provides a better awareness of *what* the emotionally ill person experiences. This is less tedious than attempting to elicit unexplored "unconscious" factors behind *what he professes to believe or what he thinks he believes.*

Patient-centered hypnotherapy incisively and more rapidly reverses the negative or destructive patterns which produce faulty behavioral responses. Thus, the goal of this type of hypnotherapy is not so much to find or manipulate a "cause" as to discover effective intervention to break up the vicious cycle of faulty conditioning.

After almost 30 years of clinical practice, the author is convinced that the neuroses and functional psychoses are due to disturbed cortical dynamics following continued stress rather than to unconscious conflicts. My thesis, at the risk of oversimplification, is that emotional illness and health are conviction phenomena that are "programmed" into the neural circuits by negative, destructive and harmful experiential conditioning; positive, constructive reconditioning results in health. Such reconditioning by hypnosis mobilizes the "built-in" responses and the adaptive processes that already are present in the organism. This effects homeostatic adjustments and stimulates the recovery forces by raising the threshold to specific or nonspecific stressors.

Teaching contacts with several thousand physicians have made clear the need for a work on hypnotherapy that would enable the professional man to have access to the actual clinical setting. Many of the technics are verbatim transcripts recorded at the author's office, hospital or classroom.

I am grateful to the many patients described in this volume who enabled me to develop more insight into the interrelationships of hypnosis to that magnificent "computer"—the brain. Also, I am indebted to the numerous physicians attending my workshops in hypnosis who pointed out those areas of instruction and knowledge that are particularly germane for the practice of clinical hypnotherapy.

It is hoped that this volume will stimulate the reader to test the methodologies discussed and to further his knowledge by studying the references listed at the end of the various chapters. In addition to the didactic material presented in this book, a practical introduction to the fundamentals of hypnosis at any one of the recognized medical school training centers is recommended. With training, the mature physician who already has the clinical judgment, the experience, the intuition and the diagnostic acumen to practice medicine can employ hypnotherapy. It can be "prescribed" as a medicine because it is in reality the "art of medicine" based on the fundamental tenets of Faith. No one will deny that the greatest ally every psychotherapist has is faith.

Finally, to quote from Hippocrates, "Nothing should be omitted in an art which interests the whole world, one which may be beneficial to suffering humanity and which does not risk human life or comfort."

9735 Wilshire Blvd.
Beverly Hills, California

WILLIAM S. KROGER, M.D.

Acknowledgments

It would be impossible to write a book of this magnitude without the consecrated help of friends and the courtesies of the many authors and publishers who granted me permission to quote from their works.

I am particularly indebted to Robert S. Starrett, a member of the American Medical Writers' Association, who freely gave of his own writing time to aid me in editorial matters, and to his wife, Marion Starrett, for secretarial aid far beyond the call of duty. I am also deeply grateful to Drs. Bernard Saltzberg, J. Wesley Edel, Martin Orne and Milton Brutten for help in assembling special material in the sections on cybernetics, radiology, criminology and speech correction, respectively. Dr. Deszo Levendula was helpful in the criminology section; Dr. Norman Mellor contributed to the chapter on juvenile delinquency; Dr. Aaron Moss contributed the chapter on dentistry, and Dr. Meyer A. Perlstein collaborated on the chapter on Hypnotherapy in Physical Rehabilitation of Neuromuscular Diseases.

The following authors and publishers have generously given me permission to use quotations, and I wish to thank them:

L. W. Davis and R. W. Husband for the use of their scale in "A study of hypnotic susceptibility in relation to personality traits," Journal of Abnormal and Social Psychology 26:175-182, 1931.

Grune & Stratton, Inc., and J. Bordeaux and L. M. LeCron for the LeCron-Bordeaux System for Indicating Depth of Hypnosis, from *Hypnotism Today*, 1947.

Milton V. Kline for a description of the picture visualization technic from *Hypnodynamic Psychology*, Julian Press, Inc., 1955.

Aaron A. Moss for a description of the blackboard technic from *Hypnodontics*, Dental Items of Interest Publishing Company, 1952.

John G. Watkins for a description of various technics from *Hypnotherapy of War Neuroses*, The Ronald Press Company, 1949.

I am also obligated to Rabbi Samuel Glassner for quotations from his publications on "Allusions to Hypnosis in the Bible and Talmud."

I acknowledge the permission of the Society of Clinical and Experimental Hypnosis to reprint its code of ethics.

I wish to express my sincere admiration to Dr. Milton H. Erickson from whom I learned a great deal about hypnotherapeutic technics in our many years of teaching together.

Also, I am obligated to Drs. T. X. Barber, Milton V. Kline and Edward R. Pinckney who were kind enough to read the entire manuscript with a critical eye.

Finally, I am deeply appreciative to Walter Kahoe, Brooks Stewart and Stanley A. Gillet of the J. B. Lippincott Company for their patience and valuable advice in the preparation of this book.

W. S. K.

Contents

1. HISTORY OF HYPNOSIS 1

2. PHENOMENA OF SUGGESTION AND HYPNOSIS 6
   Types of Suggestion 6
   The Nature of Suggestibility in Hypnosis 6
   The Nature of Hypnosis 7
   Everyday Aspects of Suggestion and/or Hypnosis 8
   The Hypnoidal "State" 9
   Animal Hypnosis 10
   Autohypnosis 10
   Rapport 10
   Catalepsy 11
   Ideosensory Activities 11
   Ideomotor Activities 11
   Posthypnotic Suggestions and Conditioning 12
   Amnesia 13
   Dissociation 14
   Depersonalization 14
   Hypermnesia or Memory Recall 14
   Revivification and Age Regression 15
   "Age Progression" 16
   Hypnotic Analgesia and Anesthesia 17
   Hyperesthesia 17
   Posthypnotic Hallucinations 18
   Somnambulism 18
   Automatic Writing 19
   Time Distortion 19
   Summary 20

3. THEORIES 22
   Atavistic Hypothesis: Immobilization Theories 22
   Hypnosis as a State of Hysteria 23
   Theories Based on Changes in Cerebral Physiology 23
   Hypnosis as a Conditioned Process Leading to Sleep 23
   Ideomotor Activity and Inhibition Theory 24
   The Dissociation Theory 24
   The Role-Playing Theory 24
   The Regression Theory 25
   The Hypersuggestibility Theory 25
   Miscellaneous Theories 26
   Psychosomatic Theories 27

4. MISCONCEPTIONS 30
   Loss of Consciousness 30
   Surrender of Will 30
   Weakmindedness 31
   Revelation of Secrets 31

4. MISCONCEPTIONS—(*Cont.*)
    Fear of Not Being Dehypnotized 31
    Confusion Between Hypnotizability and Gullibility 31
    Dominant Personality Required 31
    Summary 31

5. SUGGESTIBILITY TESTS 33
    The Handclasp Test 33
    The Postural-Sway Test 33
    The Forward Postural-Sway Test 34
    The Eyeball-Set Test 34
    The Hand-Levitation Test 35
    Modified Hand-Levitation Test 35
    The Hand-Drop Test 35
    The Thermal Test 36
    The Olfactory Test 36
    The Kohnstamm "Test" 36
    Chevreul's Pendulum Test 36
    Disguised Tests 37
    Discussion 38

6. FACTORS WHICH INFLUENCE SUSCEPTIBILITY TO HYPNOSIS 39

7. LAWS OF SUGGESTION 41
    The Law of Concentrated Attention 41
    The Law of Reversed Effect 41
    The Law of Dominant Effect 42

8. RECOGNITION OF THE DEPTH OF THE HYPNOTIC STATE 43

9. CLINICAL OBSERVATIONS AND MANAGEMENT OF VARIOUS DEPTHS OF HYPNOSIS . 45
    Eye Changes 45
    Movements of Head 46
    Character of Breathing 46
    Limpness of Limbs 46
    Lid Catalepsy 46
    Arm Catalepsy 47
    Following Posthypnotic Suggestions 47
    Development of Glove Anesthesia 47
    Following Positive and Negative Hallucinations 47
    Somnambulism 47

10. HINDRANCES TO HYPNOTIC INDUCTION 49

11. PRACTICAL HINTS FOR HYPNOTIC INDUCTION 50

12. PREINDUCTION TALK 53

13. AUTHORITARIAN OR DIRECT TECHNICS OF HYPNOSIS 55
    Motivational Technic Utilizing Progressive Relaxation 55
    Technic for Posthypnotic Suggestions 57
    Eye-Fixation Technic With Sleep Suggestions 57
    Eye-Fixation Technic Without Sleep Suggestions 58
    Handclasp Technic 59
    Postural-Sway Method 59
    Stare Technic With Sleep Suggestions 62
    Stare Technic Without Sleep Suggestions 62
    Repetitive Technic for Handling Resistant Patient 63

14. PERMISSIVE OR INDIRECT TECHNICS 64
    The Arm-Levitation Technic 64
    Watkins' Progressive-Anesthesia Technic 65
    Handling of Resistance in Levitation Technics 66
    Combinations of Technics 67
    The Sensory-Imagery With Arm Levitation Technic 67
    Visual-Imagery Technics 69
    The Eye-Opening-and-Closing Technic 70
    The Eye-Closure and After-Image Technic 70
    The Progressive-Relaxation Technic Utilizing the Handclasp and the
      Postural Sway 70
    The Tension-and-Relaxation Technic 71
    The Hyperventilation Technic 71
    The Cataleptic Technic 71
    The Confusion Technic 72
    The Disguised Technic 72
    Pressure on "Nerve Centers" 73
    "Blood-Pressure" Method 73
    Mechanical Technics 73
    Other Technics 74
    Drug Hypnosis 74

15. DEEPENING TECHNICS 76
    Weitzenhoffer's Technic 77
    Hand-Rotation Technic 77
    Vogt's Fractionation Technic 77
    Escalator Technic 77
    Helpful Hints in Deepening 78
    Maintaining Deep Hypnosis 79

16. AUTOHYPNOSIS 80
    Methodology of Autohypnosis 80
    Dynamics of Autohypnosis 80
    Instructions to the Physician for Autohypnosis 81
    Instructions to the Patient for Autohypnosis 82
    Deepening the Autohypnotic State 83
    Dehypnotization 84
    Recognition of Autohypnosis 84
    Handling of Resistance in Autohypnosis 84
    Dangers In and Contraindications to Autohypnosis . . . 85
    Summary and Discussion 85

17. AUTOGENIC TRAINING 87

18. GROUP HYPNOSIS 89
    Preliminary Discussion for Group Hypnosis 89
    Technic for Group Hypnosis 91
    Verbalization for Group Autohypnosis 91

19. ANTISOCIAL ASPECTS OF HYPNOSIS 93
    Dangers from Stage Hypnosis 94

20. DANGERS FROM HYPNOSIS 95
    Theoretic Dangers from Medical Hypnotherapy 97

21. PRECAUTIONS IN THE USE OF HYPNOSIS 99
    Contraindications 99
    Dangers of Symptom-Removal 99
    Dangers to the Operator 99
    Dangers to the Method 100

22. PRECAUTIONS IN DEHYPNOTIZATION 101
    Precautions 101
    Dehypnotizing the Difficult Patient 102

23. MEDICAL TRAINING, LEGAL AND ETHICAL ASPECTS OF HYPNOSIS 104
    Medical Training 104
    Hypnosis and the Law 105
    Malpractice and Insurance Aspects 105
    Ethical Aspects 106

24. RELIGIOUS ATTITUDES: COMPARATIVE EVALUATION WITH HYPNOSIS 108
    Attitude of the Roman Catholic Church Toward Hypnosis 108
    Comparative Evaluation of Other Religions and Hypnotic Phenomena . . . 109

25. MAGIC, SPIRITUALISTIC FAITH-HEALING AND HYPNOSIS 115
    Role of Magic in Healing 115
    Spiritual Faith-Healing 115
    Development of Faith-Healing from Hypnosis 116
    Rise of Other Faith-Healing Movements 116
    The Rise of Christian Science 117
    The Attitude of Christian Science Toward Hypnosis 118

26. THE DYNAMICS OF FAITH, PLACEBO EFFECT AND HYPNOSIS 119
    Faith in Religion and Hypnosis 119
    Placebo-Effect Concept 120
    Drugs and the Placebo Effect 121
    Placebo-Effect in Psychotherapy 122
    Hypnosis and the Placebo Effect 122

27. NEUROPHYSIOLOGIC MECHANISMS IN MEDIATION OF EMOTIONS AT NONHYPNOTIC
    AND HYPNOTIC LEVELS 125
    Role of Cortex 126
    Role of the Interpretive Cortex 126
    Role of the Limbic System 127
    Role of the Hypothalamus 129
    Role of the Reticular Activating System 129
    Neurophysiologic Mechanisms in the Mediation of Emotions During Hypnosis 130

28. PSYCHOPHYSIOLOGIC MECHANISMS IN THE PRODUCTION OF HYPNOTIC PHENOMENA:
    RELATION TO BELIEF AND CONVICTION 134
    Reality and Perceptual Awareness 134
    Psychophysiologic Mechanisms in Hypnotic Phenomena 135
    Relationship of Belief and Conviction to Hypnotic Phenomena 135
    Relationship of Conviction to Depth of Hypnosis 137
    Light Stage of Hypnosis 137
    Medium Stage of Hypnosis 137
    Somnambulism or Deep Hypnosis 137
    Dehypnotization 137

29. Relationship of Semantics, Communication and Perception to Hypnosis . 139
    Role of Hypnosemantics in Therapy 139
    Role of Communication in Psychotherapy 140
    Role of Communication as a Control Mechanism in Psychotherapy 141
    Helpful Hints on How to Communicate Effectively in Psychotherapy . . . 142
    Role of Perception in Hypnosis 143
    Psychophysiology of Perception 144
    Role of Learning in Hypnosis 144

30. Some Relationships of the Physical and Behavioral Sciences to Psychotherapy and Hypnosis 146
    Cybernetic Applications 146
    Cybernetic Models of Learning 147
    Comments on Adaptive Control Systems as They May Relate to Psychotherapy 154
    Neurophysiologic Theories of Memory 155
    Importance of Psychocybernetics to Therapy 157

31. Hypnosis in Internal Medicine 160
    Reasons for Use 160
    Psychosomatic Cardiovascular Disorders 161
    Psychosomatic Gastrointestinal Disorders 164
    Summary 169
    Other Psychosomatic Disorders 169
    Hypnotherapy in Metabolic Diseases 172
    Obesity 173
    Hyperthyroidism 177
    Anorexia Nervosa 177
    Bronchial Asthma 177
    Allergy 179

32. Hypnosis in Surgery and Anesthesiology 183
    History 183
    Recent Developments 183
    Advantages and Disadvantages 184
    Indications and Review of the Literature 185
    Mechanism of Hypnoanesthesia 186
    Technics for Surgery 186
    Rehearsal Technic 187
    Maintenance of Hypnoanesthesia During Surgery 187
    Postoperative Verbalization for Dehypnotization 188
    Disguised Technic 188
    Case Reports 189
    Conclusions 191

33. Hypnosis in Obstetrics 192
    Susceptibility of the Subject 192
    Personality Factors in Suggestive Anesthesia Methods 192
    Comparison Between Hypnosis, "Natural Childbirth" and Psychoprophylactic Relaxation 193
    Advantages of Hypnosis 193
    Disadvantages and Contraindications 194
    Preparation of Patient 195
    Determining Responsiveness 195
    Reasons for Choosing Hypnoanesthesia 196
    Training in Hypnosis 196

33. HYPNOSIS IN OBSTETRICS—(*Cont.*)
  Management of Labor 197
  Helpful Suggestions During Labor 198
  Helpful Suggestions for Postpartum Period 199
  Induction of Labor by Hypnosis 199
  Group Training 200
  Nausea and Vomiting 200
  Emotional Spontaneous Abortion 202
  Heartburn of Pregnancy 203
  Lactation 203
  Late Toxemias of Pregnancy: Pre-eclampsia and Eclampsia 203
  Discussion 204

34. HYPNOSIS IN GYNECOLOGY 206
  Psychosomatic Factors 206
  Amenorrhea 206
  Pseudocyesis 207
  Dsyfunctional Uterine Bleeding 208
  Functional Dysmenorrhea 208
  Infertility 209
  Frigidity 210
  Low Back Pain 211
  Pelvic Pain 212
  Premenstrual Tension 212
  Menopause 213
  Intersexuality 213
  Miscellaneous Psychogynecic Conditions 214
  Summary 215

35. HYPNOSIS IN DERMATOLOGY 217
  Emotions and Skin 217
  Hypnosis in Dermatologic Disorders 217
  Hypnotherapeutic Methods 218
  Verbalizations for Authoritarian Hypnotic Technics 218
  Contraindications to Symptom-Removal 219
  Permissive Hypnotic Technics for Symptom-Removal 219
  Use of Sensory-Imagery Conditioning 219
  Use of Glove Anesthesia 220
  Symptom Substitution 220
  Specialized Hypnotic Technics 220

36. HYPNOTHERAPY IN PHYSICAL REHABILITATION OF NEUROMUSCULAR DISORDERS . 223
  Effects of Placebo Therapy 223
  Psychosomatic Factors 224
  Hypnotherapy in Physical Rehabilitation 224
  Epilepsy 229
  Discussion 229

37. HYPNOSIS IN OPHTHALMOLOGY, OTOLARYNGOLOGY AND RHINOLOGY 232
  Ophthalmology 232
  Otology 234
  Laryngology 236
  Rhinology 237

38. HYPNOSIS IN GENITOURINARY CONDITIONS 240
  Postoperative Urinary Retention 240
  Chronic Bladder Irritability 240

38. HYPNOSIS IN GENITOURINARY CONDITIONS—(*Cont.*)
    Premature Ejaculation and Impotence 241
    Cystoscopy and Surgical Procedures 243
    Vasectomy 243
    Male Infertility 243
    Female Infertility 244

39. HYPNOSIS IN ONCOLOGY 245
    Effect of Emotions 245
    Personality Factors and Emotional Reactions 245
    Psychophysiologic and Biochemical Factors 245
    Spontaneous Remission and the Adaptive Responses 246
    Hypnotherapeutic Management of Cancer Patient 246

40. HYPNOSIS IN PEDIATRICS 249
    Nocturnal Enuresis 250
    Tics or Habit Spasms 254
    Stuttering 254
    Mental Retardation 259
    Thumb-sucking 259
    Behavior Disorders 260
    Juvenile Delinquency 262
    Asthma 262
    Hysterical Symptoms 263
    Miscellaneous Conditions 263

41. HYPNOSIS IN ORTHOPEDICS 265
    Torticollis 265
    Hysterical Contractures 266
    Vertebral Neuroses 266
    Psychogenic Rheumatism 267
    Miscellaneous Applications 267
    Hiccoughs 267

42. HYPNOSIS IN THE REMOVAL OF HABIT PATTERNS 269
    Alcoholism 269
    Excessive Smoking 274
    Insomnia 276
    Narcotic Addiction 276

43. HYPNODONTICS: HYPNOSIS IN DENTISTRY 279
    Dental Applications of Hypnosis 279
    Types of Suggestion 280
    Hypnodontic Indications and Applications 280
    Contraindications for Hypnodontics 281
    Limitations of Hypnodontics 282
    Hypnodontic Procedures 282
    Hypnodontic Technics 283
    Elimination of Gag Reflex 285
    Control of Salivation 286
    Preinduction Procedures 286
    Audio-Analgesia Technic 286
    "Sealing" the Patient Against Hypnosis 287
    Dehypnotization 287
    Operative Hypnodontics 288
    Pediadontics 289

43. HYPNODONTICS: HYPNOSIS IN DENTISTRY—(*Cont.*)
    Disadvantages of Hypnodontics 289
    Advantages of Hypnodontics 289
    Conclusions 290

44. MISCELLANEOUS INDICATIONS FOR HYPNOSIS 291
    Hypnosis in Electroconvulsive and Nonconvulsive Therapy 291
    Improvement in Learning and Perception 291
    Perception During Anesthesia 292
    Hypnosis in Radiology 293
    Hypnosis in Geriatrics 294
    Hypnosis in Sports 295
    Hypnosis in Space Travel 296
    Homosexuality 296
    Multiple Personality 297
    Hypnosis in Criminology 298
    Hypnosis in Military Medical Practice 299
    "Port-of-Last-Call" Patient 300

45. PRACTICAL HINTS IN HYPNODIAGNOSIS 303
    Clinical Manifestations of Anxiety 304

46. PRACTICAL HINTS IN HYPNOTHERAPY 306
    The Emotional Needs 309

47. SPECIALIZED HYPNOTIC TECHNICS 312
    Brief Hypnotherapy by Symptom-Removal 312
    Handling Resistant Patients by Brief Hypnotherapy 314
    Psychobiology Hypnotherapy 319
    Reciprocal Inhibition Psychotherapy 319
    Miscellaneous Specialized Technics of Hypnotherapy 321
    Hypnosynthesis 322
    Hypnoanalysis 322
    Applications of Contraindications and Indications for Hypnoanalysis . . . 322
    Other Uncovering Hypnoanalytic Technics 324

48. EVALUATION OF VALID AND INVALID CRITICISMS OF HYPNOTHERAPY 330
    Do We Know How Hypnosis Works? 330
    Hypnotherapy Is Not a Panacea 331
    Does Strong Dependency on the Therapist Exist? 331
    Does Hypnotherapy Sexualize the Doctor-Patient Relationship? 331
    Is Analysis of the Transference Necessary in Hypnotherapy? 332
    Are Free Associations Necessary? 333
    Does Hypnotherapy Overcome Resistances? 333
    What Is the Role of Psychodynamics in Psychotherapy? 334
    Are Interpretations Valid? 335
    Is Symptom-Removal Dangerous? 336
    Is Insight Really Necessary? 336
    Do Defenses Have To Be Analyzed? 337
    Is Autohypnosis Dangerous? 337
    Summary 337

49. FAILURES IN HYPNOTHERAPY 340
    Failures During Induction 340
    Failures During Hypnotherapy 342

INDEX 347

1

History of Hypnosis

The history of hypnosis, going back to antiquity, has been reviewed by many writers.[2-4, 7, 8] Hypnosis has been practiced under numerous labels in different places since time immemorial. Tribal medicine men, witch doctors and religious leaders have employed it in various forms to heal the sick. The cures usually were ascribed to miracles performed by the gods. The Ebers papyrus, over 3,000 years old, describes how Egyptian soothsayers used hypnoticlike procedures similar to those practiced today. Centuries ago, the Greek oracles, the Persian magi, the Hindu fakirs and the Indian yogi used hypnosis without realizing it. The earliest medical records describe miraculous healing by priests or demigods who induced a sleeplike state by ceremonial rites in the Aesculapian temples.

There are many allusions in the Talmud and in the Bible[1, 5] to the laying on of hands and to other hypnoticlike technics. Later, several religions introduced healing through touch and prayer. For many centuries, especially during the Middle Ages, kings and princes healed through the "royal touch." This method was instituted in England by Edward the Confessor and in France by Francis I. It was exploded by William III, at the beginning of the 18th century, when he said to his well-wishers, "May God give you better health and common sense."

The 17th century spawned healers such as Valentine Greatrakes (1628-1683), the "great Irish stroker," who attracted a huge following. At the same time, Francisco Bagnone was operating in Italy in a similar manner and with equal success. He had only to touch the sick with his hands, or with a relic, to accomplish astonishing cures. Hardly less famous than these two was Johann Gassner (1727-1779), a Catholic priest, who believed that most diseases were caused by evil spirits and could be exorcised by conjuration and prayer.

Paracelsus (1493-1541) was among the first to point out the healing effect of the astral bodies and the magnet. His views on animal magnetism were shared by Glocenius, Burgrove, Helnotius, Fludd, Kircher, van Helmont, Balthazar Gracían, Porta and Maxwell. All propagated the same doctrine: the magnet could cure most diseases. Dr. Maxwell, the Scot, assumed that a universal and vital spirit affected all humans. However, he recognized the influence of the imagination and of suggestion. It was from these sources that Franz Mesmer, a physician with little scientific insight, got his idea of a "universal fluid."

About 1771, Father Hell, a Jesuit in Vienna, became famous for magnetic cures obtained by applying steel plates to the naked body. Mesmer borrowed these ideas from Father Hell's work and Maxwell's doctrine, but applied them by means of contact and passes. The "new" method, which he called animal magnetism, attracted a large following during the latter part of the 18th century. Later, to treat the huge crowds that sought treatment by his methods, he developed a *baquet* or large tub filled with iron filings. Patients grasped the iron rods attached to this contraption to receive the "magnetic" flow. Thirty or more persons also were connected with each other by cords and were magnetized as Mesmer touched each person with a glass rod; many developed seizures or crises similar to those observed among some religious sects. At first he contended that the magnetism emanated from the astral bodies and later that it was transferred from himself to the patient by his magnetic wand.

A commission exposed Mesmer in 1784, stating that the cures were due to the imagination, not to magnetism. However, Mesmer unwittingly laid the cornerstone for present-day group psychotherapy, and such strange bedfellows as spiritualistic healing and psychoanalysis. His later disciples were Petètin, the discoverer of catalepsy; the Marquis de Puységur, who first described artificial somnambulism, and de Barbarin, who magnetized without paraphernalia and whose followers called themselves Barbarinists. In Sweden and Germany, the latter group were called Spiritualists; the mesmeric cures were acts of God. Those who followed de Puységur were called Experimentalists, and they considered themselves the disciples of the Paracelsus-Mesmer fluidism theory. Mesmerism soon spread all over the world.

The next phase was ushered in by Abbé Faria in 1814-1815, who came to Paris from India and gave public exhibitions without manipulations or a *baquet*. He induced over 5,000 persons, and expressed the opinion, still valid today, that the cures were not due to magnetism but *to the expectancy and co-operation of the patient*. Following Faria, Bertrand and Noizet paved the way for James Braid's doctrine of suggestion. Mesmerism flourished for a time in Germany, but by 1840 it was on the wane.

The first recorded uses of hypnoanesthesia were in 1821, by Recamier, who performed operations on patients under mesmeric coma. Cloquet performed a breast amputation before the French Academy of Medicine in 1829, using mesmerism. At about the same time, in the United States, Wheeler did a nasal polypectomy employing mesmerism, its first reported use in this country.

Through the influence of Dupotet in 1837, John Elliotson, one of the ablest physicians in England, and the first professor of medicine at the newly founded college hospital attached to the University of London, became an enthusiastic advocate of the little-known science of mesmerism. Elliotson, afraid of neither innovations nor criticism, was severely censured by editorials in *Lancet* for alleged charlatanism. Though he had introduced the stethoscope to Eng-

land, he was called a quack and an impostor. Subsequently, the university banned the use of mesmerism. The Church also opposed its use. Elliotson, a dedicated and fearless scientist, promptly resigned. For many years he published the *Zoist*, a journal in which numerous painless operations and other mesmeric phenomena were reported.

However, mesmerism grew and attracted many other disciples. Among them was James Esdaile, a Scottish surgeon practicing in India, who reported hundreds of painless operations between 1840 and 1850. In 1849, Crawford Long, who pioneered the use of ether in America, stated that many reputable physicians were recommending mesmerism for pain relief during surgery.

James Braid, a Scottish physician who merits the title "Father of Modern Hypnotism," became interested in mesmerism in 1843 when he attended a demonstration in Manchester by La Fontaine, the Swiss magnetizer. Braid scoffed at the ideas of the mesmerists. He contended that the degree of expectation increased the subject's susceptibility to suggestion. He eschewed the occult and the mysterious and instead emphasized clinical observation and experiment. Unfortunately, he coined the terms "hypnotism" and "hypnosis" from the Greek word *hypnos*, meaning sleep. Later, he recognized that hypnosis was not sleep, but the term had gained common currency. He also made the basic discovery, ignored for over a century, that hypnosis could be induced without a formalistic induction.

In a brief résumé, it is impossible to mention the many contributions and contributors of this period. However, some stand out, such as Liébeault of Nancy, whose book *Du Sommeil* was published in 1866. He has been called the real founder of suggestive therapeutics. Though a poverty-stricken country doctor, Liébeault, to avoid being branded a charlatan, said to his poor patients, "If you wish to be treated by drugs, you will have to pay my fee; if, however, you allow me to treat you by hypnotism, I will do it free of charge!" His integrity, selflessness, devotion to the needy and success with hypnosis attracted the attention of Hippolyte Bernheim, a renowned neurologist from Nancy, who, at first skeptical, later became an ardent proponent of hypnosis. Together they developed Braid's theories, and without the theatrical-like legerdemain of Charcot, treated over 12,000 patients! Bernheim and Liébeault, the legitimate innovators of modern psychotherapy, considered hypnosis a function of normal behavior and introduced the concept of suggestion and suggestibility. They also believed that symptom-removal was effective and harmless. They triumphed over the views of Charcot, who stoutly maintained that hypnosis was a form of hysteria and that it was dangerous!

Charcot's theories, based on working repeatedly with only a dozen hysterical patients at the Saltpêtrière, an insane asylum, were completely discredited. However, because of his great scientific standing, his interest in hypnosis helped to make it respectable. Charcot, like many eminent scientists today, did not realize that some degree of hypnotizability could be induced in nearly everyone. Also, he did not recognize that hypnotic responses were a part of everyday subjective happenings and were not the kind of dramatic occurrences that he took great delight in demonstrating. Nor did he appreciate the broad therapeutic potentialities that Liébeault and Bernheim achieved in their impressive series of cases.

Although slowly accepted, hypnosis emerged as a science around 1886, when Bernheim published his book *De la Suggestion*. As did Braid, he recognized that suggestion was the basis for hypnosis. His unimpeachable reputation spurred the growth of the science. Hypnotherapy came into its own, and many recognized scientists such as Bramwell, Tuckey and Wingfield in England; Janet, Bérillon, Pitres in France; Moll, Dessoir and Vogt in Germany; Forel in Switzerland; Van Renterghem in Holland; and Morsell in Italy became interested in its clinical applications. Later, Heidenhain, Broca, Pavlov, Babinski, Krafft-Ebing, and Prince and Sidis in the United States, accepted its validity.

Freud and Breuer became interested in hypnosis; the former had studied with Charcot and Bernheim. However, he *avoided* hypnosis for several reasons. First, he was embarrassed because he could not hypnotize very many patients to a sufficient depth; second, the cures were temporary, inasmuch as the posthypnotic suggestions could not be maintained, and he could not elicit buried traumatic material because of the patient's resistances. He also felt that hypnosis stripped the patient of his defenses. Freud's abandonment of hypnosis did not discredit its validity as a valuable psychological tool, but rather indicated his inability to incorporate hypnosis into his own authoritative hypnotherapeutic approach. Whether or not hypnosis is too seductive a technic and covers up the resistances is open to question. A recent treatise, *Freud and Hypnosis,* refutes many of Freud's subjective reasons for "side-stepping" hypnosis.[6] These reasons will be discussed more fully in Chapter 48.

However, Sidis, Prince and Janet demonstrated that hypnosis could be utilized for intensive exploration of the personality. They did not believe that deeply repressed emotional forces were obscured by hypnotic suggestion, as contended by Freud. The failure of many of his followers to accept hypnosis today is due largely to their emotionally conditioned blind adherence to the position assumed by Freud rather than to critical evaluation through personal experience.

Further criticism generally comes from those who naïvely regard hypnosis as belonging to a specific school of psychotherapy. They seldom realize that hypnosis is a meaningful interpersonal relationship involving real patient participation because of increased receptivity, and that the productive involvement of the patient with the therapist results in readier acceptance of suggestions. Contrarily, the hypnosis they rightfully criticize was the dramatic symptom-removal type used at the turn of the century, which was essentially commanding and authoritative. Today, however, the technics are permissive and oriented around the patient's needs rather than being "doctor-directed." These factors, together with the utilization of autohypnosis and autoconditioning, have resulted in a type of hypnotherapy that is vastly different from the hypnosis that Freud rejected. Illogically, too, he equated hypnosis with suggestion instead of realizing that suggestibility is a complex modality involving the whole field of behavior dynamics. Additionally, he apparently did not know that hypnosis was a *subjective* phenomenologic experience.

The history of hypnoanesthesia and its relationship to the inhalation anesthetic drugs is interesting. Both were used by the street-corner "professors" and the tent-show exhibitors of chemical and psychic phenomena. Induction of hypnosis and lectures on the wonders of chemistry were favorite amusements, which often ended with the entertainer's demonstrating the effect of nitrous oxide or "laughing gas."

It is of historical importance that one of these showmen, Gardner Q. Colton, gave such a performance in Hartford, Connecticut, on December 10, 1844. Horace Wells, a dentist, who was in the audience, saw one of Colton's subjects, who had inhaled the gas, stumble against a chair and badly bruise his legs. When the young man sat down, Wells asked if he had hurt himself. He answered that he had not and was astonished that his legs were bloody. He stated that he felt no pain until the effect of the gas wore off. Wells immediately thought of using nitrous oxide for dental extractions, and the next day Dr. Riggs, a colleague, extracted one of Well's own teeth after Colton had administered the gas. On regaining consciousness, Wells exclaimed, "It is the greatest discovery ever made. I did not feel so much as the prick of a pin!"

Thus, when hypnosis was commonplace, anesthesia was a curiosity. Now, after more than a 100 years, anesthesia is the vogue and hypnosis is the anomaly. Janet, the great French psychologist who at first opposed hypnosis and later advocated its use after his epochal investigations on relaxation, stated: "If my work is not accepted today, it will be tomorrow when there will be a new turn in fashion's wheel which will bring back hypnotism as surely as our grandmother's styles." That his prophecy, made at the turn of the century, is now being fulfilled is evidenced by the expanding literature on the medical, dental and psychological applications of hypnosis.

The need for rapid treatment of war neuroses during World Wars I and II and the Korean conflict led to a tremendous interest in hypnotherapy. The merger of hypnotic technics with psychiatry was one of the important advances to come out of these conflicts. Since the pioneering work of Pavlov and his disciples in the Soviet Union, and Clark Hull's classic experiments at Yale, a spate of books has been published on the subject, chiefly by psychologists and physicians. More reports are appearing in scientific publications exclusively devoted to hypnosis all over the world in nearly every discipline, indicating the increased interest in this age-old science.

From a historical viewpoint, it is interesting that many nostrums and other medical fads have passed into the limbo of discredited procedures, but hypnosis has survived, and, at present, scientific interest is stronger than ever. This salient point alone indicates the indispensable value of hypnosis. Its powers, medically applied, to cure and to relieve pain have been greatly underestimated or ignored by the medical profession because of irrational prejudice. This is not surprising, since *prejudice is ignorance educated,* and it is difficult for any individual, in any given era, to see through the "smoke screen" of his own culture.

Clinical and experimental investigations into the scientific applications and the limitations of hypnosis are being conducted by well-trained investigators in nearly all the medical, psychological and ancillary disciplines. Hypnosis is being taught at an ever-growing number of universities and medical schools. In addition, many thousands of physicians, dentists and psychologists in the United States have received training in the introductory workshops on hypnosis conducted by leaders in the field.

The British Medical Association, on April 23, 1955, reported its approval of hypnosis for treatment of the psychoneuroses, and of hypnoanesthesia for relief of pain in childbirth and surgery. The report also advised that all physicians and medical students receive fundamental training in hypnosis. The Council on Mental Health of the American Medical Association, on September 13, 1958, recommended that, in view of our increasing knowledge, instruction in hypnosis be included in the curricula of medical schools and postgraduate training centers.

It further emphasized that there are definite and proper uses for hypnosis in medical and dental practice in the hands of those who are properly trained, and that those who use hypnosis should be aware of the complex nature of the phenomena involved. The report ended with the statement that certain aspects of hypnosis still remain unknown and controversial, as is true of many other areas of medicine and the psychological sciences. Therefore, active participation in high-level research by members of the medical and of the dental professions was to be encouraged. The use of hypnosis for entertainment purposes was vigorously condemned. In a subsequent report in 1961, the A.M.A. Council on Mental Health recommended that 144 hours of training be given over a 9- to 12-month period at the undergraduate and postgraduate levels.

At present, clinical and experimental investigations into hypnosis are being conducted by numerous serious research workers in many countries. They are gathering data which it is hoped will shed further light on the nature and clinical applications of hypnosis. It is unfortunate that, throughout the long history of hypnosis, it has been the favorite whipping boy of those who at one and the same time espouse the value of psychological and placebo therapy, but yet deny the obvious correlation with hypnosis. However, it is true that hypnosis has been hurt more by the extravagant claims of its ardent proponents than by its opponents. The American Society for Clinical Hypnosis and the International Society of Clinical and Experimental Hypnosis have established sections in many countries throughout the world to maintain high ethical and training standards and to prevent the abuses that caused hypnosis to fall into oblivion twice during the past century and a half.

During its tortuous history, and in spite of the many obstacles confronting those intrepid enough to risk hearing their thoughts called absurd, hypnosis has emerged as a valuable adjunct to medicine. At last its therapeutic and psychological value are being recognized by many sober-minded scientists. The author believes that the links forged by Paracelsus, Mesmer, Bernheim and Liébeault, which led to Freud, ultimately will be joined with those contributed by the physical scientists to make hypnosis a well understood and fully accepted modality.

REFERENCES

1. Bowers, M., and Glasner, S.: Auto-hypnotic aspects of the Jewish cabbalistic concept of Kavanah, J.C.E.H. 6:50-70, 1958.
2. Bromberg, W.: Man Above Humanity, Philadelphia, Lippincott, 1954.
3. Conn, J.: On the history of hypnosis *in* Introductory Lectures on Medical Hypnosis, The Institute of Research in Hypnosis, 80-89, 1958.
4. Cutten, G. B.: Three Thousand Years of Mental Healing, New York, Scribner, 1911.
5. Glasner, S.: A note on allusions to hypnosis in the Bible and Talmud, J.C.E.H. 3:34-39, 1955.
6. Kline, M.: Freud and Hypnosis, New York, Julian Press, 1950.
7. Rosen, G.: History of medical hypnosis *in* Hypnosis in Modern Medicine, 25, Springfield, Ill., Thomas, 1959.
8. Wolberg, L.: Medical Hypnosis, New York, Grune and Stratton, 1951.

2

Phenomena of Suggestion and Hypnosis

TYPES OF SUGGESTION

Suggestion can be defined as the uncritical acceptance of an idea. It is the process by which sensory impressions are conveyed in a meaningful manner to evoke altered psychophysiologic responses. One cannot necessarily equate suggestion with hypnosis unless it is accompanied by diversion or "misdirection of attention." How this is done will be described below. However, the acceptance of ideas by suggestion must be differentiated from logical persuasion. *Persuasion is not suggestion and suggestion is not persuasion!*

Suggestions provide sensorial data input or information to the higher centers. All sensory input routes continually receive data from verbal, nonverbal, intraverbal or extraverbal communications. This is done not only via the five senses, but through other sources, as thermal, pressure sensations, kinesthetic, etc. Verbal, which includes preverbal, refers to communication by sounds and words. Nonverbal refers to gestures and grimaces. Intraverbal is concerned with modulation of the voice. For example, an orator with emphatic vocal inflections holds his audience's attention more readily than one who speaks in a monotone. Extraverbal deals with the implications of words or phrases more apt to reduce criticalness. Thus, the harsh command "stand up" is likely to produce resistance to carrying out a suggested act. Contrarily, if one softly asks, "Are you *not tired* of sitting down?", the chances are that the person will stand up, especially if the request is accompanied by a gesture symbolic of the desired act. Thus, the whole complex of mannerism, inflection of voice and implied meaning of the words employed plays an important role in facilitating perception, suggestibility and response. Aristotle's maxim, "Nothing is in the mind that did not pass through the senses," is literally true.

THE NATURE OF SUGGESTIBILITY IN HYPNOSIS

Nearly all subjects believe that their responses are produced by the hypnotist. In reality, it is the subject who involuntarily initiates the acts in response to previously experienced conditioning. Where criticalness is reduced as the result of misdirection, a suggested act is automatically carried out without the individual's intellectual or logical processes participating in the response. And when one suggestion after another is accepted, more difficult ones are accepted, particularly if the sensory spiral of belief is compounded from the outset. This is called abstract conditioning and, in part, helps to explain the role that suggestibility plays in the production of hypnotic phenomena.

Suggestibility is further enhanced by a favorable attitude or mental-set that establishes proper motivation. It depends on the technic utilized to produce it, but more on the quality of the relationship established between operator and subject—the rapport. Thus, mere suggestibility per se does not account for hypnotizability, but rather increased suggestibility is a constant feature of hypnosis. However, the concept of increased suggestibility does not explain the complex neuropsychological processes that occur with hypnotic behavior. These processes are learned but are, in part, basically an essential feature of the organism.

There is an extensive literature on the qualitative nature of suggestibility in hypnosis. Investigations[20, 43, 44] reveal that, with a male operator, suggestibility is slightly greater in females than in males.[43] However, since hypnotic suggestibility depends on motivation, it varies from person to person and even changes in the same person, depending on his needs. Therefore, it cannot be correlated significantly with the sex or the character traits of the subject. The degree of suggestibility is determined rather by the way an individual reacted to suggestions from others in the past, by the structuring or setting, by the prestige of the person who gives the suggestions, and by the way the suggestions are interpreted. A subject may be highly suggestible to stimuli affecting his health, yet he may be nonsuggestible to persuasive salesmanship. In the latter area, his critical faculties are aroused. Yet the same person may be very suggestible to political and religious persuasion, especially if the exhortations seem to fit in with his cultural and value systems.

Often the degree of suggestibility cannot be evaluated in advance because of the duration and the extent of neurotic involvement. Some investigators believe that psychoneurotics are more suggestible than emotionally healthy persons,[44] and that even psychotics are extremely susceptible to suggestion. This has not been the author's experience, as disturbed psychotics seldom can concentrate sufficiently to follow even simple suggestions. Most neurotics, also, are reluctant to part with symptoms that fulfill a defensive need in their personality functioning. However, those neurotics who submit to hypnosis for entertainment purposes, particularly exhibitionists, are very suggestible because they know they are not going to lose their symptoms.

Of particular interest is the paradoxical reactor, who believes he is not susceptible to suggestion, but who, because of his innate stubbornness, always reacts with positive suggestibility. Of course, suggestibility always must be differentiated from gullibility, which implies the use of deception.

THE NATURE OF HYPNOSIS

It has been postulated that hypnosis is a condition of emotional readiness during which perceptual alterations can be induced. Another viewpoint[30] conceptualizes it as "an altered state of the organism originally and usually produced by a repetition of stimuli in which suggestion is more effective than usual." This definition is more descriptive than explanatory. Hypnosis has been described as a "dissociation of awareness from the majority of sensory and even strictly neural events that are taking place."[43] While this is partially true, it does not help us understand the actual nature of hypnosis. Dissociation characterizes not only hypnosis but many other altered states such as dreams, hypnogogic states, "highway hypnosis," reverie states, the detachment or depersonalization seen in many types of religious worship, and many other mental phenomena.[45] These theoretic considerations and relationships will be described in succeeding chapters.

Another explanation of the nature of hypnosis is that it is not a "state," but rather a "descriptive abstraction" referring to a number of interrelated and overlapping processes.[2] It is my belief that the proper motivation induces a favorable mental set or attitude; that hypnosis is produced on the basis of misdirection of attention, belief and expectation—all catalyzed by the imagination.[17] Operationally, hypnosis results from a restructuring in perceptual and object relationships. This involves a reorganization of what constitutes reality for the subject. The dimensions of reality, when altered, depend on the reciprocal interplay of psychophysiologic forces between subject and hypnotist. However, in the response to sensory alteration the hypnotic state must not be confused with the complex processes that occur in hypnotic behavior.

It can be concluded that, whenever a suggestion is repeated over and over again, this usually leads to a conditioned reflex, which, in turn, is dependent upon previously established associative bonds or processes in the cortex. The effects of reflex conditioning have much in common with hypnotic conditioning.[5] Conditioning by suggestion and/or hypnosis has masqueraded under a multiplicity of healing terms from time immemorial and relies heavily on misdirection of attention. This term, as it relates to hypnosis, will be more fully discussed now.

Misdirection of attention is merely a diversionary maneuver or "smoke screen" to obscure the fact that suggestion in one guise or another is used to influence an individual. The ritual of a formal hypnotic induction procedure makes full use of misdirection; the operator "slips in" suggestions when the subject is least expecting them. For instance, during induction, the subject's attention is fixed upon his eyelids by the remark, "Your eyes are getting very, very heavy." If his eyes actually become very heavy, then he is ready to believe other suggestions that he attributes to the operator's "powers." The subject does not realize that the lid heaviness actually was induced by the constant and fatiguing position of the eyes, staring upward at the ceiling. Rather, he believes that his eye fatigue resulted from the operator's suggestions of heaviness.

EVERYDAY ASPECTS OF SUGGESTION AND/OR HYPNOSIS

Suggestion by misdirection of attention accounts for the success of many types of "therapy." For example, when the emotionally disturbed patient is told, "Your trouble is in your second cervical vertebra," he may ask, "What do you do for that?" The healer may say, "You will need 20 adjustments to correct your condition." Now it is well known that, when one adds a little truth to an assumption, the whole supposition sounds logical. Does not the patient hear the "crack" or the adjustment of his neck? And is this not *prima facie* evidence that something was done? The "adjustment" thus becomes the misdirection of attention!

Likewise, whenever a patient with a psychogenic complaint develops a favorable mental-set that a particular type of therapy will help, he is aided *not* so much by the therapeutic modality as *by his inner conviction or faith that he will be helped.* The effects are greater if he has been referred to the doctor by a person who has obtained results from similar "treatments." Here, misdirection in the form of a placebo effect brings about the favorable mental-set so essential for enhancing the subject's expectation of success.

Thus, one of the most important ingredients for hypnotic suggestibility is the expectation of help from one who is in a prestige position. If convinced of the truth of this person's words, the subject *behaves differently* because he *thinks* and *believes differently.* From time immemorial, all healing by suggestion and/or hypnosis has been based on this mechanism. If the idea is accepted that increased suggestibility is produced by a favorable mental-set or attitude, catalyzed by the imagination, then hypnotic responses fall into the realm of conviction phenomena. As such, they are due to *subjective* mechanisms inherently present, to a degree, in all individuals. They result from the subject's imagination compounding the sensory spiral of belief until conviction occurs. Hence, it is indeed a wise hypnotist who knows who is hypnotizing whom!

An extreme degree of suggestibility is illustrated by medical students who, due to their imagination, develop the signs and the symptoms of many of the diseases they study. The role of the imagination in the production of psychological symptoms is generally admitted, and it seems reasonable to infer that what is caused by the imaginative processes may be reversed by the same means. At the risk of oversimplification, we may say that conviction of illness leads to illness, and *conviction of cure results in cure!*

The hypnotic state, depending upon the degree of selective attention to a given stimulus, occurs as the result of a wide variety of stimuli. All factors accounting for it are not known. Even consciousness, reverie, sleep or wakefulness, which are fluctuating states of attention or awareness, are poorly understood at present. A mother can sleep through a thunderstorm, yet hear the cry of her baby —so, is she really asleep? In a reverie or a daydream, one does not hear what is going on, even though ostensibly "awake." Everyone has had the experience of "listening" attentively to another person and yet not hearing a word. For all practical purposes, we were "asleep" at the time. Data indicate that discussions that take place while a patient is anesthetized can be recovered postoperatively through hypnotic recall.[5] Sensory impressions noted subliminally can be reproduced—a song heard over and over again eventually can be hummed without our being aware of how it was "learned." Repetitive stimulation of any of the sensory input organs can induce a state of increased receptivity to suggestion. Therefore, if a stimulus is sufficiently maintained, the desired response eventually will be produced.

We are, knowingly or unknowingly, continually bombarded by suggestions. Since there is no fine line of demarcation between suggestibility and hypnosis, where suggestibility ends and hypnosis begins is not known. It is obvious that suggestions leading to hypnosis in its broadest sense occur as a part of everyday existence. This begins during our formative years—when a child hurts his hand, his mother's kiss usually relieves the pain. And, as an adult, he re-enters a hypnotic relationship whenever he is placed in a situation that contains some or all of the elements that were present during his conditioning as a child.[40]

The capacity to be hypnotized is, in reality, an adaptive response, probably "programmed" into the central nervous system as the result of a billion or more years of inheritance. One portion of the brain, the neocortex, deals with reality. During hypnosis there is a special kind of awareness, characterized by the ability of the brain to respond to ideas, images and feelings which may or may not be related to reality. For example, in a dream one can float out of the window and land on the roof. Here, distortion of reality occurs because of complete lack of discrimination or cortical inhibition. It is likely, therefore, that when cortical functioning is selectively inhibited, as it is apparently during hypnosis, the altered perceptions can be organized into a wide variety of thought patterns wholly unrelated to reality.

There is a wide field in which to maneuver when one uses hypnotic suggestions to "tap" the brain's capacities. According to neurophysiologists, the human brain has about 10 to 15 billion neurons in which to process and store information. Each neuron, in turn, has the capacity to store a tremendous number of "bits" of information or memories. Furthermore, a single neuron has one or more synapses or "switches." The sum total of these limitless possibilities, associations or potential interactions for memories, feelings, ideas and attitudes simply staggers the imagination!

It is estimated that the brain by the age of 50 contains some 70 trillion "bits" of information or memories as part of what is referred to as the total experiential background. This gives us some idea of the magnitude of the field that is capable of responding to the proper input. No wonder the brain has been referred to as an "enchanted loom"!

THE HYPNOIDAL "STATE"

Hypnoidal refers to a precursor of hypnosis, usually induced by nonformalistic technics. Through fixation of attention, the monotonous stimulus of a white line on the highway induces a tiring effect upon the driver. This eventually leads to some degree of dissociation that can produce a hypnoidal effect, and this, in turn, can merge with true sleep. Depending upon the degree of dissociation, it resembles hypnosis. Moreover, there is no sharp cleavage between the two. The hypnoidal "state" is characterized by some detachment as well as by physical and mental relaxation. The attention span fluctuates more toward abstractionlike states. Since critical thinking is reduced, enhanced suggestibility results.

Our lives are full of hypnoidal contacts and relationships that are referred to by psychologists as "waking hypnosis." Repetitive radio and TV commercials, advertising propaganda and a good orator or actor heighten the attention span in a meaningful manner and enhance our suggestibility. When watching an interesting motion picture, our attention is focused on the screen and we soon enter into a hypnoidal stage. Varying degrees of emotion are registered as we identify with the action in the film. *Reality is made out of unreality.* Whenever the necessity for reality thinking is obviated, a type of waking hypnosis occurs. After walking out of the theater, we usually blink our eyes for a moment to orient ourselves. Without realizing it, we were in a hypnoidal state and on the way to being effectively "hypnotized." Waking hypnosis here occurs as the result of utilizing ordinary experiences.

Mass suggestion, mass hypnosis, subliminal projection, brain-washing, propaganda and evangelistic appeals leading to altered behavior are also produced by nonformalistic hypnotic technics. Thus, a knowledge of the everyday aspects of scientifically applied suggestion—hypnosis—has profound implications for an understanding of all mental functioning and responses.

ANIMAL HYPNOSIS

Animal hypnosis displays some of the phenomena noted in humans. A chicken placed in a horizontal position develops a tonic immobility characterized by an extensor rigidity of the limbs—catalepsy— when a line is drawn from the eye that is closer to the ground. The immobility may be due, in part, to restriction of activity. The individual who "fights" an alligator strokes the reptile until it develops catalepsy; this renders the animal harmless. Other illustrations of hypnoticlike phenomena are seen throughout the animal kingdom; the female spider, which is much larger than the male and ordinarily kills him, is rendered immobile by stroking her belly just before copulation; a snake is deaf but is "hypnotized" or charmed by the to-and-fro movements of the flutist; and the bird that sings the sweetest attracts the most potential mates.

The older literature posits a similarity between animal hypnosis and a hypnoidal stage, the latter being a primitive type of resting stage noted in animals. The more primitive the animal, the more hypnoidal-like is its sleep state.[39] From a phylogenetic standpoint, sleep and hypnosis may have evolved from primitive hypnoidal mechanisms. However, it should be stressed once again that the capacity of a human to enter into hypnosis is due primarily to the relationships induced by the symbolic or experiential meaning of words and other stimuli. In animals, on the other hand, hypnosis is produced chiefly by physical manipulations.

AUTOHYPNOSIS

Autohypnosis or self-hypnosis usually is produced by *previous posthypnotic suggestions* made by the operator. Every autosuggestion was originally a heterosuggestion. Varying degrees of autosuggestion and autohypnosis in no small measure account for the success of the metaphysical "sciences" and religious spiritual-healing movements.

Suggestions have a much greater chance of being followed when they appear to originate from the self rather than being instituted by another person.[32] If the patient feels that he can facilitate recovery by such therapy, he develops more motivation. The resultant self-pride in this achievement strengthens the confidence essential for recovery. Autohypnosis also makes available a tremendous reservoir of unrecognized potential strength—the "forgotten assets." Diligent practice, however, generally is necessary to obtain a satisfactory depth; lesser degrees are attained more readily.

RAPPORT

Rapport has been defined as a harmonious relationship between two persons. In hypnosis, it results from restricted attention to some or all stimuli residing in the field of awareness.[13] Thus rapport, as it relates to the hypersuggestibility produced by the hypnotic situation, is a special kind of relationship in which the operator's suggestions are followed more readily. This is due to the great belief and confidence established in him. This definition will be used in this book.

When greater attention is paid to the words of the operator, a subject usually responds with almost a pinpoint literalness or specificity to suggestions, especially if they are in accord with his wishes and needs. Thus, wherever a "pipeline of communication" is established between a sender and a receiver, a suggestion or "message" will be understood if there is no interference, noise or static on the circuits (garbling or unintelligibility).

Some subjects in good rapport even will respond to an operator's posthypnotic suggestions as a printed or written order, such as "Go into a state of deep relaxation." Others respond to the voice of the operator over the telephone, providing they have been appropriately "cued" for this posthypnotic suggestion beforehand. Even an associate without prior knowledge of hypnotic technics, upon a prearranged signal, can readily produce deep hypnosis in a willing subject.

It has been contended that the rapport in hypnosis is due to emotional dependency on the operator. There is no more dependancy in the hypnotic situation than in any other psychotherapeutic relationship. When autohypnosis is incorporated into therapy, whatever dependency exists is minimized or eliminated. The success of all psychotherapy is based on a good interpersonal relationship, which is essentially a shared experience. Because of the intense and close interpersonal relationship produced by the hypnotic stage, both operator and patient enter into good rapport, since it provides each with an emotional satisfaction that otherwise could not be obtained.[28] More research should be directed toward one of the most essential psychological phenomena of hypnosis—the shared qualities of rapport.

One can conclude from the above that patient rapport denotes the ability and willingness of the patient and the operator to enter into an intensified emotional relationship with each other. As a result, the subject is motivated to accept the beliefs that are so necessary for the establishment of conviction. These are the special requisites for hypnotic induction, utilization of the hypnotic state for production of behavioral responses and subsequent behavioral changes.

CATALEPSY

Catalepsy, an interesting phenomenon of hypnosis, is characterized by a peculiar involuntary tonicity of the muscles. The limbs remain in almost any position in which they are placed; the waxy molding of the fingers and the extremities is known as *flexibilitas cerea*. During eyeball catalepsy, the eyes do not move when the head is turned slowly—they remain "frozen" or "fixed" when the head moves. At nonhypnotic levels, there generally is a quick darting of the eyes, which is associated with a time lag or an economy of motion.

Catalepsy usually denotes that a light or a medium stage of hypnosis has been achieved, and its presence enables the operator to determine the depth at which he is working. Very few psychophysiologic investigations have been made of this common hypnotic phenomenon.

IDEOSENSORY ACTIVITIES

Ideosensory activity refers to the capacity of the brain to develop sensory images, which may be kinesthetic, olfactory, visual, auditory, tactile or gustatory. A common example of ideosensory activity is looking at a fire and "seeing" the "face" of one's beloved. During negative ideosensory activity, there is a denial of actual sensory experiences, such as *not* seeing or hearing something that actually is present, e. g., looking for one's pencil and finding it in front of one. A typical example is the complete absorption in an interesting book that produces a selective type of "deafness" to irrelevant stimuli. Imagining the "smell" of a certain odor that does not actually exist is an example of a positive ideosensory activity.

Ideosensory activities are used as misdirection to obtain a somatic response. The subject must be involved in as many ideosensory experiences as possible, as this facilitates hypnotic conditioning. The subject must think of these in terms of his own memories, ideas and sensations, that is, those that he has already experienced. For example, when the author wishes to induce hypnoanesthesia, he has found the following suggestion to be helpful, "Your hand is getting just as numb as if it were frozen, or as if you had been sitting or sleeping on it." Nearly everyone has experienced this sensation. Naturally, to elicit ideosensory activities, the posthypnotic suggestions must revive responses previously experienced by an individual — his experiential background. For instance, the mention of a specific food to a hungry individual is likely to produce salivation only if he has experienced the taste of that particular food.

The section on technics will illustrate how ideosensory activities are employed to effect somatic responses. Comprehension of the nature of ideosensory processes is necessary to understand the *modus operandi* of hypnosis.

IDEOMOTOR ACTIVITIES

Ideomotor activity is one of the phenomena used to facilitate suggestibility. It refers to the involuntary capacity of muscles to respond instantaneously to thoughts, feelings and ideas. These built-in responses are necessary for survival. An example of ideomotor activity is seen when a mother puts a spoonful of food up to a baby's mouth and her own mouth opens. Leaning in the direction of the ball carrier on a favorite football team, and the backseat driver's stepping on the brakes of the careening car, are other ideomotor activities spontaneously produced without the awareness of the individual.

All induction technics depend on the subject's being unaware that he has made such physical responses to suggestion. He does not realize that they are the result of his own thoughts. In the section on induction technics, it will be shown how ideomotor activities are utilized to invoke the subject's belief and thus lead to the expectation of hypnosis.

Chevreul's pendulum test, described in Chapter 5, the operation of the Ouija board, oil- and water-witching, clairvoyance, and even extrasensory perception to a degree, depend upon the involuntary or ideomotor muscular responses associated with the ideosensory processes of the individual. Subcortical mechanisms are responsible for the primary or inherited responses, manifested as involuntary reflexes. These are not learned, and include blinking, pupillary dilatation or contraction, endocrine responses, peristalsis, breathing and cardiac functioning. Even though breathing and blinking can be controlled volitionally, most of the vital functions are under autonomic control.

However, it is possible to "build in" other reflexes upon those that are involuntary and make these increasingly subject to volitional control. For instance, the pupil can be conditioned and made to contract to a hallucinated light. Thus, the autonomic nervous system is *not* as autonomic as we have been led to believe. The greater control of autonomic functioning accounts for the feats of Yoga and the transcendence of normal voluntary capacity achieved by posthypnotic suggestions.

At nonhypnotic levels, the autonomic nervous system attempts to act in response to all new situations and it is corrected by awareness of reality. For instance, in the case of the back-seat driver, the discriminatory portion of the cortex appraises reality and returns the conviction that he is *not* in danger. Without such awareness, *he would produce responses as if he were the*

driver, as happens in dreams, hallucinations and psychoses.

Reality results whenever incoming information in the form of sensory percepts can be validated with previously stored data; this results in automatic behavior and response. During hypnosis, however, the operator's suggestions are accepted as reality because of selective cortical inhibition; the incoming information does not have access to the stored data; therefore it cannot be validated. Thus, the increased suggestibility leading to production of hypnotic phenomena is brought about by the resultant of two forces—automatic activity (ideomotor and ideosensory) and selective cortical inhibition. Stated simply, when ideas that lead to "ideoid" (idea-like) actions are interpreted as reality, the resultant convictions lead to hypnosis!

POSTHYPNOTIC SUGGESTIONS AND CONDITIONING

Acts carried out after the termination of hypnosis in response to specific suggestions are called posthypnotic phenomena.[42] A suggestion given during hypnosis serves as the stimulus and the act becomes the response. A posthypnotic suggestion and a conditioned reflex serve a similar purpose except that the former is not established by repetitive trial and learning in the classic sense. Rather, a posthypnotic act is a complex task, often carried out as the result of a single session of "learning"; it is more durable and not as rapidly extinguished as a conditioned reflex.

The posthypnotic act, even though carried out long after it is suggested, probably is a spontaneously self-induced miniature replica of the original hypnotic situation. The difference, if any, is in degree rather than in type. A posthypnotic suggestion may last for minutes to years.[13-15, 18, 22] It is generally agreed, however, that on the average it may remain effective for at least two months.[23, 33] During this period, decrement occurs in the strength and the quality of the posthypnotic performance. Periodic reinforcement, however, tends to increase its effectiveness; repeated elicitation does not weaken it.

Posthypnotic suggestions usually are followed irrespective of the depth of the hypnosis. Completion depends more upon the nature and the difficulty of the suggested task than upon the depth of the hypnosis.[41] Internal or external factors, of one type or another, can prevent fulfillment. When this happens, profound anxiety may be produced. Therefore, a posthypnotic suggestion should not be of a bizarre nature, but in keeping with the subject's needs and goals.

Some subjects develop a complete amnesia for the posthypnotic act and yet readily follow the original suggestion. Others can be aware of the original suggestion as they carry it out. Still others remember the suggestion only after the completion of the act. Response to posthypnotic suggestions might be compared with the compulsive behavior noted in all of us at times. We know what we are doing, but do not know *why!* If the setting in which the posthypnotic suggestion occurs is altered, or if the expectant attitudes change between the time of the suggestion and the time when it is about to be carried out, then deeply hypnotized persons can cancel even the original suggestion.[14]

Unless the subject is a volunteer for the stage hypnotist, ridiculous suggestions usually are rejected. Most of these volunteers are exhibitionists and seldom mind carrying out suggestions that are compatible with their usual behavior. Whether or not a suggestion is carried out also depends upon the wishes and the intentions of the subject.[4, 27] The type and the quality of the operator's communication also affect the response. When working with a subject in hypnosis, an extraverbal approach, such as, "You wouldn't mind opening the window after you come out of this relaxed state, would you?" minimizes resistance. If the posthypnotic suggestion is not followed, a remark such as, "It's stuffy inside. I wonder how we can get some fresh air in the room?" is usually effective. A cue of this type often reinforces a posthypnotic suggestion given during hypnosis.

When a posthypnotic suggestion that is not fully in accord with the subject's desires is carried out, he usually rationalizes the unusual behavior. Purposeless posthypnotic suggestions are as readily forgotten as other instructions given at nonhypnotic levels.[37]

The greater tenacity of posthypnotic suggestions stems from the graded effects of prior invoked beliefs such as lid heaviness and limb catalepsy, which, when compounded by ideosensory responses, lead to automatic conviction. Since the subject felt the operator's initial suggestions, he naturally believes and follows other and more complex posthypnotic suggestions. The subject, just as during the induction, is wholly unaware that his own ideomotor and ideosensory responses initiated the sensory spiral of belief that was processed into conviction.

Hence, in further amplification of the explanation on page 8, the complex mechanisms involved in the fulfillment of a posthypnotic suggestion are the resultant of a series of conditioned sensory impressions and muscular activities. The subject develops a belief in the reality of a subjective experience and response following a posthypnotic suggestion. He accepts its reality as readily as any belief associated with dreaming, thinking and perceptual recognition. One investigator[2a] thinks there is no *essential* difference between behavior in the "hypnotic" and "posthypnotic" period, that is, all phenomena elicited by means of posthypnotic suggestions are seen during hypnosis. However, the reverse is not always true.

AMNESIA

Amnesia may or may not occur spontaneously during hypnosis. More often it is produced through posthypnotic suggestions. When it has occurred, there is a selective loss of memory following dehypnotization. The subject is "unaware" of what has transpired during hypnotically produced amnesia; however, the recollections are only held in abeyance. Most good subjects, when rehypnotized, can remember nearly everything that happened during the hypnotic session; others gradually forget some or all of their experiences. Still others, even though deeply hypnotized, have an inordinate need to maintain control and will not develop amnesia.

The phenomenon of amnesia occurs as an

everyday experience. For instance, the name of an old friend can be forgotten temporarily when an introduction is being made. Either spontaneous or suggested amnesia can be used for evaluating the depth of hypnosis; the former generally is indicative of deep hypnosis—somnambulism. Here loss of memory for whole segments of an individual's life is produced; the dissociation is analogous to the fugue states noted in amnesia victims. Suggested hypnotic amnesia is somewhat comparable with the everyday experience of repressing painful experiences. The duration of the amnesia is not predictable.

Amnesia is obtained as follows: "You may find it very convenient to forget everything that I suggested. Imagine that your mind is like a blackboard that has just had everything erased" Another method is to say, "After you open your eyes, you will have no recollection of what I said to you while you were in a relaxed state. However, all the suggestions I gave you will be effectively carried out as specified."

DISSOCIATION

Dissociation is somewhat similar to hypnotic amnesia. It refers to the inherent ability of a hypnotized subject to "detach" himself from his immediate environment. This phenomenon occurs at nonhypnotic levels, as in reverie states. An individual may be completely dissociated and yet retain his capacity to function adequately. This dissociated state is similar to dreaming, when one "sees" himself performing many activities. Nearly all situations produced in dreams can be attained in the dissociated state by appropriate posthypnotic suggestions.

A well-conditioned subject can "step out" of himself and see himself sitting on the other side of the room. Dissociation frequently is used to induce hypnoanesthesia. The following remark to a deeply hypnotized patient in the dental chair automatically will raise the pain threshold: "You would not mind going out to the ball park, would you? It is such a nice day for a baseball game, isn't it?"

A portion of the body, such as a limb, can be "anesthetized" through dissociation; the person does not feel the "separated" part. This can be produced as follows: "You can feel and see both arms in your lap, can't you?" This suggestion may be given while the subject has his arm extended in rigid catalepsy. Obviously, if a positive visual and tactile hallucination is produced by the suggestion to "see" *both* arms resting comfortably in his lap, then *the extended cataleptic limb becomes the dissociated* arm and it *automatically becomes impervious to pain* without any mention of anesthesia!

DEPERSONALIZATION

Depersonalization can be induced readily in a good subject through posthypnotic suggestions. He can be told to forget his own identity and assume that he is another person. This is accomplished most easily by asking him, "Who is your favorite person?" The operator then suggests that *he is* that person. Depersonalization can be used for psychotherapeutic purposes that are similar to those mentioned under dissociation.

HYPERMNESIA OR MEMORY RECALL

Hypermnesia refers to the retrieval of information or an increase in memory recall greater than that achieved at volitional or nonhypnotic levels. This phenomenon, too, is seen in some degree as a part of everyday life. How often, when walking along a certain street, one thinks: "Whatever happened to my old buddy, Jim? I can remember when we used to play on this very block." All memories, no matter how trivial, are stored in the brain and leave an indelible impression. Most of these can be recovered when the proper association pathways are stimulated.

Under hypnosis, a good subject apparently can recall long-since-forgotten memories. One investigator believes that the magnitude of recall or retrieval of information obtained under hypnosis is increased only slightly,[32a] whereas another thinks it is much greater than at nonhypnotic levels.[37] However, the material recalled may be inaccurate, and one must realize that hypnotic subjects can confabulate material readily. Hypermnesia must be differentiated from revivification, which is essentially an actual reliving of an incident at the time at which it occurred. Memory recall is obtained by posthypnotic suggestions, such as, "Perhaps you might like to tell me all about your graduation from grammar school and what did you say *was* the name of your school?" The emphasis here is on the past tense, whereas in revivification the question would be asked in the present tense.

The author has used hypermnesia for recall of pertinent information that has helped solve crimes and legal matters. In one instance, a policeman, wounded by bandits, recalled the license number of their automobile several months after the event. In another, involving a large sum of money, a subject remembered where he had been on a specific date eight years prior to the hypnotization. In each instance, recall of the facts was verified.

REVIVIFICATION AND AGE REGRESSION

Revivification must be differentiated from age regression. In revivification, the hypnotized person actually relives earlier events of his life; all memories following the age to which the subject is regressed are ablated. On the other hand, in age regression, the subject plays a role; there is a simulated pattern of acting out of past events in the framework of the present;[34] this type of age regression is called psuedorevivification.

The phenomenon of revivification is produced by posthypnotic suggestions directed toward progressively suggesting disorientation as to the year, the month and the day; then, by appropriate suggestions, an earlier age level is reached. Some investigators believe that long-forgotten memories are not reactivated, but rather are simulated; that nonregressive elements are present.[32a] However, it has been demonstrated frequently that in revivification the subjects exhibit many of the personality traits of that period in their lives. For instance, intellectual functioning, indicated by the manner of speaking and the choice of words, is childlike; the handwriting changes; and there are other objective manifestations that corroborate the validity of the revivification.

However, it is possible that much of the descriptive material revealed during revivification is due to role-playing or "screen memories." This "misremembering" can occur in response to a prior suggestion that a specific act took place; later the act is reinstated as if it were an original memory. It appears that recall is not improved for unimportant mnemonic material, but is improved greatly under hypnosis when strong emotional elements are associated with the memories.[10] The meanings and the motivations associated with spontaneous revivification during hypnotherapy have been described.[6]

The best way to obtain revivification is for the operator to identify himself with a surrogate figure that the subject once knew. For example, if the operator plays the role of a friendly person, he can remark: "You are now in the fourth grade. I happened to be talking to your teacher and she told me how well you are doing in school." Some subjects will respond with genuine affection and warmth.

Psychophysiologic revivification is supposed to be authentic if the Babinski reflex is elicited.[16] A spontaneous Babinski may also appear whenever the subject's perceptions and sensations are compatible with the regressed chronologic age.[25] However, neither of these investigations used naïve subjects—a crucial point. Revivification is not valid if the subject's vocabulary is incompatible with his present chronologic age level. Other observations[31] at nonhypnotic levels indicate that revivification in the form of complex somatic changes can occur during drug-facilitated abreactions. However, here too, the reliability of the results is open to serious question.

There are various degrees of revivification and regression that can occur simultaneously, depending on the depth of hypnosis. This accounts for the diversity of opinions as to their distinguishing features. Nevertheless, the effects of either revivification or regression can produce meaningful emotional experiences that are compatible with earlier age levels.[36] It seems that most spontaneous age regressions contain some facet of revivification as well as regression.[25] This has been referred to as retrogression[24] or dynamic regression.[35] An interesting example of simulation once occurred while a female patient was being regressed to a very early age level. She imitated a neonatal position, became mute and appeared to be sucking the breast. Fortunately, this patient had been given two sets of cues for dehypnotization: (1) she could terminate it herself, or (2) she could respond to the shoulder signal (a touch on the left shoulder). Both sets of signals should be given to all patients who are being regressed to ensure that the situation can be controlled if communication at the verbal level is lost. This should be done even if simulation or role-playing is suspected.

To obtain revivification, the subject is told that, upon a given signal, "You are soon going to be 10 years of age, and you can see yourself clearly at that age and everything that is happening." (A few minutes are allowed to elapse to allow sufficient time for the reorientation to take place.) The signal is now given. The subject is asked, "What is the date today? How old are you today? What are you doing? Who are some of the people around you?" Additional conversation in the past tense will help to establish the regression more firmly.

How the handwriting changes in a good hypnotic subject who has achieved revivification is illustrated by the following:

"AGE PROGRESSION"

It is believed that both hypnotic age regression and "age progression" are a form of psychological activity that involves disorientation for the subject and a reorganization of his perceptual equilibrium and control mechanisms, with particular reference to time-space perception.[24] The term "age progression" refers to the artificially induced disorientation of a hypnotized subject who hallucinates living in the future, but who still retains his present chronologic age. It does not refer to reversing a regression (making a person return to his present chronologic age), as when a regressed subject is told during hypnosis, "You are now growing older: 10; 12 years of age; and now you are 14 years old."

Research concerned with "age progression" into the future periods has been reported by Israeli.[21] It is difficult to accept the data on age progression without checking the subject's ability to simulate advancing years at nonhypnotic levels. Also, the possibility of role-playing has not been ruled out. It is hard, too, to understand how an individual can relate material that he has never experienced or that has never been "programmed" into his experiential background as data or information.

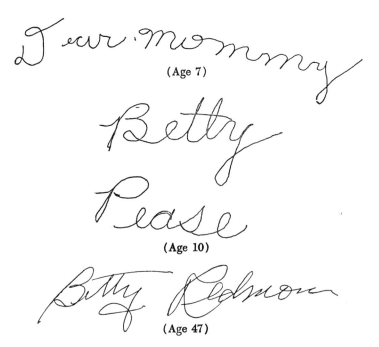

(Age 7)

(Age 10)

(Age 47)

Furthermore, the fact that an individual can be regressed to a previous age by no means indicates that the opposite, namely, age progression, can be achieved. However, a form of "age progression," i.e., pseudo-orientation in time, can be of great clinical value in understanding how a hypnotized subject might react in the future to stressful situations that are suggested at his present chronologic age.

A good example of pseudo-orientation in time from the author's clinical practice is the case of an apprehensive and tense individual who came for consultation for the advisability of having a vasectomy. In deep hypnosis he was told that the actual surgery had been performed five years ago; an amnesia for the posthypnotic hallucination was given. He was then asked, "How have you been feeling since you were sterilized?" He replied, "Oh, Doctor! I haven't had a good night's sleep since my operation. It's made me very tense and nervous." After dehypnotization and removal of the hallucinatory experience, he was advised to postpone surgery until deeply repressed and meaningful material could be worked through. By such measures he was able to accept the consequences of the proposed surgery and ultimately achieved better personality integration.

HYPNOTIC ANALGESIA AND ANESTHESIA

Analgesia, or the first stage of anesthesia, is characterized by a lack of startle reaction, facial flinch and grimaces. Although insensitivity to pain can be simulated readily, hypnotized persons seem to withstand more discomfort and pain than would otherwise be possible. Hypnoanalgesia is more effective than the "built-in" or voluntary control of pain. Soothing verbalizations suggesting insensitivity often can result in analgesia and occasionally in anesthesia. Hysterical anasthesia is obviously the "other side of the coin" of hypnoanesthesia.

Anesthesia refers to a complete lack of awareness of pain. The question arises as to whether hypnoanalgesia and hypnoanesthesia are due to amnesia, or whether the sensory threshold is increased due to roleplaying. Electromyographic studies indicate

that in hypnosis the pain is present in the tissues, but there is no awareness of it. Theories of pain transmission have been revised on the basis of comparison between relief of pain by lobotomy, opiates, placebos and hypnosis.[1]

Since the physiologic reactions to painful stimuli, such as increased heart rate, respiration and galvanic skin reflexes, are diminished, hypnoanesthesia apparently is genuine.[12, 38] It has been shown further that there is a positive relationship between the depth of hypnosis and the degree of induced anesthesia.[46]

HYPERESTHESIA

Hyperesthesia refers to increased sensitivity to touch. It is noted commonly in hysterics. That there is a wide variability in pain perception indicates that subjective interpretation of pain is not a reliable indicator of hyperesthesia or, for that matter, of anesthesia. Hyperesthesia may be due to a lowered threshold to discomfort.[1]

Hyperesthesia is produced hypnotically as follows: "Imagine that you are in your own bathroom. Would you mind describing the location and the color of your bathtub?" ("It is next to the toilet, and it is a white one.") "Now you will turn the hot water faucet on. Which one is it?" ("It is the left one.") "Notice the steaming *hot* water filling up the tub." (The patient nods.) "Now will you place your toes in the water to see how *hot* it is?" A good patient will grimace with discomfort. If he states, "I didn't feel the heat," one can use a posthypnotic suggestion, such as, "You will feel a sensation of warmth when you are able to imagine your foot in the tub of hot water. Perhaps it will be at the next session."

Cutaneous hyperesthesia usually is induced readily in emotionally disturbed individuals. Those who have organic pain syndromes are more sensitive to hypnotically suggested discomfort. Thus, it can be hypothesized that pain is not necessarily a fixed response to a hurtful stimulus, but rather that its perception is modified by our past experiences and expectations, and more subtly by our cultural attitudes. Thus, pain is synthesized out of present thoughts, fears and motivations. In support of these views, it has been noted that placebos are more effective in persons whose stress and anxiety are greatly intensified.[3a] Their effectiveness is due largely to reducing the anxiety component associated with pain.

POSTHYPNOTIC HALLUCINATIONS

Negative and positive hallucinations involving any one of the senses can be produced, as in dreams, by appropriate suggestions. In deep somnambulism, the eyes may be opened without affecting the depth of the hypnosis. A good subject can be made to "see" a person, to "hear" a voice, or to be "deaf" to spoken words, as discussed on page 11.

During deep hypnosis, there is a hyperacuity of all the senses, at least for the suggestions of the operator. As a result, there apparently is an increase in vision, hearing, touch and smell, which is greater than can be demonstrated at nonhypnotic levels.[11] Color-blindness, tubular vision, scotomata and even "total blindness" have been induced. "Deafness," in varying degrees, involving one or both ears, has been described.[26, 29] Similarly, taste and smell have been altered.

Many of the hallucinations are difficult to distinguish from those produced by everyday experiences and distortions. It is contended that the hallucinations are due to elicitation of organic reaction patterns or, in some instances, to simulation[2b] or roleplaying.[9] Since various brain formations, as the temperature center, may be influenced by posthypnotic suggestions involving hallucinatory experiences of coldness, the first explanation may be correct.

Posthypnotic hallucinations are produced as follows: "Perhaps you might enjoy opening your eyes and still remain in a deep, relaxed state. You will see everything that is suggested to you. At first everything will be blurry, and then the various things I suggest will get much clearer." It is a good idea to begin first with simple hallucinations of objects which fit into the immediate environment, such as an imaginary ashtray or desk.

One can first suggest, while the subject still has his eyes closed, that he "see" the ashtray on the operator's desk (it is vividly described), and he is to indicate when he sees it. It is then suggested: "After you open your eyes, you will see the ashtray on my desk just as I described it. Also, you will be able to walk around and look at it, pick it up, examine it and describe it."

SOMNAMBULISM

Somnambulism is one of the deepest stages of hypnosis. It also is observed in sleepwalkers who have no recollection of their nocturnal experiences. Nearly everyone has had a roommate who talked in his sleep. A conversation can be carried on for some time without any recollection on the part of the sleeper. He can even respond to posthypnotic suggestions. It is surprising how many such individuals will perform various acts later without ever realizing how they were suggested. Most of these individuals are "natural" somnambulists who exhibit many hypnotic phenomena *without* going through formalistic hypnotic induction. These persons can develop spontaneous analgesia and anesthesia, dissociation and depersonalization. Some are classified erroneously as multiple personalities.

Somnambulism generally is associated with amnesia; acts are performed without subsequent recollection. The subject appears to be in a dreamlike state; however, somnambulism is not sleep. Recognition of the objective signs of the somnambulistic stage are described below.

The somnambulist still retains generalized memory but cannot remember the events that occurred during hypnosis. Hypnotically inserted suggestions automatically become convictions in the somnambule. Because of the extensive cortical inhibition, the subject has no knowledge of how the convictions were established. As a result, the hypnotically induced convictions prevent incoming sensory information from being tested against reality! This inability of the subject to appraise the operator's suggestions, together with the amnesia, explains somnambulism.

The first thing to do when developing somnambulism is to get the subject to open his eyes without affecting the depth of hypnosis. The method for this was described above. Next, an amnesia must be produced if it has not occurred spontaneously. Finally, the subject must be cued to respond to a specific posthypnotic suggestion.

The nature of the cue can vary, depending upon whether hetero or autohypnosis is utilized. In the former, a touch on the right shoulder can be the signal to reinduce somnambulism at the next session. Frequently, without saying a single word, the author makes use of a cue such as merely lifting the subject's arm. If it becomes cataleptic (the arm-drop test), deep hypnosis has been induced. The subject can use a count-down method from 100 to zero—as the numbers decrease, the hypnosis will get deeper and deeper until somnambulism is reached. Somnambulism often can be transformed into sleep, and vice versa.

AUTOMATIC WRITING

Automatic writing, too, occurs at nonhypnotic levels. "Doodling" while conversing on the telephone is a common manifestation of this phenomenon. The material produced by a good subject's automatic writing has considerable meaningfulness to the hypnotized patient. The hypnotherapist can make good use of its symbolic meaning, especially when working with those who cannot express themselves.

Specifically, the subject is told that the dissociated hand holding the pencil will write even while he is engaged in conversation. It will do so without any attempt being made by him to control its movements. He is also instructed that he will have no knowledge of what is being written; that after being dehypnotized he will understand that the significance of the material appears nonsensical or cryptic, and that it can be interpreted by the subject in a subsequent session.

The actual verbalization for establishing dissociated handwriting is: "Your hand will get numb and cold; it is losing all feeling, all sensation and all movement. You do not feel your hand as I rub it—it is getting very numb, and the hand no longer feels attached to your wrist. Now, as you raise your arm, it will feel as if the hand is no longer attached to your arm. You no longer have any control over your hand. However, your hand can remember everything about you. If you cannot remember something in particular about yourself, your hand will be able to remember it, and write out the answer. If it is too painful for you to face or talk about it, your hand will write it. If you do not tell the truth, your hand will write the correct answer without you controlling it. Nor will you know what the hand is writing. However, after the relaxed state is terminated, you will easily recognize what you have written."

TIME DISTORTION

Time distortion is one of the most interesting and clinically valuable phenomena of hypnosis. It refers to the remarkable capacity of the human brain to appreciate time, condense time or expand time.

Everyone has a "clock" in his brain that is capable of judging time with extraordinary accuracy. All of us have had the experience of arising at a much earlier hour than usual to do something we enjoy, and often we can wake up within several minutes of the designated hour. This indicates, of course, that many of us can estimate time at nonhypnotic levels with great precision.

Time can drag while one is waiting for a cab on a cold, rainy day, even though it is due in two minutes. In this instance, two minutes can seem like 20 minutes (time expansion). Contrarily, when one is pleasantly engaged in conversation with an old friend while waiting for a cab, 20 minutes can pass as if they were only two minutes (time contraction). It is maintained that a drowning man recapitulates whole segments of his life in a few split seconds. Thus, the brain obviously has the capacity to condense a considerable amount of memorial data even at nonhypnotic levels.

In a good subject, time distortion can be induced readily through posthypnotic suggestions. Briefly, one minute of subjective or experiential time can be equated to 10 minutes of world or clock or chronologic time (time lengthening). Or, 10 minutes of clock time can be condensed to one minute of subjective or experiential time (time contraction). The phenomenon of time distortion utilized in hypnotherapy has been described by Cooper and Erickson.[7]

Posthypnotic suggestions to induce time distortion are given as follows: "Every minute of actual time will *seem* like 10 minutes to you. Time will go by very, very slowly; it will seem like an eternity. Every five minutes that you remain in this deep and relaxed state *seem* almost as long as an hour. If you wish, in less than 10 minutes you can see almost an entire motion picture again, and *really* see it better than when you actually saw it."

SUMMARY

The important phenomena associated with hypnosis have been discussed briefly. Since they also occur at so-called nonhypnotic levels, hypnotic phenomena follow the natural laws of thought and behavior. Current and past literature is replete with many ingenious methodologies for obtaining hypnotic phenomena. Their fundamental characteristics have been discussed. These phenomena are elicited in various combinations, depending upon the therapeutic or experimental situation, the personality and the motivations of the subject, and also, of course, upon the skill, the empathy and the personality of the operator.

REFERENCES

1. Barber, T. X.: Toward a theory of pain: relief of chronic pain by prefrontal leucotomy, opiates, placebos and hypnosis, Psychol. Bull. *56*:430-460, 1951.
2. ——: Hypnosis as perceptual–cognitive restructuring: I. Analysis of concepts, J.C.E.H. *5*:147-166, 1957.
2a. ——: Hypnosis as perceptual–cognitive restructuring: II. Post-hypnotic behavior, J.C.E.H. *6*:10-20, 1958.
2b. ——: The after images of "hallucinated" and "imagined" colors, J. Abnorm. & Social Psychol. *59*:136-139, 1959.
3. ——: The good hypnotic subject, Science Digest *43*:36-41, 1958.
3a. Beecher, H. K.: Role of stress in placebo and drug effectiveness, Science *132*:91-92, 1960.
4. Birenbaum: Den Vergessen einer Vornahme; Isolierte seelische Systeme und dynamische Gesamtbereiche, Psychol. Forsch. *13*:218-284, 1930.
5. Cheek, D. B.: Unconscious perception of meaningful sounds during surgical anesthesia as revealed under hypnosis, J. Am. Soc. Clin. Hypnosis *1*:101-113, 1959.
6. Conn, J. H.: Meanings and motivations associated with spontaneous hypnotic regression, J.C.E.H. *1*:21-44, 1958.
7. Cooper, L. F., and Erickson, M. H.: Time Distortion in Hypnosis, Baltimore, Williams & Wilkins, 1954.
8. Dittborn, J.: Expectation as a factor of sleep suggestibility, J.C.E.H. *6*:164-170, 1958.
9. Dorcus, R. M.: Modification by suggestion of some vestibular and visual responses, Am. J. Psychol. *49*:82-87, 1937.
10. ——: Recall under hypnosis of amnestic events, International J.C.E.H. *7*:57-61, 1960.
11. Doupe, J., et al.: Vasomotor reactions in the hypnotic state, J. Neurol. & Psychiat. *2*: 97-106, 1939.
12. Dynes, J. B.: An experimental study in hypnotic anesthesia, J. Abnorm. & Social Psychol. *27*:79-88, 1932.
13. Erickson, M. H., and Erickson, E. M.: Concerning the nature and character of posthypnotic behavior, J. Gen. Psychol. *24*:95-133, 1941.
14. Fisher, S.: The role of expectancy in the performance of posthypnotic behavior, J. Abnorm. & Social Psychol. *49*:503-507, 1954.
15. Fontan, J., and Segard, C.: Eléments de Medecine suggestive, Hypnotisme, et Suggestion: Faits Cliniques, Paris, C. Douin, 1887.
16. Gidro-Frank, L., and Bowers Buch, M. K.: A study of the plantar response in hypnotic age regression, J. Nerv. & Ment. Dis. *107*: 443-458, 1948.
17. Gindes, B. C.: New Concepts of Hypnosis, New York, Julian Press, 1951.
18. Gurney, E.: Peculiarities of certain posthypnotic states, Proc. Psych. Res. Soc. London *4*:268-323, 1886-7.
19. Guze, H.: The involvement of the hypnotist in the hypnotic session, J.C.E.H. *4*: 61-68, 1956.
20. Hilgard, E. R., et al.: Individual differences in susceptibility to hypnosis, Proc. Nat. Acad. Sc. *44*:125-159, 1958.
21. Israeli, N.: Experimental study of hypnotic imagination and dreams of projection in time: 1. Outlook upon the remote future extending through the quintillionth year, J.C.E.H. *1*:49-60, 1953.
22. Janet, P.: L'Automatisme Psychologique, Paris, F. Alcan, 1889.
23. Kellogg, E. R.: Duration and effects of posthypnotic suggestion, J. Exper. Psychol. *12*:502-514, 1929.
24. Kline, M. V.: Hypnotic retrogression: a neuropsychologic theory of regression and progression, J.C.E.H. *1*:21-28, 1953.

25. ——: Hypnotic age regression and psychotherapy: clinical and theoretical observations, International J.C.E.H. 8:117-136, 1960.

26. Kline, M. V., *et al.*: An experimental study of the nature of hypnotic deafness: effects of delayed speech feedback, J.C.E.H. 2:145-157, 1954.

27. Lewin, K., *et al.*: Mit Vorbemerkungen über die psychische Kräfte und Energien und die Struktur der Seele, Psychol. Forsch. 7:294-385, 1938.

28. Lindner, H.: The shared neurosis, hypnotist and subject, Internat. J.C.E.H. 7:61-71, 1960.

29. Malmo, R. B., *et al.*: Electromyographic study of hypnotic deafness, J.C.E.H. 2:305-318, 1954.

30. Marcuse, F. L.: Hypnosis: Fact and Fiction, Baltimore, Penguin, 1959.

31. Moody, R. L.: Bodily changes during abreaction, Lancet, 254-964, 1948.

32. Moss, C. S.: Therapeutic suggestion and autosuggestion, J.C.E.H. 6:109-115, 1958.

32a. Orne, M. T.: The mechanism of age regression: an experimental study, J. Abnorm. & Social Psychol. 46:213-225, 1951.

33. Patten, E. F.: The duration of posthypnotic suggestions, J. Abnorm. & Social Psychol. 25:319-334, 1930.

34. Rubenstein, R., and Newman, R.: The living out of "future experiences" under hypnosis, Science 119:472-473, 1954.

35. Schneck, J. M.: Dynamic hypnotic regression, Am. J. Psychiat. 113:178, 1956.

36. ——: Special aspects of hypnotic regression and revivification, Internat. J.C.E.H. 8:37-42, 1960.

37. Sears, A. B.: A comparison of hypnotic and waking recall, J.C.E.H. 2:296-305, 1954.

38. Sears, R. R.: An experimental study of hypnotic anesthesia, J. Exper. Psychol. 15:1-22, 1932.

39. Sidis, B.: The value of the method of hypnoidization in the diagnosis and treatment of psychopathic disorders, Medical Times, 47:245-250, 1919.

40. Solovey, G., and Milechnin, A.: Hypnosis in everyday life, Dis. Nerv. System 28:1-7, 1957.

40a. Von Neumann, J.: The Computer and the Brain, Yale Univ. Press, New Haven, 1958.

41. Weitzenhoffer, A.: A note on the persistence of hypnotic suggestion, J. Abnorm. & Social Psychol. 45:160-162, 1950.

42. ——: Posthypnotic behavior and the recall of the hypnotic suggestion, J.C.E.H. 5:41-58, 1957.

43. Weitzenhoffer, A. M.: Hypnotism: An Objective Study in Suggestibility, New York, Wiley, 1953.

44. Weitzenhoffer, A. M., and Weitzenhoffer, G. B.: Personality and hypnotic Susceptibility, Am. J. Clin. Hypnosis 1:79-82, 1958.

45. West, L. J.: Psychophysiology of hypnosis. J.A.M.A. 172:672-675, 1960.

46. West, L. J., Niell, K. C., and Hardy, J. D.: Effects of hypnotic suggestion on pain perception and galvanic skin response, A.M.A. Arch. Neurol. & Psychiat. 68:549, 1952.

ADDITIONAL REFERENCES

Christenson, J.: An operational approach to hypnosis, J.C.E.H. 4:89-91, 1956.

Solovey, G., and Milechnin, A.: Concerning the nature of hypnotic phenomena, J.C.E.H. 5:67-76, 1957.

SUPPLEMENTARY READING

As, A., and Lauer, L. W.: A factor-analytic study of hypnotizability and related personal experiences, Inter. J. Clin. Exper. Hypnosis 10:169-183, 1962.

Barber, T. X.: The concept of "hypnosis," J. Psychol. 45:115, 1958.

——: Hypnotic age regression: a critical review, Psychosomatic Med. 24:286-300, 1962.

Friedman, H., *et al.*: Direct current potentials in hypnoanalgesia, Arch. Gen. Psychiat. 7:193-198, 1962.

Gebhard, J. W.: Hypnotic age-regression: a review, Am. J. Clin. Hypnosis 3:139-169, 1961.

Lerner, M.: Comparative aspects of human and animal hypnosis, Am. J. Clin. Hypnosis 5:52-57, 1962.

McCord, H.: The "image" of the trance, Inter. J. Clin. Exper. Hypnosis 9:305-309, 1961.

Weitzenhoffer, A. M.: Some speculations regarding the nature and character of hypnotic behavior, Am. J. Clin. Hypnosis 4:69-90, 1961.

3

Theories

Even though hypnosis has always been an enigma, it is still one of the seven wonders of psychology. As in the fable of the elephant who was touched in different places by the four blind men, each investigator formulates a different theory. As long as theories differ about the nature of human behavior, there will be different theories about hypnosis. This reasoning is based on the premise that hypnotic phenomena are an integral part of all human behavior and, since this is not understood as yet, we must try to explain what we can deal with objectively.

Then, too, nearly all current theories mistakenly attempt to explain the induction procedure and the resultant hypnotic responses together. This is patently impossible, since they are separate and distinct entities which involve both the hypnotist and the patient. Not to recognize its dual nature is like trying to include a surgical procedure and an anesthetic induction in a unified theory. The following review covers the more important theories on hypnosis.

ATAVISTIC HYPOTHESIS: IMMOBILIZATION THEORIES

Kroger and Freed[20] suggested that hypnotic behavior or response is an atavism that at one time may have been necessary in humans as a protective defense mechanism to ward off fear or danger. This theory was based on Pavlov's[24] observation that "the phenomenon represents a self-protecting reflex of an inhibitory character." He observed that an animal's only chance of salvation is to remain *immobile* in order to escape detection. From observations in dogs, he recognized that hypnosis is an adaptive response mechanism involving higher nervous activity, which evolved to its present form dur-

ing the course of phylogenetic development. His theory is discussed more fully below.

More recently, the atavistic hypothesis was reinstituted by Meares,[22a] who mentions that "hypnosis was a return to a more primitive form of mental functioning in which suggestion plays a major role. . . . Anything, word or act, which tends to aid in this regression, will aid the induction of hypnosis." The atavism hypothesis, the subjective nature of hypnosis, and other formulations will be discussed in the light of the development of brain-computer analogies and functioning in Chapter 30.

Hypnosis has been compared with the catalepsy or tonic immobilization noted in animals. Though induced differently in animals, tonic immobilization is produced chiefly by physical and instinctual factors. In humans, it results from these factors interacting with the symbolic meaningfulness of words. Human and animal hypnosis are dissimilar in that repetitive induction in the animal decreases hypnotic susceptibility, whereas in humans it increases it.

In general, any powerful stimulus such as fright causes certain animals or humans to "freeze up." Thus, the "death-feint" theory[26] postulates that minimal self-awareness is experienced when environmental contact is reduced or eliminated; a more primitive level of psychophysiologic functioning is developed. It is also contended that the retention, to some degree, of this capacity to achieve hypnosis, either with or without external measures, is not limited merely to humans but is characteristic of other biologic forms of life. However, this theory does not explain how hypnosis occurs. Similarly, hypnosis has been defined as "a state of readiness for emotional action increasingly subordinated to cortical influence as one ascends phylogeny, but nonetheless consistently present in animal organisms in a variety of forms."[14]

HYPNOSIS AS A STATE OF HYSTERIA

Hypnosis was once considered to be a symptom of hysteria—only hysterical individuals were hypnotizable.[7] The formulations leading to this conclusion were made on only a few cases in a pathologic setting, and the hypothesis was discredited by the fact that susceptibility to hypnosis is not pathognomonic of neurosis: normal individuals are readily hypnotizable.[6] Although hysterics are more suggestible than normal individuals, it does not necessarily follow that increased suggestibility is a sign of hysteria.

THEORIES BASED ON CHANGES IN CEREBRAL PHYSIOLOGY

Many theories contend that hypnosis is due to a changed physiology of the cerebral cortex: inhibition of the ganglion cells of the brain;[16] inhibition of one set of mental functions and excitation of others;[35] cerebral anemia;[15] shift of nervous energies of the central nervous system to the vasomotor system;[22] and vasomotor decerebration involving anemia of the frontal lobes.[28] Others[21] contend that hypnosis is due to a focus of central excitation with surrounding areas of inhibition (or nonexcitation). Another theory[10] posits that hypnosis is due to "synaptic ablation": neural impulses are directed into a smaller number of channels (selective attention).

Psychophysiologic data are lacking to substantiate that anemia of the brain or a shift of nervous impulses accounts for hypnosis. If hypnosis is due to a shift of one set of mental functions, what produces it? If it is due to anemia, then anemic individuals should be readily hypnotizable. Finally, if the cerebral blood flow is decreased during hypnosis, fainting rather than somnambulism should be produced.[21a]

HYPNOSIS AS A CONDITIONED PROCESS LEADING TO SLEEP

A large body of evidence can be adduced to indicate that hypnosis is due to alterations in cortical neuron fields, primarily because of its similarity to sleep, dissociative states and conditioned reflexes. Pavlov[24] says that in hypnosis we are *not dealing with complete sleep,* but only with "partial sleep." He noted that spreading and deepening of the localized areas of inhibition over the cortex produced varying degrees of hypnosis, which ultimately led to *real sleep.* Since pavlovian concepts are exerting a profound effect in the Western world, the reader is strongly urged to read Pavlov's contributions to hypnosis, and those of his disciples, rather than the writings of those who misquote these researchers.[24, 24a]

According to Pavlov's classification, those stimuli directly affecting the sense organs constitute the primary signal system of both men and animals. Those signals or words belonging to the secondary signal system are characteristic for man alone and exert their conditioned effects via the primary signal system. Thus, words can become conditioned stimuli, which may in turn produce physiologic reactions. For example, a word (signal or cue) becomes the stimulus for conditioned reflexes of a physiologic nature. These in turn are copies of built-in or organic reflexes already present in the organism. Both systems are governed by similar laws. Pavlov correctly observed that the various gradations of hypnosis hardly differed physiologically from the wakeful state and that its ever-increasing mobility depended on even insignificant variations of environmental stimuli. In accord with recent findings described in later chapters, Pavlov hinted that lower brain stem mechanisms were involved in hypnotic conditioning.

Another theory,[4] similar in part to Pavlov's hypothesis, contends that hypnotic phenomena result from the symbolic or experiential conditioning by words. Such a theory of conditioning is inadequate to explain hypnosis, because it has to postulate that some degree of hypnosis is present so that successful conditioning can take place. The proponents of this theory do not elucidate whether the phenomena occur from conditioning of a preexisting hypnosis or whether the hypnosis is produced by conditioning.

Just as many authorities[18] believe that there is no relationship between sleep and hypnosis and that the latter is due merely to hypersuggestibility. If there is any similarity between sleep and hypnosis, then it would be better to start an induction procedure with the individual asleep! Even though some investigators[3] have been able to convert light sleep to hypnosis, this does not prove that the two are identical. Hypnosis is not a transitional state between sleeping and waking: Experimental data show a rapid decrement in motor response and reflexes during sleep. During deep sleep, conditioned reflexes or physiologic responses to a repeatedly given stimulus cannot be established, whereas in hypnosis the learning of conditioned reflexes is enhanced over and above that of the nonhypnotic state.

During normal sleep, suggestibility is decreased markedly, rapport is lost and memories are ablated. The whole concept of sleep, when it is applied to hypnosis, obscures rather than clarifies the issues. The subject appears to be asleep because he thinks that he should look and act as if he is asleep. Also, there is a considerable amount of literature on blood pressure, reflexes and physiochemical studies which further indicates that hypnosis more closely resembles complete wakefulness.

A hypnotized person is more alert to his environment than when he is asleep. Kline[19a] remarks, "A patient in hypnosis becomes more critical, more articulate; he is not to be thought of as stuporous even though he may have, as Freud describes it, an expression of stuporification. Behind the sleeplike characteristics of some hypnotic states lies an acuteness, an intensity, and a productivity that far exceed those of the nonhypnotic state." This is why it is a helpful adjunct in therapy: a relaxed patient concentrates more effectively and thus becomes increasingly more receptive to the communications and feelings of the therapist as well as to his own thoughts. The most convincing evidence that hypnosis is characterized by hyperacuity is that nearly all hypnotic phenomena occur as everyday happenings. However, if the operator uses a technic which emphasizes sleep, then the individual, because he responds experientially to the word "sleep," is apt to enter into a sleeplike state. Thus, in such persons, the EEG findings might resemble those associated with sleep. On the other hand, for the same reasons, an entirely different result is obtained when the word "sleep" is not used.

IDEOMOTOR ACTIVITY AND INHIBITION THEORY

It is contended by several authors[1, 11, 36] that the effects of suggestibility are the resultant of ideomotor action and inhibition; also that suggestibility is merely an experience of imagining that which is actualized through ideomotor activities.[1] Although this theory, to a degree, accounts for physical reactions and even for some of the psychological reactions noted during hypnosis, it fails to explain the complex psychological reactions elicited during hypnosis.

THE DISSOCIATION THEORY

For many years it was contended that the hypnotized individual was in a dissociated state: certain areas of behavior were split off from the main stream of awareness. Accordingly, hypnosis abolished volitional control and, as a result, the individual responded only with autonomic behavior on a reflex level. If the dissociation theory were valid, then amnesia could not be removed by suggestions of the operator. Furthermore, the amnesia would always occur spontaneously.

This theory fell into oblivion when it was demonstrated that more often, instead of amnesia or dissociation, there was a hyperacuity and a better co-ordination of all the senses during hypnosis. Thus, although some degree of dissociation occurs in amnesia, it by no means indicates that dissociation produces hypnosis or is similar to it.

THE ROLE-PLAYING THEORY

One current theory,[33] widely held by psychologists, is that the person in hypnosis plays a role, that is, he acts as he believes a hypnotized person should act. Esdaile,[9] who had such remarkable success with hypnoanesthesia, once made these particularly cogent remarks:

I see two ways only of accounting for it. My patients, on returning home, either say to their friends, similarly afflicted, "What a soft man the doctor is! He cut me to pieces for 20 minutes and I made him believe that I did not feel it. Isn't it a capital joke? Do go and play him the same trick," or they may say to their brother sufferers, "Look at me; I have got rid of my burden"—20, 30, 40, 50, 60 or 80 lb., as it may be (scrotal tumors)—"I am restored to the use of my body and can work for my bread. This, I assure you, the doctor did when I was asleep, and I knew nothing about it."

Hypnosis is not wholly the result of goal-directed striving, but is due rather to sensory proof of the reality that an altered state has been produced. The role-playing theory does not explain how the pupils can be conditioned under hypnosis to contract involuntarily to a hallucinated light.

Although some simulation occurs through identification with that which the patient has seen, the role-playing theory does not explain how hypnosis can raise the sensory threshold during hypnoanesthesia. Nor can it account for a naïve subject's spontaneously developing a Babinski reflex (which is present up to the age of 2 or 3) when regressed to a very early age. Also, if hypnosis were due to role-playing, then psychoneurotics, in desperate need of hypnotherapy, would ordinarily make the best subjects. That this is not so negates this theory. Multiple personalities, who are not actors, readily switch from one role to another. The greatest Thespian would be ashamed by the facility with which this is accomplished during hypnosis.

THE REGRESSION THEORY

Another theory[12] still held currently is that hypnosis is essentially a regression to infancy, in which the operator assumes the role of a parent. This concept implies that, if the therapist assumed the character of the favored parent, he could readily hypnotize his patient. This is not borne out by objective observations. Theoretically, the child who had a domineering father should be easily hypnotized by an authoritarian approach. If his parents were kind, then a permissive technic should prove highly effective. This theory is based upon naïve speculations, and its proponents are unable to correlate either the depth or successful incidence of hypnotic induction with the supposed parent-child relationship. Furthermore, if this theory were valid, men would be better hypnotists than women. Experimental data[30] indicate little difference: a good subject is hypnotizable by either a male or a female operator. Also because this theory disregards hypnosis as a subjective response, it cannot account for autohypnosis and those spontaneous alterations in awareness which simulate hypnosis.

However, even though hypnosis in certain instances might involve transference phenomena (the process by which the patient transfers to the therapist emotions which he felt for some other person), they are very likely only incidental to it. Transference probably is facilitated by the intense interpersonal relationship or rapport rather than by irrational submission to a father-figure with abandonment of executive control.[27]

Another theory[8] postulates that, as the result of increased motivation and retrogression, greater manipulation of the subject is possible; the elicited phenomena occur because of the peculiar responsiveness in the subject at the time. Since actual retrogression is not always present unless specifically suggested, hypnotic phenomena can in part be attributed more to motivation than to retrogression.

There are many combinations of the transference theories that have just been described. Some stress fascination or sensual attraction as an important factor; others consider that hypnosis is due to erotic elements in the doctor-patient relationship. If this were true, then a male hypnotized by a male operator would be a potential homosexual. If there is anything to this theory, then a necessary prerequisite for successful hypnosis would be fascination or sensual attraction. If it were true, all lovers would swoon into mutual hypnosis! The sensual-attraction theory thus cannot serve as a generalization for the hypnotic state or hypnotic relationship.[21a]

THE HYPERSUGGESTIBILITY THEORY

Hypersuggestibility has been a popular theory[18, 31] for explaining hypnosis. The fact that the attention span is narrowed to the words of the operator and, as a result, his suggestions become more effective only explains the phenomena and not how hypersuggestibility actually occurs. It does not explain the spontaneous occurrence of amnesia or other bizarre nonsuggested symptoms as hallucinations. The hypersuggestibility theory, by inference, also implies that only gullible people are suggestible. This is not the case.

It has been suggested that hypnosis is due to direct or prestige suggestion involving heightened receptive states, that the effects of suggestion during such emotional states are identical with those obtained in hypnosis. As proof, the influence of demagogues on mob psychology and the persuasive effect of orators and salesmen have been compared with hypnosis. Although strong persuasion is one factor for successful salesmanship, salesmen do not produce somnambulism, actual hallucinations or anesthesia.

MISCELLANEOUS THEORIES

Another theory[17] states that words are represented in consciousness as symbolic processes to control internal functionings, particularly those which are inhibited by the cranial and the sacral subdivisions of the autonomic nervous system. These mechanisms are integrated through the rhinencephalon (visceral brain) and the subcortical structures. This theory is, in part, similar to the Bechterew[4] hypothesis.

More speculative formulations contend that hypnosis is due to psychokinetic field forces, involving cortical areas through extrasensory perceptions in a manner similar to oscillating electromagnetic fields.[23] Various psychophysiologic theories[25, 32] have been proposed. Roberts[25] contends that the suggestions of the operator become the positive content of mental experience, which the subject cannot check against his own percepts because these have been blocked out of awareness. Interruption between the brain-stem reticular formation and the specific sensory, parasensory and co-ordinated neuronal channels results in hypnosis. Blocking of the neural channels between cortex and midbrain results in inhibition.

Roberts believes that the central nervous system is thus immobilized because the activating system has been deprived of the data—sensory, somesthetic, sensorimotor, affective, intentive, mnemonic—requisite to the normal direction of psychic activity and responses. The capacity for integration,

higher elaboration, and response, however, is maintained by means of the continued activity of the brain-stem reticular formation and the elaborative and effector areas of the cortex.

Similarly, West[32] believes:

The information inserted into the restricted area of the subject's awareness by the hypnotist, through his suggestions, is accepted as reality to a greater or lesser extent, depending on the subject's dissociation of other information from awareness, moment by moment.

These formulations have considerable merit. The brain functions similarly to a data-processing apparatus, which, when unable to validate incoming information (sensory percepts) against stored data (memories, impressions) causes unreality to be interpreted as reality. The degree to which hypnosis occurs depends to a great extent upon the degree of cortical inhibition. This constitutes the dynamism of hypnotic behavior brought about by the intricacies of the hypnotic interpersonal relationship.

Such mechanisms correlate closely with behavioral manifestations such as the misdirection of attention proposed by Gindes[13] which is nothing more than the reduction of the subject's critical faculties—an aspect of cortical inhibition. He believes that misdirected attention (getting the subject to concentrate his attention upon something irrelevant to the actual hypnosis so that he is unable to harbor doubt), together with belief and expectation—all catalyzed by the imagination—produce hypnosis. The sensory changes or the phenomena become effective through distortion of the imaginative processes.

It has been suggested by Barber[2] that hypnosis is not a "state" or a "trance," nor is it due to "subconscious motivation." It is not "unconscious awareness" nor produced as the result of "suggestion."[2] Rather, it is based upon an interpersonal relationship (belief and faith)* in which the operator restructures the "perceptions" and the "conceptions" (imagination)* of the subject because the subject is relatively inattentive to his environment (misdirection of atten-

* The parenthetic explanations are those of the author of this book.

tion).* This results because the subject (due to an expectant attitude) is ready, willing and able to "literally think as the operator wants him to think." Such "perceptual-cognitive restructuring" rather than "suggestion" is the essential element responsible for hypnosis.

In hypnosis, the subject behaves differently because he "perceives and conceives differently and thus his behavior is in strict accordance with his altered conceptions of his self and his surroundings."

PSYCHOSOMATIC THEORIES

An elaborate theory[29] hypothesizes that suggestibility and hypnotic phenomena have a multiple origin that is based on psychosomatic processes. The basis for this theory is that suggestibility is ideomotor action, which, in itself, is a form of abstract conditioning. Everything is included "in dissociation of awareness," except the words of the operator, whose voice becomes an extension of the subject's psychic processes, resulting in a large variety of perceptual alterations.

Another author[34] states that hypnotic phenomena are due to a psychosomatic reaction consisting of a reciprocal and a dynamic interaction of physiologic and psychological factors. It is considered that, in the hypnotic relationship, the individual obtains gratification of earlier dependency needs. Thus, Wolberg[34] states:

In hypnosis, the later adaptational processes are wiped away by the regressive process associated with inhibition of the higher cortical centers.

An ego-psychological theory of hypnosis has been formulated recently.[5] Hypnosis is seen as a special type of self-excluding function of the ego. A change occurs from conscious perception to preconscious functioning, akin to the performance of routine activities, and this is regarded as a "topological regression."

Most of the above theories, even though inadequate in many respects, contain some facet of truth. However, hypnosis cannot be explained by any single factor, as cortical inhibition, hypersuggestibility, atavism, regression, death-feint, dissociation, dependency or transference because, like any behavioral process, it cross-fertilizes with many areas of human thinking. Also, many psychological and physical factors, acting reciprocally through the imaginative processes, induce the perceptual response called hypnosis.

Hypnosis cannot be produced with greater frequency in individuals with passive, infantile needs. Nor does a regression of the personality necessarily occur from the hypnosis per se. The dependency relationship is no more an essential feature of hypnosis than that present in all doctor-patient relationships, even at nonhypnotic levels.

From the foregoing, it is apparent that hypnosis is not literally a sharply delineated state, but a fluctuating process which, like any altered state of awareness, depends upon the degree of arousal or perceptivity induced by the hypnotist. What is referred to as the hypnotic state must be differentiated from the hypnotic interpersonal relationship, even though the latter developed from the hypnosis. The capacity to enter into hypnosis is as subjective and naturalistic a phenomenon as sleep; both presumably developed as phylogenetic adaptive response mechanisms.

During hypnosis, the excitatory cortical areas can be conditioned to remain selectively "awake" to specific sensory percepts (selective attention), while other cortical areas which are partially or completely inhibited prevent access to the stored or experiential data (selective inattention).

In the presence of the proper mental-set, new conditioned responses can be "built in" the organism on the basis of new convictions compounded upon prior invoked beliefs (the ideomotor and ideosensory responses). Under these conditions, "unreality becomes reality" and the "conviction of hypnosis leads to hypnosis," as there is no other way to think.

The processing, storage and retrieval of information in hypnosis can be understood better from the study of brain-machine (computer) analogies. The brain acts in hypnosis according to the same principles set down by the physical sciences for the design of communication equipment. Thus, greater receptivity (produced by fixation of attention, relaxation and concentration) in a receptor (the subject) enables messages (sensory inputs or percepts, i.e., information) to be received clearly from a transmitter (the operator) with a minimal degree of interference (noise), either in the external environmental communication pathways (channel) or in the internal sensory receptors of the subject. This allows greater self-objectivity and self-exploration of subjective thoughts, feelings and attitudes. Thus, hypnosis is an adaptive response mechanism which enhances the transmission of ideas and their understanding in a more effective manner than at ordinary waking levels, at which attention is scattered. For a more complete exposition of this hypothesis, the reader can refer to Chapters 29 and 30.

REFERENCES

1. Arnold, M. B.: On the mechanism of suggestion and hypnosis, J. Abnorm. & Social Psychol. *41*:107-128, 1946.
2. Barber, T. X.: Hypnosis as perceptual-cognitive restructuring: I. Analysis of concepts, J.C.E.H. *5*:147-166, 1957.
3. ——: The concept of hypnosis, J. Psychol. *45*:115-131, 1958.
4. Bechterew, W. V.: What is hypnosis? J. Abnorm. & Social Psychol. *1*:18-25, 1906.
5. Bellak, L.: An ego-psychological theory of hypnosis, Internat. Psychoanalysis *36*:Part 6, 1955.
6. Bernheim, H.: Suggestive Therapeutics, New York, Putnam, 1902.
7. Charcot, J. M.: Lectures on Diseases of the Nervous System, London, New Sydenham Society, 1889.
8. de Milechnin, G. S.: Concerning a theory of hypnosis, J.C.E.H. *4*:37-46, 1956.
9. Esdaile, J.: Mesmerism in India, Hartford, England, S. Andrus & Son, 1850.
10. Estabrook, G. H.: Hypnotism, New York, Dutton, 1943.
11. Eysenck, H. J.: Dimensions of Personality, London, Kegan Paul, 1947.
12. Ferenczi, S.: Introjektion und Uebertragung, Jb. Psychoanalyse *1*:422-457, 1909.
13. Gindes, B. C.: New Concepts of Hypnosis, New York, Julian Press, 1951.
14. Guze, H.: The phylogeny of hypnosis, J.C.E.H. *1*:41, 1953.
15. Hart, E.: Hypnotism and Humbug, Nineteenth Century (as reported by Bramwell), January, 1882.
16. Heidenhain, R.: Hypnotism or Animal Magnetism, London, Kegan Paul, Trench, Trubner, 1906.
17. Howarth, E.: Postscript to a new theory of hypnosis, J.C.E.H. *2*:91-92, 1954.
18. Hull, C. L.: Hypnosis and Suggestibility—An Experimental Approach, New York, Appleton, 1933.
19. Janet, P.: Major Symptoms of Hysteria, New York, Macmillan, 1920.
19a. Kline, M. V.: Freud and Hypnosis, New York, Julian, 1958.
20. Kroger, W. S., and Freed, S. C.: Psychosomatic Gynecology; Including Problems of Obstetrical Care, Chicago, Free Press, 1956; reprinted, Los Angeles, Wilshire Book Co., 1962.
21. Kubie, L. S., and Margolin, S.: The process of hypnotism and the nature of the hypnotic state, Amer. J. Psychiat. *100*: 611-622, 1944.
21a. Marcuse, F. L.: Hypnosis: Fact and Fiction, Baltimore, Penguin, 1959.
22. McDougall, W.: Outline of Abnormal Psychology, New York, Scribner, 1926.
22a. Meares, A.: A System of Medical Hypnosis, Philadelphia, Saunders, 1960.
23. Muftic, M. D.: A contribution to the psychokinetic theory of hypnotism, Brit. J. M. Hypnosis *10*:24-30, 1959.
24. Pavlov, I. P.: Experimental Psychology, New York, Philosophical Library, 1957.
24a. Platonov, K. I.: The Word as a Psychological and Physiological Factor, Moscow, Foreign Languages Pub., 1959.
25. Roberts, D. R.: An electrophysiologic theory of hypnosis, Internat. J.C.E.H. *8*: 43-55, 1960.
26. Schneck, J. M.: A theory of hypnosis. J.C.E.H. *1*:16-17, 1953.
27. Spiegel, H.: Hypnosis in transference, A.M.A. Arch. Gen. Psychiat. *1*:96-101, 1958.
28. Volgyesi, F.: Menschen- und Tierhypnose, Leipzig, Füssli, 1938.
29. Weitzenhoffer, A. M.: Hypnotism—An Objective Study in Suggestibility, New York, Wiley, 1953.
30. Weitzenhoffer, A. M., and Weitzenhoffer, G. B.: Sex, transference and susceptibility to hypnosis, Am. J. Clin. Hypnosis, *1*: 15-24, 1958.
31. Wells, W. R.: Experiments in waking hypnosis for instructional purposes, J. Abnorm. & Social Psychol. *18*:389-404, 1924.
32. West, J. L.: Psychophysiology of hypnosis, J.A.M.A. *172*:672-675, 1960.

33. White, R. W.: A preface to the theory of hypnotism, J. Abnorm. & Social Psychol. *36*:477-505, 1941.
34. Wolberg, L. R.: Medical Hypnosis, Vol. I. The Principles of Hypnotherapy, New York, Grune & Stratton, 1948.
35. Young, P. C.: Experimental hypnotism: a review, Psychol. Bull. *38*:92-104, 1941.

ADDITIONAL REFERENCES

Arnold, M. B.: Brain function in hypnosis, Internat. J.C.E.H. *7*:109-121, 1959.
Barber, T. X.: "Sleep" and "hypnosis": a reappraisal, J.C.E.H. *4*:141-159, 1956.
Das, J. P.: A theory of hypnosis, Internat. J.C.E.H. *7*:69-79, 1959.
Leuba, C.: A reality of hypnotic phenomena—a critique of the role-playing theory of hypnosis, J.C.E.H. *1*:32-39, 1957.
Schneck, J. M.: Transference in hypnotic behavior, J.C.E.H. *3*:132-136, 1955.
Takahashi, R.: An experimental examination of the dissociation hypothesis in hypnosis, J.C.E.H. *6*:139-151, 1958.
Watkins, J. G.: Trance and transference, J.C.E.H. *2*:284-291, 1954.
Weitzenhoffer, G. B.: Femininity and Susceptibility to Hypnosis. In press.

4

Misconceptions

LOSS OF CONSCIOUSNESS

It is imperative to remove *all* the most popular misconceptions about hypnosis before attempting an induction procedure. The most common one held by the laity is that an individual is asleep, unconscious or in a "knocked-out" state. Public exhibitions by the professional stage hypnotist have contributed to the widely held notion that hypnosis is a "trance," "sleeplike" or an "out-of-this-world" state.

Apprehensive patients should be informed that they will never lose their full sense of awareness or fall asleep. Rather, they will be more awake! One should explain carefully that all levels of hypnosis, including the deeper stages, are characterized by *increased attention* to the operator's suggestions, and that this concentration facilitates receptivity to suggestions. Also, that the profound concentration achieved is one of the principal reasons for the use of hypnosis.

Actually, hypnosis has little resemblance to true sleep. Most ideas equating sleep to hypnosis stem from motion-picture films portraying a hypnotized individual with his eyes closed. An explanation that the eyes are closed to facilitate concentration can be be amplified by the following remarks: "Have you ever noted how a music lover at a concert often has his eyes closed while he is listening appreciatively to the performance? Even though he *looks relaxed and asleep,* he is *more alert;* he can even follow a single theme through many variations." This analogy is useful for differentiating between sleep and hypnosis.

The author seldom uses the term "sleep" in his verbalization technic to induce hypnosis, as it only creates confusion. However, many good operators use the word "sleep" as part of their induction technic. Most subjects are intuitively aware, nevertheless, that they are not expected to fall asleep. If, during the induction technic, the term "sleep" is used inadvertently, it can be qualified by stating, "You will feel *as if* you could go to sleep, or *as if* you are about to fall asleep."

Frequently, even after it has been emphasized repeatedly that the hypnotized individual does not fall asleep, patients state, "Doctor, I know I wasn't hypnotized. I heard everything you said." I often remark, "That's right. I wanted you to hear everything that was said. If you heard 100 per cent of what I suggested, you then have a 100 per cent chance of absorbing these suggestions and if you absorbed *all* of these suggestions, there is a much better chance that you will follow these suggestions." This statement, when made in an affirmative manner, clears up any misconception that sleep and hypnosis are synonymous.

SURRENDER OF WILL

Another misconception is that the subject "surrenders his will" to the all-powerful hypnotist. Unfortunately the Svengali-Trilby novel, comic strips and television programs have perpetuated this myth. Since the capacity to be hypnotized is a *subjective* experience, nothing could be further from the truth. Many patients state, "I always thought that under hypnosis I could be made to do anything against my wishes." It is helpful to emphasize that subjects are not dominated by the will of the hypnotist as they are fully capable of making decisions at all times.

Those who fear that hypnosis can weaken their moral code or permanently change their attitudes can be informed that strong persuasion, mass psychology and propaganda (subtle forms of suggestion) are thoroughly capable, especially during wartime, of changing attitudes and behavior. However, it is conceivable that an unscrupulous hypnotist, by producing a total amnesia and establishing a valid motive, could get an individual, already predisposed to lie, steal or kill, to commit a criminal or a social act. Naturally, such circumstances do not exist in the doctor-patient relationship. This will be discussed in more detail in Chapter 21.

WEAKMINDEDNESS

Some still believe that morons, imbeciles and weakminded persons make the best hypnotic subjects. This, too, is a misconception. Rather, it appears that people of above-average intelligence, who are capable of concentrating, usually make the best subjects. Motivation can be increased by stating, "If you are readily hypnotizable, this indicates that you are above average in intelligence."

In this connection, constant hypnotic induction does not weaken the mind nor make an individual more suggestible. Thousands of subjects have been hypnotized hundreds of times without the slightest demonstrable harm.

REVELATION OF SECRETS

Few patients reach the deeper stages of hypnosis if they think that intimate secrets will be revealed, as might occur under anesthesia or truth serum. They should be informed that they will be *aware of everything* while hypnotized and afterward, unless a specific amnesia is suggested. As a result, guilt-laden subjects relax and become more amenable to hypnosis.

FEAR OF NOT BEING DEHYPNOTIZED

Some subjects fear that they will not be "brought out of it." A common question is, "Doctor, what happens if you can't get me out of this?" Another is, "What happens if you should drop dead while I am hypnotized?" These fears can disrupt the interpersonal relationship, and may cause a real resistance to being hypnotized. As mentioned, the patient actually induces the hypnosis through his own convictions. There-

fore, he can readily dehypnotize himself in a split second, if necessary. The author points out that, when posthypnotic suggestions contrary to the wishes of the patient are given, invariably spontaneous dehypnotization occurs and breaks the rapport. One must remember that hypnosis is an *interpersonal* relationship between the therapist and the patient and that it is an *intrapersonal* one for the patient. Often, if the operator merely leaves the room, this causes deeply hypnotized subjects to dehypnotize themselves. Inasmuch as nearly all my patients are taught autohypnosis, they can terminate it at any time. Emphasizing this fact allays their fears, anxieties and tensions.

CONFUSION BETWEEN HYPNOTIZABILITY AND GULLIBILITY

Some persons believe that, if they are hypnotizable, this indicates that they are gullible and believe everything told to them. The difference between the two states has already been explained. Mental discrimination is not impaired with regard to stimuli which threaten the integrity of the organism.

DOMINANT PERSONALITY REQUIRED

Another widely held misconception is that one has to have a strong personality to be a hypnotist and that, therefore, males are better hypnotists than females because they are supposedly dominant personalities. This is not true, as a male hypnotist also can be an excellent subject for a female hypnotist.

SUMMARY

All misconceptions should be removed by adequate explanations during the initial visit. This discussion should be conducted at the level of the patient's intelligence. Readily understood examples should be used for illustrative purposes. Although this is time-consuming, the results are rewarding. Mentioning that the phenomena of hypnosis occur as a part of everyday life is helpful in the removal of the commoner misconceptions.

The author finds that it is particularly helpful to have all new candidates observe an induction procedure in a well-conditioned subject. A few minutes of observation will save hours of explanation. A well-conducted induction also corrects the false impressions derived from stage hypnosis. The fallacious ideas about hypnosis, originating from uninformed sources, have to be removed.

In summary, as repeatedly mentioned, hypnosis is not a "sleep" state, "trance" or state of unconsciousness. Rather, it closely resembles the waking state. Nor is the will surrendered. Intelligent individuals usually make the best subjects; a hypnotized person does not lose control nor reveal intimate material unless he wishes to do so; susceptibility to hypnosis is not related to gullibility or submissiveness; hypnosis can be terminated readily by either the subject or the operator; and, finally, many other misconceptions, such as being helpless to resist undesirable posthypnotic suggestions, stem from outmoded and wholly unscientific tenets. Removal of all doubts and misconceptions helps establish a closer rapport and the motivation necessary for successful hypnotic induction and therapy.

5

Suggestibility Tests

There are tests that presumptively can determine the degree of susceptibility to suggestion. Sophisticated hypnotherapists seldom use these, however, as they are time-consuming. Nevertheless, it is a good idea for the beginner to use any one of the following suggestibility tests. If he doubts his ability to hypnotize a patient, under the pretext of testing he can proceed immediately with an induction technic instead. If hypnosis is obtained, one can say, "I started to test you, but I recognized that you would be an excellent subject. Therefore, I continued hypnotizing you." Contrarily, this can be a welcome face-saving device for the novice in case hypnosis is not obtained.

THE HANDCLASP TEST

The handclasp test is excellent for quickly selecting suitable volunteers when using group hypnosis. Patients can be either in a standing or a sitting position and instructed to clasp their hands firmly together, either above their heads or at eye-level. Before beginning, the operator clasps his own hands in the desired manner, explaining where the subjects' hands should be placed. Then they are asked to close their eyes tightly.

The following verbalization is used to determine which subjects will, in all probability, be hypersuggestible: "Please lock your hands tightly together. Press your fingers *tighter* and *tighter* together. Imagine, if you will, that your hands are glued together; that they are *sticking tighter* and *tighter* together . . . and the *tighter* they stick together, the better you will respond to all suggestions. I am going to count slowly from 1 to 10, and with each number that I count, and with each breath that you take, you will find your fingers sticking *tighter* and *tighter* together. When I reach the count of 10, if you *really* wish to follow all other suggestions, you will feel your hands sticking *tighter* and *tighter* together. The *tighter* you can imagine that your hands are sticking together, the better you will be able to follow all other suggestions. Your fingers are locked so *tightly* that it would be difficult to pull your hands apart." (A pause of a second or two.) "Now, your hands are tightly locked together." If a subject has difficulty in unclasping his hands, this indicates a high degree of suggestibility.

There are modifications of this test, one of which is to have the subject place his hands above his head with the fingers interlocked and the palms facing outward. Either of these methods tests the subject's ability to concentrate, as well as his capacity to respond to suggestion. A direct authoritarian approach or a permissive one can be used. The latter is preferred.

THE POSTURAL-SWAY TEST

The subject is asked to stand erect with his feet together, his hands at his sides and his eyes closed. The operator stands behind the subject with the palms of his hands resting lightly on the subject's shoulders. "I am going to count from 1 to 10, and you will feel yourself falling backward, backward. One, you are falling backward, backward. Two, your body is getting rigid from your head to your toes. Three, you are falling backward! Your body feels stiff and rigid. Four, as I relax my hands on your shoulders, you will feel yourself being pulled backward. . . b-a-c-k-w-a-r-d. Five, you are f-a-l-l-i-n-g . . . f-a-l-l-i-n-g. . . ." The hands now can be drawn backward; at this point the subject usually begins to sway backward and, as this occurs, the tempo of the suggestions is increased. "You are falling backward, backward. You are beginning to lose your balance. You're beginning to fall! I will catch you. That's right. Let yourself go." Naturally, one must be ready to catch the patient as he falls backward. Before beginning the test, have the subject fall backward 2 or 3 times for assurance that he will be caught.

The ease and the manner in which he falls indicates whether or not the subject is trying to resist the operator's suggestions. A good subject will fall backward without any difficulty. By placing his hands lightly on the subject's shoulders, the operator can detect readily the slightest sway of the body. If the subject sways forward when the command to fall backward is given, or vice versa, this indicates either that the subject is not co-operating or that he has much involuntary resistance.

A variation of this test is for the operator to extend his arms, with his fingertips in front of the patient's face as he stands directly behind the patient. As mention of falling backward is made, the hands are moved forward slowly, producing the illusion in the patient that *he is actually falling backward.* This modification is especially valuable for resistant subjects.

THE FORWARD POSTURAL-SWAY TEST

This test is also a fine one for "crossing up" the resistant subject. The verbalization is as follows: "Close your eyes and listen to my voice. If you really wish to go into a nice, deep, soothing, pleasant state of relaxation, you will notice yourself *falling, falling* forward, forward, forward." Any slight forward sway indicates positive suggestibility, provided that the movements are not voluntary on the part of the subject. If there is resistance, he will sway backward. At this point, to circumvent patient negativism, one can "reverse the field" and say, "You are falling backward." If he starts to sway backward, then the operator can remark, "See, you are falling backward." This increases the subject's suggestibility and also utilizes his resistance to achieve positive suggestibility.

THE EYEBALL-SET TEST

This test is not only a suggestibility test but also an important one for rapid establishment of belief in the operator's "power" or suggestions. The subject is asked to look at a spot directly above his forehead. He is told to stare intently at this spot. The following verbalization is used: "Your eyes are getting *heavier* and *heavier*, and *the heavier* you can *think, feel and imagine* your eyes getting, the sooner you will close your eyes. The more *relaxed* your eyes get, the more deeply relaxed you will become. Your lids are getting *heavier* and *heavier*." If the patient begins to blink, one should say "Your eyes are blinking, blinking. That is a good sign. It shows that your are beginning to relax. Your eyes are blinking still more, as you relax deeper and d-e-e-p-e-r. I will now count from 1 to 3. Promptly, precisely and exactly at the count of 3, if you really wish to learn how to relax deeply, you will close your eyes tightly together. . . . One, your eyes feel as though they are closing. Two, your eyes are closing . . . c-l-o-s-i-n-g. Three, shut your eyes together and let your eyeballs roll up into the back of your head for just a few seconds." Then the following is said all in one sentence: "You can feel your lids sticking *tighter* and *tighter* together, and the *tighter* they stick together, the better you will be able to *relax* and follow my suggestions. You can feel your lids sticking *tighter* and *tighter* together. See, the suggestions are beginning to work! Your lids are really stuck tightly together."

This test is actually based upon physiologic factors rather than psychological ones. The patient does not realize that it is extremely difficult to open the lids with the eyeballs rolled back into the head; he thinks that the effect is due to the operator's suggestions. This initiates the compounding of belief into conviction.

Another variation of this test is to have the subject turn his eyeballs upward as far as possible and close his eyes tightly. One can lightly press the forefinger of each hand on the subject's forehead just above the eyes, and instruct him to "Look up at the spot where my fingers are placed." While he is doing this, one suggests, "Keep looking at this spot. You will find that it is extremely difficult to open your eyes now." Simultaneously, several downward passes over the closed eyes by the open palm reinforces lid closure. If the individual is unable to open his eyes, this generally indicates that he will be an excellent subject.

THE HAND-LEVITATION TEST

This test can be used not only as a means of determining whether or not an individual will make a good hypnotic subject but also for the indirect or permissive type of induction of hypnosis by hand levitation. The subject is told: "Place your hands in your lap. Would you mind looking steadily at one or the other of your hands? And as you keep looking at them, you will soon feel some type of sensation in one hand or the other. Perhaps at first it might be a prickly sensation, or a numb feeling, or perhaps one of your fingers will begin to move or separate. Or perhaps one of the fingers may begin to twitch. Do not interfere in any way with the movements of your fingers but simply observe *any* and *every sensation* that occurs." One might remark, "You can speculate about the texture of the cloth of your trousers. Perhaps, as you keep pressing down, you can feel the warmth of your skin. As you keep pressing down and building up tension in your fingers, you may even begin to notice that one of your fingers will move." Call the subject's attention to even the slightest movement of his fingers. Invariably, some movement of one of the fingers will occur in time. Naturally, the subject does not realize this. To facilitate levitation, one can explain that the finger is beginning to move because it wishes to respond; that the opposite of tension is relaxation (this is a perfectly logical remark). "As your finger gets more relaxed, it will begin to rise up into the air" (another logical remark). "As your finger begins to *lift*, it will get *lighter* and *lighter*—so light, in fact, that the other fingers will also get *lighter* and *lighter*. See? Your fingers are beginning to lift up, up, up . . . *higher* and *higher*. Your hand now is getting *lighter* and *lighter* and pretty soon the arm will begin to get *lighter* and *lighter*. And, as the arm gets *lighter* and *lighter*, it will lift higher and higher." The operator continues to suggest lightness, rising or floating sensations. Then he suggests that the hand will continue to lift until it touches the face. Perhaps the subject might be willing to accept

the suggestion that, when any portion of his hand touches any part of his face, this will be a signal that he will drop into a deep, deep state of relaxation. If the rising of the hand is slow, smooth and steady, this usually indicates that the subject is co-operating. If the hand and the arm are lifted rapidly, or if the movements are spasmodic or jerky, it usually indicates resistance. One should always attempt to correlate the lifting of the arm with the subject's breathing and state: "As your arm lifts *higher* and *higher*, your breathing becomes slower, deeper, more regular . . . slower, deeper, more regular." If the subject carries out these suggestions and his arm drops back into his lap with a thud after it has touched his face, one can be reasonably certain that the individual will be an excellent subject.

MODIFIED HAND-LEVITATION TEST

There are several modifications of this test. In one, the subject is asked to place the palm of his hand on his knee, and the following verbalization is used: "As I stroke your hand lightly, you will feel your hand getting *lighter* and *lighter*. And the *lighter* it gets, naturally, the higher it will float up into the air. As I stroke your hand, it is getting *lighter* and *lighter*. Your hand is beginning to *lift*, it is *lifting*, *lifting*, l-i-f-t-i-n-g, as if it is weightless. And as it lifts higher and higher, it gets *lighter* and *lighter*." If the hand does not move, this indicates resistance. Here, one can press lightly against the subject's palm and gradually release the pressure to give the illusion of lightness.

THE HAND-DROP TEST

An excellent test for choosing likely subjects from a group is the following: "Would you all put your arms out in front of you? Now, close your eyes and visualize in your 'mind's eye' or imagine that you have a 10-pound bag of sugar on the back of the palm of your right hand. Now, you can feel it getting *very, very heavy*. It is so *heavy* that your right hand is beginning to fall, beginning to get *heavier* and *heavier* as the heavy bag of sugar is getting *heavier* and *heavier, very, very heavy*. Your right arm is getting very, very tired because it is so difficult to support this heavy weight." (Positive suggestibility is indicated by the right arm's being well below the other). "Now open your eyes. See, there is a difference of at least a foot between the right and the left arm."

THE THERMAL TEST

Even the heat- or the cold-illusion test can be used to predict the degree of suggestibility. An ordinary block of wet wood such as a child's wet alphabet block will suffice for this test. The subject is asked to close his eyes and extend his hand forward, palm down. The block is placed on the back of the palm and, in a confident tone of voice, the operator remarks, "I am placing this ice cube on the back of your hand. It is getting colder and colder. You can feel the chilling, paralyzing numbness of the ice cube as it begins to melt. You can feel your skin getting numb." The block is then removed. If the individual is convinced that this was an ice cube, he has a high degree of susceptibility.

In order to produce the illusion of heat, one can strike a match and tell the subject, while his eyes are closed, that a quarter or a half dollar is being heated. After a few seconds, the coin is placed on the back of the subject's hand, while his eyes are shut tight. If he winces or withdraws his hand, one can be fairly certain that the subject is susceptible.

This test can also be performed in another manner. The subject is given a coin to hold in his clenched fist. Remark, "The coin is getting warmer and warmer. It is now getting *hotter* and *hotter,* and the longer you hold it, the hotter it will get. It is getting hotter all the time. It is actually getting very, very hot. Don't hold it too long as it is apt to burn you. If it gets too hot, let the coin drop to the floor." If this happens, the subject is obviously a good one. The test can be made more plausible by explaining that the heat of the metal is produced by the sweat of the hand.

THE OLFACTORY TEST

The olfactory test also is an excellent one for choosing good subjects out of a group. For this test, a stoppered perfume bottle, filled with colored water, is used. The operator holds the perfume bottle up so that everybody can see it and, as he takes the stopper out, he says, "The odor of this perfume is drifting toward the back of the room. It is beginning to become more and more pronounced. Will those who smell this odor please raise their hands?" As a rule, those who do so make excellent candidates for hypnosis.

THE KOHNSTAMM "TEST"

This is not a test but rather a maneuver, which produces a favorable mind-set. It involves physiologic muscular mechanisms rather than suggestion per se. It is very convincing and enables the subject to understand the mechanism of arm levitation. The subject is instructed to press the back of his tightly clenched fist against the side of a wall, with his entire arm held very stiff. He is informed that he should try to push against the wall only with his arm and not with his body. After several minutes he is asked to step away from the wall and allow his arm to hang freely at his side. The arm will begin to rise spontaneously until it reaches a horizontal position. It will feel weightless as it is rising. This is known as the Kohnstamm phenomenon. The subject does not know that contraction of the muscles of the arm naturally follows relaxation. He believes that the arm lifts because of the operator's suggestions; this heightens his susceptibility to further suggestions. This is a good technic to employ as a precursor to induction of hypnosis by an arm-levitation technic.

CHEVREUL'S PENDULUM TEST

For this test one can utilize a heavy ring or a glass ball on a string, which the patient holds in his hand, arm outstretched, over a piece of paper upon which is drawn a circle about 8 or 10 inches in diameter with a cross inside. The subject is told not to make any conscious attempt to help or hinder the movements of the ball (or ring), but that the ball will move spontaneously by just thinking about it. He is informed that the mere concentration upon the ball's moving from left to right, forward or backward, clockwise or counterclockwise, will cause it to swing in accordance with his thoughts.

The subject is instructed to let his eyes travel around the circle, or up and down the cross, or from one side to the other of the horizontal line. It is again suggested that he will not be able to control the swing of the ball. If the ball follows the operator's suggestions, this indicates a positive suggestibility. When the swing is well developed, the subject is asked to concentrate on the ball's swinging in a clockwise direction. After this has been accomplished, it is suggested that it might swing in a counterclockwise direction or up and down. Individuals who are extremely susceptible to suggestion react in full accordance with the suggestions because of involuntary ideosensory activities. This is also the principle of the Ouija board. However, it should be emphasized that, regardless of the degree of his reaction to the suggestions, the subject's suggestibility can be enhanced by remarking convincingly, "Your reaction definitely shows that you will make an excellent subject. I know that you can be hypnotized."

DISGUISED TESTS

For patients who remark, "I doubt if anyone can hypnotize me," there is one disguised test that is particularly suitable for the physician's use. If the outcome of the "test" is successful, a favorable mind-set leading to positive suggestibility is produced. This ordinarily facilitates induction.

This disguised test is based on prestige suggestion. When the patient comes into the office, he is immediately given a placebo with the casual remarks: "This drug facilitates hypnotic induction. It takes exactly 30 minutes to act. Let me see, it is now 11 A.M. If you will wait in my reception room for one half hour, you will be ready to go easily into a nice relaxed state at that time." This, of course, generally produces an expectant attitude, with subsequent hypersuggestibility. In about half an hour, the patient, who in the meantime has been sitting in the reception room building up his expectancy level, comes into the office. Then the right or the left eye is inspected in the following manner: The operator places his thumb just below the outer canthus of the eye to evert the lower lid. With the patient either sitting or standing, he carefully scrutinizes the conjunctiva in a professional manner. After intently looking at the eye for several seconds, he nods his head approvingly and exclaims confidently, "Yes, it's beginning to work. You will be an excellent subject." The patient naturally does not understand how this conclusion was reached; yet he cannot fail to be impressed by the operator's self-assurance and confident demeanor.

One can use other disguised tests to determine susceptibility to hypnosis. The following one makes use of ideomotor and ideosensory activities. One places the blood-pressure cuff around the patient's arm and remarks, "Now as I relax the pressure and as you hear the air escaping, you will go *deeper* and *deeper* relaxed. You will go *deeper* and *deeper* relaxed." (The subject closes his eyes.) "That's wonderful. You are going *deeper* and *deeper relaxed!* That's fine." Now, as the cuff loosens and the air escapes simultaneously, the ideomotor effect of the deflated cuff and the sound of the escaping air (ideosensory) are conducive to even deeper relaxation. Usually, as the pressure falls, a good subject will relax readily. The effects of this test are dramatic.

This test can also be extended into an induction technic: "Now that's fine. I want you to relax still more; you are going deeper and deeper relaxed. As the pressure drops and as the cuff loosens still more on your arm, you are going *deeper* and *deeper* relaxed." Here, one can test for arm catalepsy.

Meares[1] has described an interesting disguised method that is based on the repeated elicitation of the tendon reflexes which, in itself, aids in relaxation. The method has the advantage not only of estimating suggestibility but also of acting as a reliable guide to the best technic for the induction of hypnosis. The patient is unaware that he is being tested for hypnosis. If he proves to be unsuitable, the subject of hypnosis need not be discussed. The patient is not disappointed, nor does the therapist lose face. Since the rapport is not broken, the therapist is free to use another method. The association of the reflex movement of the limb with the verbal suggestions of movement accustoms the patient to the involuntary motions of his limbs in response to suggestion, and so paves the way for hypnotic suggestibility.

DISCUSSION

The fact that subjects respond positively to suggestibility tests does not imply that every one of them will enter the hypnotic state. However, where there is no response, this is presumptive evidence of negative suggestibility. Most of these tests depend on elicitation of ideomotor and ideosensory activities and, since hypnosis is contingent on other factors, such as confidence and expectation, all tests have certain deficiencies.

Furthermore, they do not indicate what method will enable the subject to be hypnotized effectively. Also, they give little information as to what may be the deterrent factors contributing to negative suggestibility. Various modifications of most of the above tests have been described by others.[2-5]

If all tests are unfavorable, this naturally interferes with the rapport. Often there is a distinct disadvantage in using tests to determine the subject's degree of susceptibility, because many subjects might have been hypnotized readily without them. However, irrespective of the subject's reactions to the tests, he always should be informed that he responded favorably, and that he will do much better the next time!

REFERENCES

1. Meares, A.: The clinical estimation of suggestibility, J.C.E.H. 2:106-108, 1954.
2. Moss, A. A.: Hypnodontics—Hypnosis in Dentistry, Brooklyn, Dental Items of Interest Publishing Co., 1952.
3. Weitzenhoffer, A. M.: Hypnotism—An Objective Study in Suggestibility, New York, Wiley, 1953.
4. ——: General Techniques of Hypnotism, New York, Grune & Stratton, 1957.
5. Wolberg, L. R.: Medical Hypnosis: The Principles of Hypnotherapy, vol. 1, New York, Grune & Stratton, 1948.

6

Factors Which Influence Susceptibility to Hypnosis

Generally, highly motivated, intelligent individuals are the best hypnotic subjects because of their ability to concentrate;[5] exhibitionists, with the exception of those who use resistance as an attention-getting device, are easy to hypnotize. Imbeciles, morons, senile persons, certain types of psychotics and children under six years of age, who are incapable of concentrating, are difficult or impossible to hypnotize.

Casually mentioning that persons of low mentality seldom are good hypnotic subjects increases motivation. Even though this statement is not strictly true, all patients wish to be regarded as above average in intelligence. Therefore, the remarks, by inference, increase their susceptibility. However, individuals with a real intellectual deficiency usually are insusceptible and tax the ingenuity of the operator.[1] Scientifically minded individuals are often poor subjects because of internal "noise"—self-analysis of their emotions.

Misdirection, by getting the subject's attention diverted to his own ideosensory or ideomotor responses, increases susceptibility to the operator's suggestions. The misdirection can be employed during the induction procedure as follows: "Would you mind shifting your attention to your toes and feet? As you do this, notice how very, very heavy your shoes are getting. Your shoes are getting heavier and heavier." (The subject invariably becomes aware of the heaviness, and this begins to build up his conviction that the operator's suggestions are producing changes within his own body.) After a pause, the operator remarks, "You are now becoming aware of the watch on your left wrist. It, too, is getting heavier and heavier .. very heavy! Notice that you are no longer aware of the pressure of the shoes; is that

not true?" (Nods.) "You now can feel the watch, can you not?" (Nods again.) "So, you see, you can either be aware of, or ignore, sensations that are constantly present within your own body." As mentioned, if the subject experiences one sensation after another, the conviction that other suggestions will be followed is enhanced.

Psychotherapists know that neurotics seldom relinquish the symptoms used to get attention. Such mechanisms are pleasurable. Naturally, this is vehemently denied. Instead, they ardently protest that they wish to be cured of their symptoms. However, once rapport has been established, they tend to be more suggestible than "normal" individuals.[2, 3, 9] On the other hand, as just mentioned, exhibitionists are easily hypnotized by the professional entertainer. The hypnosis is not produced by him, but, rather, because the subject expects it to happen. The stage hypnotist likes to give the impression that his passes, staring eyes and verbalizations produce the hypnosis. He is very anxious to make his audience believe that he is an all-powerful person, so he uses the usual gesticulations and the "mumbo jumbo" to heighten this illusion. Such "window dressing" merely obscures the fact that the hypnosis occurred as a result of the subject's expectation and imagination! The stage hypnotist relies on the subjects to please not only him, but the audience as well.[7]

Another factor which determines the degree of susceptibility to hypnosis is the ability to the restrict the attention span to a given idea. Braid tried to change the name of hypnosis to monoideism—the ability of a person to concentrate on one idea at a time to the exclusion of others.

Cultural factors often determine the depth

of and the susceptibility to hypnosis.[4, 8] The feelings and temperament of the operator also determine the outcome of the hypnotic induction; intuitive subjects respond in a positive manner to the operator's empathy and self-confidence. If they develop a good mental-set, they effectively concentrate on his suggestions; if not, they are refractory to all suggestions. For instance, if the operator is absorbed in his personal problems during the induction procedure, this adversely affects the intraverbal and meaningful aspects of his communications.

Susceptibility is definitely enhanced by motivation.[6] Though poorly motivated subjects are invariably insusceptible, this does not imply that they cannot be hypnotized. Frequently, the person who is not highly motivated may have an inordinate need for hypnosis. Even though he uses the lack of motivation as a defense, often he, too, is very susceptible to suggestion. If rapport is established quickly, there is greater motivation. It should be impressed upon all subjects that their full co-operation is essential, that they must be willing to respond to suitable suggestions, and that coercion will not be used. This also helps to increase motivation.

The specific technic for handling poorly motivated subjects is similar to the "misdirection of attention" approach described for extremely introspective or analytic persons. Also, saying "Even if your mind wanders, you will still hear my suggestions—this will help you to relax" is more effective than saying "Just make your mind a blank." Many subjects have been told that it is necessary to concentrate intensively in order to be hypnotized. Since some doubt their ability to do so, they should be informed that only ordinary concentration is required.

The factors which determine susceptibility depend on the manner in which prior invoked beliefs are processed into convictions. These influence susceptibility to hypnosis more than any other factor. The author cannot emphasize strongly enough that *conviction of hypnosis leads to hypnosis!*

REFERENCES

1. Beigel, H. G.: Some signs and causes of unsusceptibility, Brit. J. M. Hypnotism 4: 34-41, 1952.
2. Ingham, J. G.: Body sway suggestibility and neurosis, J. Ment. Sc. *100*:432-441, 1954.
3. ——: Psychoneurosis and suggestibility, J. Abnorm. & Social Psychol. *51*:600-603, 1955.
4. Kline, M. V.: Toward a theoretical understanding of the nature of resistance to the induction of hypnosis and depth of hypnosis, J.C.E.H. *1*:32-41, 1953.
5. Martin, R. M., and Marcuse, F. L.: Characteristics of volunteers and nonvolunteers for hypnosis, J.C.E.H. 5:176-180, 1957.
6. Meares, A.: A note on the motivation for hypnosis, J.C.E.H. 3:222-228, 1955.
7. Schneck, J. M.: Relationships between hypnotist–audience and hypnotist–subject interaction, J.C.E.H. 6:171-181, 1958.
8. Secter, I. I.: Considerations in resistances to initial induction of hypnosis, J.C.E.H. 5: 77-81, 1957.
9. Weitzenhoffer, A. M.: A note concerning hypnotic susceptibility and maladjustment, J.C.E.H. 6:182-184, 1958.

7

Laws of Suggestion

THE LAW OF CONCENTRATED ATTENTION

There are several important principles or "laws" that should be followed when employing hypnotic suggestion.[*] The first is the *law of concentrated attention:* Whenever attention is concentrated on an idea over and over again, it spontaneously tends to realize itself. Repetitive radio and TV commercials that cause people to buy the advertised products are typical examples of this law. In many commercials, the listener's attention is gained without his knowledge through subliminal stimulation. This is even more effective than persuasion, as critical faculties are reduced.

THE LAW OF REVERSED EFFECT

The second is the law of reversed effect: The harder one tries to do something, the less chance he has of success. For instance, trying to recall someone's name often can be a difficult task. Regardless of how hard he wills himself to remember the name, he cannot. It seems that, whenever the imagination and the will are utilized, the imagination supersedes the will.

This law applies to the insomniac who tries to go to sleep, and to the food, drug or alcoholic addict who cannot stop by making an appeal or inner "speech" to his will. These respond more readily to imagination power than to will power! The sophisticated hypnotherapist employs technics which make full use of the principles embodied in the law of reverse effect.

It is difficult to negate the effects of the

[*] Davis, L. W., and Husband, R. W.: A study of hypnotic susceptibility in relation to personality traits, J. Abnorm. & Social Psychol. 26:175-182, 1931.

imagination, which comprises all an individual's past associations, feelings and ideas. A typical illustration is the individual who lacks confidence in public speaking. When in bed at night, he "sees" himself walking up to the rostrum and "hears" himself delivering his address. The mere thought of the future talk causes palpitation, sighing, holding of the breath and a panicky feeling. Thus, the imagination produces the same effects *as if* the speaker were in front of the audience. This process is referred to as sensory imagery. If his imagination is negatively "programmed" in this manner, time after time, night after night, it is only natural that he will develop anxiety when he gets up to speak. Continually thinking negative, harmful and destructive thoughts eventually leads to their realization *because of expectation and belief that they will happen.* Having an idea of an action often results in that action.

Therefore, one never resorts to the will to attain desired physiologic changes! The organism will not respond as well to direct authoritative commands as it will to permissive manipulation of the experiential background via the individual's imagination. For instance, when one is trying to develop glove anesthesia, it is incorrect to suggest, "I want your hand to get numb." Rather, one must use a descriptive sensory-imagery type of verbalization, such as: "Imagine that you are putting your hand in a pitcher of very cold ice water. As soon as you can visualize this, you will feel your hand developing a numb, heavy, wooden feeling, the same as if you had been sitting on it, or the same as if you had had an anesthetic injected into it." Stimulating the imagination in this manner is more likely to produce the desired response.

THE LAW OF DOMINANT EFFECT

The law of dominant effect also plays an important role in enabling suggestions to be received in a more meaningful manner. It is based on the axiom that a strong emotion tends to replace a weaker one. Attaching a strong emotion to a suggestion tends to make the suggestion more effective. Thus, when a person is having a pleasurable emotional experience and danger is imminent, the stronger emotion of danger displaces the former, which disappears instantly if the danger is pronounced.

Another illustration of this law is the use of a strong physiologic effect to reinforce a psychological suggestion. Suggestions of relaxation are increased by massage or gentle stroking. The effect of this principle is noted when a child slams the door on his finger and his mother remarks, "Oh I'll just kiss it and the pain will go away." Here the mere touch of her lips becomes the more dominant suggestion and makes the finger feel better. Thus, at an early age, we become responsive to this fundamental principle or law.

8

Recognition of the Depth of the Hypnotic State

It is difficult to measure the depth of hypnosis objectively. At best, all rating scales are arbitrary divisions. Catalepsy is indicative of light to medium stages. Amnesia usually connotes deeper stages. However, amnesia may be present in lighter stages.

Thus, it is difficult to tell where one of the various stages begins and ends. Sometimes it is difficult to state with certainty that one has achieved a light or a medium stage of hypnosis. An experienced operator, however, can often make a close approximation.

For teaching purposes, 5 divisions of the various stages of hypnotic susceptibility are satisfactory, with 3 of these being sufficient for clinical purposes.

1. Insusceptible
2. Hypnoidal—precursor to hypnotic state—no symptoms
3. Light stage
4. Medium stage
5. Deep stage

The Davis and Husband[1] classification depends on a point-scoring system and is the rating scale most commonly referred to in the literature.

LeCron and Bordeaux[2] have developed a more involved scoring chart separated into 6 divisions instead of 5, the last being a deeper stage which is seldom seen—the plenary or hypnotic coma state. Based on 2 points for each symptom exhibited, a total score would indicate the depth of trance reached. From 2 to 12 points would be hypnoidal; from 14 to 36 would show a light trance; from 38 to 54, a medium stage; 56 or more, a deep or somnambulistic trance.

On the basis of objective and subjective clinical signs, the first part of the light stage is characterized by a pleasant state of restfulness. The subject hears surrounding sounds, is well able to control his thoughts,

DAVIS AND HUSBAND SUSCEPTIBILITY SCORING SYSTEM

Depth	Score	Objective Symptoms
Insusceptible	0	
Hypnoidal	2	Relaxation
	3	Fluttering of lids
	4	Closing of eyes
	5	Complete physical relaxation
Light trance	6	Catalepsy of eyes
	7	Limb catalepsies
	10	Rigid catalepsy
	11	Anaesthesia (glove)
Medium trance	13	Partial amnesia
	15	Posthypnotic anaesthesia
	17	Personality changes
	18	Simple posthypnotic suggestions
	20	Kinesthetic delusions; complete amnesia
Somnambulistic (deep) trance	21	Ability to open eyes without affecting trance
	23	Bizarre posthypnotic suggestions
	25	Complete somnambulism
	26	Positive visual hallucinations, posthypnotic

and there is no impairment of the senses. After spontaneous eye closure, muscle tension is slightly decreased and motor activities of limbs are easily carried out. This is followed by drowsiness and lassitude; the carefully lifted arm drops limply. There is some difficulty in opening the eyes or moving the limbs.

As the hypnosis deepens and the so-called medium stage is reached, the relaxation becomes more marked; the respirations become deeper and regular; some loss of motor activity occurs; the lifted arm remains upright but slowly falls (light catalepsy), and there is a loss of interest in extraneous environmental sounds. As this stage deepens, catalepsy of the limbs is more marked; spontaneous analgesia can be augmented by ap-

LeCron-Bordeaux Scoring System for Indicating Depth of Hypnosis

Insusceptible
0   Subject fails to react in any way

Hypnoidal
1   Physical relaxation
2   Drowsiness apparent
3   Fluttering of eyelids
4   Closing of eyes
5   Mental relaxation, partial lethargy of mind
6   Heaviness of limbs

Light Trance
7   Catalepsy of eyes
8   Partial limb catalepsy
9   Inhibition of small muscle groups
10 Slower and deeper breathing, slower pulse
11 Strong lassitude (disinclination to move, speak, think or act)
12 Twitching of mouth or jaw during induction
13 Rapport between subject and operator
14 Simple posthypnotic suggestions heeded
15 Involuntary start or eye twitch on awakening
16 Personality changes
17 Feeling of heaviness throughout entire body
18 Partial feeling of detachment

Medium Trance
19 Recognition of trance (difficult to describe but definitely felt)
20 Complete muscular inhibitions (kinaesthetic illusions)
21 Partial amnesia
22 Glove anesthesia
23 Tactile illusions
24 Gustatory illusions
25 Olfactory illusions
26 Hyperacuity to atmospheric conditions
27 Complete catalepsy of limbs or body

Deep or Somnambulistic Trance
28 Ability to open eyes without affecting trance
29 Fixed stare when eyes are open; pupillary dilation
30 Somnambulism
31 Complete amnesia
32 Systematized posthypnotic amnesias
33 Complete anesthesia
34 Posthypnotic anesthesia
35 Bizarre posthypnotic suggestions heeded
36 Uncontrolled movement of eyeballs—eye co-ordination lost
37 Sensation of lightness, floating, swinging, or being bloated or swollen; detached feeling
38 Rigidity and lag in muscular movements and reactions
39 Fading and increase in cycles of the sound of operator's voice (like radio station fading in and out)
40 Control of organic body functions (heart beat, blood pressure, digestion)
41 Recall of lost memories (hypermnesia)
42 Age regression
43 Positive visual hallucinations, posthypnotic
44 Negative visual hallucinations; posthypnotic
45 Positive auditory hallucinations; posthypnotic
46 Negative auditory hallucinations; posthypnotic
47 Stimulation of dreams (in trance or in natural sleep)
48 Hyperesthesias
49 Color sensations experienced

Plenary Trance
50 Stuporous condition in which all spontaneous activity is inhibited. Somnambulism can be developed by suggestion to that effect.

---

propriate suggestions; the subject's thoughts begin to wander, and he now concentrates more on the words of the operator. Inability to move the limbs is noted at this stage, and the automatic movements become more pronounced.

In the deep stage, negative and positive hallucinations can be produced readily; partial or complete amnesia is present, and suggestions of active and passive motor reactions are easily affected. As this stage deepens, positive and negative hallucinations of all types can occur with the eyes open, and these can be maintained posthypnotically; total amnesia is generally present as are age-regression, revivification and other phenomena characteristic of the somnambulistic state.

REFERENCES

1. Davis, L. W., and Husband, R. W.: A study of hypnotic susceptibility in relation to personality traits, J. Abnorm. & Social Psychol. 26:175-182, 1931.
2. LeCron, L. M., and Bordeaux, J.: Hypnotism Today, New York, Grune & Stratton, 1947.

9

Clinical Observations and Management of Various Depths of Hypnosis

From the clinical aspect, the experienced operator can observe the signs and symptoms characterizing the progress of an induction. As belief is compounded into conviction, there is, in good subjects, a steady progression toward more obvious relaxation and alertness to the operator's suggestions.

EYE CHANGES

First, during the initial stages of the induction, the responsive subject generally closes his eyes promptly upon command. If there is a momentary lid lag or delay in eye closure, this often indicates resistance, poor motivation and possible failure. The next objective is to produce a catalepsy of the smallest muscles of the body—those of the eyelids. The eyelid muscles are the easiest to catalepse. All suggestions are directed toward this objective in the manner described earlier.

After lid catalepsy has been achieved, the operator can assume that the subject will follow all the remaining suggestions, because it has already been emphasized that the final result will depend on how well he co-operates. Later, the individual is asked to count backward from 100 to zero; this is one of the elementary suggestions. One can remark, "I have no way of knowing whether or not you are going to count backward and, if you do not count in this fashion or do *not* follow these simple suggestions as they are given, then, of course, you will not enter into hypnosis. The responsibility, then, for not entering the hypnotic state is due to your failure to follow my suggestions in a specific manner." Thus the onus for entering hypnosis is placed on the subject rather than on the operator.

Other signs indicative of increasing depth are the blinking and the involuntary drooping of the eyelids. The trembling of the eyelids after closure usually indicates further deepening, contrary to the belief of inexperienced operators. After the suggestions are made that the lids are getting heavier and heavier, one notices some blinking and tiring of the lids. The subject, as mentioned earlier, does not know that the lids tire because of the upward position in which the eyes are held. The operator utilizes this blinking, saying, "The blinking indicates that your lids are *really* getting *heavy*, getting *heavier* and *heavier*." The next step is based on the operator's judgment, experience and intuition. When there is an increased amount of blinking and fatigue, it is suggested in the following manner that the subject can close the eyes: "At the count of 3, if you *really* wish to go into a *deep*, deep state of relaxation, all you have to do is just let your lids close and let them close *tight*, very *tight*. That's right, closing, closing, closed. You will close your eyes not because you *have* to, but because you *want* to do this. Now, let your eyeballs roll comfortably up into the back of your head for a few moments so that you are 'looking' at your own hair. That's right. I can see your eyeballs moving up beneath your lids." The next suggestion is given in a casual manner: "If you *really* wish to go into a nice, deep, pleasant, soothing state of relaxation, it is *really* so easy. All you have to do is just close your eyes and let your eyeballs roll up into the back of your head." This is much more effective than saying, "I want you to close your eyes promptly and exactly at the count of 3." (This peremptory command mobilizes a critical attitude. So does: "No matter how hard you try, you *cannot* open your eyes." Here you are challenging the subject; with the intonation of your voice or the intra-verbal aspects of your communication, you arouse antagonism.)

One can evert the upper lid and, if the eyeballs are rolled upward, be sure that a considerable depth has been reached. If there is no lid reflex when the eyelashes are lightly touched by the tip of the finger, this is indicative of a good response—at least a medium stage of hypnosis has been reached. The production of lid catalepsy is described below.

MOVEMENTS OF HEAD

If the head of the subject spontaneously rolls sideways or forward, the hypnotic depth is increasing. When this occurs, the operator should support the head, as a strained posture usually results in spasm, which can prevent the hypnosis from becoming deeper. However, some individuals do not seem to mind the abnormal position and sink deeper and deeper into relaxation. If the jaws relax limply, this, too, is significant of increasing depth.

CHARACTER OF BREATHING

Shallow, diaphragmatic breathing usually is associated with lighter stages, while slow, deep, regular abdominal breathing generally is characteristic of deeper stages of hypnotism. One can remark, "You will go *deeper* and *deeper* with each breath you take. Your breathing is getting slower, deeper and more regular." The second phrase can be correlated with the rhythmicity of the breathing. To heighten the effect of this suggestion, the operator can breathe deeply in unison with the subject.

If the eyes have not closed, one should say, "Your lids are beginning to close and, as they close, they are closing *tighter* and *tighter;* getting *very, very* heavy; *getting heavier* and *heavier*" (ideosensory activity). The more ideomotor and ideosensory activities the individual is involved in, the more readily will he enter into hypnosis—another illustration of misdirection of attention.

LIMPNESS OF LIMBS

While hypnosis is being induced, an arm or a leg can be lifted to see how it falls. If the limb falls slowly, it indicates voluntary control and that not too great a depth has been reached. The test for depth is made by gently clasping the wrist of the patient between the forefinger and the thumb and slowly lifting the arm. If the arm is allowed to fall, and it falls with a thud to the side or the lap, this denotes optimal relaxation and at least a medium stage of hypnosis.

To achieve heaviness of the lower extremities, one remarks: "Your toes are getting *very, very heavy.* If you really wish to go *deeper* and *deeper* relaxed, you can feel a numb, heavy, woodenlike feeling moving up, up, up to your feet, and then to your legs, and then to your thighs. Just imagine, if you will, that you are sitting on your legs, cross-legged. Your legs, beginning with your toes and feet, are really getting heavier and heavier. Your legs are *relaxing* more and more from your toes, up, up, up to your feet, up, up, up to your legs, and up, up, up to your thighs. And you can, if you *really* wish to go deeper, tell yourself that your legs from your toes to your thighs are really relaxed!"

LID CATALEPSY

Inability to open the eyes may occur in either light or deep stages. It indicates that the subject can become deeply relaxed. To induce lid catalepsy, one can remark (when the lids are closed), "Your lids are locked *tight, tighter* and *tighter.*" At the very second that the eyeballs roll upward, one can remark emphatically, "Your lids are closed tight. Roll your eyeballs up into the back of your head." This is the eyeball-set. The subject is unaware that it is difficult to open the lids with the eyeballs rolled upward. He attributes this to the operator's suggestions, and this is another instance of misdirection of attention. These nuances of induction technics are picked up only with experience.

This important maneuver can also be accomplished in this way: "At the count of 3, you will close your eyes, not because you have to, but because *you want* to close your eyes. Do you not? And *after* you close your eyes, if you *really* wish to go into a nice, deep, soothing state of relaxation, you will do so. You can now, if you wish, close your eyes tightly—1 . . . 2 . . . 3. . . . Now, roll your eyeballs up into the back of your head. Very good. You're doing fine." It is always a good idea to praise the patient's efforts because most subjects wonder if they are responding adequately to the suggestions.

At this point, the individual may attempt to open his eyes. If the suggestions have been given properly, he will not be able to open them. This difficulty is evidenced by the furrows on the brow. If there is any doubt, one says, "If you really wish to go deeper and deeper, just imagine that the harder you try to open your eyes the less chance you have of opening the eyes." Motivation is being established each step of the way to coax the patient to go deeper by telling him that, if he really wishes to benefit from future suggestions, he must follow the preliminary suggestions. In other words, one must motivate the subject or use "bait" each step of the way. By the use of such measures, the desire and the responsibility for achieving hypnosis are put on the patient.

ARM CATALEPSY

Arm catalepsy is manifested by the arm's being extended straight up, with the fingers outstretched. The entire arm appears to be drawn up as far as it can stretch. A cataleptic limb resists counterpressure involuntarily and is usually indicative of a medium to deep hypnosis.

The individual is asked to raise the arm upward slowly. He is told that, if he wishes to relax still more, with each motion of the arm upward he is to think and to imagine that "with each motion of my arm upward, I am going deeper and deeper relaxed." By means of this suggestion, the subject associates the idea of relaxation with the resultant ideomotor activity. For instance, the following is helpful: "With each motion that the arm moves upward, if you think, imagine and feel that you are *really* going deeper and deeper relaxed, you will indeed go *deeper* and *deeper* relaxed." This makes full use of ideosensory and ideomotor activities and invariably results in arm catalepsy.

Catalepsy is characterized by an increased tonicity of all the muscles of the arm from the fingertips down to the wrist and from the elbow to the shoulder. The whole body can be made cataleptic. The muscles are balanced against each other, and certain muscles become very rigid *without the subject's knowledge.* The fingers remain for long intervals in any position in which they are placed. There is an associated waxy flexibility—*flexibilitas cerea.*

FOLLOWING POSTHYPNOTIC SUGGESTIONS

This is a good sign of medium hypnosis. Telling the subject that, after being dehypnotized, he cannot count the even numbers from 1 to 10 is a good test. Some subjects will remember that the suggestion was given and can still count, but without omitting the alternate numbers. This indicates that no more than a light stage has been reached. Ways to induce the patient to follow posthypnotic suggestions are given in Chapter 2.

DEVELOPMENT OF GLOVE ANESTHESIA

Although this is an objective finding associated with the medium stages, glove anesthesia is often characteristic of deep hypnosis. The entire hand can be made insensitive in a circumscribed area from the fingertips to the wrist. This area of the hand will be numb, woodenlike and "anesthetic." It will feel just as completely "numb" as if an anesthetic had been injected. As proof, a large bore needle can be placed through the skin without a facial flinch or grimace on the part of the patient. The technic for its production also is described in the obstetric section in Chapter 33.

FOLLOWING POSITIVE AND NEGATIVE HALLUCINATIONS

When patients accept the validity of hallucinatory suggestions, it indicates that a profound hypnotic depth has been achieved. A negative hallucination, as described in Chapter 2, is produced by making suggestions that an object that is present cannot be perceived (through any of the senses). A positive hallucination is produced when a suggestion is made that something is there that is not present.

SOMNAMBULISM

In somnambulism, patients can walk, talk and engage in all types of activities with their eyes open, yet be in a deep stage of hypnosis. Due to the spontaneous amnesia, patients seldom recall what occurred during somnambulism. Anesthesia, hyperesthesia and dissociation are readily induced.

Somnambulism is one of the deepest stages of hypnosis, easily recognized by the immobility of the features, the staring eyes, the widened palpebral fissures, the flattened nasolabial folds, the masklike countenance and the dreamy look. There is also an economy of motion or a time lag between the giving of a suggestion and the following of it; the speech is slow and slurred. There is loss of the startle reflex. The individual is in a state of fixed attention, and there is also a concomitant absorption in his own physiologic processes.

Somnambulism occurs at the nonhypnotic level, too, as in the sleepwalker, or in the individual who spontaneously develops a fuguelike state, without having undergone a formalized hypnotic procedure. During somnambulism, the subject generally responds automatically to nearly all suggestions.

10

Hindrances to Hypnotic Induction

The emotional status of the subject may be a hindrance to hypnotic induction. It was mentioned previously that a skeptical or an analytic attitude toward hypnosis is not conducive to the establishment of hypnosis. In others, over-co-operation often may be a defense against being hypnotized. Some subjects are merely curious or are unable to concentrate because of the fear of being hypnotized. All these factors decrease rapport and the ability to be hypnotized. Trivia, such as the pipe or the cigarette which the doctor is smoking, may be objectionable. These and other factors can produce resentment and interfere with successful induction.

Apprehensive individuals also show other elements of conflict, such as excessive giggling or laughing, sweating and trembling, weeping or crying; these are indicative of profound tension and anxiety. Unless the operator is experienced, induction should not be continued in such emotionally disturbed individuals, because chagrin, a sense of failure and other depressive reactions can be brought to the surface. Although induction of hypnosis depends, to a degree, on the strength of the interpersonal relationship, it must be emphasized again that it is a subjective and intensely intrapersonal problem for the subject.

Hypnotic response usually is facilitated by making the subject comfortable and eliminating all distracting influences; freedom from interruption helps to promote relaxation. However, many therapists do not have soundproof offices; some have consultation rooms that overlook busy intersections. Often certain types of distractions can be utilized to facilitate a hypnotic induction. The monotonous traffic hum or sounds can be incorporated in the induction technic as follows: "With every car that goes by, you will go deeper and deeper relaxed." If a secretary's typing is audible, one says: "With each click, click, click of the machine, you will go *deeper* and *deeper relaxed.*"

An office near the author's was being remodeled and the hammering was continual. Several patients were hypnotized by using this distraction, as follows: "With each *beat, beat, beat* of that hammer you will go *deeper* and *deeper relaxed.* With each pounding of that hammer you will feel that *you are being pounded into a deeper* and *deeper relaxed* state." So one has to use what one sees, and see what to use! One utilizes everything and anything that the patient manifests to build up his confidence and reduce his resistance to hypnosis.

The room must not be too hot or too cold. Even a draft will be uncomfortable enough to interfere with the induction procedure. The posture of the subject is important. If he prefers a chair, his feet should be flat on the floor and his hands on his lap. The back of the head should be well supported, as neck strain becomes unbearable and interferes with induction. If the subject lies down, he should assume his usual position for sleeping. Some subjects much prefer to lie on their sides.

Noises such as those made by a chiming clock should be eliminated from the room. Naturally, all outside noises, such as loud talking, should be discouraged. Subjects with a severe cough or a head cold should not be induced for the first time, as they often are disturbed by sneezing, coughing or the need to clear their throats. Others may have a postnasal drip, and this can be a distinct hindrance to induction. All disturbing situations should be under control before any type of induction procedure is attempted with any individual.

Practical Hints for Hypnotic Induction

Before beginning an induction procedure, describe as simply as possible what the subject is supposed to feel, what you are going to do, and what you expect of him—this raises the expectancy level.

Next, stress that the more attention directed to the operator's suggestions, the more successful the induction.

Naturally, all misconceptions regarding surrender of the will, loss of consciousness, inability to "wake up," and revelation of secrets must be removed.

Mentioning that only suggestions compatible with the subject's wishes will be followed increases rapport. It is axiomatic that induction is more successful in the presence of good rapport and motivation.[3]

Confidence is most essential, since most subjects, on the basis of subliminal cues, pick up the operator's insecurities and hesitancies. Therefore, the operator must approach every induction with the expectation of success. The experienced operator is readily recognized and there cannot be even a modicum of success in the absence of the conviction of success on his part.[1]

Modern technics seldom require challenges. Unsophisticated operators generally use them and, when subjects defy the challenges, the operator "loses face." This can be avoided by not giving the patient the impression that the suggestion will be acted upon. Rather, he should be given a wide latitude of choices to follow.

All suggestions should be made on the basis of logic and common sense rather than by deception. Subjects should be controlled, not fooled.

Failures during induction often are due to inability to understand the full meaning of the operator's suggestions. Hence, clarity and simplicity in the verbalizations are mandatory.

Never appeal to the will, but stress that *willingness* to co-operate and to use the imagination induces hypnosis. Maximal effects are achieved if the patient's own ideational activities are utilized to the utmost. This depends on the subject's being involved in as many ideomotor and ideosensory activities as possible.[2] An individual must be kept so busy thinking about the heaviness of his lids, the heaviness of his toes, his legs and his thighs, the counting backward with each breath he takes in order to relax, that he figures he might as well escape all this intense mental work, and instead enter into hypnosis.

When an individual is deliberately switched from one type of ideomotor and ideosensory activity to another, the resultant misdirection is conducive to induction of hypnosis. This approach works on analytic or too introspective subjects. It also is of distinct value for the over-curious and over-co-operative patient; these are resistances against being hypnotized. Changing the suggestions or switching to a different technic minimizes the resistance. That is one reason why all skillful hypnotherapists must be conversant with a variety of technics. These must be adapted to the needs and the personality of the subject and the operator.

The following 10 practical hints are useful:

First, make sure that the subject is absolutely comfortable. When an individual is sitting in an uncomfortable position, he may interrupt the induction by saying, "My neck hurts. Can't you stop talking until it relaxes?" This distraction is "noise," and such interference prevents the subject from focusing his attention on your suggestions. If your "message" does not come through, failure in the induction is inevitable. The room should be free from distracting influences, and, if this is impossible, one can use the distractions as reinforcement as described on page 49.

The second is: "If you follow the simple ABC suggestions, such as looking at a spot above your eyes, counting to yourself, *imagining*, *thinking* and *feeling* that your legs are getting heavier and heavier, you will follow other and more complex suggestions."

The third is: "The ability to achieve hypnosis is within you. I do not hynotize you. You do! I cannot force you into hypnosis. However, if you *really* wish to be hypnotized at your own pace and by your own effort, all you have to do is to follow the ABC suggestions. If you follow these in sequence, you should readily develop a nice, pleasant state of relaxation, provided that you really wish to reach the ultimate goal of very, very *deep* relaxation."

The fourth is: Monotonous, repetitive stressing of key words such as "heavy" and "relaxed" increases relaxation.

The fifth is: Sequentially building up ideosensory and ideomotor responses first by simple suggestions, then by more complicated ones, helps limit voluntary movements and is conducive to hypnotic relaxation. For instance: "With every breath (ideomotor) you take and every number you count backward (ideosensory), *you will go deeper and deeper relaxed.*" (The author never uses the word "sleep" in his induction technics for reasons discussed on page 24.)

The sixth is: Reinforcing a psychological suggestion (ideosensory) by a physiologic effect, such as lightly stroking a limb (ideomotor), facilitates acceptance of suggestions.

The seventh is: Suggestions must be given slowly, with sufficient time allowed for their assimilation and response.

The eighth is: Never tell the subject that he is difficult to induce. Using positive conditioning such as, "You did very well considering that it was the first time; you will do better the next time," facilitates future inductions.

The ninth is: Fearful subjects never should be traumatized by too early testing for anesthesia; be certain that this phenomenon has been obtained.

The tenth is: Never blame the patient for his inability to enter hypnosis, as this only mobilizes resistances. Fear over failure to enter hypnosis, and subsequent anxiety, can be allayed by a confident, sympathetic and reassuring approach, rather than by a condemnatory one.

The skillful operator closely observes his subject's responses to use every voluntary or involuntary manifestation to reinforce the subject's expectancy and belief that hypnosis will be induced. Here, too, the dictum bears repeating: *One must use what he sees and see what to use.* If the subject's eyelids tremble involuntarily during the induction, remark: "Trembling of your lids is a good sign that you are becoming deeper relaxed." If the patient voluntarily swallows, say, "You just swallowed. That's good; it shows you are relaxing!" Every inconsequential movement, even the uncrossing of the patient's legs, *is a good sign.* Constant reassurances, if made convincingly, especially during the initial phases of induction, are helpful to unsophisticated subjects. These promote relaxation in subjects who doubt the effectiveness of the suggestions.

If a suggestion is not followed, the experienced operator should use another one so that the subject thinks that he is progressing nicely. If the subject refuses to close his lids, one can suggest: "The harder you try to keep your eyes open, the deeper relaxed you become." Always emphasize that better results are obtained if the sequence of the suggestions is not broken.

This author finds that it is helpful (whenever possible) to have a new patient observe an induction procedure on a well-conditioned subject—a few minutes of observation are worth hours of discussion. Through identification with patients who successfully enter hypnosis, the subject now knows what to expect; this helps to overcome resistances due to misconceptions. Most patients have little or no reluctance when asked, "Would you mind allowing me to demonstrate the technic of hypnotic induction? After my new patient has seen you induced, he will leave the room." Since this was the way he was introduced to hypnosis, the old patient does not mind showing the uninformed how easy it is to attain hypnosis. He also feels a sense of achievement by collaborating. And it must be remembered that many individuals are retreating from the world because they feel inadequate, insecure, frustrated and lonely. This gives the unhappy and disturbed individual the feeling that he is finally being noticed and is capable of helping a fellow sufferer. Furthermore, this saves valuable time that would be lost in talking to uninformed and skeptical patients.

REFERENCES

1. Blumenthal, L. S.: Confidence—the keystone of the physician-patient relationship: how hypnosis is based on this confidence, Am. J. Clin. Hypnosis *1*:169-173, 1959.
2. Solovey, G., and de Milechnin, A.: Concerning the attributes of the hypnotic state, J.C.E.H. *4*:115-126, 1956.
3. Wagner, F.: A dynamic approach to the problem of hypnotic induction, J.C.E.H. *4*: 93-98, 1956.

12

Preinduction Talk

It is advisable in nearly every instance to have a preinduction discussion, especially with the skeptical or apprehensive patient. The following is helpful in achieving a favorable mind-set: "Physicians, dentists and clinical psychologists are becoming seriously interested in medical hypnosis, which is not a state of 'trance,' 'sleep' or 'unconsciousness.' Rather, it is an exaggerated state of being awake! More simply, it is *selective attention* to my words, with *selective inattention* to distracting noise and everything else around you. Now, if you wish to relax, imagine and feel all of my suggestions. Do not try too hard. Just try to concentrate on my suggestions to the best of your ability. Don't press, just relax! Remember that if you do this you will relax, and then, the better you relax, the better you will concentrate on what I am saying. As a result, you will respond more effectively to those suggestions which are for your benefit.

"Medical hypnosis is different from entertainment hypnosis. The entertainer-hypnotist makes you think that he hypnotizes you because he is a powerful person. Physician-hypnotists know that hypnosis is effective because of the patient's desire and expectant attitude. The physician uses this tool with respect, realizing that every patient is an individual personality who should be treated with dignity both in and out of hypnosis.

"I really do not hypnotize you, and I have never hypnotized a single human being in my life! However, many individuals have entered into deep hypnosis *because they really wanted to do so.* I cannot make you close your eyes by suggesting eye closure unless you *wish* to close your eyes. I cannot make you count to yourself if you do *not wish* to count. And I have no way of know-ing whether or not you are counting to yourself. I cannot make you lift your arm, can I, if you do not care to lift it? Our relationship, therefore, is a co-operative one and *not* a mental 'tug of war.' For instance, you will raise your arm, not because you have to, but *because you want to.* Also, if I suggest that you drop your arm limp, relaxed, that is the way it will drop—limp." The operator can lift the arm and let it slip from his fingers. If the arm is relaxed, he can remark, "That's just the way you will relax.

"Hypnosis is a learning process and, of course, as in any other learning procedure, one begins with very simple suggestions. Isn't that logical? Is this clear? And if you follow the simple suggestions, then naturally you will follow complicated ones. May I repeat, you will not really be in a trance, even though we refer to it as such for want of a better term.

"Actually, we are being hypnotized continually as a part of everyday life. When I sit in a rowboat, fishing, the monotonous ripples relax me and time passes by rapidly. The first thing I am apt to say is, 'Have I been here for 6 hours?' It seemed like 3 hours, because a part of that time I was in a reverielike state. Or how many times have you been in a theater, engrossed in a movie? As you looked at that screen, you became fixated on the movie and registered all types of emotions just as if it was real. You forgot who was sitting on your left and who was sitting on your right. Because you identified with the picture on the screen, you may even have forgotten what city you were in at the time. Next time you are at the theater, turn around and notice the 'glassy' stare in everyone's eyes. Of course, after it was over, you realized that what made you cry and laugh was not reality. Yet, for an hour and a half, you reacted to what you saw and heard as if it was real—yet it was an illusion. In other words, you were 'entranced,' but you did not think of this as hypnosis. However, is this any different from when a stage hypnotist tells you that you will itch because 'ants' are crawling all over your body?

"Attainment of deep relaxation is easy, if you follow my suggestions. The capacity to be deeply relaxed is already present within you. I merely bring it to the surface, and only act as a guide. Is that clear?"

In addition, it should be emphasized, "You will do nothing to violate your moral code; you will not reveal information of a personal nature unless you wish to do so; you will be completely aware of what is said; and you will not act contrary to your wishes. Finally, every suggestion will be for your benefit."

With this preliminary talk, the operator can remove the apprehension, fear, anxiety and tension that are naturally present in all individuals undergoing a hypnotic induction for the first time.

13

Authoritarian or Direct Technics of Hypnosis

In general, even though variants are used, the methods most commonly employed for inducing formal hypnosis are: direct or authoritarian; indirect or permissive, with or without arm levitation; confusion technics; mechanical technics. All technics utilize ideosensory and ideomotor conditioning. The formalistic technics described in this chapter make full use of ritual and expectancy of success. Hence, the technic which the patient expects to be hypnotized by is the most satisfactory one. Since one of the principal features of hypnosis is a regression to a primitive level of mental functioning, it can be initiated best by relaxation.[1] Therefore, it is imperative to establish belief that relaxation will occur during the initial portion of the induction. The simplest and best method for establishing this belief is to induce the feeling of lid heaviness or catalepsy that results from eye-fixation. All direct induction methods—and there are innumerable combinations—depend on eye-fixation with resultant fatigue and relaxation of various muscle groups, first small, then large. The following technic, which the author prefers, is illustrative.

MOTIVATIONAL TECHNIC UTILIZING PROGRESSIVE RELAXATION

The verbalization is as follows: "Now get as comfortable as possible. Rest your head on the back of the chair. Fix your eyes directly above your forehead. Keep looking directly above your hairline at one spot on the ceiling. Notice now that your eyes are getting very, very *heavy*, your *lids* are getting very, very, very *tired*. Your lids are getting *heavier* and *heavier*, and the heavier that your lids get now, the better you will relax your lids. The better you relax your

eyelids, the better you will follow all subsequent suggestions." (Note the motivation for eye-closure implied here.) "Your lids are getting *heavier* and *heavier*. They are getting *very, very tired*. Your lids are getting *very, very heavy*. Your eyelids are blinking. That is a good sign that the lids are getting *heavier* and *heavier*. Your lids are blinking a little more. That is right. If you really wish to go into a deeper state of relaxation, all you have to do is to let your lids close *tightly*, very tightly, at the count of 3. You will close your eyes not because you have to but because you really wish to go deeper and deeper relaxed. One—your eyelids are getting *heavier* and *heavier*. Two—getting much heavier. Your lids are blinking still more." The following must be said as if it were all one sentence: "Three—now, *close your eyes tight* and let your eyeballs roll up into the back of your head. As your eyeballs roll up into the back of your head, notice how your lids are sticking tighter and tighter together. You feel the tightness, do you not?" (Subject nods head.) "This shows that it's really beginning to work. And your lids continue to stick tighter and tighter together. And as your eyeballs are rolled up toward your forehead for a few moments longer, you will go deeper and deeper relaxed. And if you *really* wish to go deeper, all you have to do is to slowly count backward from 100 to zero. With each number that you count backward (ideosensory activity) and with each breath that you take (ideomotor activity), you will go *deeper* and *deeper relaxed*." (More motivation to relax.) "And if you wish to go *deeper*, just think of a numb, heavy, wooden-like feeling that is beginning in your toes. Just imagine, in your 'mind's eye,' if you will, that you are sitting on your legs in tailor-fashion or cross-legged; or think, if you will, of the heavy, numb feeling that you may have had when you fell asleep on your arm; or think of a numb, heavy, stiff feeling similar to that which occurs when your dentist injects procaine into your gums." (Such suggestions really tap the subject's experiential background.) "The numb, heavy feeling is moving *up, up, up* from your toes, up to your feet, up to your legs, up to your thighs. With every breath, you will go *deeper* and *deeper* relaxed. Now, it is *your* privilege to go into as deep a state of relaxation as you wish. It's really so easy to let yourself go *deeper* and *deeper relaxed*. You will do so only *after* you raise your arm straight toward the ceiling. So if you *really* wish to go deeper, at the count of 3, slowly raise either your right arm or your left arm, whichever arm you choose." (Motivation for raising of arm.) "It is very important to concentrate on the idea that as you raise your arm you say, think and imagine with each motion of your arm upward, 'I am falling deeper and deeper relaxed.' So, at the count of 3, you will slowly raise either the right arm or the left arm. You can now decide, 'Which arm am I going to raise *slowly* straight toward the ceiling?'" (Arm begins to rise.) "1 . . . 2 . . . 3 . . . Now slowly raise your arm, slowly, just a half inch or so at a time. And with each movement of the arm upward, just think to yourself that 'I am going *deeper* and *deeper* relaxed.' And if you really wish to go deeper after your arm has reached a perpendicular position, you will notice that you will go into a nice, deep, pleasant state of relaxation. The stiffer your fingers become, and the stiffer your arm becomes from the wrist down to the elbow, the deeper relaxed you will get. You will now feel yourself going deeper and deeper relaxed, and *you just can't wait* until your arm is stretched straight toward the ceiling. That's right, straight as an arrow, just as stiff and rigid as an iron bar! *After* your arm is raised straight toward the ceiling, you will go deeper and deeper relaxed!" (Motivation for limb catalepsy.) "That's fine. Now straighten out your fingers *stiff, stiffer. Spread them apart! Stiff* and *rigid, stiff* and *rigid.* And now, as I stroke the arm, if you really wish to go deeper, the arm becomes *stiffer* and *more rigid, stiffer* and *more rigid, stiffer* and *more rigid.* Now

straighten out your arm, straighten out the fingers. That's right! Just say to yourself, 'I cannot bend my arm. My arm is *stiff* and *rigid.*' You are not asleep, unconscious or in a trance, but are completely awake! Thus you will derive more benefit from my suggestions because they will 'sink' in more readily." (Thus far there is no need for challenges. These often can handicap the inexperienced operator because, if the subject succeeds in meeting the challenge, the rapport is broken.)

The technic is deepened as follows: "Now, if you really wish to go deeper, all you have to do is to *slowly,* and I do mean *slowly,* allow your arm to fall a half inch or an inch at a time. At the count of 3, perhaps, you might say to yourself, 'I am going deeper and deeper relaxed with each motion of my arm downward. I will go *deeper* and *deeper* relaxed.' Now, at the count of 3, let your arm fall. 1 . . . 2 . . . 3 . . . And as your arm falls, you too will fall into a *deeper* and *deeper* state of relaxation. As your arm falls, you will fall *deeper* and *deeper* relaxed. And now, perhaps, you might be willing to give yourself a suggestion, providing you wish to *really* relax deeper, that the moment your arm or any portion of your hand touches any portion of your body, you will go *deeper* and *deeper relaxed* (more motivation). You might be willing to accept this suggestion as a cue that every muscle and every fiber in your body will relax completely. Every muscle will relax. You are going to relax completely. Now, as I lift your arm, it is just as *heavy* as lead. And when I drop your arm, you are going to drop *deeper and deeper relaxed.* Your eyelids will remain *tightly* closed and you will feel yourself going *deeper* and *deeper* into a nice, pleasant, soothing state of relaxation. As I lift your arm, you are going to *relax* still *deeper.*" When the arm is slowly lifted, it is gently clasped at the wrist by the thumb and the forefinger of the operator. He lifts the arm gently and remarks: "As I lift your arm, it is getting *heavier* and *heavier.* It is going to get *heavier* and *heavier,* and it is going to slip out of my grasp. When it drops to your thigh, it will drop with a resounding *thud,* just like a towel heavy with water, and then you will drop even *deeper relaxed.* At the count of 3, I will drop your arm. 1 . . . 2 . . . 3 . . . deeper, way down!" Here, too, a psychological suggestion reinforces a physiologic effect. Some subjects drop the arm slowly. This indicates resistance. The subject may be only in a hypnoidal state—a precursor to actual hypnosis. If catalepsy has been obtained or if there is a waxy flexibility of the fingers (*flexibilitas cerea*), a somnambulistic state may have been achieved. In this state, subjects are very alert. They characteristically respond with pinpoint precision or literalness.

This technic continually motivates the subject. You are, in reality, always in a "one-up position," but he seldom realizes this fact. The subject is always given an opportunity to co-operate, and, if he agrees to follow the suggestions, he will go deeper. The lid closure was our number one objective. Because some motivation was used every step of the way, the subject had to follow the suggestions. When I said, "If you really wish to go deeper, you will close your eyes," I was really saying, "If you don't want to co-operate, you don't have to close your eyes, and you won't enter into hypnosis." I generally preface my remarks by stating emphatically, "This is not a case of 'mind over matter.' It is your wish to enter into hypnosis, not mine. Now, if you wish to go still deeper, it's up to you."

TECHNIC FOR POSTHYPNOTIC SUGGESTIONS

If you wish to give your subject posthypnotic suggestions, the following remarks are conducive to the retention of these suggestions: "Everything that you wish to remember will be retained with remarkable ease. It will *all* be remembered as if it has been indelibly etched on your mind; just as if a carbon copy had been made and imprinted on your mind! Because you are going to store all this information, you will be able to recall it more readily. Perhaps you won't remember all of it today or tomorrow, but you certainly will during the next week, month or year. None of it ever will be forgotten! You are going to retain more than you would ordinarily.

"At this time, may I give you a posthypnotic suggestion that you will always re-member? At any time that you wish to have hypnosis induced, and remember it will occur only with your permission, I shall touch you on the *right* shoulder. This will be a cue for you to drop promptly into a deep state of relaxation. Simultaneously, you will close your eyes, let your eyeballs roll up into the back of your head and experience this exact state of complete muscular relaxation. I will repeat the suggestion. At any time in the future that I touch you on your right shoulder, you will relax completely, and this will occur only if and when you wish to relax. I can't induce hypnosis unless you desire it. Remember, a touch on your *right* shoulder will be a prearranged signal to close your eyes, let your eyeballs roll up into the back of your head and promptly fall into a deep state of relaxation. Remember, you will not go to sleep, be unconscious or even be in a trance. Also, you will hear everything, actually more than usual. A touch on the *left* shoulder will be the signal for dehypnotization. You will open your eyes, feel wonderful, very refreshed, relaxed and aware of everything that happened." It is very important to give suggestions conducive to the patient's well-being. Many subjects develop a headache as a result of the intense mental concentration.

Before bringing a subject out of hypnosis, always compliment him on how well he co-operated and then say: "Now, I am going to touch you on the *left* shoulder. You feel fine! You will open your eyes, feeling *perfectly wonderful*. Open your eyes wide. That's right."

Also, always compliment the subject after the hypnosis is terminated: "Thank you for being such a wonderful subject." Expressing your gratitude at both the hypnotic and the nonhypnotic level motivates the subject for the next session.

EYE-FIXATION TECHNIC WITH SLEEP SUGGESTIONS

This is a favorite technic of many operators who use the words "sleep" or "asleep."

1. "In gazing at that spot you will *relax quickly* and *deeply*." Pause 10 seconds.

2. "Your legs will grow *heavy—very heavy*." Pause 10 seconds.

3. "Your arms will grow *heavy—very heavy.*" Pause 10 seconds.

4. "Your entire body will grow *heavy—very heavy.*" Pause 10 seconds.

5. "And now your legs are heavy, your arms are *heavy*, and your entire body is *heavy*. You are deeply relaxed. You are relaxing *more* and *more* all the time." Pause 10 seconds.

6. "You are so *deeply* relaxed that your eyes are now growing *heavy* and they are becoming *tired*, very *tired*. You will want to close your eyes. As you close your eyes, you will enjoy perfect relaxation." Pause 10 seconds. It is very important at this point, or at any point previous to this, to note and observe carefully the movement and the condition of the patient's eyes. Failure to do this may result in "loss of patient." If the patient's eyes close at this time, or at any time previous to this, skip 7 and proceed with 8. **THIS IS VERY IMPORTANT.**

7. "Your eyes are growing *heavier* all the time. They are closing—closing—closing. They are so *very heavy* and *tired*, you cannot keep them open—closing—closing—closing." At this point the eyes will close in about 70 per cent of the subjects. If the eyes do not close, repeat these words for another minute or two. Then, if they still have not closed, direct the patient to close them by saying, "Close your eyes, please," which he will do presently. In rare instances, the patient may already be in a hypnotic trance at this point, and the operator should gently place a finger on each eyelid to close his eyes. No matter whether the eyes close spontaneously as suggested, or as instructed, it is important to proceed precisely at the moment that the eyes close, quickly and emphatically, without a second's delay:

8. "*Deep, deep asleep.*" This phrase is uttered in a decisive and emphatic voice, forcefully and yet not too loud, instead of in the previous lulling and soothing tone. Repeat the phrase "Deep, deep, asleep" every 2 or 3 seconds, 4 or 5 times. This will tend to narrow down consciousness to only one idea, namely, "*deep, deep, asleep*"—as in fact the patient will be at this point in one of the several stages of hypnosis.

EYE-FIXATION TECHNIC WITHOUT SLEEP SUGGESTIONS

The following is a more rapid and direct authoritarian technic:

The patient is seated comfortably with his eyes fixed on a given spot slightly forward and upward. As in the previous technic, there should be no strain on any part of the neck or the body; the hands should be unclasped, resting comfortably in the lap. The patient is instructed to close his eyes any time he feels like it, and then to keep his eyes closed.

"I will teach you to relax. You will *relax every fiber, every muscle in your body.* When I raise your right hand, let it fall limply into your lap." (Pick up one hand and let it slip out of your fingers slowly.) "Let your hand fall as though it is as *heavy* as *lead*, just like a wet dish towel. Your arm is completely relaxed." (It is necessary to accomplish this before proceeding further.) Then continue: "Breathe in deeply and relax your diaphragm. Again." (This must be said 5 or 6 times in unison with the patient's breathing. Hyperventilation will tend to produce even deeper relaxation.) "Now relax your feet and legs the same as you did your hands. Make them *very, very heavy*. I want you to feel a very pleasant tingling, relaxed feeling in your toes. It will travel up from the soles of your feet, up your legs to your abdomen and chest." (Pause.) "Take another deep breath and relax still more. Again." (Repeat this 3 or 4 times, coinciding with the patient's breathing.) Then continue: "Now relax your lower jaw . . . more . . . Relax your cheeks." (By this time the eyes usually are closed.) If the eyes are not closed, say: "Now your eyes are very tired and heavy. They are closing, closing, closing." (The eyes will probably close.) If the eyes still are not closed, say: "Let your eyes close." If the eyes still remain open, request the patient to close his eyes by simply saying, "Close your eyes, please."

Occasionally a patient may be in a hypnotic state with a fixed stare, in which case it will be necessary to draw the lids gently over his eyes. Then continue: "Relax your forehead. Listen only to my voice. You can think of anything you wish, but you will

Eye fixation induction technic.

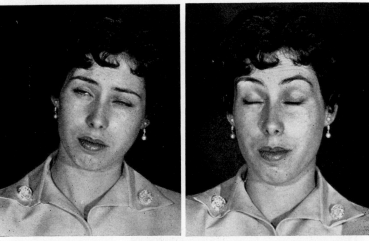

(*Left*) Beginning eye closure.
(*Right*) Eye closure complete. Inability to open eyes.

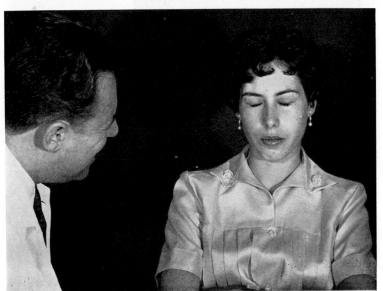

Suggestions for eye catalepsy.

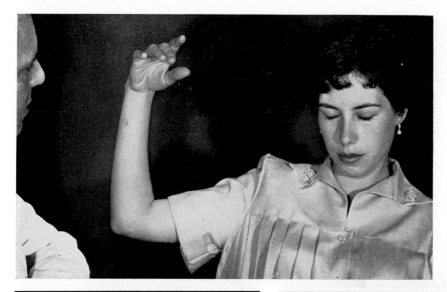

Suggestions for limb catalepsy.

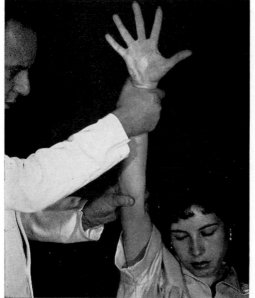

(*Left*) Testing for limb catalepsy.
(*Right*) Subject just dehypnotized.

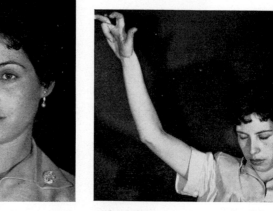

Somnambulism.

Flexibilitas cerea—waxy flexibility of fingers.

concentrate on my voice. I want you to go into an even *deeper* state of relaxation. 1, 2, 3 . . . deep, *deeply relaxed* . . . every muscle from your head to your toes is completely relaxed. You will remain relaxed until I ask you to open your eyes. When you open your eyes, you will be completely relaxed and full of confidence for your next visit. Each time, when you come back for your appointment, you will always relax quickly and deeply with this method. You will never forget these suggestions."

The patient is "alerted" as follows: "When I count 3, you will open your eyes and be completely relaxed, feeling fine. 1 . . . 2 . . . 3."

HANDCLASP TECHNIC

With the patient sitting in a comfortable position, tell him: "Close your eyes. Now clasp your hands together and make them as tight as you can." There is constant repetition to utilize sensory-imagery conditioning, as follows: "Think to yourself, 'I should like to make my hands stick tightly together.'" This is interspersed with "Keep your eyes closed until I ask you to open them. Imagine how nice it would be to develop self-relaxation." When the hands tighten, the operator adds, "Now you feel the pressure in your fingers as your hands tighten and *tighten* still more!" The operator watches the hands; if they do not tighten, he waits, as this is indicative of resistance. If the hands are tightly stuck together, he continues: "Your fingertips are getting numb, very numb! Your hands are sticking tighter and tighter together, and you feel a pleasant sensation in your thumbs as they press down tightly upon one another." When the hands appear to be tightening from pressure, he proceeds: "Your hands are now so tightly stuck together that you cannot tell your left fingers from your right. Your hands feel as if they are a solid piece of wood. They are now sticking together without any effort. You have no desire to take them apart. *YOU DON'T WANT TO TAKE YOUR HANDS APART.*" From here on, if the patient does not separate his hands, he is deepened in the usual manner.

POSTURAL-SWAY METHOD

The following method has been described by Watkins[3]:

The therapist speaks to the patient as follows: "Now Jones, I'd like to have you stand here with your heels and your toes together and your body erect, shoulders back. That's right. Breathe comfortably and easily with your hands at your sides. Now close your eyes. Just imagine that your feet are hinged to the floor and your body is like a stick pointing upward in the air, free to move back and forth. You will probably find after a while you will become unsteady. Don't worry, if you should fall, I'll catch you." (This last remark is given in a rather matter-of-fact way, almost as a side comment. If previous suggestibility tests have been given, and the therapist is quite certain the patient will enter the trance, he may modify this statement by saying, "Don't worry, I will catch you *when* you fall.")

The therapist then continues: "Now while you are standing there, breathe very calmly and easily. Just imagine that your body is floating up into space. Don't try to do anything, and don't try *not* to do anything. Just stand there and let yourself drift." The therapist is then silent for a time, perhaps 15 seconds up to a minute. If the patient is suggestible, he will sway back and forth slightly.

The therapist should place himself at the side of the patient where he can line the back of the patient's head or the tip of his nose against a mark on the opposite wall so that a slight backward or forward swaying movement can be easily detected and measured. It is even convenient to have a card against the wall on which black vertical lines have been ruled about an inch apart, thus making it easier to determine the amount of sway. Usually the therapist will soon detect the rhythm of the swaying, since it is almost impossible for anybody to stand perfectly still. There will always be some swaying, although it may be slight in the more unsuggestible patients. One will generally find that the more suggestible the patient, the greater will be the amplitude of the swaying arc.

The therapist next begins to reinforce this swaying by timing his remarks to coincide with it. As soon as the patient has reached the extreme forward part of the arc and begins to sway backward, the therapist says, "Now you are drifting backward." Frequently this will cause the patient immediately to catch himself and to reverse the direction, whereupon the therapist instantly follows it with, "Now you are drifting forward." As the swaying continues the therapist reinforces it with "Drifting forward, drifting backward and forward, backward, forward, backward, etc." The tone is low, soft, and firm. The therapist should be about 1 to 2 feet away from the patient's ear and should repeat the suggestions in a low, soft monotone from which all harshness has been deleted. It should have an almost pleading quality, monotonous like the drone of a bee. There should be no change in pitch, and the patter should be continued steadily. Occasionally it may be varied from "drifting forward" to "swaying forward, swaying backward, swaying over backward, now swaying forward," or "leaning forward, backward, forward, backward," etc.—on and on in a monotonous, repetitious voice.

As the therapist observes the amplitude of the swaying arc increasing, he may make the voice somewhat less pleading, less soft, and more dominant and controlling, even injecting some emotional pitch into the "forward, backward, forward, backward."

When the amplitude of the swaying arc has become quite substantial—6 or more inches—it is probable that some light degree of trance has been induced. Suggestibility should then be checked by beginning a command of "forward, backward" a little before the patient has reached the maximum sway of the arc. If the patient is suggestible, and there is a degree of hypnotic trance, he will interrupt the natural sway in order to follow the therapist's suggestions. The past remarks of the therapist have so closely followed the patient's swaying behavior that the patient begins to think to himself, "What this man says is true, I am swaying backward. Then I do sway forward." Consequently, the therapist's prestige is increased, and the patient begins to follow the suggestions instead of leading them. From this point on, the therapist can usually assume the more dominating role and direct rather than follow the swaying of the patient.

To induce deeper trance the voice tone is now made much firmer and the swaying suggestions are given somewhat more rapidly, "Swaying forward, swaying backward, forward, backward," the volume of the voice growing stronger and stronger. Finally, an attempt is made to induce the patient to fall over backward into a deep trance. The emphasis on the "backward" is increased, and on the "forward" diminished, and the verb is changed from "drifting" or "swaying" to "falling, *falling backward*, falling forward, *falling backward*, falling forward, *fall-over backward*, falling, falling, *falling, falling*" rather rapidly and in a higher-pitched and more emotional tone. If a deep trance has been induced, the patient will increase the amplitude of

his sway until he can no longer stand erect. He will then fall over backward in a deep trance where he may be caught by the therapist and eased into a waiting chair.

If the patient is in a light trance only he may start to fall backward, but catch himself by placing one of his feet back, or attempt to sway sideways or steady himself voluntarily in some manner. This indicates to the therapist that a deep trance has not yet been induced and he can then do one of two things: he may either continue the monotonous repetition of "falling forward, falling backward," etc., to induce a deeper degree of trance; or he may reassure the patient that he will not fall by placing a hand lightly behind his shoulder. This allays fears which might arise and interrupt the hypnotic process. After the patient realizes that he will not be permitted to fall and hurt himself, he tends to loose the signs of anxiety which may have begun to appear. He may then allow himself to fall back against the therapist's arm, whereupon the therapist continues the suggestions, "Falling over backward, falling backward, falling back into a deep sleep, back into a deep sleep, deep sleep, deep sleep," and then eases the patient gradually over into a chair. This, preferably an armchair, should have been placed behind the patient. He can also be gradually lowered back upon a couch which has been located conveniently near.

If the patient is either completely limp or in a stiff catatonic state when he is placed back on the chair or cot, it is evident that a fairly deep degree of trance has been induced. If, however, he is able to help himself either by taking steps backward or by putting his hands on the armchair and guiding himself into it, then only a light hypnoidal trance has been induced.

THE COIN TECHNIC

The coin technic can begin with the eyes open. This is a very rapid and direct method.

Here the thumb is used as a fixation point. Instructions are given that at the count of 3, two things will happen: the eyes will close tight and, at the same time, the fingers which tightly clasp a coin will open and allow the coin to drop. The sound of the coin hitting the floor will be a signal that the eyes are closed tight, *very tight*. At the moment of eye closure, the outstretched arm is lightly stroked to produce limb catalepsy or rigidity, a sign that a medium stage of hypnosis has been reached. To ensure success, the instructions to close the eyes and simultaneously allow the coin to drop can be repeated several times.

The following is one verbalization of the coin technic: "All you have to do in this technic is to look at your thumb and keep your arm stretched out at eye level. There are only *two* things you have to do if you *really* wish to go into a *deep* state of hypnosis. All you have to do if you *really* wish to go into a *deep* state of relaxation is to keep staring at your thumb. Remember there are only *two* things you have to remember. Number *one*, when I count to 3, *open your fist* and *close your eyes* simultaneously! Remember that! Open your fist and close your eyes at the count of 3. These are the only *two* things you have to remember. And when you hear the coin drop and hit the floor, let that be a signal that you *can't* open your eyes. Now remember, if you *really* wish to go into a *nice, deep, pleasant, soothing, refreshing state of relaxation*, there are only *two* things you have to do. Simultaneously, at the count of three you *open* your fist and close your eyes. 1 . . . remember there are two things you are going to do. 2 . . . 3 . . . *straighten out* the *fingers, stiff* and *rigid, spread them apart;* that is right, stiff and rigid, like a bar of steel. And as they stiffen, you go *deeper* and *deeper*, way down, *deeper*, and *deeper relaxed!* The arm is now cataleptic." (The operator can lightly stroke the outstretched arm to deepen the catalepsy.)

THE COIN TECHNIC WITH EYES CLOSED

"If you will follow my instructions exactly as I give them to you, you will go into a deep, deep state of relaxation. Take this coin in the palm of your hand and close your eyes tightly together. Now clasp your fingers tightly together so that the coin will not fall out of your fist. Place your arm in front of you. Keep your fingers tightly closed on the coin until I tell you to drop it.

"Notice, now, how the coin is grasped tightly between your fingers. I am going to count from 1 to 10. As you feel the fingers around the coin, you will notice your fingers relaxing. They will relax and open so that the coin will fall to the floor at the count of 10.

"Now close your eyes. Your eyes are closed very tight, tighter and tighter. When the coin drops to the floor at the count of 10, you will straighten out your hand and arm. The sound of the coin hitting the floor will seal your eyes still tighter. 1 . . . your fingers are opening. Your fingers are relaxing and your eyes are tighter and tighter. 2 . . . your fingers are opening a little more and your eyes are closing tighter and tighter. Your eyes are stuck so tightly together, it feels as if they are glued shut. And the tighter they stick together, the more comfortable and relaxed you will go. 3 . . . you are doing fine. Your fingers are opening a little more and I notice that one of your fingers is beginning to open still more. That is fine. First one and then another. 4 . . . all the fingers are beginning to open, just a little more, as you go deeper and deeper relaxed. 5 . . . with each breath you take, your fingers are opening a little more. Remember that when the coin hits the floor, that will be the signal that your eyes will be closed tightly together. 6 . . . also remember that when the coin hits the floor, you will straighten out your fingers stiff and rigid. Your right arm will get stiff and rigid from the fingers to the wrist, from the elbow to the shoulder. 7 . . . your fingers are opening still more and the coin is about to drop to the floor. 8 . . . just a little more. You are going deeper and deeper relaxed. With every breath you take, you will go deeper and deeper relaxed. 9 . . . remember that when the coin hits the floor, your right arm will become just as rigid as an iron bar and your eyes will be stuck tightly together. 10 . . . open your fingers. Your arm is as stiff as an iron bar from your fingers up to your wrist to your shoulders." At this point, a deft stroking of the arm from the fingers up to the shoulder is sufficient to induce catalepsy.

This aspect of the coin technic can be made part of a deepening procedure, as follows: "At the count of 3, you will let your arm fall, and with each inch that it falls, you will fall deeper and deeper relaxed. 1 . . . 2 . . . 3 . . . your arm is falling. Slowly. That's right. And as your arm falls, you fall deeper and deeper relaxed. And when your arm returns to your lap, every muscle, every fiber in your body will be completely relaxed. (Patient's arm falls to his lap.) "I am going to pick it up and, as I let it fall, you will fall even deeper relaxed."

HANDLING RESISTANCE IN COIN TECHNICS

"As your arm remains outstretched, just tell yourself, 'I can't bend my arm to the right and I can't bend it to the left. I can't raise it and I can't drop it.' It just remains out there as you go deeper and deeper relaxed. Now it seems like it's lifting, lifting, higher and higher. And as it keeps lifting, the palm of your hand gets lighter and lighter. That's right." (The arm remains in the same position.) "Remember, if your arm falls, you will fall deeper and deeper relaxed." (The patient does not realize that the arm is bound to fall eventually.)

If resistance is still present, the following is helpful: Rapidly suggest different and contradictory sensory changes—that the right arm is getting lighter, the left arm is getting heavier, the right arm is getting heavier, the left arm is getting lighter. Similar suggestions referable to the lower limbs are made, interspersed with suggestions that the subject can move the arm upward if he wishes to remain "awake," or move it downward if he wishes to go deeper, or that one arm will spontaneously lift if his "subconscious" wishes to resist, or will fall if he wishes to go deeper. In addition, attention is called to the pressure produced by the shoes or by other objects such as a wrist watch, a ring or a tight collar. I have the subject count backward, but I instruct him to use only even numbers from 100 to 70 and odd numbers from 75 to 45. Finally, from sheer mental exhaustion or in desperation, the subject "escapes" from the myriad suggestions and accepts the suggestions to be hypnotized.

STARE TECHNIC WITH SLEEP SUGGESTIONS

Many physicians object to using the direct stare—looking directly into the eyes of the subject—because it is associated with the stage performer who makes full use of dominance, submission and seductiveness. In our culture, the "evil eye" is taboo. However, it often is effective when all other methods fail. It is simply ridiculous to outlaw this method merely because of irrational prejudice. The stage technic with eye stare is a very powerful authoritarian technic which is effective on those who expect to be hypnotized by such a method. It should be used only when a very dominating approach is indicated.

"Look in my eyes, and do not take your eyes off mine. . . . Keep looking at me. Let yourself go. That's right, look at me. Think of nothing but sleep. Your eyes are beginning to feel *heavy;* your eyes are closing . . . closing . . . closing. Close your eyes!" At this point the patient's eyes will close if they haven't already done so. (It is important that the operator does not return his gaze to the patient's eyes but fixes his gaze at the base of the nose between the eyes. The patient will not know the difference.) Then the operator continues: "Your eyes are now closed, they are heavy, you are going to sleep. Your arms are heavy, your legs are heavy, your entire body is heavy. You are going deeper into sleep all the time." The operator continues now with a deepening procedure. If the patient does not close his eyes at the point mentioned previously, the operator continues with: "Your eyes are growing heavier all the time. Your vision is getting more and more blurry. You will go to sleep, you cannot do otherwise. You cannot feel anything; your body is growing heavy and numb." And then he adds, in a commanding tone, "*Sleep, deep sleep.*" This usually turns the balance, and the eyes close; the patient goes into a hypnotic state. If, on the other hand, the patient does not shut his eyes, it may be because of rigid fixation. The operator slowly closes the patient's eyes and continues with suggestions of sleep, heaviness, etc. The operator removes his fingers from the patient's eyes after a minute or so and then makes his test for catalepsy.

STARE TECHNIC WITHOUT SLEEP SUGGESTIONS

Some subjects respond better to the stare approach because it is *what they expect!* The stare technic is described here to show that it is really the conviction of the subject that leads to hypnosis. There are many modifications of this approach. The reader is referred to an excellent description by Meares.[2]

Stand directly opposite the subject and have him stare into your eyes as you focus your own eyes from the bridge of the subject's nose to the tip. This causes dilation and contraction of your pupils and fixes the attention of the subject.

"Now, just look into my eyes. Now you feel a ray between my eyes and yours and you feel yourself irresistibly being pulled toward me. Irresistibly being pulled right toward me. A terrific pull. Can't hold yourself up." (In the stare technic, *no* challenges are used.) "At the count of 3 you will close your eyes. That is right. 1 . . . 2 . . . 3 . . . Let your eyes close tight, and your head fall forward. Your head gets heavier and heavier as it falls forward. You are going deeper and deeper relaxed. Way down. Your head is getting *heavier* and *heavier. Heavier* and *heavier.* Your head gets just as heavy as lead as you drop deeper and deeper relaxed. Your head is falling forward. That's a good sign that you are going deeper and deeper relaxed. And now, at the count of 3, raise both arms straight out toward your side. 1 . . . 2 . . . 3 . . . *Stiff* and *rigid* like a bar of steel. Stiffer. And the stiffer your arms get, the deeper relaxed you will go. Stiff and rigid. Like steel, like stone." (To deepen the state, gently rotate the subject in a small arc.) "And you drop deeper and deeper as you feel yourself swaying around and and around in a circle, and the arc is getting larger and larger as you sway around and around." (Place both hands on the subject's shoulders and gradually increase the arc as he is swayed to and fro or around and around.) "Around and around you sway in an ever-increasing arc. And as you sway more and more, you feel yourself going deeper and deeper, deeper and deeper. And now at the count of 3 you will just let your arms drop right to your side. 1 . . . 2 . . . 3 . . . and you will go deeper after you drop your arms." (His arms drop to his sides.)

"That's right. Now, at the count of 3, you will open your eyes and feel fine. Feel fine. 1 . . . 2 . . . 3 . . . ."

REPETITIVE TECHNIC FOR HANDLING RESISTANT PATIENT

Meares[2] has described an excellent technic for dealing with resistance in direct induction procedures. The patient who resists pulls his arm backward when a forward movement is suggested. He is asked to close his eyes and move his arm to and fro, with the elbow supported on a table or couch. This is maintained until a rhythmic motion is well established. There is a gradual withdrawal of contact after the arm movements become automatic. The subject is then asked to open his eyes and to try to stop the repetitive movement. At the same time, the suggestion, "Your arm goes to and fro, to and fro," is kept up, only now the suggestion is really synchronized with the movements, whereas at first it was at variance with the movements of the arm.

There are several variations of this technic, as, "Your arm is stiff as a board as it goes round and round, round and round."

These technics illustrate an interesting point, namely, that the resistant patient is resistant only to the second idea if two different ideas are suggested simultaneously— the first idea is uncritically accepted because the subject is thrown off guard by the second idea. In this variation of the method of repetitive movement, the first idea is the rigidity of the arm. The second idea is the movement of the arm. For a while many patients resist the suggestion of movement, but the fact that they have accepted the suggestion of rigidity of the arm means that they are well on the way to satisfactory hypnosis.

REFERENCES

1. Kroger, W. S.: Techniques of hypnosis, J.A.M.A. *172*:675-680, 1960.
2. Meares, A.: A System of Medical Hypnosis, Philadelphia, Saunders, 1960.
3. Watkins, J. G.: Hypnotherapy of War Neuroses, New York, Ronald, 1949.

14

Permissive or Indirect Technics

In this chapter, arm-levitation and miscellaneous technics of various types are described. These may be used in conjunction with sensory-imagery or picture-visualization technics. The levitation technics are best adapted to emotionally disturbed individuals who require more permissive approaches. As mentioned, the psychoneurotic has resistances to yielding his symptoms and therefore is often refractory to an authoritarian approach.

All levitation technics make use of the subject's ideomotor and sensory activities. The author's technic differs from those herein described[1, 6, 8] in that the patient is motivated each step of the way. Also, the term "sleep" is never employed. The subject never realizes that he is being controlled at all times by carefully graded suggestions to slowly deepen the hypnotic state.

Levitation technics are initially time-consuming, but any posthypnotic suggestion or cue to reinduce hypnosis obviates the need for reinduction. Glove anesthesia is induced more readily than states requiring authoritarian technics. Watkins'[6] progressive anesthesia technic, when combined with arm levitation, is excellent for those patients requiring anesthesia.

THE ARM-LEVITATION TECHNIC

The advantages of the author's modification of this technic are that the subject is not rushed and he is convinced that the responses result from the operator's suggestions. It is time-consuming and frequently taxes the patience of the operator.

The verbalization is as follows: "Would you mind placing your hands on your thighs, and, if you please, just look down at your fingers, at your hands as they rest lightly on your knees. Perhaps you wouldn't mind pressing down real *hard;* if you will, just *press down hard,* just as *hard* as you *can,* as if you are pushing your knees and feet through the floor. Of course, this is impossible! Perhaps you can press a little harder and still harder. And, as you press harder and harder, become aware, if you will, that you are building up a great amount of tension in your fingers. Notice the tension building up in your fingers as you press *harder* and *harder.* Just keep pressing *harder* and *harder.* And, perhaps, you can feel an increased sensitivity in your fingertips. And notice, if you will, please, the texture of the cloth of your trousers. And maybe, as you keep pressing, you will notice the warmth of your body as it comes through the cloth of your trousers. And keep pressing, *harder* and *harder.* And, of course, you know that the opposite of the tension that you are building in your fingers is relaxation. So, any time that you might wish to relax, it is really so simple; all you have to do is just close your eyes and visualize, if you will, that one of the fingers on either the left hand or the right hand is getting lighter than all the others. Remember, the opposite of tension is relaxation; I am sure that you will agree to that. And if you *really* want to relax, one of the fingers on *either* the *left* hand or the *right* hand is getting lighter than all the others. And as it gets lighter than all the others, perhaps one of the fingers will begin to lift up in the air. And one of the fingers will begin to move on either the left hand or the right hand. Which finger will it be? Maybe it will be the little finger of the left hand or perhaps it will be the ring finger of the right hand. It might even be the forefinger of the left hand. And I notice the forefinger of the right hand is beginning to lift. And it's *lifting, lifting, lifting.* And as it gets lighter than all of the other fingers, the other fingers of that hand can begin to lift. And very soon, if you wish, you are going to notice the most wonderful sensation—a floating, soothing sensation. The right hand is lifting in the direction of your face. Lifting, lifting, lifting. And perhaps you might be willing to give yourself the suggestions that 'With each motion that my arm lifts upward I will go deeper and deeper relaxed; my arm is lifting not because it has to, but because it wants to. I will soon reach a *deep* state, a *deep state of relaxation.*' The right hand is now lifting, lifting lifting, lifting, lifting! And perhaps you can visualize a balloon tied around your wrist, and now another balloon, 3, 4 balloons are tugging at your wrist. And then you can visualize still another balloon. A red balloon, a blue balloon, and the arm is now *lifting, lifting, lifting, lifting!* And as soon as it touches your face you might be willing to give yourself a suggestion that the moment any portion of your hand touches any portion of your face that will be a signal, perhaps, for you to be willing to drop into an *even deeper* state of relaxation. As your arm lifts, you are going *deeper* and *deeper relaxed.* That's fine. You are doing just fine. You are really willing to learn, are you not? Hypnosis is a learning process. And if you learn these simple, elementary ABC suggestions, then you can learn other suggestions that are so necessary for complete mental and physical relaxation. And as the hand draws closer and closer to the face, just think of that wonderful feeling of relaxation that is going to come over your body. Just as if you have had a couple of drinks of whisky or beer; that wonderful tired, *relaxed* feeling that's coming over your body." (The subject touches his nose with the back of his palm; the arm drops limply into his lap as his head falls forward.) "You drop even deeper relaxed; way down; deeper and deeper. Complete relaxation. That's right. And now I am going to lift this arm and you will go even *deeper* and *deeper.* And if you wish to go really deeper, just let it *plop* right in your lap with a resounding thud. Now I will let it go at the count of 3. Can't wait. 1 . . . 2 . . . 3 . . . plop." (His arm drops to his lap.) "That's fine. Now, as long as your arms and hands remain in that position you will go

deeper and deeper relaxed. And as I raise your arm, it will get stiff and rigid." (Catalepsy is induced by a deft stroke.) *"Stiff* and *rigid;* your arm is just as *stiff* and *rigid* as a bar of steel. Now it's *rigid.* And now, if you wish to go deeper, you may go still deeper by letting your arm drop even more relaxed into your lap. That's fine."

MODIFIED ARM LEVITATION

Christenson[1] uses a levitation technic with *sleep suggestions.* He informs the subject that relaxation will deepen with each number he counts. Simultaneously, the more relaxed he becomes, the more his hand will lift; the degree of lifting will determine the degree of relaxation. The lifting, the relaxing and the counting are all cleverly tied in, one with the other, and their interdependence is stressed. He cues the touching of the hand to the face to complete hypnotic relaxation. He also uses sleep suggestions. Wolberg's[8] modification of Christenson's technic uses a more permissive approach.

WATKINS' PROGRESSIVE-ANESTHESIA TECHNIC

Watkins[6] has described an effective method which may start out as a hand-levitation technic.

As soon as there is a change of feeling in one finger, the operator points out that this finger not only tends to tingle but also loses its feeling and becomes numb. At the same time the finger is stroked. Suggestions may be given as follows: "You can feel the numbness coming into it. It gets more numb and more stiff. It begins to uncurl. Watch that numbness as it spreads. It moves around from this finger to this one." The therapist has been stroking the one finger and now moves his finger on and starts stroking the adjacent one, continuing the suggestions of numbness at the same time. In turn, each of the other fingers is stroked until all the fingers are stiff and numb. The suggestions are next directed in turn to the whole hand, the wrist, the arm, the shoulder, etc. "Now the whole hand begins to feel as if it is a block of wood with nails sticking out of it. It loses its feeling. Now you feel the numbness move up into the elbow. Isn't it interesting how this moves across the shoulders and starts down into the other arm? Now the hand, and all the fingers, and the other arm become stiff." The stroking continues. "Now the whole body feels heavy. The heaviness moves down the neck, the chest, into the legs. Your body feels like a log." Use the kind of words that people think of. How does a log feel? How does a block of marble feel? How did it feel when one was anesthetized? These are the cues which make the patient respond. Suggest to the patient that, as the feeling spreads down into his legs, "They feel heavy, enormously heavy. They get stiff. You feel as if everything below the neck is devoid of feeling and sensation. Now the numbness goes up into the head, and this too gets heavier, like a solid block of marble. Everything is going out except the eyes. Now the eyes get so heavy, tired and sleepy. They close, and you have a feeling as if it is night-time. The sun is setting; it is getting more and more twilight."

This method of progressive anesthesia is very effective. One of the technics which derives from it is the "magic-finger" approach. After you have anesthetized the finger of a good subject you can tell this person that he may rub any part of his body and that part of the body will then be anesthetized. This works wonders with children. They love to have a magic finger. If a child rubs a tooth with it, it is as effective as a shot of procaine.

HANDLING OF RESISTANCE IN LEVITATION TECHNICS

As emphasized, when resistance is encountered, one should switch technics. If what started to be a permissive technic, with arm levitation, seems not to be successful, say, "That's fine. You have done your part very well. Now you will raise your arm directly overhead." Few patients will realize that the switch has been made. Because the ultimate goal is limb catalepsy, it is important to get the arm raised to the position where this phenomenon can be induced quickly. Expectation leads to hypnosis and, if that expectation is not instantaneously fulfilled, both the operator and the subject will be concerned. The time to switch to a different technic is before the patient senses that failure is inevitable. Thus the rapport is maintained.

Enlightened patients understand that a rather high order of concentration is necessary to achieve hypnosis, and that it also requires more than a moderate degree of in-telligence. Thus, if the operator emphasizes this point at some time during the induction, it becomes quite apparent to the subject that he is not utilizing his concentration to its fullest capacity. Some resistant patients may say, in the midst of an arm-levitation induction, "I guess I'm no good, Doctor. My arm wouldn't go up. I just don't have what it takes." Here, reassurance that the subject is intelligent and can concentrate is helpful. The operator can remark, "Perhaps you are trying too hard; I am sure that if you try again you will relax."

When a subject's arm does not levitate, the operator can remark, "And as your arm remains comfortably in your lap, you can feel yourself going *deeper* and *deeper* relaxed with every breath you take. *Deeper* and *deeper* relaxed. Now I will raise your arm straight upward, and as it moves upward you will become more relaxed." (The arm is moved slowly to an upright position.) "Now, straighten the fingers, spread them apart. That's right. Spread them apart. That's fine. And now the entire right arm will continue to get *stiff* and *rigid!* Like a bar of steel! *Stiff* and *rigid.* Like a bar of steel. *Stiffer* and more *rigid. Straighten* out the fingers. *Stiff* and *rigid.*" (The arm is lightly stroked from the fingertips down to the shoulder.) "And now, if you wish to go deeper, just say to yourself, 'I can't make a fist,' and the more that you really believe that you can't make a fist, the *deeper* relaxed you will go. And I notice that now you swallowed. That is a very good sign that you will reach a *deep, deep* state of relaxation. Go *deeper* and *deeper.* Real deep. Deeper and deeper. Way down. *Deeper and deeper* relaxed. That's right. Just close your eyes and let your eyeballs roll up into the back of your head."

Resistance is often manifested by the subject's raising his arm too quickly. Here again, the operator must not be disturbed but, rather, should remark, "That's right. Your hand has reached your face. Now you can slowly allow your arm to fall toward your lap and, as it falls, you will go deeper and deeper . . . ," etc.

Frequently, subjects do not close their eyes but keep them in a fixed and staring position. These individuals are in a somnambulistic state. The sophisticated hypnotherapist recognizes this immediately and proceeds with appropriate posthypnotic suggestions.

Another technic[7] for handling resistance in the negatively suggestible subject is as follows:

This hand is going to get increasingly light, but I am going to put my hand on it and hold your hand down. I will not allow your hand to come up. It keeps on getting lighter and lighter, but I force it down. You can sense the lightness as it is pushing up against my hand. I am in great difficulty trying to hold it down. In fact, it seems ultimately as if it would force my hand up in spite of my efforts to hold it down. You will prevail over me. I cannot keep your hand from rising into the air, and I cannot prevent you from *relaxing*. You go into a *very deep relaxed* state in spite of my efforts to stop you.

In this case the motivation to oppose the doctor is used in the actual hypnotic induction.

Often the arm may lift halfway and remain in a horizontal position. Then the following suggestions are valuable: "Your arm is now extended straight in front of you. You can move it upward, downward, or you can move it from side to side." This confuses most individuals; they do not realize that there is no other direction in which the arm can move. If they still resist, invariably they will move the arm in one direction: up, down or sideward. If so, quickly remark, "That's right, you are moving it in the right direction, just as I suggested. Now all you have to do is to move it upward (if that is the direction) until it is extended straight toward the ceiling." If the arm moves downward, similar suggestions are made, ending with, "Return it to your lap or side" (where it inevitably must go).

COMBINATIONS OF TECHNICS

The sensory-imagery technics, with or without arm levitation, are excellent for the establishment of deeper hypnotic states. The principle of nearly all of them is to involve the subject in as many ideosensory activities as possible. Through this type of misdirection of attention, the suggestions of the operator are accepted more readily.

The eye-opening-and-closing, the pro-gressive-relaxation and the tension-and-relaxation technics stress ideomotor activity, although ideosensory involvement is an essential feature of all these technics. Most technics of this type are ideal for the induction of children and also for handling the refractory individuals who state, "I doubt if you can hypnotize me because I have a strong mind." "Playing a game" appeals to the former group, and the latter group are caught "off guard." Nearly all can be used in various combinations, and the verbalization described can be altered to fit the needs of the subject and the operator.

The tension-and-relaxation, the hyperventilation and the cataleptic technics are dependent largely on physiologic effects to reinforce the psychological suggestions (the law of dominant effect).

The disguised technics are too numerous to mention. Many methods, such as progressive relaxation, psychoprophylactic relaxation and natural childbirth are disguised technics employing "waking hypnosis" or the alterations of awareness characteristic of hypnoidal states.

THE SENSORY IMAGERY WITH ARM-LEVITATION TECHNIC

This is an excellent technic, especially applicable for children. Kline[2] has described a similar technic which involves "picture visualization." My technic is as follows:

"I understand you become very frightened when you have to go to the dentist. I don't blame you. I used to dread it, too. And I would rather play baseball anytime than go to the dentist, wouldn't you?"

"Now, how would you like to go into a nice, deep, relaxed state so that you can sit in the dentist's chair without worrying about being hurt? You would like that, wouldn't you? Suppose you just close your eyes and tell me what the outside of your house looks like. You are standing on the curb, and I want you to tell me what the outside of your house looks like. I want you to see it very clearly; I want you to describe the color, where the front door is and everything about it." (The subject describes the house.) "Well, that's very good. Suppose you walk up to the front door and walk into the house. Now tell me in detail what you see. And I want you to see yourself walking into that front door now." (The child describes the interior of the living room.) "Is there a television set in the living room?" ("Yes, it's a black one.") "You didn't tell me about the furniture in the living room. Is there a couch?" ("Yes, it's a green one.") "What does the couch look like? Do you like to sit on it? Suppose you see yourself walking into the living room and lying down on the green couch; stretch out on it, and it really feels good, doesn't it? You can also turn on the television set if you wish to see your favorite program or a baseball game. Now as you keep looking at the TV screen, you are going to get the most wonderful feeling of floating away. Your lids are going to get *heavier* and *heavier*. You can see yourself stretched out on that couch, in your mind's eye, and every muscle and every fiber is relaxing, and your lids are getting *heavier* and *heavier*. I notice now that your breathing is getting *slower, deeper* and *more regular*. Slower, *deeper,* and more regular with every breath you take. *With every breath you take, you can feel yourself going into a deep,* pleasant state of relaxation. It is getting so hard to look at that television set, because you are getting so very, very tired. You are getting very, very drowsy and it's so relaxing to just lie there and just feel as if you are floating away. Now if you wish to go into a *deeper* and *deeper* state of relaxation, all you have to do is to imagine that you have a great big balloon tied around either your right wrist or your left wrist and that the balloon is just tugging and pulling your arm upward." (The same suggestions are given as in the arm-levitation technic until the subject's hand touches his face.)

"And now if you wish to go *deeper,* you can. You do not have to do anything you do not wish to do. If you wish to go deeper, that's your privilege. All you have to do is to let your arm drop about a half inch, or an inch at a time. And as your arm drops, say to yourself, 'The next time I sit in my dentist's chair, I'm going to develop this same feeling of relaxation.' Or perhaps you would enjoy seeing your favorite television program or a ball game. You can be very interested in the ball game and forget all about the dentist. You won't even hear the buzzing of the drill. Now as your arm drops, you feel

yourself going *deeper* and *deeper relaxed.* And when your arm touches the side of the chair you will relax every muscle. Every muscle will be *deeper* and *deeper* relaxed, and go limp just like a dish towel, just like a wet dish towel. I'm lifting your arm and it's just as heavy as lead, completely and thoroughly relaxed! That's right. And now I'm going to let it drop right into your lap. Your arm is getting heavier and heavier. It is slipping right out of my fingers, getting very, very heavy. When it drops, it is going to drop so completely relaxed, just completely relaxed! And perhaps you are willing to agree that the second it hits your lap every muscle and every fiber in your body will relax completely. You are now going into deep, deep relaxation. That's right. Just let it slip right out of my fingers, getting heavier and heavier. At the count of 3, it's going to drop into your lap and you too will drop deeper. 1 . . . 2 . . . 3 . . . ." (The child's arm drops limply to his thigh.) "That's fine. Very good. I'd like to have you work with your doctor so he can continue training you in hypnosis. Is that all right? You wouldn't object to that, would you? You are a good subject. You are going to do very well.

"May I give you a suggestion that you will never forget?" "Yes." "All right. Now, any time that your dentist touches you on the right shoulder you will promptly fall into a *deep, deep* state of relaxation. However, this won't happen unless you give your permission. Remember that from now on, you will go into this nice state of relaxation after you close your eyes and let your eyeballs roll up into the back of your head. And each time that you enter this *relaxed* state, you will find that you will go just a little *deeper,* a little faster, and a little better. It's like practicing any sport. The first time you swung a bat you were awkward. After you swung the bat a few times you were pretty good. It's the same way with this type of relaxation. You have to practice.

"A touch on the *left* shoulder will be the signal to come out of it. Of course you could come out of it any time you wanted to but, since you wish to get the most benefit out of all my suggestions, you will not come out of the hypnosis until I touch you on the left shoulder. You know that if you think hard enough, long enough, and strong enough, your dental work is not going to hurt. If you say over and over again, 'Well, I'm relaxed. This is not going to hurt. I'm going to tell myself that the drill is not even in the same room with me. This will allow me to relax and, if I relax, then I will not be tense, and if I am not tense then I will not have any more discomfort than I am willing to bear.' So if you tense up, the drill will hurt. But if you relax it will not hurt.

"There is no question that dental work is painful. I certainly won't deny that, but it isn't going to hurt very much if you think that it won't. Remember, too, you need have no more discomfort, no more pain than you are willing to bear. Remember, too, that every time you sit down in the dentist's chair you will just turn on that television set in your mind's eye and watch your favorite program. You will find this most comforting. And don't forget about the baseball bat and how you are going to swing it. Keep looking at it right now. Just see yourself hitting a triple. Where did you go? To third base? All right now, I am going to touch you on the left shoulder and you are going to open your eyes." (The child's eyes blink and open slowly.) "Thank you for being such a wonderful patient."

VISUAL-IMAGERY TECHNICS

THE BLACKBOARD TECHNIC

The individual is asked to see how well he can concentrate on all instructions. This technic appeals primarily to the subject's imagination and is an excellent method for developing amnesia.[5] The following is the verbalization:

"Just visualize in your 'mind's eye' a blackboard in one of your high school classrooms. You are beginning to see it, are you not? When you do, nod your head to indicate that you see the blackboard." (The subject nods his head.) "Now you may imagine that you are walking over to the blackboard. You are picking up a piece of chalk. Write the numbers from 1 to 10. You will see each number on the blackboard. After you have done this, you will let me know by nodding your head." (The subject nods his head.) "Now, erase all of the even numbers. You see a smudge between each of the odd numbers. You do see it, do you not? All of the even numbers from 1 to 10 are now dropping out of your mind, are they not? You can see only the odd numbers, can you not?" (The patient nods his head, indicating that he is responding.) "You will remember now that when you are requested to count you will *not* be able to remember any even numbers. You are going *deeper* and *deeper relaxed. Deeper* and *deeper relaxed* with every breath you take, and with each breath that you take, all the even numbers are dropping out of your mind. And now, since all the even numbers have dropped out of your mind, you may find it difficult to count out loud." (If the patient does not block, he may or may not be hypnotized. If he blocks but has not forgotten the even numbers, he may be in a light hypnotic state. Of course, if he is not able to remember the even numbers and merely counts "1, 3, 5, 7, 9," then you can be fairly certain that he is in a deep state of hypnosis and is capable of developing posthypnotic amnesia as well as of following other suggestions.)

THE TELEVISION TECHNIC

This is a form of the picture-visualization technic that is excellent for the induction of children. They close their eyes and visualize a favorite television program. As soon as they say they have "turned the TV on" and are seeing the scenes changing, the operator remarks:

"You will pay more and more attention to the television screen. Keep looking at it. As you are looking at it, you will notice that your right arm will begin to lift up into the air by itself. That's right. It is beginning to lift. It is lifting, lifting, lifting. Higher and higher. Just keep looking at the picture. Your arm is lifting still higher. Listen to everything that is said and, as you keep looking at the screen, you are getting *very, very tired.* And now your arm is raised straight toward the ceiling. If you wish, you can go deeper relaxed. Just say to yourself, think to yourself, 'My arm is getting *stiffer* and *stiffer.* Rigid!' And, if you wish to go *deeper,* slowly allow your arm to fall, and as it falls you too will go deeper and deeper." (The same deepening procedure is used as in the blackboard technic.)

THE EYE-OPENING-AND-CLOSING TECHNIC

The following verbalization is used:

"Would you mind fixing your eyes on a spot directly above your forehead? Keep looking at a spot directly above your forehead. As you keep looking at that spot, perhaps you would not mind opening and closing your eyes." (The eyes open and close.) "That is right. The more you open and close your eyes, the more you will be able to relax." When the lids begin to droop, the operator suggests: "Your lids are very tired now. If you keep them closed, you will relax. You may now let your eyeballs roll up into the back of your head and, as your eyeballs remain in this position for a few seconds, notice how your lids are sticking tighter and tighter together." If the subject is unable to open the eyes, this indicates success—manifested by furrowing of the brows and trembling of the lids. The lid catalepsy can be made more complete by saying, "If you really wish to go deeper and deeper relaxed, you will notice that your lids are *really* stuck tightly together. Your eyes can only be opened with difficulty." This does not leave the operator "out on a limb" and, in fact, he has not challenged the subject. The rest of the verbalization follows a standardized direct technic.

For resistant individuals who keep their eyes open, I remark: "You see, your eyes remain open; you *cannot close your eyes.* If you do close your eyes, you will certainly go deeper and deeper relaxed." Most subjects do not realize that eventually they must close their eyes; when this occurs, they attribute it to hypnosis instead of fatigue of the eyelids.

THE EYE-CLOSURE AND AFTER-IMAGE TECHNIC

In this technic, the subject is asked to gaze at a light directly in front of him. He is instructed that, as the operator counts from 1 to 10, he will close his eyes following every even number and he will "see" or visualize the light (which may be red or blue). He is instructed to open his eyes on the odd numbers and concentrate his gaze on the light. When his eyes begin to show signs of fatigue, evidenced by flickering of the lids, I say, "Keep your eyes open. You will notice it is more and more difficult to keep your eyes open." When it is noticed that he is having difficulty keeping his eyes open, he is instructed to close his eyes and keep them closed a little longer at each successive even number. If the subject has difficulty in opening his eyes after they have been closed, I say: "Your eyes are closed tightly; you will notice that they are very, very heavy. This same heavy feeling will move up over your entire body from your toes to your head. You will let your mind think about any subject that you care to, yet you will follow my suggestions. And, as you follow my suggestions, you will relax and go deeper and deeper relaxed." At this point, I generally attempt to test for limb catalepsy. I lightly clasp the subject's wrist between my thumb and forefinger and slowly lift the arm upward about an inch at a time, remarking: "As I lift your arm upward, you will notice that you will go deeper and deeper relaxed and, when your arm reaches a straight up-and-down position, you will observe that the *stiffer* your arm gets from your fingers to your shoulder, the *deeper relaxed* you will go." After the arm has reached a perpendicular position, a slight stroke from the fingers downward is sufficient to induce catalepsy. The hypnotic state is deepened as in the direct technic. I seldom mention the words "sleep" or "hypnosis" but, rather, prefer to use the terms "relaxation"—"soothing"—"restful"—"calm"—"sleeplike."

THE PROGRESSIVE-RELAXATION TECHNIC, UTILIZING THE HAND-CLASP AND THE POSTURAL SWAY

The subject is asked to close his eyes tightly; a light touch on the lids is usually sufficient to give the impression that they are sealed tight, especially if the operator remarks, simultaneously, "Your eyes are locked tight, glued together, tightly, very tight." The operator now takes the subject's hands and clasps them together, saying, "If you really wish to go deeper relaxed, you will think, 'I cannot open my eyes and I cannot unclasp my hands no matter how hard I try.'" Simultaneously, he is gently swayed around and around, and it is suggested, "If you really wish to go still deeper, just image that you are on a boat, and the waves are rocking you deeper and deeper relaxed." The operator can easily discern the degree of relaxation by the ease with which the subject sways. At this point, he remarks, "Your body is relaxing still more and you feel as if you could go into a deep, deep sleeplike state, almost like nighttime sleep. If I ask you to open your eyes, you will see everything that I suggest, nothing else." This is accomplished by slipping from ideomotor to ideosensory suggestions. Since belief is invoked with each suggestion, as the result of conviction, sensory reality becomes unreality. Because he is convinced that the relaxation, the eye-closure and the inability to open the fingers were due to the operator's suggestions, the subject will readily develop sensory hallucinations. This is a good technic for developing somnambulists.

THE TENSION-AND-RELAXATION TECHNIC

The subject is asked to close his eyes and press his feet down on the floor as firmly as possible. It is suggested: "Press your feet firmly on the floor. Just as if you were trying to push your feet through the floor. Now press your hands tightly on the sides of the chair, as hard as you can. Real tight! Keep pushing your feet down on the floor and grip the chair *tighter* and *tighter* with your hands. You are building up tension in your hands and arms. I am sure you will agree that the opposite of tension is relaxation. Therefore, the more tension you build up in your arms and legs, the more you will relax." When the subject shows appreciable evidence of strain, the operator remarks: "Now, because your arms are so tense, they will relax more than they ordinarily do. It will also feel so good to relax your legs. Your whole body is going to relax, deeper and deeper relaxed." If necessary, this procedure can be repeated with other parts of the body. As the procedure advances, the subject gradually develops limb catalepsy and follows the suggestions mentioned under deepening technics.

THE HYPERVENTILATION TECHNIC

In this technic, the subject is asked to close his eyes. He can be rocked to and fro as in the postural-sway technic, with his eyes tightly closed. The following verbalization is used:

"Your eyes are tightly closed together. Take a deep breath and hold it. Hold it as long as you can. Take another deep breath and hold it! Now inhale deeply. Let all the air out of your lungs. Do it again. That is right. With each deep breath you take, you will notice that your head will get lighter and lighter. You are getting very lightheaded. The longer you hold your breath, the more light-headed you get." This is kept up, together with suggestions that he will continually go deeper and deeper as he gets more and more light-headed. Naturally, the subject is not aware that he is getting lightheaded because of the hyperventilation. He thinks that all the sensations are due to the operator's suggestions.

Light to medium hypnosis usually appears, even if no other suggestions are given. As long as the regular and deep breathing is maintained, the subject will remain relaxed and hypersuggestible. The operator must be on guard for syncope produced by hyperventilation. Usually hypnosis is achieved before signs of this occur. The literalness with which such suggestions as "Breathe deeper and more rapidly" are followed is indicative of relaxation; a person in syncope develops shallow respirations and is unaffected by any type of suggestion. If fainting should occur, the hyperventilation is terminated automatically. The associated carpopedal spasm and muscular twitching are more awesome than serious. However, they are a good indication against further use of this technic.

Catalepsy and deepening are produced as with other conventional technics.

THE CATALEPTIC TECHNIC

The eyes are closed tightly and the subject is asked to press his hands against his sides. The operator remarks, "Your arms are getting stiff, stiff and rigid—like an iron bar." At the same time, he deftly runs his hands from the shoulders down past the tips of the fingers, emphatically stating, "Your arms are getting stiffer and stiffer." The subject is gently rocked back and forth and, as his body begins to relax, he is gently allowed to sink into a chair. The operator says, "You are going deeper and deeper relaxed. Your head is getting heavier and heavier and it soon will fall toward your chest." To facilitate this, he can state, "As your head gets heavier and heavier, you will go deeper and deeper relaxed."

A modification of this technic is to have the subject keep his arms stretched horizontally in front of him. He is asked to keep his eyes open and to concentrate on the idea that his arms are getting stiffer and stiffer. At the same time, his arms are lightly stroked from the fingers to the shoulders. It is now suggested that the arms are getting heavier and that they are beginning to fall, that it is difficult for him to hold his arms up. Also, it is suggested that the arms are increasing in weight. This feeling actually results from weariness induced by the extension of the arms, but the subject believes that it is due to the operator's suggestions. As the arms sink downward, it is suggested that he close his eyes tightly and sink deeper and deeper relaxed; that the moment his arms return to his body, he will be deeply relaxed.

THE CONFUSION TECHNIC

This technic, which is highly effective and rapid, is performed as follows: The individual is asked to stand erect, feet together, eyes closed. The operator's hands are placed lightly on his shoulders and his body is swayed gently in a circular direction. At the same time, he is asked to count backward slowly and aloud from 100 to zero. "You will pay no attention to anything that I am saying. Your eyes are rolled up into the back of your head. You are going *deeper* and *deeper relaxed. Deeper* and *deeper relaxed. You* can imagine that you are on a boat and the waves are gently making you feel more and more relaxed. Keep counting backward, backward, and soon your arm will begin to lift. It will lift higher and higher and, as you feel yourself being rocked from side to side, you will go *deeper* and *deeper* with each number that you count backward; you will feel yourself going *deeper* and *deeper.* Your arm is lifting, higher and higher. Keep counting backward."

As the subject counts backward and his arm starts to levitate, he begins to lose track of the count and usually enters a deep state of relaxation, which can be discerned readily by the operator. At this point, a bewildering barrage of suggestions, some mutually contradictory, facilitates a more relaxed state. The operator must talk continually, and the subject eventually becomes confused by the multiplicity of suggestions given in rapid sequence. He enters hypnosis partly to escape the mental "gymnastics" and also because of the somnolent effect produced by the verbalizations and postural changes. This technic is indicated for highly resistant subjects but requires considerable experience on the part of the operator.

THE DISGUISED TECHNIC

A disguised technic, which can also be used as an induction procedure, is performed in the following manner: If a small child or an adult with an extensive laceration of the thigh is seen and you wish to induce a hypnotic state without having anyone, especially the subject, know it, just place a towel over the subject's eyes and say: "Now close your eyes and keep them tightly closed! If you *really* wish to go into a nice state of relaxation so that you won't feel any discomfort, just relax. You will go *deeper* and *deeper* with each breath you take. The more you relax, the less it is going to hurt you. Now, here comes the first stitch." (Gently place the needle on the edge of the wound without pressure.) Now you say, "See, stitch number 1 didn't hurt, did it? Stitch number 1 is a 'hallucinated' stitch." (This is misdirection.) "You are going deeper and deeper relaxed. Here comes stitch number 2. That's fine. You are relaxing wonderfully. You are going into a deeper and more pleasant state of relaxation. The more you relax, the less discomfort you will have. There, I just put in stitch number 2." (Again there is only light pressure against the wound.) Three, 4 and 5 are "put in" in a similar manner. When the patient develops rigidity or limb catalepsy, and the breathing gets slower, deeper and more regular, you can be fairly certain that the hypnotic state has been induced. Now, stitch number 1 can be painlessly inserted. (This is a nice, naturalistic approach for induction of hypnosis.)

PRESSURE ON "NERVE CENTERS"

Nearly everyone has heard that there are nerve centers which, when pressure is applied in the proper place, will produce paralysis. The following method makes use of this myth: The operator explains that the nerve centers for inducing deep relaxation are situated in the back of the head and above the nose. He presses lightly on the lower part of the back of the occiput and, at the same time, he presses his left forefinger and thumb on the forehead just above the nose. The pressure is maintained as equally as possible on both areas. At the same time, the operator states, "You feel yourself sinking deeper and deeper relaxed, into a deep state of relaxation." When the eyes begin to droop and the head slumps forward, the pressure at the base of the nose can be released. Simultaneously, the pressure upon the back of the head is increased, so that the head slumps further forward. This is imperceptible to the subject. Apparently all that he is aware of is the tilting of the head, the drooping of the body and the increasing heaviness and limpness of the body. When the head has dropped upon the chest and the eyes are tightly closed, the operator can release the pressure posteriorly. Now he can suggest, "Your head is falling forward, your body is getting limp as you go deeper and deeper relaxed."

The usual tests of depth of hypnosis will demonstrate how successful either of these disguised technics has been. They are very effective on refractory subjects. Frequently, one can state, "I am only going to see how well you can relax. All you have to do is merely let yourself go. By pressure on certain nerves, you will be able to go into a deep, deep state of relaxation—not sleep— just relaxation, where every muscle, every fiber in your body will relax so completely."

"BLOOD-PRESSURE" METHOD

The author has used a blood pressure apparatus to induce hypnosis by a nonformalistic approach. The method is as follows: The cuff is placed around the arm and is inflated to produce a pressure sensation. Then, as it is slowly released, the operator remarks: "You feel yourself going deeper and deeper relaxed. You can hear the air escaping and feel the pressure relaxing around your arm as you become deeper and deeper relaxed. Now close your eyes," etc.

MECHANICAL TECHNICS

Any steady, monotonous sound has a tendency to induce relaxation. Any regular sound, such as the ticking of a watch, a metronome or a clock, the constant falling of drops of water, or even listening to the heartbeat (a stethoscope is placed in the subject's ears) will induce hypnorelaxation. The operator must explain how and why the sounds will induce relaxation. He can suggest that the eyes will be opened and closed alternately with every sound of the watch or beat of the metronome or the heart.

A small microphone can be used to amplify and conduct the subject's own heart and respiratory sounds to his ears.[4] The rhythm of the heartbeat acts as a monotonous fixation stimulus and the monotonic effect of the breath sounds serves as a conditioned stimulus for sleep. A verbalization technic also can be employed with this method. Another variation is to use intermittent visual stimuli, such as is provided by a flashlight, which can go on and off in synchrony with the metronome. Counting backward or forward is also helpful with either of these technics.

Passes of the hands over the face and the body often fit the expectancy of the subject. Frequently they facilitate induction. A rotating mirror or a brightly colored fish lure can accomplish the same effects. All of these technics can be combined with appropriate suggestions for relaxation. There are many other devices, such as hypnodisks and tape and record players, which can induce some degree of hypnosis in susceptible individuals. Recordings are valueless unless rapport with the operator is established first. However, as yet there is no device *per se* that is 100 per cent effective in inducing hypnosis. Invariably a standard verbalization technic is necessary.

The author helped to develop the brain wave synchronizer, an electronic instrument designed to induce various levels of hypnosis, probably by photic stimulation of the brain waves.[3] The instrument can be used alone or in conjunction with a tape recording of the therapist's induction and dehypnotization technics. It definitely increases receptivity to suggestion and has been tested clinically on many subjects, including obstetrical patients attending group hypnosis prenatal training classes. The apparatus induced light to deep hypnotic levels in over 90 per cent of the subjects. Hypnotic response is more readily produced if a favorable "mental-set" is created. Therefore, to some extent, the expectant attitude created by the structured situation enhances the hypnotic response, but about 30 per cent of the subjects, who had received no explanation or verbalization and who had no knowledge of what the brain wave synchronizer would do, were hypnotized to various degrees ranging from light to deep stages. The apparatus has remarkable potentialities for deepening a previously fixed hypnotic level and for facilitating and speeding up hypnotic induction, which often can be time-consuming, especially in refractory subjects. A distinct advantage is that no physical connections or attachments are placed on the patient. The author has noted that refractory subjects with whom little rapport exists often are easily induced by the apparatus.

All mechanical technics depend to a degree on expectancy and rapport. The prestige factor is very important. If a subject expects to be hypnotized by a device and has confidence in the person who controls the instrument, then hypnotic relaxation can be induced readily in a susceptible subject.

OTHER TECHNICS

Two other technics are mentioned only to be condemned. The *carotid sinus method,* which is achieved by pressure on the carotid artery, is dangerous, as it may stop the heart. In the *shock technic,* a subject is caught off guard by the command, "Go to sleep, deep, deep sleep," accompanied by a snap of the fingers and a very authoritarian approach. Both of these methods smack of the entertainer, who uses them because of their dramatic appeal.

The passive use of the direct stare can be combined with a permissive or indirect approach. The patient is asked to look into the hypnotherapist's eyes. There is no outward display of authority or overpowering of the patient. Rather, he is to get the feeling of confidence that he can let himself go into a nice deep state of relaxation. The therapist says: "You just let yourself go. It is easy. It is easy and calm and comfortable. Look at me, and you can let yourself go more completely. You let yourself go utterly. Everything lets go. Everything lets go, and your body works automatically. Good, your eyelids get heavy, automatically heavy. Yes, they close automatically with the heaviness. It is all through you. Good. Your whole body works automatically. Let yourself go completely relaxed. That's right. Let every muscle, every fiber in your body relax. Just look into my eyes and you will notice a deeper state of relaxation coming over your body. Your whole body is getting very, very relaxed as you look into my eyes. And when you feel yourself completely relaxed, just close your eyes." (From here, any one of the other technics can be used to deepen the hypnosis.)

Incorporating the direct eye stare into a permissive technic readily produces hypnosis. It also can be incorporated for use with any other of the hypnotic technics. The advantages are that the patient is not dominated, nor does it arouse any resentment. The only disadvantage is that there are some people who just can't look someone else in the eye. Whether a direct or a passive eye-stare technic is used, they look the other way or shut their eyes. However, as they develop more confidence, they are able to look at the therapist's eyes.

DRUG HYPNOSIS

It has been the author's experience that a drug seldom induces hypnosis by itself. However, some of the tranquilizing agents, such as the phenothiazine derivatives, can be helpful in decreasing central autonomic reactivity while maintaining a good cortical arousal pattern. Meprobamate preparations and phenobarbital often relax and facilitate induction in patients with musculoskeletal tensions.

Patients who are insusceptible to hypnosis are seldom made more suggestible by narcotics. On numerous occasions, the author has used Sodium Amytal or pentobarbital intravenously, carbon dioxide and nitrous oxide, ether, scopolamine and Trilene with equivocal results. This may be due to his personal bias against drugs. It is difficult to assay the value of drugs for facilitating hypnosis with any degree of accuracy unless double-blind studies are utilized.

The success of all hypnotic technics depends upon the strength of the interpersonal relationship. When one operator cannot hypnotize a subject, a successful induction is not precluded by another one; his personality and approach appeals to the patient or may fit in with the latter's need.

The nuances of induction technic are learned by experience. For example, the manner in which the arm is slowly being lifted is often indicative of whether or not the individual is going into hypnosis. Frequently, light stroking or the deft touch which reinforces a psychological suggestion by a physiologic effect instantaneously facilitates catalepsy. One can feel muscles that develop rigidity as they are stroked; the increased tonicity cannot be simulated.

An induction procedure can be initiated with the subject's eyes shut tight. The only reason for initial eye-fixation is that the heaviness heightens the belief that other "suggested" phenomena will result. No one aspect of induction is as important as the dictum "Belief of hypnosis leads to hypnosis." Therefore, one must never arouse a critical attitude or resistance by using "loaded" words such as, "You are going to lie there perfectly still as if dead." To a hypochondriac, this would interrupt the necessary concentration for achieving hypnosis.

From a practical standpoint, no one technic is superior to any other but, rather, the technic used must fit the *needs* of the subject at that *particular* time, his personality, and, most important, the ongoing relationship manifested by his behavior. If the patient believes that you are going to hypnotize him, then nearly any approach, formal or nonformal, will be successful. As a matter of fact, nonformalistic technics, as utilized by spiritualistic healers, are extremely effective inasmuch as criticalness is reduced. Also, any technic which uses breathing exercises

and a religious-philosophic approach, as Yoga and Buddhist meditation, is effective for similar reasons.

An extremely authoritative type of induction is seldom as efficacious as the permissive approach. Use of the patient's total experiential background, with all his feelings, ideas and attitudes, allows him to decide *what he wishes—not what you wish!* This places the onus or responsibility for achieving the phenomena of hypnosis upon his shoulders.

When using hypnosis in a child, always talk to him at his intellectual level. If possible, make the induction procedure a sort of game. Use his imagination to "look" at a TV program. Get him to play a role in it or have him resort to some type of daydreaming fantasies. Imagery technics are more effective if the ideas are incorporated into the child's imagination. Let him think that he controls the situation by having him decide if he wishes to play baseball while getting an injection; there will be less discomfort if he is engrossed in the ball game. Most children go into hypnotic states readily through such naturalistic technics, especially if ideomotor and ideosensory involvement are fully utilized.

REFERENCES

1. Christenson, J. A.: Dynamics in hypnotic induction, Psychiatry *12*:37-54, 1949.
2. Kline, M. V.: A visual imagery technique for the induction of hypnosis in certain refractory subjects, J. Psychol. *35*:227-228, 1953.
3. Kroger, W. S., and Schneider, S. C.: An electronic aid for hypnotic induction, Internat. J.C.E.H. *7*:93-99, April 1959.
4. Kubie, L. S., and Margolin, S.: A Physiologic method for the induction of states of partial sleep, and securing free association and early memories in such states, Tr. Am. Neurol. A.: *10*:136-139, 1942.
5. Moss, A. A.: Hypnodontics—Hypnosis in Dentistry, Brooklyn, N. Y., Dental Items of Interest Publishing Co., 1952.
6. Watkins, J. G.: Hypnotherapy of War Neuroses, New York, Ronald, 1949.
7. ——: Introductory Lectures in Medical Hypnosis, pp. 40-41, New York, The Institute for Research in Hypnosis, Oct., 1957.
8. Wolberg, L. R.: Medical Hypnosis, vol. I., New York, Grune & Stratton, 1948.

15

Deepening Technics

Deepening is achieved by establishing a definite goal for each step of the induction procedure by such phrases as, "As you raise your arm higher and higher, and with every motion of your arm upward, you will go deeper and deeper relaxed." Linking these suggestions with on-going physiologic processes is helpful here, too. For example: "With each beat, beat of your heart, you will go deeper and deeper relaxed."

It is relatively simple to incorporate a deepening procedure into an induction technic, as follows: "If you *really* wish to go deeper, you will slowly raise your arm. With each motion of your arm upward, you will say to yourself, 'I'm going deeper and deeper relaxed.' In this way you will learn to coordinate your bodily functioning (ideomotor) with your thoughts (ideosensory)." Such suggestions of self-mastery appeal to the patient and effectively motivate deepening of the hypnosis. Achievement of arm catalepsy also is indicative of greater cooperation.

Even before the arm is raised, or while it is being lifted, one can remark, "If you really wish to go deeper, your arm will become stiffer, and the stiffer your arm becomes, the deeper relaxed you will go." This obviously implies that the stiffer the arm, the deeper the hypnotic state. One can then say, casually, "All you have to do if you *really* wish to go deeper is to tell yourself that you are going deeper and deeper relaxed with each motion of your arm upward." If the suggestions are incorporated as the subject's own ideas, there is a better chance of obtaining catalepsy.

After the extended arm is cataleptic, the hypnosis can be deepened by the following verbalization: "If you wish to go deeper, all you have to do is to let your arm drop slowly to your lap, and with each motion that your arm makes toward your lap, if you will suggest to yourself that you will drop deeper and deeper relaxed, indeed you will drop deeper and deeper relaxed. Remember that with each movement that your arm falls downward, if you imagine that you are falling deeper and deeper, you *will* fall deeper and deeper relaxed. Perhaps you might be willing even to give yourself the suggestion that 'The moment my arm returns to my lap, this will be a signal that I will go even deeper and deeper relaxed. And with each breath that I take, I will go deeper and deeper relaxed.'" (The arm slowly drops toward the lap about one-half or one inch at a time.) "Now your hand has returned to your lap. That's good. I notice that your breathing is slower, deeper and more regular. Slower, deeper, more regular. With each breath that you take, you will go deeper and deeper relaxed. Every muscle, every fiber in your body is becoming completely relaxed." Here the operator's breathing is co-ordinated with the rhythmicity of the subject's breathing; this facilitates deepening.

In general, the procedure for deepening is first to suggest that the relaxation is becoming progressively deeper and deeper; second, to allow periods of silence in order to allow it to deepen spontaneously. Finally, having the subject follow a variety of responses associated with ideomotor and ideosensory activities is conducive to greater relaxation and depth.

With reference to this last point, the most practical suggestions are as follows: "If you really wish to go deeper, just think, feel and imagine that with each breath you will go *deeper* and *deeper* relaxed." (There is a period of silence.) "As long as your arms rest comfortably at your side, and as long as they remain in a comfortable position, and with every breath that you take, you will go deeper and deeper." (Silence.) This bewildering array of ideomotor and ideosensory activities automatically deepens the hypnosis.

To achieve even greater depths of hypnosis, visual-imagery suggestions are helpful, such as: "If you really wish to go still deeper, would you mind thinking of one of the most relaxing experiences that you have ever had? Perhaps it might be lying on a beach, nuzzling in the hot sand. Or, perhaps you can recall, after a particularly hard day, when you crawled in between the sheets of your own bed. It felt so good to let every muscle in your body relax. You are s-o t-i-r-e-d. It will be s-o good to go d-e-e-p-e-r and d-e-e-p-e-r relaxed." Here, too, it is most helpful to tap the experiential background of the individual for other memories involving relaxing experiences. Do not use such phrases as "blacker and blacker" or "Your legs will feel as if they are paralyzed," because such phrases can be misinterpreted by psychoneurotics.

A method that is particularly useful for deepening the arm-levitation technic is to suggest: "If you will imagine that each time you move your hand in the direction of your face you will go deeper and deeper, indeed, you will go *deeper* and *deeper* relaxed. And perhaps *you* might be willing to give yourself the suggestion that when any portion of your hand touches any portion of your face, you will go deeper and deeper relaxed."

WEITZENHOFFER'S TECHNIC

For many other modifications involving induction technics and deepening procedures, the reader is advised to refer to Weitzenhoffer's comprehensive presentation on this subject. He has described an excellent procedure, which utilizes suggestion of sleep and challenges.[1]

HAND-ROTATION TECHNIC

Another method to effect deepening is to start the hands moving around and around one another. After the movements are well established, it is suggested, "As you move your hands around faster and faster, you go deeper and deeper." This technic is par-

ticularly effective if a person who has not been able to develop deep hypnosis observes another subject who is capable of deepening the hypnosis in this manner.

VOGT'S FRACTIONATION TECHNIC

Another deepening technic that can be utilized is Vogt's[2] fractionation technic. Before dehypnotization, the subject is asked to relate the thoughts, feelings and sensations he experienced at the moment of his maximal relaxation. The individual is then dehypnotized by the shoulder cue. Then these sensations are fed back when rehypnotized. He is told that he will go deeper with *each* rehypnotization. For instance, if he states, "I felt that I was floating on fleecy white clouds," this is incorporated into the next induction procedure by stating, "You will go deeper and deeper as you feel yourself floating on fleecy white clouds." If he remarks, "I saw all kinds of colored flashes of light," tell him, "Now as soon as you see these colored flashes, you will relax deeper and deeper." The elicited subjective information is repetitively utilized for immediately deepening each phase of the induction until a deep state is attained. Vogt's fractionation technic simply depends on the subject's being dehypnotized, questioned and then reinduced by feeding in those relaxing sensations which he has just described. This procedure is repeated again and again until a deep state of relaxation is achieved. This technic is effective because it obviates the possibility of suggesting sensations which may antagonize the subject. Another advantage is that the information used is conducive to deep hypnotization. The fractionation method can be used in conjunction with the hand-levitation method for subsequent inductions.

ESCALATOR TECHNIC

This technic is used frequently as a deepening technic in conjunction with a direct or an indirect approach. The following verbalization is used after light hypnosis has been produced: "Visualize, if you will, that you are in an elevator on a high floor. Notice the number of the floor. Perhaps it is the sixteenth floor or the twentieth floor. Notice the number on the landing. And now the elevator is beginning to fall, and as you feel it *falling,* you, too, will feel yourself *falling deeper* and *deeper relaxed.* As each number on the landing gets smaller and smaller, you will fall *deeper* and *deeper relaxed. Deeper* and *deeper relaxed.* When the elevator stops at the ground floor or the lobby, you will be in a *real deep, deep state of relaxation.* Not asleep, not unconscious, not in a trance, but just a deep, pleasant, soothing, refreshing state of relaxation, in which you will listen to every suggestion that you wish to follow." Here, as in the blackboard technic (p. 69), the hypnotic state can be deepened by lifting the arm and allowing it to fall to the subject's lap.

HELPFUL HINTS IN DEEPENING

Before deepening, the patient is informed that in case anything should happen to the operator he will be able to dehypnotize himself upon a split-second's notice. This allays the anxieties of apprehensive patients who fear being left in hypnosis. The suggestions must be given slowly and deliberately so that ideas of deep relaxation influence the subject in a positive manner.

Watch the patient and time the suggestions to coincide with the patient's objective responses. For example, remarking "Your breathing will get s-l-o-w-e-r and more r-e-g-u-l-a-r" with the rise and fall of the chest is most conducive to deep relaxation. Let the patient deepen the hypnosis at his own pace. Inform him: "You have the privilege of going just as deep as you wish to go and through your *own* efforts." This places the onus for deepening the hypnosis on the patient. An experienced operator can recognize the depth by the manner in which the arm falls. If it drops limply and with a "thud" into the lap, a fairly deep stage has been attained.

When only a light state has been attained, a kindly noncondemnatory approach maintains good rapport for the next session. The successful operator knows that giving a posthypnotic suggestion, "You will go deeper the next time," usually begins to work in the second, third or fourth session. Respect must be maintained at all times. Thus, thanking the individual for co-operating, at both hypnotic and nonhypnotic levels, results in better motivation and no loss of rapport.

As was said before, to deepen hypnosis, one should establish a goal to motivate the subject each step of the way: "After your arm is extended straight toward the ceiling, only then will you go *deeper* and *deeper* relaxed. You will do so, as I stroke your arm from the fingers to the wrist, if you *really* want to go deeper and deeper." By tying up your suggestions with other physiologic effects—"With each breath you take you will go *deeper* and *deeper*"—you make use of the dictum that a physiologic effect always reinforces a psychological suggestion. When stroking the arm to deepen the hypnosis, use a light, featherlike caress.

Counting forward and backward in multiples, as 2 or 4, has a deepening effect: "Each time I count, you will go deeper. 2 . . . 4 . . . 8. . . . You are going deeper. 8 . . . 12 . . . 16. . . . You are going still deeper relaxed. Now, going backward, as: 12 . . . 8 . . . 4. . . . You are going deeper and deeper," often is effective.

It is also important, when deepening the hypnosis, to make full use of intraverbal suggestion (intonation of words) and to stress certain words. It has been said that, if you wish to be a good Hamlet, you actually have to *believe that you are Hamlet!* Therefore, *one must fully and emotionally participate in* the hypnotic interpersonal relationship. Put yourself in the subject's place. If you say, "Your lids are getting very tired, *getting heavier and heavier*," you *really have to feel these sensations yourself.* If you say, "I want your eyes to get tired, or your lids to get heavy," this does not effect the patient. But, if you state emphatically, "You will feel a numb, heavy, woodenlike sensation, the same kind of a sensation you may have had when your gums were anesthetized, or the same sensation you had from freezing the side of your face when walking against an icy, cold wind"—these are meaningful suggestions to a subject.

IMPORTANCE OF CONFIDENCE ON THE PART OF THE OPERATOR

It has been glibly stated that anyone can learn easily how to induce hypnosis. This is not quite true, as some operators are better than others. However, it requires years of clinical training, good judgment, intuition and experience to be an accomplished hypnotherapist. One cannot read the description of an induction technic in a book and expect always to hypnotize someone successfully: the intraverbal aspects of the communication process will not sound real. A hollow approach seldom inspires the belief, the faith, the confidence and the expectant attitudes that are so necessary for successful deepening of hypnosis. Also, each patient reacts differently; therefore the deepening technic cannot be standardized.

Reproaching the patient because hypnosis was not deepened usually alienates him. Likewise, remarking, "Well, you didn't go deep enough today. Maybe it was my fault," only weakens the relationship. Rather, say, "You did very well! You were excellent. You co-operated very well. Next time you will go much deeper. I'm really satisfied with the depth you reached." Speak in the same confident tone of voice that you use when you are handing a prescription to a patient.

MAINTAINING DEEP HYPNOSIS

To maintain deep hypnosis, as already mentioned above, merely suggest, "As long as your arms remain comfortably relaxed at your sides, and with every breath you take, you will remain in this very, very deep state of relaxation." Ideosensory and ideomotor responses are reinforced by these suggestions. Every individual must, of necessity, continue breathing; as long as he keeps breathing, and as long as he keeps his arms in this nice, comfortable position, he will go deeper and deeper with each breath. This sounds perfectly natural to the subject. Thus, by *extraverbal measures*, one can imply that the subject should go deeper. This obviates saying, "*I want you to go deeper and*

deeper." The first way appeals even to a refractory subject.

Frequently hypnosis can be deepened by leaving the subject alone after making the following posthypnotic suggestions: "I shall return in a few minutes. As long as you continue breathing slowly, deeply and more regularly, you will remain in a deep, deep, relaxed stage as each minute goes by. And with each breath that you take, you will find yourself becoming more deeply relaxed. Upon my return, you will be in a deep, deep state of relaxation." Absenting oneself for 10 minutes is usually adequate. Longer periods may break the rapport—apprehensive subjects usually dehypnotize themselves spontaneously. A metronome, a flashing light and any other monotonic stimulus can be utilized in such a situation.

The foregoing observations have been instrumental in achieving deeper stages of hypnosis than ordinarily would have been obtained. Naturally, every experienced operator has to "play it by ear" and change his technics to suit the personality needs of his subject and the various situational factors, as they arise.

REFERENCES

1. Weitzenhoffer, A. M.: General Techniques of Hypnotism, p. 213, New York, Grune & Stratton, 1957.
2. Vogt, O.: Zur Kenntnis des Wesens und der psychologischen Bedeutung des Hypnotismus, Zeitschrift f. Hypnotismus, 1894-95: pp. 3, 277; 1896: pp. 4, 32, 122, 229.

SUPPLEMENTARY READING

Erickson, M. H.: Naturalistic techniques of hypnosis, Am. J. Clin. Hypnosis 1:3-9, 1958.
Levitsky, A.: Some additional techniques of hypnosis, Am. J. Clin. Hypnosis 3:231-235, 1961.

16

Autohypnosis

Autohypnosis is a highly suggestible state wherein suggestions can be directed to the self. It is a powerful tool in any therapeutic process, and well-trained patients often can parallel the success of heterohypnosis through their own efforts. When judiciously used, it can alleviate many distressing symptoms, substitute strong behavioral responses for weaker ones, help overcome bad habits, and also promote relaxation, concentration and self-confidence.

In achieving autohypnosis, self-control is not relinquished, as is commonly believed. Actually, *more* control is gained. Its effectiveness depends upon strong motivation, the intelligent application of the autosuggestions, and diligence: these are the essential prerequisites. The time necessary to achieve autohypnosis varies: some subjects learn it in a half hour and others require much longer periods.

One question often asked is: "If I am under hypnosis, how can I give myself suggestions?" The patient can be told: "You are always aware of what is going on, and, therefore, you can think, reason, act, criticize, suggest or do whatever you imagine or believe you need. You can give yourself the suggestions aloud or mentally." Another frequent question is: "How do I bring myself out of the autohypnotic state?" The patient can be informed: "You can terminate autohypnosis immediately upon specific suggestions or a prearranged cue."

Coué[2] and others[1] once unwarrantably hailed autosuggestion and autohypnosis as cure-alls. These are not panaceas, even though they often account for the cultists' success in curing psychogenically based symptoms. Spiritual religious healing modalities combine autohypnosis with various types of self-reflection, breathing exercises and muscular relaxation technics. However, autohypnosis is not a religion. Autoscience, positive thinking, self-affirmation—all are modifications of self-hypnotic technics. It is interesting that criticism is never leveled at autohypnosis when used in a religious framework. Nor are there any objections when recovery ensues without the basic causes or underlying conflicts being resolved. No one can deny that many emotionally disturbed individuals are helped and live well-adjusted lives through various "do-it-yourself" or autosuggestive technics.

METHODOLOGY OF AUTOHYPNOSIS

Generally, autohypnosis is induced as a specific technic taught by the physician. A tape recording or record with the appropriate posthypnotic suggestions often is satisfactory for autohypnosis. Occasionally, some patients can induce autohypnosis without prior conditioning; this is the exception rather than the rule.

Autohypnosis chiefly depends upon the nature and type of posthypnotic suggestions given to the self. In this regard, all patients must be given specific instructions (see below).

DYNAMICS OF AUTOHYPNOSIS

Percepts which require reasoning and decision-making when tested against reality are seldom accepted uncritically. On the other hand, our imaginative processes, through fantasies, dreams and wishful thinking, are often accepted as realities. In other words, as our ideational processes shift more toward imagery-activity, our mental images become more variegated and potent as they can be formulated, controlled and utilized for purposeful behavior.

Thus, all purposeful behavior depends on

a dynamic and reciprocal reaction between our reality perceptions and our innermost feelings, needs and goals. The personality structure of an individual is determined, in part, by this behavior. Hence, if the inner feelings of an individual are stimulated in a beneficial manner, healthful reality factors allow the organism to become more responsive. Autohypnosis is most useful in precisely this area of personality functioning by effectively increasing the potentialities for modifying behavioral responses. Nothing could be simpler!

A well-conditioned patient can hypnotize himself by a prearranged cue. The cue acts as a stimulus for the conditioned response—the autohypnosis. After the subject has been properly conditioned, he usually can bring this stimulus-response mechanism into action rapidly. It appears that autohypnosis produces increased receptivity to ideas and the capacity to examine these ideas for their inherent values. This self-objectivity is one of the reasons why autohypnosis is used.

When a person suggests thoughts to himself, this is much more meaningful than when they are given to him by someone else. For instance, when a person imagines himself to be in love, he seldom listens to another person's advice, even if it is logical.

INSTRUCTIONS TO THE PHYSICIAN FOR AUTOHYPNOSIS

1. The signal or cue for inducing autohypnosis must be one that will work only with the patient's permission. This prevents him from inadvertently responding to a similar cue or signal from another person.

2. It must be emphasized that, if optimal conditions for the safety of the patient are not present, the cue will be ineffective.

3. The patient should be trained in the method of suggesting actions to himself. Explicit directions should also be given as to how the suggestions can be carried out both during and after the termination of autohypnosis. Suggestions must be of a positive nature and oriented toward his own welfare.

4. Time limitations on the duration of the autohypnosis can be specified beforehand. However, even if only the slightest possibility of danger exists, the patient must be assured that he will be able to terminate the autohypnosis instantaneously and react to any environmental threat as he would at non-hypnotic levels.

5. The time for subsequent autohypnotic induction can be shortened by time distortion (20 minutes can seem like 1 minute).

6. Complete amnesia developing spontaneously during autohypnosis is impossible. Partial amnesia, if it persists after dehypnotization, follows the usual laws for forgetting: One can forget or remember almost everything on the preceding page after reading it.

7. Autohypnosis is a learned conditioned response; therefore, one must try to practice as much as possible every day. Half a dozen sessions of 2 or 10 minutes each throughout the day are more practical than lengthier sessions. However, longer sessions may be required if deeper stages or hypnoanesthesia are desired.

8. A somewhat similar format must be followed to "stamp in" the learning. The best one is a progressive type: from smaller to larger groups of muscles, i.e., eyelids to limbs to body.

9. If specific relaxation of any part of the body cannot be developed, concentration on ideosensory responses in these areas should be singled out for additional practice.

10. When a specific idea is suggested, the patient should try revivifying an association that once produced this idea (if one wishes to make the arms heavy, he can recollect how his arms felt after lying on them for several hours). Therefore, the patient must associate actual experiences with the desired responses as much as possible. The more vividly these are imagined, the better the effect.

11. The patient must be certain to end each session by stating that he will go into autohypnosis more readily with each practice session; that he will follow all the autosuggestions to the best of his ability; and that he will terminate each session by suggesting that he will feel relaxed, motivated and confident. This obviates any "hangover" feelings as headache, nervousness and tension.

12. The patient may also suggest that autohypnosis can merge with actual sleep. If this happens before bedtime, he will awake in the morning feeling just as he would after

a normal night's sleep—refreshed and alert.

If the above instructions are discussed in detail, and the patients are reasonably intelligent, there is little possibility that danger will ensue from the mere production of autohypnosis per se.

INSTRUCTION TO THE PATIENT FOR AUTOHYPNOSIS

The technic and verbalization the author uses are as follows: "Confucius once stated that one picture is worth a thousand words. Picture images are much more important than words. For instance, if you say, 'I will be confident,' the words must be implemented by a picture of yourself as the confident person you want to be. If you keep fortifying this image with appropriate suggestions, eventually these mental impressions will give rise to the confident feelings that you seek.

"I know that this technic seems too simple, but if you keep implanting positive images into your mind, they will become a part of your personality. Do not expect immediate results when you begin to use autohypnosis and don't ask, 'What's wrong?' All you have to do to attain autohypnosis is to use what we call sensory- or visual-imagery conditioning. This is an old technic that has been the basis for many different types of prayers.

"Any one can learn and practice autohypnosis, but to achieve the best results you must carefully consider what you wish to accomplish. Through self-exploration you can establish reasonable goals for improvement. Don't think that you have to be 'out of this world' to be in autohypnosis. This idea is produced by novels, comic strips and motion pictures. Actually, you only will be in a very deep state of relaxation and concentration. You may develop a feeling of detachment or you may experience a very pleasant sinking feeling, or you may get a feeling of peace and serenity. At times you may not even feel a definite change: it may just seem as if you had your eyes closed and heard everything at all times. However, if you aim for a deeply relaxed state, you will reach it.

"After you are satisfied that you have achieved autohypnosis you may give yourself further suggestions to deepen it if you wish. Also, remember that it is not too important to reach a deep state on your initial attempts. Just realize that you are trying to establish a conditioned response which will cause you to react instantly to any cue that you wish to use. Through frequent repetition, the cue will bring on the autohypnosis.

"During every attempt to achieve autohypnosis, visualize yourself going deeper and deeper. At first you may experience some difficulty, but as you stick to it you will be able to picture yourself deeply relaxed. Always use the visual imagery technics whether or not you think you are under hypnosis. The images will become clear as you constantly repeat the appropriate suggestions. As you continue to work with yourself, you will develop confidence in giving yourself suggestions. To be effective, they cannot be given in a hesitant manner. They must be given with enthusiasm and anticipation. If you follow these instructions you will see tangible results of your suggestions and efforts.

"Begin by selecting a quiet place and arranging to spend an uninterrupted half hour a day practicing there. Seated in a comfortable chair with your hands resting in your lap and your feet on the floor, fix your eyes on a spot on the ceiling above the level of your eyes.

"Then begin counting to yourself slowly from 1 to 10. Direct your attention to your eyelids and, between numbers, tell yourself repeatedly that your eyelids are getting *very, very heavy* and that your eyes are getting *very, very tired*. Again and again say: 'My lids are getting *so heavy*. I feel as if I want to close my eyes at the count of three. My lids are getting *heavier* and *heavier*. I feel my lids getting so *heavy*, and the *heavier* they get, the *deeper relaxed* I will become and the better able I will be to follow all suggestions I give myself. Now my lids are getting *very heavy*. It's going to feel so good to close my eyes.'

"By the time you count to 2, think of enough suggestions like the ones just mentioned so that you actually 'feel' the heaviness of your eyelids. When you are sure that your lids are indeed heavy, count to 3 and let your eyes roll up into the back of your head for a few seconds. Then say: 'My lids are now locked so tight that I doubt very much that I can open them. My lids shut tighter and tighter, and as my lids lock tight, I begin to feel a nice, calm, soothing, relaxed feeling beginning in my toes, moving into my legs and into my thighs—as I keep counting. It's the same feeling that I have in my jaws when my dentist injects procaine into them—the same feeling that I have when I fall asleep on my arm—the same feeling that I have when I sit too long in one position—the identical feeling that I would have in my legs if I sat cross-legged on them. A numb, wooden-like feeling starting in my toes is beginning to move up, up, up from my toes into my legs.'

"Next, count to 4 and say: 'By the time I have counted to 5, my legs from my toes to my thighs will be just as heavy as lead. I can feel my legs relaxing from my toes to my thighs. I can feel them getting *heavier* and *heavier* and *heavier*. 5. They are so *heavy* now that I don't think I can move them.' Then double back for purposeful repetition. 'My eyelids are locked tight, so tight that I don't believe I can open them. My legs from my toes to my thighs are completely relaxed.' Each time you retrace these autosuggestions, you stamp in the learned response pattern.

"You continue in this way: 'By the time I have counted to 6 and 7, my fingers, hands and arms will be very, very heavy. I am beginning to feel that same numbness moving up from my fingers to my shoulders. A heavy, detached feeling is moving up from my fingers to my hand, to my wrist, past my elbows, up to my arm, to my shoulder. Both my arms, from my hands to my shoulders, are getting very numb—a heavy, wooden-like numbness. When I have counted to 7, my arms will be just as heavy and relaxed as my eyelids, and as numb as my legs are now. My arms feel just as if I have been sleeping on them.'

"Do not worry if you forget the exact words. They are far less important than the effect that you are trying to achieve—a feeling of numbness all the way from the fingertips to the wrist, to the elbow, to the shoulder, to the neck. In practice, this may be a bit more difficult to accomplish in the first few sessions at home, but the feeling will come faster in subsequent attempts. It is most important that you never become discouraged

and that you not tire yourself by spending more than the half hour a day in practice.

"When you finally reach the point where, by the count of 7, your limbs are sufficiently relaxed, you repeat again all the suggestions you have given yourself, adding: 'My legs are so heavy that I don't believe I can move them. My eyes are locked so tight that I doubt that I can open them. My arms are so heavy that I cannot lift them, and, by the time I have counted from 7 to 8, my trunk will be relaxed.'

"Now go back to the lids, legs, and arms. Then say: 'By the time I count from 8 to 9, my chest will have relaxed, too. With every breath I take, I can just feel myself going deeper and deeper into a relaxed state. My back and abdomen are getting very, very numb. I can feel the muscles in my chest relaxing. 8. My entire body, from my neck down, is relaxed. 9. I am completely relaxed . . . I can't open my eyes . . . I can't move my legs . . . I can't move my arms. I feel my whole body relaxed, thoroughly and deeply. It is so refreshing to remain in this deep, quiet state.

" 'I will now relax my neck and head, so that, at the count of 10, I will be completely relaxed from my head to my toes. I can feel that with every breath I take I am becoming calmer and deeper relaxed . . . deeper and deeper relaxed . . . into a calm, soothing, refreshing state. Everything is just getting more and more relaxed. I feel as if I am floating away . . . falling deeper and deeper . . . not asleep, but just thoroughly relaxed. 10. I am completely relaxed. My eyes and limbs are as heavy as lead. My entire body feels numb, heavy, woodenlike, as I go deeper and deeper.' "

DEEPENING THE AUTOHYPNOTIC STATE

The key to deepening autohypnosis lies in the use of visual-imagery technics. The patient can be informed: "By picturing yourself deeply relaxed in your 'mind's eye,' you will go deeper. If you can imagine yourself in your own bed comfortably relaxed, this can be a stimulus for deepening the relaxation. If you think of this again and again, you set in motion a conditioned response mechanism that ultimately will allow you to achieve a profound state of relaxation.

"It is well to remember that you deepen the autohypnosis by your own efforts and that the depth depends largely on how well you follow the principles which you are going to learn. It also is most important to have the proper frame of mind if you wish to achieve effective autohypnosis. If you approach it with a 'prove-it-to-me' attitude, nothing will happen. To attain ultimate success, self-confidence, persistence and systematic conditioning are necessary.

"Instructions for autohypnosis, as well as deepening verbalization technics, have been described by Salter,[5] Rhodes,[3] Powers[2a] and Weitzenhoffer.[6] The escalator technic described on page 77 is an excellent procedure for deepening autohypnosis. Further relaxation can be obtained by giving yourself the suggestion that when you think of a color (soothing green, perhaps), you will instantly become relaxed. You may select any other color that relaxes you."

DEHYPNOTIZATION

During autohypnosis, all patients are actually more alert to internal and external stimuli than at nonhypnotic levels; except for sight, all sensory inputs are increased. When reassured that, if necessary, they can terminate even a deep introspective state in a split second and that no untoward effects will occur, the depth of autohypnosis usually can be increased.

The apprehensive individual's fears that he will not be dehypnotized can be further allayed by describing what it feels like to be in autohypnosis. Autohypnosis is often confused with sleep. Therefore, it is imperative to distinguish between it and sleep. Remark: "If you are asleep, you will only remember some of your dreams instead of your suggestions. Actually, it feels as if you are about to fall asleep, and yet you know you are completely awake. Time may pass by rapidly or it may drag. At times, you may feel as if you are observing your own behavior.

"If you should not be able to open your eyes, don't worry. Just repeat the suggestions again, and emphasize that at the count of 3 you will absolutely, positively be able to open your eyes very easily and will feel fine.

Should you not be able to come out of it, keep calm and give yourself the dehypnotizing suggestions with more emphasis."

Failures in self-dehypnotization are rare. The author has never had a case. However, occasionally some patients become so relaxed that they wish to enjoy this pleasant sensation. When this occurs, the patient may go into real sleep and will eventually come out of it.

RECOGNITION OF AUTOHYPNOSIS

Some patients may have difficulty recognizing subjectively whether or not they have achieved autohypnosis. In good subjects there is extreme responsiveness to autosuggestions. Other subjects who, in reality, are able to produce autohypnosis, vehemently protest that they "felt nothing"; they think that they have to be "knocked out." Still others, even though they initially think they are merely role-playing and going along with the autosuggestions, suddenly realize they are spontaneously executing specific and relevant autosuggestions.

Autohypnosis can fluctuate from reverie-like states or alteration in the body image to the complete detachment of the Yoga state. When these sensations are subjectively experienced, this is sensorial proof of autohypnosis.

HANDLING OF RESISTANCE IN AUTOHYPNOSIS

The most commonly encountered resistance in autohypnosis is that of the patient who feels that it did not work for him. One can suggest: "Even if you were not under autohypnosis, if you practice again and again, eventually you *will* slip into autohypnosis. After this has been accomplished, it will become automatic."

Those who are unable to develop autohypnosis are seldom aware of the needs for their resistances. The therapist must find out the reasons. This might well be compared with the removal of a neurosis in a disturbed patient. He certainly wishes to get rid of his symptoms, yet, because of the secondary gain value of the symptoms (neurotic needs for the symptoms), he is unable to "let go" of them.

The best way to dissipate the resistances is

to agree that attainment of autohypnosis is difficult for some persons. However, *some degree* of suggestibility must be present in every intelligent person. If the patient agrees to this, the therapist should resort to Chevreul's Pendulum Test (see page 36). The highly resistant patient will remark, "I am sure I didn't make it move." Upon the successful accomplishment of this task, one can say: "If the pendulum moves without volitional direction, you have successfully influenced your mind. Autohypnosis involves the same procedure. The goal is to voluntarily cause an involuntary reaction. If the experience does not work with your eyes open, try it with your eyes closed for about 5 minutes. You will be pleasantly surprised with the results. Should you want to prove to yourself that you are suggestible with your eyes open, practice the technic every day for a week or two. The idea of the practice sessions is to reinforce and increase the response of the involuntary movements until you develop proficiency. If, after several weeks, you should still not be successful, use the role-playing technic. Consciously make the object revolve. After a while, it will move automatically whenever you attempt the experiment.

"When this happens, you will have proof of your suggestibility. It is highly improbable that you will not be successful. It would be a rare occurrence. By the same systematic efforts, I can assure you that you can achieve autohypnosis."

DANGERS IN AND CONTRA-INDICATIONS TO AUTOHYPNOSIS

The author has taught hundreds of *selected* patients autohypnosis by the above technics. In these, or for that matter, any other patients, he has yet to see any of the dangers described by Rosen[4] (one of the few psychiatrists who repeatedly warns against the use of autohypnosis), who states:

The desire for self-hypnosis, whatever the rationalization advanced by its practitioner, when investigated frequently turns out to be a desire to further fantasy formation, to facilitate sinking deeper and deeper into a dream world of one's own, and to indulge in fantasied or actual "acting out" of a type not allowable to the individual and for which, as a result, he may posthypnotically be amnestic. While it may be used for constructive purposes, it may be utilized self-destructively.

There are few carefully documented cases that one or many autohypnotic sessions *per se* can cause regressive and harmful acting-out tendencies. Thousands upon thousands of patients have been taught autohypnosis by many thousands of physicians, dentists, psychologists and even pastoral and spiritual healers—all without dangerous sequelae. Autohypnosis merely is an intensification of the capacity of an individual to examine his own mental processes in order to make the best "bets" as to how he should act.

Those few who regard autohypnosis as dangerous fail to recognize that an individual is in an almost identical state during profound prayer. If autohypnosis is dangerous, then prayer, religious ecstasy, the meditative states taught by Buddhist priests and Yoga are also dangerous. The only theoretic danger is in teaching autohypnosis to a person who is already detached or depersonalized. No physician would think of pushing an individual who is already "out of this world" into autohypnosis. Nor would he allow an individual who spends a great deal of time in autistic thinking or introspection to learn all about autohypnosis.

SUMMARY AND DISCUSSION

The rules for teaching autohypnosis are similar to those for heterohypnosis. The operator must give all patients accurate instructions as to specifically *where* and *how* the autohypnosis is to be practiced. Also, definitive suggestions for its termination must be given with the utmost clarity. Naturally, just as the use of hypnosis is often contraindicated as a form of psychotherapy for emotionally disturbed individuals, so is the *teaching of autohypnosis to narcoleptic and schizoid patients by untrained lay or professional individuals to be strongly condemned.* The real danger is that the patient might coincidentally be entering an unrecognized psychotic state, and the hypnotherapist would be held culpable. The limitations of autohypnosis should be stressed; it is not a panacea. Rather, it is a means of developing sensory-imagery conditioning. However, hypnotherapists should recognize the limitations of autohypnosis and not oversensationalize its clinical applications.

REFERENCES

1. Baudouin, C.: Suggestion and Autosuggestion, London, Allen, 1920.
2. Coué, E.: Self-mastery Through Conscious Autosuggestion, 1922; London, Allen, 1951.
2a. Powers, M.: Practical Guide to Self-Hypnosis, Los Angeles, Wilshire Book Co., 1961.
3. Rhodes, R. H.: Therapy Through Hypnosis, New York, Citadel Press, 1952.
4. Rosen, H.: Hypnosis, mental hygiene, and the dental hypnotist, J.C.E.H. 5:121-122, 1957.
5. Salter, A.: Three techniques of autohypnosis, J. Gen. Psychol. 24:423-438, 1941.
6. Weitzenhoffer, A. M.: General Techniques of Hypnotism, pp. 327-329, New York, Grune & Stratton, 1957.

17

Autogenic Training

Autogenic training was developed in Germany by Schultz, of Berlin, approximately 50 years ago.[2] He trained patients to go into self-induced hypnoticlike states. Autogenic training consists of a graduated series of mental exercises designed to produce a general psychobiologic reorganization. The resultant changes improve the individual's capacity for introspection and purposeful activity, which help to modify maladaptive behavior processes.

Schultz, as does Vogt, uses definitive bodily sensations reported by the subject during induction. For instance, most subjects develop an abnormally *heavy* sensation of the limbs and/or the body, or a *warmth* that diffuses through the organism, and *lightness* of the extremities. He suggests that the subject correlate the sensation of heaviness with muscular relaxation. Thus, the development of self-relaxation invariably produces a sleeplike state. As a prerequisite, subjects must be motivated, co-operative and capable of a certain amount of self-direction and self-control. Introspection on ideomotor and ideosensory activities is enhanced while the subject is in a relaxed position. Distracting stimuli are reduced to a minimum, and monotonic auditory stimuli are used to facilitate self-concentration; as a result, psychophysiologic changes occur.

The posture is similar to that used for hypnotic induction. The subject leans backward in an armchair with his arms held limply at his sides or resting on his thighs; or he can slump forward or lie on his back. The eyes are closed at the start and the subject emphasizes at the very beginning, "I am very relaxed." Then it is suggested that the subject can relax still more if he associates the thought of deep relaxation with memories of when he was actually relaxed, as, for example, the experience of dozing while sunbathing. In this way, mere words such as "relaxed" become fused into meaningful experiences. This is identical to hypnotic sensory-imagery conditioning.

After the subject attains relaxation readily, he is taught, through suggested ideosensory and ideomotor activities, to concentrate on making one arm very, very *heavy*. Here, too, stroking the arm facilitates a feeling of heaviness, which automatically spreads by generalization to the other arm, the lower limbs and the rest of the body. The right arm is chosen because most people are right-handed.

Schultz advises that at first this should be performed for only 10, 20 or 30 seconds at a time. Subjects described their feelings as "sleepy," "detached" and "dizzy."

He terminates this relaxed state by having the subject take a deep breath, and flex and extend his arms several times in quick succession. The subject breathes deeply several times more, and then opens his eyes. The importance attached to posture, concentration, an expectant attitude, a favorable mental-set and the use of a ritualistic procedure shows that all are modifications of hypnotic technics. Systematic practice of the exercises invariably results in a graduated mastery of bodily functioning.

Autogenic training is a kind of mental gymnastics; its principles are similar to Yoga, Buddhist meditation and Kavanah. The mental exercises are practiced 2 or 3 times a day. The relaxation spreads whether or not patients were informed that it would happen. Schultz's technics are rather elaborate, and the reader can study his excellent book *Autogenic Training* for the specific steps involved.[2]

The importance of autogenic training is

that hypnotic phenomena are not a mere matter of heterosuggestion, that is, of one person suggesting certain things to another. As used clinically, hypnosis is structured around autosuggestion and heterosuggestion. Thus, when a person is in hypnosis, something happens to enable him to do a great many things which often are not suggested. One may not know what to suggest for a specific purpose. Yet some patients develop the capacity to meet their somatic needs in an autonomous fashion. With autogenic training, some people learn to develop complete anesthesia automatically without its being specifically suggested. One must remember, however, that 5 per cent or more of the population can develop some degree of anesthesia without autogenic or hypnotic training.

Schultz also demonstrated that many individuals could induce self-relaxation without the instructor's presence. As they learned to relax deeply, many became interested in sensory changes such as feelings of heaviness, coldness or warmth of the extremities. He cites data to prove that, if warmth was produced in the right arm, a rise of one degree centigrade occurred, as measured by a thermocouple. The other arm was unaffected. Eventually, he had subjects learn as many hypnotic phenomena as possible.

The clinical applications of autogenic training have not been explored in this country, one reason being that we are oriented more toward dynamic psychiatry. Schultz's method has proved to be a rational and practical psychotherapeutic modality in Europe, where orthodox psychoanalysis has lost much of its former popularity. The method has been employed primarily as an adjunctive procedure for relief of a wide variety of psychosomatic conditions such as asthma, hypertension, ulcers, female disturbances and numerous others. He does not claim that he can cure asthmatics simply by autogenic training. However, in conjunction with other therapeutic measures, it is indispensable in their cure.

Autogenic training is very useful in that it teaches the patient to be self-reliant and enables him to feel that *he* is now doing something helpful. This undoubtedly builds up the patient's self-esteem. As happens when autohypnosis is utilized, the dependency situation is minimized.

The author has been able to duplicate Schultz's results. Autogenic training has given some individuals the feeling that they have learned something with which they can externalize their tensions. It can be used not only for relaxation, but for rather involved and complicated psychotherapeutic procedures such as relief of impotency, or as in surgery (see Chapter 32). Autogenic training indicates that hypnosis is more than mere suggestion. It also beautifully illustrates that hypnotic behavior is primarily *a subjective experience* based on the inner conviction and the expectant attitude induced by the hypnotic state. This capacity resides within every person.

Autogenic training is a rather interesting aspect of hypnotherapy and Schultz's work is timely and provocative. For many years the author of this book had been using similar technics for autohypnosis without being aware that they were a modification of Schultz's methods. Many therapists, unfamiliar with autohypnotic technics, fail to realize that psychotherapeutic results often can be attained almost wholly as the result of the patient's own efforts.

Edmund Jacobson's[1] progressive relaxation is similar to Schultz's autogenic training, and Schultz points out the similarity. Even though the "misdirection" for these methodologies is different, sensory-imagery conditioning and motivational strivings are the principal features responsible for the recoveries. Tantra Yoga used similar technics centuries ago. The relaxation, meditation and self-absorption produce some degree of dissociation, and the resultant cortical inhibition, similar to that which occurs in prayer, narrows the attention span to the imaginative processes. The more one responds to his own healthy mental pictures, the more likely his healthy fantasies will become healthy realities!

REFERENCES

1. Jacobson, E.: Progressive Relaxation, Chicago, Univ. Chicago Press, 1938.
2. Schultz, J. H., and Luthe, W.: Autogenic Training, New York, Grune & Stratton, 1959.

18

Group Hypnosis

Mass suggestion or mass hypnosis is relatively easy to establish in a group. The reasons for this are: There is an "emotional contagion" that takes place with other members of the group; persons identify with what they see. The inherent competitiveness is mobilized, and there is usually an intense desire to please the leader (father-figure) of the group.

The beginner should use a suggestibility test such as the handclasp method to find out which persons are likely to make the best subjects. Those whose hands stick together are asked to act as volunteers. It is also advantageous for an inexperienced operator first to induce hypnosis in one whom he has already hypnotized. This produces a favorable mind-set and is highly motivating to the rest of the group.

Following demonstration of successful hypnosis in a volunteer, the group can be hypnotized as a whole, or from 6 to 10 persons can be taken at one time. A comfortable sitting position is preferred, as deeply hypnotized persons are likely to fall off their chairs if not carefully observed. The audience is invited to ask questions about hypnosis. This not only enlightens the individuals but also helps facilitate rapport for those who volunteer.

The following is a verbatim transcript of the preliminary discussion with a group, and some of the typical questions asked of the medical hypnotist. The actual induction technic is not included, but one similar to the author's progressive relaxation technic is used. Also included is the author's technic for inducing autohypnosis.

PRELIMINARY DISCUSSION FOR GROUP HYPNOSIS

"All of you know that hypnosis and autohypnosis are being used for group training for childbirth, obesity and other psychotherapeutic medical conditions.

"First, understand that there are many misconceptions about hypnosis. (These, as well as everyday aspects of hypnosis, are discussed.) There are many different degrees of hypnosis. May I enlighten you to the best of my ability about these matters? Please ask any questions you have regardless of how elementary they may seem to you."

Q. "In autohypnosis, do I get the impression that I am inducing myself? And in such a situation, can I bring myself out of it, or is it necessary for someone else to do so?"

A. "You will always bring yourself out of autohypnosis. If you can produce it yourself, you can readily come out of it."

Q. "What makes a person go into a hypnotic state?"

A. "It's your belief, your faith, your confidence, your willingness to co-operate with my suggestions and the attention that you pay to my words that produce the necessary susceptibility leading to hypnosis."

Q. "Doctor, could you make me do something contrary to my moral code?"

A. "I can't make you do a single thing against your wishes."

Q. "What do I have to do, Doctor, in order to be hypnotized? That is, besides being co-operative?"

A. "If I ask you to close your eyes, you close your eyes—not because you have to but because you want to. If I say to you, 'Raise your arm,' you do not have to do it, but you raise your arm under your own control because you want to raise it. Now, why do we have you go through these simple exercises? Because hypnosis is learned exactly as you learn your ABC's in school. First, you learn simple, elementary words. You start with A . . . B . . . C. If you learn

A . . . B . . . C . . . , then you will learn X . . . Y . . . Z. It's as simple as that."

Q. "Are all people suggestible? Also, how does hypnosis help one to get better?"

A. "We are all suggestible. Have you not had the experience when someone casually mentions, 'Say, you are looking bad. Are you working too hard?' Or, if another person says, 'Are you losing weight?' and if a third person says, 'You look awfully pale; are you getting enough sleep?', you are apt to look at yourself in the mirror, be horrified by what you see, and then make an appointment with your doctor. Actually, you can be 'sales-talked' into being healthy! And it's much better if you do it through autohypnosis—the really scientific 'power of positive thinking.' Here your own affirmations that you will get better are accepted uncritically, and also you can better explore the nature of your problems."

Q. "Doctor, do you also give us medication?"

A. "Yes. Usually, if indicated, I use a comprehensive approach. Hypnotic suggestion can be combined with drugs and medical procedures. A combined approach is better than either alone."

Q. "Once I'm hypnotized, will I know everything that is happening?"

A. "You are always in control. You will remember everything you say unless a loss of memory for specific events is produced."

Q. "What is the difference between entertainment and medical hypnosis?"

A. "The stage hypnotist makes it appear as if he induces the hypnosis. The medical hypnotherapist knows that the patient really induces the hypnosis. Also, medical hypnosis is used for serious purposes, so naturally you will not be made to bark like a dog or perform other 'shenanigans,' as in entertainment hypnosis."

Q. "Suppose you have a problem that requires the use of autohypnosis. Can I still perform my normal duties afterward?"

A. "Yes, an individual can perform his normal duties and often can carry them out more effectively after posthypnotic suggestions."

Q. "Why not use suggestion instead of hypnosis? What is the difference?"

A. "Performance can be enhanced by hyp-nosis. Sometimes it is difficult to determine where suggestion ends and hypnosis begins. Between halves, a good football coach gives a strong pep talk that inspires the players. This is a mild form of hypnosis. Hypnosis is the acme of scientifically applied suggestion. However, I can't promise you that hypnosis is going to change your attitudes toward a given problem, but let us assume that you are only 10 per cent better. This is still 10 per cent better than nothing, is it not?"

Q. "Does one go to sleep at all during hypnosis?"

A. "No, you do not. Under hypnosis, you are more alert and better able to follow all suggestions because you are concentrating."

Q. "Why is hypnosis more effective than ordinary persuasion?"

A. "The purpose of hypnosis is to get an individual to respond with a pinpoint literalness. If you can get another person's attention just as a good orator or entertainer does, then the other person can be influenced by what you say because he does not realize that he is being persuaded. Otherwise he would have his guard up. This is the technic of an effective salesman. He gets his suggestions through without you realizing that you are being given a 'soft sell.' This is the reason why hypnosis is more effective than strong persuasion."

Q. "Could I not use my will power instead of hypnosis?"

A. "No. Hypnosis is better than will power; it uses the imagination. You can't *will* yourself into salivating or goose-pimpling, but you can salivate or develop goose-pimples if you can imagine the experiences or memories which once produced such responses. A fundamental law of hypnotism is that you can't beat the will. You can't will yourself into a sickness, but you can imagine yourself into or out of an emotional sickness! Hence, we always use the imagination."

Q. "How do you account for having chronic pains when my doctor tells me it's all in my head? How is hypnosis going to help that?"

A. "Once an idea is launched in the central nervous system, it becomes like a 'satellite' which 'orbits' around the nerve pathways of the brain. Just as the rocket site for launching a rocket loses its importance and is forgotten, so is the original cause forgotten. Often a chronic discomfort is due to what is referred to as a conditioned pain pattern. The painful event which originated the response is no longer present, but its aftermath remains as a reflex. Often hypnosis can break up the chronic pain pattern by reversing or interrupting what we call a conditioned reflex."

TECHNIC FOR GROUP HYPNOSIS

The direct technic is the best for group hypnotherapy. The levitation technic is impractical because varied responses occur with each patient. Furthermore, one might have to wait 35 or 45 minutes for the arm to levitate.

VERBALIZATION FOR GROUP AUTOHYPNOSIS

"If you all are interested in going into a nice, deep state of relaxation, get as comfortable as you can.

"Now I want you all to listen to me because I am going to show you how hypnosis can be readily induced in all who wish to follow my suggestions. (The author's progressive relaxation technic for autohypnosis, described on pages 82 and 83, is employed.)

"Now, what is the purpose of going into this state of relaxation or meditation, self-reflection, contemplation or absorption? It is to give yourself positive, healthy, constructive suggestions in order to neutralize negative, harmful and destructive suggestions.

"In the case of the young lady who wishes to have a delivery under hypnosis, she can imagine, 'I'm going to look forward to having my baby with a feeling of joy and happiness. I will not have the slightest dread or fearful anticipation. It's going to be a wonderful, wonderful experience and I need not have any more discomfort than I am willing to bear. Pain-killing drugs, too, will be available if I should need them. I will not hesitate to ask my doctor for these drugs. I am not going to feel guilty in asking for them. If the hypnosis does not work, I may have to have drugs. However, I will relax and, the more I relax, the less tension I will have. And the less tension I will have, the less discomfort I will have.' And really, childbirth is not a terrifying procedure unless you make

it that way in your imagination. You can look forward to its being a beautiful experience in your imagination. It's as simple as that.

"And all of you can give yourselves positive suggestions for your own benefit. Now one more thing. While you are in this state of relaxation, it's remarkable with how much clarity and with how much precision you can think. It's almost like praying in church. It's almost like concentrating on your studying before an examination in a sound-proof room. As a result of this 'retreat into yourselves' right now, whatever you are thinking about is going to stick. And since you are planting ideas in your mind, you can rest assured that these eventually will become positive and constructive suggestions.

"Now, how are you going to bring yourself out of this? It's very simple. All you have to do is to count to 3. At number 1, you will say to yourself, 'I am going to go deeper the next time that I try this.' Number 2, 'I am going to try to the best of my ability to follow all suggestions.' Now in this state of introspection, reflection, meditation or contemplation (it doesn't make a bit of difference what you call it), these suggestions really stick. This is more effective than when suggestions are given while there is noise and distraction around you. When you are concentrating, tell yourself, 'I'm going to follow suggestions to the best of my ability.' And the third thing that you will think is, 'I will open my eyes and feel perfectly wonderful, free from all tensions, completely relaxed.'

"There are also two other suggestions you might like to follow. And that is, when your doctor wishes to rehypnotize you, he will touch you on the right shoulder—and this will happen only with your permission—it will be your cue for re-entering hypnosis. Remember, you are always in charge. When he touches you on the right shoulder, that will be a cue for you to drop into a deep stage of relaxation. At first you will close your eyes, then let your eyeballs roll up into the back of your head, and then you will feel a real, deep state of relaxation coming over you. Not sleep, but deep relaxation or hypnosis. A touch on the left shoulder will be the signal to open your eyes. So now you have two ways to enter into hypnosis; one in which the doctor can induce it and the other in which you do it yourself. That is all there is to it."

The author's methods of handling large groups for prenatal training are described elsewhere in this book (Chapter 33). Invariably, one third of those who are observing the volunteers being hypnotized will be hypnotized in varying degrees themselves.

They will all dehypnotize themselves when the signal is given.

Group hypnosis has been employed effectively for stutterers, alcoholics and those afflicted with headaches. However, group hypnosis reaches its greatest potential in relieving pain in obstetric patients and in the therapy of obesity. There is no reason why it could not be utilized in dermatology and anesthesiology, especially if conducted in a hospital setting.

19

Antisocial Aspects of Hypnosis

Considerable controversy exists as to whether or not a hypnotized individual will commit an antisocial act following posthypnotic suggestions. Many investigators[1, 3, 10, 14, 15, 17] believe it possible, whereas others[2, 4, 8, 18] do not think the evidence warrants such assumptions. Still others[6, 7, 13] take a position between the two camps. Most of the experiments to show that antisocial behavior can be induced have not been carefully structured—the experimental setting suffering from a pseudoreality situation.

Furthermore, since only a relatively few cases have been studied, more controlled clinical data is needed. Erickson,[4] who believes that the possibilities for antisocial behavior are nonexistent, says that there are people "who will discount the theoretical possibility of hypnosis, yet will insistently attribute miraculous, effective, antisocial powers to even a single hypnotic suggestion."

Soldier volunteers in a military setting have performed antisocial acts through posthypnotic suggestions.[15] It has been pointed out that such subjects were strongly motivated to act in this manner because of the "demand characteristics" of the situation; they intuitively or subliminally knew what the experimenter was trying to prove. They also felt that the hypnotist, usually a superior officer, would ensure the safety of all involved irrespective of their actions.

In similar experiments, a college professor in a psychology class has asked a student to shoot a supposedly loaded gun. The student, on more than one occasion, pulled the trigger and thought he was "shooting" the professor. However, the subject recognized the surroundings and the professor's voice. No professor has handed a student a loaded gun and put a bullet-proof vest on himself and said, "Shoot me." To evaluate the contradic-

tory data that antisocial behavior can occur under hypnosis, one must consider many other factors as motivation, role-playing and exhibitionism, as well as the needs of the hypnotist.

There is a well-documented case in which a person ostensibly committed murder as well as other criminal acts at the behest of a hypnotist.[5] This crime obviously was perpetrated because the subject, over a long interval, had developed a close emotional attachment to a mentally unbalanced hypnotist. In another case, a prisoner of war committed criminal acts through a posthypnotic suggestion.[12] Judging from his relationship to the hypnotist and the nature of the subject's acts, however, it seems possible that the antisocial behavior could have been performed just as easily through strong persuasion without the use of hypnosis. The consensus of opinion is that the antisocial behavior induced in an unwilling subject is primarily dependent upon the hypnotist and the extent to which he participates in the act himself. The subject is but a part of the newly created, structured hypnotic relationship.[9]

Because only 3 documented cases of actual criminal behavior involving hypnotic suggestion have been reported in the last 25 years, Orne[11] does not think that a cunning hypnotist could force another individual to do his criminal bidding purely by hypnotic suggestion. When a subject develops a strong personal attachment toward a hypnotist as in the above-mentioned cases, it is not extraordinary for such a subject to become involved in an antisocial act which might benefit another individual. He concludes that, "An explanation which purports to account for such behavior by singling out one aspect of the relationship, i.e., hypnosis, must be viewed with skepticism."

The explanations that characterize virtually all the experimental studies on antisocial behavior to date have been summarized as follows: The subjects believed that there were protective measures taken, since they knew it was only an experiment; they trusted the hypnotist either because they had confidence in him or because there were legitimate reasons for the hypnotist's requests; or the subjects had latent criminal tendencies. After studying all the available data, it is concluded that "hypnosis alone is incapable of causing antisocial behavior; that criminal behavior can be induced only if perceptual alterations are produced so that the act is not considered antisocial."[16]

DANGERS FROM STAGE HYPNOSIS

Considering the thousands of people hypnotized daily by entertainers, there are remarkably few documented cases of harm. The author of this book, however, is unalterably opposed to the entertainer-hypnotist's using hypnosis in any manner. Irrespective of his technical proficiency in inducing hypnosis, *he does not know the emotional make-up of the person he is hypnotizing.* Without this knowledge, he invites trouble for himself and his subject. Often the person hypnotized by the entertainer may have an emotional upset after he suffers embarrassment while on the stage. Frequently, some members of the audience will be hypnotized inadvertently. However, these are only temporary reactions.

Stage hypnotists supposedly have induced depressive reactions in some subjects. However, in most instances they failed to remove the suggestions which upset the subject. Typical is the following: "You will cry and feel sad because your husband is very sick." Inexperienced entertainer-hypnotists also fail to recognize that some subjects will *overreact physiologically* to psychological suggestions. For instance, if a deeply hypnotized subject is asked to imagine that he is hanging from a 10-story window ledge, and that his strength is ebbing, it is possible that he could easily develop a cardiac collapse if he has a bad heart. Entertainers are going to give medical hypnosis a "black eye" until

pending legislation prohibits them from using it for amusement purposes. The various bills in the state legislatures for these purposes recently have been reviewed.*

The amateur operator often may encounter violent hysteric outbursts which he is poorly equipped to handle. Naturally, when this occurs, the hypnosis should be terminated immediately. Prompt removal of the subject from the stage, together with strong reassurance, will invariably remedy this difficulty. Heavy sedation may be necessary for those who overreact.

Age-regression in the hands of the inept hypnotist is potentially the most dangerous of all hypnotic phenomena; here, deeply buried traumatic memories can erupt and result in panic reactions. If the resulting acting-out behavior is not handled properly, or if the regression cannot be removed, the hypnotist can identify with someone that the subject liked at an earlier age level. In the role of a benevolent surrogate figure, he can request the subject to return to his present chronologic age. It should be suggested that the subject will feel none the worse for his experience after dehypnotization.

Entertainer-hypnotists are not familiar with such technics, nor are they competent to handle conflictual material as it emerges. Therefore, the entertainer has no right to meddle with raw human emotions. Then, too, there are many amateur hypnotists and a few entertainer-hypnotists who treat a wide variety of medical conditions in which hypnosis is not indicated. Their inability to make a diagnosis can cause delay in effective medical assistance.

For over 25 years, the author of this book has requested the A.M.A. and the federal authorities to ban hypnosis by the stage hypnotist because, as long as it is identified with entertainment, professional men will hesitate to employ hypnotherapy. This is particularly true where the physician must practice medicine according to the dictates of public policy.

Unfortunately, irrational prejudices about hypnosis are still held by the laity. It is sincerely hoped that healthier public attitudes toward hypnosis and appropriate legislation

* Newsletter of the Society for Clinical and Experimental Hypnosis 4:9-13, May 1961.

will eventually make it an exclusive medical tool. Yet it is regrettable that many serious-minded scientists who use hypnotherapy have to fight a two-front war—on the one hand, the mountebanks who are promising quick cures with hypnosis and, on the other hand, those colleagues who utterly disbelieve in its utility.

REFERENCES

1. Bernheim, H.: Suggestive Therapeutics, New York, Putnam, 1902.
2. Bramwell, M. J.: Hypnosis, Its History, Practice and Theory, Philadelphia, Lippincott, 1930.
3. Brenman, M.: Experiments in the hypnotic production of anti-social and self-injurious behavior, Psychiatry 5:49-61, 1942.
4. Erickson, M. H.: An experimental investigation of the possible anti-social uses of hypnosis, Psychiatry 2:391-414, 1939.
5. Estabrook, G. H.: University of Colgate Symposium on Hypnosis, April 2, 1960.
6. Heron, W. T.: Hypnosis as a factor in the production of crime, Brit. J. M. Hypnotism 3:15-29, 1952.
7. Hollander, B.: Methods and Uses of Hypnosis and Self-Hypnosis, New York, Macmillan, 1928.
8. Hull, C. L.: Hypnosis and Suggestibility—An Experimental Approach, New York, Appleton, 1933.
9. Kline, M. V.: The dynamics of hypnotically induced anti-social behavior, J. Psychol. 45:239-245, 1958.
10. Marcuse, F. L.: Anti-social behavior and hypnosis, J.C.E.H. 1:18-21, 1953.
11. Orne, M. T.: Book review of Reiter (12), Internat. J.C.E.H. 7:133, 1960.
12. Reiter, P. J.: Antisocial or Criminal Acts and Hypnosis, Springfield, Ill., Thomas, 1959.
13. Schilder, P., and Kauder, O.: Hypnosis, Nerv. & Ment. Dis. Monogr. Ser. No. 46, 1927. (New edition in press, International Universities Publishers.)
14. Schneck, J. M.: A military offense induced by hypnosis, J. Nerv. & Ment. Dis. 106:63-102, 1941.
15. Watkins, J. G.: Anti-social compulsions induced under hypnotic trance, J. Abnorm. & Social Psychol. 42:256-259, 1947.
16. Weitzenhoffer, A. M.: Hypnotism: An Objective Study in Hypnotizability, New York, Wiley, 1953.
17. Wells, W. R.: Experiments in the Hypnotic production of crimes, J. Psychol. 11:63-102, 1941.
18. Young, P. C.: Is rapport an essential characteristic of hypnosis?, J. Abnorm. & Social Psychol. 22:130-139, 1937.

SUPPLEMENTARY READING

Barber, T. X.: Antisocial and criminal acts induced by "hypnosis," Arch. Gen. Psychiat. 5:301-312, 1961.

20

Dangers From Hypnosis

A wise man once stated, "It is much easier to ignore the obvious than to renounce the traditional." Thus, thousands upon thousands of persons all over the world are hypnotized daily without harm and yet the method is considered dangerous simply because the Svengali-Trilby myth has been perpetuated for years.

However, an infinitesimally small number of dangerous sequelae following hypnotherapy have been reported. These isolated cases have been brought to the attention of the laity and of the profession chiefly because of the ill-advised and promiscuous use of hypnosis by untrained and unqualified lay and medical hypnotists.[9, 10]

This situation is certainly deplorable, and adequate precautions to avoid the misuse of hypnosis are indicated. Yet a sober and objective evaluation of these cases show that it is *not* the hypnosis, but many other variables, as psychotherapeutic mismanagement and misdiagnosis, that are etiogenic. The lack of documentation, personal bias, operator attitude and hearsay evidence, together with the necessary warnings against the unwarranted current use of hypnosis—all contribute to exaggerated claims that hypnosis is dangerous. It is safe to say that hypnosis is the safest of all psychotherapies. Deaths and considerable permanent damage have been reported with shock therapy, steroid administration, narcosynthesis and hallucinogenic agents. Yet no one has ever died from hypnosis!

Another issue is made of the proper criteria for selection of patients on whom hypnosis can be used safely. This author firmly believes that the sole criteria are the training, the judgment and the experience of the operator and the motivation and the willingness of the patient to be hypnotized, provided there is, of course, a specific indication.

The British Medical Association[2] has reported:

The dangers of hypnotism have been exaggerated in some quarters. The subcommittee is convinced, however, that they do exist, especially when it is used without proper consideration on persons predisposed constitutionally or by the effects of disease, to severe psychoneurotic reactions or antisocial behavior. The commission of crimes involving even danger to life is not entirely to be ruled out.

The initial approval by the Council on Mental Health of the A.M.A.[1] stated:

The surgeon, obstetrician, anesthesiologist, internist and general practitioner may legitimately utilize these technics within the framework of their own particular field of competence.

Whereas the report stresses that all who use hypnosis should be cognizant of its complex nature, it points out that controversy exists as to the hazards of hypnosis. There were few dissenting voices to contend that hypnosis was a dangerous medical tool. Yet the American Psychiatric Association report,[11] and the most recent "Report on Training" issued by the Mental Health Council of the A.M.A.,[8] while making many worthwhile recommendations on training, indicate that the minority opinion of the original 1958 A.M.A. report has been accepted. It is hoped that the present studies on possible dangers being made by Wolberg and others will shed more light on this problem. The reader is also referred to a recent publication by the author of this book.[6]

The A.M.A. was queried about their stand. The question:

"Has the A.M.A. Committee on Hypnosis ever published officially any statement defining or implying the dangers in the use of hypnosis by physicians?" elicited the answer that it had not done so, nor had it authorized one, and that a member of the committee who states this is "expressing his own personal opinions."

Platonov,[7] an associate of Pavlov, who has used hypnosis for over 50 years in over 50,000 cases, reports as follows in one of the most remarkable books written on hypnosis.

We have never observed any harmful influence on the patient which could be ascribed to the method of hypnosuggestive therapy, presumably leading to the development of an "unstable personality," "slavish subordination," weakening of the will, increase in suggestibility, pathological urge for hypnosis, etc.

The author is in accord with Cheek,[3] who has had a vast experience, when he states:

The mechanisms by which hypnosis can do harm are not different from the tools which Lady Macbeth used on her husband, which Cassius used on the honorable Brutus, which Iago used on Othello.—We can do more harm with ignorance of hypnosis than we can by intelligently using the forces of suggestion.

Julius Grinker[4] long ago stated:

The so-called dangers from hypnotism are imaginary. Although I have hypnotized hundreds of times I have never seen any ill effects from its use. Bernheim, Liebault, Ford, Wetterstrand, and a host of others who have practiced suggestive methods in thousands of instances have had similar experiences.

Similarly, Pierre Janet,[5] who at first opposed hypnosis and later became an ardent advocate, stated: "The only danger to hypnosis is that it is not dangerous enough."

Words can be more devastating than bacteria. During a physical examination, for instance, symptoms can be produced by merely placing a stethoscope over a patient's heart and carelessly saying, "Humph." The frightened and apprehensive patient is apt to ask, "What's the matter, Doctor, is there something wrong with my heart"? No amount of persuasion can convince this patient that his heart is perfectly normal. One would not indict the stethoscope or the physical examination as being responsible for the iatrogenic condition produced. But what was said and how it was done could be held culpable.

THEORETIC DANGERS FROM MEDICAL HYPNOTHERAPY

Seldom considered also is the fact that disturbed subjects can fabricate material as well as "acting-out" behavior in and out of hypnosis if they desire either to please or displease the experimenter. This can lead to dangerous conclusions on the part of the therapist. Also, it is not so easy to change behavior by hypnosis. If so, a team of hypnotherapists could be sent into our penal institutions to hypnotize every hardened criminal into becoming a law-abiding person. This just could not be done. Thus, if wanted changes are difficult to obtain by hypnosis, certainly unwanted changes are not going to occur.

Not to belabor this point, in the usual doctor-patient hypnotherapy relationship, it is extremely difficult to hypnotize a patient without his consent or to induce untoward behavior in a subject from hypnosis per se. It is conceivable, however, that an unscrupulous physician, under the guise of giving vitamin B injections, could make an addict out of a patient by repeatedly giving him morphine and telling him that it was vitamin B. Likewise, through very devious and circuitous routes, it is theoretically possible to engraft an experimental conflict, covered over by an amnesia, in a somnambulist, and to give him posthypnotic suggestions to commit an amoral act. This "contrived" situation admittedly does not apply, however, in the doctor-patient relationship.

Wolberg[13] states:

Employed by a reasonably trained professional, within the context of a structured therapeutic program, with proper awareness of limits of its application and with appropriate timing . . . the dangers inherent in its use are few or nonexistent, if it is skillfully employed by a responsible operator.

Another authority[12] believes that there is no foundation for the belief that hypnosis weakens the will, leads to overdependency or causes neuroticism. This author is in complete accord with this statement. The incontrovertible fact is that it is doubtful if, when properly used, there is another modality *less* dangerous in medicine than hypnosis.

Yet there is no medical technic which makes a better "whipping boy" than hypnosis!

REFERENCES

1. A.M.A. Council on Mental Health—Committee on Hypnosis: Training in Medical Hypnosis, Report approved by Council on Mental Health, February, 1960.
2. British Medical Association, Medical Use of Hypnotism: Report of Subcommittee Appointed by Psychological Medicine Committee, British Medical Association, British Medical Journal *1*:1019-1020, 1955.
3. Cheek, D. B.: Hypnosis: an additional tool in human reorientation to stress, Northwest Med. *6*:177-182, 1958.
4. Grinker, J.: Quoted in Quackenbos, J. D.: Hypnotic Therapeutics, p. 109, New York, Harper, 1908.
5. Janet, P.: Psychological Healing, London, Allen & Unwin, 1925.
6. Kroger, W. S.: It is a wise hypnotist who knows who is hypnotizing whom, West. J. Surg., Obst. & Gynec. *69*:132-137, 1961.
7. Platonov, K.: The Word: As a Physiological and Therapeutic Factor, Moscow, Foreign Languages Publishing House, 1959.
8. Plunkett, R. J.: Medical Use of Hypnosis, J.A.M.A. *168*:186-189, 1958.
9. Rosen, H.: Hypnosis and self-hypnosis in medical practice, Maryland M. J. *6*:297, 1957.
10. Rosen, H., and Bartemeier, L.: Hypnosis in medical practice, J.A.M.A. *175*:128-131, 1961.
11. Ross, M.: Regarding Hypnosis: a Statement of Position by the American Psychiatric Association, Feb. 15, 1961.
12. Weitzenhoffer, A. M.: General Techniques of Hypnotism, p. 424, Grune & Stratton, New York, 1957.
13. Wolberg, L. H.: Hypnoanalysis, New York, Grune & Stratton, 1945.

SUPPLEMENTARY READING

Meares, A.: An evaluation of the dangers of medical hypnosis, Am. J. Clin. Hypnosis *4*:90-98, 1961.

21

Precautions in the Use of Hypnosis

CONTRAINDICATIONS

The two most important contraindications to the use of hypnosis by the nonpsychiatrist are the queerly acting or unstable "crackpot" and the psychotic. The prepsychotic is difficult to recognize. He usually can be discerned by the intensity of his mood swings. The psychotic, especially the withdrawn, apathetic type, whose thinking is unreal, will be a liability for anyone but the trained psychotherapist. Conn[1] says: "Neither one nor many hypnotic sessions can precipitate psychoses if no psychotic process has been at work." Of course, organic conditions amenable to medical therapy should be given a careful differential diagnosis and not treated exclusively by hypnosis.

DANGERS OF SYMPTOM-REMOVAL

Conn[1] believes that there is no danger in the removal of a symptom, and that one symptom is not replaced by another except in very disturbed, unstable persons. It is best, however, to use permissive suggestions oriented around the needs of the patient when hypnotherapy is employed for symptom-removal. Symptom-substitution or "trading down" to a less disturbing one enables the well-established symptom to be manipulated more readily, and this prevents other symptom-equivalents from being substituted. Recent data indicate that even if hypnosis is used for direct symptom-removal there is very little danger that the original symptom will recur. Dorcus,[2] in a 5-year follow-up study of two groups of patients who had phantom limb pain and hiccoughs, respectively, noted that *not a single one of these symptoms returned when hypnotherapy for symptomatic relief was employed.*

The dangers attributed to hypnotic removal of symptoms are grossly exaggerated. Such reasoning is not applied to generalists at nonhypnotic levels when symptomatic therapy is used. Furthermore, since other symptoms often make their appearance concomitantly during any form of psychotherapy, how can a new symptom necessarily be related to the "symptom-removal"? And is not the bulk of nonpsychiatric treatment directed toward symptom-removal? Furthermore, there are no accurately controlled data to prove that other symptoms replace those that have been removed by hypnosis, especially when autohypnosis and permissive technics are employed. Often symptom relief is as good as it is when so-called insight is given to the patient.

It is often stated that repeated hypnotization can lead to emotional instability. There is no reliable evidence to substantiate this statement. Individuals who have been hypnotized hundreds of times have exhibited absolutely no harmful effects.

DANGERS TO THE OPERATOR

However, there are certain dangers to the operator, such as a charge of unethical conduct. These can be obviated if a third party, such as a nurse, is present. Tape-recording each session is also helpful. Permission of parents should be obtained when employing hypnotherapy in children. The inexperienced therapist should have another individual present when hypnotizing a disturbed female, or a subject who one suspects might be hysteroid, psychopathic or psychotic; psychopathic personalities often resort to confabulations characterized by wishful thinking, deceit or actual fabrications.

A female patient may develop a spontaneous hypnotic amnesia and claim that the physician had raped her (this unfortunate situation can also occur at nonhypnotic levels) and because of the oft-associated idea that hypnosis can overpower the will, the hapless operator may find himself charged with unethical conduct. Many, aware of such possibilities, obtain a signed release if unable to have a third person present. Three malpractice cases stemming from hypnosis were reported in a recent survey.[3] In each, the defendant was accused of assault during a hypnotic session; each case was later dropped by the prosecution, and each patient was subsequently judged insane.

Fortunately, most malpractice insurance policies protect medical men and psychologists against such lawsuits (see Chapter 23).

DANGERS TO THE METHOD

To protect hypnotherapeutic methods from adverse criticism, the therapist should not promise more than can be accomplished, and a guarantee of cure should not be made. However, if there is a valid indication, one can state that everything will be done to help the patient recover. All patients should be informed that the results obtained in hypnosis are based wholly on the patient's cooperation and willingness to co-operate. The following remark is helpful: "You are *not* being treated *by* hypnosis but rather *in* hypnosis. Hypnosis by itself does not cure but merely facilitates the understandings so necessary in all successful therapy. You are

the one who developed the condition that you wish removed; therefore, it can be accomplished only by reversing those faulty thinking patterns which produced the symptom. Naturally, this will require your utmost concentration, receptivity, self-objectivity and understanding."

Hypnosis should always be employed for definitive goals. The dictum that "Hypnosis should be used for the good of the patient, not to enhance the prestige of the operator" must be kept in mind. It should never be used for entertainment by a physician or a dentist. Otherwise, respect for the method and the operator is destroyed. Finally, as emphasized, the inexperienced operator must never attempt to elicit deeply repressed and traumatic material unless he has been trained to recognize it and to know what to do with it when it appears. Otherwise, the patient will develop what has been referred to as "traumatic insight."

REFERENCES

1. Conn, J. H.: Preparing for hypnosis in general practice, Roche Report 3:3, 1961.
2. Dorcus, R. M.: The treatment of symptoms with special reference to removal by hypnosis. Read before University of Kansas Symposium on Hypnosis Research and Clinical Psychology, May 8, 1960.
3. Could you use hypnosis in your practice?, Medical Economics, May 22, 1961.

22

Precautions in Dehypnotization

PRECAUTIONS

There are certain precautions that one should use when dehypnotizing a patient. As the result of the increased amount of concentration required for successful hypnosis, many subjects state, upon termination of the hypnosis, "I have a terrible headache." Therefore, the operator should remark, "Your eyes will open at the count of 3; you will feel perfectly wonderful; you will be completely refreshed and relaxed."

Always give posthypnotic suggestions so that hypnosis can readily be reinduced. The touch on the right shoulder is a good one, because one can remember "right" to induce, and "left" for dehypnotization. The same standardized procedure for each patient should be used in order not to become confused.

All posthypnotic suggestions, as anesthesia or hyperesthesia induced over any part of the body, should be removed by the statement, "You are going to feel fine. All of the suggestions that I have given you except the ones you wish to retain will disappear." Even though a subject is in control, one also should suggest, "Nobody can ever induce hypnosis without your permission, and this includes myself." This pleases most individuals, as so many patients fear they will be hypnotized against their will. This procedure nullifies the unfounded criticism that hypnosis can be produced against a subject's wishes.

Also, reiterate *over* and *over*, "Now, remember, you were *not* asleep, you were *not* unconscious, you were *not* in any kind of trance, and *you heard everything I said.*" In spite of these clear-cut suggestions, subjects who were deeply hypnotized, but who do not understand the nature of hypnosis,

state, "Doctor, I know I wasn't hypnotized. I heard everything you said." On the other hand, those who are conversant with hypnosis remark afterward how alert they were and how everything was heard clearly. I assure patients that this hyperacuity is characteristic of hypnosis. Patients who confuse hypnosis with sleep should be informed: "I am using hypnosis because I want you to be *more* 'awake.' If you are paying full attention to me, I can get more meaningful suggestions across to you." Patients then understand more about the nature of hypnosis.

All patients can be dehypnotized readily. This author, in several thousand patients and lecture demonstrations, *has never had a patient who would not or could not come out of hypnosis.* However, there are several reports on difficulties of dehypnotization.[1-3] The author remembers when an amateur hypnotist could not dehypnotize a patient because he neglected to remove a suggested anesthesia from a subject's arm. The patient, naturally, did not wish to have a part of the body anesthetized. It was only when he informed the hypnotist about the arm that he allowed himself to be dehypnotized. Therefore, one must be careful to recheck all suggestions whenever a patient cannot be dehypnotized.

There is also the rare possibility that a somnambulist, who has been deeply hypnotized for a long period, may spontaneously re-enter hypnosis unless completely dehypnotized after the initial induction. Therefore, it is always wise to keep such patients in the office for an hour or more, especially if they have to drive. Failure to do this might invite a law suit if an accident occurred. Even though it would be difficult to prove negligence, the situation could prove very troublesome. Often, too, subjects who are reacting to a posthypnotic suggestion are not fully dehypnotized; some look "sleepy." Therefore, here too, sufficient time must be allowed for the relaxing effects of the hypnosis to be dissipated.

The pattern of actual sleep and the ease of awakening may be related to the ease of dehypnotization; heavy sleepers theoretically dehypnotize slowly. The particular mood of the subject at the time of dehypnotization can determine the way he feels and acts after the induction is terminated. Some cry, while others laugh—either is dependent on the type of associations stimulated during the hypnosis. Often the specific personality needs of the hypnotized subject can be correlated with the manner in which dehypnotization occurs. This is affected by the ability of the subject to face reality—a person who has a difficult life situation to face may prefer to remain in hypnosis.

Williams[23] has described the difficulties associated with dehypnotization. He points out that some individuals are only partially dehypnotized and then can lapse into deep hypnosis spontaneously. He also cites[2] three cases in which dehypnotization was delayed by the subjects' refusal to terminate the hypnosis. One subject became belligerent but finally was dehypnotized; another, who had been given a posthypnotic suggestion to misspell his name, was dehypnotized only after he had carried out the suggested act. The third subject refused to be dehypnotized because some preservation of highly charged emotional material of the preinduction period persisted during the hypnosis.

Bramwell[1] cites 2 cases in which the subjects were reluctant to terminate the hypnosis (in both, disagreeable posthypnotic suggestions had been given). Williams discusses other cases in which the hypnotist attempted to reinstitute an aphasia while the patient was being treated for hysteric aphasia. One patient told the physician-hypnotist that, if he persisted, she would refuse to "wake up." Another wanted to see a hallucinated movie again. He told the hypnotist he intended to remain in the hypnotic state.

Williams reviewed 30 cases in which difficulty in dehypnotization had occurred. In some, carry-over of the preinduction mood, malingering, incompetency of the hypnotist and other factors were responsible. Only scant data are available as to the exact time required for dehypnotization, but the periods ranged from one to several hours, despite medical intervention.

One of the "psychological" factors responsible for difficult dehypnotization is that the subject often deliberately attempts to test the hypnotist's ability to dehypnotize him. Frequently there is collusion with friends merely to embarrass the hypnotist. Errors and ambiguities in instruction, as well as omission of a relevant detail which is disturbing to the subject, can be responsible, as, for instance, failure to remove a suggested paralysis of the limbs, as mentioned above. Other factors are: aggression toward the therapist, reliving of highly charged emotional material, association with what happened on television or in the movies associated with hypnosis, or combat fatigue treated by hypnoanalysis.

When some psychoneurotics fail to dehypnotize, the responsible factors often can be those which are also behind their symptoms—the behavior in hypnosis fits in with their emotional needs. This is borne out by the cases just described: the subjects were in control and decided how they wished to react.

DEHYPNOTIZING THE DIFFICULT PATIENT

Treat every patient with respect, as hypnosis is a dignified procedure which should be used only for medical reasons. Understanding the emotional needs of the patient who is to be dehypnotized is imperative. If an individual refuses to be dehypnotized, one can do several things. One can suggest that the hypnosis will merge with true sleep and that the subject will awaken from it none the worse for the experience, or that he will come out of it spontaneously.

If these measures fail, one can use time distortion, as follows: He can be informed that 1 minute of subjective or experiential time will *seem* like half an hour of clock or chronologic time. If 1 minute is equated to a half hour, then if he remains in hypnosis for 10 minutes it will *seem* as if 5 hours have elapsed. Thus, he will have had his full measure of revenge. Now he will dehypnotize himself, because he has proved his point. If these methods are of no avail, one can resort to mild electroshock or Metrazol.

The best method is to superinduce another hypnotic state and make every effort to recognize and understand the specific behavior involved in the subject's refusal to be dehypnotized. If the hypnosis still cannot be terminated, another hypnotist can deepen the hypnosis and then impose his own conditions for dehypnotization. Sometimes fur-

ther psychotherapy must be promised to get disturbed individuals, who demand more attention from the therapist, out of hypnosis.

REFERENCES

1. Bramwell, J. M.: Hypnotism, London, Rider & Son, 1921.
2. Williams, G. W.: Difficulty in dehypnotizing, J.C.E.H. *1*:3-12, 1953.
3. ——: The termination of the hypnotic state *in* Introductory Lectures in Medical Hypnosis, pp. 62-69, New York, The Institute for Research in Hypnosis, 1958.

23

Medical Training, Legal and Ethical Aspects of Hypnosis

MEDICAL TRAINING

The question of medical training in hypnosis is being considered at the present time.[2-4] The A.M.A. Council on Mental Health's Committee on Hypnosis, consisting largely of psychiatrists, stresses that a knowledge of psychodynamics, defined as the motivational basis of human behavior, is essential for practicing hypnotherapy. Other reports[1-3] indicate that their authors consider hypnosis to be a technic that should be limited primarily to psychiatrists. These recommendations are worthy of consideration as many psychiatrists were unfamiliar with hypnotic technics until recently.

Inasmuch as hypnosis, in one form or another, recognized or unrecognized, cross-fertilizes with all the healing arts, it is not clear which of the numerous schools of psychotherapy should teach it. Since clinical practice and applications encompass the broad field of suggestion and behavior dynamics, it simply cannot be broken down into psychiatric, obstetric or medical or psychological hypnosis. Progress in hypnosis might be retarded for another 50 years if training in hypnosis is oriented around the concepts of the schools of "popular" psychotherapy that are currently being challenged.

Hypnosis cannot be claimed by any school of psychotherapy. Have not suggestion and/or hypnosis been responsible for the placebo effect in medical and psychological therapy for years? Waking hypnosis, together with other factors, accounts for the success of most religious and spiritual healers. Even though they have had no medical training in psychodynamics, can anyone deny the latter's successes?

The mature physician, successful in his practice of medicine, already has demonstrated his capacity to deal adequately with emotional disturbances. Since psychosomatic illness comprises the bulk of his practice, it is inexcusable for any physician, oriented or trained in hypnosis, *not* to be able to conduct adequate hypnotherapy when it is indicated. This should be done within the usual restrictions on the basis of his medical training, judgment, intuition and experience. Hypnosis can be used much like any drug, especially as an adjunct to supportive therapy of psychosomatic disorders.

Because of the inadequate numbers of psychiatrists, physicians are demanding a less time-consuming psychotherapy. This has led to the current worldwide interest in hypnotherapy as an adjunctive psychotherapeutic procedure for *selected* patients. Therefore, those who assume the responsibility for training future physicians should recognize that hypnosis must be incorporated into a more scientific frame of reference.

It is hoped that the behavioral sciences, which are assuming a greater role in medical education, especially in psychotherapy, will incorporate hypnosis in their teaching programs. Until recently, much of the teaching available to physicians was offered by workshops sponsored by medical schools and scientific societies. These were only intended to orient the doctor in this field. However, many of these physicians, including a considerable number of psychiatrists, have continued their interest and made notable contributions to the clinical and experimental applications of hypnosis.

The workshops, however, have served their purpose, as they not only developed a grass-roots interest in hypnosis, but ultimately contributed in no small measure to the establishment of the A.M.A. Committee on Hypnosis. This Committee has formulated a curriculum on hypnosis to be taught in medical schools.[4] To be sure, this is the logical way to teach clinical hypnosis. One school, the University of Pennsylvania School of Medicine, is now offering a 66-hour course. When other centers institute courses, this should eventually bring hypnosis to its full medical acceptance.

Physicians, until further clarification, are urged to seek training in medical schools, and to adhere to the recent British and A.M.A. reports on medical hypnosis.[2, 5]

HYPNOSIS AND THE LAW

Due to the striking character of hypnotic phenomena, serious questions for legal consideration may arise. The legal aspects of hypnosis recently have been discussed from 3 standpoints: (1) the criminal law, (2) hypnosis and the law of evidence and (3) the regulation of hypnosis.[6]

As mentioned in preceding chapters, several criminal cases involving hypnosis have reached the courts, consisting of women claiming rape or seduction while hypnotized. Nearly all have been dismissed on the basis of insufficient evidence or fabrication. Commission of other crimes has been recorded, as murder, robbery and assault following posthypnotic suggestions. In practically every instance, hypnosis was used as an alibi. In Chapter 19, it was emphasized that in the ordinary doctor-patient relationship, it would be extremely difficult to perpetrate a crime under hypnosis and that, if sufficient criminal intent was present, the act could be performed just as readily by strong persuasion. The number of such cases decided is small. Now, however, with the medical acceptance and greater application of hypnosis, the law will be called upon more frequently to cope with the medical uses and abuses of hypnosis. In some instances, present legal principles are adequate; in other cases they are inadequate.

The most important claim is that hypnosis can induce extreme suggestibility. However, as discussed, extreme suggestibility and/or hypnotizability exists in varying degrees in all humans. Furthermore, hypnosis is as readily induced by nonformalistic technics. Hence, current notions regarding suggesti-

bility and hypnotizability need considerable revision. This is especially true with reference to the subtle suggestibility produced by all media of communication, as television, radio and motion pictures. Standardized statutes are therefore needed, based on enlightened court decisions dealing specifically with hypnotic suggestibility, its limitations and its contraindications.

MALPRACTICE AND INSURANCE ASPECTS

Physicians using hypnosis, as well as any other forms of psychotherapy, are naturally concerned about malpractice. Most state and county medical societies completely protect the physician who uses hypnosis. At present, Lloyd's of London issues malpractice coverage for physicians using hypnosis.

Citing a 1959 statement by the A.M.A. legal department, physicians were warned that they would be faced with malpractice suits over hypnotic treatment if they were unable to establish their competence; two malpractice suits had been filed.[1a]

Yet one of the largest insurance companies which handles malpractice for physicians and dentists states:

that it has no restrictions on the use of hypnosis, nor are any contemplated. No additional premiums are being considered by the underwriters for those who use hypnosis in the practice of their profession. At a recent meeting of the Professional Liability Underwriters, none had encountered any malpractice claims predicated on the use of hypnosis by dentists or physicians who were not trained psychiatrists. Not a single one knew of any difficulties whatever, and all recognized that hypnosis was being used to a great degree in the practice of medicine and dentistry—and quite successfully.

In response to a recent query to the leading malpractice insurance company in Los Angeles, which has the highest number of malpractice claims in the nation, the following reply was received:

As far as we can determine at the Nettleship Company there has not been a physician in California sued for hypnosis, and as far as we are aware, there has only been one physician other than a psychiatrist sued for hypnosis in the United States.°

Nevertheless, the same precautions employed to prevent malpractice claims in any other branch of medicine should be used. A generalist certainly would not perform a brain tumor operation. Similarly, without special training in handling psychotics at nonhypnotic levels, the hypnotist-physician might find himself in a hazardous position. He might be blamed for complications wholly unrelated to the hypnotherapy. As emphasized, improper suggestions easily can upset and embarrass disturbed individuals. Therefore, the hypnotist-physician must at all times assume full responsibility for what he says to his subject.†

In summation, from the medicolegal standpoint the important precautions are: Hypnotherapy should be restricted to those qualified by experience and training for diagnosing and treating medical and psychological disorders. The physician should not exceed his competence; even then hypnosis must be used only for *selected cases*. The operator should never promise more than can reasonably be expected from hypnotherapy and should emphasize that it is by no means a panacea. Sometimes it is advisable to obtain permission for hypnotization from zealots and potential troublemakers as well as from the parents of children to be hypnotized.

Unfortunately, some malcontents may blame the physician on any pretext when they fail to recover. Therefore, it should be emphasized that hypnosis is being used primarily as an adjunct to psychotherapy and medical therapy in relation to the patient's needs. Hence, the degree of recovery is wholly dependent upon the patient's own motivations and co-operation and the extent of his emotional involvement.

With reference to a psychosis developing in a severely disturbed person, it is extremely doubtful that this can be attributed to the hypnosis per se. The onset of a psychotic breakdown is more temporal than causal; that is, as a iatrogenic remark either

° The Nettleship Company of Los Angeles in a letter dated May 16, 1961.
† Bloomquist, E. R.: Parlor hypnosis: a game for fools, Gen. Practice *19*:120-124, 1959.

at hypnotic or nonhypnotic levels, can be disturbing to an apprehensive person, especially the person on the verge of collapse.

If the above precautions are kept in mind, medicolegal difficulties will be reduced or eliminated.

ETHICAL ASPECTS

Since hypnosis is rapidly becoming a dignified medical tool, a physican should not employ it in the parlor for entertainment or self-laudation. The following ethical code has been adopted by the Society for Clinical and Experimental Hypnosis:

Inasmuch as hypnosis is particularly susceptible to popular misunderstanding and to sensationalism and inasmuch as membership in the Society is open to many professions (dentists, physicians, psychologists, psychiatrists, etc.), the code of ethics governing the behavior of any member, whether hypnosis be used experimentally or clinically, shall include the following points to which individuals, by virtue of their membership in the SCEH, shall subscribe:

I. (a) A person who uses hypnosis shall continue in good (ethical) standing in his own professional organization. (e.g. APA, ADA, etc.) If the individual is not a member of his own professional organization, he may be requested to obtain such membership or show cause as to why he should not meet such a requirement.

(b) A person who uses hypnosis shall neither claim directly nor imply professional qualifications that exceed those that he has actually attained.

(c) A person who uses hypnosis must refer his patient to an appropriate specialist when there is evidence of a difficulty with which he is not competent to deal.

(d) A person who uses hypnosis shall not employ any procedure, which in the informed opinion of competent persons, is likely to mislead a patient or subject. A cardinal obligation is to protect the welfare and respect the integrity of the individual with whom one is working.

(e) Guarantees of easy solutions or favorable outcomes must not be made nor may one claim to have secret techniques.

(f) A person who uses hypnosis shall not offer his services for the purpose of public entertainment or advisement via newspapers, magazine articles, radio, television or similar media. Such a person, if he makes public announcement of his services, is obligated to describe such services with accuracy and dignity, adhering to professional rather than commercial standards. Direct solicitation is unethical.

(g) Demonstrations should only be conducted for serious purposes, such as the training of professional workers. It is unethical to display subjects or patients to satisfy casual curiosity.

(h) The supervisor of the research of a student in training should be sufficiently familiar with procedures and data to insure that principles of good research and good ethics are observed.

(i) Only when a problem is significant and can be investigated in no other way, is the person who uses hypnosis justified in exposing human subjects to stress. Should he do so he is obligated to provide such services as may be required. Research at all times will be conducted within a framework of moral, judicial and socially accepted principles.

(j) Exaggerations, sensationalism, superficiality, and premature reporting of new developments should be avoided; modesty, scientific caution and due regard for the limits of our knowledge should characterize all statements.

(k) Reference to membership in the SCEH for activities involving hypnosis should not be made unless endorsement by the SCEH does in fact exist. Where doubt exists such a statement should be followed by "For identification only"

(l) Should any activity occur in conjunction with the use of hypnosis, such activity should in no way put hypnosis in an unfavorable light

Procedure for Instituting Complaints

II. (a) Initiation of charges by one or more members. Should charges be brought by only one member, they must be signed and agreed to by at least one non-member who is to be identified as to occupation.

(b) Submission of specific charges in writing to the Executive Body.

(c) Referral of such charges to the Committee on Ethics.

(d) Notification of member concerning charges pending.

(e) Hearing of charges at a meeting of the Executive Body with opportunity for member to present his case in person, by writing, or to be represented by a person of his choice.

(f) Right of appeal by defendant to Executive Body to reconsider its action.

Possible Action

The Committee on Ethics (a standing committee whose chairman is appointed by the president) may recommend to the Executive:

III. (a) That charges be dropped.

(b) That the individual be apprised of the fact that his behavior resulted in the initiation of charges and bordered on violation of principles for which the SCEH stands. Should the member be warned, under the provisions of this section, on more than two discrete occasions he will be deemed guilty of violating SCEH principles and Section III (c), III (d) or III (e) will automatically be invoked.

(c) That the individual be suspended for one year.

(d) That the individual be asked to resign.

(e) That the individual be expelled.

REFERENCES

1. Rosen, H. and Bartemeier, L. H.: Hypnosis in medical practice, J.A.M.A. *175*:128-131, 1961.

1a. Rosen, H.: A.M.A. News June 29, 1959.

2. Plunkett, R. J.: Medical use of hypnosis: Council on Mental Health Report, J.A.M.A. *168*:186-189, 1958.

3. Training in Medical Hypnosis: A.M.A. Council on Mental Health, Committee on Hypnosis, Approved Feb., 1960 by A.M.A. Council on Mental Health. J.A.M.A. *180*: 693-698, 1962.

4. Regarding Hypnosis: a statement of position by the American Psychiatric Association, Feb. 15, 1961.

5. British Medical Assoc.: Medical use of hypnotism, Report of Subcommittee appointed by Psychological Medicine Group Committee of Brit. Med. Assoc., Brit. Med. J. *1*:1019-1020, 1953.

6. Solomon, J.: Hypnotism, suggestibility and the law, Nebraska Law Review *31*:575-596, 1952.

24

Religious Attitudes: Comparative Evaluation With Hypnosis

The only major religious groups objecting to hypnosis are the Christian Scientists and the Seventh-day Adventists. The former strenuously deny that their system of healing was or is associated with hypnosis, while the latter defend their opposition to it on ethical and moral principles. However, the Seventh-day Adventists admit that hypnosis has medical value if performed by qualified practitioners.[18] Their objection is that it deprives humans of freedom of the will. Without getting involved in an epistemologic discussion on free will, several[6, 11, 15, 17] writers question whether man can be deprived of his will. Bridgman,[1a] a Nobel prize-winning physicist, asks if there is objective proof that we really are free. And has not the nervous system before birth been subjected to an elaborate preconditioning?

There are also unwarranted misconceptions about the ethical and moral use of hypnosis by uninformed lay Roman Catholics as well as clergy and physicians, who remark, "I always thought that the Catholic Church was against hypnosis." Actually, there never has been a blanket condemnation of hypnosis by the Roman Catholic Church at any time. The historical attitude of the Church toward hypnosis will be summarized from a theological frame of reference.

ATTITUDE OF THE ROMAN CATHOLIC CHURCH TOWARD HYPNOSIS

The first proclamation of the Holy See on this subject was a decree of the Sacred Congregation of the Holy Office, July 28, 1847:[7]

Having removed all misconceptions, foretelling of the future, explicit or implicit invocation of the devil, the use of animal magnetism (hypnosis) is indeed merely an act making use of physical media that are otherwise licit and hence *it is not morally forbidden*, provided that it does not tend toward an illicit end or toward anything depraved.

Aertnys-Damen,[1] Jone[12] and Davis[8] are in essential agreement, and are favorably disposed toward the medical use of hypnosis. The chief objection to hypnosis, according to the above theologians, is that, if hypnosis is not used in accordance with a person's wishes, it may deprive him of his free use of reason. However, St. Thomas Aquinas[20] specifically says "that the loss of the use of reason is not a sin in itself (*secundem se*) but only by reason of the act (*secundem actum*) by which one is deprived of his use of reason; thus, if the act is inordinate concupiscence by the use of wine, there will be a sin of intemperance pertaining to gluttony. But if the act that deprives one of his use of reason is licit in itself and is done for a just cause, there is no sin; if no just cause is present, it must be considered a venial sin."

Thus, the use of hypnosis for a definitive reason is not a venial sin. In the light of the recent pronouncements of the Holy See given below and the opinions of other qualified moral theologians, a properly trained Roman Catholic physician can use hypnosis where it is indicated.

A theologian, J. T. Mangan, S. J.,[14] recently investigated the subject of hypnosis with the intention of making a medicomoral evaluation. He interviewed six leading Catholic and five non-Catholic psychiatrists. The author of this book also participated in the preparation of the questionnaire material. Mangan noted that hypnosis is not a state induced by so-called "occult" practices, nor is it associated with witchcraft, black magic, spiritualistic séances or the like. Nor is it fakery, foolishness, a game or a form of entertainment. After a careful review of the various authoritative directives issued by Catholic ecclesiastical authorities in Rome, he, too, concluded that they *condemn the abuse but not the legitimate use of medical hypnosis.*

His conclusions list the following requirements: (1) The hypnotherapist should be a competent and conscientious practitioner. There is a need today for a professionally recognized standard for hypnotherapists, stressing high integrity, good moral character and judgment. It is wise to have a third person present to protect the interests of both the patient and the doctor, especially when the patient is a woman. (2) An indication is required. (He believes that we are not permitted, without a compensatory reason, to give up our dominion over the rational faculties of understanding and will. When a competent and conscientious doctor advises that hypnosis is medically indicated, we may accept that it is for the benefit of his patient.) (3) The consent of the patient must be procured. (No one has the right to deprive another against his wishes of the full use of his faculties.) It is not necessary, however, always to obtain the explicit consent of the patient. (4) There should be no risk of harm to the patient. (5) Professional secrecy concerning the information obtained under hypnosis must be maintained.*

Mangan's erudite study should be read *in toto* by all Roman Catholic physicians who still think that hypnosis violates the moral and ethical values decreed by the Church. There are only two points on which we disagree with Mangan, namely: hypnotized patients are *never* bereft of their will or reason and the patient's critical faculties are *not* reduced. Rather, they are increased!

In recent years, His Holiness, the late Pope Pius XII, made two statements about hypnosis, the first in his address to an audience for obstetricians and gynecologists, on January 8, 1956.[13] The Pope referred to deep hypnosis in delivery and suggested that one danger might be "emotional in-

* Mangan, J. T.: Hypnosis: A Medico-Moral Evaluation, Linacre Quarterly, 26:39–49, 1959.

difference" of the mother toward her child. He was careful to add, however, that some doctors thought this indifference need not be attributed to the use of hypnosis. Moreover, the danger could be avoided. The manner in which the Holy Father spoke of hypnosis in this context showed that he considered this primarily a medical question and that the judgment of its morality would ultimately be based on sound medical opinion. The papal statements are in complete accord with the views of nonreligious leaders in the field of hypnosis.

The progressive attitude of the Roman Catholic Church has fostered considerable interest in hypnosis among Catholic physicians. The subject has been taught to many Catholic hospital staffs. Courses on hypnosis are given at the Seton Hall Postgraduate School of Medicine, a Roman Catholic medical school, and the Marquette University School of Dentistry has conducted workshops in hypnosis. Many Catholic psychiatrists and psychologists recently have been trained to use hypnotherapy. Obstetric patients have been delivered under hypnoanesthesia at Catholic hospitals. Its use in other branches of medicine is increasing in other Catholic hospitals. Also, many prominent Catholic physicians and psychologists have made contributions to hypnosis in medicine, dentistry and psychology.

COMPARATIVE EVALUATION OF OTHER RELIGIONS AND HYPNOTIC PHENOMENA

BUDDHISM

Buddhist meditation is another modification of autohypnosis. Siryananda,[22] a psychiatrist who practices in Bangkok, points out that hundreds of Buddhist priests use a primitive form of psychotherapy that is similar to actual hypnosis. He states:

I believe that they obtain this method from Buddhist meditation. Most of them seem to believe this primitive method works through their supernatural powers or is a miracle cure.

Buddhist priests treat neurotic patients and are regarded as family doctors in many villages.

Buddhists practice meditation (Zen) upon

one's own self, and this leads to insight and wisdom, to self-realization and lasting peace. In autohypnosis as in Zen, the meditation leads to increased concentration, turning of attention on the self, and increasing receptivity to healthy ideas. As a result, the corrective emotional processes are speeded up. Viewing the self with greater objectivity (insight) allows an appraisal of one's needs and this leads to deeper understanding (self-realization).[24]

After meditation, a Zennist receives instruction wherein a series of problems are presented to him. They deal with difficult and universal questions. It sometimes takes years to get the right answers to the 1,700 or more prepared questions. This approach contains the "misdirection of attention" which prevents Zen from being recognized as hypnosis.

YOGA

The fundamental principles of Yoga are, in many respects, similar to those of hypnosis. It probably originated between 700 and 500 B.C. Yoga is a Sanskrit word meaning "union." Yoga is not considered a religion, but a "science" to achieve mastery of the mind and cure physical and emotional sickness. It works for the followers of any religious system or for an atheist. There are many systems to Yoga, but the central aim—union with God—is common to all of them and is the method by which it achieves cure. There are four principal steps which one must master sequentially. There is a cognitive approach (*nirvanam*) for the person who merely seeks intellectual fulfillment. There is also a dynamic active approach (*pratyahara*), a metaphysical (*samkhya*) and a reflective or meditative approach (*samadhi*). Their similarity to hypnosis and its associated phenomena will be discussed later.

The aims of Yoga appear to be similar to the goals achieved by Zen Buddhism. From an analysis of Mishra's authoritative book on Yoga,[16] his description of Yoga and its technics are compared with hypnosis. The following are his statements and my interpretations:

Mishra	*Kroger*
Never doubt your ability to control your mind.	Autohypnosis.
Be positive that you have eternal existence, knowledge and bliss.	Positive, constructive, healthful conditioning.
Always observe silence, according to your leisure, and make powerful dhāranā, dhyāna and samādhi (fixation, suggestion and sensation).	Fixation of attention with narrowing of the perceptual fields to outside stimuli.
Follow the instructions given in each lesson.	Heterosuggestions.
Never become excited when you are in an unfavorable situation.	Relaxation and avoidance of negative attitudes.
Never say "I will try to concentrate my mind," but say, "I will control my mind. I will concentrate."	Concentration necessary for hypnotic induction.
Do not become discouraged in your failure. You will eventually be successful in your practice.	Confidence; set realistic goals.
Be sure that you can do anything and everything—whatever has been done by any liberated souls. Have full confidence in yourself.	Belief and faith.
Understand exactly the science and the psychology of Yoga to become successful.	Expectant attitude.
Make a firm determination to control your mind. This is the first step or yama.	Motivation.
Follow strict rules to accomplish your determination. This is the second step, or niyama.	Practice.

Mishra	*Kroger*
Place your body in a firm and steady posture. This is the third step, or āsana.	Posture to facilitate sensory-imagery conditioning.
Practice control of your breathing. This is the fourth step, or prāṇāyāma.	Ideomotor activity in the form of slow, deep, regular breathing to produce relaxation.
Withdraw your conscious energy from the external world and external contact and identify yourself with supreme consciousness. This is the fifth step, or pratyāhāra.	Depersonalization.
Fix your mind for local concentration on particular cakras and limbs which you choose, and for general concentration on the entire body. This is the sixth step, or dhārana (fixation).	Narrowing the perceptual fields; fixation on ideomotor and ideosensory activities.
Send strong suggestion after fixation. The suggestion depends on your intention, whatever you want, such as anesthesia, cold like ice, hot like fire, and so forth and so on. This is the seventh step, or dhyāna (suggestion).	Ideosensory activities; the law of dominant effect.
Feel the sensation of your given order, whether your subconscious mind is able to follow your command or not. After due practice it will follow your order. This is the eighth step, or samādhi (sensation).	Sensory-imagery conditioning.

After carefully studying Mishra's technics, I have concluded that the last three steps—fixation, suggestion and sensation—are analogous to the ideosensory and ideomotor responses during autohypnosis. The first five steps involve the creation of a favorable mental-set or attitude. This creates the expectancy so necessary for the imagination to catalyze the entire process. The misdirection of attention is obtained through the various postural and breathing exercises, the rhythmicity of the breathing being conducive to complete relaxation. The goal of ultimate reality or nirvana—the state of complete liberation—is strikingly similar to depersonalization and to other dissociated states characteristic of hypnosis. Naturally, I have respect for all religious systems, whether or not they are so classified—but belief compounds belief! The faith or religion that helps is the one that the individual has been taught to believe in.

Arthur Koestler, in *The Lotus and the Robot*, after an exhaustive survey of the various types of Yoga, concludes it is "neither more nor less miraculous than the blisters and stigmata, the anesthesias, catatonias and hallucinations produced under hypnosis . . ."

In regard to Yoga, it should not be surprising that there are various types when one considers that we have many spiritual healing religions, many of which are mentioned in this chapter.

I have observed Yoga as practiced in India. They readily attain a deep stage of hypnosis comparable to somnambulism and the plenary state. Deeply religious persons, with experience in meditation, and introverts make the best subjects because of their self-objectivity. The Y-state is discussed in Chapter 47.

Variations of Yoga were also used by Jewish priests and, in the next section, this similarity between Jewish ritual and prayer, Yoga and autohypnosis will be discussed.

JUDAISM

Bowers and Glasner,[3] the latter a rabbi-psychologist, have compared the Jewish cabbalistic state of kavanah with autohypnosis. Glasner noted that the experiences during prayer were strikingly similar to the phenomena observed in his hypnotic subjects. The common element in all the successful Jewish worship experiences and other ritualistic practices seemed to be reminiscent of autohypnotic phenomena. Both are crystallized in the concept of kavanah.[5]

The word kavanah contains the suggestion of empathy, rapport, righteousness and steadfastness; its verb root is found in the context of "a heart properly attuned."[9] However, in the Talmud, kavanah implies concentration—correct intention (motivation). In Jewish theology the efficacy of ritual or prayer is wholly dependent on achieving kavanah.[3] Maimonides declared that a prayer without kavanah is no prayer at all. Kavanah was used to induce a state of religious ecstasy and also a state of deeper understanding and experiencing of God in inner reality.

Scholem[21] describes in his book, which gives the impression of a Judaized treatise on Yoga, how Abulafia, a cabbalistic philosopher and mystic, developed a method of concentration upon the magical and mystical properties of the Hebrew letters, arranging and rearranging them, starting with the name of God and developing further names of God. Bowers and Glasner[4] were impressed with the autohypnotic nature of Abulafia's experiences; the various letter combinations produced hypnotic fantasies which accounted for the new truths and insight achieved.

The development of a proper emotional state in preparation for devout prayer or ritual (kavanah) is similar to Yoga, Buddhist meditation and autohypnosis. In all, posture and breathing play an important role. Centuries before, the Chinese used similar technics to conjure the spirits of the departed.[23] Here, too, posture and prolonged eye fixation on the navel produced ecstatic states, which were autohypnotic in nature.

Prayer, particularly in the Jewish and the Christian religions, has many similarities to hypnotic induction. There is the regular cadence and intonation in the prayers (chanting), a relaxing environment, and the fixation of attention on the altar or religious leader. In Judaism, there is a rhythmic rocking of the body back and forth in time to the chanting which is hypnogogic. Finally, the contemplation, the meditation and the self-absorption characteristic of prayer are almost identical with autohypnosis.

The Prophets probably utilized both auto-hypnotic and mass-hypnotic technics.[10] Talmudic scholars note that kavanah was used to produce depersonalization so that the Prophet could see himself elsewhere. At this early date, the hypnotically dissociated self was recognized as such and was not regarded as a miraculous revelation of God himself.[3] Bowers and Glasner also point out that earlier generations had to describe and explain many experiences which would be regarded as autohypnotic in character by modern descriptive terms. This is what might be expected, as the concept of hypnosis is a very recent one. On the basis of their findings, they state that hypnotic research could possibly provide us with an operational understanding of prayer and its effects. On a nonreligious basis, Rund[19] has described how prayer may be used as a method of induction for dental analgesia.

Studying the underlying tenets of all the major religions, the scholar oriented in the phenomenology of hypnosis as well as in theology cannot help being impressed by the observation that suggestion and/or hypnosis are being utilized at many different levels of awareness. One need not refer to the Bible, the Talmud, the Koran, or any other religious work to realize that hypnosis in one form or another is practiced in nearly all religions. Our daily newspapers carry announcements of religious worship conducted in churches of all the major faiths. There are literally hundreds of other types of faith-healers—all use suggestion and/or hypnosis. The very fact that there are so many religions which cure emotional ailments indicates that they all have the same common denominator. As proof, the religion that does the most good is the one in which sufficient evocation of prior belief and conviction has been established. A Buddhist is not going to be helped by Catholicism and a Protestant is not going to be helped by Buddhist meditation.

The author is by no means trying to derogate religion, but wishes to illustrate that the *raison d'être* of all religions is positive, constructive conditioning. If one observes pilgrims expecting to be healed at a shrine, one is immediately impressed by the fact that the majority of these individuals, as they walk toward the shrine, are actually in a hypnotic state. Shrine-healing is extremely helpful in many cases; however, it is not the shrine that actually cures the individual with a psychogenic disorder but *his belief, faith and conviction that the shrine will be effective.* Therefore, such healing falls into the realm of conviction phenomena that are strikingly similar to those of hypnosis. There are about two thousand religions among the two billion people in this world, and the more one studies the various religions, from the most "primitive" to the most "civilized," the more one realizes that there is an astonishing relationship between religious phenomena and hypnosis.

Bowers[2] states:

The religionist can no longer hide his head in the sand and claim ignorance of the science and art of the hypnotic discipline. . . . Whether he approves or disapproves, every effective religionist, in the usages of ritual, preaching and worship, unavoidably makes use of hypnotic techniques, and is therefore subject to the same responsibilities as known and acknowledged by the scientifically trained hypnotist.

In religious and medical healing relationships, the deeper understandings that we refer to as faith, influence the body processes. The recognition of these age-old forces in the healing arts demands an explanation. It is obvious that both prayer and hypnosis are intrapsychic phenomena involving either dissociation or depersonalization while one is in communication with one's self or with God.

The rise of Christian Science and other metaphysical religious healing movements attest to this fact. A review of the past and the current attitudes of the Christian Science Church and that of its principal founder, Mary Baker Eddy, indicates that it was indissolubly linked with the spiritualist movement which began in Europe, through the influence of the Chevalier de Barbarin. Without paraphernalia, he successfully magnetized people during the latter part of the 18th century. His influence spread to the Scandinavian peninsula, where Emanuel Swedenborg, the Swedish scientist-mystic, embraced his method. Phineas Quimby, whose manuscripts were recently published,[8a] practiced almost similar methods in America.

Another famous disciple of Quimby's, in addition to Mary Baker Eddy, was Rev. W. F. Evans, a Swedenborgian clergyman, who visited him in 1863. Evans became a noted and voluminous writer on mental healing, whose views were incorporated into the New Thought movement. The principles of New Thought are that the mind has an influence on the body, that good thoughts have a salutary effect and bad thoughts are injurious. Such views are similar to those currently held in some areas of psychosomatic medicine.

REFERENCES

1. Aertnys-Damen: Theologia Moralis, Secundum Doctrinam Sancti Alfonsi de Ligurio, Doctoris Ecclesial, No. 432, vol. 1, p. 360, Torino, Italy, Marietti Press, 1947.
1a. Bridgman, P. W.: The Way Things Are, Cambridge, Howard Press, 1959.
2. Bowers, M.: Friend or traitor? Hypnosis in the service of religion, Internat. J.C.E.H. 7:205-217, 1959.
3. Bowers, M., and Glasner, S.: Auto-hypnotic aspects of the Jewish cabbalistic concept of kavanah, J.C.E.H. 6:50-70, 1958.
4. *Op. cit.*, p. 51.
5. *Op. cit.*, p. 136.
6. Budd, W. C.: Is free will really necessary? Am. Psychologist 15:217-218, 1960.
7. Collectanea Sanctae Congregationis de Propaganda Fide, No. 1018, editio anni 1907.
8. Davis, H.: Moral and Pastoral Theology, New York, Sheed & Ward, 1946.
8a. Dresser, H. W.: The Quimby manuscripts, New York, Julian Press, 1961.
9. Enelow, H. G.: Kavanah—the struggle for inwardness in Judaism in Enelow, H. G.: Selected Works, vol. 6, pp. 252-288, 1935.
10. Glasner, S.: A note on allusions to hypnosis in the Bible and Talmud, J.C.E.H. 3:34-39, 1955.
11. Hartman, W.: Is determinism useful? being published in Am. Psychologist.
12. Jone, H.: Moral Theology, Westminister, Maryland, Newman Press, 1948.
13. Kelley, G.: (Quoted) Hypnosis as anesthesia in Medico-Moral Problems, Chap. 32, p. 289, St. Louis, Mo., The Catholic Hospital Association of the U.S. and Canada, 1958.
14. Mangan, J. T.: Hypnosis: A Medico-Moral

Evaluation, Linacre Quarterly 26:39-49, 1959.

15. Maier, N. R. F.: Maier's law, Amer. Psychologist 15:208-212, 1960.

16. Mishra, R. S.: The Fundamentals of Yoga, New York, Julian Press, 1959.

17. Nettler, G.: Cruelty, dignity, and determinism, Am. Sociol. Rev. 24:375-385, 1959.

18. Provonsha, J. W.: Ethical implications of medical hypnosis, Med. Arts and Sciences, vol. XIV, No. 4, Fourth Quarter, 1960.

19. Rund, J.: Hypnosis and Prayer, J. of Hypnosis & Psychology in Dentistry 1:24, 1957.

20. St. Thomas Aquinas: Summa Theologica, 2, 2, qu. 153, Art. 4, ad 2.

21. Scholem, G. G.: Major Trends in Jewish Mysticism, pp. 133-134, Jerusalem, Schochen.

22. Siryananda, C.: Medical hypnosis in Thailand, Brit., J. Med. Hypnosis 10:41-46, 1948.

23. Stoll, O.: Suggestion und hypnotismus in der Voelkerpsychologie, pp. 49-50, 1940.

24. Suriyabongs, L.: Buddhism in the Light of Modern Scientific Ideas, Bangkok, 1954. (Quoted in Ref. 226.)

SUPPLEMENTARY READING

Bryan, W. J., Jr.: Religious Aspects of Hypnosis, Springfield, Ill., Thomas, 1962.

Wittkofski, J.: The Pastoral Use of Hypnotic Technique, New York, The Macmillan Company, 1961.

25

Magic, Spiritualistic Faith-Healing and Hypnosis

ROLE OF MAGIC IN HEALING

Magic is the pretended art of performing wonders by using misdirection of attention. The use of magic and faith-healing from earliest recorded history to the development of modern psychotherapy from mesmerism and spiritualism has been reviewed.[1]

The history of medicine closely parallels the development of magical healing, which was practiced when no rational physical cause for disease could be demonstrated. The magical healing was produced by amulets, herbs, naturalistic forces and/or exorcism. Over the last several thousand years, magical healing became the special province of priests and, to a degree, it still is practiced as faith-healing. Only during the latter half of the last century has science infiltrated into the healing arts.

Just as primitive man developed the expectation that some type of magical gesture would heal him, so has his descendent, modern man, searched for a miraculous cure to relieve his suffering. The modern physician's role often is similar to the one played by the tribal medicine man. The latter's prestige is enhanced by his costume and headdress and, likewise, the physician's, by his garb, or, if he is a psychotherapist, by his couch and/or consultation chamber. The physician's instruments, prescriptions, reputation, skill and bedside manner—all often are essential ingredients for recovery. Cultural factors such as the psychosocial attitudes toward the latest fad, wonder drug, or psychotherapeutic procedure potentiate healing; those methods of therapy that occupy the limelight seem to be the most effective. Therefore, as true scientists, we should determine the relationship between magical methods, suggestibility and hypnosis.

We might also investigate if and how magical procedures can kill. *Susto* or *aspanto*, in which the victim falls "dead," and then is revived following ritualistic procedures by a magician, has been described among the half-castes of Guatemala. In that country, a susceptible individual can go into coma and be cured of it almost instantaneously by a magical system of faith-healing.

SPIRITUAL FAITH-HEALING

In all magical healing one must distinguish between faith-healing, carried out through the confidence of the healer in his secular power, and spiritual healing, in which the healer may act as an intermediary in a spiritual process initiated by a deity. The faith-healer believes that his power is akin to drugs, rational psychotherapy and other measures; the spiritual healer believes that he is a divine instrument of God and therefore is capable of healing solely through a religious approach. Both types of faith-healing are related to suggestibility and/or hypnosis, as discussed on page 111.

Faith is a difficult parameter to measure as it affects man's health; yet it is perhaps the most curative power on earth. Every physician has witnessed its force, and he can ill afford to ignore this valuable ally in his therapeutic approach. Since almost every organic condition has a psychological component, faith-healing can be successful in certain psychosomatic entities. Ulcers, neurodermatitis, arthritis and asthma are often helped by faith in a certain medicament or procedure. However, it is doubtful if organic ailments can be cured by faith-healers. This in spite of the testimonials invariably produced following an emotionally charged impact on the participant. Faith-healing is not in any sense miraculous healing, but rather a method involving known psychological forces. However, some have exploited faith-healing for their own selfish purposes, thus destroying the subject's belief in faith. This is not an indictment of religious faith, but of those charlatans who feed on human misery.

Nearly all religious denominations agree that, when a person is ill, scientific procedures should be utilized together with faith. The latter merely supplements the doctor's therapy. Lack of faith can lower the patient's morale and adversely influence the course of a disease. No one can deny the power of the mind in any type of healing and say that faith is not the best antidote for despair.

DEVELOPMENT OF FAITH-HEALING FROM HYPNOSIS

To understand the rise of faith-healing during the past century, it is necessary to amplify its historical development in Europe and America. As mentioned in Chapter 1, its modern history began in 1765 with Franz Mesmer, whose observations were discredited. Those who were interested in animal magnetism divided into two groups. One became interested in phrenology. The other, led by physicians, Drs. Braid and Liébeault, began to pay more attention to the psychological aspects of healing and steadfastly adhered to the practice of hypnotism. They believed that the cures of their patients were obtained solely by suggestion. Later, many prominent neurologists and psychologists, as mentioned in Chapter 1, began to study hypnotism. The role of hypnosis in personality dissociation was elucidated by Janet, Prince, Sidis and others.

RISE OF OTHER FAITH-HEALING MOVEMENTS

The other offspring of mesmerism in Europe, the phrenologists, were led by Franz Gall and his associate Spurzheim. The former was discredited and the latter came to America, where Stanley Grimes introduced the concept of phrenomagnetism in 1845. By pressing a skull protuberance which he assumed to be responsible for the mesmerizing "propensity," he was able to invoke mesmeric trances directly. The uniting of mesmerism with cerebral manifestations excited scientific investigators for many years, and then

died. Nevertheless, many other pseudoscientific healers, who followed, employed magic, physical measures and hypnosis to effect a cross-fertilization between medical science and psychic phenomena. Cures were obtained by mesmeric clairvoyance, telepathy and spiritism.

Just as the newly honored sciences of astronomy and physics led to mesmerism and its various "scientific" faith-healers, who used a religious approach, so did metaphysical neoreligions provide the matrix for faith-healers with no scientific pretensions. Among these were the mind-curers or spiritualists, who seldom realized that their cures resulted from the imagination, as postulated by the medical-hypnotists.

Spiritualism, together with slight deviations acquired from various oriental religions, became the background for the various sects devoted to mental- or faith-healing in America. All focused their attention on the psychical-religious side of healing through faith. This faith has not diminished materially, and, even today, there is an ethical and co-operative therapeutic effort between theologians and psychiatrists in the form of "pastoral psychology."

Pastoral psychology had its origin in the Emmanuel movement.[12] This was a sincere spiritual movement for psychotherapeutic purposes developed by a Boston minister, Elwood Worcester. He, in conjunction with S. Weir Mitchell, a famed neurologist, introduced the healing ministrations of Jesus through religio-suggestive procedures. The Emmanuel Church aimed to inculcate suggestions from the Scriptures on the basis that a temporary dissociation of the personality facilitated acceptance of faith-laden ideas.[21] The advocates of the Emmanuel movement admitted that suggestion and hypnosis were utilized. The Dubois method of persuasion was considered good psychotherapy, and to this they added the serenity afforded by "surrender to God."

Men like Emerson, the essayist, and William James, the psychologist,[9] who was cured of melancholia, believed that strengthening the will or educating it was the object of our existence; James emphasized that ideas and emotional excitement could "energize" a man and release inhibitions which habitually cut down his capacity for work and enjoyment.

This new alignment of Christian faith within a clinical atmosphere continued its growth. During the past 3 or 4 decades a spate of books has appeared emphasizing the effect of spiritual life on the mind of man. Many scientists became impatient with the attempts to make disguised hypnotism serve religion, and refused to be associated with the numerous neoreligious movements which were springing up. But hypnotism could not be stifled. That this modality has received the attention of healers, generation after generation, and is today stronger than ever, is one of the most interesting phenomena in the history of mental-healing.

One of the first mental-healers to use magnetism in the United States was Phineas Quimby, a clock-maker's apprentice, who had little schooling. In 1838, he was impressed by a lecture on mesmerism by Charles Poyen. After briefly studying with him, he began to experiment in this new "science," and became a professional mesmerist in Portland, Maine, in 1859, giving public demonstrations and successfully treating disease by magnetization.

Soon Quimby dispensed with magnetization, convinced that the patient's mind could be influenced directly through persuasion. He reasoned that if disease is due merely to belief, it was only necessary to refute the idea that disease existed; all disease was a delusion. Though not an adherent of Christianity, he believed that his methods were similar to those by which Christ healed. At various times he referred to his doctrine as the "Science of Christ," "Christian Science," "Science of Health" and/or the "Science of Health and Happiness." He was the first of the mental healers to align mind and soul with Christ. Nearly all the later religious sciences which supposedly healed physical ailments originated from Quimby's remarkably perceptive formulations. He stated, "Higher spirit . . . is God spirit and healing is Christ's method."[15] Again he stated:

I give no medicine and make no outward applications. I tell the patient his troubles, and what he thinks is his disease; and my explanation is the cure. If I succeed in correcting his errors—I establish the truth, or health.

The world will not remember Quimby for his writings—10 volumes written in longhand—but rather for the indelible imprint he made on his pupils. One was the Rev. W. S. Evans, whose influence still persists among the adherents of the New Thought movement. Evans often propounded the following: "Disease being in its root a wrong belief, change that belief and we cure the disease." Borrowing further from Buddhism, his disciples stated, "All that we are is the result of what we have thought." The characteristic feature of all the spiritualistic mind-cures was a happy mental outlook—an optimism found in the gospel of modern spiritualists—and a belief that all things work together for good through a perfect Divine Universal Spirit.

THE RISE OF CHRISTIAN SCIENCE

The other famous pupil of Quimby's was Mary Baker Eddy, who transformed his "Science of Health" into a religion and a psychotherapy which have attained enormous proportions throughout the world.

The relationship between mesmerism and Christian Science has been fully documented.[10] Also on record is the history of Mary Baker Eddy's career from the time that she discovered that she possessed considerable ability as a spiritualist and took part in séances, occasionally going into trance states and receiving "spirit communications" from her deceased brother Albert.[10] The various testimonies, the substance of a new philosophy espoused by Mary Baker Eddy, the characteristic defects and the nature of her psychic "explorations" have also been detailed.[9]

Mary A. Morse Baker, afterward known successively as Mrs. Glover, Mrs. Patterson, and now as Mrs. Eddy, has been subjected to deification by her disciples and to the cold objectivity of unsympathetic critics. Possessing strong drives and great organizing ability, she combined religious inspiration and mystical poesy into a movement that has influenced the lives of millions.

Mrs. Eddy (then Mrs. Patterson) first consulted Quimby in 1862 for the relief of a "spinal disease." She improved, and became so enthusiastic about his methods that she asked him to teach her his "science." For several years she taught from one of his manuscripts and she praised him in a letter published in the *Portland* (Maine) *Courier* on November 7, 1862, explaining that he healed her neither by spiritualism nor by animal magnetism.[11]

The main tenet of Mary Baker Eddy's "divine" metaphysics, which started in 1862, posits the all-comprehensiveness of mind and the nonexistence of matter. If bodies do not exist, diseases cannot exist and must be only mental delusions. If the mind is freed of these delusions, the disease is gone. This was, in essence, Quimby's doctrine.

THE ATTITUDE OF CHRISTIAN SCIENCE TOWARD HYPNOSIS

Mrs. Eddy castigated all medical therapy and psychotherapy as hypnotism—these belonged to "mortal mind" and hence were inherently in "error." Hypnotism (magnetism) in particular earned Mrs. Eddy's condemnation. She found herself hampered by the passes and the manipulations included in the theories of Quimby.[13] Animal magnetism was not on a scientific basis; rather, it was criminal, subtle, ubiquitous and enslaving, and must be dealt with as evil. She stated that the effect of animal magnetism, called hypnotism, was the effect of illusion.[6]

The ready acceptance of Mrs. Eddy's teachings was due to a half century of belief in the exaltation of the spiritual over the material, via faith healing. Both were phases of the movement initiated by Mesmer. Mesmer's tragic mistake was that he believed that the healing occurred as the result of *his efforts*. The spiritualists, as disciples of God, thought that they healed through His methods. Neither group realized that it was the favorable mind-set of the patient that raised the adaptive responses to produce the results.

Contrary to the practice of religious healers, however, physicians and other nonreligious healers do not treat organic conditions by suggestion. Rather, they will use suggestive procedures only after ruling out the presence of organic disease. It is the author's object in this chapter to show that no healers have a monopoly on the use of faith and spiritual forces; that faith is another valuable arrow in the therapist's quiver; that sus-

ceptibility to hypnosis is based on faith, and is largely brought about by conviction. Although it is not a panacea, it is especially effective in the case of emotionally disturbed individuals—*those who wish to have faith*. The references that follow are for those who wish to pursue further the subject of Magic, Spiritualistic Faith-Healing and Hypnosis.

REFERENCES

1. Bromberg, W.: Man Above Humanity, Philadelphia, Lippincott, 1954.
2. *Op. cit.*, p. 131.
3. *Op. cit.*, p. 137.
4. Eddy, Mary Baker: Miscellaneous Writings, 1883-1896, p. 284, Boston, Stewart, 1917.
5. *Op. cit.*, p. 107.
6. Eddy, Mary Baker: Science and Health with Key to the Scriptures, (from authorized version of 1873) Boston, Stewart, 1917.
7. *Op. cit.*, p. 107.
8. *Op. cit.*, p. 109.
9. James, William: The Energies of Men, New York, Holt, 1916.
10. Podmore, F.: Mesmerism and Christian Science: A Short History of Mental Healing. Philadelphia, Jacobs, 1909.
11. *Op. cit.*, p. 253.
12. Powell, L. P.: The Emmanuel Movement in a New England Town, p. 6, New York, Putnam, 1909.
13. Eddy, Mary Baker: A Life-Size Portrait, p. 109, New York, Macmillan, 1950.
14. Provonsha, J. W.: The Healing Christ, Current Medical Digest, 1958.
15. Quimby, P. P.: The Quimby Manuscripts, Showing the Discovery of Spiritual Healing and the Origin of Christian Science *in* (ed.): Dresser, H. W., p. 31, New York, Julian Press, 1962.
16. Shapiro, A.: Hypnosis, miraculous healing, and ostensibly supernatural phenomena *in* A Scientific Report on "The Search for Bridey Murphy," p. 148, New York, Julian, 1956.
17. Stetson, A. E.: Reminiscences, Sermons and Correspondence, New York, Putnam, 1913.
18. Twain, Mark: Christian Science, p. 72, New York, Harper, 1907.
19. Wilbur, Sibyl: The Life of Mary Baker Eddy, ed. 4, p. 87, Boston, Christian Science Publishing Society, 1938.
20. *Op. cit.*, p. 95.

26

The Dynamics of Faith, Placebo Effect and Hypnosis

FAITH IN RELIGION AND HYPNOSIS

When therapeutics began to divorce itself from magic and superstition, all mental healing split into religious and nonreligious movements. The latter group consisted primarily of physicians, who used suggestive procedures in one form or another to heal. The former group, however, maintained that all cures were due either to metaphysical factors or divine faith. "Faith" is a loaded word and difficult to define. However, because it plays a significant role in all forms of psychotherapy, the dynamics of faith and its relation to religious and hypnotic types of healing will be discussed.

All faith is built up by conviction and the imagination, as described. Deslon, the successor to Mesmer, discerned that conviction and imagination were responsible for the curative effects of mesmerism. He asked, "But since the medicine of conviction and imagination cures, why do we not use it?" In spite of his cogent observations almost 200 years ago, healers, both medical and nonmedical, do not use it as such, but unwittingly stimulate the imagination by some type of misdirection in the form of a new approach or method over which the public becomes enthusiastic, especially if it is mysterious and fashionable.

Faith-healing also depends to a degree on psychosocial and cultural factors. The savage expects to be healed by the incantations of the shaman because he is *convinced that he will help him.* For similar reasons, the civilized person is aided by the belief and faith engendered by the rapport and prestige suggestions from the omniscient figure—the doctor.

When an emotionally disturbed individual sees a religious healer, his faith is strong because of a previous conviction that "God heals." In other words, his faith in a cure has been continually validated or computed by the already thought-out conviction that the clergyman-healer is an emissary of God. He recovers, often as the result of a single session, because *he expects to recover.*

Now when the average person consults a physician initially for psychotherapy, he comes in with *uncomputed* conviction because he does not have the powerful built-up faith in psychiatry that he has in religion. However, with successive visits, a positive rapport develops and eventually his uncomputed conviction becomes computed conviction leading to faith in the therapist. He recovers for the same reason as with the religious healer—expectant faith in a cure.

When a patient sees a physician-hypnotist healer, his *uncomputed convictions* or negative attitudes are generally increased. Not only does he have to establish confidence in the doctor, but he has to be "sold" on the hypnosis; it invariably connotes something "magical." His *uncomputed* convictions become *computed* convictions as the result of the hypnotic-induction procedure; he attributes the ideosensory and ideomotor responses, as lid and limb heaviness and arm levitation, to the hypnotherapist's suggestions. After these convictions are established, then he readily believes other suggestions even though they may be at variance with reality. Thus, hypnotic healing does not require faith in a cure but only faith in the fact *that he was hypnotized!*

The question as to whether religious or hypnotic faith-healing is more effective obviously relates to previous conditioning of the subject. There is no ideal method applicable to all persons, nor is there a preferential religious approach. All heal—the specific one being the one for which the person has been "programmed."

Paracelsus shrewdly observed: "Whether the object of your faith is real or false, you will nevertheless obtain the same effects." It is amazing that there are relatively few scientific observations on the relationship between faith-healing and hypnosis. One would expect that a medium which has such a pronounced effect on human emotions, autonomic functioning, mood changes, mental associations and sensory imagery would be worthy of further investigation.

On the basis of the observed data, all faith healing makes use of suggestion by effecting a temporary dissociation produced by selective cortical inhibition—the attention is diverted through misdirection—and the favorable attitude or the mental-set resulting from prior-invoked beliefs allows the acceptance of faith-laden ideas. The misdirection is obtained by the ritualism that accompanies all religious healing. This also occurs as well in hypnotic procedures, but differs as mentioned above.

For instance, when a headache is relieved by hypnosis, the conviction that hypnosis has been established causes the subject to accept the hypnotherapist's suggestions as *true statements.* Then he behaves differently because he *thinks and believes* differently through the alteration in his beliefs. The power of hypnosis is the power of belief! Thus, hypnosis is merely a catalytic agent through which conviction phenomena can be established. As such, hypnotic behavior is a particular branch of faith phenomena.

Most faith-healers and even unsophisticated medical hypnotherapists have the tendency to "play God"; they usually are unaware that psychogenically based symptoms are removed by activation of the latent recovery forces.[14] The sick person usually has his own mental representation of the disease, of the recovery he hopes to achieve and, often, even of the psychotherapeutic procedure he desires.[11]

An attempt has been made to explain how most cases of miraculous faith-healing, which appear in the professional and the nonprofessional literature, follow the principles of faith described in this section.

However, occasional cures of organic illnesses occur in which faith is only part of the rationale. At Lourdes, for instance, most of the countless "miracles" can be explained as the result of the subjects' expecting to be cured. However, 51 official miraculous cures have been recognized by the Church, a Canonical Commission, the Medical Bureau, and the International Medical Commission.

Shapiro[19] states:

If they are indeed produced by faith, then they are certainly not dependent on the intensity of faith. The devout and saintly believer may remain unhealed while the skeptic who suffers the same disease may be miraculously cured.

(When this happens, the skeptic usually becomes a devout believer.)

Again Shapiro states:

But the time, the circumstances and the person who evaluates the miracle always modify the description of the nature of the event. One man's religion is another man's superstition, and one man's magic is another man's science.

The only scientific explanation of this type of faith-healing is that a nonformalistic technic of hypnosis by misdirection would tend to mobilize the recovery processes that are inherently present in every individual. Here too, a placebo action, described in the next section, would exert an influence.

The rise of pastoral psychiatry is evidence of the ability of faith to help large numbers of mentally ill individuals because of their prior-invoked beliefs in the religionist. As a result, some psychiatrists are working hand in hand with theologians to utilize the latent capacity for faith that is inherently present in all humans. Both a religious and a psychiatric approach are appealing to blind faith rather than to logical reasoning or persuasion. If the latter were better for mentally sick people, then more people would be cured by appealing to logic and common sense. Every psychotherapist knows that this is not the case.

PLACEBO-EFFECT CONCEPT

There is a growing recognition that the placebo effect plays an important role in drug therapy,[4, 13, 15] and also applies to all forms of psychotherapy as well as hypnosis. In this section, emphasis will be placed on an explanation of the placebo effect of drugs and psychotherapy as these relate to suggestion and hypnosis. The clinical applications and ethics of the placebo effect will not be stressed. If one substitutes "placebo effect" for "faith" one finds that in many instances the cause of the physicians' dramatic cures of today is similar to the cause of the miraculous healing of yesteryear.

DRUGS AND THE PLACEBO EFFECT

Osler[16] points out that doctors often are ignorant of their own faith cures when prescribing medications and are just a wee bit too sensitive about those performed outside their ranks. This observation hints that most drugs have no more value than a placebo. This dynamic placebo force sustained the medical profession for centuries, even when drugs were physiologically detrimental. One cannot help being impressed by the fact that placebo action has been the one constant in medicine—by whatever term it was called. And it is certain that our present cure rate for many of the psychogenic entities would not differ appreciably from that of any other period.

Chiefly responsible for the physician's placebo effect is the enthusiasm and the faith inculcated by his approach. This is transmitted to the patient, who develops the necessary confidence and faith for recovery. Thus, the physician himself is still the most important therapeutic agent. The term "the art of medicine" means nothing more than the rapport that exists between the patient and the physician. If the common denominator in medicine is the placebo effect (faith), then its chief ally is the imagination, for without imagination there would be no placebo cures. Oliver Wendell Holmes was cognizant of this when he stated that the greatest benefit can accrue to the patients "through the influence exerted on their imaginations." Voltaire once stated, "There is probably more cure in the doctor's words than in many of the drugs he prescribes."

Factors other than rapport which contribute to the "success" of the placebo are not only the suggestive effect of prescribing a drug but also the spontaneous recoveries which occur in any illness. Environmental factors and cultural attitudes toward new drugs and procedures also enhance the placebo effect. Another interesting factor recently postulated is that all placebos are more effective in the presence of stress or in pain due to organic causes. All these factors simply illustrate the power of words!

At present, enthusiastic physicians are prescribing "wonder drugs" in all fields of medicine; the patient often obtains the effect that he has been told to expect. This is not to imply that the author is a therapeutic nihilist; he is not. It has been noted that whenever a new drug loses its popularity, its effect is markedly reduced. Conn[7] remarked:

This is what occurred after the introduction and initial wide acceptance of bromides, chloral hydrate and the barbiturates, each of which was hailed as a "wonder" drug, and it also will happen to the "tranquilizers."

Trousseau[5] facetiously advised, "You should treat as many patients as possible with the new drugs while they still have the power to heal."[11]

One of the most difficult things for any individual, living in any period, is to be able to shake off the rigid dogmas of his own culture. Future historians may laugh at what we consider modern-day therapies. The author has often wondered, after each new "wonder" drug has been exploded, how and why the honest and conscientious investigators were misled. Obviously, these drugs, despite statistical validation, acted by virtue of their placebo effect. Usually such variables as the emotional relationship, the dosage, the choice of subject, the use of inadequate controls, an improper assay of the data, the operator's attitude or bias, and other factors, influenced the results. One author[10] significantly states, "The ability of inert compounds . . . to modify a variety of conditions . . . has begun to have a serious impact on medical thinking." Others believe that much time and money would be saved if placebo effects were analyzed before it was assumed that a drug had value.

In an excellent review of a history of the placebo effect, Shapiro[20] writes that until recently, there was virtual silence about the placebo effect in spite of the fact that this effect is the unwritten therapeutic agent in almost every prescription. The effect of placebos can be very powerful and often permanently modifies physiologic functioning. These effects are not superficial or transient. Yet their everyday use has been neglected.

PLACEBO EFFECT IN PSYCHOTHERAPY

The fact that there are contradictory theories being employed with identical results, in a wide variety of psychotherapies indicates that here, too, a placebo effect is in operation! Psychiatrists need to know more about placebo effects because their rapport with patients is great and, as a result, the placebo potential of their therapy is thereby enhanced. With every physician, this potential consists of the patient's confidence, faith and belief, operating on the basis of the therapist's personality. In the hypnotic situation, there are the mystery, the ritualism, the repetitive conditioning and the other suggestibility factors.

Recently, several authors[9a, 17a] have noted that hope and faith on the part of the patient, and suggestion and persuasion on the part of the therapist constitute some of the universal factors operative in mental healing. Curiously, however, hypnotic suggestion was not distinguished from persuasion, and hypnosis from classic conditioning.

Most authorities do not even mention the placebo effect in psychotherapy, and those that do seldom equate it with their cures. Bromberg,[6] who discusses faith-healing and suggestibility, does not mention it as it applies to medication or psychotherapy, past or present. Although there is a subtle placebo effect in many forms of psychotherapy, yet nothing has been done about it despite the fact that more therapeutic methods have been introduced into psychiatry than ever before. Using more knowledge of the placebo effect, modern-day psychiatry could more objectively understand its failures and eliminate ineffective methods.

Rosenthal and Frank,[17] who have studied the placebo effect in psychotherapy, believe that all forms of psychotherapy, including hypnosis, uniformly yield successful results in about 60 per cent of cases. They stress the effects of the interpersonal relationship, and that psychotherapists fit their results into their theories and therapeutic rationale, indicating that "the efficacy of any particular set of therapeutic operations lies in their analogy to a placebo in that they enhance the therapist's and patient's conviction that something useful is being done."

A placebo effect accounts for psychotherapy by nonpsychiatrists as well as for intensive psychoanalysis.[2] In short, improvement does not prove the correctness of the theory on which the therapy was based, nor the efficacy of a specific technic employed, unless the improvement is greater than that produced by the patient's faith in the efficacy of the therapist and his technic—"the placebo effect."

On this basis, the old family doctor was a good psychotherapist because of his humanistic approach and willingness to listen to a patient's story. An analysis of the placebo effects of "homespun" psychotherapy should help to elucidate the roles of suggestion, waking hypnosis and hypnosis in all forms of psychotherapy.

HYPNOSIS AND THE PLACEBO EFFECT

The nature of the placebo effect as it operates in hypnotherapy has been described by several investigators.[7, 20] In the light of newer knowledge gained from the placebo effect, the nature of the therapeutic deficiencies of early concepts now can be understood. During the period when mesmerism and hypnosis reached their peak, emphasis was on a very authoritative approach directed toward symptom-removal. Even today, authoritarian methods employing suggestion or hypnosis by an omniscient father-figure are successful in helping some patients, at least temporarily. It has been observed, "It is surprising how frequently these so-called 'transference cures' persist even if no further treatment is administered." Genuine recoveries have been observed in patients "without any psychodynamic insight into their condition."[11] There is no experimental study which indicates that therapeutic effects based on insights or perceptual reorganization are less superficial or less transitory.[17]

Although suggestion and hypnosis are related to the placebo effect and have much in common, they differ from each other in some ways. The difference is analogous to the comparison made between religious and hypnotic healing. Healing by hypnosis requires belief in the validity of the induction of hypnosis, that is, in the "power" of the hypnotist. Cortical-inhibition produced by misdirection of attention is common in hypnosis but not in placebo administration. Faith in the placebo merely indicates faith achieved by prior-invoked belief in all drugs as well as the prestige of the physician. Here, there is a proper mental-set, based on a high degree of enthusiasm or motivation, belief, confidence and an expectant attitude.

From the above, we can conclude that all human beings need motivation, self-esteem and something to believe in so that they can face their everyday tensions. The emotionally ill patient's value systems have failed him. As a result, he is ready to accept the therapist's, especially if they are presented with confidence, and it appears that they have a chance of helping him. It is also surprising how, on the basis of conviction, the incorporation of the therapist's suggestions can help large numbers of patients.

It is a sad commentary that those who now subscribe wholeheartedly to the concept that psychotherapy operates through a placebo effect still avoid hypnotherapy. The cumulative effect of successive and successful suggestions often results in a conviction of cure that cannot be achieved as rapidly by other psychotherapeutic modalities, especially if the therapy is directed to establishing the need of a symptom in a patient's emotional economy. When indicated, every psychotherapist owes it to his patients to utilize his unquestioned placebo effect at the highest level—hypnosis. Although hypnotherapy cannot be successfully applied to all disturbed individuals, there are certain cases which respond to hypnotherapy which orthodox psychotherapy cannot treat.

Considerable attention has been given to the placebo effect in psychotherapy, religious healing and drug therapy. Obviously, the most suggestible patients will be the best reactors. However, response will vary from individual to individual and will even change in the same individual from time to time. Many psychiatrists[15] are opposed to placebos because they feel they should never be substituted for psychotherapy, even though there is a placebo effect in the latter.

Recently, the placebo effect of tranquilizers has been noted.[3] According to uncontrolled and subjective methods of evaluation, from 53 to 80 per cent of the patients benefited from the new "drugs" (both drugs given were placebos, but patients were informed that one was real and the other a placebo). The authors[13a] point up the dubious value of the studies which do not employ double blind and other controlled procedures.

The capacity to respond to what is believed and accepted as true is simply amazing and, as hypnotic phenomena attest, is very valuable. The success of charlatans in beguiling the public is an unfortunate by-product of the placebo. Yet this only indicates how powerful the placebo is in the use of drugs and psychotherapy. Our thesis is that if the placebo is effective, then hypnosis employed prudently by a competent physician for a valid indication will serve the patient's best interest.

REFERENCES

1. Alexander, F.: Discussion by Hoch, P. H.[11]
2. Appel, K. E., *et. al.*: Long term psychotherapy *in* Psychiatric Treatment, (A.R.N.M.D. series), vol. XXXI, Baltimore, Williams & Wilkins, 1951.
3. Baker, A. A., and Thorpe, J. G.: Placebo response, A.M.A. Arch. Neurol. & Psychiat. 78:57, 1957.
4. Beecher, H. K.: The powerful placebo, J.A.M.A. *159*:1602, 1955.
5. Bernheim, H.: Translation from Trousseau's Dictionnaire, 1833, Paris, Librairie de la Faculté de Medecine, 1889.
6. Bromberg, W.: Man Above Humanity: A History of Psychotherapy, Philadelphia, Lippincott, 1954.
7. Conn, J. H.: Cultural and clinical aspects

of hypnosis, placebos, and suggestibility, Internat. J.C.E.H. 7:179, 1959.

8. *Op. cit.*, pp. 181-182.
9. Feldman, P. E.: The personal elements in psychiatric research, Am. J. Psychiat. *113*: 52, 1956.
9a. Frank, J. D.: Persuasion and Healing: A Comparative Study of Psychotherapy, Baltimore, Johns Hopkins Press, 1961.
10. Gliedman, L. H., *et al.*: Reduction of symptoms by pharmacologically inert substances and by short term psychotherapy, A.M.A. Arch. Neurol. & Psychiat. 79:345, 1958.
11. Hoch, P. H.: Aims and limitations of psychotherapy, Am. J. Psychiat. *112*:321, 1955.
12. Holmes, O. W.: Medical Essays, 1842, 1892, Cambridge, Mass., Riverside Press, 1891.
13. Lasagna, L.: Placebos, Scient. Am. *193*: 68, 1956.
13a. Loranger, A. W.: The Placebo Effect in Psychiatric Drug Research, J.A.M.A. *170*: 920-925, 1961.
14. Milechnin, G. S., and Milechnin, A.: Concerning the criterion of recovery, J.C.E.H. 6:1, 1958.
15. Modell, W., and Houde, R. W.: Factors influencing clinical evaluation of drugs, J.A.M.A. *167*:2190-2200, 1958.
16. Osler, W.: Medicine in the Nineteenth Century in Aequanimatas, Philadelphia, Blakiston, 1905.
17. Rosenthal, D., and Frank, J. D.: Psychotherapy and the placebo effect, Psychol. Bull. *55*:294, 1956.
17a. Sargant, W.: Battle for the Mind, New York, Doubleday, 1957.
18. Shapiro, A. K.: *in* Kline, M. (ed.): A Scientific Report on the Search for Bridey Murphy, p. 133, New York, Julian, 1956.
19. *Op. cit.*, p. 147.
20. Shapiro, A. K.: A contribution to a history of the placebo effect, Behavior Science 5:109-135, 1959.

SUPPLEMENTARY READING

Barber, T. X.: Death by suggestion, Psychosomatic Med. *23*:153-156, 1961.
——: "Hypnosis," analgesia, and the placebo effect, J.A.M.A. *172*:680, 1960.
Bowers, M.: Hypnotic aspects of Haitian voodoo, Internat. J. Clin. Exper. Hypnosis 9:269-283, 1961.
Glass, L. B., and Barber, T. X.: A note on hypnotic behavior, the definition of the situation and the placebo effect, J. Am. Ment. Dis. *132*:539-542, 1961.
Psychiatry and Religion. Formulated by the Committee on Psychiatry and Religion of the Group for the Advancement of Psychiatry, 104 E. 25th St., New York, 1960.

27

Neurophysiologic Mechanisms in Mediation of Emotions at Nonhypnotic and Hypnotic Levels

Little is known of the brain's dynamic properties and even less of the neuropsychological meaning of its anatomic structures. As a result, there are few studies to explain the precise nature of drives and other behavioral phenomena. Another reason for this lack is that the ideational processes, which distinguish humans from other living organisms, as self-experience, imagery and creativity, as yet cannot be measured and analyzed because it is difficult to understand what makes up an emotion or an idea. Only the physiologic effects of a stimulus, as it affects behavior, can be explored in terms of cause-and-effect or input-and-output relationships. Thus, vegetative reflex, conditioned responses, learned behavior and problem-solving can be measured to some extent. Before one can predict, however, what specific areas of the brain will do in response to a specific emotional stimulus, more must be known about the biologic roots of creativity processes initiating it. Microbiologists believe that what takes place, as new organizing activity or creativity, is in essence a reduplication and amplification of those biologic processes that take place at the microcellular level. More succinctly, "micro-events in the genes produce macro-events in those new activities which man imposes upon his environment."[6a] The entire process at both biologic levels is based on codified information and is self-regulated by feedback control—a concept which plays an important role in the organization of adaptive responses and behavior of all living and nonliving systems.

In this presentation, brain structures have been separated into arbitrary divisions but, unfortunately, simple spatial separations into discrete centers, each representing a specific function, do not explain how almost similar stimuli from respective regions contribute to differences in psychological functioning. More important, what interplay of forces in the central nervous system accounts for "spontaneous" activity, and what happens in the time between the initiation of an ideational stimulus and its resultant response? Is the reflex monitored by the "control of feedback"? Where and why are the ideas or mental images which are responsible for the diversity of drives in the organism produced? How are they influenced by motivation or expectation, mood swings, and changing life situations? What produces such fluctuating degrees of attention as sleep, wakefulness and hypnosis?

These and other questions, especially that of localization, which only answers the "where" of higher nervous activity, have to be worked out before we can thoroughly understand "how" and "why" the brain works at hypnotic (selective attention) and nonhypnotic (less selective attention) levels. Until newer research sheds light on the organization of behavior, we are handicapped in our full understanding of brain functioning. However, in this chapter, we shall, for descriptive purposes only, discuss the more important brain structures separately and what is known about their *neuropsychological* functioning.

There is virtual agreement among neurophysiologists that the vertical or two-brain "concept" of a core system surmounted by a cerebral mantle, in contrast to classic "horizontal" types, represents a major change toward clarification of neuropsychological and neurophysiologic mechanisms.

Thus, the two arbitrary divisions of the brain, the cortical and subcortical portions, are complementary and interdependent. This dynamic and reciprocal interaction helps to maintain the purposeful goals necessary for survival. In achieving this optimal state of equilibrium, some of the brain's structures tend to influence the function of others by regulating and dominating these. An integration of cerebral mechanisms subject to the regulation of one another and ultimately dominated by one of them is called a hierarchy. Self-regulation of the hierarchic functioning enables the brain to become not only more adaptive but also more discriminative in its behavior. In this respect, the brain can be compared with an efficient, automatically regulated machine.[2] However, brain functioning not only attempts to maintain self-regulation by feedback control but also to produce something new. Thus, its function is not only adaptive but also creative.

An attempt to reconcile the two speculative concepts—control of feedback and hierarchy—may provide a crude model for understanding the relation between behavior and higher neural organization. One significant drawback is that it is difficult to make definitive analogies to psychological processes. It is hoped that the development of modern computers will provide the tools required for simulating such brain processes as creativity and other poorly understood mechanisms.

At this point, the important brain structures involved in the mediation of emotional stimuli and their chief neurophysiologic functions at both hypnotic and nonhypnotic levels will be discussed.

ROLE OF CORTEX

In man, the cerebral cortex has evolved to its highest neural level of integration. As a result, discriminatory thinking has been developed to a maximum with the ability to meet the present and anticipate the future in terms of past memory experiences stored as codified information. Though the biologic needs of an organism initiate behavior, behavioral patterns are integrated through higher neural levels and are also influenced by past learning.

The cerebral cortex represents a huge network of intricate and interlacing systems in which storage, comparison and coding of impulses can occur to provide perception, memory and learning. Wakefulness, sleep, hypnosis and a wide variety of complex emotional affects depend upon varying degrees of arousal. These are a property of the midbrain or diencephalic level in which attention recently has been focused on the differences in organization and function of the ascending reticular activating system (A.R.A.S.) as it is involved in somatovisceral adjustments.[20]

Also at this level, research has been concentrated on clarifying the functions of the thalamocortical and hypothalamic systems which connect with the A.R.A.S.[4-9] Others[14, 18, 21] have differentiated the functions of the medial and basal "limbic" formations of the forebrain from those of the more laterally located portions of the cerebral cortex.

ROLE OF THE INTERPRETIVE CORTEX

Penfield[28] has electrically stimulated certain areas of the temporal lobes of epileptics to activate memory sequences which may be classed as experiential and interpretive. An experiential response occurs as a flashback to a seemingly random event in the subject's past; it ceases when the stimulus is removed. Such scanning or interpretive "signaling" is manifested by strange emotional reactions such as fear, loneliness, panic and a false sense of familiarity or the *déjà vu* phenomenon.

These scanning mechanisms functioning reciprocally with other specific brain areas are unquestionably involved in age-regression, revivification, amnesia, hyperamnesia, negative and positive sensory hallucinations and other hypnotic phenomena.

Although access to the past is available from either temporal lobe, both the experiential and interpretative responses indicate the existence of a permanent ganglionic recording of the stream of consciousness that is formed and preserved in a constant pattern of electrical impulses projected from a hypothetical integrating system for thought in the upper brain stem—the centrencephalic system.[29] This pattern is a sort of neuronal record in which present experience is preserved for life by means of successive facilitation through the cells and synapses which constitute this pathway. It seems likely that some of this same record is used when recurring judgments are made in regard to familiarity with and the meaning of each new experience. The actual recording of the stream of consciousness may be utilized for the purpose of comparison long after it has been lost to voluntary control.

ROLE OF THE LIMBIC SYSTEM

Recent research on the neurophysiologic mediation of emotions has pointed more clearly to the importance of a series of older cortical structures given the name "Papez action circuit" or, more recently, the limbic system.[26] Structurally, this system constitutes the inner core of the brain concealed by the convolutions of the neocortex or the new brain. This ancient structure, the rhinencephalon, was the primitive "nose-brain." Experimental evidence indicates that it may serve as a nonspecific activator for the cortex, facilitating or inhibiting learning, memory, overt behavior and internal feelings, even though it is under neocortical control.[8]

Thus, the limbic system is to feeling states what the reticular system is to somatovisceral adjustments. The presumed primacy of the role of the limbic system in emotional behavior supports the assumption that it is here that the important neural mechanisms for "feeling drive" and "conceptual will" are located.[17] In this regard, the role of the limbic system, as it functions in the brain's hierarchic order, helps to elucidate the nature of hypnosis, hysteria, schizophrenia and psychosomatic diseases.

Behavioristically, the limbic system gives expression to the visceral needs of the body rather than to its purely ideational functions. It interprets experience in terms of feeling rather than in terms of intellectualizing symbols. The latter type of interpretation is presumed to be predominantly under neocortical control. However, the modulating influence of the limbic system is not exclusively concerned with the mediation of subjective emotional expressions, but it also acts in correlating primitive motivational-emotional processes. Homeostatic and adaptive centers also are abundantly located around the third and fourth ventricles; these, too, react to neocortically directed activities in general as, e.g., during voluntary physical work or during intense intellectual concentration, or when we voluntarily induce ourselves to relax, or, as described below, to enter into hypnosis.

Since both the striated and the smooth muscular systems are under the influence of the limbic system, this helps to explain the close relationship between voluntary and involuntary control of visceral functions during hypnotic behavior. The involuntary system is not as involuntary as it is believed to be, and portions of the voluntary system can come under neocortical control with appropriate conditioning, as by Yoga or hypnosis.

The controls which the limbic system exercises are massive and diffuse, and, as a result, entire organ systems as well as the body image appear to be symbolically represented as a whole rather than specific muscles or movements. This is different from the sharply exercised controls in the neocortex.[12] Thus, because of the interconnections among the various structures of the limbic system, this subcortical region acts as a sort of "automatic pilot," and, together with the reticular formation, seems to provide a mechanism in which:[6]

. . . sensory afferents and symbolic representations of the outside world, and sensory afferents from the symbolic representations of the bodily structures plus all the autonomic components of experience can become integrated. It is here that a triple linkage may occur involving the "I" or self, the "non-I" or non-self, and the intermediate or communicating worlds.

For instance, the amygdaloid complex, an important structure of the limbic system, together with the reticular formation and the intralaminar systems, is capable of exerting a diffuse regulatory influence on the cortex.[5] As evidence of the hierarchic relations, the electrical activity recorded from the amygdaloid complex changes when an animal is startled or when, as a result of conditioning, its "attention" is focused on some environmental event.

When the hippocampus—still another subdivision of the limbic system—is inhibited, the electrical activity from the amygdala changes whenever the animal touches, hears or sees any environmental event.[24] Hippocampal seizures result in catatoniclike states similar to catalepsy.[18] Alterations in hippocampal activity also reflect the presence of a mechanism by which limbic system structures contribute a "staying" quality to emotion and pain. One important function of the hippocampus is to keep the brain attentive to carrying out goal-directed behavior and to prevent it from being shunted haphazardly by every fluctuation in the environment.[3a]

EEG findings indicate that the cortex can be desynchronized during arousal. Simultaneously, the hippocampus changes its electrical pattern in a way that has generally been associated with sleep. Livingston[15] poses an interesting hypothesis to explain what appears to be a paradox. He thinks that the limbic system plays a trophic role to restore and conserve energy to maintain visceral well-being. In the presence of anxiety-evoking arousal in which energy is expended rapidly, the temporary "going to sleep" of the involved nervous structures may be protective to the organism. Might not this mechanism also explain the effectiveness of Pavlov's protective "sleep" inhibition therapy (hypnosis)? The limbic system apparently also can develop an odd type of memory loss. When large lesions of the limbic system are produced, execution of complex action sequences cannot be carried out. Also, an interference with feeding, fighting, mating and maternal behavior may occur.

Although many seemingly unrelated effects on behavior have been attributed to limbic system activity, it can be hypothesized on the basis of the above data that these systems comprise the substrate concerned with motivational and emotional behavior: primitive, instinctual and "visceral" reactions. The kind of effect obtained depends on which of the major divisions of the limbic systems are involved.[24]

Heath,[7] via lobotomies and related operations, observed a consistent reduction in "emotional overflow from memories" following removal of a part of the prefrontal cortex connected with a rhinencephalic region below the corpus callosum (septal region). Stimulation of this area speeds movement and alerts the animal, whereas stimulation of the caudate nucleus has an opposite effect. Most important, his data indicated that the same emotional response always accompanied stimulation of a specific region. Such findings lend general support to ideas expressed by Herrick,[8] Papez,[26] Klüver[10] and others who opened up this line of investigation.

The above data indicate that ideational processes which occur as a function of neocortical and limbic lobe activity reach peripheral nervous pathways via the R.A.S. Heath's work may have some connection with the increased alertness, the vividness of sensory-imagery and the facilitation of ideomotor activity noted during hypnosis. How else can we explain the alert behavior of the person who is ostensibly "asleep" or detached while in hypnosis or the person who is "awake" while supposedly asleep? And what about dreaming when cortical activity is completely inhibited? Does the rhinencephalon act as a "watch dog" to protect the dreamer? Even though their functional significance is different, the similarity between schizophrenic symptoms and states of reverie, hypnosis and sleep is well known.

In this section we have attempted to show how limbic system activity relates primarily to the execution of complex goal-directed emotional activities, and *how* and/or *where* these goals originated in the brain. The decision to execute a sequence of operations undoubtedly begins by transfer of control from the posterior "association areas" to the frontal "association areas" which have been referred to as the "organ of civilization." These are intimately connected with the limbic system to "serve as a working memory" in which plans can be retained temporarily when they are being formed, transformed or executed.[24] Thus, selecting a goal from memory is largely a function of the primitive portions of the brain. The subjective experiencing of associated emotional affects in turn requires mediation by cortical portions of the brain.

ROLE OF THE HYPOTHALAMUS

The hypothalamus receives a complex pattern of afferent connections from higher brain areas such as the limbic and reticular activating systems. There are also two-way neural pathways, reverberating circuits or feedback mechanisms that reciprocally connect the hypothalamus and cortex via limbic system structures.[4] It is generally accepted that the expression of emotions is mediated by the hypothalamus—not only the autonomic reactions, such as those which result in pallor, blushing, palpitation, elevation of blood pressure, sweating and/or peristalsis, but also the responses involving striated muscle, such as the grimaces and trembling of rage. The hypothalamus mobilizes the body for emergencies—co-ordinating the necessary build-up of breathing and other autonomic functions. It also regulates hunger and sexual activities.

The emotional influence of both the A.R.A.S. and the limbic system are expressed in part by modulating the functions of the hypothalamus; all three systems overlap. Thus, the thalamus and the hypothalamus occupy an important position in the maze of intricate connections between the neocortex and the subcortical structures.

ROLE OF THE RETICULAR
ACTIVATING SYSTEM

The reticular formation is the central axial core of the brain stem, which acts as a neuron pool and seems to have an influence on almost all sensory inflow to the higher centers as well as their motor outflow. Besides participating in vital autonomic responses, it elicits generalized inhibition of movement. It also reduces, or may eliminate, incoming sensory impulses at the level of their entrance into the brain stem.

Magoun, *et al.*[19] found that sensory stimuli reach the cortex by two pathways: the classic lemniscal pathways to the primary receptive areas, and "a series of ascending relays coursing through the mesencephalic tegmentum, subthalamus, hypothalamus and ventromedial thalamus to the internal capsule." It is this collateral network that is called the A.R.A.S.[14, 18, 19, 21]

Activation of the brain stem reticular formation may cause generalized cortical arousal; that is, it induces electrical and behavioral manifestations of alertness. For this reason, it has been called the reticular activating system (R.A.S.). Corticofugal projections of the cortex, acting through the ventromedial nucleus of the hypothalamus, have some measure of reciprocal control of the reticular formation by exerting an inhibiting or deactivating effect so that painful stimuli are diminished or eliminated. Thus the R.A.S. is able "to burn the nervous system's candle at both ends."[15]

Impulses also reach the R.A.S. from the cerebellum. The R.A.S. is activated by epinephrine and acetylcholine and by other adrenergic or cholinergic substances. It modifies muscle tone and movement and visceral regulatory mechanisms. Hence, stimulation, inhibition, arousal and depression can be reciprocally exercised simultaneously in different areas by the A.R.A.S.[19] When the cortex is prevented from being stimulated by impulses from the R.A.S., the brain is quiescent. Wakefulness is then maintained by lower brain centers which are activated by incoming afferent stimuli. As more of the R.A.S. is eliminated, the electrocortical activity changes from a waking to a sleeplike state.

Operationally, the relative quiescence of the brain may be observed in the variations of electroencephalographic patterns that occur in the transition from sleep to wakefulness. The arousal function of the R.A.S. and the thalamus have *specific* activating influences on the cortex. This may have relevance for the phenomena of hypnosis—it maintains wakefulness while some degree of cortical inhibition occurs. Although no significant alterations in the wave patterns have been noted in hypnosis, there may be sufficient basis, depending on the degree of cortical excitation and inhibition, to posit that the A.R.A.S. is an important screening mechanism for a continuum of sleep, hypnosis and wakefulness.[23]

NEUROPHYSIOLOGIC MECHANISMS IN THE MEDIATION OF EMOTIONS DURING HYPNOSIS

The preceding section stressed that one difficulty in assaying cerebral functioning at any level of awareness is that the simplest neural event becomes enormously complex. Also that the neuronal correlates responsible for hypnotic behavior are not likely to be found in the action and the interaction of systems, nor in the activity of single brain structures. The reason for this is that hypnosis is a part of everyday behavior dynamics. Like other instinctual defense mechanisms, it is a phylogenetically determined adaptive response.[11] The basis for this assumption is that the activity of an inherited network of neuronal synapses to produce altered states of awareness can be modified by experience through learning. There is evidence[13] that inherited ingredients enter into every learning process, and that in turn an extensive modification of these inherited ingredients may occur through the process of learning and conditioning, so that these overlapping determinants constitute broad bands on a continuous spectrum. The capacity to enter hypnosis is already built into the organism and is merely elicited on the basis of altering the subject's "perceptions" and interpretations of himself and his surroundings.[3]

There are several other recent studies[1, 33, 36] which have tried to elucidate the neural mechanisms by which hypnosis affects human thinking and behavior. Arnold[1] believes that, when irrelevant action impulses are excluded, the subject develops a set or a state of expectancy to accept what the hypnotist is describing, with the result that the flow of sensory impressions is reduced. On a neurophysiologic level, cortical inhibition occurs in which the "set to imagine" is mediated by the limbic system; more specifically, the hippocampal action circuit connected with the diffuse thalamic system. The latter, in turn, mediates the reduction or the intensification of neural conduction to the limbic cortex and the hippocampus and is instrumental in excluding sensory impressions. The resultant distortion and/or exclusion of sensory information may help to explain negative or positive sensory hallucinations.

It is contended by Arnold that suggestions given for complete neuromuscular relaxation (cataplexy), even though characterized by full awareness, are mediated via the limbic system connecting with the premotor and the motor cortex, and represent motor imagination (ideomotor)* transformed into action. Suggested sensations (ideosensory)* are mediated via the limbic system which connects with the frontal "association areas" and the primary sensory receiving areas. These represent projected memory images which are accepted as real because the impulse to appraise and evaluate has been excluded. Suggested goal-directed actions (posthypnotic suggestions)* flow from the suggested situation (suggestions given during hypnosis)* and are mediated via the limbic system just like any action carried out without hypnosis.[1]

However, Roberts[33] questions the role of the diffuse projection of the thalamic reticular formation in the production of hypnotic phenomena, as it cannot be safely posited that this area could serve as a vehicle of perception. The pronounced loss of sensory-motor activity which occurs during hypnosis is consistent with the theory that perception may occur through a secondary system. This system may be in the upper part of the brain stem, where a switching over to the cortex occurs—that is, in the A.R.A.S. and the surrounding areas of the dorsal hypothalamus. Psychic excitement radiates from this center and probably has something to do with a central "pacemaker" of the cerebrum, possibly the centrencephalic system.[29]

Because of the resultant inhibition produced by electrodynamic factors (selective activity of brain rhythms of delta frequency), Roberts[33] postulates:

During hypnosis the central nervous system is immobilized because the activating system has been deprived of the data—sensory, somes-

---

* The parenthetic expressions are the author's interpretations.

thetic, sensorimotor, affective, intentive, mnemonic—requisite to the normal direction of psychic activity and response. However, the continued activity of the A.R.A.S. and elaborative and effector cortical areas maintains the capacity for integration, higher elaboration and response.

In accord with the principle of selective inhibition, he believes that the subject cannot check incoming information against the stored data because these have been blocked. As a result, the subject uncritically accepts the suggestions of the hypnotist.

West,[36] considers hypnosis to be a controlled dissociated state, maintained through "parassociative" mechanisms mediated by the A.R.A.S., and which probably involves the thalamocortical projection system, the corticofugal systems, both excitatory and inhibitory, and other integrated regulatory systems known to function in connection with the A.R.A.S. The A.R.A.S. performs a scanning operation to focus on as well as to screen information, so that, when the subject is in the hypnotic state, alertness is maintained relative to the restricted area of the subject's awareness so that the hypnotist's suggestions are accepted as reality to a greater or lesser extent, depending on the subject's dissociation of other information from awareness, moment by moment. He believes that recently observed bioelectric variations during the hypnotic state, as well as differing reactions of hypnotic subjects to drugs under various circumstances, are compatible with this theory.

According to Muftic[25] hypnosis originates as the result of individual psychokinetic force-field impulses which influence other "somatic individual bodies." His complex theoretic formulations are based on a mixture of present-day neurophysiologic data, extrasensory perception, electrophysics and a unified field concept.

Recently, neurophysiologists and behavioral scientists have attempted to understand hypnosis in terms of the psychology of cognitive processes. The brain is considered as a data- or information-processing system programmed by ideas, and these are executed according to a Plan. Despite the contentions of learning theorists, human cognition and activity is not understood as a chain of reflexes, nor can it be explained by the naïve oversimplification that new reflexes can be formed through experience.

Miller, *et al.*[24] have postulated the TOTE unit (test-operate-test-exit) to show the relation between the *Image* (the experiential background) and a *Plan* (a hierarchic process which controls the order in which a sequence of operations is to be performed). The TOTE concept, which incorporates the important notion of feedback, is a fundamentally different explanation of behavior from that provided by the reflex arc. This author, however, cannot agree with their concept of hypnosis, because hypnosis is a subjective phenomenon. It is not true that a hypnotized person has stopped making his own Plans, and, therefore, executes the hypnotist's version of the Plan, since this is the only one he has. However, the reader is strongly urged to read their excellent book, which helps to elucidate the neuropsychological mechanisms involved in thinking, memory, personality, motor skills, intention, instincts, problem-solving and hypnosis.

Ravitz[31, 32] also attempts to explain the possible neural basis of hypnosis and its biologic significance as the result of electric force fields; also, that hypnotic states can be "distinguished from sleep by the development of characteristic force field shifts with preservation of a waking EEG configuration." He also reported changes in direct current potentials at the point of induction of hypnosis and at the point of termination of hypnosis.

Ravitz's theories appear to have no operational utility since they provide no hypothesis which can be meaningfully tested in terms of neurophysiologic functioning or behavior. They are couched in language borrowed from electromagnetic theory that is so abstruse as to confound even specialists in this area. References are made to electric force field changes during sleep, and the shifting of certain EEG rhythms in response to drugs as supporting evidence for applying electrodynamic field theory to the problems of biology, psychiatry, medicine and hypnosis. Although the author is totally in accord with Ravitz's noble goal, it appears that his approach does not resolve any problems or even point to a clear approach which others can understand, much less pursue.

In the next section, attempts will be made to clarify what determines the brain's acceptance of suggestions in a noncritical manner during hypnosis, and also why some individuals at nonhypnotic levels have little or no difficulty in accepting suggestions uncritically. In the next chapter, a practical understanding of how a hypnotherapist induces an attitude of belief in his subject to alter his psychological processes in a particular way will be discussed.

REFERENCES

1. Arnold, M. B.: Brain function in hypnosis, Internat. J.C.E.H. 7:109-119, 1959.
2. Ashby, W. R.: Design for a Brain, p. 6, New York, Wiley, 1954.
3. Barber, T. X.: The concept of hypnosis, J. of Psychol. 45:115-131, 1958.
3a. Brazier, M. A. B. (ed.): Central Nervous System and Behavior, Trans. of second conference, Feb. 22-25, 1959, New York, J. Macy, Jr. Foundation.
4. Fields, W. S.: Hypothalamic-Hypophyseal Interrelationships, p. 80, Springfield, Ill., Thomas, 1956.
5. Feindel, W. and Gloor, P.: Comparison of electrographic effects of stimulation of the amygdala and brain stem reticular formation in cats, Electroencephalag. & Clin. Neurophysiol. 6:389, 1954.
6. Glaser, G. H.: Recent concepts of central neurophysiology, Psychosomatic Med. 17:337-346, 1955.
6a. Gutman, H.: The biological roots of creativity, Genetic Psych. Monog. 64:417-458, 1961.
7. Heath, R. G.: Correlations between levels of psychological awareness and physiological activity in the central nervous system, Psychosomatic Med. 12:383-395, 1955.
8. Herrick, C. J.: The amphibian forebrain: VI. Necturus, J. Comp. Neurol. 58:1-288, 1933.
9. Jasper, H.: Diffuse projection systems; the integrative action of the thalamic reticular system, EEG Clin. Neurophysiol. 1:405-420, 1949.
10. Klüver, H., and Bucy, P. C.: Preliminary analysis of functions of the temporal lobes in monkeys, Arch. Neurol. & Psychiat. 42:979-1000, 1939.
11. Kroger, W. S. and Freed, S. C.: Psychosomatic Gynecology, Chicago, Free Press, 1956; reprinted, Los Angeles, Wilshire Book Co., 1962.
12. Kubie, L. S.: The central representation of the symbolic process in psychosomatic disorders, Psychosomatic Med. 15:1-7, 1953.
13. ——: Appendix I: Body symbolization and development of language (Reprinted from Psychoanalytic Quart. 3:430, 1934), Cybernetics, New York, Macy, 1951.
14. Lindsley, D. H.: Emotion *in* Stevens, S. S. (ed.): Handbook of Experimental Psychology, pp. 473-516, New York, Wiley, 1951.
15. Livingston, R. B.: Some brain stem mechanisms relating to psychosomatic functions, Psychosomatic Med. 17:347-353, 1955.
16. MacKay, D. M.: The epistemological problem for automata *in* Shannon, C. E., and McCarthy, J. (eds.): Automata Studies, Princeton, Princeton Univ. Press, 1956.
17. MacLean, P. D.: The limbic system and its hippocampal formation; studies in animals and their possible application to man, J. Neurosurg. 11:29-44, 1954.
18. ——: Limbic system ("visceral brain") in relation to central gray and reticulum of brain stem: evidence of interdependence in emotional processes, Psychosom. Med. 17:355-366, 1955.
19. Magoun, H. W.: The ascending reticular activating system, Res. Publ., A Nerv. & Ment. Dis. 30:480-490, 1952.
20. ——: An ascending reticular activating system in the brain stem, A.M.A. Arch. Neurol. & Psychiat. 67:145, 1952.
21. ——: The ascending reticular system and wakefulness *in* Brain Mechanisms and Consciousness, pp. 1-15, Springfield, Ill., Thomas, 1954.
22. ——: Paper read at Third World Congress of Psychiatry, Montreal, June 10, 1961.
23. Marmer, M. J.: Hypnosis in Anesthesiology, Springfield, Ill., Thomas, 1959.
24. Miller, G. A., Galanter E., and Pribram, K. H.: Plans and the Structure of Behavior, New York, Holt, 1960.
25. Muftic, M. K.: A contribution to the psychokinetic theory of hypnotism, Brit. J. Med. Hypnotism 11:28-38, 1959.
26. Papez, J. W.: A proposed mechanism of emotion, Arch. Neurol. & Psychiat. 38:725-743, 1937.
27. Pavlov, I. P.: Selected Works, Moscow, Foreign Languages Pub. House, 1955.

28. Penfield, W.: Memory mechanisms, A.M.A. Arch. Neurol. & Psychiat. *67*:178-191, 1952.

29. ——: The interpretive cortex, Science *129*: 1719-1726, 1959.

30. Pribram, K. H.: A review of theory in physiological psychology *in* Annual Review of Psychology, pp. 6-7, Palo Alto, Calif., Ann. Rev., 1960.

31. Ravitz, L. J.: Application of the electrodynamic field theory in biology, psychiatry, medicine, and hypnosis, Am. J. Clin. Hypnosis *1*:135-151, 1959.

32. ——: Electrometric correlates of the hypnotic state, Science *112*:341, 1950.

33. Roberts, D. R.: An electrophysiological theory of hypnosis, Internat. J. C. E. H. 8:43-57, 1960.

34. Shaefer, H.: Physiology and psychosomatic medicine, Med. Arch. Gen. Psychiat. 3:99-110, 1960.

35. Snezhnevsky, A. V.: Paper read at World Psychiatry meeting, Montreal, June, 1961.

36. West, L. J.: Psychophysiology of hypnosis, J.A.M.A. *172*:672-675, 1960.

SUPPLEMENTARY READING

Anokhin, P. K.: Electroencephalographic analysis of cortico-subcortical relations in positive and negative conditioned reactions, Ann. New York Acad. Sci. 92:899-938, 1961.

Arnold, M. B.: Emotion and Personality, New York, Columbia Univ. Press, 1960.

Bailey, P., and von Bonin, G.: The Isocortex of Man, Urbana, Ill., Univ. of Illinois Press, 1951.

Barber, T. X.: Physiological effects of "hypnosis," Psychological Bull. 58:390-420, 1961.

Brazier, M. A. B.: Brain and Behavior, Proc. 1st Conference of the Brain Research Institute, Univ. of California, L. A., Washington, D. C., Am. Inst. Biol. Sci., 1961.

Crasilneck, H. B., and Hall, J. A.: Physiological changes associated with hypnosis: a review of the literature since 1948, Inter. J. Clin. Exper. Hypnosis 7:9-50, 1959.

Diamant, J., *et al.*: An electroencephalographic study of the waking state and hypnosis with particular reference to subclinical manifestations of sleep activity, Inter. J. Clin. Exper. Hypnosis 8:199-213, 1960.

Gorton, B. E.: Physiological aspects of hypnosis, *in* Schneck, J. M. (ed.): Hypnosis in Modern Medicine, Springfield, Ill., Thomas, 1953.

——: The physiology of hypnosis, *in* The Annual Review of Hypnosis Literature, New York, The Society for Clin. and Exper. Hypnosis, 1953.

Simon, A. (ed.), *et al.*: The Physiology of Emotions, Springfield, Ill., Thomas, 1961.

28

Psychophysiologic Mechanisms in the Production of Hypnotic Phenomena: Relation to Belief and Conviction

REALITY AND PERCEPTUAL AWARENESS

The current psychiatric literature postulates that there are two "minds," the conscious and the unconscious (subconscious). "Consciousness" is defined as awareness to one's own existence, self and actions. It requires effort and is invariably referred to as the part of the brain which maintains critical faculties. It accounts chiefly for the cognitive aspects of most mental functioning. "Consciousness" and its associated mental states all involve discriminatory activities, are of necessity dynamic functions heavily dependent on the cortex.

The other portion of the brain is "nonconscious" and, at its lowest levels, is devoid of awareness even though it is never inoperative, either during sleep or wakefulness. Thought influenced by the neural centers below the cortex is egocentric, dreamy and wishful. Its functioning depends largely on the activity of subcortical structures, which, as already described, play a role of equal or even greater importance in cognitive functioning.[8]

However, subcortical structures are not in continual strife, at lower levels, with the cortex. Since these subcortical centers apparently lack discriminative ability, they initiate rather than attempt to control the goal-directed activities of the organism. This reciprocal and dynamic interaction of the two arbitrary divisions of the brain makes up the experiential background of the individual—past and present. Without the subcortical centers, the cortex could not receive memories or current percepts. On the other hand, without the cortex, the lower centers cannot receive the necessary information essential for validating reality.

When any one of the senses is stimulated, the information is first received in the lower centers and then forwarded to the cortex for correlation with data from the other senses. After the information has been validated as reality, the original percept is then filed as information in the subcortical centers. Later, when a similar percept is received, these centers transmit not only this information to the cortex for validation, but the memory of percepts related to the original reality situation. This forms the basis for convictions. Incoming percepts may differ, so as to require different convictions, but earlier convictions influence the current ones. As past convictions accumulate, they become available for consideration of current problems as these relate to reality.

Hence, thought is the association of new percepts with past data, and past convictions afford possible solutions to new situations. In other words, reality is based on sensorily received information, which of necessity has to be continually validated against previously stored memories. Convictions result from acceptance of reality and, unless new reality situations are introduced, the older sensory impressions cannot be changed.[6] One might say the brain is guided by reality as it perceives reality, but this freedom is limited by past and present realities.

Studies in perception[3] indicate that awareness of reality *comes from within us*, not from our environment. This would fit in with the operational definition that hypnosis is a subjective phenomenon processed out of prior-invoked beliefs which create a *readiness to believe*. All perceptual awareness in hypnosis is altered by compounding of beliefs, and this leads to conviction independent of reality.

PSYCHOPHYSIOLOGIC MECHANISMS IN HYPNOTIC PHENOMENA

The phenomenon of posthypnotic amnesia depends upon the type and degree of cortical inhibition. During deep hypnosis, the cortex is not even "aware" that such memories are accessible. Posthypnotic amnesia does not actually eliminate the memories but merely prevents information processed out of what constitutes reality for the subject from reaching the mnemonic data in the higher sensorium. In other words, instead of *reality, there is unreality*. It must be emphasized, however, that any sensory distortion negates reality for only that particular posthypnotic suggestion, that is, the amnestic material. The conviction of amnesia is brought about first by the reality of hypnosis, and then this is followed by the belief that amnesia will occur.

Posthypnotic suggestions that are carried out successfully are those capable of instilling convictions at variance with the prior-invoked beliefs. However, conviction can be accepted without question even at non-hypnotic levels; this is noted in religious faith-healing and in the blind trust of children. Such conviction, deduced through normal thought processes, is, of course, subject to change unless altered by other information.

Hence, the function of all ideational activities is to process sensory information for the most useful combinations possible out of our experiential background. The importance of understanding the psychophysiologic basis of hypnosis as a phenomenological experience is set not only by what information the brain contains, but also by what it will receive in terms of awareness or "consciousness." Kline[4] states:

. . . when one studies hypnotism and when one works with it, he is working with an important element for controlling and determining aspects of consciousness.

He believes that more than the element of suggestion is involved, and emphasizes that "one must not confuse the hypnotic state with hypnotic behavior and with the nature of neuropsychologic processes in the hypnotic state."

It has been emphasized previously that words have the power to produce associative conditioning, that belief is based on experiential conditioning, and when the sensory spiral of belief is cumulative, it leads to hypnotic conviction. As the author[5] stated in a recent publication, "Conviction of hypnosis leads to hypnosis."

Some psychosomatic disorders may be due to increased susceptibility of the cortex induced by partial cortical inhibition. This is brought about by the inability of the integrating centers to interpret correctly new sensory information or data. This can occur whenever repetitive destructive conditioning activates faulty associations or whenever the resultant harmful emotional responses ultimately lead to adverse somatization reactions based on *conviction*. In the former, the beliefs can be changed only by correcting the faulty information through re-education; in the latter, deeply ingrained convictions can be reversed best by implanting constructive conditioning through meaningful suggestions. Such reconditioning to alter the disturbed cortical dynamics is more readily achieved under hypnosis.

RELATIONSHIP OF BELIEF AND CONVICTION TO HYPNOTIC PHENOMENA

After the production of hypnosis, the need for reality testing is obviated. West[9] states:

When there occurs a marked narrowing of focus of awareness on a particular aspect of reality, to the exclusion of much of the rest (as in the initiation of a hypnotic trance), then sensory data (verbal suggestions) taken in through an open channel (rapport) become effective because they are not subjected to ordinary reality testing.

It is precisely for this reason that post-hypnotic suggestions can be carried out. The degree of effectiveness of a posthypnotic suggestion is based on the degree of suspension of cortical discrimination. Arnold[1] states:

The connection of the hippocampal action circuit (which seems to be the repository of neuronal mechanisms that preserve the stream of consciousness) which mediates recall of the memory image together with the diffuse thalamic system allows the inhibition of irrelevant impulses from the visual area and thus prevents a correction of the hallucinations by the visual impression—as long as the singleminded concentration lasts he is incapable of seeing any incongruity either in his actions or perceptions.

Thus, if a suggestion seems to be a certainty because of belief and conviction, it has the power to effect an appropriate response in the organism. Conviction consists of two types, one based on pooling present and past information. In this type, the brain functions logically because the validation results from past and present circumstances *which are real*. The other type, hypnotic or nonvalidated conviction, requires no checking against stored information because the suggestions are accepted with a literalness *as if they are real*.

The degree of "conscious" response depends on the manner and the number of beliefs necessary to establish conviction. Hence, if we hear something long enough and strongly enough, we can build up conviction, as in religious faith. And a faith in brand names built up by advertisers! It is no wonder that conviction can be put to work in hypnotherapy so admirably.

It is known that, in the presence of the appropriate mental-set, thoughts based on conviction can heal or kill. Conviction of illness can lead just as readily to hypochondriasis as to sickness. No more forceful example can be found than that of voodoo death. Cannon[2] describes how sorcery and witchcraft kill young, healthy people in spite of all modern medical care. Conviction of death processed into the brain may invoke the sympathetico-adrenal system, which supersedes volitional control and leads to death!

Whenever distortion of reality is slipped into awareness through hypnotically induced heterosuggestions, it takes precedence over reality-testing even in well-adjusted individuals. It is by such measures that conviction at hypnotic and often at nonhypnotic levels can occur without volitional participation. The reverse is undoubtedly the mechanism for paranoid trends. The aberrant behavior characterizing the psychoses and the psycho-

neuroses is due, in part, to distortion of reality by the patient's autosuggestions. The phenomena of hypnosis temporarily mimic, in almost pure culture, the manifestations of deranged thinking and behavior. This does not imply that hypnotic behavior *is* psychotic behavior, but rather that they are opposite sides of the same coin.

If we can comprehend the relationship of belief and conviction to hypnosis, we should be able to achieve better insight into the basic causations of irrational mental functioning. Posthypnotic suggestions afford a remarkable experimental tool for studying the ontogenesis of many different types of neurotic behavior. Just as hypnotically produced suggestions are difficult to resist if they are in keeping with the individual's desires or rationalizations, so are delusional tendencies well-nigh impossible to eradicate by appealing to volition.

The following material has been mentioned in other chapters; however, in this context it warrants repetition. One can produce physiologic effects only if the corresponding imaginative processes are used to invoke the necessary sensory data. The fundamental principle of the law of reverse effect here holds true, namely, that the imagination is more powerful than the will. In this regard, imagining a posthypnotically suggested sensation results in its being experienced, provided contradictory impulses are excluded. The positive gustatory hallucination of "eating a steak" results because the needed data are available in the cortex. However, human beings cannot imagine ideomotor and ideosensory responses that have not been previously experienced.

Ideomotor and ideosensory responses are the *sine qua non* for facilitation of hypnosis. These activities depend on past experiences, which endow the organism with automaticity and require little cortical discrimination. When conviction becomes reflexlike and when it is accepted at this level, the resultant conviction leads to uncritical acceptance of other suggestions.

Briefly, then, an induction procedure makes full use of cortical and subcortical mechanisms. The technic, regardless of the methodology, provides the validation necessary for acceptance of beliefs.

Hypnotic susceptibility also has a high content of thought-out conviction. For instance, if a person expects to be hypnotized by someone in a prestige position, his expectancy level is raised. Subjects who are analytical or who know a considerable amount about hypnosis are difficult to induce by any technic because the prestige factor so necessary for conviction is not present. Furthermore, the initiated anticipate the carefully contrived sensory illusions. Because they cannot exclude irrelevant thoughts, they cannot give their full and continuous attention to the operator. As a result, the necessary diminution of sensory reality never occurs.

In summation, the ability to achieve hypnosis is often based on a single "learned" response, and once it has been achieved it is easy to develop more complex response. The induction of hypnosis results from conditions which preclude logical thinking. If an individual has the conviction that he has been hypnotized, then further beliefs wholly or partially unrelated to reality are accepted as convictions. Stated simply, acceptance of hypnosis allows acceptance of all that follows, provided that the beliefs do not mobilize critical attitudes. First, cortical awareness is required to establish the sensory meaningfulness of the stimuli leading to hypnosis. This, in turn, allows the summation of convictions to gain control over critical faculties. Now, with reality held in abeyance, information that cannot be checked can be directly implanted to produce appropriate responses.

RELATIONSHIP OF CONVICTION TO DEPTH OF HYPNOSIS

The various hypnotic depths, as has been mentioned, are at best only arbitrary delineations, and no two individuals respond in a similar fashion to identical suggestions because reality varies from person to person and even changes in the same person from time to time. This accounts for the variations in hypnotic response often noted in even well-conditioned subjects.

It was pointed out that, in some highly suggestible individuals, conviction often can be instilled without hypnosis. For these, the need for conviction of hypnosis is obviated.

Hence, the concept of "trance" really has no basis in fact, because nearly all "trance" phenomena can be produced without the necessity for inducing a formalistic state of hypnosis!

LIGHT STAGE OF HYPNOSIS

The fundamental principle in achieving any degree of hypnotic depth is to get the subject to accept the validity of simple suggestions first, and then build up to more complex suggestions (see Chapter 15).

MEDIUM STAGE OF HYPNOSIS

After limb catalepsy is attained, further belief is established by the suggestion of deep relaxation. As the depth increases, subcortical centers take over, much as in sleep.

SOMNAMBULISM OR DEEP HYPNOSIS

Here conviction is complete and there is no need for reality testing. The operator's suggestions are received with a literalness because no modification or distortion of the incoming information occurs. Furthermore, the suggestions cannot be compared with previous data, so they are accepted as convictions even though they are at variance with reality. If it is not present, amnesia is produced by a command to forget.

Negative and positive sensory illusions or hallucinations are readily produced because the subject's beliefs grow with *conviction!* In short, the brain can screen impressions selectively from awareness, or inhibit and distort sensory impressions so as to produce visual, auditory and other sensory hallucinations. Often as a result of these impressions, there is an increase in voluntary performance.

DEHYPNOTIZATION

When good subjects are dehypnotized they usually follow most posthypnotic suggestions, since they cannot recall how or why the commands were issued to them in the first place because of the associated amnesia. If they are able to remember, they can resist because the suggestion is no longer a deeply implanted conviction. If they obey the posthypnotic suggestions, subjects offer innumerable rationalizations for their actions.

Not to belabor the point, the nature of posthypnotic suggestions is similar to that of compulsive acts. Like compulsive behavior, which does not follow logical or reality thinking, a posthypnotic suggestion will be resisted only and after recall that the command was given during hypnosis. Here the reality of the situation is recognized, thus negating the effects of the command. For an explanation of other posthypnotic phenomena such as hypermnesia, age regression or revivification, the reader is referred to Chapter 2. Not all posthypnotic suggestions will necessarily be followed if the subject's convictions are at variance with the reality of the situation. Also, every individual has different convictions as to what is right and what is wrong.

In conclusion, the phenomenology of hypnosis as well as the degree of hypnotizability depend more or less on how the brain has been "programmed" by previous beliefs and convictions. Thus induction of hypnosis is the induction of conviction![6]

REFERENCES

1. Arnold, M. B.: Brain function in hypnosis, Internat. J.C.E.H. 7:109-119, 1959.
2. Cannon, W. B.: "Voodoo" death, Psychosom. Med. 19:182-190, 1957.
3. Kelley, E. C.: Education is Communication, ETC: Rev. General Semantics 12: 248-256, 1955.
4. Kline, M. V.: Clinical and Experimental Hypnosis in Contemporary Behavioral Sciences, Introductory Lectures in Medical Hypnosis p. 1, N.Y., Institute for Research in Hypnosis, 1958.
5. Kroger, W. S.: Techniques of hypnosis, J.A.M.A. 172:675-680, 1960.
6. Lacey, H.: Beyond Hypnosis, Whittier, Calif., Independent Publishing Co., 1952.
7. Penfield, W.: Some mechanisms of consciousness discovered during electrical stimulation of the brain, Proc. Nat. Acad. Sc. 44:51-66, 1958.
8. Rowland, V.: Conditioning and brain waves, Scient. Amer. 1959. Vol. 201, pp. 89-96, Aug. 1959.
9. West, L. J.: Psychophysiology of hypnosis, J.A.M.A. 172:672-675, 1960.

Relationship of Semantics, Communication and Perception to Hypnosis

In this chapter there will be a brief description of how communication, the chief tool of the hypnotherapist, relates to semantics, perception and learning, as well as of the contemporary developments that the behavioral and physical sciences have made in the comparative study of the messages of control and communication in man and machine—cybernetics. These disciplines regard man as a highly evolved and complex automaton or "servomechanism," regulated by the transmission of feedback data—that is, a process by which error-correcting information is fed back to maintain homeostasis. Cybernetics suggests new hypotheses for understanding neurophysiologic functioning and, perhaps, such behaviorial responses as hypnosis.

ROLE OF HYPNOSEMANTICS IN THERAPY

It has been stressed that words are important tools in the arsenal of the hypnotherapist. Responses during hypnosis are due to the manner in which words are interpreted by the subject. Most hypnotized persons respond with a literalness to the meaning of words. For instance, if a nonhypnotized person is told, "Raise your right hand," he usually *lifts the entire arm*. The hypnotized individual invariably *raises his hand because he responds exactly as suggested*.

The anxiety-ridden patient, however, is likely to attach a different connotation to certain words, particularly during the induction. Therefore, such phrases as "going down, down," "falling deeper and deeper," "you are in a sleeplike state" should be avoided, as they may be equated to sexual or death fantasies. Illustrative is the phrase,

"Imagine that your body is like a 'dead weight.'" Those who regard hypnosis as a deathlike or a "suspended animation" phenomenon will generally respond unfavorably, but proper orientation will negate this misconception.

Others, with a low threshold to anxiety will overreact even to harmless words. The degree depends on previous associations. At the first sign of an untoward reaction to a word or a phrase, corrective measures must be instituted. Words that might shock the patient should be eliminated from the vocabulary of the hypnotherapist, especially in obstetrics. Instead of asking a hypnotized patient in labor, "How are your pains?" the word "contractions" should be substituted for "pains." In surgery, lack of "word-watchfulness" often can interfere with recovery. The calamitous effect of words in the production of hypochondriasis is well documented.

It is also easier to make a disturbed person sicker by words, or even grunts or gestures, than to make him well. It is not without reason that it has been said, "A word can make or break a man," and *it is this which accounts for most of the dangers attributed to hypnosis*. Much difficulty can be obviated by the careful measurement of words. The science of measuring words is called semantics—the systematic study of the meaning of words. General semantics is the study and the improvement of human evaluative processes to language with special emphasis on their relationship to signs and symbols, including language.

The semantic significance of words for psychophysiology is that they constitute real, conditioned stimuli. Thus, patients can be habituated to key words which will invariably evoke behavioral responses, as in hypnosis. Pavlov[20] bound up speech, hypnosis and the conditioned reflex in a statement which the years have done nothing to alter. He said:

Speech, on account of the whole preceding life of the adult, is connected up with all the internal and external stimuli which can reach the cortex, signalling all of them and replacing all of them, and, therefore, it can call forth all those reactions of the organism which are ordinarily determined by the actual stimuli themselves. We can, therefore, regard "suggestion" as the most simple form of a conditioned reflex in man.

In other words, the mere mention of a word associated with a certain physiologic or psychological reaction elicits that reaction even though the original stimulus has been forgotten. Thus, a word does not become meaningful until a conditioned reflex between it and some conditioned or unconditioned stimulus takes place in the cortex. For instance, in the child, the word "hurt" acquires a definite meaning only after it has been associated with real pain. After that, the appropriate conditioned reaction to the word "hurt" can be evoked to reproduce the exact conditioned response (pain reaction). Once a conditioned reflex is established, the person automatically reacts without thinking to the nongenuine stimulus that has become a part of the reflex. In the example just given this would be the word "hurt."

It even has been observed that a verbal stimulus alone provokes a stronger reaction in hypnotically conditioned subjects than an actual pinprick.[22] Pavlov's conditioning, in the classic manner, is somewhat analogous to the effects obtained by repetitive posthypnotic suggestions. The only difference is that, in the latter, full use is made of the inborn feedback mechanisms—the ideomotor and ideosensory responses. These do not require learning.

Also, during autohypnosis, the mere thought of a word or a phrase elicits the same responses that it ordinarily would following posthypnotic suggestions. In hypnotic sensory-imagery conditioning, the words act in the "mind's ear" as "inner speech," because subcortical structures cannot differentiate between a vividly imagined experience and a real one. The reason is that the only information available to the cortex for validation about a given situation is *what one believes to be true about it!*

Illustrative is the work of Hudgins,[13] who conditioned the pupillary reflex to voluntary control. When the verbal command "Contract" was given to a group of hypnotized subjects, together with a light (unconditioned stimulus) and a bell (conditioned stimulus), the pupils contracted without the light or the bell. In other subjects, pupillary contraction occurred at the *mere thought of the word!* This response remained as long as 2 months without reinforcement. The importance of this work indicates that conditioned responses achieved through posthypnotic suggestions have great durability and tenacity. Similar conditioning, achieved at nonhypnotic levels, is more rapidly extinguished.

Conditioning by certain words can also "ring bells" to produce other psychophysiologic changes; the suggestion of "ice" or "snow" causes shivering and often a temperature drop in susceptible subjects. Everyone apparently "possesses verbally conditioned bells waiting to be rung."[26] However, it must be emphasized that physiologic responses are not obtained by the meaning of the word per se but rather by the image that is conjured up.

The importance of semantics for hypnosis is that words establish associational reflexes which automatically activate ideomotor and ideosensory responses. The more the subject is involved in one ideomotor and ideosensory response after another, the more he will respond, and, as a result, the more dissociation from reality occurs: every suggestion is now accepted as a belief. Thus, the subject now accepts the hypnotist's words as reality, and unreality is readily transformed into reality.

ROLE OF COMMUNICATION IN PSYCHOTHERAPY

To achieve a better understanding of the roles of thinking and learning, one must know how communication of information occurs. A comparison between the electrical transmission of messages and the exchange of information between humans will be described in more detail in the next chapter. The former, developed by telecommunication engineers, may help us to understand the psychology of the cognitive processes, especially hypnosis. Communication in the ordinary sense, however, is particularly important in psychotherapy and will now be discussed.

Communication has been defined as any process that leads to an exchange of information.[27] It is not a technic but, rather, an attitude directed toward the sharing of information for a purpose.[2, 4, 11, 25, 27] Whenever there is an overlapping of experiences, as in the doctor-patient relationship, both understand, accept and adjust to each other's communications more readily. Therefore, effective communication in psychotherapy makes full use of the patient's capacities to respond experientially to meaningful suggestions of the operator. Also, greater response occurs if the operator recognizes the patient's needs and motivations.

Yet few physicians exploit the communication processes to their maximal potential. Still fewer recognize that the hypnotic relationship affords a vehicle for effective communication of ideas and understandings which can unlock the hidden recovery forces present in the patient. Skilled hypnotherapists, who utilize the nuances of permissive but yet directive communication, are aware that clarity and warmth in the semantics and the sounds of words distinctly benefit their patients. So essential is good physician-patient communication that an updated course in therapeutic semantics should be mandatory for students in medicine and psychology.

The semantic approach has corrected spurious identifications, mis-evaluations and recently acquired harmful conditioned reflexes through strong persuasion based on Korzybskian principles.[14] Ruesch and Bateson[23] point out that "communication is the link that connects psychiatry with all other sciences." They note that "jamming of the networks" or overloading of the neural pathways leads to disruption (anxiety). Continual exposure to semantic confusion, along with other factors, may produce schizophrenia in predisposed persons.[1]

The objectives of psychotherapeutic communication can be accomplished at the interactional level by "either reducing the number of confusing messages or by prevention of jamming."[24] There are two major problems in any type of psychotherapeutic communication. First, the depth of one's feelings must be meaningfully conveyed so that they can be understood and accepted by the patient. Second, the doctor must listen attentively. The important notion of the feedback of information is relevant to both patient and therapist as it automatically answers the questions, "How am I doing?" and "To what extent will I permit myself to share with another?" The insecure, anxiety-ridden patient usually cannot share or express himself effectively because of his own inadequacy. Other disturbed persons, as the affect-blocked individual, fear self-revelation and subsequent loss of respect. To obviate these, the therapist, on the basis of the information available, must put the patient at ease and build up the patient's self-confidence and self-esteem.

Whenever communication bogs down to superficialities, rapport is decreased. As an unintentional defensive mechanism, many patients stray from the subject. Thus, to obviate resistance, the discussion should be relevant to the patient's problems. It is in the handling of the disturbed patient that the physician's ability to communicate reaches its greatest potential. Since the hypnotic situation induces greater receptivity, more information is available for the understanding necessary for personality integration.

ROLE OF COMMUNICATION AS A CONTROL MECHANISM IN PSYCHOTHERAPY

Haley[6] contends that the therapist and the patient try to control different areas of the psychotherapeutic relationship. The therapist does this by *setting the rules* for therapy, thus being "one up" while, at the same time, denying his superior position; the patient attempts to defeat the therapist by his symptomatic behavior. However, the therapist always wins because he can impose a "double bind." This refers to a situation in which an individual is confronted by two contradictory messages which prevent him from successfully protesting or leaving the field.[7] In the struggle to circumscribe each other's behavior, the person imposing the symptomatic double bind must win. An example of a double bind is the wife who asks her husband to wash the dishes because she claims that she is dizzy. She, of course, denies controlling the behavior of her husband but blames it on her symptom.

In a typical double-bind maneuver during therapy, a patient's insistence that he cannot help himself is *accepted* rather than opposed. He is directed in such a way that he must stop behaving in the way he does or stop denying that he is behaving in that way. There is a similarity between symptomatic behavior of the patient and the tactics of the therapist. When the patient behaves in a symptomatic way and uses the double bind, he is met by an opposing double bind. The patient can quit, comment on a contradiction posed to him, or cease suffering double-bind maneuvers himself.[8] Whatever he does, he loses. If he leaves, he remains sick; if he comments, he is trying to control the therapist; and if he abandons his own double-bind maneuvers, he gives up his symptomatic behavior. From this point of view the patient is forced by the therapist to behave differently, whether he likes it or not, particularly when the therapist is most permissive.

Resistant maneuvers are dissipated by accepting them and redefining them as co-operation by double binds. Suggestions can be concealed or given in the form of a double bind so that the patient will not be aware of their implications.[9] For example, if a patient has a pain, he can be told, under hypnosis, "Any pain that can be increased can be decreased," and then asked, "You do wish to have less discomfort, do you not?" If the pain is increased, the patient is accepting the premise that the pain can be decreased. Phobic reactions can be relieved in a similar fashion. As Haley aptly put it, "Hypnosis might be defined as the art of getting someone to do what you tell him while indicating that he isn't doing it."[9]

Psychodynamicists contend that they do not employ a directive approach. Yet, according to Haley,[10] communication on a non-directive basis is an impossibility, because the therapist, by continually redefining the therapeutic situation, maintains control of the relationship. The "nondirective" therapist makes the patient communicate in an indirect way—much as the patient once used symptoms to control others (secondary gains). This also permits the therapist to deny that he is in control of the relationship. In addition, the patient always hands control over to the therapist when he hangs onto his every remark, and especially when he asks him to interpret his dreams, thoughts and free associations. Also, he must change his maneuvering voluntarily, on the slightest indication of the therapist. On the other hand, he cannot use the therapist's maneuvers because he is always in a "one down" position.

HELPFUL HINTS ON HOW TO COMMUNICATE EFFECTIVELY IN PSYCHOTHERAPY

1. In handling resistance, ask questions such as, "You can see my point of view, can you not?" Or ask a question that either leaves a choice or is good for the therapist's position. Still another approach is, "Do you mean that this is so?" This makes the patient feel accepted, and he will usually elaborate on the query in another way.

2. Remember that words have more than one meaning; therefore, rephrase the patient's statements in order to get his meanings.

3. Realize that words represent only a few selected details of what the patient really perceived. Therefore, when listening to the description of an object, an event or another reality situation, or when describing something to the patient, remember that important particulars usually are omitted.

4. Never make dogmatic judgments on insufficient facts. However, a decision often must be risked from an incomplete collection of facts. Take such risks only when absolutely necessary.

5. Never think in terms of black and white only; shades of gray may exist. Always examine the middle ground between two opposing ideas, since there is more than one way of doing a thing. The possibility of alternatives must always be kept in mind.

6. Think before speaking. An inadvertent

remark *often* is a common cause of a communication breakdown.

7. Being too friendly when conveying therapeutic explanations inevitably will cause a loss of prestige.

8. Never give a patient carte blanche with a phrase like "You know what I mean?" The patient usually does not understand!

9. Be brief, and discuss one specific topic at a time. This avoids "scattering" or distraction.

10. Watch for the psychological moment or the proper timing for therapeutic interpretations. Then *get across* what you want to get across and what you *mean to get across.*

11. Discuss the patient's explanations, so that you can be sure that they convey his point of view.

12. Remember that actions speak louder than words; note the implications of nonverbal communications in both yourself and the patient.

13. Listen to what the patient is trying to say. Inattention is disturbing. Never intimate beforehand that you know everything that is going to be said.

14. Avoid dogmatism. Be flexible and reasonable when voicing your differences. A handy formula to prevent being considered opinionated is to use the phrase "it seems to me" rather than stating flatly "it is a fact."

15. Never directly challenge what is patently a falsehood. Rather, if the issue is important, ask subtle questions to ascertain the truth.

ROLE OF PERCEPTION IN HYPNOSIS

The problem of perceptual discrimination is pertinent for learning theory, and particularly important for understanding the nature of hypnosis. Recently, several investigators[5, 15, 25] have increased our understanding of the ways in which we learn to perceive. However, no one ever perceives "all" of any situation, but only enough to deal with it. What is perceived is based on the "functional probabilities" or the "best bets," based on the individual's past experiences. Hence, two or more individuals' perceptions will be similar only if their past experiences and motivations are alike. Thus, differences in views, kinds and rapidity of

environmental change, and cumulative effects of experience mold perception. Bridgman[3] observes that, since no one can get away from himself, there are limitations on our understanding of perception and reality. Hence some of the major paradoxes of modern science have arisen. Actually, there is no absolute free will and no absolute determinism. Absolutes are human concepts and have no basis in fact.

Some learning probably occurs through the process of redintegration, which may be defined as the "triggering" of imaginative identifying impressions representing specific situations of prior experiences. Thus, the brain has the freedom to manipulate and to be *guided by reality as it perceives reality.* In hypnosis, there is an increased capacity for redintegrative processes. This is the basis for hypnotic sensory-imagery conditioning. Neurophysiologic observations indicate that an original experience can be recalled irrespective of whether or not it was a fact, a dream or a fantasy.[21]

Until recently, little was known about the psychological interrelationships within which hypnotic phenomena could be considered. We are indebted to Kline[16] for his penetrating insights into these fruitful areas for research. He believes that there is no such thing as a hypnotic state per se, but rather that it manifests itself as a fluctuating phase of awareness closer to hyperacuity than to sleep. To be sure, however, there are hypnotic phenomena and hypnotic relationships, and these do not require a formalistic induction procedure for their establishment.

Therefore, it is obvious that hypnosis cannot be explained in terms of such constructs as "consciousness," "unconsciousness" or "deep sleep." Kline thinks that consciousness, too, is an illusion, which, though very real, cannot be separated from physical happenings, as it merely reflects the meanings conceptualized within one's own sensory order, namely, with existence or reality. He contends that reality is determined by a number of impressions, principally arousal, which are converted into behavior and become meaningful through the associations, the experiences and the involuntary reactions that characterize the nature of responsiveness.[16]

Since illusions constitute an important part of reality, they produce exceedingly complex reactions. This is demonstrated during a great dramatic moment in the theater when the entire audience is, in reality, "hypnotized." Here a meaningful illusion is created, and each person's change in reality perception occurs as the result of his own experiential reactions to himself and his environment. New meanings and associations are brought forth which cause a subject to *behave differently because he thinks and believes differently.*

PSYCHOPHYSIOLOGY OF PERCEPTION

The psychophysiologic mechanisms by which past and present impressions blend into perceptual realities are not too well understood. Suffice it to say that under the affective influence of a comparison of an imagined future with an experienced past, the brain attempts continuously to predict the goals that will help maintain equilibrium. As Kline[16a] notes:

All of this infers a dependency upon those stimulus-response modalities which go into the organization and creation of self-equilibrium. Equilibrium starting on a molecular basis rises to equilibrium on a molar (whole entity as contrasted with molecular), self-concept, body image basis.

The temporal lobes are in the center of perceptual activities. These areas with their deeper limbic structures mediate the integration of instinctual, affective and autonomic processes. To this, the activities of the sensory and premotor cortex add the processes of perception, their apperceptive integration, and the fantasy formation which is built around the central core of the instinctual drives. Ostrow[19] also suggests that temporal lobe afferents may mediate the controls which pleasurable affects exercise on psychic functions. However, much more data must be obtained before these concepts can be validated.

The neural mechanisms capable of recognizing visual and auditory forms have been described by Pitts and McCulloch.[17] They postulate a system of impulses which sweep up and down over interlacing fibers in the cortex and thereby provide a scanning arrangement for the recognition of patterns of incoming sensory stimuli. The methods by which hypnosis utilizes these scanning mechanisms for maintaining increased perceptual awareness or selective attention are discussed in Chapter 30.

ROLE OF LEARNING IN HYPNOSIS

The interaction between perception and learning is called a microgenetic process.* The cognitive theories of learning assign an important place to perception. Motivation based on needs and drives of the individual, as well as exploration, reinforcement and trial-and-error learning play an important role for all goal-seeking organisms.[12]

Attempts to explain learning have developed into behavioral theories of varying degrees of complexity and sophistication, beginning with Pavlov's conditioned reflex theory and extending to Watson[29] and others who immediately followed him and who incorporated his principles into psychological theory. They failed to realize that they were dealing with simple and elemental units of behavior. In their desire to introduce scientific rigor into psychology, they created their image of man and involved few variables of behavior beyond the stimulus-response sequence. Other behavioral learning theories avoided hypothesizing what might occur within the organism.

Although important proponents of learning theory still maintain this parsimonious view, the main stream of learning theory recognizes that there are intervening variables before and between the time a stimulus impinges and a response occurs.[18] It is becoming self-evident that the reflex arc is not representative of the elemental unit of behavior. Rather, the fundamental building block of the nervous system is the feedback loop which follows the laws of electrical activity and cybernetic principles. The relationship of these important concepts to physiologic psychology and hypnosis will be discussed in the next chapter.

* Arieti, S.: The microgeny of thought and perception. Arch. Gen. Psych. 6:454-468, 1962.

REFERENCES

1. Bateson, G., et al.: Toward a theory of schizophrenia, Behavioral Science *1*:251-264, 1956.
2. Bois, J. S.: Explorations in Awareness, New York, Harper, 1957.
3. Bridgman, P. W.: The Way Things Are, Cambridge, Mass., Harvard Univ. Press, 1959.
4. Dollard, J., and Miller, N. E.: Personality and Psychotherapy, New York, McGraw-Hill, 1950.
5. Gardner, R. W.: Cognitive control principles and perceptual behavior, Menn. Clin. Bull. 23:241-248, 1959
6. Haley, J.: Control in psychoanalytical psychotherapy *in* Progress in Psychotherapy, vol. IV, pp. 48-65, New York, Grune & Stratton, 1959.
7. *Ibid.*, p. 50.
8. *Ibid.*, p. 64.
9. *Ibid.*, p. 55.
10. *Ibid.*, p. 61.
11. Hayakawa, S. I.: Language in Thought and Action, New York, Harcourt, Brace & Co., 1940.
12. Hilgard, E. R.: Theories of Learning, New York, Appleton-Century-Crofts, 1956.
13. Hudgins, C. V.: Conditioning and the voluntary control of the pupillary light reflex, J. Gen. Psychol. 8:3-51, 1933.
14. Kelley, E. C.: Education for What Is Real, New York, Harper, 1947.
15. Kilpatrick, F. P.: Perception theory and general semantics. ETC.: A Review of General Semantics *12*:257-264, 1955.
16. Kline, M. V.: Clinical and experimental hypnosis in contemporary behavioral sciences *in* Introductory Lectures in Medical Hypnosis, New York, Institute of Research, 1958.
16a. ——: Freud and Hypnosis, New York, Julian Press, 1961.
17. McCulloch, W. S., and Pitts, W.: A logical calculus of the ideas imminent in nervous activity, Bull. Math. Biophysics 5:115-133, 1953.
18. Miller, G. A., Galanter, E., and Pribram, K. H.: Plans and the Structure of Behavior, New York, Holt, 1960.
19. Ostow, M.: Psychic contents of brain processes, Psychosomatic Med. *17*:396-406, 1955.
20. Pavlov, E. P.: Twenty Years of Objective Study of the Higher Nervous Activity Behavior of Animals, p. 376, Medzig Publishing House, Moscow, 1951.
21. Penfield, W.: Memory mechanisms, Arch. Neur. & Psychiat. 67:178-191, 1952.
22. Platonov, K.: The Word as a Physiological and Therapeutic Factor, Foreign Languages Publishing House, Moscow, 1959.
23. Ruesch, J., and Bateson, G.: Communication: The Social Matrix of Psychiatry, New York, Norton, 1951.
24. *Ibid.*, p. 19.
25. Ruesch, J., and Prestwood: Communication and bodily disease *in* Life Stress and Bodily Disease, Assoc. Res. Nerv. Ment. Dis. 29:211-230, 1950.
26. Salter, A.: What Is Hypnosis: Studies in Conditioning, New York, Farrar, Straus Co., 1955.
27. Sondel, B.: The Humanity of Words, Cleveland, World Press, 1958.
28. Santos, J. R., and Murphy, G.: An odyssey in perceptual learning, Menn. Clin. Bull. *24*:6-17, 1960.
29. Watson, J. B.: Psychology from the Standpoint of a Behaviorist, Philadelphia, Lippincott, 1919.

SUPPLEMENTARY READING

Chase, S.: The Tyranny of Words, New York, Harcourt, 1938.
Korzybski, A.: Science and Sanity, New York, Dutton, 1933.
Lee, I.: Language Habits in Human Affairs: An Introduction to General Semantics, New York, Harper, 1941.
Meyers, R.: The nervous system and general semantics, E.T.C.: A Review of General Semantics 5:14-21, 1948.
Miller, G. A.: Language and Communication, New York, McGraw-Hill, 1951.
Rapoport, A.: Science and the Goals of Men, New York, Harper, 1950.

30

Some Relationships of the Physical and Behavioral Sciences to Psychotherapy and Hypnosis

CYBERNETIC APPLICATIONS

The development of a more scientific psychology has increased the need for mathematical models or symbolic representations of the most recent learning theories. These are mechanistic in nature and are classified under the general concept of cybernetics, which attempts to describe control processes in precise mathematical terms. The term cybernetics comes from a Greek word *Kybernetes,* which means pilot or governor. Much has been written on this discipline in relation to the study of control processes in machines, organisms and social groups.

On a broader basis, cybernetics combines the views from different but related fields of knowledge, including engineering, mathematics, physiology, biology and psychology. Cyberneticians contend also that principles of learning and purposeful behavior characteristic of machines apply to human functioning. The theory does *not* imply that electronic or mechanical analogues can adequately represent the functioning of the central nervous system, but, rather, that living organisms parallel the over-all stimulus-response behavior patterns of automatically controlled machines (servomechanisms).

The central principle, as defined in the last chapter, is that goal-directed organisms as well as machines utilize *error-correcting* information to achieve purposeful behavior or equilibrium. This indicates that the system is in *negative feedback.* If the information fed back in an automatically controlled machine or organism causes the error to *increase,* with a resultant instability or breakdown, the system is said to be in *positive feedback.*

These principles are similar to Bernard's and Cannon's views on homeostasis. However, what is new is that dynamic equilibrium involves a perpetual exchange of energy with the environment. What leaves the organism is called "output," and what goes into it, "input." Man, as an open control system, therefore, receives from his environment and makes his contribution to it—but input and output do not interact.

With this model in mind, it appears that the hypnotic interpersonal relationship, as well as the resultant hypnotic conditioning procedure, depends largely on the manner in which the subject is willing to have his perceptual mechanisms restructured. If the subject incorporates the therapist into this system, the type of feedback is altered in the control process. This concept allows us to understand some of the fundamentals of behavior. It is hoped that the life sciences will join forces with the behavioral sciences to reveal other hidden factors in the tangled areas of human behavior. Hypnosis, because of its discriminative ability, affords an experimental device for penetrating this bewildering maze.

From the rapid strides of the engineering and mathematical sciences, cybernetics is providing newer applications for the older concepts of self-maintenance or equilibrium. These applications should lead to a better understanding of higher nervous system functioning, especially in reference to hypnotic behavior. Also, it is more apparent that research possibilities and new insights into the psychology of learning and the processing of information (thinking) will ultimately be developed to understand the complex neuropsychologic mechanisms of human relationships, responses and behavior.

Critics of cybernetics believe that it, like behaviorism, is an excellent theory from the viewpoint of scientific methodology, but that, like most of the behavioristic theories, it is inadequate since it neglects the role of man's creativeness (something no machine yet possesses). Overlooked, too, is the role of the essential meaningfulness which underlies man's experiences, past and present.

CYBERNETIC MODELS OF LEARNING

There are several models for understanding the mechanisms involved in learning, especially as it applies to the communication of information in man and the machine. Outstanding among these are the feedback, information theory and probability theory models. The first two are related to the design of telecommunications equipment—all are concerned with goal-directed behavior, probability and decision making. The probability theory developed from the strategy of games and has been used in the prediction of behavior in several other fields. Already it is being suggested that, if human specifications can be recast into machine-compatible specifications, this "could give clarity and rigor to the language and concepts of psychology, and open the possibility of man-machine comparisons, cross-simulation studies, and substitution experiments."[24] Also, these experiments would make possible the scientific validation of hypotheses, and would be especially valuable if one wishes to use the machine to study any factor which is not accessible in people.[25]

The following hypotheses are presented with due regard to the dangers involved in contending that there might be a comparative relationship between the machine and man. Nevertheless, there seem to be no objections when engineers attempt to design better machines by studying the behavior of living organisms. This new science is known as *bionics*. The physical and behavioral sciences are now revising our notions of communication processes as they relate to physiologic signal analysis, neural control and self-regulating features of brain functioning. These disciplines are destined to play an ever-increasing role in medical education. It is for this reason that cybernetic principles are presented in this chapter.

THE FEEDBACK MODEL

The feedback principle, though not new, is a unique method for viewing things: it introduces a new model for *thinking about thinking*.[23] A good example of negative feedback is its use in walking. Kinesthetic and postural feedbacks from muscles, joints and tendons automatically make the corrective movements necessary for effective locomotion. The gait of an alcoholic or a tabetic is illustrative of disequilibrium or positive feedback. Here, some of the necessary feedbacks are missing, and this results in in-coordinated muscular activities of an oscillatory rather than a purposeful character. The placing of the feet has to be controlled visually—a less satisfactory substitute feedback.

In learning and adaptive responses to everyday life situations, the feedback principle constantly "monitors" behavioral response; the success or the failure of the results modifies future behavior. In other words, learning is by trial and error—adaptive. For instance, we have emphasized that, during hypnotic induction, the motivated subject automatically makes full use of his own internal feedback mechanisms (the ideosensory and ideomotor activities) for achieving a goal (hypnotic relaxation). Also, in the hypnotic interrelationship, patient and therapist use feedback mutually to improve their respective reactions to one another's communication processes. As these aspects of feedback mechanisms and cybernetics become more applicable to behavior disorders, the fundamental role and technics of hypnotherapy may greatly expand in this respect.

THE INFORMATION THEORY MODEL

It is not possible in a book of this type to treat the mathematics of information theory and its quantitative applications to the problems of information transmission, storage or its retrieval. For a deeper understanding of the scope and the application of information theory, the classical work of Shannon and Weaver[22] is recommended for those with mathematical training. However, an understanding of the principles of information theory is valuable even though one lacks a knowledge of higher mathematics. The following discussion will, therefore, avoid abstract mathematics, and will be directed to those with little or no previous acquaintance with probability or information theory.

The relevance of information theory to psychiatry has been described.[4] In psychotherapy, particularly in hypnosis, we are interested in meaningful measures of the *subjective or semantic value* of the information conveyed to a patient or to a therapist. If such measures are available, there is a possibility that scientific methods can be applied to a field which must otherwise remain an art. Therefore, it might be instructive to compare the technics employed by physical scientists in measuring and studying information, in the hope that information theory, allied with other theoretic and experimental work, will in the near future help to explain human communication processes on a more scientific basis.

In the physical sciences, the information in a message is defined in a purely statistical way without any reference *to the importance of the message*. The amount of information gained from receipt of a message is measured in terms of the amount of uncertainty removed by the message.* The resultant information, which leads to a reduction of uncertainty, enables decision making based on knowledge rather than on guesses. These ideas are intuitively obvious, but, until they are translated into the exact language of mathematics, it is not possible to formulate the concepts in other than loose verbal terms.

* Information gained $= \log \dfrac{\text{Probability of knowing the state of a system after receipt of the message}}{\text{Probability of knowing the state of a system before receipt of the message}}$

In engineering design, information theory answers some very basic questions as to the ability of a communication system to transfer information from sender to receiver in the presence of "noise"—defined as any type of interference. Even the clearest message can lose some of its meaningfulness before its reception. This is known as *entropy*, and some entropy occurs at all levels of human communication. However, the theory allows one to state explicitly how information is lost due to noise in the communication channel. Also it allows one to determine the extent to which the signal must be strengthened in order to transmit the desired amount of information in the presence of noise. This is a fundamental consideration in design of all communication or telemetry systems.

At the risk of oversimplification, these concepts seem particularly germane to the objectives of psychotherapeutic communication, especially during hypnosis. The hypnotherapist, acting as a transmitter, wishes to communicate or encode information to the patient as accurately and reliably as possible in the presence of noise. The noise may take the form of disturbing sounds in the environment or internal noise generated in the "receiver" (the patient) by virtue of his unreceptive attitudes or preoccupation with irrelevant thoughts. Understanding the technics used by the physical scientist to cope with the problems of noise may offer interesting possibilities for improving the two-way communication* during any interactional relationship.

The following simple illustrations show how the amount of information possessed (the ability to select from a large number of alternatives) allows correct predictions or decisions to be made. The unit of information is the binary digit or "bit." It represents the amount of information necessary to resolve two equally likely alternatives. Symbolically, these two alternatives may be represented as "yes" or "no," or "1" and "0." Using such a pair of symbols, it is possible to encode any message—a printed page, a symphony, a picture—with any de-

* For example, correlation technics are very effective in reducing the deleterious consequences of noise in electronic communications equipment.

sired degree of detail. For instance, a message which gives a person's sex contains one bit of information, since there are only two equally likely alternatives. To resolve 8 equally probable alternatives, a message containing 3 bits is required. The first bit reduces the alternatives from 8 to 4, the second bit from 4 to 2, and the third from 2 to 1. Thus, in general, each bit reduces the number of alternatives by one half.

It is believed that all of man's experiences, memory and thought are based on such simple particles of information. Every perception is a pattern of impulses—unique only in that certain nerve fibers "fire" digitally ("all," "yes" or "1"), while others do not ("none," "no" or "0").

McKay[14] believes that general information theory may provide a mathematical description of the nature of human behavior, that is, a reduction of all communication processes to statistical data. He further contends that the *thought processes of living organisms may soon be imitated by mechanical means.* Already it has been applied usefully to learning problems which involve discrimination, judgment and decision making.[13]

Our interest in this fascinating area is particularly relevant during hypnosis communication, in which the prime objective is to convey meaningful verbalizations in order to narrow the attention span to a given idea and, as a result, eliminate "noise" in the form of semantic confusion. This reduces *entropy* or the number of possible meanings or alternatives.

For example, messages which have a high specificity contain more bits of information than do generalities. Suggesting to a subject that he is not "asleep," "unconscious" or in a "trance" does not effectively convey information. On the other hand, telling the subject that *he is* in a state of relaxed attention identifies hypnosis as a positive state, and eliminates all alternatives. Hence the therapist must be *specific in saying what he means as well as meaning what he says!* One might say that the heightened perception or acuity characteristic of hypnosis acts as a filtering "device" similar to that used in machines for screening out irrelevant signals.

Communications systems which stress accuracy in the receipt of a message utilize a high level of redundancy (repetition of the same information). This applies particularly to hypnotic induction, in which, for instance, a phrase such as, "Your legs are getting heavier and heavier," is used again and again to obtain the correct ideosensory and ideomotor responses. Once these are identified as correct, the chances that the subject will make the same responses again will be greater than ever. With sufficient repetition, the correct responses will become a virtual certainty, that is, they will be learned automatically and become a "habit." It is by such "ideoid" phenomena that one's beliefs are processed into convictions.

This section has dealt primarily with some of the basic aspects of information theory. Very few comments have been made regarding semantic information, not because this subject is unimportant, but rather because there is at present no sound quantitative theory for treating semantic information. Statistical information theory, however, has relevance to semantics insofar as it tells us what confidence we can place in the information received as truly representing the information sent.

One might conclude that information theory provides insight for analyzing and improving storage and communication processes, but does not unravel the bewildering complexities associated with significance, meaning or value judgments.

THE THEORY OF GAMES MODEL

Von Neumann's[26] mathematical theory not only estimates the probabilities of outcome but makes decisions (best "bets") based upon a course of action which has the greatest *value* or *utility.* Since both of these are involved in motivation, the theory may have relevance to the psychology of individual learning. It may help to treat, in meaningful quantitative fashion, the outcome of an action that is not *completely determined.*

This theory closely parallels the field approach used in co-operative engineering. The old concept of cause and effect has been abandoned. A phenomenon is understood not as an effect but as an event taking place in a field, and every force in it, whether active or not, has some relationship to it. In order to produce a change, it is desirable to *ascertain which of the forces can be altered or eliminated to bring about the desired effect.* The goal is not to find the "cause" but rather *to discover a means of intervention.*[5] The physical scientist considers that we do not know the meaning of a concept unless we can detail the specific operations used in applying the concept in a concrete situation. Any abstraction which cannot be duplicated in terms of what the scientist does is considered unscientific. Thus such abstractions as "the underlying psychodynamics" or "hypnosis is nothing but suggestion" would be ruled out as meaningless constructs.

This approach is the essence of a relatively new concept called "operational analysis." It has much in common with the probabilistic game theory. Although developed independently, both are applicable to all situations in which a large number of variables have to be considered for increasing efficiency. This is particularly significant for medicine, especially psychotherapy, which is essentially a two-person interactional "game." Since game theory has apparently developed an approach to give the results of outcomes with certain theoretic assumptions for an unlimited number of multivariant processes, it may be that the "probability theory" can help us to evaluate how imaginative processes build up a notion of probability, calculate the odds and learn which decisions are most favorable based on these odds.

If higher nervous activities are to perform the task of making continuous predictions under the affective influence of a comparison of an imagined future with an experienced past, the brain must have available "counters" or images as the data ("bits" in the computer) for its computations.[17] These represent the elements of behavior patterns. Glaser[5a] states:

Among these are: (1) the image of the subject himself (the "I"); (2) an image of the "Non-I"—that is, of external objects, past and prospective; (3) an image of the somatic apparatus by which the individual contacts or makes an interchange with objects in the environment; (4) images of the instinctual apparatus; and (5) images of the entire constellation of instinctual processes. These are represented as tendencies either toward or away from the gratification of underlying instinctual needs, as well as the objects, through which this gratification can be either achieved or thwarted. There are images (6) of the individual's role, whether active or passive, (7) of the technics of consummation of need, (8) of the searching for the object, and (9) the operational processes. These make up the data (or counters) which the psychic computer manipulates. Finally all must be generalized and the final images are (10) the symbols representing these generalized concepts, and becoming the building blocks of fantasies, with their attendant affects which when pleasurable lead to the reinforcement of action, and when unpleasurable lead to repression or other forms of defense.

It is evident that such abstract properties of mind are supposed psychological entities. Modern neurophysiology ultimately must deal with physiologic units of brain function in terms of brain-computer analogies. For instance, the brain seems to function like a highly sophisticated model of a digital-analogue computer. By way of explanation, the digital machine performs numerical computations with incredible speed when the problems can be reduced to conventional arithmetic operations. The digital computer loosely approximates those of brain processes concerned with awareness and those which involve autonomic or reflex activities. The analogue machine attempts to solve a problem by recreating within the machine the physical circumstances which give rise to the problem and thus determine its outcome. It is useful for handling relatively complex situations. The cerebral mechanisms for those psychological functions which we now call, for want of a better name, unconscious and certain preconscious functions, approximate more closely the digital type of computer in their functioning.

There are other similarities of the brain to the digital machine. Control of an organism by thought processes is largely mediated by discrete or different distinct levels of neural functioning (digital). The execution of the digital "commands" are carried out in analogue fashion. For instance, humoral and endocrine functioning resembles the continuous levels of activity characteristic of analogue computers. It has been postulated that Pavlov's distinction between a primary signal system concerned with directly perceived stimuli and a secondary signal system devoted to verbal elaborations seems to parallel the above distinction between digital and analogue computers.[22a]

Because cybernetics has disregarded nonoperational and useless constructs, it is making rapid strides in explaining, not only how information is processed in the machine, but also how perception, learning and concept formation are processed in the nervous system. Therefore, brain-computer operational analogies will be discussed more fully in an attempt to explain the phenomenology of hypnosis—its evolution and function as an adaptive response mechanism not as a singular thing, but rather as a process basic and fundamental to the organism, which, like behavior, is multifaceted as well as fluctuating. The author fully realizes the speculative nature of these assumptions, but believes that they constitute a rational hypothesis that will help place the understanding of hypnosis on a more scientific basis.

ANALOGY BETWEEN COMPUTER AND BRAIN FUNCTION

As of now, machines are not capable of thinking. However, from a purely mechanistic standpoint, devices capable of a wide range of selective behavior based on evaluation of a large number of variables are being developed, but they are incapable, even remotely, of equaling the tremendous capacity of human recall, learning and perception.

Those who embrace the present highly formalized schools of psychology may object to a mechanistic approach since humanistic elements are ignored. But to conclude that research on the simulation of human behavior with a machine is wrong is somewhat analogous to saying that research on the simulation of the human heart with an artificial one is wrong because the latter organ is not a living one.

Let us examine some of the properties of living organisms which machines are capable of simulating. One of the key features of the behavior of living organisms is adaptability. This property can be simulated on the machine. Such a device automatically changes its internal structure in accordance with the environmental stimuli (input information signals) to function in a purposeful manner. This same adaptive property enables the mechanism to change from a positive to a negative feedback system by sensing and correcting its own performance. In the human, this trial and error process of learning causes physiochemical changes in the structure of the feedback networks to enable the organism to respond normally to the class of stimuli to which it has become adapted.

THEORETIC EVALUATION OF HYPNOTIC RESPONSES AND CONTROLLED ADAPTIVE BEHAVIOR BASED ON COMPUTER ANALOGIES

In the past, vague and nontestable formulations have been advanced to explain the nature of hypnosis and hypnotic responses. The reasons are obvious—these are built-in mechanisms—the resultant of responses developed during our genetic endowment and continually refined to give the organism greater adaptability.

My hypothesis is that hypnotic response was at one time a primitive adaptive mechanism which was necessary for survival. Its evolutionary development can be descriptively equated with that of the origin and behavior of modern computers.

Modern electronic "thinking" machines were originally developed as *special purpose computers* (S.P.C.) for solving relatively simple problems. As the physical sciences developed, it became necessary to perfect a machine that would solve a large variety of complex problems. Since the S.P.C. was inadequate, it inevitably evolved into the present large and complex *general purpose computer* (G.P.C.). However, in achieving this flexibility, the G.P.C.'s capability far exceeded the demands of limited problems. Nevertheless, when the G.P.C. is committed to limited problems it can solve them with amazing speed—but at a high cost for this increased celerity.

Although one cannot as yet demonstrate that analogies exist between computers and subcortical neurophysiologic systems, the evolutionary development of this model of automatic control closely parallels the evolutionary development of brain function before it is capable of analytic thinking, a comparatively recently acquired function. Early man had a primitive mechanism—the "nose-brain"—for sensing the world around him. Its function was specialized to receive nonverbal signals or impressions only through olfactory sensations. This was the only sense which provided information for coping with his environmental problems. In this respect, the simple behavior of the primitive nose-brain mechanism might be compared with that of the S.P.C.

As man's brain continued to evolve, other sensory stimuli, in the form of subverbal or preverbal suggestions, helped to shape his mental processes before he had the ability to think analytically and to adapt with a greater degree of affective feeling to environmental changes. A stage of development comparable with this archaic level of functioning is the behavior of anencephalic monsters and decorticated humans and animals, who apparently, in a primitive way, see, hear, taste, smell, utter crude sounds, cry and smile and react with pleasure or displeasure to pleasant and unpleasant stimuli.[3]

In this evolutionary process, as the cortex expanded from the ancient smell centers, the simple adaptive responses were integrated into the lower or the subcortical centers to provide an automatic system for maintaining vital functioning of the organism—homeostasis. One of the adaptive physiologic response mechanisms manifesting this "mechanical calming" of the organism was hypnosis, which has been known under various appellations from "nirvana" to "suggested sleep." The fact that spontaneous hypnoticlike behavior is noted, to a degree, in animals and humans strongly indicates that it is still largely dependent on autonomic functioning, and as such, therefore, is an inherited behavioral response mechanism in the human. It is also known that neural control of behavior, when it becomes more complex in the process of evolution, retains simpler mechanisms as higher centers are added.

In primitive man, before the development of analytic processes, simple ideas must have been accepted by primitive mechanisms. Suggestions must have been the process which fulfilled this function.[15] It is also at this psychophysiologically regressed level of mental functioning that suggestions are uncritically accepted and acted upon with precision by the human. Here, hypnotic response is strikingly similar to the limited-goal behavior of the S.P.C., that is, when arousal or perceptivity is high, and when the cognitive processes are directed toward a special purpose, a hypnotic subject behaves like an efficient S.P.C. This regression is in rather sharp contrast with the logical and highly analytic but generalized mental functioning characteristic of nonhypnotic states.

Therefore, it is plausible to conclude that when an organism can have its sensing apparatus respond selectively to specific inputs, with its *fullest* cognitive capacities, as during hypnosis, such functioning is a reversion to a more primitive adaptive level. The evidence cited below points to hypnosis as being an atavistic state or psychophysiologic regression serving as a substratum for the latter development of more complex life experiences. The author was among the first to postulate the atavism or regression hypothesis as an explanation for hypnotic behavior.[9] He stated:

The hypnotic state at one time may have been necessary in humans as a protective defense mechanism . . . the hypnotic state may be an *atavistic reversion* analogous to the inanimate state of catalepsy so commonly observed in frightened animals when they "freeze to the landscape" in order to escape detection, the difference being that the presence of fully developed cortex in the human now makes unnecessary various instinctive defense mechanisms.

Later, several theoretic concepts based on a phylogenetic core were proposed: The hypnotic state was visualized as a condition which represented the most primitive form of psychophysiologic awareness of individual environment differentiation attainable among living organisms; this capacity was to some degree retained in all biologic systems.[21] Guze[6] states that hypnosis may be defined as "a state of readiness for emotional action increasingly subordinated to cortical influence as one ascends phylogeny but nonetheless consistently present in animal organisms in a variety of forms."

The concept that suggestibility is an archaic mental function thus can be used to explain the nature of hypnosis. According to Meares,[16] the regression is not at the *behavioral* level but rather at the perceptual or *mental functioning* level. It is not implied that primitive man lived in a constant state of hypnosis; rather, that in the phylogenetic development of the nervous system, higher functions retained the ability to control the more primitive functions to a greater or a lesser degree. Hypnosis was one of these autonomic primitive functions to maintain homeostasis or a "steady state" in the organism.

The ability of man to survive is due largely to these autonomic functions built into the lower brain centers for selectively handling incoming information. This frees the cortex for the more specialized complex problems of adaptation. Similarly, when hypnosis is used to increase adaptive cortical responses, a comparison can be made with the G.P.C. operating with its total capacity directed toward a specific problem. This, too, represents an operational regression or purposeful reversal in computer operation, that is, a highly developed device (G.P.C.) being used instead of an S.P.C. to solve an elementary or primitive problem.

RELATIONSHIP OF NEUROPHYSIOLOGY TO
PSYCHIC PROCESSES AND HYPNOSIS

Neurophysiologic data[11] which tend to confirm our hypothesis are as follows: The reticular activating system (R.A.S.), phylogenetically speaking, is an ancient brain structure. Before the full development of cortical structures, the R.A.S. played an even more important role in regulating behavior, probably that of maintaining greater arousal. However, in the modern brain, the ascending reticular activating system (A.R.A.S.) can now selectively filter incoming sensory stimuli not only for maintaining selective arousal but for integrating incoming sensory information with awareness. This is significant in regard to autonomic responses, movements and sensations.

With reference to adaptive ability, higher nervous activity is apparently Pavlovian in type. As proof, Anokhin[1] showed that the A.R.A.S. specifically and selectively involved *only some* of the synaptic endings in the brain stem. He demonstrated this by involving biologically opposite activities, as eating and defense, which could occur only through different functional systems. The importance of this observation is that all biologic activities consist of continuous formation of newly established conditional reflexes on the basis of unconditioned stimuli of different quality.

This implies that the A.R.A.S. and the limbic lobes, to some degree, in the brain's hierarchy of other structures, govern discriminatory functioning during hypnosis. This is obtained by maintaining arousal of the cortex (selective attention or excitation), while simultaneously excluding irrelevant stimuli from awareness (selective inattention or active, concentrated inhibition). (See Chap. 27.)

The arousal results either when narrowing of the attention span occurs in response to monotonic stimuli, or when there is an input-overload. In the latter instance, the high degree of arousal induced by strong emotions or vigorous stimulation tends to prevent extraneous sensory stimuli from reaching cortical awareness. Here, the law of dominant effect is followed; a strong stimulus displaces a weaker one.

It seems also that whenever the integrity of the organism is threatened by imminent danger, the A.R.A.S. allows such vital and important information to be forwarded to the cortex for discrimination and instantaneous arousal. For instance, a sleeping person generally awakens in response to a strange sound such as a footstep, but is able to sleep through much louder noises such as routine traffic.

Likewise, in hypnosis, arousal is maintained by limiting the patient's attention-span to specific input information from the operator. The limiting process may be due to a summation effect reaching threshold levels or saturation of the A.R.A.S. Here there is full utilization of its pathways. West[27] contends that feedback mechanisms limit "nearly all additional information regardless of its significance under ordinary circumstances of adaptation."

However, it appears that a feedback process is not necessary to explain the functioning of the A.R.A.S. under such conditions. It may be that the saturation is analogous to what happens under similar circumstances in electronic systems which filter information at their input to exclude less important or unnecessary information. In short, the A.R.A.S. reduces the saturation threshold to zero for all sensory inputs except those selectively permitted to get through to higher centers. As a result, selective attention exists—as mentioned above, to the exclusion of reality, i.e., internal inhibition.

In Chapter 3, it also was pointed out that Pavlov was the first to note this neural mechanism—internal inhibition—as it related to the neurophysiology of hypnosis. He observed that hypnosis had an inhibitory character; that is, the cortical neurons became, as it were, weaker and less efficient, the maximum limit of their possible excitability diminished. This hypothesis, too, fits in with the saturation threshold hypothesis.

The inhibitory character of internal inhibition during hypnosis also has a *protective* feature similar to the nonspecific therapeutic effect of sleep and tranquilizers in emotionally disturbed individuals. This has been borne out by recent Russian experiments involving toposcopic examination.[*] In this procedure, oscilloscopic representations of the brain's electrical potentials make a bioelectric mosaic or pattern of different cortical areas. In well-adjusted persons, the resultant bioelectric mosaic shows continual and rapid changes in potential distributed at random over the cortex. In severely disturbed individuals, such as psychotics, the changes in the mosaic are greatly reduced. Tranquilizers, sleep (generalized inhibition) and hypnosis (partial inhibition) increased the activity of the

bioelectric mosaic (converted it to a normal pattern).

Particularly interesting in this respect is the use of hypnotic suggestion to inhibit specific or nonspecific stressors, such as harmful words, thoughts and memories. Hypnotic suggestion directed to elimination of conditioned and unconditioned stimuli results in their inhibition.[†] The stimulation excluded by the suggestion acquires the characteristics of conditioned inhibition (neutralization of a harmful conditioned or unconditioned **stimulus.**)

The neurophysiologic data supports Pavlov's thesis that emotional disorders are brought about by increased excitation of neurons, and that hypnosis (*protective sleep inhibition*) or even actual sleep prevents exhaustion or destruction of neurons, with consequent improvement.

Leading neurophysiologists are now urging reconsideration of internal inhibition as the neural mechanism which can be utilized in psychotherapy. Magoun[‡] points out that "If the inferences drawn from these many contributions (Pavlovian concepts) are correct, this is a brain mechanism whose function psychiatry must ultimately incorporate into its conceptions of inhibitions in mental activity and, I urge it, in understanding of the wellness and illness of the the mind."

COMMENTS ON ADAPTIVE CONTROL SYSTEMS AS THEY MAY RELATE TO PSYCHOTHERAPY

In order to gain some insight into the complex processes which take place in psychotherapy, it is instructive to compare the subject's response in psychotherapy with the response characteristics of adaptive servomechanisms. Since some modern electronic systems have the ability to adapt to their environment, these comparisons are becoming more meaningful.

In comparing electronic and human systems, the environment consists of the signals

[*] Snezhnevsky, A. V.: Paper delivered at First Conference on Higher Nervous Activity, Medical News, Nov. 9, 1960.

[†] Korofkin, I. I., and Suslova, M. M.: On the Neural Mechanisms of Hypnosis *in* Psychotherapy in the Soviet Union (Winn, R. B., ed.), New York Philosophical Library, 1961.

[‡] Magoun, H. W.: Discussion of Ref. No. 1. (Anokhin.)

(stimuli) as well as the electrical noise and interference (specific or nonspecific stress), which appear as inputs (afferent stimuli).

The internal structures of these systems are allowed to vary so that the systems can learn from previous experience how to process the input information ("think") in an optimal way (successful adaptation). For example, if the positive feedback or the noise input to the system in a given frequency range is excessive, the system will reject this noise by means of a rejection filter centered at the noise frequency (scanning mechanisms). The system does this at the risk of rejecting useful information which may be centered at the same frequency. However, the system design essentially is based on the decision that it is preferable to run the risk of losing useful signals in a given frequency range rather than to allow the system to be swamped by noise which would prevent it from accepting useful information at other frequencies. This is rather similar to the physiologic functioning of the A.R.A.S.

Thus, these adaptive systems react to interfering signals (stress) in a manner much like that of physiologic systems. For example, if an interfering signal causes instability, the system detects its own unstable behavior and causes the adjustable components in the system to change values so that the instability is decreased. In other words, after the system has been exposed to the signal environment for a period of time, it has learned where to place its rejection filters and how to adjust its internal structure to prevent unstable modes of behavior.

Automatic control systems used in engineering, like many analogous physiologic control systems, are stable in behavior when the input signal or stimuli are of one type and unstable when these signals or stimuli are of another type. In the adaptive control system, the system is required to adapt so that its mode of behavior will be stable when subjected to either type of input signal. The significance for psychophysiology, in studying the engineering uses of adaptive systems, is that it now appears possible to attempt a quantitative study of adaptive

psychophysiologic behavior with simulated physiologic control systems.

The communications which take place between the psychotherapist and the subject, irrespective of whether the approach is permissive or directive, may be looked upon as a rather complex form of directed adaptive behavior. The psychotherapist may be thought of as providing the input signal environment, while the subject may be considered as the adaptive system which adjusts its behavior parameters (psychophysiologic variables) to conform with the environmental stimuli (inputs). As in engineering systems, the ability of the subject to adapt is a strong function of his present state. Also, if the range of adjustment required to cause stable behavior is very large, the parameters of the system may be unable to change their values enough to achieve stability. In engineering systems, such a situation would necessitate revision of the adaptive system to allow its adjustment parameters to be varied over wider ranges. The speculative implications to be drawn from this in the case of psychotherapy suggest that those subjects who do not respond require another approach, perhaps a revision or a restructuring of the therapeutic design.

NEUROPHYSIOLOGIC THEORIES OF MEMORY

Older theories of memory and learning maintained that experiences left "etchings" on the brain as traces. Still others contend that memory traces depended upon decreased synaptic resistances, with the resultant establishment of well-grooved pathways. These have been invalidated by pavlovian "learning," which is not confined to the cortex. Nor is memory limited to the midbrain or the brain stem, although some storage of information takes place in these areas. Localized memory traces apparently have been demonstrated also as a function of the temporal lobes.[18] However, the data are inconclusive as yet. Other theories are that "experiences establish perceptual patterns of potential gradients in cortical electrical fields" or "resonance patterns occur in neural loops to produce altered physio-chemical changes."[10]

The recently developed complex general computer stores "bits" of information as electrical pulses, which continually revolve until needed for computation. Since these pulses are not specifically located, they are referred to as "functional" or random memory; changes are not stored in a definite manner. Recent neurophysiologic data[23] also indicate that human memory is random in nature, because no special part of the brain stores it—a wise provision in case of accident.

As further evidence that memory is random, it has been hypothesized that the two-way feedback or reverberating neuronal chains are capable of manipulating thought according to symbolic or mathematical logic.[12] Lashley's[10] alternative theories are that memory is due to "potential gradients in electrical fields" or that "resonance patterns in neural loops" account for it. Pringle[19] postulates a model of closed chains of neurons which act as "loosely coupled oscillators," similar to those occurring in the brain. Irrespective of the validity of the above theories involving reverberating neural loops, it is certain that physiochemical alteration takes place in the circulating neuron chains to preserve "memories." This is more in accord with the most recent theory that every incoming percept leaves its trace by alterations in the arrangement of the large protein molecules of the neuron.

Hyden[7] has demonstrated that some stimuli alter the ribonucleic acid (RNA) molecules of the neurons which cause the synthesis of altered protein molecules that are stored as "bits" of information or memory traces. It is believed that the frequency modulation set up in a neuron by a specific stimulus may prescribe the arrangement of the RNA components (and thus of proteins) which acts as a code to pass on information to other neurons. In this way, whole chains of neurons can be molecularly conditioned to react to the repetition of a stimulus. From a statistical viewpoint, the molecules furnish the required permutation possibilities for the storage of all the bits of information received in a lifetime. Thus, the recall of past experiences as memories is made possible.

The best clinical data on the recovery of memory traces is Penfield's[18] work, cited earlier. It is interesting that a single recollection was recalled, not a mixture of memories or a generalization, as in ordinary memory. The evoked reaction was an exact reproduction of what the patient saw, heard, felt and understood.

It seems that the memory records of all experiences are recorded by patterns of previous passage of nerve impulses. The patterns of neuronal memories are duplicated in both hemispheres since the removal of most of one lobe does not interfere with recollection. It is believed that these records are located in the centrencephalic circuits in the higher brain stem. Every experience seems to have access to both temporal lobes and evidently remains unchanged with the passage of time.

As discussed in Chapters 28 and 29, this may be the explanation for age-regression, revivification, sensory-imagery conditioning and hypnotic self-exploration. Scanning mechanisms unite stored memories with selected ideas, former experiences, and relate them to the incoming sensory percepts. Since peculiar disorders of memory also occur with lesions around the third ventricle, there are two other areas involved in various types of memory in addition to the temporal lobes, namely, the upper brain stem and the periaqueductal region.

These memory mechanisms also operate during dream states, reverie, hypnosis and other dissociated states, the degree depending on selective "filtering," mediated chiefly by the reticular activating system. Since hypnosis is a state of hyperacuity, one would infer that greater arousal is being maintained to a selected input than during ordinary attention. The only difference is that, in hypnosis, the discriminatory ability of the cortex is held in selective inhibition. Normally, the cortex does not accept incoming information without prior computation. If stored data are not available for computation, unreality is accepted as reality—hypnosis.

Raginsky[20] described how the symptoms of syncope and temporary cardiac arrest were induced under hypnosis in a patient who had been operated on for a so-called Stokes-Adams syndrome and who had, until the time of the experiment, remained free of such symptoms. Since the memory was sequential (always moved forward) in this patient as well as in several others, it was felt that hypnotic recall closely parallels electrical stimulation. If this is true, then hypnotic recall is purer or more accurate than the recalls elicited by psychotherapy, in which patients bring up generalized memories or those that have been modified by subsequent thinking or experiences (screen memories).

IMPORTANCE OF PSYCHOCYBERNETICS TO THERAPY

It has been pointed out that what the learner does in successive trials is regulated by the results of his performance—feedback. Incorrect responses usually are replaced by successful responses and, when these are remembered and automatically reinforced, they become adaptive or maladaptive habit patterns. However, incorrect responses or failures usually are forgotten and replaced by successful ones. There are numerous examples of how feedback modifies faulty behavioral responses. For instance, constructive self-criticism can correct maladaptive behavior to bring about a desirable state or goal. However, too much criticism is disastrous and is synonymous with psychological inhibition.

Kline[8] has demonstrated that a continual delayed-speech (positive) feedback at nonhypnotic levels, with the inability to defend oneself against this feedback, produces acute emotional disorganization and signs of stress and psychopathologic behavior. These reactions to positive or excessive physical feedback can be inhibited by hypnosis. He believes that not only does the importance of hypnosis lie in the fact that it is a perceptual mechanism, but also that hypnosis is capable of blocking and masking many of the effects of feedback.

Extreme carefulness or fear of error is a form of excessive feedback. This dynamism is noted in the stutterer who, in the presence of increased fear, develops bad motor response patterns because of inhibition. By having the stutterer listen to his own voice, negative auditory feedback automatically monitors correction of the speech. In the section on stuttering in Chapter 41, it is suggested that the patient listen under hypnosis to the playback of a tape recording of his own voice, speaking *normally*. Faulty enunciation, tone and such other impediments as blocking are quickly discerned and therefore readily corrected. Optimal functioning is established more effectively under hypnosis because the learned responses make use of the built-in reflexes, and, as a result, are eventually utilized automatically in a more spontaneous manner. The only danger is that overcorrection makes the stutterer too self-conscious, and, as a result, he worsens (inhibition).

Autohypnosis and sensory-imagery conditioning can alter behavioral responses either positively or negatively. If positively, purposeful behavior is brought about by healthy autosuggestions (input), which result in proper physiologic responses (output), and then a part of these regulate further "input" to control the behavior of the system to achieve equilibrium.

In a previous chapter it was noted that the brain can only process sensory percepts and correlate them with stored impressions. If the resultant computations are perceived as harmful, then a negative self-image is produced. Everyone has special images of himself and the environment, and behaves as though the images were real rather than imagined. At the risk of oversimplification, if an individual can imagine himself sick, he also can imagine himself well. Under hypnotic sensory-imagery conditioning, many "dry runs" can be processed to implant healthy convictions based on the stored data. A new image of the self is achieved by replacing negatively stored images by positive ones. As a result, new reaction patterns are formed which become available for involuntary functioning to maintain healthy adjustments. The well-adapted individual no longer has to check his mental (How am I doing?") feedbacks, but, rather, can be more concerned with goal-directed activities. In general, it is the purpose of positive hypnotherapeutic suggestions to make available the *healthy stored data* in order to inhibit harmful impressions (disinhibition). This allows the subject to perceive and cope with reality in a more effectual manner.

With the advent of recent cybernetic concepts, the capabilities ascribed solely to humans are being chipped away slowly. Computers designed to model human mental processes can now simulate problem-solving, learning and decision making. Computers are making possible a much more intensive search for factual observations of multivariant functional relationships. It is hoped that these developments not only will give us a theoretic explanation of corresponding human behavior, but will help also to explain memory mechanisms, the bridge between nerve impulses and thought, and the continuum of awareness ranging from hypnosis to sleep.

REFERENCES

1. Anokhin, P. K.: Paper delivered at First Pavlovian Conference on Higher Nervous Activity, Medical News, Nov. 9, 1960.
2. Ashby, W. R.: Design for a Brain, New York, Wiley, 1952.
3. Cairns, H.: Disturbances of consciousness with lesions of the brain stem and diencephalon, Brain 75:109, 1952.
4. Crider, D. B.: Cybernetics: a review of what it means and some of its applications to psychiatry, Neuropsychiat. 4:35-38, 1956-57.
5. Dunbar, H. F.: Anxiety, stress and tuberculosis *in* Sparer, P. J. (ed.): Personality, Stress and Tuberculosis, p. 211, New York, Int. Univ. Press, 1956.
5a. Glaser, G. H.: Panel Discussion: Recent concepts of central neurophysiology; their bearing on psychosomatic phenomena, Psychosom. Med., Sept.-Oct., 1955.
6. Guze, H.: Hypnosis as emotional response, J. Psychol. 35:313, 1953.
7. Hyden, H.: Paper read at symposium, Control of the Mind, Univ. of Calif., Feb. 27, 1961.
8. Kline, M. V.: An experimental study of the

9. Kroger, W. S., and Freed, S. C.: Psychosomatic Gynecology, p. 127, Phila., W. B. Saunders, 1951; reprinted, Los Angeles, Wilshire Book Co., 1962.
10. Lashley, K. S.: In Search of the Engram, Soc. Exper. Biology Symposia 4: Physiological Mechanisms in Animal Behavior, C.U.P., Cambridge, 1950.
11. Livingston, R. B.: Some brain stem mechanisms relating to psychosomatic functions, Psychosomatic Med. 17:351, 1955.
12. McCulloch, W. S., and Pitts, W.: A logical calculus of the ideas imminent in nervous activity, Bull. Math. Biophysics, vol. 5, 1953.
13. McGill, W. J.: Applications of information theory in experimental psychology, Bull. New York Acad. Science 19:343-350, 1957.
14. McKay, D. M.: In Search of Basic Symbols, Cybernetics, New York, J. Macy Found., 1951.
15. Meares, A.: A System of Medical Hypnosis. Phila., Saunders, 1961.
16. *Ibid.*
17. Ostrow, M.: Psychic contents and processes of the brain, Psychosomatic Med. 17:396-406, 1955.
18. Penfield, W.: The role of the temporal cortex in certain psychical phenomena, J. Ment. Sc. 101:451-465, 1955.
19. Pringle, J. W. S.: On the parallel between learning and evolution, Behavior, vol. 3, 1951.
20. Raginsky, B. B.: Temporary cardiac arrest induced under hypnosis, Int. J. Clin. & Exper. Hypnosis 7:53-68, 1959.
21. Schneck, J. M.: A theory of hypnosis, J. Clin. Exper. Hyp. 1:16, 1953.
22. Shannon, C. E., and Weaver, W.: The Mathematical Theory of Communication, Urbana, Ill., Univ. of Ill. Press, 1949.
22a. Simon, B. (ed.): Psychology in the Soviet Union, Stanford, Calif., Stanford Univ. Press, 1957.
23. Sluckin, W.: Minds and Machines, England, Pelican Books, 1954.
24. Uhr, L., and Vossler, C.: Suggestions for self-adapting computer models of brain functions, Behavioral Science 6:91, 1961.
25. *Ibid.*
26. Von Neumann, J., and Morgenstern, O.: Theory of Games and Economic Behavior, Princeton Univ. Press, 1944.

nature of hypnotic deafness: effects of delayed speech feedback, J. Clin. & Exper. Hyp. 2:145-156, 1954.

27. West, L. J.: Psychophysiology of Hypnosis, J.A.M.A. *172*:673, 1960.
28. Wiener, N.: Cybernetics, New York, Wiley, 1948.

ADDITIONAL REFERENCES

Coburn, H. E.: The brain analogy, Psychological Review, vol. 58, 1951.

Craik, K. J. W.: The Nature of Explanation, C.U.P., Cambridge, 1943.

Hilgard, E. R.: Theories of Learning, Appleton-Century-Crofts, New York, 1948.

McCulloch, W. S.: The brain as a computing machine, Electrical Engineering, vol. 68, 1949.

MacKay, D. M.: Mentality in Machines, Proceedings of the Aristotelian Society, 1952.

Rashevsky, N.: The neural mechanism of logical thinking, Bull. Math. Biophysics, vol. 8, 1946.

Thomson, R., and Sluckin, W.: Cybernetics and mental functioning, Brit. J. for the Philosophy of Science, vol. 3, 1953.

Walter, W. G.: Possible features of brain function and their imitation, Symposium on Information Theory, London, Ministry of Supply, 1950 (reprinted 1953).

Wisdom, J. O.: The hypothesis of cybernetics, Brit. J. for the Philosophy of Science, vol. 2, 1951.

SUPPLEMENTARY READING

Blum, G. S.: A Model of the Mind, New York, Wiley, 1961.

Hebb, D. O.: The Organization of Behavior: A Neuropsychological Theory, New York, Wiley, 1949.

Reiff, R., and Scheerer, M.: Memory and Hypnotic Age Regression: Developmental Aspects of Cognitive Function Explored Through Hypnosis, New York, International Universities Press, 1959.

Rosenblatt, Frank: Principles of Neurodynamics. Perceptions of Neurodynamics. Perceptions and the Theory of Brain Mechanisms, Washington, D. C., Spartan Books, 1962.

Sheer, D. E. (ed.): Electrical Stimulation of the Brain: An Interdisciplinary Survey of Neurobehavioral Integrative Systems, Austin, Tex., Univ. of Texas Press, 1961.

31

Hypnosis in Internal Medicine

REASONS FOR USE

Suggestion (in its most potent form—hypnosis) establishes the capacity for conditioning and formation of habit patterns that exceeds those that are developed at ordinary levels. Thus, reassurance, re-education and deconditioning are more durable than when employed at nonhypnotic levels. When repetitive reinforcement through autohypnosis is utilized, healthy responses become autonomous. It is this self-sustaining feature of hypnotic conditioning that reverses faulty thinking processes and behavior patterns responsible for maintenance of stress associated with a wide variety of psychosomatic disorders.

There is no reason why hypnotic conditioning cannot be combined with drugs when the latter are indicated as part of a comprehensive treatment program. For instance, hypnotic conditioning can reduce the fears and anxieties which exacerbate attacks in cardiacs to instill optimism and feelings of well being. This can mean the difference between life and death. Recognized, but not generally appreciated is that preoccupation with structural heart disease can spark a chain reaction leading to generalized anxiety and harmful sequelae.

However, even when hypnotic conditioning is used alone for symptomatic control, it can be employed *in the same judicious manner as a drug.* Is not the bulk of medical therapy directed toward symptom relief? And why should not psychogenically based symptoms removed by hypnosis respond similarly to those eliminated by physical and drug measures? There are no well-controlled studies to support the contention that other symptom-equivalents take the place of the original one.

For refractory cases, hypnotic conditioning can be incorporated with uncovering types of psychotherapy by psychiatrically oriented physicians to provide an understanding of what the *symptom means to the patient* (secondary gain value); how much of it he wishes to yield; and, most important, how he can face his problems and life situations in a more realistic and mature manner rather than resorting to infantile methods of coping with them.

Hypnotic conditioning also modifies or ameliorates organic conditions having a large psychogenic component; this occurs irrespective of whether the latter produced the illness or is the result of an organic disease. Each case is different because of the individual peculiarities of man's adaptive responses, conditioned as he is by the complexity of life's experiences. Therefore, whenever possible, a detailed life history is necessary to disclose the degree of emotional involvement, the conditions under which the pathophysiologic processes developed, and the strengths and weaknesses of the personality. This helps determine the degree of emotional support that will best motivate the patient during the initial phases of therapy when progress is imperceptible. Such an approach also helps structure the therapeutic goals.

Hypnotherapy should be used in carefully evaluated cases that have been screened by a thorough physical examination to establish the diagnosis. However, it is *not* a panacea for the illnesses of mankind. What is seldom realized is that hypnotic conditioning is a naturalistic behavioral property inherently present in humans. Recognized or unrecognized, it is part and parcel of most therapeutic procedures.

Hypnorelaxation generally expedites therapy, particularly in those who are affect-blocked; the increased concentration and co-operation allow them to talk more freely about their problems. As a result, the greater self-objectivity provides new ideas and understandings of the nature of their symptoms. Where indicated, in suitable subjects, posthypnotic suggestions temporarily can suppress a symptom or "hold it on leash" until the inordinate need for the symptom is understood and ready to be relinquished.

Autohypnosis also can be employed for self-exploration—when the symptom is removed by the patient rather than by the therapist, this accomplishment leads to longer lasting results. Artificially hypnotically induced conflicts, in amenable subjects, often help resistant individuals recognize the "how" and "why" of their emotionally based disorders. After this knowledge is obtained, appropriate posthypnotic suggestions can be used to channel the harmful drives produced by a symptom-complex into more constructive outlets. Often, "trading down" or substituting a more innocuous symptom is helpful in this regard (see Chapter 47).

A prime indication for hypnotherapy is the hypochondriasis induced by alarmist health columns, magazine articles or remarks of well-meaning friends. The doctor, too, by ill-considered statements, a "polypragmatic" approach, an inadequate history or a careless physical examination, can unwittingly generate anxiety.

Another distinct advantage of hypnotic conditioning is that firmly established rapport acts to "bind the anxiety-ridden patient in therapy" during the initial phases of any psychotherapeutic relationship. It is at this crucial period that most emotionally disturbed individuals, through one rationalization or another, defeat the therapist by prematurely breaking off treatment, with the result that they then can cling to their neurotic behavior patterns without guilt and tension.

PSYCHOSOMATIC CARDIOVASCULAR DISORDERS

Essential Hypertension

In essential hypertension, stress due to chronic and inhibited rage is considered *one*

important factor. The symptom often represents the individual's "cold war with his environment," manifesting itself as a sympathetico-adrenal, salt-retaining, blood-pressure-raising response. Since relaxation, sedatives and tranquilizers temporarily reduce the blood pressure, a stress factor apparently is operative.

Posthypnotic suggestions, together with sensory-imagery conditioning under autohypnosis, potentiate drug therapy to reduce the blood pressure. This cannot lightly be dismissed "as nothing but suggestion," as, in this state, conditioning phenomena, as disturbed feedback mechanisms, faulty associative learning patterns, and harmful stimuli, can be significantly altered. Thus it can be understood why this type of hypnotherapy is more effective than directive hypnosis. This new approach also is far superior to the old bromides such as, "You must take it easy and learn to relax." Or, "Why don't you just quit worrying?" Individuals with other types of hypertension can be taught specifically how to relax and to develop a better comprehension of their problems as well as their capabilities to cope with their everyday tensions.

Often, a disarming façade of calm co-operativeness in hypertensives obscures their aggressive drives. Many are depressed, threatened and easily frustrated because of their hostile dependency needs. However, modification or correction of these needs is often a difficult task with almost any type of therapy; relapses are commonly noted. In cases in which physical rest has been prescribed, the psychic stress of merely being inactive often raises the blood pressure. Here, modified activity and mental rest by sensory-imagery conditioning is an ideal combination for all types of hypertensives.

The following case, though briefly discussed, is illustrative of technics directed toward limited goals:

A young man was rejected for insurance because of essential hypertension which occurred especially when he was examined. His blood pressure fluctuated between 150/80 and 170/100. The history revealed that he had a frigid, demanding wife, a passive nature, dominating parents and a sadistic employer. His wife related that "My husband is more of a mouse than a man. I've lost all my respect for him and also all my sexual feelings." The need to assert himself with his wife, parents and employer was discussed. Taking his blood pressure frequently while he was hypnotized also had the effect of deconditioning him; it stabilized around the 140/80 level. Autohypnosis and sensory-imagery conditioning, together with the adoption of healthy attitudes toward those whom he feared and resented, reduced his tensions. Three months later he was accepted for insurance. Posthypnotic suggestions were employed to have him imagine the memory of a relaxing experience whenever his blood pressure was checked. During the third visit, his blood pressure dropped to 130/70.

Hypnotic conditioning, combined with supportive psychotherapy, was most effective. Autohypnosis should be reinforced at necessary intervals.

PSYCHOGENIC CARDIAC DISORDERS

Arrhythmias, Effort Syndrome and Palpitation

Paroxysmal tachycardia, extrasystoles and arrythmias can be produced by spontaneous recall of traumatic memories. Doubt as to the integrity of the heart can result in alteration of the rate and rhythm. Fright, anxiety and sudden shock are commonly associated with precordial pain.

Deconditioning, consisting of pleasant associations under hypnosis, often can relieve functional chest pain and associated symptoms in tense and anxious patients. Reflex conditioning of the heart to produce a rise in blood pressure and tachycardia, or bradycardia, has been demonstrated (the Danini-Aschner phenomenon).[36a]

Other functional disorders of the heart respond to hypnotic conditioning directed primarily to symptom-removal.[28] To illustrate:

A young man who became "heart conscious" after being told that he had a "murmur," was helped by strong reassurance and explanation under hypnosis that his heart was in good condition, and that he could expect to live out his natural life span. He was convinced of this only after appropriate posthypnotic suggestions accelerated the heart, and reproduced the same oppressive precordial feelings that had caused his worry.

Hypnotic age-regression has been successfully utilized to re-experience and relieve arrhythmias due to rheumatic fever in childhood.[56] When the symptoms are functional in origin, hypnotic symptom-removal is particularly effective.[27]

If the arrhythmias can be related to specific situations, the results are excellent if the patient is conditioned not to overreact to strong emotional stimuli: This is not surprising, as cortical regulatory mechanisms acting through specific nuclei of the hypothalamus affect the rate and rhythm of the heart, and are responsible for premature beats and paroxysmal tachycardia.

Suggesting conflictual situations to hypnotized patients has resulted in either the production or the elimination of extrasystoles. Creation of serene feelings eliminated the extrasystoles. Revivification of a combat scene, which resulted in abreaction of an affect-charged experience, produced complete recovery in a case of psychogenic heart disease.[44] These cases, as well as others discussed in this volume, apparently confirm Pavlov's observations that *traces of past experiences are indelibly "etched" in the brain, and can be activated by the proper associational reflexes.* It also appears that when some degree of abreaction of highly charged emotional material is relived under hypnosis, the resultant deconditioning significantly aids recovery.

In many instances, doctor-patient rapport is as effective as most of the vasodilating drugs in relieving even the pain of angina pectoris.[3a] The placebo effect of pharmacologic agents in cardiac disorders is well recognized. Therefore, if placebos are effective, then hypnotic inhibition of excitatory stimuli should afford even greater relief.

The author recently treated a colleague who had functional chest pain and extrasystoles, which began after he was unable to collect a large sum of money loaned to a friend. He generally developed the precordial pain at night, while thinking of how he could retaliate against his friend. Although intellectually aware of the associations responsible for the discomfort, there was no response to superficial psychotherapy or drugs. Temporary relief occurred only after he had been taught to develop glove anesthesia under autohypnosis. Complete relief was established only after repeated posthypnotic suggestions were given to decrease the significance of the incident.

Direct suggestions under hypnosis have relieved cases of chronic palpitation.[50] Raginsky[39] reinduced a stoppage of the heart in a patient who had been operated for a carotid sinus syndrome several years before. The cardiac arrest had not occurred since the surgery. It was reproduced by posthypnotic suggestions to revivify the "attack," and it was re-experienced with all its original manifestations and intensity. In spite of the absence of the carotid bodies, the objective findings of cardiac arrest were demonstrable in the serial electrocardiograms!

Coronary Disease

Raginsky[40] performed an immediate "hypnotic leukotomy" on several patients with coronary occlusion. In one case, a man developed a massive cardiac infarct while he was at the patient's home. Prompt hypnotization reduced the pain, anxiety and shock, and the patient was rushed to the hospital. Subsequent electrocardiograms indicated definitive improvement. He attributed the successful outcome to the hypnotic relaxation, as no other measures were employed. Of course, recovery could have been due to coincidental factors.

Recent data[42] indicate that acute or chronic stress is an important factor in the production of coronary disease, especially if obesity, hypertension and hypercholesteremia are present. Emotional tension per se can elevate serum cholesterol up to 35 mg. in an hour. In some cases of coronary insufficiency, it is difficult to understand how a patient can do a large amount of physical work at times and yet be unable to walk up a flight of stairs. Some sufferers have attacks while performing light physical duties and yet have no difficulties during more strenuous tasks. Levine[31] remarks, "There is much about all this that makes one think of a conditional reflex. The number of foot-pounds of work is not the whole story." In this regard, Platonov[36a] describes how cardiac output can be improved by appropriate hypnotic conditioning.

Particularly pertinent to coronary disease are recent studies[10] made possible by hypnotic conditioning and sensory-imagery technics to indicate that induced depression, anger and fear are associated with an increase in the free fatty acids in the blood stream. The emotions equaled those experienced as reality situations in the past. Here is proof positive that the ability to experience sensory distortion in hypnosis is correlated with the ability to respond physiologically to hypnotically suggested emotion.

Many heart sufferers can live out their life span if they recognize their limitations, learn how to relax and develop new interests. To minimize acute anxiety produced by aggravating situations, positive hypnosuggestions can augment tranquilizers and sedatives. Hypnosis also mobilizes faith and the "will to live." Unfortunately, not every heart victim is susceptible to deep hypnosis. However, even light hypnosis potentiates narcotics and sedatives, and can help those who react poorly to these drugs. Unquestionably, thoughts of death and impending doom take their toll. Extreme mental anguish, by production of hyperventilation, interferes with blood oxygen tensions, increases norepinephrine output and sets the stage for acute exacerbations. These can be reversed by "transmarginal inhibition" or catalepsy.

Postcoronary Syndrome

The author has had gratifying results in a selected number of patients with postcoronary syndrome. Strong reassurance and re-education under hypnosis directed toward achieving better adjustment to their condition, together with development of glove anesthesia, relieved or reduced their fears and anxieties and thereby raised their pain threshold. Those whose symptoms were ameliorated were advised to live within their limitations. They were carefully informed that the onset of shortness of breath and anginal pains was a warning signal to be heeded. All were checked and kept on routine medication by their physicians. Dietary control as well as salt reduction can be maintained by posthypnotic suggestions in those who have obesity, diabetes or hypertension. It would be interesting to compare a group of acute coronary and postcoronary cases treated as above with those treated by standard medical procedures.

Though hypnosis was not employed, Dunbar[9] demonstrated that postcoronary patients, who had received some type of psychotherapy, outlived those who had not been similarly treated. This area offers a fertile field for investigation.

Congestive Heart Failure

In congestive heart failure, the attacks of dyspnea are more frequent during the night when the sensory threshold is lowered. Everyone advocates complete mental and physical rest, but no one teaches patients specifically how the former can be attained. During periods of increased emotional tension, patients with congestive failure have increased sodium and water retention. The sodium output may be 20 per cent less than normal, thereby leading to decreased cardiac reserve.

In these patients, hypnorelaxation decreases stress, hyperventilation and electrolyte retention, and often can stimulate the recovery forces to their maximal potential.

PSYCHOSOMATIC GASTROINTESTINAL DISORDERS

Numerous investigations[9] indicate that psychic influences can produce spasms in the gastrointestinal tract. Inability to recognize and treat these influences accounts for failures in many patients with gastrointestinal dysfunctions. The combination of hypnotherapy with a medical regimen in properly prepared patients readily offsets noxious cortical influences, and thus ameliorates the disordered mood and resultant disturbed motility.

The imagination plays an important role in digestive upsets; for instance, merely hearing a description of a nauseating smell or even thinking about swallowing castor oil can induce vomiting in highly susceptible persons. Radiographically, it has been demonstrated that gastric activity of the stomach can be varied with emotional affects.[36a] Physiologic correlates of emotions also have been induced by hypnotic conditioning. In

all probability, such emotions exert their influence on the gastrointestinal tract by a combination of hormonal and neural routes which act reciprocally with a local tissue vulnerability to result in functional symptomatology.

Emotional influences are transmitted to the gastrointestinal tract by way of the anterior hypothalamus and the vagus nerves. Another route is by way of the posterior hypothalamus and the pituitary-adrenal axis. The cortex not only actively participates in all visceral and autonomic activity, but also maintains equilibrium between the parasympathetic and the sympathetic systems.

The more common gastrointestinal disorders with a large emotional overlay that are amenable to hypnorelaxation are peptic ulcer, spasms of the bowel, gastritis and duodenitis, mucous colitis, diarrhea, pylorospasm, spastic constipation and biliary dyskinesia. Other associated conditions are glossitis and bizarre tastes in the oral cavity, globus, dysphagia, cardiospasm, dyspepsia, aerophagia, anorexia, ptyalism, nausea and vomiting, pyrosis, bloating and flatulence; all of these have a high content of severe anxiety.

Patients with such symptoms usually state, "I have always had a nervous stomach." Repeated physical examinations seldom reveal the cause of their difficulties. Many have had some type of abdominal surgery, a long history of digestive upsets and/or food intolerance, as well as severe symptoms of chronic anxiety and tension.

Since vacations, hospitalization, removing the patient from his family or business worries often bring about a sharp reduction in symptoms, psychic factors obviously play an important role. In addition to medication and dietary measures, hypnotherapy directed toward relaxation and correction of faulty behavior patterns is often successful. Reassuring the patient that an organic involvement does not exist improves gastric function in many chronic dyspeptics.

Refractory individuals generally require hypnotherapeutic measures directed toward a reduction of their anxieties and tensions, and then a discussion of their problems, such as that described below under peptic ulcer

PEPTIC ULCER

It has been well established that peptic ulcers occur following severe burns, shock and anoxemia—thus, stimuli mediated via the cortex and reticular formation apparently excite the adrenals, and the resultant corticotropin output increases the activity of the parietal cells in the stomach. Other diverse factors such as heredity, age, conditioning by previous exposure to stress, and the nutritional state can affect both the production of the adrenal hormones and their feedbacks to the higher centers, and thus affect the gastric mucosa.

Before instituting therapy, a careful history and physical examination should be made. Several multi-evaluation sessions are required to select patients for hypnotherapy. Initially, therapy should elicit the relationship between the character of the emotional upsets and the symptoms. If the patient is seen during an attack, questioning should be directed to the type of mood, thoughts or environmental stimuli that preceded the onset of the symptom. In good hypnotic subjects, one can "trigger" the symptoms by suggesting specific situations or thoughts that obviously are etiologic. In this manner, the subject obtains a clearer understanding of the manner in which stressful stimuli exacerbate and maintain the chronicity of the symptom.

It is helpful initially to tell the patient: "There are persons who can get rid of their angry feelings and promptly forget about it. Others cannot do this and develop a great deal of aggravation and they get terribly upset. No wonder that their stomachs act up." The patient can be motivated for hypnosis by being asked, "How would you like to learn not only how to control your nerves, but to relieve your stomach symptoms?"

The patient is asked to identify and enumerate those emotional situations connected with his symptoms in order of their importance. Under hypnosis, reciprocal inhibition technics described in Chapter 47 are used to "immunize" him against their harmful influences. He is asked to think and discuss the least aggravating conditions first and the more serious ones later. He is also advised that while under autohypnosis he can use self-exploration to assay his needs for the symptom. Then a constructive plan that will enable him to meet his future needs without frustration, anxiety and tension is discussed with him. Also, posthypnotic suggestions to associate pleasurable reactions with partaking of foods that were formerly upsetting is helpful.

Since most ulcer patients crave love and affection in the form of recognition, hypnotherapy must be directed toward building up these strong emotional needs. After these, as well as those necessary for healthy functioning of the personality have been dealt with, the patient can be made relatively independent of the operator by training him in autohypnosis and sensory-imagery conditioning. Moody,[35] using controls, noted improvement in 20 patients treated *only* by directive hypnosuggestive procedures.

Hypnosis in the form of prolonged "sleep" is excellent for some refractory ulcer patients. Wennerstrand, the great Swedish hypnotherapist, kept his patients almost continuously under hypnosis for several weeks. Andreev[1a] recently described how prolonged hypnotic "sleep" is more conducive to relaxation than is continuous intravenous Amytal. The only disadvantage is that a trained person has to be in constant attendance. The patient is dehypnotized only for evacuation and feeding. In this way, the organism is maintained at complete physiologic rest. Stress is eliminated, and the ulcer has a good chance to heal. Long-term follow-up psychotherapy is necessary to prevent relapses.

The rapid mobilization of faith and confidence by hypnosis, together with the establishment of healthy emotional attitudes, and the meeting of his needs—all play an important role in facilitating recovery. Most ulcer patients will respond to relaxation, reassurance, re-education and hypnosuggestions for symptom-removal when this approach is incorporated with a medical regimen. Those who cannot be helped by any type of psychotherapy require environmental manipulation, change of occupation, hospitalization and/or surgery.

COLITIS

Emotional maladjustments are closely related to colitis. Fear and tension usually aggravate such bowel symptoms as pain, diarrhea, bloating and bleeding. These are often associated with depression, migraine-like headaches, irritability and anorexia. Most sufferers with colitis have fears and unresolved anxieties; they are characteristically referred to as "having no guts." The bowel, for reasons unknown, becomes the target organ for displacement of unexpressed anxieties and tensions.

Hypnorelaxation, with strong posthypnotic suggestions involving reassurance, helps some colitis sufferers face their conflicts; these generally involve social and occupational maladjustments. However, the majority respond poorly to hypnotic conditioning as well as to other psychotherapeutic procedures. They usually improve on any regimen, but relapse rapidly. The ideal approach consists of permissive hypnotic technics, sensory imagery, autohypnosis, a dietary regimen and tranquilizing agents. Surgery should be recommended for unresponsive patients.

The following illustrates a combined therapeutic approach in a *selected* case of colitis:

Mrs. E. H., aged 34 and the mother of 2 children, complained of persistent bowel spasm, bloating, diarrhea and lassitude, which had been present for 6 years. Medications were of little help. Her father was a top industrialist, who had been too busy to spend much time with her; her mother was a very aggressive woman who had completely dominated the patient all of her life. As a result, she feared and resented her parents. After marriage, she tried to displace her tensions to her husband but since he, too, was very dominating, she began to "clam up" and suppressed her ambivalent feelings toward him. It was at this time that her symptoms became unbearable.

Under hypnosis, the patient was taught to relieve her pain and spasm by glove anesthesia. It was suggested that her symptoms would decrease in intensity if she thought of pleasant and relaxing thoughts via sensory-imagery conditioning. This enlisted her active participation and, after she mastered this technic, some of her symptoms improved. It was further suggested that she remember the specific emotions associated with the onset of symptoms. After becoming aware of the patterns which seemed to initiate the symptoms, she utilized her innate capacities to learn, react and respond to her feelings without suffering the severe abdominal cramping. Under autohypnosis, she imagined speaking up to her hypercritical and demanding spouse. Within a month she was able to talk to her husband without anxiety, guilty fears or self-recrimination. These needs were worked through on a surperficial level, and it was pointed out that if she wished to be free of her bowel symptoms she would have to "quit beating her head against the wall." The following pointed question was asked: "How much of your symptoms *do you really need to keep?*" After several months of therapy at hypnotic and nonhypnotic levels, she began to understand the real significance of this question, and what it meant in terms of her unhappy domestic situation. She discussed the possibility of divorce with her husband if he would not change his attitude. Her bowel upsets became less frequent but never completely disappeared. Therapy was suggested for the husband, but was refused. Although this patient was not cured, she at least made a partial adjustment to a difficult life situation by learning how to assert herself. Hypnosis was used as an adjuvant to superficial psychotherapy.

ULCERATIVE COLITIS

Nearly all investigators agree that psychogenic factors play an important role in the cause and the maintenance of ulcerative colitis, especially with reference to the exacerbations of the symptoms. The physical aspects of the disease are serious and should not be neglected. Here, too, as in the colitis sufferer, one must find out how and why the patient reacts to his deep-seated emotional problems with his gut. A combined medical and psychological approach is always indicated. Hypnotherapy includes sympathetic understanding of the patient's plight, strong reassurance, even stronger persuasion and encouragement, and a thorough discussion of the patient's problems. Many of these patients feel that their prognosis is hopeless, so the major objective is to continually reinforce their confidence and outlook toward life. They deteriorate rapidly unless intensive psychotherapy is instituted. Without controls, it is difficult to determine how much these patients are helped by any type of psychotherapy. A few have been arrested, probably temporarily. Others go rapidly downhill and require successive resections of the bowel. On the surface, these individuals wish to live, but the majority have unrealized death wishes. Many are caught in marital or occupational "traps." As a group they are easily frustrated, ambitious and compulsive. Illustrative is the following case:

Mr. L. S., a 40-year-old writer, developed all the signs and symptoms of ulcerative colitis when faced with a scenario assignment. He worried over his inability to write (he was considered excellent). In spite of his wife's encouragement, and medical therapy, his attacks became more frequent.

When first seen, he was resistant to hypnotic induction. It was suggested that the same emotional factors which prevented him from being hypnotized undoubtedly also were associated with his symptoms. He revealed that he feared being controlled by another person. It was emphasized that the hypnotherapy would not be doctor-centered but, rather, *that he would control it.* Following this explanation, he readily entered a medium state of hypnosis. Since there seemed to be a clear-cut connection between his work and his symptom, it was decided to limit the therapy to overcoming the frustrations brought about by his work. Posthypnotic suggestions were utilized to give him more confidence in his creativity and writing ability. Sensory-imagery conditioning allowed his imagination full rein. As expected, he developed a better attitude toward his work, his superiors and his family. His bowel symptoms decreased in intensity. Unfortunately, he was transferred to another city and had to terminate the therapy.

Emotional Diarrhea

Nervous or emotional diarrhea responds to hypnotherapy. It generally occurs in sensitive and unstable persons. Episodes usually follow stress, tension and anxiety. The urge to defecate immediately after eating or drinking suggests a triggerlike gastrocolic reflex mediated by cortical and subcortical centers.

In addition to dietary and medical measures, hypnorelaxation is particularly beneficial in mild cases when it is combined with direct suggestions, anticholinergic drugs and tranquilizers. Those refractory to this approach require correction of the autonomic imbalance. This is best achieved by supportive psychotherapy under hypnosis. Many of these individuals already have had deep probing of their personalities without affecting the chronicity of the symptom.

One of the most refractory cases the author has seen responded to intensive hypnotherapy when it was directed toward enabling the patient to face his problems.

A very successful business executive, aged 46, had diarrhea and painful abdominal spasms immediately after eating or drinking. The symptoms generally occurred when dining in restaurants or away from home. As a result, he was unable to eat out, to travel or to perform many of his duties unless he was close to a lavatory. His symptoms began after he discovered that his wife, who had been frigid toward him, had been unfaithful. Following this episode, he became guilt-laden while he was having intimate relations with his secretary. Exacerbations of diarrhea were noted whenever he had to discuss problems with his superiors or when aggressive behavior was required when dealing with business associates. Through autohypnosis he utilized self-exploration and sensory-imagery conditioning (imagining he could perform dreaded tasks). He also received psychotherapy to overcome his passive, dependent tendencies, to deal objectively with his wife's problems, and also to work through his own guilt over his extramarital relations. Less than a year after the start of hypnotherapy (approximately 30 sessions) his diarrhea subsided. He took assignments that he formerly was unable to fulfill. Glove anesthesia also materially assisted in controlling the abdominal cramps.

The crucial factor in this case was not the self-exploration under autohypnosis and sensory-imagery conditioning, but the strong interpersonal relationship that allowed the patient to act out most of his repressed anger. This helped diminish his anxiety. This grateful patient was free from all symptoms on follow-up two years later.

Postgastrectomy Syndrome

Following subtotal gastrectomy, some patients develop the dumping syndrome, consisting of anorexia, nausea, vomiting, vertigo, sweating, fatigue and weight loss. Often these symptoms become chronic, especially if associated with anxiety and tension. Cases have been treated successfully by hypnoanalysis.[38]

Dorcus and Goodwin[7] treated a small series of cases by direct posthypnotic suggestions centered on reducing tension, removing fear of the symptoms, and improving the olfactory appeal and consumption of the food itself. *Despite the fact that only direct symptom-removal was used, not a single case relapsed.*

In another study[11] on nutritional problems, directive hypnotic technics increased caloric intake, relieved certain food restrictions, allayed pain and helped remove the accompanying loss of appetite.

Good results have been attained by group hypnotherapy.[30] The author treated several cases by sensory-imagery conditioning. Posthypnotic suggestions associated with pleasant memories, involving the sight, the taste and the smell of all the foods which the patient enjoyed before his surgery, were utilized. Glove anesthesia, transferred to the epigastrium, relieved the nausea and the vomiting in susceptible patients.

CONSTIPATION

Obstinate constipation that does not respond to laxatives can be helped by posthypnotic suggestions and sensory-imagery conditioning. One cannot merely suggest under hypnosis that the patient will have a bowel movement at a certain time but, rather, that *all* the *subjective* sensations associated with a normal evacuation will be experienced; these are "rehearsed" during autohypnosis.

The rectal sphincter is under autonomic as well as volitional control, which provides this area with a "time sense." One usually develops the desire for defecation as the result of a well-established habit pattern. When this pattern is disturbed, constipation often results. Patients are first trained in hypnosis and autohypnosis. Then, during a self-induced hypnotic state, the patient describes in minute detail what a normal evacuation feels like to him. All relevant details such as the time and the nature of the "call to stool" signal, and the type of spasms or tenesmus at the rectal sphincter are elicited. It is now suggested that all these sensations will be experienced during the next few days. The exact time can be suggested.[36a]

BILIARY DYSKINESIA

Dysfunction of the gallbladder may result from disturbances of the sphincter mechanism that is regulated in part by autonomic impulses, or from functional derangements in other portions of the biliary tract. Symptoms arising from a normally functioning gallbladder without stones frequently indicate a psychosomatic involvement. Emotional factors often can upset the function of the biliary tract.

Ivy,[26a] after reviewing the literature, concludes that the choledochoduodenal mechanism can contract with sufficient force to prevent the evacuation of the contracting gallbladder and to counteract the secretory pressure of bile. An increase of intracholedochal pressure has been associated with intense emotional stress. Such a rise may be due to hypertonus of the duodenal sphincter. There is also a physiologic basis for emotional jaundice. A syndrome has been described, consisting of distention of the gallbladder secondary to spasms of the sphincter of Oddi. The contractions are mediated by vagal impulses of central origin, with symptoms of biliary colic and even jaundice. The syndrome has responded to environmental manipulation, psychotherapy and some monoamine oxidase inhibitors.

Surgeons are aware that some patients with prolonged icterus, intense pruritus, negative parenchymal tests and normal structures at laparotomy, promptly establish bile flow with relief of itching on drainage of the ducts. This must be a functional jaundice. Even if calculi are present in the bile ducts, this does not necessarily rule out the possibility of emotional factors.

Derangement in cortical dynamics, acting through limbic system activity, can trigger spasms of the duodenum and of the sphincter of Oddi. Either of these can produce distention of the gallbladder, colic and jaundice, and the resultant stasis can contribute to stone formation. This author has seen a Yoga who under fluoroscopy could voluntarily contract the duodenal sphincter. Thus far there are no reports of emotional icterus or biliary dyskinesia treated by hypnosis. However, the syndrome has responded to change of environment, mental rest and sedation.

Glove anesthesia and opiates are the methods of choice for short-term relief of pain. In the presence of intermittent substernal pain, further search for such physical factors as reflex coronary spasm should be made.

SUMMARY

Psychosomatic gastrointestinal disorders are, in part, produced by emotional factors and visceral reactions to physical stressors. Therefore, an interdisciplinary therapeutic program directed toward the psychic and the somatic factors is indicated. Hypnotherapy, judiciously employed in selected patients, can potentiate the medical therapy of gastrointestinal complaints caused or aggravated by emotional stress.

Hypnotherapy, as described, has proved to be beneficial in many patients who were unable to respond to a wide variety of medical measures. This approach has afforded considerable relief of pain, spasms and other related disorders such as heartburn, nausea, pylorospasm, eructations and other symptoms. Sensory-imagery conditioning and glove anesthesia are valuable adjunctive procedures.

Hypnosis relaxes many anxious and disturbed patients, reduces their tension, helps relieve the irritability caused by a strict dietary program, and also increases the likelihood of co-operation with the medical regimen. The dual approach provides the physician trained in hypnotherapy with a comprehensive and definitive therapy for conditions many of which are refractory to general psychotherapy.

It is unfortunate that some of our cases could not be followed. Also, that space does not permit a fuller description of the nuances of the interpersonal relationship which in any form of psychotherapy affords a bulwark of support to the emotionally disturbed patient. The reader also should not get the impression that all our cases were helped or cured. We have failures and these are discussed in Chapter 49. In this volume, we are presenting primarily our successful cases, realizing full well that a placebo effect exists in every psychotherapeutic relationship, including hypnosis!

OTHER PSYCHOSOMATIC DISORDERS

TUBERCULOSIS

Tuberculosis is, in part, a disease of maladaptation due to stress.[45] The importance of the psychologist and the psychiatrist in the therapeutic program is incalculable. Correction of human factors which defeat the ministrations of the physician is mandatory in this disease. Almost half the patients institutionalized do not take their medications, refuse surgical treatment or leave the hospital before being discharged as cured.

It is believed that adrenocortical activity plays a role in resistance to tuberculosis and that the effects of stress on the course of the disease may be mediated in part by the adrenals.[24]

The relevance of personality factors to the cause of tuberculosis has been described by many investigators.[8] Many patients are insecure, rebellious, over-assertive, hard-driving and conflict-harassed individuals. Thus, at present, the research is directed more toward the host than the bacteria. The combination of psychotherapy, energetic drug therapy and well-timed surgery can increase the cure rate in chronic tuberculosis. With reference to surgery, the need for an adequate personality study in all patients requiring thoracoplasty has been stressed.[21] Preoperative hypnosis can be useful in raising the threshold to shock, especially in debilitated patients or in those who have a "will to die."

Hypnosis can facilitate relaxation and feelings of well-being in subjects who require complete bed rest for months.[1] It can also be employed to stimulate the appetite, promote sleep and rest, and change the patient's unhealthy attitudes.

The author has had very little personal experience with hypnotherapy in tuberculosis, but believes that this area affords another promising area for research. Osler once said that, when you see a patient with tuberculosis, do not treat his chest, but rather his head. The reader interested in one of the best interdisciplinary studies made on tuberculosis should read *Personality, Stress and Tuberculosis*.[45] The resigned attitudes of consumptives to the disease itself must be taken into consideration.

Hypnosis has been used individually and by group therapy for tuberculars in the Soviet Union to alter the patient's outlook toward his misfortune, to inculcate cheerfulness and confidence in his recovery. Specific posthypnotic suggestions are: "You will eat everything with relish because your full recovery depends on it, especially butter, milk and rich food. Recollection of your difficulties no longer troubles you as you will maintain your interest in life." Such encouragement can invariably stimulate the adaptive processes and help the tuberculosis patient in the successful struggle against his disease.

Migraine Headache

Etiology

Although the precise mechanisms responsible for migraine headache have not as yet been elucidated, there seems to be little doubt that emotional tensions are precipitating factors in most instances. Likewise, the existence of a "migraine personality" cannot be satisfactorily substantiated even though many migraine sufferers are compulsive, rigid, hostile and perfectionistic.

Many causes have been suggested, such as vasoconstriction,[55] vasodilatation of blood vessels, leading to a combination of distention and altered sensitivity which results in pain,[36] heredity[16] and allergy.[51] Miscellaneous factors that have been suggested are electrolyte imbalance, histamine sensitivity, elevated serotonin levels,[35a] anoxia, vitamin and hormonal deficiencies, ocular malfunctions and chronic intestinal disorders.[14]

The author wishes to advance a speculative hypothesis for the currently accepted vascular basis for migraine headache. He postulates that, when we once walked on all fours, the head or cephalad portion of the body was functionally significant, especially for feeling states involving fight and rage reactions (head lowered to charge at an opponent). During our evolutionary development, the somatic manifestations of emotions involving rage continued to be displaced cephalad. Thus, this deeply repressed response may occur as an atavism in those unable to express rage. In such predisposed individuals, the blood rushes to the head, with chronic vasodilatation and subsequent vasoconstriction. The blood vessels become hard, tender and rigid, and this produces a steady ache accompanied by spasm and pain of the neck muscles.

Treatment

The possibility of such physical factors as brain tumor, sinusitis and other organic conditions must be ruled out before instituting any type of therapy. The psychogenic factors involved in tension headache or migraine respond readily to hypnotherapy, particularly cluster headaches (atypical facial neuralgia). There are numerous reports on this approach.[1, 10, 20, 26, 37, 49, 54] The author has utilized directive hypnotherapy for menstrual migraine and for headaches associated with premenstrual tension.

The purpose of all treatment is to relieve tension and raise the pain threshold. Should analgesics or local methods of therapy fail, hypnosis is the method of choice, especially if it is combined with autohypnosis and glove anesthesia.

The generalist who is familiar with hypnotic technics is in an enviable position for treating such individuals, as he knows the longitudinal life history of his patients and has already established a good rapport. Rarely is formalized depth psychotherapy indicated in resistant cases of migraine, as the results are about the same as with directive hypnotherapy, which is less time-consuming and less expensive.

Hypnotic relaxation, supportive psychotherapy, education and adjunctive pharmacotherapy can reduce the frequency and the intensity of tension headaches, especially if the patient is enabled to understand how he is reacting to his life situations and what he can do about facing his problems with more equanimity.

Many drugs recommended for migraine headache have little more than a placebo effect. Friedman[15] states:

In treatment of headache it is well to remember that the efficiency of any drug depends upon many factors. The emotional factors influencing results of treatment depend upon the personality of the patient, the method in which the medicine is applied and the doctor-patient relationship. The personal influence of the physician is most important.

The following is an interesting case of intractable migraine which responded favorably to hypnotic intervention:

The patient was a 33-year-old married woman who had recently lost an 8-year-old daughter from cancer. Headaches developed soon after this unfortunate occurrence. Hypnosis and glove anesthesia were only partially effective, but within 2 months the following data were elicited: She had conceived the daughter before marriage and always felt that she "had to marry her present husband." She became guilt-laden and frigid following her tragedy and believed that "God took my child from me because I sinned." Her deep-seated resentment of her mate as well as her faulty sexual responses were worked through, the latter under hypnosis.

The patient improved and at present is still being treated for codeine addiction.

Ostfeld[35a] sums up the current attitude toward therapy by stating:

For prevention of migraine headache, the simplest and most effective remedy is still a sympathetic relationship with the patient and a kindly helpful attitude on the part of the physician. A more penetrating relationship can be one in which some attempt is made to have the patient recognize those factors in his life that may be causing him to go in the wrong direction or at the wrong pace. Two out of 3 patients with migraine can be greatly helped by any physician who is interested in human problems and is willing to spend a minimum of time with a patient in reviewing them with him.

Arthritis and Rheumatism

There is a large body of literature on the psychosomatic factors in arthritis and rheumatism.[18] A high percentage of the patients who complain of pain have minimal radiologic findings; contrarily, those who show extensive damage often have little discomfort. Most drugs and procedures employed to treat these conditions have little more than a placebo effect.[47] Data indicate that aspirin and salicylates are as good as steroid medication even in rheumatoid arthritis. Hypnotic suggestion is often effective for symptom-relief and dramatically relieves the distress in the milder attacks. Hypnosis is of little value in osteoarthritis.

Pain can be controlled by the production of glove anesthesia and sensory-imagery conditioning; these reduce narcotics, steroids and analgesic drugs. Hypnosis should always be directed toward relaxing the musculoskeletal "armoring" which characterizes many arthritics. Even at rest, their muscles are in a continual state of spasm. Autohypnosis to promote relaxation and mobility of joints can be most effective. Dissipating the discharge of strong emotions which maintain chronic muscular tension often can prevent an attack.

Even strong suggestion per se can help many chronic arthritis sufferers, especially those who have a large psychogenic component to their ailment. Shrines and faith healers cure many such individuals. The value of spa therapy is due to the relaxation produced by separation from adverse environmental factors plus a nonspecific placebo effect.

The author has had gratifying success in ameliorating discomfort in small groups of arthritics by merely teaching the patients glove anesthesia and how to relax by autohypnosis. Contributory conditions such as overweight and dietary indiscretions are controlled by appropriate hypnotic suggestions.

Raginsky[40] points out that attacks of arthritis can be either relieved or reinduced through hypnosis when the proper stimulus is applied. He states:

The emotional stimulus appeared to be almost specific for the individual so that he would become embroiled in a conflict which resulted in symptom formation. What is of interest here is that once the attack of rheumatism or gout developed in these patients, the attack could be shortened immeasurably through hypnotherapy.

The author recollects the following interesting case:

A 65-year-old school teacher, who had been an active homosexual the greater part of her life, was relieved of a chronic stiffness and discomfort in her hand of over 20 years' duration in 4 visits. She was able to enter a somnambulistic state in the first session, in which autohypnosis and glove anesthesia were taught. Additionally, through sensory-imagery conditioning she was able to develop warmth in her hand by imagining its insertion in a tub of hot water. A posthypnotic suggestion, given during the second session, directed her to use the "warm" hand to remove the discomfort. With practice, she was readily able to achieve this result. Suggestions were also given to increase the mobility of the hand. During the third visit, she related how she feared being exposed because of her homosexuality (she lived with another homosexual who also was a teacher). It was pointed out that she was doing a good job as a school teacher, that she was not seducing others, that there was no reason to feel guilty over her homosexuality, and also that she would wish to live out her life in the current pleasant relationship. She reported back at the end of a month, stating that she was relieved of all pain, and that she had full use of her hand.

It must be emphasized that arthritis is a disease of unknown etiology with protean manifestations involving all systems of the body. The spontaneous remissions and unexplained exacerbations which characterize the course of the disease make it difficult to evaluate critically the results of hypnotherapeutic management of this condition.

HYPNOTHERAPY IN METABOLIC DISEASES

DIABETES MELLITUS

The emotional factors in diabetes were recognized in the 17th century when Thomas Willis, describing the sweet taste of diabetic urine, said that the disease was due to "prolonged sorrow." Recently, an extensive literature has pointed out that the effects of stressful life situations[4, 8, 22, 23] are a contributing cause of diabetes.

The relationship to diabetes of fear and other psychic factors in anxiety has long been recognized by numerous investigators. These may interfere with therapy or indirectly affect the disease. Thus, emotional stimuli originating in the cortex affect the hypothalamus via the limbic system. As a result, overestimation of the adrenals causes impairment of glucose tolerance, increased insulin resistance and sometimes ketosis.

Hypnotherapy can be directed toward a reduction of the stress component by achieving relaxation. Also, it can be helpful indirectly by maintaining weight reduction in obese individuals. Posthypnotic suggestions or autosuggestions enable poorly motivated persons to limit their dietary intake to prescribed foods.

Much more can be done for the diabetic than just keeping his urine sugar-free by means of diet and insulin. An appreciation of the patient's personality make-up, his strivings and frustrations, his home environment and relationships as well as recognition of how to cope with current stresses, allows a wider scope for the physician in the treatment of this condition. In selected cases, the use of hypnotherapy can reduce the quantity of insulin needed to keep the urine sugar-free and also can reduce the frequency of the attacks of ketosis.[39]

The author remembers several patients whose diabetes improved after emotional adjustments to domestic and sexual difficulties had been made. In one, a 42-year-old male who developed impotency, hypnotherapy directed toward this condition modified the course of the disease. In another, a very sick diabetic, drastic weight reduction through hypnosis alleviated the disease. In still another, re-establishment of potency materially reduced the need for insulin.

In general, hypnotherapy finds its greatest utility in the treatment of the psychic factors contributing to the diabetes. From recent experimental evidence there are strong indications that diabetes is not limited to being a dysfunction of carbohydrate metabolism, but rather is a multifaceted disease. For instance, some patients are diabetics but have normal fasting blood sugar levels and their urine examinations consistently are aglycosuric. Hence, insulin deficiency need not be the only factor involved in the production of lesions characteristic of diabetes. It is logical to postulate from this that unknown endocrine or metabolic processes secondary to corticohypothalamic dysfunctions may be implicated. It is in such cases that attention to the psyche by hypnosuggestive procedures is indicated.

Particularly germane to this discussion is the influence of the cortex on carbohydrate metabolism studied under hypnosis. When a hypnotized subject is given a concentrated solution of sugar, and is told it is distilled water, the blood sugar does not increase but may sharply diminish. Obviously, under the influence of suggestions at the verbal level, a strong unconditioned stimulus loses its force or provokes an unusually distorted action. This paradoxical phenomena is well known among pavlovians and may be the "unknown factor" accounting for unrecognized diabetes as well as explaining the results obtained by hypnosis. Foa[10b] recently described how the mediation of psychic stimuli, and regulation of endocrine function resulted in diabetes.

OBESITY

Overweight is one of the common problems that are brought to the physician's attention. It accounts for a high percentage of degenerative diseases; therefore, its treatment by hypnosis will be discussed in detail. Numerous authors have discussed the importance of psychic factors in stimulating the drive to eat. This is particularly pronounced during the evening, and has been referred to as the "night-eating" syndrome.

PSYCHOLOGICAL FACTORS

It has been demonstrated that, in addition to the deeper psychological forces at work, the ordinary vicissitudes of daily living contribute to the desire to overeat and to the inability to diet. Thus, domestic upsets, fatigue, sexual problems, economic worries and many other such common sources of tension interfere with the reduction of food intake. The treatment of overweight is much easier if tensions are eliminated. It has been noted that most of the patients who feel well as a result of reduced tension and frustration achieve successful weight reduction.[12] Only those who are emotionally stable should undertake a drastic reducing regimen.[2]

As has been mentioned, tension and frustration often lead to excessive caloric intake and subsequent obesity. These reactions usually depend on early developmental patterns. For example, the hungry infant soon learns that frustration is relieved by the pleasurable experience of nursing, thumb-sucking or playing with a rattle. Although these earlier tension-relieving mechanisms are repressed, the individual always "remembers" the route by which gratification was once afforded.

Other oral methods for the relief of tension are chain-smoking, chewing gum and nail-biting. Insecure adults, when faced with frustration, resort to one of these tension-allaying outlets. This "return-to-the-breast" mechanism now involves the use of food to satisfy the oral cravings, since the bottle, the nipple and/or the thumb are no longer acceptable. Contrarily, many individuals lose weight following stress.

Excessive food intake can also result from other causes. For instance, in certain "food addicts," overeating is often a substitute for suppressed hostile impulses. Since they cannot express anger toward those around them, they take it out on food, which is smashed to pieces. In homes where food is hard to get, the children eat everything available today, for tomorrow there may be no food. Many parents warn against wasting food, and also praise their children for being good eaters. Even after becoming wealthy, such individuals must "always clean the plate." Parental attitudes and other psychosocial factors determine one's eating habits. Thus, a child brought up on large, rich meals usually imitates the parents' eating habits. This tendency is more often responsible for obesity than hereditary factors.

Overeating due to tension may follow the death of a friend or a relative. Frequently, food is used as a substitute for love. For example, people who are alone and who feel unwanted and unloved, substitute the pleasure of eating for affection. Their attitude is: *As long as no one loves me, I will be good to myself.* Unwanted children often become obese. To relieve their guilt feelings, some mothers become overprotective and stuff the children with food as a proof of their "love." Then, being concerned about their children's weight, they seek the physician's help. They refuse psychotherapy, however, because of their own emotional problems.

Adult obesity is a sign of social prestige and a "badge of wealth" in many races, who overfeed a child to make it fat, not only because "big babies are healthy babies" but also because a plump baby is highly esteemed.

An occupation sometimes is the primary cause of obesity. In high-strung individuals such as actors, singers or executives, eating may be used for relaxation. Conversely, people who lead a dull life eat more often than usual to relieve the monotony. This is commonly noted in housewives who "raid the icebox" between meals to lessen the drudgery of their work. There are many fat women who remain obese because their spouses prefer them fat! Since these husbands usually have an inferiority complex, they feel more secure with plump, unattractive wives. Sterile women often use obesity as a symbol of the wish for pregnancy.

Persons with heightened sexual impulses

often displace these drives by food intake and eat ravenously. Sooner or later this type of individual reacts toward eating with the same feelings as he or she had about sex—namely, shame, guilt and anxiety—and then more food is required to alleviate the tension. Many emotionally insecure individuals unconsciously believe that a heavy layer of body fat is a protective armor against a hostile world. For instance, the young girl, guilty over her sex drives, often retreats behind the "wall of obesity." By doing this, she now has a ready-made alibi for not being attractive to men. She can safely say, "I am so fat, no wonder boys are not interested in me."

Many young athletes enjoy eating large quantities of good food, but they do not gain weight when they are physically active. As they grow older and their lives become more sedentary, their caloric intake exceeds their energy requirements, yet their level of satiation is raised because of their previous eating habits. This type loses weight with difficulty.

The rationalizations proffered for overeating are many. Some of these are: *It runs in my family; it's my glands; others eat twice as much as I do.* However, the actual causal factors are hostility, anxiety, guilt, self-pity, self-punishment and depression. These are usually found in combination and are often repressed from awareness.

Obviously, with psychological factors so frequently at the root of obesity, the difficulties of weight reduction cannot be overcome on the level of general practice unless pharmacologic agents can provide powerful assistance. Amphetamines are the most effective appetite depressants in current use. The action of the amphetamines can be negated by severe emotional tension, premenstrual tension, untreated menopause, impotency and other symptoms.

In addition to those resistant to medication, there are the paradoxical reactors who require much larger doses of sedatives, antihistamines and other drugs than the average person to achieve any type of pharmacologic response. In these individuals, one can use hypnotherapy as an adjunctive procedure.

The preliminary discussion is usually conducted after the physical examination and before the induction of hypnosis. It is as follows: "Our approach is a threefold one. First, it is axiomatic that you cannot lose weight unless you take in fewer calories—this means that you will have to follow a diet. All diets are good, but they are only as good as the way they are followed. You will be helped to avoid fattening foods through various hypnotic technics. Please be assured that you will not be hungry and that you will be able to eat an adequate amount of nutritious and healthful foods. Diets, as you know, can actually refer to eating *more* food, but of the right type.

"The second approach consists of medication. However, all types of medications, as appetite-suppressing drugs, have their limitations. They are useful, nevertheless, until proficiency has been developed in following the posthypnotic suggestions. They are particularly advantageous to get you started and motivate you to continue with other procedures. In addition, drugs will help overcome many depressive feelings that cause you to overeat. These drugs seldom produce nervousness, sleeplessness and palpitation of the heart. If you should by any possibility develop any one of these reactions, report to me at once and you will be given other medications.

"The third or hypnotherapeutic portion of the treatment consists of training in hypnosis and autohypnosis, wherein you will give yourself appropriate autosuggestions. The degree of success will be in direct proportion to the amount of effort you put forth in the practice sessions. If you practice autohypnosis faithfully, you can expect better results. You additionally will be helped to understand what your *need to overeat* represents. You will also be taught how you can face your problems on a more adult level instead of putting food in your mouth to allay anxiety-provoking tensions in the same manner you once used a rattle, a nipple or a bottle."

The verbalization after hypnotization that has been found applicable to most patients is: "If you really wish to lose weight, you will roll the food from the front of the tongue to the back of the tongue and from side to side in order to obtain the last ounce of satisfaction and the 'most mileage' out of each morsel and each drop that you eat. By doing this you will more readily satisfy the thousands of taste cells that are located all over your tongue (there is an appetite center located in the hypothalamus), and, as a result, less food will be required and your caloric intake will be immeasurably curtailed.

"Secondly, you will 'think thin,' that is, you will keep an image uppermost in your mind of how you once looked when you were thin. Perhaps you have a picture of yourself when you weighed less. If so, place this in a prominent position so that you will be continually reminded of the way you once looked. There is considerable basis for this suggestion. You undoubtedly are aware that, if a woman imagines or thinks that she is pregnant, her body will develop the contour of a pregnant woman; her breasts will enlarge and she may, in many instances, stop menstruating. Also, you may have at one time experienced a great deal of inner turmoil and lost weight in spite of the fact that you ate excessively. Cannot a frustrated lover also 'pine away' for the beloved?

"Thirdly, you might like to think of the most horrible, nauseating and repugnant smell that you have ever experienced. Perhaps it might be the vile odor of rotten eggs. In the future, whenever you desire to eat something that is not on your diet, you will immediately associate this disagreeable smell with it. Also, you might like to think of the most awful and disgusting taste that you may have had in the past. This, too, can be linked up with fattening foods even when you merely think of them.

"Finally, for this session, remember that you cannot will yourself to lose weight. The harder you try, the less chance you have to accomplish your aims. So relax—don't press. The imagination determines this struggle, so would you mind purchasing the most beautiful dress that you can afford, hang it up in your bedroom where you can see it every morning and imagine yourself getting into it within a relatively short time. You can speculate how soon this will be. Now this is important! The dress that you buy should be at least one or two sizes too small for you."

The above 4 suggestions are given after the operator is certain that hypnosis has been induced. Following dehypnotization, the rationale for these suggestions may be discussed if the patient is inquisitive about them: "There is no question that there is a close association between the thousands of taste buds and the impressions that they convey to the higher brain centers for interpretation."

The "think thin" suggestion makes use to a degree of the alteration in body image secondary to strong emotional stimuli. It is well recognized that emotions can alter metabolic and endocrine activities to produce weight gain. This has been illustrated vividly in phantom pregnancy or pseudocyesis. If the autonomic nervous system can "trick" endocrine activities and bodily processes, into responding with a weight gain to expressed or unexpressed wishes regarding pregnancy, then it is conceivable that these same pathways can produce loss of weight.

The association of fattening foods with disagreeable tastes and odors to produce an aversion is based on classic conditioning methods. While the organs of taste and smell are distinct, the impulses from each reach the cortex by different pathways. However, the two senses are closely associated psychophysiologically. They should be designated as chemical senses because chemical rather than physical stimuli act on the receptors in the higher centers. The most important aspect of flavor is due to the sense of smell rather than of taste. Olfaction is sensitive to small changes because it is capable of ascertaining the location of the source. In addition to these chemical sensations, smoothness and roughness, temperature, and pressure sensations originating in the mouth contribute to taste impressions.

Some attempts have been made to explain how various tastes can give rise to nerve impulses, but there is still insufficient knowledge to formulate a working hypothesis. However, in man the sense of smell remains closely associated with the motivation of the individual to eat. As described in Chapter 30, the close association of the limbic system (cortical areas, nuclei and fiber tracts philogenetically associated with the sense of smell) with the emotions is now generally accepted. Perhaps no sense is more provocative of moods and memories than that of smell, and so the smell of food may enhance or diminish the appetite. The close association of taste and smell with feeling states is further reflected in the words that we use to express our reactions to things—we speak of a "sweet" girl, a "salty" character and "sour" grapes. In particular, we use the idea of "taste" to express our feelings.

The fourth suggestion has a twofold meaning. First, it is highly motivating, as it stresses the value of a nice figure by indirection or extraverbal suggestions. This approach does not mobilize a critical attitude. It makes full use of the imagination. One must be careful to suggest that not all these affirmations or aids will be utilized immediately, but that continual repetition through autohypnosis eventually will enable the overweight person to respond to these autosuggestions.

If the subject has had some modicum of success, the following verbalization is used on subsequent visits: "You will, if you really wish to lose more weight, consider the following suggestions: Do not plan on more than a 6- to 8-pound weight loss per month, but set a deadline for this weight loss. You will try harder when you have to meet a deadline. Wonder whether you will reach your objective before or after the deadline date.

"The desire to eat results when the appetite center in the brain is stimulated, whereas hunger is brought on by contractions of the stomach. If you wish temporarily to delay eating your next meal for several hours, all you have to do is to employ glove anesthesia over the pit of the stomach in order to 'knock out' the hunger contractions which are initiated in this area. Another suggestion that might appeal to you, especially if you are interested in having a trim figure, is to think of your ultimate goal in terms of the actual weight desired. Let us assume, for instance, that you would like to get down to 130. This will be what I call a 'food stamp' suggestion, that is, every time you even think of eating something you are not supposed to, you will see the number 130 in blue encircled by a blue ring, much as the price of an item is stamped on the food can in a grocery store. You will give yourself this suggestion particularly at night if you get extremely hungry before retiring.

"Finally, if you find that you have ex-

ceeded the required food intake and you are still hungry, you can place yourself in hypnosis and *imagine* that you are eating enough pleasurable food to satisfy yourself."

During future visits the patient is asked to repeat the affirmations until they are remembered, and also for purposes of reinforcement. New suggestions to reduce caloric intake can be incorporated with the old. These consist of strengthening the patient's desire for weight loss by stressing the health, the social and the beneficial appearance of a trim figure; these act to reinforce the patient's own specific reasons for losing weight. Posthypnotic suggestions may be given to eliminate "eating between meals," "nibbling," and munching on such items as peanuts while watching television. For those who have a full social life, suggestions can be given to resist inordinate demands for eating and drinking. Suggestions for a specific type of diet, such as one high in protein but low in fats, carbohydrates, sodium and liquids may be employed at hypnotic levels. Likewise, suggestions at hypnotic levels may be given to induce proper alimentary functions.

Some of the above suggestions have a psychophysiologic basis. There are hypothalamic centers mediating hunger and satiety. They not only have separate anatomic locations but also different behavioral consequences. Appropriate lesions made in these brain areas in experimental animals result in bulemia, and they eat ravenously. Recent clinical studies suggest that either a decreased satiability or an increased hunger drive accounts for obesity.[12]

It has been established that one of the principal physiologic centers for initiating hunger contractions is just below the xiphoid process in the region of the epigastrium. Many obese individuals are not hungry but eat because the hunger contractions are conditioned to a time schedule. It is recognized that following the old adage, "Tighten up your belt a notch," can assuage hunger.

The deadline suggestion is obviously only to increase further motivation. This applies also to the "food-stamp" suggestion. Many of the other suggestions are based upon the correlation between taste and the visual senses being stimulated. Visual senses develop appetite at the expense of taste and smell. The tongue and the connecting brain centers are continually stimulated by the reciprocal feedback connections. No wonder one unidentified wit said, "One tongue may have three times as many taste buds as another and the empire of taste also has its blind men and deaf mutes."

Hypnoanalytic technics (Chap. 47) to elicit the needs for overeating are generally required. A strong rapport, a noncondemnatory attitude and encouragement when failure occurs facilitate psychotherapy. When permissive technics are employed and it is emphasized that it is a "do-it-yourself program," dependency is avoided. Furthermore, as described above, hypnotherapy is used as part of a total approach consisting of a sensible diet and appropriate medications.

Group hypnosis for obesity is even more rewarding than individual sessions. The same factors described in group training for childbirth apply. The author sees 4 to 5 patients for one hour, at first weekly and then biweekly. After the patients have learned autohypnosis and how to modify their eating habits, medication is discontinued. The use of psychotherapy is helpful in maintaining the optimal weight after it is reached. About 40 per cent relapse and require periodic reinforcement to prevent further weight gain.

HYPERTHYROIDISM

Stress plays an important role in altering thyroid function. Overrelaboration of the thyroid-stimulating hormone (TSH) is often secondary to cortical-hypothalamic factors. Though the etiology of this condition is a multicausal one, emotional factors can modify thyroid function.[29] Nearly all patients are easily upset, sensitive to their environments and exceedingly intolerant. Hypnotherapy must be directed toward a reorganization of the personality functioning. Not only can it implement medical therapy and achieve this, but strong hypnotic rapport can also alter the individual's reaction to fears and other environmental stresses.

Hypnorelaxation is particularly valuable in the pre- and postoperative emotional preparation of the patient who requires thyroid surgery. Anxious patients can be conditioned for thyroid surgery by a "rehearsal" or a "dry-run" technic of the proposed surgery

(see Chapter 33). The combination of hypnorelaxation and medication after surgery is better than either one alone. Clinicians are aware that the treatment of hyperthyroidism only begins after the surgery is finished. When such individuals are taught to relax, face and understand their difficulties through hypnotherapeutic technics, they become more stabilized, with a better prognosis.

ANOREXIA NERVOSA

The chief symptoms of anorexia nervosa are the loss of appetite and weight, and amenorrhea. Untreated cases have a high mortality. The condition occurs in very high-strung individuals, chiefly women. It must be distinguished from pituitary dysfunction, in which pubic and axillary hair is lost.

Hypnotherapy can be used to keep the patient relaxed in bed, and the appetite can be increased through posthypnotic suggestions associating food with pleasant memories. Concomitantly, feelings of aggression, disgust and hostility should be ventilated. The value of any type of therapy in this condition is based on the rapport fostered by the hypnotic relationship.

In 2 cases recently seen by the author, one patient lived and one died. Posthypnotic suggestions of an increase in appetite were accepted by one patient, and there was a subsequent weight gain. This patient, who came in regularly, faced the problems contributing to her depressive reactions. The patient who died of malnutrition did not come in regularly. She had profound guilt feelings and remorse because she had driven her daughter away from home. The daughter became a prostitute, and the mother never forgave herself and masochistically developed an intense need to punish herself.

BRONCHIAL ASTHMA

There is extensive literature on the psychogenic aspects of asthma.[8, 13, 51] Characteristically, these patients suppress all intense emotions involving threats to their dependent relationships, deprivation and insecurity induced by sexual conflicts. As children, they are anxiety-ridden, lack confidence and are dependent to an extreme degree. Developmental failures in the functioning of the reticular formation, exacerbated by repeated allergic reactions in the brain stem, have been implicated as an etiologic factor.

TREATMENT

Numerous authors have treated asthma by hypnotherapy.[1, 33, 34, 40, 41, 48] Abreaction under hypnosis may reduce attacks of status asthmaticus. For chronic cases of asthma, autohypnosis together with steroids and evocation of conflicts is often helpful. Asthmatics who became "adrenalin-fast" have been relieved by hypnotherapy directed toward understanding the responsible psychogenic factors.[40]

In children afflicted with asthma, it has been reported that, in a control series, reassurance by psychotherapy was slower and less certain in its effects than hypnotherapy.[33] In both series, parents had to be treated concurrently. Reinforcement suggestions under hypnosis are usually necessary long after recovery has occurred. Parents can be taught to give suggestions to neutralize the anxiety-provoking situations. For adults, a superficial uncovering type of hypnotherapy often is successful. Prolonged "sleep" can alleviate severe asthmatic attacks. The author uses relaxation to regulate the breathing, and trains all patients in sensory-imagery conditioning. About 60 per cent of carefully selected cases can be helped by these methods. The reader should not infer that our results are always as dramatic as in the following cases:

A 42-year-old male who had failed to respond to cortisone and psychoanalysis was cured in several sessions. The patient was induced into somnambulism on the first visit. It was suggested that any time that he felt an attack coming on, he would induce autohypnosis. While in this state, he was to re-experience an actual relaxing episode from the past. Much to the patient's surprise (as well as the author's), he was promptly relieved of all the symptoms such as wheezing, coughing and choking sensations. It is possible that his bronchial manifestations may have been a conversion-hysteria reaction and, as such, dramatically responded to a "magical gesture." This patient was seen over a period of 3 years, and no significant relapses occurred. It is conceivable that his exaggerated response to tension and anxiety (later a marital conflict was uncovered) was due to a conditioned autonomic excitability. The hypnosis interrupted the conditioned pattern, and the subsequent superficial psychotherapy under sensory-imagery conditioning served to reinforce the apparent cure.

Even more dramatic was the case of a 78-year-old woman who was seen in consultation at a distant hospital. This patient was in an oxygen tent and was *in extremis*; coarse rales were audible in the hospital corridor. Hypnosis, autohypnosis and sensory-imagery conditioning were taught to her at the first session, which lasted 4 hours. Immediately, the labored breathing subsided and rales were no longer heard except in stethoscopic examination. She was removed from the oxygen tent and, much to the surprise of her 4 consultants, she left the hospital the next day. She was "cued" to enter hynosis over the telephone because she lived in another city. This patient was seen monthly during the past year and there has been no return of her symptoms. She also lost 35 pounds with a dietary and hypnotic approach. When last seen, she was quite active for a person of her years, very happy and looking forward to a useful life. No attempt was made to understand her personality difficulties, and not even superficial exploration was attempted.

MacLaren and Eisenberg[33a] studied a group of 50 carefully selected asthmatics who showed no response to medical therapy, and who had overt signs of emotional instability. Hostile, skeptical individuals or those who had advanced lung disease were rejected. They noted that if suggestions directed toward the patient's breathing in unison with the operator's counting was followed, the breathing soon became slower and quieter. Strong suggestions of the chest's relaxing usually eliminated breathing difficulties. Sensory-imagery conditioning involving relaxing experiences were employed. Posthypnotic suggestions that the bronchial tubes were opening helped relax the breathing. Scene-visualization technics oriented around the patient's seeing himself in a protected and comfortable position were most effective.

Their results, however, showed a high number of relapses brought about by exposure to a strong antigen, or respiratory infection. In the emotionally disturbed asthmatics, stress precipitated severe attacks. They concluded that, for more lasting results, threats to the individual's emotional stability had to be uncovered or the person's fears of the threats had to be corrected by psychotherapy.

When fear of choking, which is commonly noted in these patients, was neutralized by reassurance and relaxed breathing exercises, 75 per cent of the relapsed patients improved. Others were asked to ventilate their emotions prior to the attacks. Using an abreactive technic, they had their patients relive anxiety-provoking situations, but without effects. One in 8 could not be hypnotized readily, and 1 in 3 can be hypnotized but gets little if any benefit. Two out of 3 get relief, varying from temporary to sustained effects.

Many deaths occur with steroids, and this alone makes the assessment of the potentialities of hypnosis more rather than less urgent. Edwards[9a] reports that hypnosis worked by decreasing airways' resistance or by a psychological effect (decreased awareness of airways' resistance). Another report extolled the effect of dramatically saving an elderly man's life by hypnosis for a severe case of status asthmaticus.[44a]

Recent observations[36a] deserve mention: typical attacks of bronchial asthma were hypnotically produced, and the attacks thus provoked were immediately terminated by appropriate hypnotic suggestions. This indicates that bronchial asthma results from a conditioned reflex to harmful external and internal stimulation. African natives, who have a high incidence of tuberculosis, almost never have asthma.

Therefore, bronchial asthma is a "neurosis of the lungs." The expiratory phase in humans is particularly "overloaded" because it underlies the entire complex of speech; hence, breathing is the first manifestation of suffering. The involvement expresses itself as an alteration in the tonus of the smooth muscles of the bronchi.

There are numerous reports of asthma treated by short-term hypnotherapy. Soviet scientists believe that the results achieved by hypnosis may be due to

. . . liberation of the functions of the physiologically lower divisions of the central nervous system and that this may be achieved by inhibition of the higher divisions which normally regulate their work.[36a]

ALLERGY

Allergic reactions are frequently associated with stress.[17, 25, 43, 46] Urticaria can be precipitated by traumatic life situations. There are significant differences between acute and chronic urticaria; specific allergens are not present in the latter.[39]

Hypnosis has been employed to prevent asthmatic attacks in individuals susceptible to certain allergens, even though skin tests remained positive and attacks were produced when these patients were shown an artificial rose or a picture of this.[19, 53] Wheals resulting from a cutaneous reaction to eggs have been suppressed by hypnosis.[3] The suppression of allergic skin reactions by hypnosis has not been confirmed.[57] However, some[6] have concluded that hypnotic suggestion influences cutaneous allergic reactions.

The above data indicate that the widespread use of injections may be because of a placebo effect. Lowell[32] believes that the rationale for injection therapy has not been validated to exclude coincidental factors, chance or bias. He states:

. . . we cannot rule out the possibility of a happy coincidence—the initiation of treatment in a year of less intense exposure to pollen, instruction in allergic cleanliness and in the intelligent use of drugs, the allaying of anxiety, the spontaneous lessening of the patient's level of clinical sensitivity and, last but by no means least, the suggestion that accompanies the ritual of injection therapy. These, individually or in combination, might explain many a success without invoking any specific therapeutic or prophylactic merit for the solution that we put into the syringe.

The author is not surprised at these remarks. When he first began his practice, several hay-fever victims had complete relief from placebo medications. He has recently seen patients with angioneurotic edema, hives and urticarial reactions who responded to hypnotherapy. He well remembers the case of a 12-year-old boy, a nephew of the man with asthma whose case was discussed on page 178.

The boy was allergic to cats, weeds and candy. His uncle, who had been aided in a remarkable fashion, brought the patient to me. Because of the prestige factor, he was readily hypnotized and given posthypnotic suggestions that he could play with his cat, walk through a weed patch and eat chocolate candy. He was seen again in one week and, to my surprise, he reported that he no longer reacted to these agents. He was presented at a workshop almost 1 year later, with a history of no attacks. At this time, an amnesia was engrafted for the fact he had ever been hypnotized. Upon dehypnotization he ate a candy bar and, as expected, developed numerous hives about his face, neck and torso. Rehypnotization, together with appropriate suggestions, caused the hives to disappear. The amnesia was removed, and now, following termination of the hypnotic state, he ate candy without difficulty—a case which might be designated as fulfilling a psychological Koch's postulate.

Once again, the author wishes to emphasize that those who benefited from hypnosis are being presented in this section. Failures do occur, and at times the handling of such cases taxes the patience of both patient and therapist. Goldman[15a] noted that, in most allergic patients, the benefits from hypnosis are not proportionate to the effort involved. However, in tense and anxious asthmatics, hypnosis reduced fright reactions. He wisely advocates that pulmonary function tests be used to record actual progress. The reader must realize that results in any condition depend on many variables in the physician and patient rapport. One man gets recoveries and results while another using the same approach gets only failures.

REFERENCES

1. Ambrose, G., and Newbold, G.: A Handbook of Medical Hypnosis, London, Baillière, Tindall & Cox, 1958.
1a. Andreev, B. V.: Sleep Therapy in the Neuroses, New York, Consultants Bureau, 1960.
2. Bruch, H.: The Importance of Overweight, New York, Norton, 1957.
3. Clarkson, A. K.: The nervous factor in juvenile asthma, Brit. M. J. 2:845-850, 1937.
3a. Cole, S. L., Kaye, H., and Griffith, G. C.: Assay of antianginal agents—the rapport period, J.A.M.A. vol. 168, Sept. 20, 1958.
4. Daniels, G. E.: Emotional and instinctual factors in diabetes mellitus, Am. J. Psychiat. 93:711-724, 1936.
5. de Moraes Passos, A. C.: Do Mesmerismo a Hipnolgia e ao Sono Prolongado Sugerido, Rev. Psycol. Norm. e Patalog., pp. 167-192, 1957.
6. Diehl, F., and Heinichen, W.: Beeinflüssung allergischer Reaktionen, München. med. Wchnschr. 78:1008-1009, 1931.
7. Dorcus, R. M., and Goodwin, P.: The treatment of patients with the dumping syndrome by hypnosis, J. C. E. H. 3:200, 1955.
8. Dunbar, H. F.: Emotions and Bodily Changes, New York, Columbia, 1938.
9. ——: Emotions and Bodily Changes, ed. 3, New York, Columbia, 1946.
9a. Edwards, G.: Hypnotic treatment of Asthma, Brit. Med. J., pp. 492-498, Aug. 13, 1960.
10. Eisenbud, J.: The psychology of headache: a case studied experimentally, Psychiat. Quart. 11:592-619, 1937.
10a. Elkins, M.: Paper delivered at Amer. Soc. of Clin. Hypnose, Oct., 1960.
10b. Foa, P. P.: The mediation of psychic stimuli and regulation of endocrine function in Kroger, W. S. (ed.): Psychosomatic Obstetrics, Gynecology and Obstetrics, Springfield, Thomas, 1962.
11. Fogelman, M. J., and Crasilneck, H. B.: Food intake and hypnosis, J. Am. Dietetic A. 32:519, 1956.
12. Freed, S. C.: Psychic factors in the development and treatment of overweight, J.A.M.A. 133:369, 1947.
13. French, T., and Alexander, F.: Psychogenic factors in bronchial asthma, Psychosom. Med. Monog. Ser. 2:34, 1941.
14. Friedman, A. P.: Migraine and Other Common Headaches, World-Wide Abstracts, September, 1959.
15. Op. cit., p. 17.
15a. Goldman, S. T.: Paper read at Am. Coll. Allergists, 1961.
16. Goodell, H., Lewontin, R., and Wolff, H. G.: The familial occurrence of migraine headache: A study of heredity, Res. Pub. A. Nerv. & Ment. Dis. 33:346, 1953.
17. Grant, R. T., Bruce-Pearson, R. S., and Comeau, W. J.: Observations on urticaria provoked by emotions, by exercise and by warming the body, Clin. Sc. 2:253-272, 1936.
18. Halliday, J. L.: Psychological aspects of rheumatoid arthritis, Proc. Roy. Soc. Med. 35:455, 1942.
19. Hansen, K.: Analyse, Indikation und Grenze der Psychotherapie beim Bronchialasthma, Deutsche med. Wchnschr. 55:1462-1464, 1927.

20. Harding, H. C.: Hypnosis and migraine or vice versa, Paper read at the 11th Annual Scientific Meeting of the S.C.E.H. San Francisco, August, 1959.

21. Hartz, J.: Thoracoplasty and claustrophobia, Psychosom. Med. 7:34, 1946.

22. Hinkle, L. E., Jr., Conger, G. B., and Wolf, S.: Studies in diabetes mellitus: the relation of stressful life situations to the concentration of ketone bodies in the blood of diabetic and nondiabetic humans, J. Clin. Invest. 29:754, 1950.

23. Hinkle, L. E., and Wolf, S.: Experimental study of life situations, emotions and the occurrence of acidosis in a juvenile diabetic, Am. J. M. Sc. 217:130-135, 1949.

24. Holmes, T. H., et al.: Psychosocial and psychophysiologic studies of tuberculosis, Psychosom. Med. 19:134-143, 1957.

25. Hopkins, J. G., Kasten, B. M., and Hazel, O. G.: Urticaria provoked by heat or psychic stimuli, Arch. Dermat. & Syph. 38:419-422, 1938.

26. Horan, J. S.: Hypnosis and recorded suggestions in the treatment of migraine, J.C.E.H. 1:7-10, 1953.

26a. Ivy, A. C.: Motor dysfunction of biliary tract: analytical and critical consideration (Caldwell lecture 1946), Amer. J. Roentgenol. 57:1, 1947.

27. Kline, M. V.: Situational cardiovascular symptomatology and hypnosis, Brit. J. M. Hypnotism 1:33-36, 1950.

28. Kupfer, D.: Hypnotherapy in a case of functional heart disorder, J.C.E.H. 2:186-191, 1954.

29. Lidz, T.: Emotional factors in etiology of hyperthyroidism, Psychosom. Med. 11:2, 1947.

30. Leonard, A. S., et al.: Treatment of postgastrectomy dumping syndrome by hypnotic suggestion, J.A.M.A. 165:1957-1959, 1957.

31. Levine, S. A.: Some notes concerning angina pectoris, J.A.M.A. 171:1838, 1840, 1959.

32. Lowell, F. C.: American Academy of Allergy: Presidential Address, J. Allergy. 31:185, 1960.

33. Magonet, A. P.: Hypnosis and asthma, Int. J.C.E.H. 8:121-127, 1960.

33a. MacLaren, W. R., and Eisenberg, B. C.: Hypnosis in the treatment of asthma, Paper read at the Pan American Med. Assoc., May 5, 1960.

34. Marchesi, C.: The hypnotic treatment of bronchial asthma, Brit. J. M. Hypnotism 1:14-19, 1949.

35. Moody, H.: An evaluation of hypnotically induced relaxation for the reduction of peptic ulcer symptoms, Brit. J. Med. Hypnotism 5:23, 1953.

35a. Ostfeld, A. M.: Migraine headache, J.A.M.A. 174:110-112, 1960.

36. Ostfeld, A. M., Chapman, L. E., Goodell, H., and Wolff, H. G.: Studies in headache: A summary of evidence implicating a locally active chemical agent in migraine, Tr. Am. Neurol. A., 81st Meeting, p. 356, 1956.

36a. Platonov, K.: The word as a physiological and therapeutic factor, Moscow, Foreign Language Publishing House, 1955.

37. Raginsky, B. B.: in Schneck, J. M. (ed.): Hypnosis in Modern Medicine, Springfield, Ill., Thomas, 1959.

38. Op. cit., p. 37.

39. Op. cit., p. 41.

40. Raginsky, B. B.: The Use of Hypnosis in Internal Medicine, presented at Pan American Med. Assoc., May, 1960.

41. Rosen, H.: Hypnotherapy in Clinical Psychiatry, New York, Julian Press, 1953.

42. Russek, H. I.: Role of heredity, diet and emotional stress in coronary heart disease, J.A.M.A. 171:503-508, 1959.

43. Saul, L. J., and Bernstein, G., Jr.: The emotional settings of some attacks of urticaria, Psychosom. Med. 3:349-369, 1941.

44. Schneck, J. M.: Psychogenic cardiovascular reaction interpreted and successfully treated with hypnosis, Psychoanalytic Rev. 35:14, 1948.

44a. Sinclair-Gieben, A. H. C.: Treatment of status asthmaticus by hypnosis. Brit. Med. J. 2:1651-1652, 1960.

45. Sparer, P. J.: Personality, Stress and Tuberculosis, New York, Internat. Univ. Press, 1956.

46. Stokes, J. H., Kulchar, G. V., and Pillsbury, D. M.: Effect on the skin of emotions and nerves; etiologic background of urticaria with special reference to psychoneurogenous factors, Arch. Dermat. & Syph. 31:470-499, 1935.

47. Traut, E. F., and Passarelli, E. W.: Placebo and the treatment of rheumatoid arthritis and other rheumatoid conditions, Ann. Rheumat. Dis. 18:21, 1957.

48. Van Pelt, S. J.: Hypnotherapy in medical practice, Brit. J. M. Hypnotism 1:8-13, 1949.

49. ——: Hypnotism and its importance in medicine, Brit. J. M. Hypnotism *1*:19, 1949.

50. ——: Some misconceptions met with in hypnotic practice, Brit. J. M. Hypnotism *1*:33, 1950.

51. Vaughan, W. T.: Practice of Allergy, St. Louis, Mosby, 1939.

51a. Winklestein, C.: Nonspecific ulcerative colitis, Roche Report *3*:1, 1961.

52. Wittkower, E.: Studies on the influence of emotions on the functions of organs including observations in normals and neurotics, J. Ment. Sc. *81*:533, 1935.

53. Wittkower, E., and Petow, H.: Beitrage zur Klinik des Asthma Bronchiale und Verwandter Zustände. V. Zur Psychogenese des Asthma Bronchiale, Ztschr. f. klin. Med. *119*:293-306, 1931-1932.

54. Wolberg, L. R.: Medical Hypnosis, vol. 1, New York, Grune & Stratton, 1948.

55. Wolff, H. G.: Headache and Other Head Pain, New York, Oxford Univ. Press, 1948.

56. Yanovsky, A. and Urbach, J.: Address at Colgate Symposium.

57. Zeller, M.: Influence of hypnosis on passive transfer and skin tests, Ann. Allergy *2*:515-516, 1944.

SUPPLEMENTARY READING

Blumenthal, L. B.: Hypnosis in the treatment of headache and related disorders, presented before Am. Soc. of Psychosomatic Medicine and Dentistry, March 1960.

de Moraes Passos and Farina, O., (eds.): Aspectos Atuais de Hipnologia. São Paulo, S.P., Brazil, Linografica Editora Limieada, 1961.

Edmonston, W. E.: Hypnotic age-regression: an evaluation of role-taking theory, Am. J. Clin. Hypnosis *5*:3-8, 1962.

Ikemi, Y.: Experimental Studies on the Psychosomatic Disorders of the Digestive System, Proc. Wld. Cong. Gastroent., Washington, D. C., Williams and Wilkins, 1959.

Mann, H.: Group hypnosis in the treatment of obesity, Am. J. Clin. Hypnosis *1*:114-117, 1959.

Svorad, D., and Hoskovec, J.: Experimental and clinical study of hypnosis in the Soviet Union and the European socialist countries: bibliography, Am. J. Clin. Hypnosis *4*:36-47, 1961.

Yanovski, A. G.: The feasibility of alteration of cardiovascular manifestations in hypnosis, Am. J. Clin. Hypnosis *5*:8-17, 1962.

32

Hypnosis in Surgery and Anesthesiology

HISTORY

In this section, the "newer" clinical applications of hypnosis in surgery will be presented. Voltaire once said, "What is new is old, and what is old is not new." No further proof of this adage is needed than the following:

I put a long knife in at the corner of his mouth, and brought the point out over the cheekbone, dividing the parts between; from this, I pushed it through the skin at the inner corner of the eye, and dissected the cheek back to the nose. The pressure of the tumor had caused the absorption of the anterior wall of the antrum, and on pressing my fingers between it and the bones, it burst, and a shocking gush of blood, and brain-like matter, followed. The tumor extended as far as my fingers could reach under the orbit and cheekbone, and passed into the gullet—having destroyed the bones and partition of the nose. No one touched the man, and I turned his head into any position I desired, without resistance, and there it remained till I wished to move it again: when the blood accumulated, I bent his head forward, and it ran from his mouth as if from a leaden spout. The man never moved, nor showed any signs of life, except an occasional indistinct moan; but when I threw back his head, and passed my fingers into his throat to detach the mass in that direction, the stream of blood was directed into his wind-pipe, and some instinctive effort became necessary for existence; he therefore coughed, and leaned forward, to get rid of the blood; and I suppose that he then awoke. The operation was by this time finished, and he was laid on the floor to have his face sewed up, and while this was doing, he for the first time opened his eyes.

Although it may come as a surprise to the reader, this formidable procedure was performed by James Esdaile in India before 1850![8]

To undergo the knife during this period was tantamount to signing one's death warrant. Fear of pain was equally as strong as fear of a fatal error by the surgeon. Many preferred death to the excruciating agony experienced during surgery. Those willing to undergo the ordeal usually screamed and struggled, which frequently affected the outcome. Some cursed, prayed, wept or fainted. The operation invariably produced severe shock, depressive reactions and other sequelae which delayed convalescence and wound-healing. Most operations were also a frightening procedure even for the calloused surgeon. Pain dominated the scene. Dupuytren summed up the situation for this period: "Pain kills like hemorrhage."

Four out of every 10 people died. Yet Esdaile's mortality rate was less than 5 per cent in a total of several thousand operations, about 300 of which were major procedures. The latter were all performed under mesmeric coma (hypnoanesthesia) and included the amputation of limbs and breasts and the removal of huge scrotal tumors. Even more interesting is the fact that Esdaile noted that neurogenic shock was noticeably diminished. This is remarkable, as he was without the benefit of anesthesia, modern-day asepsis, refined surgical technics, blood transfusions and antibiotics. The significance of his observations was not recognized until recently.

RECENT DEVELOPMENTS

Today, more than a century later, hypnosis has been accepted as a valuable therapeutic adjunct to potentiate chemoanesthesia. However, modern-day hynotherapists have modified the technics developed by Esdaile, Elliotson, Parker, Cloquet and other hardy pioneers of the past century. The most significant developments in this area include the use of autohypnosis, suggestions to improve the postoperative period, glove "anesthesia" and autogenic training. The last named technic, developed by Schultz,[16] employs a rehearsal or a "dry run" of the intended surgery. This type of conditioning protects the patient against surprise, fear and apprehension: the pain threshold is automatically raised by "blocking" the neurophysiologic paths that transmit the painful afferent impulses. No doubt a similar mechanism explains the marked difference in pain perception between most primiparas and multiparas; if one knows what to expect, the fear of the unknown is removed, and painful impulses are to some degree decreased in intensity.

In this connection, it is interesting that one of our patients (Case 1) complained of pain only when the towel clips were placed on her abdomen, prior to the skin incision. This apparently minor detail was inadvertently left out of the rehearsal beforehand. Several other patients operated on under hypnoanesthesia had similar experiences, indicating how well perceptual awareness can be organized into a variety of reactions, depending on the range of the adaptive processes.

The author has successfully used hypnoanesthesia for many other minor surgical procedures.

Despite its effectiveness in major surgery, hypnosis will never be a substitute for chemoanesthesia, since it can be utilized in less than 10 per cent of the cases and these must be very *carefully selected*. Its greatest use is to reduce preoperative medication and chemoanesthesia. It also has other pre- and postoperative advantages.

ADVANTAGES AND DISADVANTAGES

Since the use of hypnosis allays fear and tension, induction of inhalation anesthesia is facilitated, anoxemia is reduced and, because of the profound relaxation, less analgesia and anesthesia are required. In some patients the traditional preoperative administration of morphine, meperidine hydrochloride (Demerol), and pentobarbital sodium often can be eliminated even in those who can enter only the light stage of hypnosis. It is believed that, even in minimal doses, most analgesic agents produce some degree of respiratory depression and lower the blood-oxygen volume. Beecher[2] states, "Narcotics are not necessary for preanesthetic medication but their presence is actually harmful." He found that in patients on placebo medication (0.6 mg. of atropine sulfate), experienced anesthesiologists could not differentiate between those who had received the narcotic and those who had received the placebo. Since this form of suggestion is so effective, obviously hypnoanesthesia would be more efficacious.

Postoperatively, hypnosis is of inestimable value when it is used in suitable patients. For instance, when surgical patients wake up, they usually are afraid to cough because of excessive pain, especially those having upper abdominal operations. In good subjects, trained to enter quickly into hypnosis, fear, and often pain, may be eradicated in a matter of seconds by posthypnotic suggestion.

Through specific posthypnotic suggestions also, the breathing and the cough reflex can be regulated readily. Because of the extreme relaxation, hypnosis also facilitates aspiration through the tracheobronchial passages; this prevents pneumonitis and atelectasis. Excessive postoperative retching usually can be decreased and, in good subjects, this annoying complication can be entirely prevented by posthypnotic suggestions.

The chief disadvantage of hypnosis is its unpredictability and its effectiveness; not every patient responds as expected. Also, in those that are hypnotizable, the muscular relaxation may be less than required. As emphasized in the section on dangers, it should not be employed in severely disturbed persons, zealots or "crackpots."

Unless the hypnotic conditioning is performed in a group, the procedure can be time-consuming; several hours of preparation may be required. However, since hypnosis is seldom utilized as the anesthetic agent per se, the unpredictability is not a deterrent—even if only partially successful, its advantages outweigh its disadvantages.

INDICATIONS AND REVIEW
OF THE LITERATURE

Pharmacologic analgesia and anesthesia, with their ease of administration and effectiveness, are the methods of choice over pure hypnoanesthesia for major surgery because of their reliability. However, where there is a definitive contraindication to all types of chemoanesthesia, hypnoanesthesia is indicated.

Hypnosis, in combination with anesthesia, also can be employed routinely for the poor surgical risk as well as for the debilitated and geriatric patient undergoing major surgery. It also encourages early ambulation, acceptance of surgical deformities, as, for instance, enteric stomas, maintenance of morale during a stormy convalescent period, alleviation of bizarre types of pain and earlier intake of fluids.[9a]

The combined approach has been used by Marmer[12] for a thoracotomy for heart disease. Another patient, a 42-year-old woman, underwent mitral commissurotomy after receiving only hexylcaine hydrochloride topically for endotracheal intubation and succinylcholine chloride intravenously for muscular relaxation. This patient required no postoperative narcotics or sedatives and manifested total operative amnesia. Marmer concluded that the reassurance induced by hypnosis allays fear, anxiety and tension more effectively than the tranquilizing drugs.

Doberneck et al.[3] utilized hypnosis as a pre- and postoperative adjunct in the treatment of 99 surgical cases, including the post-gastrectomy or "dumping" syndrome, postoperative pain, obesity (treated before surgery to lessen the operative risk) and various bizarre forms of pain. Striking improvement occurred in 94 per cent of the patients with the dumping syndrome; 26 out of 32 gained an average of 5.4 pounds over an average 14-month follow-up. Posthypnotic suggestions in 31 cases before surgery significantly decreased their postoperative narcotic requirements; the patients were more co-operative and cheerful and less complaining. The relief of various forms of bizarre pain was sometimes spectacular, even occurring several times in patients who

had had 1 to 3 unsuccessful cordotomies. Hypnosis was particularly effective in unexplained low back pain and pain of metastatic cancer.

Dorcus found that hypnosis is particularly useful for phantom limb pain[4] as well as for the dumping syndrome.[5] The gastric symptoms were present from 8 to 26 months. Two to 9 hypnosis sessions were required for remission in 4 patients. Suggestions were directed toward reduction of tension, removing the fear of the illness and increasing food and liquid consumption by improving the olfactory appeal of the food itself. Fogelman and Crasilneck[9] used hypnosis in patients who had severe burns; the dressings could be changed without discomfort. Nutritional illnesses are generally helped by the increased caloric intake. Pain, flatulence and anorexia often respond dramatically.

Postoperative hiccoughs are often an annoying complication of surgery. Dorcus and Kirkner[6] observed that hypnosis produced muscular relaxation and alleviated anxiety in a series of 18 cases that were refractory to all other therapies.[6] Fourteen patients were permanently relieved, 3 were not helped, and 1 benefited temporarily. The author of this book recently cured 2 refractory cases of postoperative hiccoughs—one following removal of the gallbladder and the other following a transurethral resection—in one session of hypnosis. Postoperative urinary retention often responds to hypnosuggestive therapy.

Hypnosis is of value in plastic surgery and for dermabrasion.[7] Patients requiring extensive suturing of facial lacerations or intermaxillary wiring of fractures of the mandible and the maxilla do not have airway problems under hypnosis. In most of these cases, a general anesthetic would be hazardous. The apposition of two widely separated areas can be maintained through posthypnotic suggestions while a tissue graft is being transferred from one to the other. Kelsey and Barron[11] secured fixation by these means instead of a plaster of Paris cast, which is uncomfortable, causes sores, immobilizes the joint and produces a stiffness that may require weeks of physiotherapy. Some subjects under hypnosis can be placed in bizarre postures; their limbs remain fixed until suggestions are given for their release.

They described a patient whose right foot was to be repaired with a pedicle graft from the abdomen transported via the left forearm. Under hypnosis, the left arm was fixed in rigid catalepsy against the abdomen through posthypnotic suggestions. This was so effective that it could not be moved voluntarily, nor could it be moved by attendants until it was "unlocked" by later hypnotic suggestions. The position was maintained until released at the next operation 3 weeks later. It was astonishing that, from the moment of release, movement of the elbow and the shoulder joints was full, free and painless. A similar procedure was adopted for the transfer of the pedicle from the wrist to the forepart of the foot. The arm and the wrist were again placed in the optimal position and locked there under hypnosis. This position was maintained for 28 days, during which the patient slept sitting up! At the end of this time, the arm was unlocked by appropriate posthypnotic suggestions. Immediately, once again, the movements of all the joints, including those of the spine and the fingers, were full, free and painless. Physiotherapists and nurses were trained to reinforce the hypnosis.

A bilateral mammoplasty on a tense and fearful patient was recently reported.[13] It is believed that hypnosis is valuable for relieving the pain of injuries sustained in accidents.[10, 13] Hypnosis has been effective in the setting of fractures and the repair of lacerations.[13] Hypnosis has been used in disguised form, especially in children, to perform minor surgical procedures. With light analgesia and hypnoanesthesia, they also react better and have smoother recoveries. Vaughn[17] has performed an amazing number of all types of major surgery under a combination of light anesthesia and hypnosis. Several amputations of limbs were included in his series.

Hypnosis is a very valuable adjunct for the relief of bizarre types of postoperative pain, such as unexplained backache and abdominal pain, and for controlling the intractable pain of the terminal cancer patient. Through posthypnotic suggestion, autohypnosis and glove anesthesia, the need for opiates is markedly reduced. More important, strong faith and the "will to live" can be exceedingly helpful.

Obstinate constipation following surgery often responds dramatically to appropriate posthypnotic suggestions. Here, too, the posthypnotic suggestions must be directed toward the subjective feelings associated with the act. Werbel[18] used posthypnotic suggestions to prevent posthemorrhoidectomy pain in a series of 11 patients. Their course was compared with that of the same number of other patients who were not hypnotized and acted as a control group. The first group was advised that rectal pain would not be felt after the surgery, that they would have relaxed bowel movements. All were cued to enter hypnosis readily. Not a single person in the hypnotized group had severe pain, and 8 claimed to have less discomfort than anticipated.

MECHANISM OF HYPNOANESTHESIA

Though the mechanism of hypnoanesthesia is as yet poorly understood, current research indicates that the pain, perceived in the tissues, does not reach the pain receptors in the higher brain centers during hypnosis. With the higher cortical centers inhibited during deep hypnosis, the reticular formation and other subcortical centers prevent the intrusion of painful impulses into awareness. This raises the adaptive responses of the organism to them (painful stimuli). Further psychophysiologic investigations are needed to elucidate the mechanisms by which hypnosis reduces neurogenic shock in surgery.

From an operational standpoint, a subject is relieved of pain when he becomes "relatively inattentive and unconcerned about all stimuli to which the hypnotist does not specifically direct his attention." If the readiness to respond is minimized, "the sensation of pain" is no longer "painful"; it is an isolated "sensation" unaccompanied by pain.[1]

TECHNICS FOR SURGERY

In order to reduce the surgical candidate's apprehension, the author always has a preliminary discussion with the patient, which may be as follows: "I have taught you hypnotic relaxation. You have demonstrated that you can enter into a very deep state of relaxation and be completely oblivious to all discomfort. Remember you will relax deeper and deeper with each breath you take. You also were able to achieve glove anesthesia readily. Before being taken to the operating room, you will transfer this glove anesthesia to the right side of your abdomen (or wherever the surgical field may be). You will have no more discomfort than you are willing to bear. Should you have even the slightest amount of discomfort, an anesthetic will be available upon your request—either gas, spinal or procaine. There is no need to have the slightest anticipation because either way you will have a very pleasant experience. You can look forward to your operation without dread or anxiety. I will be present during the entire surgical procedure and will do everything possible to make you comfortable and free from tension." When using surgical hypnoanesthesia, the patient must be watched carefully. If there is any sign of severe pain manifested by a facial flinch or a grimace, supplementary chemoanesthesia is necessary. Fewer than 10 per cent of individuals can go through an entire major surgical procedure *without* chemoanalgesia or anesthesia. Therefore, pain relief should not be limited to hypnotic methods, but one must use the balanced approach—hypnoanesthesia together with chemoanesthesia.

With reference to conduction anesthesia, at least half the success of local infiltration is *vocal*. The ideal method is the joint use of hypnoanesthesia and local anesthesia. One must continually reassure the apprehensive patient in a calm, confident, reassuring voice. Each patient must be inculcated with the idea that the hypnoanesthesia is going to help alleviate his fear and anxiety. The patient picks up this confidence, and he relaxes even further.

REHEARSAL TECHNIC

During a typical rehearsal session for abdominal surgery the patient is told, "Now your skin is being sterilized." (At this time the abdomen is swabbed with an alcohol sponge.) "I am now stretching the skin and making the incision in the skin." (The line of incision is lightly stroked with a pencil.) "Now the tissues are being cut. Just relax. You feel nothing, absolutely nothing. Your breathing is getting slower, deeper and more regular. Each side of the incision is being separated by an instrument." (The skin and the muscles are pulled laterally from the midline.) "Now a blood vessel is being clamped." (A hemostat is clicked shut.) "You feel absolutely no discomfort. You are calm, quiet and relaxed. Your breathing is getting slower, deeper and more regular. Just relax! Now I am going deeper and entering the abdominal cavity." (For the peritoneum, suggestions of relaxation and assurances of complete pain relief are repeated several times.) "Just relax. You are getting deeper and deeper relaxed; your heartbeat is getting slower and more regular. Just relax. You feel nothing, absolutely nothing." The viscera are relatively insensitive to cutting—one does not have to worry about pain. However, the patient has to be prepared for the discomfort produced by pulling and torsion of the abdominal organs.

The steps for closure of the peritoneum, muscles, fascia and skin are also described in a similar manner. There are really only 3 times when pain can be expected: When the skin is incised, when the peritoneum is incised, and when one is tugging on the viscera.

MAINTENANCE OF HYPNOANESTHESIA DURING SURGERY

The following is a verbalization for maintaining hypnosis: "All the muscles in your body are relaxed, and, with every breath you take, you will find yourself going deeper and deeper relaxed. You are doing fine. Just relax all the muscles of your abdomen and chest. You are breathing slower, deeper and more regular. That's right. In and out . . . in and out. Going deeper and deeper relaxed. You feel nothing except a little pressure. The more relaxed you are, the less tension you will have, and the less tension you have, the less discomfort you will have." Frequently there is a slight trembling of the eyelids. This often is indicative of deep hypnosis. One can use this objective sign to deepen the hypnosis, as follows: "I notice that your lids are now trembling. That's a good sign. And, as they continue to tremble, you will go deeper and deeper relaxed. You feel yourself falling, falling, deeper and deeper relaxed with every breath you take. Remember, if you want to open your eyes at any time, you may. Voices won't bother you."

Production of catalepsy by light stroking of the skin frequently minimizes capillary bleeding, probably as the result of vasospasm. Here the law of dominant effect is put to use: a psychological suggestion is enhanced by a physiologic effect. As the region that is going to be operated on is stroked lightly, I remark: "This area is getting very stiff, cold and numb. Think, feel and imagine that there is an ice cube on your skin. Now it is getting more numb and colder. Numb and cold. Very, very cold." This verbalization and the stroking are most advantageous where bleeding from the skin is expected.

If the hypnosis fails during surgery, one can easily switch to intravenous or inhalation anesthesia. It is always advisable to have these available for prompt use.

POSTOPERATIVE VERBALIZATION FOR DEHYPNOTIZATION

Patients are dehypnotized as follows: "You will feel just as if you have awakened from a deep sleep, but, of course, you know you were not asleep. You will be very, very relaxed. Any time in the future when I touch you on the right shoulder, if I have your permission, you will close your eyes and let your eyeballs roll up into the back of your head. Then you will count backward from 100 to zero slowly, and you will go deeper and deeper relaxed with every breath you take and every number you count. You will find that the period after your operation will be a very pleasant one. Should you have any discomfort in and around the wound, you may use the glove anesthesia which you learned to develop to 'knock it out.' You will be able to relax and sleep soundly. Should you require medication for sleep, it will make you very sleepy. You will not hesitate to eat the food given to you and, as a matter of fact, you will relish every bite. You will be very, very hungry.

The more nutritious food you are able to consume, the faster your tissues will heal. I am going to count to 5 and you will open your eyes." Dehypnotization should be done slowly: "You will feel completely alert, refreshed and wonderful after you open your eyes. One, you are feeling fine. Two, more alert. Three, still more alert. Four, sound in mind, sound in body, no headache. Five, open your eyes. You feel wonderful."

Marmer[12a] uses posthypnotic suggestions to ensure a better postoperative recovery as the patient is emerging from the chemoanesthesia. These are repeated again and again while the patient is in the recovery room to provide additional re-enforcement.

When general anesthesia is used with hypnosis, the sense of hearing may be acute during the state of analgesia. All remarks should be guarded when in this stage, especially if heavy doses of muscle-relaxant drugs have been given with resultant controlled respiration. Some investigators believe that trauma which may adversely alter the postoperative state can be inflicted by careless remarks.

DISGUISED TECHNIC

The following disguised technic is excellent for patients requiring minor surgery. It makes use of misdirection of attention. First, a bandage or a towel is placed over the patient's eyes. I state: "You are now going to go into a deep state of relaxation. Just close your eyes. Start breathing. Breathe slowly and deeply. With each breath you take, you will feel yourself going deeper and deeper relaxed. And, if you wish to go deeper, all you have to do is start counting backward from 100 to zero. Breathe slowly, deeply and more regularly. And with each number that you count backward, and with every breath you take, you will feel yourself going deeper and deeper relaxed. Now I am inserting the first stitch." (The needle is gently placed on the edge of the wound; no pressure is employed.) "There, the first stitch is in. You did not feel any pain, did you?" (The patient shakes his head.) "Just relax deeper and deeper and deeper, and with each breath you take, you will feel nothing. Now, here is the second stitch." (Again one resorts to the same procedure—

a hallucinated stitch.) If one maintains a steady flow of words, as, "You are going deeper and deeper relaxed," the individual will enter into deep hypnosis without being aware that it is being employed. After rigid catalepsy is produced, anesthesia for the entire area can be suggested. Because belief has been compounded into conviction of anesthesia, it will now be produced automatically. On numerous occasions I have been able to sew up extensive lacerations without having the patient aware that hypnosis had been induced—all without discomfort.

CASE REPORTS

The following case reports, all recent, illustrate how hypnoanesthesia, *without the use of any type of analgesia or anesthesia,* can be employed for major and minor surgery. All the patients were prepared by autohypnosis, glove anesthesia and the rehearsal technic. During the rehearsal method, every detail in the surgery was fully described while the patient was under deep hypnosis. It should be emphasized that there are few indications for pure hypnoanesthesia. Nor does this author advocate an "all-or-none" approach. However, the following cases were performed under rigidly controlled conditions to demonstrate the authenticity of hypnoanesthesia. The patients, with the exception of Case 1, were selected carefully. This is an important point to consider, as it would be impossible to perform an abdominoperineal resection or craniotomy by hypnosis per se.

CASE 1

Mrs. E. W., an 18-year-old Negro, had an excision biopsy for a benign tumor of her left breast. This unselected patient was used to demonstrate the possibilities of hypnoanesthesia before a closed circuit telecast at the annual meeting of the New York State Society of Anesthesiologists in December, 1956.

I saw this patient for the first time the night before surgery and explained the advantages of hypnoanesthesia. On the first attempt, in the presence of the hospital's chief of anesthesiology, Dr. Vincent Collins, she was placed in a deep somnambulistic trance. An indirect and permissive hypnotic technic was employed. The patient was instructed in the method of de-veloping "glove anesthesia" in her right hand and transferring this anesthesia to her left breast. After she had demonstrated satisfactorily that she could do this with ease, a number 15 needle, about 6 or 7 inches in length, was readily passed completely through the breast from the lateral to the medial border. No sign of pain was manifested, nor was there any bleeding. The patient developed a spontaneous amnesia for the entire procedure.

The next day, the surgeon, Dr. W. Mitty, removed the tumor. The start and the finish of the surgery were shown over the telecast and in the presence of a distinguished panel of anesthesiologists. The surgeon noted the marked relaxation of the tissues, the decrease in bleeding, the complete immobility of the patient and the absence of pain or discomfort. He also stated that he could have performed more extensive surgery, adding, "I would not have believed it if I had not actually done and seen it."

Upon termination of the surgery, the patient was alerted and had absolutely no recollection of the operation. I asked her if she was ready to undergo the surgery, and she answered "Yes." On my telling her that the tumor had been removed, she evinced considerable surprise and incredulity. In this instance the posthypnotic amnesia was similar to Esdaile's mesmeric coma. The amnesia could have been removed; this is optional and depends on whether or not the patient wishes to remember any part of the surgical procedure. No preoperative or postoperative medication of any type was used for pain relief and the patient made an uneventful recovery.

This case is particularly interesting because only one training session was needed, and the entire procedure and the surgery were conducted under extremely difficult conditions. On reflection, the successful outcome can be explained by the following facts: I needed a patient for the telecast demonstration of hypnosis in surgery; this was the only one available, and I just had to induce hypnoanesthesia. It was my determination and self-confidence that established the necessary rapport between the patient and myself and this increased her inherent susceptibility to hypnosis. All these factors contributed to Esdaile's successful use of mesmeric anesthesia.

CASE 2

The case of Mrs. G. D., a 28-year-old Para II, gravida II, was recently reported.[11a] She had an elective cesarean-hysterectomy performed at the Chicago Lying-in Hospital by Dr. S. T.

DeLee, without analgesia or anesthesia. This is believed to be the first such case on record.

The patient experienced no objective or subjective discomfort. She was fully conscious and able to watch the birth of her baby, and there was no discomfort when the baby was delivered by forceps or when the uterus was extirpated. The patient made an uneventful recovery.

Case 3

Mrs. R. W., a 27-year-old white female, had a subtotal thyroidectomy *under hypnotic anesthesia per se.* This, too, is believed to be the first such case reported.* She was seen 8 times; trained to enter a somnambulistic state; and exhibited all the phenomena of deep hypnosis, such as amnesia, age regression, catalepsy, disassociation, glove anesthesia and autohypnosis.

During the last training session, a complete "dry run" rehearsal of the "removal" of the thyroid was done while deeply hypnotized. That anesthesia could be produced by disassociation or glove anesthesia indicates that a subject, even in a hypnotic state, is not at all subservient to the will of the operator.

Through preoperative posthypnotic suggestions she slept for 8 hours. The next morning, the prearranged cue induced a deep hypnotic state. No trace of nervousness was discernible, although she had been extremely fearful and tense the week prior to surgery, so much so that it was necessary to reassure her that she was "not going to die." Because of their extreme nervousness, hypnotic relaxation is particularly indicated in hyperthyroid and hypertensive individuals who require surgery.

The patient was taken to the operating room in a state characterized by profound neuromuscular relaxation. She transferred the glove anesthesia and produced complete insensibility of the neck. The entire procedure, the removal of both lobes of the thyroid, was performed without discomfort except for the period of traction on the trachea. Immediately after surgery, she sat up, talked and drank a glass of water! She was able to eat immediately and had no nausea or vomiting. The entire operation took about 70 minutes, and the patient stated, "I felt no pain at any time. I could feel only pressure and tugging at my throat. The scalpel felt like a feather being drawn across my neck." She made a completely uneventful recovery and was not confined to bed during the 5 days in the hospital. The hospital personnel were amazed at

* A documentary film of this case is available for rental from Wexler Film Co., 802 Seward, Hollywood, California.

the patient's progress; no analgesic drugs were required.

In Cases 2 and 3, not a single bleeder had to be clamped in the skin, probably because of the local ischemia induced by the rigid catalepsy usually associated with deep hypnosis. There was no sign of neurogenic shock, nor did the blood pressure fluctuate appreciably in either case! However, it must be emphasized that these patients were somnambules, and constitute a small percentage of the population. But most individuals can be hypnotized to some degree, and for these hypnosis can potentiate chemoanesthesia.

The following case illustrates how hypnosis helped to relieve a bizarre pain syndrome:

Mrs. S. K., aged 48, was seen at the Cedars of Lebanon Hospital in Los Angeles 3 weeks after a thoracotomy because of intractable pain in the incision. The patient was taught hypnosis, autohypnosis and glove anesthesia during the first session. The pain promptly subsided. During subsequent visits, a "restless-legs" syndrome that had been present for many years was suppressed by substituting the twitching of a finger, which in turn was removed. Intractable dysuria and chronic bladder dysfunction were alleviated by glove anesthesia and autohypnosis; symptoms of insomnia, nervous tension and fatigue were also helped by hypnosis. Follow-up 2 years later showed that the patient was still relieved of the above symptoms. No others had been manifested.

The author of this book has had success with surgical candidates who had an inordinate fear of "needles" or injections. In several cases, surgery was postponed until the phobic reaction was removed. Many other cases, directly or indirectly related to surgery, have dramatically responded to hypnotherapy. One patient with a throbbing in the throat following thyroidectomy was helped by intensive hypnotherapy. Another with chronic pain following removal of the gallbladder, and who had had several cordotomies, was relieved by glove anesthesia. These, and many more, attest to its value in the "port-of-last-call" patient.

CONCLUSIONS

Since hypnosis is a multifaceted tool, its effectiveness can be enhanced when it is employed in conjunction with other medical procedures. All physician-hypnotists who use hypnoanesthesia should recognize the limitations of this modality and not try to operate on every patient without careful selection, preparation and availability of chemoanesthesia. This should promote a healthier acceptance of hypnosis, especially if its advantages are utilized judiciously.

REFERENCES

1. Barber, T. X.: Toward a theory of pain: relief of chronic pain by prefrontal leucotomy, opiates, placebos and hypnosis, Psychol. Bull. 56:430-460, 1959.
2. Beecher, H. K.: Preanesthetic medication, J.A.M.A. 157:242-243, 1955.
3. Doberneck, R. C., et al.: Hypnosis as an adjunct to surgical therapy, Surgery 46: 299-304, 1959.
4. Dorcus, R. M.: Hypnosis and Its Therapeutic Applications, New York, McGraw-Hill, 1957.
5. Dorcus, R. M., and Goodwin, P.: The treatment of patients with the dumping syndrome by hypnosis, J. C. E. H. 3:200, 1955.
6. Dorcus, R. M., and Kirkner, F. J.: The control of hiccoughs by hypnotic therapy, J. C. E. H. 3:104, 1955.
7. Ecker, H. A.: Hypnosis Aid in Plastic Surgery, Factor, p. 7, January, 1960.
8. Esdaile, J.: Mesmerism in India and Its Practical Application in Surgery and Medicine, Hartford, England, Silus Andrus & Son, 1850.
9. Fogelman, M. J., and Crasilneck, H. B.: Food intake and hypnosis, J. Am. Dietet. A. 32:519, 1956.
9a. Gentry, R. W.: Hypnosis in Surgery, Paper delivered at Pan American Medical Association, May 10, 1960.
10. Goldie, L.: Hypnosis in the casualty department, Brit. M. J. 2:1340, 1956.
11. Kelsey, J. H., and Barron, R. R.: Hypnosis in plastic surgery, Brit. M. J. 1:756, 1958.
11a. Kroger, W. S., and DeLee, S. T.: Use of hypnoanesthesia for cesarean section and hysterectomy, J.A.M.A. 163:442, 1957.
12. Marmer, M. J.: Hypnoanalgesia and hypnoanesthesia for cardiac surgery, J.A.M.A. 171:512-517, 1959.
12a. ——: Hypnosis in Anesthesiology, Springfield, Ill., Thomas, 1960.
13. Mason, A. A.: Surgery under hypnosis, Anaesthesia 10:295, 1955.
14. Meerloo, J. A. M.: Suggestion and hypnosis in general practice, Am. Pract. 10: 2085-2087, 1959.
15. Owen-Flood, A.: Hypnotism and the anaesthetist, Brit. J. Anaesth. 27:398, 1955.
16. Schultz, J. H.: Some remarks about techniques of hypnosis as anesthetic, Brit. J. M. Hypnotism 5:23-25, 1954.
17. Vaughn, V.: Personal communication.
18. Werbel, E. W.: Experiences with frequent use of hypnosis in a general surgical practice, West. J. Surg. Obst. & Gynec. 68: 190-191, 1960.

SUPPLEMENTARY READING

Cheek, D. B.: Use of preoperative hypnosis to protect patients from careless conversation, Am. J. Clin. Hypnosis 3:101-103, 1960.
——: Unconscious perception of meaningful sounds during surgical anesthesia as revealed under hypnosis, Am. J. Clin. Hypnosis 1: 101-114, 1959.
Mahren, F. J.: Hypnosis and the surgical patient, Am. J. Proct. 11:459-465, 1960.

33

Hypnosis in Obstetrics

The use of hypnosis in obstetrics and surgery is not new. More than a century ago, mesmerism or hypnosis was one of the principal technics of pain relief for delivery. It was unfortunate that the discovery of inhalation anesthesia, in the middle of the last century, relegated hypnosis to undeserved oblivion.

In recent years, there has been a resurgence of interest in hypnoanesthesia.[8, 9, 11] However, as stressed throughout this book, it will never be a panacea, nor will it ever supplant chemoanesthesia in parturition. Nevertheless, as the late J. B. DeLee[3a] once stated: "The only anesthetic that is without danger is hypnotism . . . I am irked when I see my colleagues neglect to avail themselves of this harmless and potent remedy." Obstetricians are finally becoming aware of the use of hypnosis for obstetrical anesthesia as an adjunctive technic, as evidenced by the increasing number of reports.[12a, 18-20]

SUSCEPTIBILITY OF THE SUBJECT

Unfortunately, hypnoanesthesia per se is effective in less than 20 per cent of *selected* patients. However, in this group, episiotomy, forceps delivery and repair can be performed *without* analgesia or anesthesia. Approximately 50 per cent more can be carried through labor and delivery by a combination of hypnosis and drugs, preferably regional block. Where hypnosis potentiates chemoanesthesia, the combined method is better for this group than either method alone, as it permits a reduction of from 50 to 75 per cent in chemoanesthesia.

Conventional procedures are used for relieving pain in the remaining group, who are failures as far as hypnoanesthesia is concerned. However, by virtue of their exposure to prenatal hypnotic training, the majority of these are more co-operative and usually more relaxed, and regard their delivery as a most gratifying experience. Tom,[18] who believes that hypnosis has a limited use in labor, comments, "It is interesting to note that, regardless of the results, all but one (73 patients) of the patients thought that hypnosis was worthwhile and a great help during labor, and all wanted to use hypnosis again for the next delivery." The exception was a patient who had an improperly conducted labor. Thus, even when hypnoanesthesia is only partially effective, repeated suggestions with or without medications can mitigate the discomfort of labor. This is not surprising, as there are two routes for pain transmission—one physical, the other emotional. With chemoanesthesia, only the physical route for perception of painful stimuli is blocked. Strong suggestion and/or hypnosis effectively blocks the emotional pathway for apperception of painful stimuli.

PERSONALITY FACTORS IN SUGGESTIVE ANESTHESIA METHODS

Candidates for both hypnosis and the so-called "natural childbirth" method have been studied.[7] These patients often have similar personality profiles as well as an identical need for these procedures. They usually have a high degree of compulsiveness and a desire to please the father-figure (the obstetrician). Generally, their choice of these methods is based on multiple factors of which fear of childbirth is only a superficial aspect. Other reasons are fear of pain in general, fear of death while unconscious, fear of losing control of themselves and injuring the baby, fear of what might be said when they lose consciousness, curiosity as to the birth process and fear of pain as a punishment in cases in which the pregnancy is unwanted.

It has been contended that an emotionally mature attitude toward pregnancy is generally dependent on healthy psychosexual development. When a female approaches menstruation, marriage, sex and motherhood with fear, it is only natural to expect anxiety during pregnancy and labor. Also, women who have rejected the feminine role, either because of latent or overt homosexuality or fixation at earlier levels of personality development (the infantile adult), are more than likely to have inordinate need for pain relief during childbirth. Unfortunately, too few patients seek the suggestive methods which are the methods of choice for a safe labor—both physically and psychologically—for mother and child.

COMPARISON BETWEEN HYPNOSIS, "NATURAL CHILDBIRTH" AND PSYCHOPROPHYLACTIC RELAXATION

There is no doubt that the expectation of pain and fear associated with labor can be effectively relieved by suggestion and/or hypnosis. Education for childbirth by the "natural childbirth" method, aimed at establishing healthy attitudes, has the same purpose as hypnosis but cannot achieve as deep relaxation or reduce discomfort to the same degree as the latter. Even the most ardent enthusiast of natural childbirth would not advocate it for major surgery.

An experienced observer will recognize that the successful natural childbirth patients *have been hypnotized* to a degree; some have reached at least a light stage, and some a medium stage of hypnosis. For the most part, this is achieved without their being aware of it and usually without the knowledge of the obstetrician. Grantly Dick Read remarks that many of his patients appear as if in a trance during the latter part of the first stage.[14a] Thus, when natural childbirth and hypnosis are compared, it is obvious that both employ suggestion to raise the patient's pain threshold. Optimal results are attained, however, when the educational aspects of natural child-

birth are combined with hypnosis to raise the pain threshold.

Psychoprophylactic relaxation, as recently developed in the Soviet Union, is yet another method of training or conditioning for childbirth, based on the principles of hypnosis and group dynamics. Those[1a] who have observed these classes in the Soviet Union have stated that the patients become absorbed in the instructions of the doctor, that his voice and manner are those of an experienced hypnotist, and that the appearance of those in attendance resembles that of persons in various stages of hypnosis. The total picture is one of confidence and faith. Oxygen administered by inhalation also has a highly suggestive effect. Since every citizen in the Soviet Union has heard the name of Pavlov since childhood, the element of prestige is high in any indoctrination method proposed by this eminent scientist. At the very least, it affords a definitive approach to eliminate fear about labor and delivery.

In a similar manner, in thousands of women, Grantly Dick Read's methods establish a "power of positive thinking" about childbirth; a favorable mental-set. The prestige factor, along with belief, faith, confidence, mental-set and expectant attitude, provides the very basis for a hypnotic relationship. In psychoprophylactic relaxation, natural childbirth, progressive relaxation, autoconditioning and hypnosis, misdirection is produced by the various exercises learned in the classes, and these help to raise the pain threshold.

ADVANTAGES OF HYPNOSIS

The benefits and the advantages of hypnosis in obstetrics are many:

1. Reduction or eradication of fear, tension and pain before and during labor, with a consequent rise in the pain threshold.

2. Reduction of chemoanalgesia and anesthesia or their complete elimination in good hypnotic subjects.

3. Complete control of painful uterine contractions; the mother can choose to experience the sensations of childbirth or not, as she sees fit.

4. Decreased shock and speedier recovery.

5. Lessened incidence of operative de-

livery since the responsive patient co-operates more fully, particularly during the expulsive stage. Relaxation and anesthesia of the perineum are produced by autohypnosis or by direct suggestion from the hypnotherapist; this eases delivery, episiotomy and suturing of the perineum.

6. Lack of undesirable postoperative effects such as may be encountered with drug anesthesia; hypnoanesthesia is also more readily controlled.

7. Hypnosis shortens the first stage of labor by approximately 3 hours in primiparae and by more than 2 hours in multiparae.

8. Hypnosis raises the resistance to fatigue, thus minimizing maternal exhaustion.

9. Hypnosis can be used in debilitated individuals, in those who have ingested food shortly before delivery and in those who are allergic to drugs. Also, it is indicated in premature delivery.

10. Hypnotic rapport can be transferred to an associate, an intern or a nurse, or to the husband, any one of whom, without previous training, can readily induce and maintain the hypnotic state by means of a prearranged cue (this can be accomplished only with the patient's permission).

11. No elaborate education or ritualistic exercises are needed to achieve the strong interpersonal relationship essential to the success of childbirth under hypnosis. These *are* required in such pain-relieving technics as natural childbirth, and psychoprophylactic and progressive relaxation, which are merely modifications of the hypnotic method.

12. There is no possibility that harm will be done to the mother or the baby by hypnoanesthesia. On the other hand, the literature offers a considerable amount of evidence that when drugs are given for pain relief they may decrease the oxygen supply to the fetus. Combined with other asphyxial factors such as trauma or difficult delivery, this may produce fetal anoxia and, in its wake, severe brain damage. With hypnoanesthesia, the danger of fetal anoxia is markedly decreased.

13. Childbirth under hypnoanesthesia is an intensely gratifying emotional experience for well-adjusted mothers. Hearing the baby's first cry or seeing him immediately after birth are thrills that mothers can never feel if they are "knocked out."

14. Hypnosis can be life-saving for mother and baby in obstetrical emergencies.* Its successful application has been reported in abruptio placenta with delivery of a live baby.†

If these advantages were more widely known, more mothers would have their babies by hypnosis. If the pain threshold can be lowered by the anticipation of pain, it can be raised by eliminating the expectation of pain through hypnotic suggestion.

For generations, women have been "hypnotized" into thinking that they must have severe pain in childbirth by older, sadistic females who relate their "harrowing" experiences to impressionable young girls. Women do have pain in childbirth but, through appropriate training, they can be "dehypnotized" of these notions to reduce or eliminate the fear-tension-pain syndrome. In this manner, childbirth becomes a joyous experience which fulfills many of their unrecognized and unformulated needs.

Moya and James[12a] recently reported on the clinical and biochemical studies of 21 infants born to mothers under hypnosis, and compared these infants with a group of babies born under various anesthetic technics.

They stated:

Serial determination of the acid-base status after birth showed a significantly greater ability of the hypnosis group to readjust rapidly and to recover from the asphyxia of birth. . . . These data indicate a definite superiority of the hypnosis group in establishing and maintaining effective ventilation which was not revealed by careful clinical examination alone.

DISADVANTAGES AND CONTRAINDICATIONS

Hypnosis is not without limitations and contraindications:

1. Despite the high percentage of people susceptible to some type of hypnosis, maximal relief of pain and discomfort can be achieved in only 1 out of 4 patients. This

---

* Cheek, D. B.: Under Additional References.
† Hartman, W., and Rawlins, C.: Under Additional References.

limits the application of hypnosis as the sole anesthetic.

2. Hypnotic induction can be affected easily by psychological factors: well-prepared hypnotic subjects often "go to pieces" when exposed to other screaming women in various stages of labor; good subjects are often "talked out of it" by apparently well-meaning friends and neighbors.

3. The added time required to achieve the rapport and the depth of hypnosis necessary for operative procedures is a potential problem. It can be solved, however, as group training for hypnoanesthesia becomes more widespread and more trained personnel become available.

4. A trained hypnotherapist must be available throughout the entire labor unless the patient can induce autohypnosis.

5. The prevailing misconceptions about hypnosis held by the laity prevent many patients from being more susceptible to hypnotic suggestion.

6. Hypnosis is contraindicated in a deeply disturbed individual, either psychotic or borderline-psychotic, except when employed by a therapist trained in psychiatry. However, there is little possibility that hypnosis per se can precipitate a psychosis. Most psychotics are difficult, almost impossible to hypnotize, but if they prove susceptible, the dangers are minimal.

Tom[18] mentions 5 patients in whom neurosis or psychosis was exacerbated or precipitated, *all stemming from the work of one doctor,* who had been emotionally ill. These cases are not documented, and it is obvious that, if a doctor is sick, he should not practice medicine.

7. Inappropriate remarks made to a hypnotized individual or a faulty interpersonal relationship between the hypnotist and the subject can be damaging. However, these dangers can arise at nonhypnotic levels in similar circumstances and they are always to be avoided.

8. Some psychiatrists contend that hypnosis fosters extreme dependency. This may be true, but a strong bond of dependency exists in every doctor-patient relationship, especially in obstetrical practice. This dependency is only temporary, however, and can be used to advantage during the early prenatal period to establish greater confidence in the obstetrician. As the patient is taught autohypnosis, the dependency is more or less dissolved.

PREPARATION OF PATIENT

When a woman asks to have a baby under hypnosis, there are three things that the hypnotherapist must ascertain: her reasons for choosing this form of anesthesia; possible contraindications, depending on her personality type; and her responsiveness to hypnotic suggestion.

DETERMINING RESPONSIVENESS

Since some patients are not susceptible to hypnosis per se, it is important for the therapist to ascertain the degree of rapport he can achieve and to assess the potentialities for hypnosis. This can be accomplished by attempting to induce a hypnotic state and then offering a posthypnotic suggestion. If the suggestion is followed, hypnosis is established. Subsequent training for deep hypnosis is not time-consuming if a posthypnotic suggestion to go deeper the next time is made during the initial session.

Hypnosis cannot be induced in some patients, due to a lack of motivation or rapport between them and a particular therapist. Rapport may be strong with one therapist and weak with another. It may even vary with the same therapist.

Hypnosis should never be attempted until a preliminary discussion has been held to remove all misconceptions and to enlighten the patient about hypnotic childbirth. The patient should be told that hypnosis does not always work by itself; that if only 20 per cent are partially successful, this is 20 per cent better than nothing; that the degree of success depends on the motivation; and that autohypnosis and the production of glove anesthesia are phenomena achieved by the patient.

If patients are doubtful, I generally remark: "Why not come to one of my prenatal classes and see what it's all about? If you think you wish to have your baby under hypnosis, you can join a class. Naturally, the more sessions you attend, the more you will understand about hypnosis. Then you can decide if you wish to continue."

REASONS FOR CHOOSING HYPNOANESTHESIA

Often a pregnant woman's reasons for choosing hypnoanesthesia may not be apparent. Many emotionally well-adjusted women who have an ardent desire for motherhood are seeking hypnotic childbirth. The majority of these women have a strong wish to experience all the pleasant feelings associated with delivery such as hearing the baby's first cry. Others wish to be fully aware and cherish the memory of this climactic event. These are bona fide reasons for seeking this type of delivery.

On the other hand, there are some women who seek hypnoanesthesia who should be rejected because they are overzealous. Such patients usually have deep-seated feelings of inadequacy which they hope to lose by undergoing hypnosis—which is in their eyes a unique and, therefore, an ego-building experience. When these women are unable to get through labor and delivery under hypnosis alone, they feel a sense of failure and may become severely depressed. This is not an indictment of hypnosis. It is just something that every practitioner of hypnosis should keep in mind, so that he will be alert to underlying personality disorders in prospective subjects. In working up the obstetrical patient who desires hypnoanesthesia, personality appraisal should be as routine as pelvic measurement.

TRAINING IN HYPNOSIS

Training in hypnoanesthesia may be carried out in private office sessions or in group training classes. In either case, the patient does not have to read extensively, carry out elaborate exercises, or necessarily be educated in the mechanisms of labor. She must only attend a varying number of sessions with the doctor, during which her pain threshold is raised and her hopes for an easy and uneventful delivery are enhanced.

All patients should be informed that analgesia and anesthesia *will be available on request*, should they need it. Moreover, they should be advised *not* to feel guilty about asking for it. They should also be told that they do not have to go through the entire labor and delivery under hypnosis per se just to please the therapist who, it should be explained, will not feel "hurt" if they require help. It should be stressed again and again that the purpose of hypnosis is to minimize, not to eliminate, drug requirements. Since fewer than 1 out of 4 will be able to do without drugs altogether, none should be made to feel that they have to "sign a pledge" against anesthesia.

Ideally, hypnotic conditioning should begin during the third or the fourth month of pregnancy. The patient is hypnotized 2 or 3 times a month until maximal hypnosis is achieved. Exactly how many visits a patient will require before one can feel confident of satisfactory anesthesia is uncertain. It may vary from 1 to 20 or more sessions. Usually, if anesthesia is not obtained after 10 visits, the outlook for success is poor. Patients should be informed in advance that numerous sessions may be required to obviate discouragement.

During the conditioning period, the patient is taught auto- or self-hypnosis and "glove anesthesia." At each session, posthypnotic suggestions emphasize that the patient *need have no more discomfort than she is willing to bear.* Repeated conditioning enables the patient to reach deeper states of hypnosis and raises her pain threshold. Suggestions are made that she will look forward to her confinement with a feeling of joy and happiness instead of dread and apprehension. The more these posthypnotic suggestions are repeated, the more effective they become. The patient is told repeatedly that when labor begins she will promptly fall into deep hypnosis in response to a given cue—usually the touch on the right shoulder. With adequate preparation, a patient can enter into deep hypnosis in a matter of seconds by the shoulder signal. Glove anesthesia is best achieved through autohypnosis, and the area to be desensitized is chosen by the patient. This permissive approach directed toward teaching the patient to be self-reliant should stop the criticism that hypnosis fosters extreme dependency on an authoritarian figure.

Response to posthypnotic suggestions and production of autohypnosis and glove anesthesia during the prenatal training period presumptively indicates that the patient is ready for all stages of labor. An Allis clamp or a sterile needle may be used for testing the degree of anesthesia present in the perineum or the abdomen. Complete anesthesia during parturition is often accompanied by disassociation and amnesia, the active use of which is optional. For example, amnesia for part or all of the labor can be induced or removed in good hypnotic subjects according to the previously expressed wishes of the patient.

VERBALIZATION FOR GLOVE ANESTHESIA

Glove anesthesia is produced as follows: "And now you will go into a deep, hypnotic state, way down, deeper and deeper! You are going to produce glove anesthesia. As I stroke this hand, it is going to get numb, heavy and woodenlike. When you are sure that this hand has become numb just as your gums would be after your dentist has injected procaine, you will then transfer this numbness to your face. *With every movement of your hand toward your face*, it will get more numb and woodenlike." (The hand moves to the side of the face.) "When it touches your face, press the palm of your hand close to your face," (the hand lifts and is pressed to the face), "and when you are certain that that numbness has transferred from your hand to your face, drop your hand and your arm. You are going deeper and deeper relaxed with every breath you take. You can just feel that numbness being transferred from your hand to your face. That's fine. Just fine. Excellent. Now, after you are certain that the area on your face is numb, you can remove your hand and it will be normal but your face will be anesthetized."

The glove anesthesia can be transferred to the abdomen by one or both hands. A posthypnotic suggestion can be given that the anesthesia can be transferred to the perineum at the appropriate time. As each site is anesthetized, the sensory proof of anesthesia can be demonstrated to the patient. However, one should remark, "Remember, you will *know* what I am doing, but you *will feel no pain* as I test for the degree of anesthesia." This is consistent with what is known of the phylogenesis of the nervous system. Since pain is the most primitive of all sensations, it does not have as much cortical representation as the other senses. Discriminatory sensations like touch, having been acquired later, have more representation in the cortex.

MANAGEMENT OF LABOR

When labor actually begins, the patient induces autohypnosis. The physician also can induce hypnosis over the phone, or through another physician to whom he has transferred the rapport. An assistant, such as a nurse, can do it by handing the patient a written order to go into a deep state of relaxation. How it is done depends on the kind of conditioning and the cues the patient received during her training program. If the patient has not mastered autohypnosis, the doctor's presence is necessary for maintaining the hypnosis. Suggestions are given for complete anesthesia of the abdomen, the perineum and other hypersensitive areas.

The following is an actual verbalization taken from a tape recorder for the conduct of labor: "Now, Mary, you have been able to enter a deep state of relaxation through autohypnosis. Also, you have demonstrated that you can produce glove anesthesia and transfer this numb, heavy, wooden feeling to either side of the face. Now that you are in active labor, you will be able to develop the same anesthesia in both hands and transfer this numb, heavy, wooden feeling to the abdomen, in order to cut down the discomfort produced by your contractions (the word 'pains' is never used). You will also develop anesthesia of any other area of the body that I pick out, such as the area between the vagina and the rectum. This area will be without any feeling for a considerable length of time. Each time you practice producing the glove anesthesia, you will be able to maintain it for long intervals. When labor starts, you first will feel an ache which will begin in the back and then it will move around to the sides of your belly. At this time, you will be able to use the autohypnosis and place yourself in a deep state of relaxation. Remember, you need have no more discomfort than you are willing to bear. Your labor contractions will get stronger and longer, and that is a good sign that you are making progress. Even though you know that the labor contractions are there, you will not be able to feel them. If the glove anesthesia does not relieve your discomfort completely, please do not feel guilty about asking for drugs, which will be available."

Eliminating the discomfort of labor does not impair those sensations and experiences that are a healthy part of natural parturition. A well-trained and responsive patient, freed of pain and discomfort, can dehypnotize herself for as many contractions as she wishes. Although she appears relaxed and "asleep," she is actually fully aware during the labor and the delivery process, and participates emotionally in these; she can hear her baby's first cry, and see it immediately.

Subjectively, the contractions are felt as a tenseness of the abdomen and the bearing-down sensation as a slight perineal pressure. Spontaneous or operative delivery is often managed with the mother fully aware of what is going on, no matter whether the operative procedure is major or minor. Patients who are not so responsive naturally do not do so well during labor and delivery.

HELPFUL SUGGESTIONS DURING LABOR

It takes years of practice to become adept with forceps or to be a good vaginal operator. Likewise, the ability to be adept in producing, maintaining and controlling the applications of hypnosis to obstetrics requires much practical experience. The most useful suggestions are:

Misdirection of attention is used to mitigate the forcefulness of the labor contractions, as follows: "I want you to breathe deeply in the same manner in which you were trained during the prenatal classes. You will count the number of deep breaths or pants that you take with each contraction. In other words, as soon as you feel the contraction, start panting and keep a record of the number of breaths required for each contraction. Perhaps it might be 28 for the first one. In about ten minutes, you should have another contraction which may last for 30 or 40 seconds; this one may require 30 deep breaths or pants. Keep an average be-

tween the first and the second by adding the total and dividing by 2, which, in this case, would be 29. I want you to keep this average for all of your contractions. As they get closer and closer, you will notice that the average number of breaths will increase, indicating that labor is progressing nicely."

The idea is to keep the patient's attention so concentrated on the addition and the division that she doesn't have time to think of the painful uterine contractions. Such a procedure can potentiate the use of hypnosis. This preoccupation undoubtedly explains to a degree the success of the natural childbirth method in which the individual spends a considerable amount of time thinking about whether or not she is carrying out this or that exercise correctly. "Finally, when you are in the last stages of labor, you will push down when requested to do so. Naturally, the more you relax, the more effective each push will be. If you follow these suggestions you will get the most out of each contraction."

Another way to deepen the hypnosis is to employ the husband's participation and posthypnotic suggestions: "I am going to instruct your husband that each time you develop a contraction, he will squeeze your wrist with his forefinger and thumb. And, as he squeezes your wrist, this will be a cue, or a signal, that you will drop deeper and deeper relaxed with each deep breath you take."

Backache in the sacral area causes considerable discomfort, especially if the fetus is in an occiput posterior position. Here, too, the husband's aid can be enlisted: "I want you to place the palm of your hand, with your fingers fanned out, over the small of your wife's back. You will press firmly over this area. You will start this at the beginning of each contraction and release the pressure only after the contraction has disappeared." This maneuver often helps patients who complain bitterly of low back pain.

"If you do have more discomfort than you are able to tolerate, do not feel embarrassed if you have to moan. It will help relieve some of the tension. Also, if you wish to open your eyes you may do so without interfering with the relaxed state you are in.

As soon as you close your eyes, you will drop even deeper relaxed. You will not be bothered by any noises or sounds around you. As a matter of fact, you will become more and more concerned with your breathing and counting, and, as you become more involved in these, the sounds around you will fade into the distance. As the head of your baby descends down the birth canal, you will notice more of a desire to push. I have taught you how to breathe. You can grunt and bear down. Every contraction will be a signal for you to bear down harder. And, because you will be completely relaxed, you will obtain the maximal effect from each contraction. You can go through the rest of your delivery without any trouble. Remember, if you should require an anesthetic agent, it will be given to you. And, even if this is necessary, you will find that having a baby will be an exhilarating experience, especially if you are deeply relaxed."

For the actual delivery, the patient can transfer the glove anesthesia to the perineum before it has been "prepped" or sterilized. She is instructed: "This area will remain completely numb and anesthetic. As you push down, with each deep breath you take this area will become more and more anesthetic." One can also produce anesthesia by commenting: "As I stroke this area with my fingers, it will become numb and anesthetic, completely numb and anesthetic, just as if this area had been injected with procaine. It will become just as numb and anesthetic as your jaws become after the dentist has blocked off a nerve. This area is getting very numb, heavy and woodenlike."

One can enhance the anesthetic effects of the above methods, after the vagina has been sterilized and the patient is ready for delivery, by the following suggestions: "I am now freezing all the skin between my thumb and forefinger." (Considerable pressure is exerted at this time.) "Everywhere I touch my thumb and forefinger together, you will notice a numb, heavy, woodenlike sensation that will get more numb with each breath you take." This, together with the delivery of the head, produces a considerable amount of pressure anesthesia which, in some patients who have a high pain threshold, is sufficient for the performance of an episiotomy.

Approximately 5 per cent of patients have high sensory pain thresholds; the pressure anesthesia is especially effective for this group. About 10 to 15 per cent, which includes this group, can have an episiotomy performed without analgesia or anesthesia. The combination of a paracervical and transvaginal pudendal block with hypnosis is the ideal prescription for painless childbirth. It is almost 100 per cent safe and enables the mother to participate emotionally in the birth process.

HELPFUL SUGGESTIONS FOR POSTPARTUM PERIOD

The glove anesthesia technic can be effective during the postoperative period for relief of perineal pain in an episiotomy produced by swelling. In a multipara, autohypnosis and glove anesthesia can be most effective in relieving the pain of postpartum contractions. The same suggestions as described in Chapter 14 are given.

INDUCTION OF LABOR BY HYPNOSIS

Labor can be induced by appropriate posthypnotic suggestions given to selected patients. The author[11] has induced labor in the multipara capable of entering the somnambulistic state of hypnosis. The patient is regressed to her last labor and delivery. In this way it is possible to revivify all the subjective sensations associated with the onset of labor, thus "tricking" the autonomic nervous system into initiating the uterine contractions. It is difficult to do this in the primipara as she cannot imagine memories which she has never experienced. Reynolds[15] has been able to correlate the amplitude of the uterine contractions with suggestions of relaxation or contraction during deep hypnosis.

Often, premature labor can be prevented by strong reassurance and deep relaxation under hypnosis. The author of this book used hypnosis to prevent premature labor in a case of abruptio placentae reported by

Hartman and Rawlins.* The case is detailed on pages 202 and 203.

GROUP TRAINING

Group training in hypnoanesthesia is a time-saving procedure for the busy obstetrician. The classes can be conducted by a nurse or a doctor. Motivation is heightened by the emotional contagion that occurs as patients identify and empathize with each other and by the spirit of competition that is mobilized within the group. Also, most patients undergoing group training attempt to please the doctor, and this is an added motivational spur.

The author's patients attend group training classes twice a month for 2 hours in the evening with their husbands. The first half hour is devoted to questions and answers on pre- and postnatal care, labor, delivery, kinds of anesthesia and hypnosis. Patients are instructed that all questions, except those of a personal nature, are to be asked in the class. This saves valuable office time for the physician. Then several patients who have recently been delivered are asked to relate their experiences during labor. Their forthright and sincere discussion is highly motivating to the rest of the group.

Following these "testimonials" and the question-and-answer period, 4 or 5 patients who are good hypnotic subjects volunteer to illustrate how readily hypnosis can be induced. After induction, they are asked to induce autohypnosis and glove anesthesia. The way in which autohypnosis and glove anesthesia are produced is explained to the group. Once the glove anesthesia is transferred to the side of the face, the abdomen or the other arm, the insensitivity to pain is demonstrated. All patients alert or "awake" themselves; then 4 or more unsophisticated patients are asked to volunteer. Since a few minutes of observation of hypnotic induction is worth hours of talking about it, the beginner's susceptibility is increased. About 75 per cent of this group usually are hypnotized readily.

Platonov,[13a] in the Soviet Union, employed individual and group hypnosis to prepare large numbers of women for painless childbirth. He quotes numerous investigators who reported on the successful use of hypnosis with results similar to this author's. Among these are the enormous numbers of women delivered over the last 20 years in Leningrad by Vigdorovich, an obstetrician who supervised 15 "hypnotariums," which were under the jurisdiction of the Leningrad City Board of Health. Painless childbirth was effected in 4,575 cases with 91 per cent positive results; toxemias of pregnancy were relieved in 95 per cent of 400 cases, and 126 false pregnancies were treated in these hypnotariums. With this impressive array of evidence, why are obstetricians in the Western World still "dragging their feet"?

NAUSEA AND VOMITING

HYPNOTIC MANAGEMENT

The dictum to "treat the patient who has the vomiting rather than the vomiting" is important. Nausea and vomiting and even hyperemesis gravidarum are astonishingly susceptible to hypnosis.

The incidence of cure in several hundred patients seen in this author's private and clinic practice for a period of almost 30 years is approximately 85 per cent. Some, in spite of medical aid, were extremely toxic, with high icteric indexes, and some were almost moribund. Over 75 per cent of those for whom therapeutic abortion was considered were cured by hypnosis.[10] Platonov[13] treated 583 grave cases of hyperemesis gravidarum and cured over 84 per cent with an average of 7 hypnotic treatments.

The following case is illustrative:

Mrs. E. P., aged 31 years, white, was Para III, gravida II. When 2 months pregnant, she complained of severe nausea and vomiting, which did not respond to medical management. After one week of intractable vomiting, the patient lost 12 pounds. Hypnosis was induced. Directive posthypnotic suggestions failed to stop the vomiting. Superficial psychotherapy under hypnosis revealed that she had had extramarital relations with her husband's best friend, whom she held responsible for this pregnancy. After working through her guilty fears, she recognized the self-punitive need for the symptom, and

* Hartman and Rawlins: see additional references.

realized why she was rejecting the pregnancy. As a result of this "mental catharsis," and the assuaging of her guilt feelings, she felt relieved. No "deep interpretations" were made. The vomiting promptly ceased. Autohypnosis was used as a reinforcement to prevent return of the symptom. However, the remainder of her prenatal period was uneventful.

Undoubtedly the noncritical attitude and the favorable rapport relieved this patient's guilty fears. The connection between her conflict and the vomiting could have been established without hypnotherapy, but it might have taken a considerable period of time; the rapid cessation of the nausea and the vomiting could not be explained on any other basis. Later this patient divorced her husband and married the "friend." She returned for her fourth pregnancy, with which she had no nausea or vomiting.

Psychogenic factors are chiefly responsible for the majority of cases. Hyperemesis gravidarum is unknown in some cultures, as the oriental, but it develops in these peoples after assimilation into our society.

In predisposed individuals, the gastrointestinal tract is symbolically utilized as a way of showing disgust—by vomiting. This is substantiated by the observation that the gut is a common site for the expression of disgust. Many of our vomiters had a strong aversion toward sex or an overdependent attachment to the mother; there was often a history of "rejection dyspepsia."

Nausea and vomiting of pregnancy usually cease by the fourth or the fifth month, at which time the fetal movements are felt. The mother now becomes aware that the fetus is a separate individual and can no longer be "thrown up." Thus, there is insufficient time for any uncovering psychotherapy. A differentiation between the "nervous" and the "toxic" type depends not only on the history but also on the laboratory findings.

Treatment should be directed primarily toward the patient as a whole, and not toward the symptom! The judicious use of hypnotherapy to establish the need for the symptom, combined with adequate medical management, is indicated for all cases of hyperemesis gravidarum. This often has obviated the need for therapeutic abortion.

The author demonstrated this in a series of desperately ill women—the salvage rate was 85 per cent.[10]

Hypnotic Management Technic

After a patient has been hypnotized and taught autohypnosis, the following verbalization can be used: "You will notice that as you relax yourself through autohypnosis, your nausea and vomiting will decrease. You can also suggest that you will find it extremely difficult even to become nauseated or to vomit upon arising. Perhaps you might like to imagine that you are eating a delightful meal without getting sick. How about 'eating' something you like right now? You can see the food, can you not?" (The patient nods her head.) "Imagine, if you will, that you are eating the food and thoroughly digesting it. You will find that your stomach will be very, very relaxed if you look forward to eating; that it will be extremely difficult to vomit. Perhaps you would like to believe that no matter how hard you try, you cannot vomit. After you have practiced 'eating' enough times and have imagined that the food is going to stay down, you will enjoy it. However, if you really have to be nauseated, why not permit yourself to develop this sensation for 15 minutes every morning, especially in the bathroom? Then each day you can suggest that the time will be cut down by 1 or 2 minutes, so that at the end of a week or two you will wean yourself from the 'need to vomit.' Or, perhaps, you can increase the vomiting. You realize that if you deliberately increase your sickness, you are controlling it, and anything you can increase, you can decrease!

"Now there are many needs for your nausea and vomiting. Perhaps you might tell me of some of your fears, anxieties and tensions in regard to pregnancy, delivery or care of the child. If you think of any problems concerning your pregnancy and delivery, relate them to me on your next visit. Regardless of how silly or inconsequential these thoughts may seem to you, tell me all about these matters. Then you will notice that with each day you will have *less need* to get sick. You can then look forward to having your baby with a feeling of joy and happiness."

Glove anesthesia can be utilized as follows: "You have learned to develop an anesthesia of the palm of your hand. You are aware that you can transfer this sensation to any portion of your body. Every time you develop the slightest nausea, all you have to do to relieve it is to transfer this numb, woodenlike feeling to your stomach. Just press firmly on the pit of your stomach and the entire area will feel very, very relaxed."

It is really surprising how effective this type of placebo therapy—in the form of "laying on of the hands"—is in abolishing the nausea and the vomiting. The patient's confidence and self-esteem are increased when she realizes that the "power" to eradicate the symptom is hers, and that no dependency on drugs or the doctor is required.

There are cases in which the vomiting persists even after an abortion. Here, the vomiting pattern is fixed in the cortex. This is similar to the pain pattern of phantom limb pain, and indicates the importance of altering the deranged cortical dynamics. Such psychopathology is more amenable to hypnosuggestive procedures because the vicious reflex can be broken up with more certainty.

EMOTIONAL SPONTANEOUS ABORTION

The emotional factors contributing to the "abortion habit" may be similar to those of the "accident habit" of certain self-destructive individuals. Thus, the author and Dr. Freed[11] postulated that the corticohypothalamic pathway can, through alterations in hormonal balance, alter the biochemical reactions in the rapidly growing placenta. Also, there is anatomic evidence that strong emotions can contract the uterine musculature and thus cause placental separation. Data of a positive nature which implicate the emotions consist of the evidence that the uteri of habitual aborters are hypersensitive to emotional stimuli; that there is a certain personality profile; that domesticated animals abort under unfavorable emotional environment; and that reports from a number of workers indicate favorable results following psychotherapy. There is also a considerable body of unclassified data

which points to the role of emotions in abortion in patients who have miscarried during shock, fright or dangerous episodes.

More recently, proliferative changes in the placentas of spontaneous aborters, which resemble those of the collagen diseases, have been found secondary to mental stress. Gray[4] and his associates noted that antibodies similar to those found in the collagen diseases can be detected in the serum of aborters. The fluctuations in 17-ketosteroids and 17-hydroxycorticoids secondary to stress, specific or nonspecific, may produce the pathologic changes in the placenta noted by Gray.

Platonov[13a] quotes Miloslavsky's recent systematic studies which showed that hypnosis could reduce uterine excitability, terminate bleeding and salvage a large number of fetuses. This substantiates Kroger and Freed's observations made in 1951.[11]

Nearly all investigators agree that the favorable results obtained in the treatment of this condition are chiefly due to the "mental rest" and the reassurance derived from the physician-patient relationship. The author has good reason to believe that several patients would have aborted if they had not been placed in a state of hypnosis or "prolonged sleep" for many hours. Hypnosis was performed at the first signs of threatened abortion, i.e., before bleeding had occurred. The following recent case history dramatically illustrates the approach used:

A 37-year-old Para III, gravida II, began to spot during the 2nd month of gestation. Uterine contractions gradually increased in intensity, accompanied by bilateral abdominal pain and backaches. Delalutin, 250 mg. every 3 days from the 8th to the 14th week, failed to alleviate bleeding. The Aschheim-Zondek test, in spite of profuse hemorrhages, was positive at the 16th week of gestation, suggesting a live fetus.

This author saw this patient at that time. Even though the prognosis was poor, the patient was taught hypnosis and autohypnosis and placed *en rapport* with her husband, a practicing clinical psychologist who had also been trained in hypnotherapy. Following the first session, the uterine bleeding and contractions diminished in intensity for 48 hours. Mild symptoms occurred over the next 4 days. At the 18th week of gestation, the patient had a

Misconceptions about hypnosis being removed; patients are receiving preliminary instructions.

Group induction: beginning arm catalepsy.

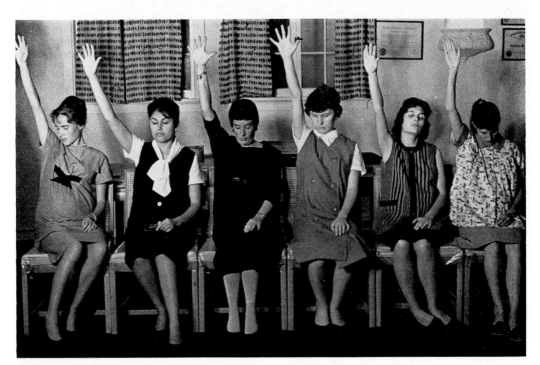

Limb catalepsy complete; medium stage hypnosis.

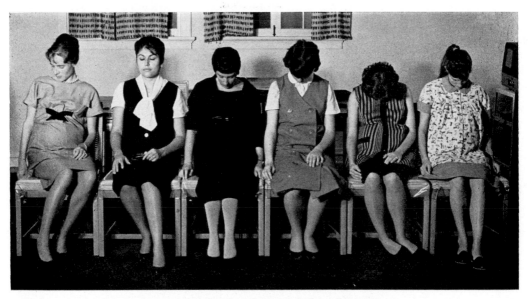

Group training for obstetrics: deep hypnosis.

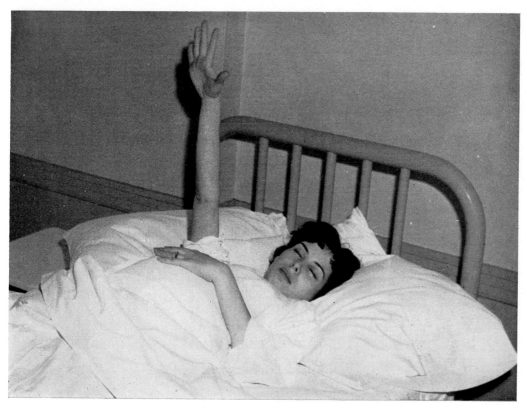
Demonstration of catalepsy in active labor.

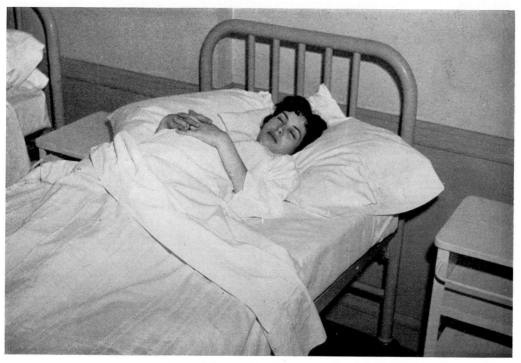
Active labor under deep hypnosis.

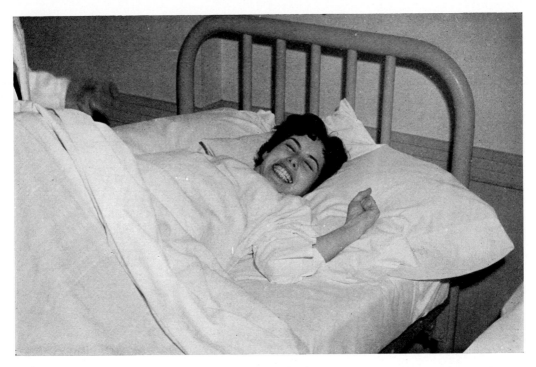

Active labor without hypnosis.

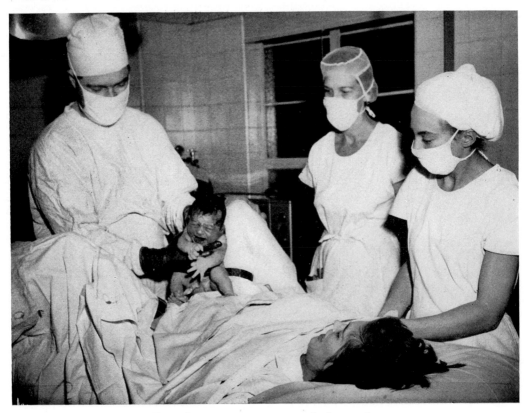

Immediate postpartum state in hypnosis.

severe hemorrhage, accompanied by sizable blood clots and strong uterine contractions. An abortion appeared to be imminent. Because the author was unavailable, another medical practitioner induced deep hypnosis. The bleeding and the contractions, as well as the pain and the discomfort, immediately disappeared. Deep, natural sleep and periods of invigorating, relaxing rest could be obtained through autohypnosis whenever premonitory symptoms of bleeding or abdominal pain occurred.

At the twenty-ninth week, the patient developed strong, regular uterine contractions, about 15 to 20 minutes apart. Following autohypnosis, the pain and the bleeding subsided for 24 hours. When these recurred, the autohypnosis was repeated with the same results. However, during the next 24 hours the uterine contractions became stronger in intensity. Hypnotic suggestions were directed toward inducing relaxation, feelings of comfort and cessation of contractions. The hypnosis was ineffective for the last. At this time the patient was hospitalized, after it was realized that she was in active labor. She delivered a 2-pound 6½-oz. live infant after a 5-hour labor, characterized by little or no discomfort. The placenta revealed evidence of an old hemorrhage, covering about three fourths of the maternal surface. The diagnosis was moderate to severe abruptio placenta. Unquestionably, hypnorelaxation was the major factor responsible for viability. The hypnosis also was used for the labor and the delivery of the premature infant.

HEARTBURN OF PREGNANCY

Heartburn of pregnancy has been termed a "monosymptomatic neurosis." Here, too, the esophagus and the stomach are symbolically selected as the expression of the pregnant woman's inability to "swallow" or "stomach" the pregnancy because of deep-seated aversion to it. The esophageal spasm is noted in apprehensive women with lowered thresholds to sensory stimuli, especially in those who harbor latent guilt feelings over their overt or covert rejection of the child.

The therapy of heartburn of pregnancy due to psychogenic causes is directed toward the relief of the anxiety and the tension. As discussed in the section on nausea and vomiting (p. 201), this may be accomplished by hypnotic exploration with a discussion and an explanation of the harmlessness of the symptom. In refractory cases, autohypnosis and glove anesthesia are beneficial.

LACTATION

Lactation often is influenced by emotional upsets. Conflicts can suppress lactogenic hormonal output via the hypothalamus, and interfere with successful mammary function. Whether the hormonal dysfunction is due to a lack of love for the baby, or whether absence of motherly feelings is a product of a general psychosomatic immaturity, has yet to be established.

The literature relative to the influence of psychic factors on lactation has been reviewed.[2] Mohr[12] treated a patient who developed a sudden inability to nurse following psychic excitement. Under hypnosis she was given a suggestion that on the way home she would feel milk flowing from her breasts. Within an hour she functioned normally, and there was no recurrence of her trouble. The French school of hypnotists—Liébeault, Bernheim and others—made innumerable observations that the flow of milk could be stopped or increased by hypnosis. Heyer,[6] in discussing the use of hypnosis during delivery, states: "Later it is very often possible to stimulate vigorously a decreasing flow of milk." More recently, Goll[3] has discussed the role of suggestion in the treatment of deficient lactation.

The effective use of hypnosis has been demonstrated in stimulating milk production in 77 cases with over 95 per cent success.[13a] The technics involve the use of sensory-imagery conditioning and posthypnotic and autohypnotic suggestions. The results depend on the manner in which the suggestions are given. Usually, direct suggestions are not as effective as those that paint "mental pictures" of the milk flow from a full breast.

LATE TOXEMIAS OF PREGNANCY: PRE-ECLAMPSIA AND ECLAMPSIA

The etiologic factors in the toxemias of pregnancy, especially pre-eclampsia and eclampsia, still remain inadequately explained. The author and Dr. Freed[11] pointed out that the psyche plays some role in the operative mechanism of this disorder. However, it is acknowledged that this condition is largely a somatic one, from the clinical standpoint, with typical pathologic findings. One finds, however, in examining the reports made by students of this subject, the suggestion that psychological factors may be involved.[17] Dieckmann[1c] states that pre-eclampsia and its complications are limited to civilized and cultured races, and that relatively primitive societies suffer from this condition only after contact with more "sophisticated" peoples. Pommerenke[14] comments, "Dr. Dieckmann hints—with a voice that is perhaps too faint—that factors which some may regard as psychosomatic or sociologic may be operative in the etiology of eclampsia."

The author and Dr. Freed[11] stated that the most likely possibilities to be considered in postulating a psychosomatic factor for this disorder are: (1) placental ischemia, (2) stimulation of the posterior pituitary, and (3) imbalance or excess of certain adrenal corticosteroids. Thus, psychosocial and other nonspecific factors potentially may lead to a disturbance of the cortical-hypothalamic–pituitary–adrenal axis, resulting in imbalance or excess of adrenal corticosteroids and/or a direct excitation or stimulation of the autonomic (pressor) nervous system, similarly mediated via a hypothalamic-pituitary-adrenal axis. Salerno[16] recently supported these observations by clinical studies.

It has long been recognized that pre-eclamptics improve when hospitalized—environmental stresses are reduced. Hypno-relaxation can also raise the adaptive responses to stress. Autohypnosis is extremely helpful for recognizing anxiety-provoking tensions. Inducing the hypnotic state several times daily for relaxation, together with intelligent prenatal care, diet, sodium restriction and proper elimination, relieves many pre-eclamptics. Resistant individuals should be placed under medical management. However, hypnosis can be used prophylactically to decrease appetite and prevent weight gain. Naturally, the acute, fulminating phase of severe eclampsia cannot be helped by hypnosis.

DISCUSSION

As a result of the medical profession's interest in relaxation procedures for painless childbirth, a marked increase in the scientific applications of hypnosis has recently become apparent. It has been a belated but welcome recognition of the usefulness of hypnoanesthesia, either as an anesthetic agent or as an adjunct to chemoanesthesia.

Hypnoanesthesia for parturition is not a panacea, nor will it ever supplant chemoanesthetic agents, but its applications are growing daily and it is proving a powerful ally in alleviating other psychosomatic conditions in obstetrics.

Hypnosis is almost a specific for relief of the psychogenic component responsible for nausea and vomiting during early pregnancy. Hypnosis and/or strong suggestion are particularly valuable in the prevention of habitual abortion. Hypnosis can frequently diminish the strength and the frequency of the uterine contractions, and miscarriage can be prevented in properly *selected* patients if placental separation has not occurred. Experience indicates that placebos are as effective as vitamins and hormones in reducing the abortion rate; contradictory theories, the varied responses to endocrine therapy, and the frequent relapses with other types of therapy, all incriminate the psyche to some extent. Hypnosis can also be employed effectively in heartburn, to promote lactation, and to curb the "eating for two" syndrome often responsible for rapid weight gain and subsequent pre-eclampsia and toxemia.

The average physician can learn to induce hypnosis for anesthesia as readily as he learns to make an abdominal skin incision. However, to use this double-edged scalpel for intensive psychotherapy he must have the intuition, the knowledge and the judgment that characterize the skill of the surgeon who wields the scalpel.

It is hoped that the foregoing will stimulate more physicians to utilize hypnosis in childbirth and other obstetrical conditions. More active participation and public education in hypnotic methodology will help dispel misunderstanding and apprehension concerning hypnosis among the laity. Since hypnosis is a very flexible agent, its utility in mitigating the pain of parturition could be broadened if it were used more often in conjunction with chemoanesthesia. Its use in this manner should have a salutary effect during pregnancy, labor and delivery. Likewise, if the disadvantages and limitations enumerated above are taken into consideration, it will not be hailed as a panacea. Most physicians initially are enthusiastic about hypnotherapy in obstetrics, but disillusionment sets in after they find that it requires years of experience to use it intelligently and successfully.

REFERENCES

1a. Ball, T. H.: Obstetrics in the Soviet Union, Tr. N. Y. Acad. Sciences, 22:578, 1960.

1b. DeLee, J. B.: Year Book of Obst. and Gynec., Chicago, Year Book Pub., p. 164, 1939.

1c. Dieckmann, W. J.: Toxemias of Pregnancy, St. Louis, Mosby, 1941.

2. Dunbar, F.: Emotions and Bodily Changes, pp. 311-315, New York, Columbia, 1946.

3. Goll, H.: Role of suggestion in hormonal therapy of hypogalactia, München med. Wchnschr. 89:55, 1942.

4. Gray, J. D.: The problem of spontaneous abortion, Am. J. Obst. & Gynec. 74:111-123, 1957.

5. Hartman, W., and Rawlins, C. M.: Hypnosis in management of a case of abruptio placenta, Internat. J.C.E.H. 8:103-107, 1960.

6. Heyer, G. R.: (Quoted by Dunbar) Hypnose und Hypnotherapie *in* Die psychischen Heilmethoden, Hrsg. von Karl Birnbaum, pp. 73-135, Leipzig, Thieme, 1927.

7. Kroger, W. S.: Natural childbirth, Med. Times, 80:152-155, 1952.

8. ——: Hypnoanesthesia in obstetrics *in* Davis, C. H. (ed.): Gynecology and Obstetrics, pp. 111-130, Hagerstown, Md., 1960.

9. Kroger, W. S., and DeLee, S. T.: The use of the hypnoidal state as an amnesic, analgesic and anesthetic agent in obstetrics, Am. J. Obst. & Gynec. 46:655-661, 1943.

10. ——: The psychosomatic treatment of hyperemesis gravidarum by hypnosis, Am. J. Obst. & Gynec. 51:544-552, 1946.

11. Kroger, W. S., and Freed, S. E.: Psychosomatic Gynecology: Including Problems of Obstetrical Care, Chicago, Free Press, 1956; reprinted, Los Angeles, Wilshire Book Co., 1962.

12. Mohr, Fritz: (Quoted by Dunbar) Psychophysische Behandlungsmethoden, Leipzig, Hirzel, 1925.

12a. Moya, F., and James, L. S.: Medical hypnosis for obstetrics, J.A.M.A. 174:80-86, 1960.

13. Platonov, M. V., et al.: Quoted by Volgyesi, F. A. *in* The recent neuropsychiatric and biomorphologic justifications of hypnotherapeutic empiricism, Brit. J. M. Hypnotism 2:6-25, 1950.

13a. Platonov, K.: The Word as a Physiological and Therapeutic Factor, Moscow, Foreign Languages Publishing House, 1955.

14. Pommerenke, W. T.: Discussion of Dieckmann, W. J., et al.: Etiology of eclampsia, Am. J. Obst. & Gynec. 58:1014, 1949.

14a. Read, G. D.: Childbirth without Fear, New York, Harper & Bro., 1953.

15. Reynolds, S. R. M.: Uterine contractility and cervical dilatation, Proc. R. Soc. Med. 44:695-702, 1951.

16. Salerno, L. J.: Psychophysiologic aspects of the toxemias of pregnancy, Am. J. Obst. & Gynec. 76:1268-1273, 1958.

17. Soichet, S.: Emotional factors in toxemia of pregnancy, Am. J. Obst. & Gynec. 77:1065-1073, 1959.

18. Tom, K. S.: Hypnosis in Obstetrics and Gynecology, Obst. and Gynec. 16:222-225, 1960.

19. Winklestein, L. B.: Routine hypnosis for obstetrical delivery, Am. J. Obst. & Gynec. 76:152-160, 1958.

20. Zuspan, F. P.: Hypnosis and the obstetrician-gynecologist, Obst. & Gynec. 16:740-742, 1960.

ADDITIONAL REFERENCES

Cheek, D. B.: Effectiveness of incentive in clinical hypnosis, Obst. & Gynec. 9:720, 1957.

Chertok, L.: Psychosomatic Methods in Painless Childbirth, New York, Pergamon Press, 1959.

DeLee, S. T.: Hypnotism in pregnancy and labor, J.A.M.A. 159:750-759, 1955.

Garcia, S. R.: Hypnosis in Obstetrics and Childbirth Without Fear, Paper read at Pan American Medical Association, May 5, 1960.

Giorlando, S. W., and Mascala, R. F.: The treatment of hyperemesis gravidarum with hypnotherapy, Am. J. Obst. & Gynec. 73:444-447, 1957.

Hartman, W., and Rawlins, C.: Hypnosis in the management of abruptio placentae, Int. J. Clin. and Exper. Hypnosis 2:103-107, 1960.

Kroger, S. W.: Hypnosis in obstetrics and gynecology *in* Schneck, J. M. (ed.): Hypnosis in Modern Medicine, Springfield, Ill. Thomas, 1959.

Kroger, W. S., and Steinberg, J.: Childbirth With Hypnosis, New York, Doubleday, 1961.

34

Hypnosis in Gynecology

PSYCHOSOMATIC FACTORS

The female generative tract is extremely susceptible to the physiologic expression of emotions. Therefore, a high percentage of gynecologic symptoms have a psychosomatic or a psychogynecic basis. Appropriate hypnotherapy can allay the anxieties and the tensions responsible for the majority of psychogynecic symptoms by altering faulty attitudes concerning femininity and sexuality.

The gynecologist, if trained in hypnosis, can use this modality much as he employs drugs for symptom-removal. Symptom-removal by hypnotherapy is not harmful, contrary to the belief of some psychiatrists. To assume otherwise is rather ridiculous when one considers that the bulk of gynecologic therapy for functional disorders is directed toward symptom-removal. This goal readily can be achieved without an understanding of the so-called "psychodynamics." The author of this book, a gynecologist, used the psychodynamic approach for years until he realized that his therapeutic results were due to an empathic relationship, reassurance and re-education rather than to the "insight" and interpretations.

Modern hypnotic technics employ autohypnosis and sensory-imagery conditioning as described in this chapter. These, together with the rapport, are utilized for most patients in preference to direct symptom-removal by authoritarian hypnotic technics. Those for whom superficial therapy is inadequate require an understanding of their neurotic needs for their symptoms. Thus, present- and future-oriented psychotherapy shortened by hypnosis is more feasible for most psychogynecic symptoms than searching for causes by uncovering the past through complex psychoanalytic technics. Our hypnotherapeutic technics now will be presented.

AMENORRHEA

Psychic factors[3, 20, 21] can prevent the release of the proper gonadotrophic hormones to produce functional or "hypothalamic" amenorrhea.[23] This form of amenorrhea can be due to fear of pregnancy, guilt feelings over masturbation and other emotional factors. A prerequisite to hypnotherapy of functional amenorrhea is not only a physical examination but also a psychological evaluation of the attitudes toward menstruation and psychosexual functioning.

Amenorrhea has been treated effectively by hypnosis.[2, 7, 11] Dunbar[2] points out:

In many cases amenorrhea can be cured by one hypnotic session. In a patient who had been suffering from amenorrhea for 2½ years, menses were induced by hypnosis, and regulated to occur on the first day of each month at 7:00 A. M. to last for 3 days.

Heyer[7] says:

Numerous authors report results from hypnotherapy in menstrual disturbances, which are beyond question, i.e., relief of pain as well as regulation of the cycle. As a matter of fact, the time of onset for menstruation can be determined in deep hypnosis to the day and hour, as, for example, one may say every 4 weeks or every first day of the month, etc. . . . In all uses of hypnosis, it is important to give not just colorless commands, but to suggest the whole experience of menstruation forcefully and vividly. Where doubts as to the efficiency of this procedure have risen, faulty technic is responsible.

Although this method does not always work, the author of this book has dramatically induced the menses by hypnosis, as in the following selected case:

Miss M. H., aged 24, had a functional type of amenorrhea of 5 months' duration. Extensive hormonal therapy failed to initiate the menses. She was taught hypnosis and autohypnosis, and her subjective and objective symptoms of menstruation were elicited. Through posthypnotic suggestions she was told that she would experience the premonitory symptoms of the menses as well as the signs and the symptoms of its actual onset in exact accordance with her description. It was further suggested that, under autohypnosis, she would revivify the entire onset of the menstrual cycle in 14 or 15 days. She did this and she reported that, to her surprise, the period was resumed exactly 2 weeks after the initial induction of hypnosis.

As mentioned, bleeding seldom can be initiated by direct suggestion. Rather, the technic is to ask the following questions: "Do your breasts get hot and heavy just before you are due to have your period? Do you feel like jumping out of your skin at this time? Is there any pain connected with the onset of the flow? If so, where is it? What is the character of the pain? Do you have a backache, or a feeling of pressure in the pelvic region? Are there any other symptoms associated with the onset of the flow?"

If the answers to the above questions are fed back to the hypnotized patient, one has an excellent chance of re-establishing the menses by this type of sensory-imagery conditioning. The verbalization used is: "In about 2 weeks, you will find it most advantageous to feel all the sensations that you previously described and associated with your periods. Think of the exact place where you have discomfort and pressure. Perhaps you might even imagine how 'jumpy' and irritable you felt just before your flow." In this technic, a "dry run" or a rehearsal of the onset of menstruation under autohypnosis helps to reinforce the appropriate posthypnotic suggestions.

Another technic is to utilize hypnotic age regression as the author did in the above-described case. The patient is regressed to her last period and asked to recall the specific sensations associated with it; if she wishes, she can choose the approximate date for the establishment of the menses. Suggestions must be made in a confident manner. However, the physician should never get himself "out on a limb" by guaranteeing that the menses will occur on a specific date. Rather, he can preface his remarks by saying, "If you are able to feel the sensations associated with your period, you have a good chance of having your period. Or, perhaps, you can begin to wonder whether it will be a day or two before the date you chose, or maybe the period will come on a week afterward."

PSEUDOCYESIS

Pseudocyesis or phantom pregnancy is characterized by some of the signs and the symptoms of pregnancy, as amenorrhea, enlargement of breasts and change in the body contour. Psychotic states, or a persistent corpus cyst, must be considered when the "pregnancy" persists.[5] This condition convincingly illustrates how psychic factors can influence the endocrine system. Cortical-hypothalamic pathways to the anterior pituitary are utilized, causing release of the corpus luteum hormones and suppression of the follicle-stimulating hormone (FSH).[22]

One should not forcefully confront the patient with her delusion but she must be aware of the neurotic *needs* for maintaining the "pregnancy." Such an individual has to be "unhypnotized" out of ideas that she has "hypnotized" herself into; therefore, permissive hypnotic technics are more likely to uncover the *need* for the pregnancy fantasy.

Pseudocyesis beautifully illustrates how the limbic system unerringly mediates impulses from the higher sensorium and transmits these repressed emotional forces to appropriate target organs. It also illustrates the astonishing susceptibility of the endocrine apparatus to psychic stimuli. It has been noted that the darkened linea alba and other signs of pregnancy occur *only* in multiparas. This indicates that the indelible imprint of an "experience" is filed away but is subject to recall at "appropriate" times.

Mrs. B. M., aged 31, presented herself with a history of 3 months' amenorrhea. An Aschheim-Zondek test and a physical examination were negative. However, she insisted that she was pregnant and could "feel life." She was taught hypnosis and autohypnosis in 5 weekly sessions. During the last session, the following issues were raised: "What are you trying to prove by maintaining the pregnancy? How much longer do you really need to keep the pregnancy?" After several sessions directed to hypnotic exploration, she stated, "My marriage is on the rocks and I thought that by having a baby I could hold my husband." After working through her neurotic needs for the pregnancy, and pointing out that it would be better to solve her domestic problem more realistically, posthypnotic suggestions were given that she would feel all the menstrual symptoms, as described in the case history in the section on Amenorrhea, page 206. In subsequent visits, some of her and her husband's important differences were worked through at nonhypnotic levels. Her menses were resumed within 4 months. She was seen one year later and was symptom-free.

Sensory-imagery conditioning under autohypnosis was a valuable adjunctive procedure in relieving this case of pseudocyesis.

DYSFUNCTIONAL UTERINE BLEEDING

Psychic shock may cause profuse vaginal bleeding. Menstruation of a bride on her wedding night often can be a defense against intercourse, fear of pregnancy and/or other fears. Irregular bleeding may be the somatic equivalent of the grief and the depression following the loss of a loved one.[6]

An increase in endogenous adrenalin can cause vasoconstriction of the endometrial blood vessels. Bleeding of psychological origin could conceivably be mediated through the midbrain to the hypophysis with a subsequent alteration in ovarian and adrenal function. Psychotics frequently manifest functional menstrual abnormalities; these are corrected after alleviation of their mental symptoms. Before treatment is instituted, an organic etiology should be ruled out. Hypnotherapy is purely an adjunctive procedure to endocrine and medical treatment of uterine bleeding. Superficial psychotherapy, consisting of education for the correction of faulty sexual attitudes and domestic and social maladjustments, and the utilization of common-sense suggestions for other anxiety-provoking tensions can often be accomplished more rapidly through hypnosis. Over 70 per cent of cases can be helped by a psychotherapeutic approach.

The following case history is illustrative of this:

Miss G. L., aged 28, had a history of irregular and painful menstruation accompanied by hypermenorrhea. Two psychotic breaks were treated by insulin and electroconvulsive shock therapy. Several curettements and vaginal smears were negative for carcinoma, hormonal imbalance and other pathologic entities. The patient became very proficient in achieving deep hypnosis and autohypnosis. A careful anamnesis revealed that she was jealous of her mother because, as she stated, "She is more beautiful than I am." Her father had died several years before, leaving her a considerable fortune. Feelings of emotional insecurity were mobilized by her mother, who constantly reminded her that she was mentally incompetent to manage her own affairs. She continually warned her about men, sexual matters and promiscuity. As a result, she masturbated excessively and also had several homosexual relationships; these produced guilt, anxiety and tension. The irregular bleeding usually occurred when she was unable to release her tensions by masturbating.

It was decided that, although masturbation was not harmful per se, it should be curbed until she had allayed the associated guilt. Under hypnosis it was suggested that she stimulate her breasts with her right index finger (the one she used for masturbation). Whenever she had a strong desire to masturbate, this relieved her genital tensions. The mother was apprised as to how she had mobilized strong guilt feelings in her daughter, and this accounted for the latter's behavior. "Trading down" or symptom-transformation, together with supportive psychotherapy, relieved the patient's anxieties. The periods were resumed within 4 months. In this case, symptom-transformation not only speeded up therapy but afforded the patient the equivalent of the sexual satisfaction which she desired and feared at the same time. She is still receiving psychotherapy for insecurity and ambivalence toward her mother.

FUNCTIONAL DYSMENORRHEA

Dysmenorrhea is a "disease of theories." Menstruation and "the curse" have been synonymous for centuries. The actual mechanism responsible for the discomfort may be due to a conditioned pain pattern in the cortex, similar to that seen in amputees who complain of phantom limb pain. The absence of gross lesions, the monthly variation in pain according to mood swings, and the frequent relapses in endocrine therapy mark it as a typical emotional disorder.[17]

It is a serious mistake to minimize pain even if it is emotionally based. Pain is pain, whether physical or emotional. One only mobilizes resentment by such bromidic statements as: "Your discomfort is all in your head. Why don't you relax? Stop worrying about it. It will go away!" In addition to sedation, analgesia and hormonal therapy, hypnotherapy is a very valuable adjunct. Autohypnosis, glove anesthesia and autosuggestions to produce a conditioned relaxation for the entire menstrual period definitely can raise the pain threshold.

Hypnosis acts to bind these patients in therapy. As discussed in Chapter 47, the strong dependency helps to overcome the initial resistances involved in yielding the symptom. Later, the dependency is lessened as the patient learns how to control the discomfort by autohypnosis. Whether one employs psychotherapy, hypnosis or just plain common sense in treating functional dysmenorrhea, one should avoid offering such "therapeutic" suggestions as "Get married," "Have a baby" or "Find a suitable lover." These are, at best, unscientific, and, at worst, extremely harmful.

Miss A. L., aged 22, presented herself with a history of primary dysmenorrhea which had appeared at the menarche. She was taught autohypnosis and glove anesthesia, which decreased the intensity of her cyclic discomfort. During the 9th session, while under deep hypnosis, she remarked, "I am very jealous of my mother; she's always at ease with everybody. I am very shy and flustered around people, especially young men. My mother is always the life of the party." Evocation of hostile envy relieved her anxiety and tension. Through further posthypnotic suggestions, directed to re-educative and supportive measures, she was able to face her life situations with more equanimity, and this in turn modified her unhealthy attitudes toward her mother. She also became more socially adaptable and began to date various young men. She soon realized that she no longer needed the cyclic discomfort to draw attention to her inadequacy as a female. This approach significantly alleviated her painful menses.

INFERTILITY

Many factors are responsible for psychosomatic infertility.[19] The author evaluated a series of infertile patients by psychological tests.[10] Behind the outward desire to get pregnant was the deeply repressed wish not to get pregnant, on the basis of emotional immaturity associated with fear of motherhood or feelings of inadequacy. Such conflicting emotions, mediated through autonomic, somatic, behavioral and endocrine mechanisms, often can affect the physiology of ovulation implantation and, perhaps, even the viscosity of the cervical mucus, to produce the so-called hostile cervix. Other factors are avoidance of coitus during ovulation; transitory or persistent tubal spasm; and conflicts in the male which may affect the fertilizing capacity of the sperm.

About 35 per cent of infertile women get pregnant soon after treatment is begun. Often the enthusiasm with which the infertile patient is investigated is therapeutic;[8] diminution of anxiety results in endogenous epinephrine suppression (an excessive amount causes infertility). A similar mechanism operates in women who conceive following the erroneous diagnosis of "blocked tubes." They stop worrying over their infertility, their tubes relax and they conceive.

The neural pathways by which emotionally conditioned disharmonic impulses produce tubal spasm have been described.[4] As proof of the validity of this hypothesis, selective denervation of the proximal tubes and the cervix readily cures this type of infertility. The fallopian tubes, the most "hysterical" portion of a woman's anatomy, also relax following sympathomimetic drugs and hypnosis. Most pharmacologic or psychotherapeutic modalities, including hypnosis, owe a large percentage of their success to the placebo effect. Since infertility often is dramatically alleviated when stress is reduced, it is not hard to see how much more effective specific suggestions would be in achieving relaxation through hypnosis.

Hypnosis can be a helpful adjunct in the treatment of infertility if the physician can understand the psychological conflicts of both partners. Posthypnotic suggestions and autohypnosis, by relaxation and healthful sensory-imagery conditioning, neutralize other anxieties and tensions. The diminution in psychosomatic factors frequently helps establish regular ovulatory cycles and probably a normal pH in the generative tract; the chemistry of the vaginal secretions can be dependent on psychogenic factors.[11] Wollman[24] recently described successful treatment of several cases of infertility by hypnosis. Increasing libido where there was very little coitus helped overcome several cases of infertility.

The author's technic is as follows: After the patient has been conditioned to enter into hypnosis, she is taught autohypnosis. Posthypnotic suggestions are utilized to induce profound relaxation immediately after coitus. Under hypnosis it is further suggested: "Do not deliberately try to get pregnant. The harder you try, the less chance you have. Just relax. Every time you have intercourse, assume that you cannot conceive." This type of suggestion, or the reciprocal inhibition therapy, follows the law of reverse effect. By such measures the patient relaxes; harmful endogenous factors are decreased; if tubal spasm is present, it may be alleviated. This reasoning may seem far-fetched, but twice the author erroneously diagnosed "blocked tubes." This achieved relaxation, mental and physical. He was not surprised to find that the patients soon became pregnant. With fear removed, relaxation of the reproductive apparatus occurs. Posthypnotic directions also can be suggested to inculcate a feeling of motherliness and to seek intercourse during the fertile period and, most importantly, to eliminate worry and tensions.

FRIGIDITY

The physician should emphasize that proficiency and complete gratification are not achieved until "there is a union of one personality with the other," or until each of the partners is capable of "giving" instead of "getting." Sexual compatibility is based on mutual respect, liking and gradually established confidence—the basis for mature *love*. Many females blame their sexual problems on physical symptoms, particularly those which bring them to the physician. Organic frigidity is rare. Pseudofrigidity due to male ineptness or ignorance of sexual matters can readily be treated by superficial psychotherapy, consisting of discussion and re-education of the male. True frigidity, including dyspareunia due to vaginismus, is not a distinct clinical entity but a symptom of faulty conditioning during early psychosexual development.[9, 13, 18]

Many women feel guilty if they do not have a specific type of pleasure response in the vagina. Sexual satisfaction cannot be reduced to a mechanical response. Kinsey contended that "orgasm is orgasm" regardless of how it is achieved, whether by digital, penile or lingual manipulation, but less superficial studies do not bear this out. Because some women can achieve an orgasm only after being beaten, it does not follow that this procedure is normal. Orgasm has little to do with the size of the penis, the position or the posture. What is important is the element of love. This entity is poorly understood and is lacking in many marriages. Since the understanding of love and sex relationships is important to any therapeutic approach, a discussion of these is indicated.

The author has classified the varieties of love.[14] Actually, there are 4 types of love. There is the "I love I" type which is seen in the child. This is primary narcissism and is in reality self-love. The child says, "This is my toy; give me this." If he doesn't get it, he gets angry, hostile and frustrated and cries or stamps off. There are adults who have never really emerged from this "I love I" period of their psychosexual development. They are totally incapable of giving in any type of sustaining relationship. Naturally, from the start, such a marriage is destined to failure.

The next type is projected self-love ("I love me—in you"). This, too, is "I love I," only these people worship themselves in another person. Like infants, these people "love" only those who do things for them. It is all incoming, not outgoing.

The third type of love is characterized by the romantic love in which sex is paramount. It is the same type of unrealistic, romantic love that is portrayed in our movies, novels and popular songs. After the initial thrill of the honeymoon, the chill sets in. The sexual ardor begins to wear off, the quarreling begins. Eventually these frustrated individuals discover that they have nothing in common except self-love. They are not willing to give to each other. Since neither gives, neither receives. The last type of love, by far the rarest, is noted in the old married couple celebrating their golden wedding anniversary. They are just as much in love as when they first met. They did not enter this relationship thinking of what they were going to get but, rather, what they were going to give to each other! Their sexual responses may have been weak at first, but increased in intensity as they sacrificed for one another. Briefly, sex is the passionate interest in another body, and love is the passionate interest in another personality! Just as whisky and soda are found together, so are love and sex found together, but they are separate ingredients!

When trying to get at the factors responsible for sexual coldness, one must inquire how the wife feels about her husband. Does she love him? Is she a warm, outgoing person, willing to give of herself to him? What reservations does she have about sex? Has sex been presented to her as wicked, sinful and dirty? Does she think that only a fallen woman has sexual climaxes?

The following case illustrates my technics:

A couple who were projecting their squabbling over their sexual tensions onto their 4 children decided to commit suicide! Her ignorance and apathy toward sexual matters were pronounced. She was a member of a very devoutly religious sect which frowned upon sex and taught that it was only for reproduction, not for pleasure. Hypnosis and autohypnosis were used. Like most women of this type, she said, "I can get plenty of satisfaction before, during or after the sex act if my husband plays with my clitoris. However, I feel very guilty about this."

Her guilt was alleviated by the assurance that any type of sex play precoitally is all right if it meets the approval of both partners and the sex act ends in genital union. Foreplay exclusively without genital-to-genital union is considered a perversion.

Sensory-imagery conditioning under hypnosis was then utilized to transfer the sensation of clitoral climax to the vagina. Through posthypnotic directions it was suggested, "You can transfer the pleasurable sensation in the clitoral area to wherever you wish to experience it." Through hallucinatory intercourse during autohypnosis, she imagined having the pleasant sensation associated with clitoral climaxes transferred to her lower pelvic region. After 3 weeks of intensive psychotherapy, often consisting of 3- or 4-hour sessions, and practice, it was suggested that she have intercourse. "Do not deliberately try to have a vaginal orgasm, but relax and don't press—it will occur eventually. The most important matter is to enjoy sex without guilt. You can wonder whether you will achieve the type of response you wish during the first month or the second month. Perhaps it may even occur earlier. Let me know. The exact pleasure responses which you experienced during the practice sessions will occur when you are least expecting them." In due time, this patient was having the type of orgasms she wished.

One can also employ time distortion[15] by suggesting, "For every minute of friction you receive during the sex act, it will *seem like 5 minutes!*" Thus, if the female requires prolonged contact and her husband has premature ejaculation, time can be "lengthened" to give them each greater satisfaction. Naturally, this mechanical adjunct, as has already been mentioned, must be combined with the over-all relationship and attitudes of love toward one another.

LOW BACK PAIN

This discussion will be limited to low back pain of psychosomatic origin. There is an "organ language" which the body uses to voice its protests, and the choice of the organ system is determined by the focal area in which the neurotic conflict occurs. To some neurotic individuals, worry is "a pain in the back," and their back symptoms only express the language of the body, saying, "I am carrying a load on my back—I cannot carry on. Can't people see how I am suffering? Why doesn't someone help me?"

If these and other questions can be answered, the emotional basis for the backache can be determined readily. A personality appraisal is generally necessary in refractory patients. Naturally, the signs and the symptoms of organic disease must be ruled out. The most common method of relieving the backache of psychogenic origin is illustrated in the following case:

Mrs. D. C., aged 20, had a severe backache for more than 3 months which was resistant to medicaments and physical therapy. There were no organic factors to account for the symptom, which had begun shortly after she had to discontinue breast-feeding. She was quickly able to relieve the discomfort by glove anesthesia, and subsequent hypnotic sessions were devoted to working through her faulty attitudes in regard to the child. Her main problem was a feeling of inadequacy concerning her ability to rear a child properly, and this had been compounded with guilt feelings when she was forced to stop nursing. She soon realized that she developed the back pain to have an alibi for her shortcomings. After 2 months of therapy consisting of reassurance, re-education and supportive measures, she felt entirely adequate as a mother and the low backache disappeared.

Low back pain of emotional origin, if its function is determined, can be treated hypnotically by symptom-transformation—switching the symptom to another less incapacitating one—but this must be only with the patient's permission. Through the induction of an artificial conflict, another target organ can be suggested for an equivalent symptom to replace the original conversion reaction. For example, it can be suggested that the low back pain be transferred to the stomach. This is not done by direct suggestion but by suggesting a conflict associated with deprivation and fear. If the patient develops the new symptom, it is indicative that she is willing to yield the old one. The fact that the symptom can be manipulated indicates a favorable prognosis. Of course, the newly acquired symptom can be removed, either by hypnosis or autohypnosis, more readily than the long-standing one. In order to use this approach one must be familiar with the hypnoanalytic technics described in Chapter 47.

PELVIC PAIN

The same factors described above apply to the diagnosis of pelvic pain. However, there can be no question of "real" versus "psychic" pain. The reproductive organs reflect the effects of emotions. Pelvic pain is treated in a manner similar to that described for backache. The cases below are typical. Many individuals with pelvic pain are "polysurgical addicts," who are making the rounds of physicians' offices seeking another operation.

Previous operations usually include an appendectomy, the removal of "ovarian cysts," "straightening of the womb," and the removal of "adhesions." Patients with polysurgical addiction are not aware of their deep-seated need for an operative assault. Such women have deep-seated guilt feelings for which the surgery serves as punishment, atonement and, finally, license to commit new offenses. As a rule, there is improvement for several months following such obtuse "therapy," after which the patient again produces symptoms and demands for further surgery.

Mrs. C. C., aged 50, had a persistent pain in the right lower quadrant. She had had numerous operations such as an appendectomy, the removal of ovarian cysts, a hysterectomy, the removal of the gallbladder and a chordotomy, without relief. On the advice of two neurosurgeons, she had had another chordotomy performed, which failed to relieve the discomfort. After she was trained in autohypnosis and glove anesthesia, she was advised to shift the pain to the left side of the abdomen by means of the latter method. Within 4 sessions, at weekly intervals, she had a well-developed pain area in the left lower quadrant. Further posthypnotic suggestions were directed toward reducing the intensity of the pain in this region. Concomitantly, the masochistic need for the pain was worked through during subsequent sessions. She revealed that she felt she had to punish herself to atone for guilty fears and aggressive reactions toward her husband, who was impotent; she felt that she was growing old and unattractive and that she was desperately *needed* attention. The secondary gain afforded by the symptom was made clear to her. This patient was seen over a period of 9 months and was one of the most challenging cases the author had ever been called upon to treat. She made a complete recovery.

PREMENSTRUAL TENSION

Women with premenstrual tension suffer from emotional symptoms such as irritability, proneness to domestic friction, crying and depression. The symptoms of physical discomfort such as backache, headache and varying degrees of edema of the breasts, the abdomen and the legs are not as important as the emotional concomitants which often disturb the patient's interpersonal relationships. In some instances, compulsive behavior, suicide and unpremeditated criminal acts are due to the breakdown of defenses and the resultant lowering of the general sensory threshold coincidental with the premenstrual phase.

Excessive estrogens, progesterone and the overproduction of antidiuretic hormones have been held responsible for the excess sodium and water in the tissues. A lowered blood sugar, following the hyperinsulinism secondary to emotional factors, was thought to increase the irritability of the nervous system. However, the use of hormones or diuretics per se cannot correct the emotional factors contributing to the difficulties.

The lack of uniformity of opinion as to what constitutes premenstrual tension, the varied methods and results reported in regard to treatment, and the frequent relapses after "cure" all indicate that there is no single causative factor. Therefore, an interdisciplinary approach directed to psychosomatic factors is indicated. Failures result if therapy is directed to only one portion of the syndrome.

The multifaceted approach should consist of amphetamines to elevate the mood, analgesic agents for the discomfort, diuretics and ammonium chloride for the edema and the correction of the electrolyte imbalance—specific therapy, however, depends on the symptomatology. Hypnosis can be used to potentiate all these approaches.

The noncritical attitude of the physician, his empathy and his acceptance of the validity of the patient's complaints are other important factors which aid in helping to correct the psychological symptoms. Supportive psychotherapy, consisting of re-education, reassurance and the development of strong rapport, through hypnosis, will enable most patients to face their life problems and not succumb to real or fancied symptoms, which often are used for secondary gain purposes —to master the world around them in a neurotic manner. Experience indicates that the symptoms of premenstrual tension disappear to a significant degree when understanding of the need for the symptom is achieved.

MENOPAUSE

The majority of clinicians attribute menopausal symptoms to estrogen deficiency. This is reflected by the large number of patients treated with estrogens and by the numerous papers reporting the success of this therapy. Severe menopausal symptoms are unknown in some cultures, and the clinical picture is confusing in our society. The cause of the flushing is a failure of the heat-regulating mechanism of the body to dissipate heat properly. There are no correlations between clinical findings and vaginal smears. Women who have the worst symptoms may have smears indicating adequate estrogen stimulation. Others, who have no symptoms, show a complete absence of vaginal cornification. Evidence exists that a "third gonad" in the adrenal gland functions long after the ovaries atrophy.

Good results have been obtained in treating numerous patients with supportive hypnotherapy, oral estrogens and sedatives.[16] Substantial improvement occurs after the ventilation of personal problems. Hormonal relief of so-called menopausal symptoms may be due, in many cases, to the placebo effect of the doctor-patient relationship. Eradication of popular fallacies by re-education, together with reassurance and the judicious use of hormones and tranquilizers, will often prove helpful. Such a psychosomatic approach serves to eliminate the "buttock syndrome," making the patient less dependent on "shots."

INTERSEXUALITY

Mrs. G. B., aged 28, had been diagnosed as a genetic male. Two testicles in the groin had been removed immediately after her birth. All her secondary sex characteristics were female. Pelvic examination revealed the presence of ovaries but the absence of a uterus. Her clitoris was slightly enlarged but was in no way a vestigial penis. The facial features were male-like. She complained, "I always feel funny, as if I don't know who I am." A psychological evaluation indicated that her drives were essentially feminine. She had considerable anxiety over the absence of menses and the inability ever to bear a child. She was working as a bookkeeper.

Posthypnotic suggestions directing her interests into more domestic pursuits were made. Her sexual responses were characterized by vaginal orgasm, and she stated that she was very much in love with her husband. Further hypnotherapy, making use of sensory-imagery conditioning involving fantasies of being very feminine, had a marked effect on resolving her conflictual attitudes over femininity.

MISCELLANEOUS PSYCHOGYNECIC CONDITIONS

The author frequently sees women who demand urethral and vaginal treatments for nonexistent diseases. These are masturbation equivalents and sexual gratification is obtained in the guise of the physician's treatment, whereas self-manipulation of the genitals is taboo.

The following case history is typical for this type of individual:

Miss C. B., aged 19, a deeply religious girl, presented herself with severe pain above the pubis. A thorough examination was negative. The patient was an epileptic and was on anticonvulsant medication. Under deep hypnosis she revealed a long history of unrequited genital tensions and a desire for intercourse and, more importantly, that she *simulated* epilepticform seizures in which she achieved orgastic relief; this obviated masturbation, which would have increased her guilt. She also admitted that she frequently requested physicians to examine her vaginally because it gave her a thrill to feel the speculum in the vagina—a masturbatory equivalent.

Unfortunately, the patient left town before further hypnotherapy could be instituted. However, this interesting case illustrates how far some women will go to develop a need for a symptom.

Retroversion of the uterus is frequently held responsible for pelvic pain. However, it has been said that the patient whose genital organs seem to be "wrong" is likely to be a patient whose psychological processes relating to sex are wrong![12] The latter can definitely influence the former. Hypnosis can be used as follows:

Miss G. C., aged 29, an asthenic and sickly looking girl, who appeared to be much younger than her chronologic age, had been informed that she had a "tipped womb." Insomnia and bloating of the abdomen and dysmenorrhea were marked. Glove anesthesia failed to relieve the symptomatology.

Her symptoms began at 16, when she was in high school and was first asked to go out on a date. She felt very embarrassed on this first date and never felt at ease with young men. Under hypnodiagnostic exploration, she related that her father was too busy ever to sit down and tell her about men and sexual matters and that her mother, who was always very busy with her club and social activities, never even informed her about menstruation. As a result, she feared men, and remained very dependent on her mother. She frequently slept with her. Posthypnotic suggestions negating her faulty attitudes toward the menses, sexuality and femininity, together with reassurance and re-education over several months of therapy achieved a dramatic relief of this patient's symptoms. Further follow-up therapy was recommended for the parents. Although this patient had appeared immature at the first meeting, she now looks, acts and feels like a mature, well-adjusted woman.

Pelvic Examination

Frequently hypnosis may be of considerable value when a pelvic examination is necessary in an obese patient. Merely having the patient enter into hypnosis usually produces adequate relaxation.

Minor Gynecologic Surgery

Hypnosis may be used as an anesthetic agent in suitable patients for performing a dilatation and a curettement, a biopsy of the cervix and a culdoscopy. It can also be employed to reduce analgesia and anesthesia for major operative gynecologic procedures (see Chapter 32).

Hysterosalpingography

Hypnosis can be used to relax a tubal spasm in an infertile patient when performing a diagnostic procedure such as a hysterosalpingography, a tubal insufflation or a hysterogram.

Pruritus Vulvae

This will be discussed in the next chapter.

STERILIZATION

Pseudo-orientation in time can be used on selected women requesting sterilization. Under hypnosis, the patient is projected "several years ahead" and asked how she feels now that her tubes were tied several years ago (the date suggested should be at least 2 years ahead). Any feelings of guilt, remorse or self-recrimination indicate the need for further investigation. Many women develop emotional disorders after sterilization; these can be obviated by projecting the patient into the hallucinated future.

SUMMARY

Any physician trained in hypnotherapy who utilizes an interdisciplinary approach can obtain gratifying results in many difficult gynecologic cases. Naturally, hypnosis here, too, is not a cure-all; there are many failures and relapses. However, autohypnosis, sensory-imagery conditioning and posthypnotic suggestions directed toward the patient's emotional needs speed up any type of psychotherapy.

Dependency is not fostered when autohypnosis is used. Since the patient, to a degree, controls the therapy, her self-esteem is enhanced. Motivation, rapport and confidence are more readily established when permissive technics that are noncritical are employed.

Dramatic symptom-removal by a doctor-directed approach is outmoded. Symptom-substitution or symptom-transformation, as discussed more fully in Chapter 47, are valuable for achieving relatively permanent results.

It is not necessary for the patient to understand the origin of the symptoms, but *how she reacts to them and how she deals with her emotional problems are of the utmost importance.* Greater therapeutic leverage can be obtained by revivification, posthypnotic suggestion, time-distortion and other hypnotic phenomena.

Hypnotherapy for psychogynecic conditions helps many emotionally disturbed females to face their problems on a more mature level by developing healthier behavior patterns. Thus, anxiety-provoking tensions can be dealt with more realistically.

Such psychotherapy usually should be combined with a medical approach for optimal results.

REFERENCES

1. August, R. V.: Paper read at 15th Annual Meeting of Amer. Soc. Study of Sterility, Atlantic City, April 5, 1959.
2. Dunbar, F.: Emotions and Bodily Changes, p. 335, New York, Columbia, 1938.
3. Fremont-Smith, M., and Meigs, J. V.: Menstrual dysfunction due to emotional factors, Am. J. Obst. & Gynec. 55:1042, 1948.
4. Friedgood, H. B.: Neuroendocrine and psychodynamic factors in sterility, West. J. Surg. 56:391, 1948.
5. Friedlander, E., and Moses, E.: Sekundare Schwangerschaftszeichen beim Chorionepitheliom des Mannes, Wien. klin. Wchnschr. 49:684-687, 1936.
6. Heiman, M.: Psychosocial influences in functional uterine bleeding, Obst. & Gynec. 7:3, 1956.
7. Heyer, G. R.: Hypnose und Hypnotherapie in die Psychischen Heilmethoden Hrsg. von Karl Birnbaum, pp. 73-135, Leipzig, Thieme, 1927.
8. Israel, S. L.: Discussion of Buxton, L.: A critical survey of present methods of diagnosis and therapy in human infertility, Am. J. Obst. & Gynec. 70:741-753, 1955.
9. Kroger, W. S.: Treatment of psychogynecic disorders by hypnoanalysis, Am. J. Obst. & Gynec. 52:409-418, 1946.
10. ———: Evaluation of Personality Factors in the Treatment of Infertility. Fertil. & Steril. 3:542-551, 1952.
11. ———: Hypnotherapy in obstetrics and gynecology, J.C.E.H. 1:61-70, 1953.
12. ———: Psychosomatic aspects of obstetrics and gynecology, Obst. & Gynec. 3:504-516, 1954.
13. ———: Psychosomatic aspects of frigidity and impotency, Internat. Rec. Med. 171:469-478, 1958.
14. *Op. cit.*, p. 471.
15. *Op. cit.*, p. 477.
16. Kroger, W. S.: Hypnotherapy in obstetrics and gynecology, J. Arkansas M. S. 55:412-416, 1959.
17. Kroger, W. S., and Freed, S. C.: Psychosomatic treatment of functional dysmenorrhea by hypnosis, Am. J. Obst. & Gynec. 46:817-822, 1943.
18. ———: Psychosomatic aspects of frigidity, J.A.M.A. 143:56, 1950.
19. ———: Psychosomatic aspects of sterility,

Am. J. Obst. & Gynec. 59:867-874, 1950.

20. ——: Psychosomatic factors in functional amenorrhea, Am. J. Obst. & Gynec. 59: 328-336, 1950.

21. ——: Psychosomatic Gynecology: Including Problems of Obstetrical Care, Chicago, Free Press, 1956; reprinted, Los Angeles, Wilshire Book Co., 1962.

22. Rakoff, A. E., and Fried, P.: Pseudocyesis: a psychosomatic study in gynecology, J.A.M.A. 145:1329, 1951.

23. Reifenstein, E. C.: Hypothalamic amenor-rhea, M. Clin. North America 30:1103-1114, 1946.

24. Wollman, Leo: The role of hypnosis in the treatment of infertility, Brit. J. M. Hypnotism 2:38-46, 1961.

SUPPLEMENTARY READING

Coulton, D.: Hypnotherapy in gynecological problems, Am. J. Clin. Hypnosis 3:95-101, 1960.

Kroger, W. S.: An integrated approach to infertility, J. Psychosomatics 3:1-12, 1962.

35

Hypnosis in Dermatology

EMOTIONS AND SKIN

The effectiveness of hypnotherapy for alopecia areata, dermatitis, eczema, hyperhidrosis, neurodermatitis, psoriasis, pruritus, lichen planus, herpes simplex, pemphigus, verrucae and other dermatologic disorders has been reviewed.[14] The psychosomatic etiology for many of these disorders is well established. The well-known phenomena of goose pimples, sweating, blanching and temperature changes in the skin following psychological stimuli constitute further corroborative evidence.

The skin mirrors the inner self. It is richly endowed with emotional symbolism. Such expressions as "thick-skinned" and "thin-skinned" may mean "insensitive" and "sensitive," respectively. "To get under my skin" and "itching to do something" are common expressions; if the latter is not carried out it may lead to actual itching and scratching. The epidermis and the nervous system originate from the ectoderm and, since both are nurtured by a mesenchymal derivative composed of vascular connective tissue, it is only logical to assume that there is a cross-fertilization between the skin and the autonomic nervous system.

Direct hypnotic suggestion has been able to produce erythema, blisters, wheals, urticaria, tumefaction, congestion, hemorrhage and various sensory effects ranging from anesthesia to hyperesthesia, cold to hot, and itching to pain.[14] However, organic skin manifestations do not respond as well to mere suggestion per se but, rather, to hypnotic sensory-imagery conditioning. This enables the individual to react to a hallucinated stimulus as if to a reality perception. However, the ability to relieve organic changes varies from one individual to another, depending upon the degree of autonomic control recovered by hypnotic conditioning.[2]

The role of the autonomic nervous system in cutaneous physiopathology has been described.[17, 21] The nervous system is capable of directing repressed emotional forces to appropriate target organs; the site selected is determined by a local vulnerability of the skin, plus a correlation between the nature of the emotional stimulus and the type of the physiologic response. Why the skin lesions vary with the type of conflict, and from person to person, appearing and disappearing during the life span of the same person is, at present, poorly understood.

HYPNOSIS IN DERMATOLOGIC DISORDERS

Hypnosis has relieved itching in refractory cases of intractable eczema, nevus, lichen planus, psoriasis and hyperhidrosis.[7] There are several favorable reports on its use in chronic ichthyosis.[15, 18] Acne has been cured by hypnosis merely by suggesting that thinking of the word "scar" would symbolize an ugly facial appearance; thus, picking and spreading of the lesions were prevented.[8]

The itching of generalized neurodermatitis has been relieved by hypnosis, probably through vasomotor alterations.[9] Others[10] have investigated the physiology of masochism in relationship to itching. A typical personality profile has been postulated.[4]

There is an extensive literature[1, 16, 24] on the psychosomatic aspects of pruritus ani and pruritus vulvae. The author[12] reported gratifying success with hypnotherapy used for direct symptom-removal in pruritus vulvae. The primitive pathways developed during infancy and childhood, when masturbation and other autoerotic tendencies were associated with guilt feelings, are often utilized during adulthood to express unrequited sexual tensions via the genitals. The pruritus occurred as often in virginal girls as in married women, and frigidity played an important role in the latter; "necking" and "heavy petting" resulted in genital tensions in the former. Some women rub their legs together to obtain relief—"onanistic prurique"—from the itching. Tickling and itching, as pleasurable sensations, only emphasize the intimate connection between sexual feelings and the modification of skin sensibility. Hence, it is not surprising that masturbation equivalents are engrafted on an actual itching dermatosis. By such measures, the scratching obviates guilt.

Some people utilize their pruritus masochistically to express inward rage over their inability to obtain love and affection. By such measures, the dependency and the subsequent hostility are denied and masked by a façade of co-operation and submissiveness. The unrelieved frustration and hostility are then activated in overt symptoms such as irascibility, insomnia, fatigue, anorexia, bodily pains and an attitude of "If I don't get some relief soon, I might just as well be dead." These typically depressive reactions only cover the real, underlying emotional difficulties.

Numerous investigators[2, 3, 6, 13] have found that 60 to 70 per cent of warts respond to suggestive therapy. Sulzberger and Wolf[20] stated: "The fact that suggestion, without recourse to any other therapy, cures an appreciable percentage of warts stands established." There have been many types of lay-healing, from "charming" away warts by bizarre and mysterious procedures to using prayers and incantations. Ullman,[22, 23] in an excellent monograph on the subject, assayed the use of hypnosis—since it emulated lay-healing—for the treatment of warts. In 8 out of 15 deeply hypnotized patients, a complete remission of the warts occurred in contrast with 2 cures in 47 patients who could not be deeply hypnotized. If a lay hypnotist had not been used, the results would have been better because the rapport would not have been divided. This work was recently corroborated in a series in which half of a group was treated and the other half was used as a control.[19] Cures were obtained in 10 out of a total of 15 patients on the treated side in from 5 weeks to 3 months. Unequivocally, directive hypnotherapy played a significant role in catalyzing the curative processes in certain patients with warts.

HYPNOTHERAPEUTIC METHODS

The intensified hypnotherapeutic relationship, combined with the therapist's ability to release a sufficiently strong affect, often results in dramatic recovery. In dermatologic disorders, it appears that the greater the patient's conviction of cure, the less the physician's suggestive "power" is required, probably because of the lability of the skin to emotions. However, lack of conviction on the part of the therapist leads to poor results and frequently makes the anxious patient worse. Hypnotherapy also can potentiate x-ray therapy, ointments and drugs.

Hypnonarcosis has been employed to relieve chronic itching dermatoses. Various types of dermatitis have been cured by prolonged hypnosis—6 or more days of continuous "hypnotic sleep." However, follow-up studies are meager. Prolonged hypnotic sleep has been used successfully for a wide variety of medical conditions.[1a] The author has had no experience with this approach in skin diseases.

VERBALIZATIONS FOR AUTHORITARIAN HYPNOTIC TECHNICS

Direct hypnotic suggestion relieves itching and scratching; the physician convincingly suggests, "Immediately upon coming out of the hypnotic state, your itching (or pain, pimples, rash) will disappear." More effective is the method of telling the hypnotized subject, "You are lying under an ultraviolet light" or "in the hot sun, and your face (if this is the area involved) is becoming very warm. This wonderful feeling will remain for several hours (or all day); your skin will feel fine until your next visit."

When this approach is used, it is advisable to enhance the psychological suggestions by the physiologic effect of touching the area with the hand or with an instrument. Reinforcement is usually necessary.

CONTRAINDICATIONS TO SYMPTOM-REMOVAL

Some psychiatrists object to symptom-removal by direct suggestion, contending that the symptom has an important defensive role in protecting the individual against further personality decompensation and a possible psychotic break. The author has never knowingly encountered such a difficulty, although admittedly many of his patients "get worse before they get better," as in any other form of psychotherapy. McDowell[14] likewise doubts if one can attribute a psychotic break to symptom-removal by hypnotic suggestion.

Pleune[25] raised the point that symptom-removal without definitive correction may be dangerous. Yet he admits that "Doctors do give drugs for colds, headaches, and so forth, without extensive investigation in every case." The whole orthodox practice of dermatology is directed to symptomatic treatment, and seldom are underlying emotional conditions treated. Most dermatologists are satisfied to get symptomatic relief.

PERMISSIVE HYPNOTIC TECHNICS FOR SYMPTOM-REMOVAL

Regardless of the hypnotherapeutic approach, itching must be controlled to prevent further scratching and aggravation of a skin disorder. Invariably, medical measures must be supplemented by explanations of the underlying disorder and the *need* for the symptom. As emphasized throughout this volume, most patients do not have to understand the origin of their symptoms, but *how they react to and face their problems in a realistic and mature manner is of the utmost importance!*

USE OF SENSORY-IMAGERY CONDITIONING

Permissive hypnotic technics which do not mobilize critical attitudes are employed to facilitate sensory-imagery conditioning. However, as has been mentioned, personality changes and the correction of faulty attitudes and habit patterns are not obtained by *fiat* or conscious exhortations to use the will. A direct frontal attack to remove the skin disorder by an authoritative hypnotic approach overwhelms the patient and achieves only temporary results. The modern permissive hypnotherapeutic approach is essentially patient-centered and makes full use of sensory-imagery conditioning. Kline[10a] describes a sensory-imagery technic for a case of psoriasis as follows:

In a light hypnotic state, the patient was told that she would be able to feel warm sensations throughout the body. Then she was told that she would be able to experience cold sensations throughout the body. Having experienced these, she was told that she would be able to feel sensations of heaviness, lightness, constriction and expansion in all the areas of the body where she had the psoriasis.

In the hypnotic state, the patient was told that she would be able to feel warm sensations only in the areas where the psoriasis was and not in the other areas of the body. Following this she was told that she would experience cold sensations but *only* in the lesion areas. This was followed by localized sensations of lightness, heaviness, constriction and expansion. Thus a regular treatment sequence of hypnotic sensation was developed: *warmth, cold, lightness, heaviness, constriction* and *expansion,* followed finally by normal sensation and relaxation.

Posthypnotic directions were given for experiencing this pattern of sensations daily, at a time when the patient would be relaxing. Thus the time was variable. In addition she was told that several times a day, again whenever it might be convenient, she would be able to visualize the areas of her body which had lesions and she would be able to visualize them as if they were going through the sequence of induced sensations. That is, she would visualize each step in the hypnotic and the posthypnotic treatment pattern. Training in visualization had been undertaken in the office during both the hypnotic and the waking states. The patient had proven herself to be able to engage in scene visualization rather easily. Imagery activity even in the waking state was easily acquired. In general, the patient was able to achieve both the posthypnotic sensations and the imagery activity with relative ease. The length of time for both the pattern of sensations and the imagery would vary somewhat but averaged about 3 minutes for the sensations (entire pattern), and about 1 minute for the imagery.

Through use of scene visualization and sensory imagery, the patient learns to control his feedback systems. This is the very essence of autogenic training and Yoga.

With these, one first learns how to control a portion of the body, and then, in a manner similar to that of Yoga, control of more autonomic functioning is established.

USE OF GLOVE ANESTHESIA

Transfer of glove anesthesia (the self-induced palmar anesthesia) to the affected area often alleviates the itching and scratching. The busy dermatologist can save time by employing group hypnotherapy in a method similar to that used by obstetricians (see p. 197).

SYMPTOM SUBSTITUTION

Another successful hypnotic technic is to exaggerate the itching. If the itching can be increased, it can be decreased! A systematic attempt then is made to "wean" the patient off the *need* to itch and scratch by symptom substitution or by symptom transformation, i.e., by "trading down." Through conditioning under autohypnosis the itch can be displaced or transferred to another portion of the body. When successful, this indicates that the patient is willing to yield the symptom. The new symptom naturally is easier to remove than the long-standing one.

An interesting technic to relieve itching is to suggest a negative sensory hallucination. This can be accomplished by the misdirection of attention as follows: The patient is to imagine, while under hypnosis, that as he looks at his lesions he "sees" that the skin looks and feels as normal as any other area of the body devoid of lesions. Unfortunately, success with this approach requires a subject who is capable of entering the somnambulistic state or one closely allied to it. One can remark: "Look at your right wrist; you can begin to speculate on whether or not that area will look like your left wrist, which does not have any involvement. Now, keep looking at the left wrist; notice the texture of the skin—it also feels perfectly normal, does it not?" (The patient nods his head in agreement.) "Every time you look at this wrist you will observe that this area on your right wrist is becoming as normal looking as your left wrist. You may also close your eyes, and in your 'mind's eye' see or imagine that the lesions have disappeared—the skin is normal

in appearance. However, you may keep just as much of the itching on the involved area of the wrist as you wish to retain. You do not have to get rid of this itching all at once but, rather, allow it to disappear slowly." The patient is given another posthypnotic suggestion such as: "You might raise the question whether you wish this lesion (on the wrist) or that lesion (one near the elbow) to disappear first. Also, you might begin to consider the possibility of just when this will occur. Will it be tomorrow, a week from tomorrow, or several weeks from now? At any rate, the more you keep thinking about this under autohypnosis, the more likely the rash will go away." Thus, the theoretic dangers attributed to symptom-removal are obviated.

Motivation, belief and confidence are readily established when permissive hypnotic technics, as sensory-imagery conditioning, symptom substitution or symptom transformation, are employed. This type of scientific hypnotherapy, through effective rapport, enables the physician to establish a beachhead on the periphery of the patient's disorder—but he helps the patient cure himself! Dependency on the therapist is minimal when autohypnotic conditioning is used to raise the adaptive response. Thus, the theoretic dangers attributed to symptom-removal therapy are obviated, the physician being merely a catalytic agent.

SPECIALIZED HYPNOTIC TECHNICS

Revivification, automatic writing, dream interpretation and other projective technics are often effective in the dissolution of refractory skin disorders. The patient is asked to revivify the disturbing experiences that preceded the onset of his symptom. Discussion of feelings associated with these experiences can help resolve emotional conflicts. Abreaction, plus education and reassurance, generally obviates the need for further working-through of conflictual material.

Of particular value is engrafting of an artificial conflict, calculated to produce a given specific emotional attitude which might elicit a given skin reaction. Unfortunately, too few patients are amenable to these complex technics. When applicable and wisely used, such hypnotherapeutic technics can alter the prognosis of many refractory cases of psychosomatic dermatologic disorders, as the following case histories show:

Mrs. M. A., aged 37, was referred by a dermatologist with a diagnosis of dermatitis factitia of 7 years' duration. She had undergone various types of dermatologic therapy without avail. The patient had had several years of intensive psychoanalytic therapy, also without appreciably success. Her entire body was scarred, particularly the face and the neck. Since extensive exploration of her personality had been fruitless, symptom substitution was employed in the following manner. After she had been taught autohypnosis, it was suggested that she should get herself a large doll made of rubber which resembled skin. Since most of the picking of her skin occurred while she was watching television or while she was trying to fall asleep at night, she was to keep the doll at her side and pick it "to her heart's content." After posthypnotic suggestions to this effect were given to her over a 3-week period, she gradually shifted the digging and the clawing from herself to the doll. The number of fresh excoriations diminished. However, the self-mutilation of the skin was still being produced during most of her daytime activities. Through further posthypnotic suggestions she was advised that she could twitch one of the fingers on either hand as often as she wished in order to obviate the intensity of the picking. Within 2 weeks all picking of her skin had stopped. It was then suggested that the frequency of the finger-twitching could gradually be reduced. At the end of approximately a month she was twitching her finger only about 2 or 3 times an hour. Concomitantly, expressive therapy of a superficial type revealed that she had always masturbated, was completely frigid with her husband and felt extreme guilt over deceiving him about this for many years. She stated that she was able to achieve considerable gratification from clitoral stimulation before and after the sex act. Through re-education and reassurance, she was informed that her guilt over her masturbatory proclivities and simulation of orgastic responses was completely unwarranted. She stated, "I like the sex act and I am very much in love with my husband, but I am not getting the satisfaction I think I am supposed to have in my vaginal area." She was informed that sexual response could not be reduced to a mechanical act; the fact that she loved her husband was of more importance than localization of the climax. Through the use of a permissive approach and further resolution of her unhealthy sexual attitudes, she stopped masturbating. Within 3 months, she realized that she no longer had a need either to stimulate her genitals artificially or to pick at her skin to satisfy unrealized masochistic needs. Although she never achieved any other type of sexual response than a clitoric one, both the finger-twitching and the face-picking subsided. At the end of a 1-year follow-up there was no recurrence. Her sexuality was still unchanged.

Mrs. R. L., aged 44, was referred with an acute neurodermatitis of the neck involving the upper portion of the chest and the back. The patient was refractory to all medicaments. Glove anesthesia was employed for relief of the intractable itching. Posthypnotic directions were given to feel sensations of warmth and coldness over the involved areas. Direct suggestion as to the improvement in her skin was not given at any time. The neurodermatitis had developed immediately after her daughter had announced her engagement to a young man of another faith; this upset Mrs. R. L. terribly. The daughter was referred to a psychiatrist in an attempt to delay the marriage; she was able to work through her feelings toward the young man and finally decided it would not be feasible to marry him. The mother's neurodermatitis promptly improved. However, during the period that her daughter was receiving psychotherapy, hypnosis afforded Mrs. R. L. considerable relief from her itching, nervous tension and anxiety. Hypnotherapy was employed only as an adjunctive procedure.

REFERENCES

1. Alexander, R. P.: Contribution to the psychological understanding of pruritus ani: report of a case, Psychosom. Med. 21:182-192, 1959.

1a. Andrew, B. V.: Sleep Therapy in the Neuroses, New York, Consultants Bureau, 1960.

2. Block, B.: Ueber die Heilung der Warzen durch Suggestion, Klin. Wchnschr. 6:2271; 2320, 1927.

3. Bonjour, J.: Cure of condylomata by suggestion, Schweiz. med. Wchnschr. 6:2272; 2320, 1927.

4. Cleveland, S. E., and Fisher, S.: Psychological factors in the neurodermatoses, Psychosom. Med. 18:209-220, 1956.

5. Delboeuf, J.: De l'Origine des Effets Curatifs de l'Hypnotisme, Étude, de psychologie expérimentale, Paris, 1887.

6. Dunbar, F.: Emotions and Bodily Changes, p. 343, New York, Columbia, 1946.

7. Fernandez, G. R.: Hypnotism in the treat-

ment of the stress factor in dermatological conditions, Brit. J. M. Hypnosis 7:21, 1955-56.

8. Hollander, M. B.: Excoriated acne controlled by posthypnotic suggestion, Am. J. Clin. Hypnosis *1*:122-124, 1959.

9. Horan, J. S.: Management of neurodermatitis by hypnotic suggestion, Brit. J. M. Hypnosis 2:43-46, 1950.

10. Kepecs, J. G., and Robin, M.: Studies on itching: I. contributions toward an understanding of the physiology of masochism, Psychosom. Med. *17*:87-95, 1955.

10a. Kline, M. V.: Hypnodynamic Psychology, New York, Julian Press, 1955.

11. Kramer, J., *et al.*: Capillary response to emotion, Psychosom. Med. *16*:393-397, 1954.

12. Kroger, W. S.: Hypnotherapy in psychosomatic pruritus vulvae (unpublished).

13. McDowell, M.: Juvenile warts removed by the use of hypnosis, Bull. Menninger Clin. *13*:124-127, 1949.

14. ——: Hypnosis in dermatology *in* Schreck, J. M. (ed.): Hypnosis in Modern Medicine, pp. 101-115, Springfield, Ill., Thomas, 1959.

15. Mason, A. A.: A case of congenital ichthyosiform erythrodermia of brocq treated by hypnosis, Brit. Med. J. 2:422, 1952.

16. Rosenbaum, M.: Psychosomatic factors in pruritus, Psychosom. Med. 7:52, 1945.

17. Rothman, S.: The role of the autonomic nervous system in cutaneous disorders, Psychosom. Med. 7:90, 1945.

18. Schneck, J. J.: Ichthyosis treated with hypnosis, Dis. Nerv. System *15*:211, 1954.

19. Sinclair-Gieben, A. H. C., and Chalmers, C.: Evaluation of treatment of warts by hypnosis, Lancet, Oct. 3, 1959.

20. Sulzberger, M. B., and Wolf, J.: The treatment of warts by suggestion, Med. Record 552-557, November, 1934.

21. Sulzberger, M. B., and Zaidens, S. H.: Psychogenic factors in dermatologic disorders, M. Clin. North America *32*:669-685, 1948.

22. Ullman, M.: On the psyche and warts: I. suggestion and warts: a review and comment, Psychosom. Med. *21*:473-487, 1959.

23. Ullman, M., and Dudek, S.: On the psyche and warts: II. hypnotic suggestion and warts, Psychosom. Med. *22*:68-76, 1960.

24. Wittkower, E., and Russell, B.: Emotional Factors in Skin Disease, New York, Hoeber, 1953.

25. Pleune, F. G.: The question of hypnosis in medical practice, Ann. of Int. Med. *52*: 1273-1278, 1960.

Hypnotherapy in Physical Rehabilitation of Neuromuscular Disorders

The object of this chapter is to describe the use of hypnosis as an potentiating agent in the physical rehabilitation of patients with various neuromuscular disorders, including multiple sclerosis, poliomyelitis, Parkinson's and cerebral palsy.

EFFECTS OF PLACEBO THERAPY

It is well known that in some of the chronic neurologic disorders, particularly multiple sclerosis[3, 4, 17-19, 23, 24] and parkinsonism,[9] exacerbations and remissions may occur, regardless of the management or the drugs employed. The beneficial effects that are often attributed to nonspecific physical measures may be due, in part, to the cause of the disease, and to a placebo effect operating at many different levels of awareness. This nonspecific or psychological portion of the various physical rehabilitation therapies can be enhanced by hypnosis or other forms of suggestive therapy. Patients are seldom aware that a nonspecific or placebo type of therapy may be camouflaged through misdirection by drugs, massage, electrotherapy and other physical measures.

Unfortunately, by omitting hypnotherapy, physicians are literally driving many patients with chronic neuromuscular disorders to cultists and faddists who, through misdirection, employ various types of suggestive procedures, including hypnosis, often with astounding success. However, the unscientific application of suggestive procedures by lay and religious healers is to be condemned because they may cause the sufferer's hopes to be raised too high and because of their inability to make a differential diagnosis. Furthermore, specific therapy for an organically based malady may be overlooked.

EFFECTS OF MUSIC THERAPY

The recent emphasis on music and rhythm therapy as an adjunct in physical rehabilitation is another example of a quasi-hypnotic procedure. It is well known that repetitive, monotonic auditory stimuli, if continued long enough, are capable of inducing relaxation and even hypnosis. Incantations of primitive tribal rituals, religious rites and some musical compositions have a hypnoticlike effect. Musical therapy readily achieves relaxation by its rhythmic and soothing qualities and is particularly successful in the mentally retarded or the brain-damaged child unable to concentrate on a standard hypnotic verbalization technic. Such patients may have their attention span increased under a combination of musical therapy and hypnosis. Music, by misdirection, may also be used as a method of defocusing attention. As an example, motor aphasics may have no trouble in verbalizing in song. At times, loud, frenzied passages isomodic with the mood of the hyperexcited, disturbed patients,[35] may be more relaxing than soft lullabies.

In relation to cerebral palsy, several investigators[5, 6, 26] have noted that if the rhythm was sufficiently slow, so that there was no strain in "keeping up" with the tempo, rigid limbs relaxed and athetoid motions noticeably decreased. Carlson[5, 6] used music therapy and corroborated Lord's findings.[6] He states, "Low rhythmic music will obviate the difficulty, or anything else which will tend to reduce the sensorial input to a minimum will be helpful."[5] He also speaks of the influence that selective inhibition or misdirected sensory stimuli have on the patient's ability to control his muscles.[6]

A close parallel has been noted between music therapy and hypnotic conditioning.[7] Thus, whenever muscular activity is satisfactorily correlated with sensory (musical) concentration, muscles react automatically. Similarly, posthypnotic suggestions are effective in promoting relaxation by a series of conditioned speech and muscle acts—ideomotor activity. It has been observed that it is possible to increase or control the severity, the rate and the stability of an athetoid tremor by means of sound (and visual) stimuli.[30]

PSYCHOSOMATIC FACTORS

The precipitating emotional triggers in many ailments are often more important than the disease itself. It is now widely recognized that, in rehabilitation centers, the combined approach, directed toward emotional adjustment of the patient, may be more important than the correction of his physical defects. Within this framework, hypnosis can be an important potentiating tool for establishing healthy motivation for recovery.

HYPNOTHERAPY IN PHYSICAL REHABILITATION

In many of the technics employed in physical rehabilitation programs, suggestion and/or hypnosis are unwittingly used. For instance, Sister Kenny employed hot packs and massage in muscles "mentally alienated" by poliomyelitis. The hot packs were of some benefit, but she also used ideo-sensory conditioning when she asked the victims to think that they were "moving" their paralyzed limbs. Though she denied any similarity to hypnosis, this conditioning may have been more effective than the physical therapy per se in facilitating the recovery of nonfunctioning muscles. She also made use of the "law of dominant effect," namely, that whenever a psychological suggestion reinforces a physiologic effect, *supramaximal motor responses* may be obtained. It might be well to call attention here to the fact that in physiology one refers to maximal effort as the largest load that a specific muscle can carry under given conditions. Then the paradoxical term of "supramaximal" is used to indicate that the maximal effort was not really the greatest but only maximal without psychological synergy.

Essentially, our thesis is that if these simple types of suggestion often help, then hypnosis, the acme of scientifically applied suggestion, should be even more efficacious in enhancing psychological synergy. The fundamental basis for my hypothesis is that hypnotized individuals respond with a pinpoint literalness or specificity to suggestion, providing that these are in full accord with their wishes and do not mobilize critical attitudes. Kline[20] points out that hypnotically motivated behavior is not due to mere acceptance of authority or to hypersuggestibility alone but to:

. . . the capacity to recognize and accept communication that centers directly into the perceptual system. This is what permits the alterations, the changes, and the reorganizations of behavior that may be observed at all levels of response, emotionally and physiologically.

Pavlov[32] showed that serial conditioning, culminating in a conditioned response, was similar to hypnotic conditioning, the difference being that often "learning" in the latter can be achieved in a single session, as described in Chapter 26. More important, a posthypnotic conditioned response lasted longer and was more difficult to extinguish than a similar conditioning at nonhypnotic levels.

The clinical improvement that followed the giving of posthypnotic suggestions in patients with neuromuscular disorders was due to elicitation of supramaximal responses. The "forgotten assets" of patients with muscular dystrophy often are not mobilized because of "fear of failure."[27]

Most patients with organic neuromuscular involvements *believe* and *think* they can no longer carry out certain activities. Therefore, they do not try because they apparently have accepted a level of performance that is actually lower than their capabilities. Improvement results after increased performance occurs. Usually, they can accomplish these acts and repeat them for some time thereafter.

Utilization of "forgotten assets" is demonstrated when a frail girl, while in a cataleptic state, suspended between two chairs and supported only by her head and heels, supports considerably more weight than at nonhypnotic levels. Here, through suggestion, a transcendence of normal voluntary muscle capacity results in a feat many athletes could not accomplish. This indicates that a potential reservoir of supramaximal strength exists in the human body and, if properly harnessed, can increase the performance of the physically disabled individual.

POLIOMYELITIS

The Delorme technic[8] of muscle-strengthening emphasizes the need for exercises by increasing gradations into the overload zone. Inasmuch as a person performs at supramaximal rather than at maximal levels under hypnosis, a more rapid and effective strengthening of muscles can be expected. In addition, the increased motivation obtained by hypnosis can also increase the skill and co-ordination of all the affected muscles and limbs. There are three effective methods for eliciting supramaximal effort by hypnosis: (1) by actual exercises carried out following posthypnotic suggestions; (2) by sensory-imagery conditioning healthy past performances during autohypnosis; (3) by vividly imagining the *successful* effort to be made. A hypnotized person acts, feels and performs in accordance with what he imagines to be *true.*

Several investigators[10, 15, 34] have demonstrated that hypnosis can reactivate earlier and healthier response patterns by the use of sensory-imagery conditioning technics, by age regression and/or revivification. The following case history illustrates the revivification technic:

A 34-year-old female had a marked weakness in both gastrocnemii muscles due to poliomyelitis during girlhood. She had reached a plateau of improvement after a long term of treatment by the orthodox technics of physical therapy. Under hypnosis, she was told that she could "relive" all the athletic activities participated in prior to the onset of her symptoms. She used this type of sensory-imagery conditioning, together with daily resistive exercises, under autohypnosis. Within 10 weeks she was able to stand on the toes of the right leg alone, something she had been unable to do prior to hypnotherapy.

This patient did not have actual regeneration of muscle as a result of hypnosis but, rather, as a result of the paralysis or weakening of some of her muscle groups, she was failing to use even her remaining, unaffected muscle groups. This naturally resulted in atrophy of disuse as well as loss of voluntary control of a muscle. Hypnosis, in this case, was effective in motivating the patient to use muscles which were still functional but which were not being used for psychological or neurophysiologic reasons. Similar beneficial results, over and above those obtained from physical therapy alone, were also obtained on three additional patients who had had poliomyelitis.

PARKINSONISM

A wide variety of therapeutic medicaments have been employed in the treatment of parkinsonism, with equivocal results. Doshay[13] states, "Probably in no other branch of medicine is psychotherapy as important or as effective as in paralysis agitans." Five cases of paralysis agitans were covered in his report: 3 patients were improved and the other 2 could not be taught to develop self-hypnosis.

A 67-year-old male, with symptoms of 15 years' duration, had progressed to a point of having a disabling tremor of the right hand. Following 6 sessions of hypnotherapy, during which he had been taught autohypnosis and sensory-imagery conditioning, he was improved. He regained his ability to write and, because of improvement in morale, was able to return to his position as a salesman. Self-hypnosis helped to control his symptoms, with marked reduction in medication, for a period of 3 years during which he was under observation.

In the other 2 patients, the improved status was not so prolonged. In a man of 57 years and a woman of 48 years, improvement lasted for 6 months and 1 year, respectively, while they were being trained by hypnotherapy. However, in both of these patients the improvement ceased when hypnotherapy ceased, indicating that no "carry over" was maintained.

No one infers that parkinsonism can be remedied entirely by hypnosis, but rather that psychological factors may be paramount in aggravating the condition. In some patients, in whom the disease is organically progressive, one would expect to get either no or only temporary improvement. In others, in whom the disease is slowly progressive, the hypnotherapeutic approach results in a clinical remission. The reader must not assume that drugs, chemopallidectomy and other procedures are only of secondary importance. Where indicated, they should be used.

MULTIPLE SCLEROSIS

Some investigators[14, 17-19, 23, 24] have postulated that a patient with multiple sclerosis reacts to his illness according to his personality make-up. These patients are characterized by a high degree of emotional immaturity. It has been contended that the exacerbations and the remissions are due to vasomotor responses in the central nervous system that are produced by psychophysiologic regression.[33]

Shapiro and Kline[40] noted that, although hypnosis did not alter the pathologic lesions, the harmful sequelae were neutralized by patients reacting in a more realistic manner. The feeling of self-confidence is particularly reinforced by the patient's ability to induce self-hypnosis at will, and this usually resulted in improved function.

The following two cases of multiple sclerosis illustrate this:

Case 1 (reported through the courtesy of Dr. M. V. Kline)

A 24-year-old man with multiple sclerosis of 6 years' duration was seen because the rehabilitation team working with him felt that he was not performing at his potential capacity. He used 2 canes to walk about the house, which he would not leave by himself at any time. On his first visit, he was brought to the office by a member of his family. Following a single session of hypnosis, his anxiety was relieved sufficiently that he made the next trip alone with the continued use of the 2 canes. Within a few weeks, he gave up one of the canes and evinced increasingly less anxiety about falling down or

being seen in public. Within 6 months, he had resumed an interrupted college career and was making plans to do graduate work in the area of rehabilitation. He eventually obtained a degree and was working toward a doctorate when last heard from.

Case 2

A 23-year-old primigravida had generalized weakness and motor in-co-ordination, greatest in her lower extremities. She also had ophthalmoplegic, bladder and bowel incontinence. Frequently she required a wheelchair to ambulate. While under hypnotic training for childbirth, her neuromotor symptoms were greatly improved. As the result of increased motivation, reassurance and neuromuscular re-education under hypnotic conditioning, her sensory, motor and associative capacities were enhanced, with a resultant diminution of her bladder and bowel incontinence, weakness, in-co-ordination and ophthalmoplegic symptoms. Most important, she was motivated to accept her physical disabilities and thus the responsibilities of womanhood. The improvement continued even after her delivery so that a wheelchair was rarely needed.

CEREBRAL PALSY

Cerebral palsy is another example of a chronic motor disorder of a nonprogressive type in which emotional factors play an important role. Practically all cerebral palsy patients improve when they are relaxed and worsen when tense. This is true of the patients with athetosis or other extrapyramidal forms of cerebral palsy in whom emotional lability is common, particularly those in whom there is aggravation of the abnormal movements during periods of psychological stress. This phenomenon accounts for the "pseudoprogression" so frequently seen in the cerebral palsied at puberty.

In the young adult with cerebral palsy, the social and the emotional handicaps may be much greater than the physical or the motor ones. In a study by Glick,[16] it was found that, in 80 per cent of the cerebral-palsied adults who were unable to obtain or hold employment, the reasons were social and emotional rather than physical or intellectual. Therefore, a combined approach utilizing hypnotherapy might be expected to afford a rapid method for relaxation and reduction of tensions. Baer[2a] recently reported that hypnosis minimized or eliminated athetoid movements in patients with cerebral palsy, with improvement in speech and voluntary motor functions. Others[6, 25] have reported on the use of hypnosis in this entity.

In a group of 6 patients with cerebral palsy in whom the hypnotic approach was employed, there was marked improvement in 5. The sixth patient was a severely involved athetoid, 8 years of age, who could not be relaxed in 2 trials. It was felt that the failure in this case was due to the fact that the child was being treated as a part of an adult group that frightened and distracted him. The 5 patients who were helped were all young women, from 18 to 44 years of age. All were treated as a group in 6 hypnotic sessions. The improvement was greater with each succeeding session, and there was a longer carry over each time.

The patients were started in this program in an attempt to teach them the technic of autohypnosis. Unfortunately, the experiment had to be terminated at the end of the sixth session. It was believed that the improvement noted in these cerebral-palsied patients resulted from the reduction in their anxiety and tension accomplished by the hypnosis, which removed the extraneous stimulation. The increased motivation and the elicitation of supramaximal responses with resultant improved motor patterns had a surprising carry over into their everyday activities.

Case 1

A 38-year-old woman, a moderately severe athetoid with an I.Q. of 77, had great difficulty in walking alone. She was able to ambulate with a weighted cane in an extremely awkward manner and had a tendency to fall, particularly when upset emotionally. Her speech was barely intelligible. She was unable to get along with other people and had been dropped out of several cerebral palsy social groups. After 5 sessions of training under hypnosis, each more productive than the preceding one, she was able to enter into fairly deep hypnosis. While in somnambulism, she was able to walk without a cane and with much greater stability than she could at nonhypnotic levels. Her speech, likewise, was also more intelligible. What was more important was that there was a carry over of

this improvement, due in part to posthypnotic suggestions and in part to the great emotional lift of succeeding where she had previously failed. She was able thereafter to keep friends and to rejoin a social group.

Case 2

A 44-year-old female was a severe athetoid of normal intelligence. She had been for several years under an intensive training program that was part of a research project which was attempting to evaluate the various methods of physical therapy. After several years of such training, she had improved only slightly in function. Her progress was adequately recorded by charts, movies and graphs. Before hypnosis, she was able to ambulate slowly and awkwardly, but only with crutches. During her first performance under hypnosis, she walked about 50 feet without crutches. Her research attending physiatrist was amazed and stated that the benefit of hypnosis was greater in 30 minutes than that of 2 years of intensive therapy. After 5 sessions (at the time of this report), the patient was able to walk without crutches and had better speech and improved hand function. She was greatly encouraged by this improvement and has been a happier person ever since.

The use of a directive type of hypnosis has significant implications for cerebral palsy patients undergoing physical rehabilitation. They are capable of developing more complex and useful patterns than had been suspected. The cases most likely to be helped are those performing below their expected potentials and in whom emotional factors are prominent. In cerebral palsy, sensory-imagery conditioning and revivification cannot be employed since these patients have never had the experience of functioning normally; the damage generally has been present from birth.

CEREBROVASCULAR HEMIPLEGIA

Shires, Peters and Krout[41] used hypnosis for neuromuscular re-education in hemiplegia acquired by adults. They hoped to regain the motion impaired by interruption of the contralateral tracts through re-education via the intact ipsilateral tracts. They used revivification or age-regression to the age of 3 or 4, under hypnosis, to re-establish the mental image of moving the limbs. The range of motion was immediately greater.

Posthypnotic suggestions were employed to encourage regular exercise, especially during periods of hopelessness and despair, as the following case illustrates:

A married woman, aged 54, was first seen 1 year after she had suffered a cerebral hemorrhage and a left hemiplegia. There were marked flexor spasms of the left hand with pain radiating up to the shoulder. Several courses of physical therapy had afforded little relief from the marked discomfort. Under a regimen of musculoskeletal relaxant drugs and hypnotic relaxation, she was able to relax her left hand sufficiently to open her fingers to shake hands. However, the functional use of the arm remained impaired.

Shurrager[42] has demonstrated that a simple form of learning is possible even in a severed spinal system. In a series of brilliant experiments, he trained spinal animals to walk. If Shurrager's hopelessly paralyzed animals could be taught to move, then one might anticipate that similar training, facilitated by scientifically applied suggestion, might be beneficial in humans with spinal injuries.

OTHER MUSCULOSKELETAL DISORDERS

Sensory-imagery conditioning under hypnosis was used as an adjunctive procedure to physical therapy in the following 2 patients with traumatic involvements of the musculoskeletal system:

A married woman, aged 56, had a postoperative ankylosis of the left knee. When first seen, she had less than 20 degrees of flexion, in spite of intensive physiotherapy. She was extremely depressed, not only over her disability but also over the recent death of her husband. Sensory-imagery conditioning under autohypnosis enabled her to "see" her knee fully flexed in her mind's eye. After 5 weekly training sessions, she regained considerably more flexion of the knee. Her morale was improved. Concomitantly, she received 45 physical therapy treatments, but the effect of the hypnotic conditioning was unmistakable. Her physician said that her range of motion was from 180 degrees of extension to 97 degrees of flexion. He felt that hypnosis had been responsible for the improvement.

A married woman, aged 45, had excruciating low back pain radiating down the left leg. She had had 2 laminectomies without relief. Large doses of opiates were required and the possibility of narcotic addiction was feared. When first seen, she required a heavily weighted cane for walking, could not get out of bed without assistance and was confined to her house. Following 15 sessions of sensory-imagery conditioning under autohypnosis, the patient improved sufficiently to walk without her cane and to perform many of her household duties. Sedative drugs were markedly reduced. A follow-up 6 months later revealed that the patient had minimal discomfort and an improved mental outlook and was able to walk without assistance at all times. At present she is being treated for her addiction.

Dr. M. V. Kline reported the following interesting case:

A 42-year-old man, a double leg amputee (one leg above the knee), was seen in connection with the use of a prosthetic device. He could not use the artificial leg because it irritated him and gave him great pain. In the opinion of the orthopedic surgeon and of the limb fitter, the prosthetic device functioned perfectly well and should not have caused irritation. Despite this, the patient was not able to use it and continued to complain of discomfort. Following the use of hypnosis, during which sensory-imagery technics were used in order to facilitate his acceptance and incorporation of the prosthetic device, the physical symptoms of irritation disappeared; within 4 weeks he was making adequate use of the artificial leg. Six months later, he was using it normally and was very gratified with the results.

This approach can be utilized for quickly learning movement patterns with a new prosthesis.

Hypnosis has been used to diminish pain in amputees.[2, 11] One group[2] refers to this as "hypnotic inhibition." They used group hypnosis with encouraging results in more than 80 per cent of the patients. These investigators did not use a deep or somnambulistic state to obtain their results. Reinforcement therapy had to be repeated every 6 months. Dorcus[11] employed autohypnosis to achieve an over-all reduction of pain in his subjects. In one case he switched the pain from the phantom limb to the stump and induced or eradicated it by hypnotic suggestion. Autohypnosis enabled the patient to control the pain.

EPILEPSY

There are 2 types of epilepsy—psychomotor and organic. Differentiating between them is accomplished best by hypnotic age-regression, which brings out the patient's ability or inability to recall seizure events.[12, 29] Patients with true epilepsy usually develop complete amnesia for all actions connected with their seizures. Also, convulsions hypnotically induced in psychomotor patients may be stopped voluntarily, while those induced in organic cases must run their course.[28, 31] This implies that epileptiform seizures could be promptly halted by an attending hypnotherapist but, inasmuch as this coincidence is improbable, treatment is prophylactic.

Evidence indicates that tension is one important cause of seizures.[1] The tension, which is alleviated by a seizure, again mounts steadily until another seizure erupts. Although drugs often relieve this tension, they are not much more effective than hypnosis and autohypnosis. Hypnotherapy, in selected patients, suppresses and eliminates the tension cycle, and a seizure can be stopped even after it is far too late for any drug to be effective. Hypnotherapy does not preclude anticonvulsant drugs, but it materially reduces their need. They should be used together to the point at which the patient has no difficulty in functioning in a normal, alert manner.

Pond[36] has postulated that psychotherapy appears to be indicated only occasionally in epileptiform seizures, but is not practicable for epileptic seizures per se. Raginsky[37] tells of a 13-year-old boy who was having from 1 to 4 epileptiform seizures per day for years. After 3 hypnotic sessions, the seizures ceased and they have not reappeared in the past 18 years. No psychotherapy or uncovering technics were used. The mere elimination of the "tension-rhythm" syndrome was enough to effect a cure.

Epileptic attacks have been induced and terminated without changing the EEG pattern.[39] Another investigator[22] was able to reproduce an epileptiform seizure with corresponding EEG changes by using age-regression. This illustrated that physiologic affects accompany age-regression and that suggestions of an emotional nature affect cerebral physiology.

Tension in women is aggravated by the menstrual cycle, and fears and anxieties concerning this function are closely connected with seizures.[21] In these cases, it is necessary to clear up misconceptions and provide reassurance.

Fortunately, most epileptics are extremely easy to hypnotize and they can readily learn autohypnosis. Armed with this knowledge, many epileptics successfully avert seizures for years. All patients, whether their epilepsy is organic or psychogenic, should be trained in autohypnosis.

Mrs. J. H., aged 32, had had grand mal epileptic seizures, often as many as 2 or 3 a week, for over 25 years. She had been on anticonvulsant drugs for years, and periodically her hypertrophied gums had to be resected. Following several training sessions in hypnosis and autohypnosis, her medication was reduced by over 50 per cent during the first month: attacks were cut to about one a week. The attacks practically disappeared as she became proficient in autohypnosis and sensory-imagery technics. All medication was stopped. Although she had considerable resentment toward her mother, who was ashamed of her condition, no attempt was made to elicit psychological factors because of the physical improvement. When first seen, the patient was slovenly, apathetic and poorly motivated. At the end of 9 months (she was seen biweekly), she was bright, alert and interested in her appearance. A dramatic change had occurred in this patient's personality merely as the result of the improvement produced by the hypnorelaxation and the rapport. The autohypnosis played a definitive role in motivating her toward recovery.

DISCUSSION

Rehabilitation of the neurologically damaged individual is primarily a relearning process. Such patients may have intellectual and emotional difficulties and are easily distracted and fatigued. A pervading depression, aggravated by a low frustration tolerance and poor motivation, frequently precludes assistance from any type of physical rehabilitation regimen. Musculoskeletal and psychological functioning may be further affected by the metabolic and negative conditioning resulting from disuse. Passive and active resistive exercises to improve the motor power may be accelerated and enhanced by the use of hypnosis, especially if directed toward more optimistic attitudes toward the self and the physical impairment. A greater attention span results from narrowing of the perceptual fields during hypnosis. In this respect, music that is hypnotic in type limits and controls sensory input and often improves muscular control.

Unfortunately, psychotherapy is seldom employed in the patient with central nervous system involvement with enough vigor and thoroughness. If permissive technics oriented around the needs of the patient are used, critical attitudes are seldom mobilized. With sensory-imagery conditioning during autohypnosis, greater psychophysiologic responses are obtained. The reflexes achieved by learning and the conditioning technics are not as readily extinguished as those induced at nonhypnotic levels.

Thus neurologic involvements are more amenable to sensory-imagery conditioning than is generally realized. The successful feats of Yogis and fakirs are due to autohypnosis. Transcendence of volitional performance is commonly noted and can be obtained in many musculoskeletal disorders. The use of hypnosis for potentiating the action of skeletal relaxant drugs has recently received attention.[12] Though the series presented is small, it is the author's hope that these observations will stimulate others to use hypnosis.

The effectiveness of a rehabilitation program for patients with neuromuscular disabilities often depends more upon psychic factors than relief of the physical disability per se. Intelligence, emotional status, motivation and attention span are enhanced by the repetitive conditioning under hypnosis. Healthy psychological and social adjustments are attained when patients can control their own organisms through reinforcement by ideomotor and ideosensory conditioning.

Hypnosis facilitates considerable associative learning and increases the capacity for stimulus transference. This may account for the increased effectiveness of neuromuscular re-education under hypnosis. Hypnosis is only a medium through which a wide variety of other therapeutic and pharmacologic procedures may be potentiated. As mentioned in Chapter 47, patients are not treated *by hypnosis but rather in hypnosis*. Its function is to catalyze the behavior dynamics associated with motivation, perception and the broad spectrum of other healthful emotional reactions. Not all physically handicapped patients respond to hypnosis. Space precludes description of the author's failures. Nevertheless, the beneficial results observed by others in selected cases indicates that hypnosis can increase the effectiveness of other forms of therapy in neuromuscular disorders. Finally, any rehabilitation program can be accomplished best through a knowledge of the reciprocal action of mind and body—that is, the comprehensive approach.

REFERENCES

1. Ambrose, G., and Newbold, G.: Medical Hypnosis, London, Baillière, Tindall & Cox, 1958.
2. Bachet, M., and Weiss, C.: Treatment of disorders of amputated subjects by hypnotic inhibition, Brit. J. M. Hypnosis 4:15, 1952.
2a. Baer, R. F.: Hypnosis, an Adjunct in the Treatment of Neuromuscular Disorders, Paper read at the 3rd Int. Cong. of Physical Medicine, Washington, D. C., Aug., 1960.
3. Braceland, F., and Giffin, M.: The mental changes associated with multiple sclerosis (an interim report), Res. Publ. A. Nerv. & Ment. Dis. 28:456, 1950.
4. Brickner, R., and Simons, B.: Emotional stress in relation to attacks of multiple sclerosis, Res. Publ. A. Nerv. & Ment. Dis. 28:143, 1950.
5. Carlson, E. R.: Neurological aspects and treatment of birth injuries, New York J. Med. 34:1-6, 1934.
6. ——: Infantile cerebral palsy: its treatment by selective inhibition of sensory stimuli, Ann. Int. Med. 11:324-334, 1937.
7. DeLee, J. B.: Year Book of Obstetrics-Gynecology, Chicago, Year Book Pub. 142, 1938.
8. DeLorme, T. L., and Watkins, A. L.: Technics of progressive resistance exercises, Arch. Phys. Med. 29:5, 1948.
9. Diller, L., and Riklan, M.: Rorschach correlates in Parkinson's disease, Psychosom. Med. 19:120-126, 1957.

10. Dolin, A. O.: Objective investigation of the elements of individual experiences by means of experimental hypnosis, Arkh. biol. Nauk. 36:28-52, 1934.

11. Dorcus, R. M.: Hypnosis and Its Therapeutic Applications, New York, McGraw-Hill, 1956.

12. Dorcus, R. M.: Personal communication.

13. Doshay, L. J.: The psychotherapy of paralysis agitans, J.A.M.A. 172:1347, 1960.

14. Gallinech, A., and Kallinowski, L.: Psychiatric aspects of multiple sclerosis, Dis. Nerv. System 2:77, 1958.

15. Gidro-Frank, L., and Buch, M.: A study of the plantar response in hypnotic age regression, J. Nerv. & Ment. Dis. 107:443-448, 1948.

16. Glick, S.: Survey of the adult cerebral palsied population, Cerebral Palsy Review, January, 1953.

17. Grinker, R., Ham, G., and Robbins, F.: Some psychodynamic factors in multiple sclerosis, Res. Publ. A. Nerv. & Ment. Dis. 28:456, 1950.

18. Inman, W. X.: Can emotional conflict induce disseminated sclerosis?, Brit. J. M. Psychol. 12:135, 1948.

19. Jelliffe, S. E.: Multiple sclerosis and psychoanalysis, Am. J. M. Sc. 161:666, 1921.

20. Kline, M. V.: Freud and Hypnosis, New York, Julian, 1958.

21. Kroger, W. S., and Freed, S. C.: Psychosomatic Gynecology, Chicago, Free Press, 1956; reprinted, Los Angeles, Wilshire Book Co., 1962.

22. Kupper, H. I.: Psychic concomitants in wartime injuries, Psychosom. Med. 7:15-21, 1945.

23. Langworthy, O.: Relation of personality problems to onset and progress of multiple sclerosis, Arch. Neurol. Psychiat. 59: 13, 1948.

24. ——: A survey of the maladjustment problems in multiple sclerosis and the possibility of psychotherapy, Am. J. Psychiat. 98:598, 1950.

25. Livingood, F. G.: Hypnosis as an aid to adjustment, J. Psychol. 12:203-207, 1941.

26. Lord, E. E.: Children Handicapped by Cerebral Palsy, Commonwealth Fund, New York, Oxford, 1937.

27. Milhorat, A. T.: Diagnosis of muscular dystrophy, Am. J. of Phys. Med. 34:103-108, 1955.

28. Moss, C. C.: A forced hypnoprojective fantasy used in the resolution of pseudoepileptic seizures, J.C.E.H. 5:59-66, 1957.

29. Owen-Flood, A.: Hypnotism in epilepsy. Brit. J. M. Hypnosis 3:49-52, 1952.

30. Palmer, M. F., and Zerbe, L. E.: in Podolsky, E. (ed.): Control of Athetotic Tremors by Sound Control in Music Therapy, pp. 187-213, New York, Philos. Libr., 1954.

31. Pasquarelli, B., and Beliak, L.: A case of co-existence of idiopathic epileptic and psychogenic convulsions, Psychosom. Med. 9:137, 1947.

32. Pavlov, I. P.: Experimental Psychology, New York, Philos. Libr., 1957.

33. Phillippopoulos, G. S., Wittkower, E. D., and Cousineau, A.: The etiologic significance of emotional factors in onset and exacerbations of multiple sclerosis, Psychosom. Med. 20:458-475, 1958.

34. Platonov, K. I.: On the objective proof of the experimental personality age regression, J. Genet. Psychol. 9:190-209, 1933.

35. Podolsky, E.: Music Therapy, New York, Philos. Libr., 1954.

36. Pond, D. A.: Psychiatric aspects of epilepsy in children, J. Ment. Sc. 98:404, 1952.

37. Raginsky, Bernard B.: The Use of Hypnosis in Internal Medicine. Presented at the 35th Anniversary Congress of the Pan American Medical Association, Section on Clinical Hypnosis, Mexico City, May 2, 1960.

38. Salter, A.: What is Hypnosis?, New York, Farrar, Strauss, 1955.

39. Schwarz, B. E., Bickford, R. G., and Rasmussen, W. C.: Hypnotic phenomena, including hypnotically activated seizures, studied with the EEG, J. Nerv. & Ment. Dis. 122:564-574, 1955.

40. Shapiro, A., and Kline, M. V.: The use of hypnosis in evaluating the physiological and psychological components in the functional impairments of the patient with multiple sclerosis, J. C. E. H. 4:69, 1956.

41. Shires, E. B., Peters, J. J., and Krout, R. M.: Hypnosis in neuromuscular re-education, U.S. Armed Forces M. J. 5:1519, 1954.

42. Shurrager, P. S., and Dykman, R. A.: Excessive and maintained conditioning in spinal carnivores, J. Comp. & Physiol. Psychol. 49:27-35, 1956.

43. Sumner, J. W., Cameron, R. R., and Peterson, D. B.: Hypnosis in differentiation of epileptic from convulsive-like seizures, Neurology 2:395, 1952.

37

Hypnosis in Ophthalmology, Otolaryngology and Rhinology

The psychosomatic entities amenable to hypnotherapy are hysterical blindness and deafness, globus hystericus, aphonia, dysphonia and certain types of dysphagia. Most resemble conversion hysteria reactions. A psychogenic component has been recognized in tinnitus, glaucoma and blepharospasm.

When a symptom has a minimal defensive function, it is readily removed by hypnosis, especially if the physical discomfort is severe and a hysterical make-up is present. This is not surprising, since most psychosomatic symptoms involving the eyes, the ears, the nose and the throat are brought about by harmful suggestions and disturb the normal functioning of the individual.

Hypnosis, together with re-education, reassurance, support, directive measures and persuasion are necessary if relapses occur. Often the symptom is needed for sympathy, absolution of guilt, escape from intolerable situations, denial of aggression, or the necessity for manipulating the environment in a neurotic manner (secondary gain) because of inability to handle problems in a healthy manner.

Relapses occur if the individual is unable to adjust to his environmental difficulties and continues to overreact to anxiety-provoking tensions. Refusal to recognize that the symptom represents a reaction to unpleasant circumstances (which only mobilizes inner conflicts) also can result in a relapse. Likewise, when the symptom provides vicarious gratification for sexual and hostile impulses, it often returns, especially if authoritative hypnosis is used for its dissolution.

These difficulties can be avoided if autohypnosis and sensory-imagery conditioning are incorporated in a permissive approach. These, together with understanding, give the individual the capacity to face his difficulties without resorting to regressive behavior, repression and the resultant symptom-formation.

OPHTHALMOLOGY

GLAUCOMA

Emotional factors affect the fluctuations of intraocular pressure, particularly in glaucoma.[2] However, a typical personality profile does not exist for individuals suffering from primary glaucoma.[3, 4] Vulnerability of the eyes as potential organs for the expression of psychic conflicts has been postulated.[4]

Most afflicted patients are elderly individuals, beset by chronic worries and anxieties over marital conflicts, ill health, unemployment, dependence on family or others, loneliness and, in particular, depression. Exacerbation of eye symptoms in association with emotional upsets is evidenced by statements such as: "My eyes get bleary when I get mad," "When I get very excited, my eyes throb," and "My eyes itch and water when I'm tense."

In glaucoma, hypnotic suggestions for relaxation effected symptomatic relief, with a drop in the intraocular pressure in one or both eyes to a level as low as, and often even lower than, previously recorded pressures.[3] The mechanism by which this occurs is not known; the tensions are affected by mood swings.[31] Posthypnotic suggestions directed toward specific symptom-removal resulted in fewer headaches, less tearing, more relaxation and sleep, and less pain. Glove anesthesia mitigates discomfort in selected patients.

HYSTERICAL BLINDNESS

Hysterical blindness is a conversion reaction to unpleasant circumstances which stimulate inner conflicts. Clinically, the condition resembles genuine blindness except that remissions and exacerbations may occur spontaneously.

Differential Diagnosis

An individual with functional blindness will react to light with pupillary contraction.[8] Hysterical blindness has been found to have no effect on the appearance or the disappearance of the alpha pattern in EEG records.[25] On the other hand, alpha activity has been recorded in hysterically blind individuals only when their eyes were shut.[23] These contradictory studies indicate that physiologic changes associated with artificially induced hypnotic phenomena and conversion reactions are not as clear-cut as those noted for well-established organic disorders.

Treatment

Wolberg[35] reported the following case:

A 27-year-old, newly married woman had had several brief attacks of total blindness before and after her marriage. Using hypnotic age-regression, it was discovered that the symptom reinforced the repression of a traumatic episode in which she had seen a man killed in a train wreck. Killing had been equated with hostility toward her mother. In repressing the traumatic event, she denied her aggression toward her mother. Her hostility stemmed from strong dependency strivings and inability to have a closer relationship with her father. Her husband's coldness reactivated these feelings of rejection, thus mobilizing her hostility and aggression toward her mother, which was linked with the killing fantasy that this entailed. Her blindness was a desperate attempt to deny the existence of her murderous impulses.

The author has seen several cases of hysterical blindness.

The wife of a colleague developed blindness when she inadvertently saw her husband kissing his secretary. Their marriage had been very unstable for years, characterized by frequent arguments and separations. The cause for the symptoms obviously was an attempt to repress the humiliation produced by the unfaithfulness of her husband. Direct hypnotic suggestion promptly "restored" her vision, and she was advised to face her life situation and decide whether or not she wished to seek a divorce. While she was making this important decision, her husband died. No other symptoms referable to the eyes occurred. However, several years later, she became a severe diabetic and died at a comparatively early age.

ORTHOPTICS

Hypnosis can be used as an auxiliary to orthoptic therapy. In squint, amblyopia and muscular disturbances involving loss of accommodation, hypnosis can shorten treatment and is less exhausting for the patients.[26]

Myopia has been improved by the Bates' system of eye training under hypnosis.[21] Concomitant psychological factors were elicited through superficial exploration. In one case, the subject felt that he looked so ugly in glasses that he hated to look at himself. Following strong suggestion, aimed at correcting these attitudes, together with the Bates' treatment under hypnosis, the individual was able to discard his glasses.

Others have reported on the value of hypnosis in amblyopia[5, 6] and in orthoptic training.[34] There is an extensive literature on the psychosomatic aspects of ophthalmologic conditions.[7, 12, 15, 20, 22, 33, 34a]

ADJUSTMENT TO CONTACT LENSES

The increasing popularity of contact lenses has opened up a new field for hypnosis. Many cannot insert the lenses because of blinking and discomfort due to a psychological block. Under hypnosis, blinking while the lens is being inserted can be reduced by sensory imagery and the misdirection of attention, as follows: "Would you mind concentrating on the pressure of your shoes on your feet. Notice that they are rather tight when you concentrate on the shoes." (The patient nods affirmatively.) "Notice the weight of your watch on your wrist. You do not feel the shoes now, do you?" (Again he nods.) "You see, in this manner you can either become aware of the lens as it comes into contact with the eyeball or you can ignore it by concentrating on your shoes." This simple procedure often obviates excessive blinking.

In others, the wearing of the lenses results

in agonizing pain, lacrimation and photophobia. If a competent ophthalmologist has ascertained that the lenses fit properly, posthypnotic suggestions can be made as follows: "Although, at first, you will have some sensitivity and discomfort, you will be able to tolerate it." All sensitivity should not be abolished, as a misplaced or a misfitted lens would not be perceived. Complete anesthesia of the eyeballs would eliminate the essential break-in time, or the lenses would be worn too long, too soon, resulting in conjunctivitis. It is much better to suggest, "You can, if possible, wear them regularly and for longer periods each day." Such suggestions under autohypnosis are even more effective.

Hypnosis in Eye Surgery

Surgery of the eye under hypnosis is still practiced in India for cataract removal. Esdaile, whose extensive experience with mesmeric coma was described in Chapter 32, described how he enucleated a diseased eye with the good eye watching the surgeon's manipulations.

Cohen[6a] recently reported an unusual use for hypnosis in surgery depending upon the ability of the pupil to contract at the right time to an appropriate suggestion. The hypnosis was used also to achieve relaxation and to relieve fear and anxiety. However, its most useful application was manifested by the conditioned reaction of the pupil which contributed to the successful outcome of the Ridley operation (insertion of a plastic lens while the pupil is contracted).

Blepharospasm

Involuntary blinking movements of the eyelids are related to tics. Ambrose[1] states, "The treatment of tics is an extremely unsatisfactory matter and there appears to be only one therapeutic measure which has any *direct* effect upon them, namely, hypnosis." This author heartily agrees with this statement, as he has cured many bizarre tics through symptom-transformation under hypnosis. The transfer to the finger twitch is employed, as described in the treatment of dermatitis factitia in Chaper 35.

One of the worst cases, involving a 65-year-old male, was cured in 4 sessions by this procedure. This patient had seen more than 18 physicians in a 10-year period. The blinking prevented him from working, and a constant conjunctivitis was present, accompanied by lacrimation and edema of the eyelids. No attempt to understand the underlying psychological factors was made in this case. A follow-up 6 months later revealed that the symptom had completely disappeared and had not been replaced by another.

OTOLOGY

Several conditions such as Meniere's disease, tinnitus, hysterical deafness and other hearing problems often respond to hypnotherapy.

Tinnitus

Etiology

The emotional factors associated with tinitus or Meniere's disease have been attributed to fear of the attacks of vertigo and nausea, fear of deafness, and excessive preoccupation over the symptom. Emotional upsets have also been implicated in the production of the vasomotor changes in the labyrinth or its connections; spasm and hemorrhage of the blood vessels occur (labyrinthine angiospasm). Edema of the labyrinth has been found with advanced involvement. Reflex irritation of the geniculate ganglion of the tympanic plexus is increased by grinding of the teeth and tension upon the jaws in association with suppressed rage.[32]

In this respect, a group of patients with Meniere's disease demonstrated that the paroxysmal attacks of vertigo, and often the onset of tinnitus and deafness, were definitely related to life stress situations.[13] Another investigation revealed that the circulation of the conjunctiva "sludged" following strong psychic stimulation; the blood clumping occluded the capillaries in the labyrinth, resulting in local disturbances. These, in turn, produced symptoms and, if the vascular pathology persisted, the labyrinthine hydrops characteristic of Meniere's disease occurred.

Treatment

A temporomandibular subluxation must be considered in all cases of tinnitus. Since many patients have bruxism, or grinding of the teeth, wearing a bite plate at night helps them. All organic factors must be ruled out before instituting psychotherapy. The author remembers a patient whom he treated unsuccessfully and who was cured after the separation between the upper and the lower jaws was increased by building up the posterior teeth.

Direct posthypnotic suggestions can be used for hysterical tinnitus. Tinnitus varies from person to person and even varies in intensity in the same person from time to time. Ask the individual what he hears. Is it a sea-shell kind of noise? Is it a high- or a low-pitched squeak? In what situation does it occur most frequently—when alone or when talking with others? Does it occur more often around certain persons than others? All of these are important.

If a clue is obtained, posthypnotic suggestions directed toward a reduction of the offending situational factors often ameliorate the symptoms. If it is intermittent, suggest that "It will occur somewhat less frequently with a longer interval of time between occurrences." If, through posthypnotic suggestion, the intensity of the tinnitus can be increased, it can be reduced, and, when this is manipulated slowly, the individual attributes the increase or the decrease to his own emotional control. Thus, he finds that the symptom can be altered. If it is changed, his confidence grows; then perhaps it can be made less annoying. And if this is accomplished, it can be made to disappear completely.

These procedures must be done slowly; specific posthypnotic suggestions must be given. Never make a general statement that "Your tinnitus is going to be less," or that "It is going to be reduced," or that "It is going to disappear," because this may not be possible. Suggest rather that the pitch is going to become lower or "When the pitch lowers, it is going to be less annoying." If taught autohypnosis, the patient can imagine via his own thought processes that the ringing in his ears is being replaced by pleasant sensations based on memories of periods when he was free of the tinnitus. The following case is illustrative:

A patient who had seen dozens of specialists consulted the author for vertigo and tinnitus. He was very depressed, unable to work, financially depleted and contemplating suicide. He stated, "This is my last hope. Every doctor says, 'I can't do anything more for you.'" On the first session, he entered a deep somnambulistic state and was taught autohypnosis. The tinnitus was promptly relieved by posthypnotic suggestions, but returned the next day. Seven sessions, together with suggestions to induce autohypnosis at the slightest indication of vertigo, resulted in marked amelioration of the symptoms. Sensory-imagery conditioning under autohypnosis to imagine pleasant sounds was also employed. He returned to work, was able to drive a car and made a complete recovery. Needless to say, he was very grateful.

Many such patients are making the rounds of physicians' offices, desperately seeking assistance. Unfortunately, the psychogenic factors are seldom treated. Mere relaxation through autohypnosis helps over 60 per cent of the patients. As is to be expected, failures sometimes occur, usually in those who are not good hypnotic subjects. Some patients, who are looking for "magic," terminate therapy too soon.

The successful use of hypnosis in tinnitus recently has been reported by others.[28, 30] Mihalyka and Whanger[28] described a case similar to the author's, which was cured by hypnosis.

A 36-year-old male with tinnitus, characterized by irregular clicking sounds, fullness in the ears and vertigo, was cured in 4 sessions. He was taught autosuggestion to relax; the tic disappeared for 48 hours. One month later the patient reported that he was "improved"; the clicking only occurred after emotional stress. He stated that he was able to control his symptoms through autosuggestions.

The investigators concluded that hypnosis, limited specifically to the reduction of tension, is often a potent tool. Hypnoanalysis has been used to evaluate the conflicts and the anxieties underlying tinnitus to establish personality integration.[16]

Tic Douloureux

The author has had very little success with tic douloureux. Of the cases seen during the past several years, he cannot remember a single one that responded permanently to hypnosis. More than half were temporarily relieved by glove anesthesia. However, Esdaile reported a successful cure. Elliotson[10] reported several cures at the London Mesmeric Infirmary at the beginning of the last century.

Hysterical Deafness

Hysterical and hypnotically induced deafness are similar in that there is no hearing loss. However, the reaction to strong auditory stimulation is significantly less in hysterical deafness. Electromyographic studies of hysterical and hypnotically induced deafness have been made, and the similarities and the differences in these two entities have been elucidated. The findings corroborated those of Kline,[18] who concluded from the study of delayed speech feedback that hypnotically induced deafness appeared "to represent a valid alteration of hearing function but not a state akin to organic deafness."

Differential Diagnosis

Abnormal audiometric readings are indicative of hysterical deafness. This type must be differentiated from organic deafness. A simple test would be to make an unexpected loud noise. If a startle reaction occurred, it would indicate that hearing was unimpaired. According to Kodman and Pattie,[19] quantitative hearing tests should be made, rather than relying on subjective reports in diagnosing cases of psychological deafness. There are several methods to measure auditory sensitivity: pure-tone audiometry (air and bone conduction thresholds), speech audiometry (speech perception thresholds and speech discrimination) and the psychogalvanic skin response (in which a conditioned skin response is set up to tonal stimuli). These investigators made hearing tests on children who showed functional hearing losses. Although their hearing was apparently normal, they complained of an inability to hear, particularly in home and classroom situations. Laboratory tests made before and after hypnotherapy indicated that improvement was brought about in every case except one. In some cases the hearing loss inexplicably involved only one ear.

Treatment

These investigators used the following suggestions while the patient was lightly hypnotized: (1) He might think that there was something wrong with his ears, but actually nothing was wrong; (2) his troubles might come from not listening well, and listening was an important part of hearing and understanding; (3) in the future he would hear and listen much better. They used no challenges except that the patient would find it difficult to open his eyes. A similar approach is described by Hurst,[17] who used strong persuasion to make patients listen more attentively.

Others have described hypnotic technics which could be used to re-educate and improve hearing acuity.[27] It is concluded, from their clinical observations, that hypnotherapy can be effective for abnormal hearing difficulties which are believed to be psychogenic in origin. Symptom-substitution was not utilized in any of the series. The hearing behavior improved in nearly all cases.

LARYNGOLOGY

Globus Hystericus

Globus commonly occurs in nervous individuals who are under severe stress. Since the mechanism is based on a conversion reaction, direct symptom-removal by hypnosis is effective. When the patient recognizes the psychogenic basis for the symptom, the emphasis should be on present and future adjustment. Other symptom equivalents are not likely to return if permissive technics are utilized.

A nervous, high-strung, 48-year-old woman, who had seen several physicians, insisted that she had "a lump in her throat." The symptom appeared after she had accidentally swallowed a peanut shell after a violent altercation with her husband. All examinations were negative. She was told that "The peanut shell is still stuck in your stomach" as there was no need to mobilize criticalness by saying, "This is all in your mind." After induction of hypnosis, post-hypnosis suggestions were given as follows: "If you *really* wish to push the peanut shell out of your stomach, take 10 deep breaths at least 6 times a day." She reported 48 hours later that the discomfort was now in her lower abdomen.

It was suggested that the peanut shell was in her intestines, and that if she took a laxative she easily could pass the peanut shell in her stool. She was to practice deep breathing under autohypnosis "in order to facilitate its passage." The patient reported that 24 hours after this session she felt free from all symptoms. The deep breathing during autohypnosis created the impression that she was doing something and actively participating in her own recovery. The results were obtained through misdirection of attention, strong rapport and building up her own self-esteem. Later, after a resolution of her domestic difficulties, her nervousness disappeared.

HYSTERICAL APHONIA AND DYSPHONIA*

There are many kinds of speech and vocal conditions that are refractory to therapy, as hysterical aphonia and dysphonia, and harsh, scratchy, rough voices that are very hard to treat. Nervous individuals who make their livings by using their voices are the ones generally affected. They know that they must sing or speak well; therefore they cannot become tense, or their vocal productions will be endangered. Many orators are nervous when they first start speaking, and the tension immediately shows itself in altered voice qualities. There may be harshness, huskiness, tremolo, or perhaps either an elevation or a depression of pitch.

Following are 2 examples of the applications of hypnosis that the author has been using in audiology:

I recall treating a popular radio announcer, who spoke perfecty well as long as he was seated. During one show he had to speak in a standing position and, for some reason, this reawakened certain memories, which later inhibited him so that, on one or two occasions, he found himself speechless before the microphone. This was an unnerving situation for him and threatened his livelihood. Hypnotherapy, utilizing sensory imagery, brought about full recovery.

In another instance, a professional singer had developed a vocal constriction and had not sung for 10 years. Although a marvelous hypnotic subject, he was a very peculiar one, as he would go immediately into a plenary or coma-

* This material was contributed by Milton Brutten, Ph.D., Audiologist at the Devereaux School, Philadelphia, Pa.

tose-like state of hypnosis. Yet no interaction between us would take place, that is, he would refuse to speak while he was very, very deeply hypnotized. I soon realized that this was what he wanted: he wished to have an opportunity to get away from reality for awhile. He accomplished this himself, without interruptions from me. He would think things over, dehypnotize himself, and say, "I feel so very much better. I thought things through and I now can understand why I have imposed such punishment upon myself." The punishment took the form of vocal constriction, preventing him from making public appearances.

He was able to work through his masochistic needs without any intervention from me except to induce and terminate the hypnosis. He relaxed and began to perform again, to his great satisfaction. One curious sidelight was that he found all his shirt collars to be loose and, when he was measured for new shirts, he found that his collar size had gone down from 16½ to 15½. I didn't understand this until I realized that he had been characteristically so very tense (probably for years) that his sternocleidomastoid muscle stood out in thick knots. Through hypnotherapy he relaxed enough to wear the smaller collar size.

Platonov[30a] described how 3 or 4 hypnosuggestive sessions cured opera singers of "footlight neuroses." Psychotherapy administered while the cortex is in a "lowered tone" made it possible to eliminate the neurosis completely.

GAGGING

Hypnosis is used to control or eliminate the gag reflex. Generally a light stage is sufficient. Many individuals, on the basis of psychological factors, believe that they will gag. Moss[29] has described several technics that are effective in almost 96 per cent of the cases (see Chapter 44).

RHINOLOGY

EPISTAXIS

Hypnosis has been used to control severe epistaxis. Edel[9] reported the following case:

A 10-year-old boy developed a sudden nosebleed and was rushed to his office for emergency aid. Packing failed to effect hemostasis. Since he had been treating the boy for another disorder, he immediately induced a deep somnambulistic state. He then suggested that the bleeding would stop if he continued breathing deeply with his "head held way back." The blood coagulated immediately. Posthypnotic suggestions were given that he could blow his nose within an hour without causing further bleeding. The patient promptly and dramatically recovered.

This case history closely parallels innumerable reports from dentists who contend that bleeding can be stopped and started by hypnotic suggestion. The author believes that more accurately controlled data are needed before the conclusion is reached that bleeding can be stopped so readily by hypnosis.

Rhinitis

Vasomotor rhinitis is astonishingly susceptible to emotional factors in its production and its dissolution. The common cold often responds to hypnosis. The author sees many patients who, coincidental to their chief complaint, have the "sniffles." Susceptible persons under hypnosis can be told, "Imagine that you are walking home. It's a very hot day, and your nose and throat are very, very dry, *real dry!* Wouldn't you give anything for a nice, cold drink of water? Your mouth and nose are getting very dry, very dry, are they not?" Or, "Imagine you are in a steam bath and the hot vapor is going up your nose. You've been in this steam bath a long time and you're very parched, etc."

As has been mentioned, physiologic effects can be obtained through hypnotic suggestion only by sensory-imagery conditioning and not by direct command. To suggest, "Your nose will stop running" is futile. Suggestions of generalized warmth can also alleviate the rhinitis. The author has often demonstrated how "goose-pimpling," sneezing, shivers and a drop in body temperature can be induced by hypnotic suggestion to a good hypnotic subject.

The fact that the common cold responds to a wide variety of medicaments implicates emotional factors even though a viral etiology has been postulated. It has been demonstrated recently that specific or nonspecific stress lowers the threshold to viral invasion.

REFERENCES

1. Ambrose, G.: *in* Schneck, J. M. (ed.): Hypnosis in Modern Medicine, p. 205, Springfield, Ill., Thomas, 1959.
2. Berger, A. S.: The emotional factor in glaucoma: a review. (In press.)
3. Berger, A. S., and Zimet, C. N.: Effect of hypnosis on intraocular pressure in normal and glaucomatous subjects, Psychosom. Med. *20*:321, 1958.
4. ——: Personality features of patients with primary glaucoma, Psychosom. Med. *20*: 389-396, 1959.
5. Browning, C. W., and Crasilneck, H. B.: The experimental use of hypnosis in supression amblyopia, Am. J. Ophth. *44*:4; 468, 1957.
6. ——: The use of hypnosis in suppression amblyopia of children, Am. J. Ophth. *46*: 1; 53, 1958.
6a. Cohen, M. H.: The use of hypnosis in the Ridley operation for cataract, J. Psychosomatics *2*:184-186, 1961.
7. Crane, M.: Mental effort in orthoptic treatment, Brit. Orthoptic J. *14*:91-93, 1957.
8. Dorcus, R. M.: Modification by suggestion of some vestibular and visual responses, Am. J. Psychol. *49*:82-87, 1937.
9. Edel, J. W.: Nosebleed controlled by hypnosis, Am. J. Clin. Hypnosis *2*:89, 1959.
10. Elliotson, J.: The Harveian Lecture, delivered before the Royal College of Physicians, London, June 27, 1846.
11. Esdaile, J.: Mesmerism in India (Hypnosis in Medicine and Surgery), New York, Julian, 1957.
12. Eyles, M. A.: Some psycho-physiological aspects of vision related to orthoptic procedure, Brit. Orthoptic J. *13*:7-13, 1956.
13. Fowler, E. P., and Zechel, A.: Psychosomatic aspects of Meniere's disease, J.A.M.A. *148*:1265, 1952.
14. ——: Psychophysiological factors in Meniere's disease, Psychosom. Med. *15*:127-139, 1953.
15. Godtfredsen, E.: Psychosomatic opthalmology, Acta psychotherap. *1*:211-219, 1953.
16. Guild, J.: Hypnosis for tinnitus, Can. M. A. J. 78:426-427, 1959.
17. Hurst, A.: (quoted by Guild, J.) Medical Diseases of War, ed. 3, Baltimore, Williams & Wilkins, 1943.
18. Kline, M. V., Guze, H., and Haggerty, A. D.: An experimental study of the nature of hypnotic deafness: effects of delayed speech feed-back, J. C. E. H. *2*:145, 1954.

19. Kodman, F., and Pattie, F. A.: Hypnotherapy of psychogenic hearing loss in children, Am. J. Clin. Hypnosis *1*:9-13, 1958.

20. Kraemer, R.: Psychotherapy of squint, Psychotherapie *1*:93-97, 1956.

21. LeCron, L.: Relief of myopia by hypnosis and eye training, Dis. Nerv. System *12*: 142, 1951.

22. Lichtenstein L, C. S.: Hipnose em Ortoptica, Arq. brasil. oft. *22*:101-109, 1959.

23. Loomis, A. L., Harvey, E. N., and Hobart, G. A.: Brain potentials during hypnosis, Science *83*:239-241, 1936.

24. Lundholm, H.: An experimental study of functional anesthesia as induced by suggestion in hypnosis, J. Abnorm. & Social Psychol. *23*:338-355, 1928.

25. Lundholm, H., and Lowenbach, H.: Hypnosis and the alpha activity of the electroencephalogram, Character & Person. *11*: 145-149, 1942-1943.

26. Luz, C. S., *et al.*: The Use of Hypnosis as an Auxiliary Orthoptic Treatment, Bull. Brazil Int. Soc. Clin. & Exp. Hypnosis *3*: 572-579, 1959.

27. Malmo, R. B., Booz, T. J., and Raginsky, B. B.: Electromyographic study of hypnotic deafness, J. Clin. & Exper. Hypnosis *2*:305, 1954.

28. Mihalyka, E. E., and Whanger, A. D.: Objective tinnitus aurium hypnotically treated, Am. J. Clin. Hypnosis *2*:85-86, 1959.

29. Moss, A. A.: Hypnodontics: Hypnosis in Dentistry, Brooklyn, Dental Items of Interest Pub. Co., 1953.

30. Pearson, M. M., and Barnes, L. J.: Objective tinnitus aurium: report of two cases with good results after hypnosis, J. Phila. Gen. Hosp. *1*:134, 1950.

30a. Platonov, K. I.: The Word as a Physiological and Therapeutic Factor, Moscow, Foreign Languages Pub. House, 1955.

31. Ripley, H. S.: Life situations, emotions and glaucoma, A. Res. Nerv. & Ment. Dis., Proc. *29*:523, 1956.

32. Schneider, D. E.: Growth Concept of Integration, New York, Nerv. & Ment. Dis. Mono., 1949.

33. Snydacker, D.: Psychosomatic Aspects of Concomitant Heterotropia, Acta V Cong. Pan. Amer. Oftal., pp. 449-452, 1956.

34. Sowden, A. S.: The value of hypnosis in orthoptic training, Optician *123*:619-620, 1952.

34a. Sukhakarn, K. V., *et al.*: A record of the discovery and investigation of how vision is attained through the cheek by the blind or blindfolded persons, Bangkok, Thailand, The Training Center for Concentration & Memory, 1960.

35. Wolberg, L. R.: Medical Hypnosis, vol. 1, p. 227, New York, Grune & Stratton, 1948.

SUPPLEMENTARY READING

Goldberg, E. L., and Kliman, G.: Improved visual recognition during hypnosis, Arch. Gen. Psychiatry *7*:155-163, 1962.

Strosberg, I. M., and Vics, I. I.: Physiologic changes in the eye during hypnosis, Am. J. Clin. Hypnosis *4*:264-268, 1962.

38

Hypnosis in Genitourinary Conditions

Selective cases of postoperative retention of urine, premature ejaculation, impotency in the male, dysuria, ureteral spasm and chronic bladder irritation respond to hypnotherapy. Pseudo-orientation in time can help emotional repercussions that might be expected with male or female sterilization. Hypnorelaxation indirectly may have an important bearing on female infertility, as the fertilizing capacity of the sperm is possibly affected by stress factors.

POSTOPERATIVE URINARY RETENTION

TREATMENT

Postoperative urinary retention, occurring after pelvic or perineal surgery, often can be completely relieved by posthypnotic suggestions.[1, 7] An authoritarian hypnotic approach such as, "You will void in exactly 20 minutes," is seldom successful. Permissive technics together with sensory-imagery conditioning are more successful. Under hypnosis it is suggested, "Perhaps you may be able to remember in detail what it felt like the last time you urinated. Try and imagine the sensations you experienced the last time you emptied your bladder." When able to do this, the patient is asked to describe the subjective sensations associated with the act of micturition. These are fed back immediately or during subsequent sessions. No time limit for carrying out the act is mentioned.

After the patient is trained in autohypnosis, he is told, "If you imagine yourself urinating again and again, then you will have no trouble starting the stream. Try not to urinate until you have re-experienced urinating in your mind first." Asking the patient to carry or not to carry out the act places him in a position in which he cannot refuse or resist the operator's suggestions. Whether or not he urinates, he is being controlled without realizing it. Since the patient does not set the terms, there is no way for him to mobilize further fears that he will not urinate. As the result of the repeated rehearsals of "urinating" under autohypnosis, confidence replaces his irrational fears. Invariably these patients will urinate within several hours, especially if deeply hypnotized and taught autohypnosis during the initial sessions.

These technics are indicated where repeated catheterizations are required. Several recent publications[3, 6] fail to mention psychogenic factors in urine retention. This is surprising, as the contraction of the bladder muscle and the maintenance of urinary continence are cortically controlled. The concepts of "voluntary" and "involuntary" control of micturition need to be modified.

The author has seen a number of patients in consultation, many of whom were used for teaching purposes in a hospital setting. In those with highly resistant symptoms, hypnosis was successful in over 80 per cent of the cases. Direct symptom-removal by command is seldom effective, as the fearful subject thinks his inability to urinate is "involuntary." The author recently saw a 60-year-old female who had not voided for 10 days after a hemorrhoidectomy. Utilizing the above-described technics, urination occurred within 4 hours after her initial hypnotic induction.

CHRONIC BLADDER IRRITABILITY

Chronic and recurrent irritability of the vesical neck of the bladder, secondary to psychogenic factors, often is noted in women.[9] The predominant symptoms are discomfort, frequency and dysuria; these respond to appropriate hypnotherapy. Many female patients use frequent micturition as a masturbatory equivalent, especially if frigid. One patient's dysuria cleared up only after correction of her husband's impotency. Another, a severe cardiac who was unable to have sexual intercourse, used glove anesthesia under autohypnosis to relieve her bladder discomfort.

PREMATURE EJACULATION AND IMPOTENCE

Premature ejaculation and impotency are so widespread in our culture that they might well be called the "emotional plague." Impotency accounts for many gynecologic symptoms—the congestion-fibrosis-hyperemia syndrome, for instance. The vascular stasis is secondary to autonomic imbalance.

Organic impotency can be established or ruled out by the history. Absence of erection, or premature ejaculation, is always noted whether the situation is copulatory or masturbatory. No nocturnal emissions or morning erections occur. Heredity, physical factors and age are predisposing factors to psychogenic impotency. Ejaculation occurs before or soon after penetration; the erection cannot be maintained.

The psychological causes may be due to anxieties produced by faulty attitudes toward sex, fear of failure brought on by intense mental activity, preoccupation, fatigue or repeated episodes of failure, hostility and lack of affection. Abstinence also leads to impotency. The idea is common that sex is wicked, sinful and not to be used to besmirch the mate whom the patient may equate with his mother; he may be potent with other women (facultative impotency). Another common factor is a deep-seated need to fail in order to reject the mate for various reasons, which are usually unrecognized. Other factors such as a too aggressive or experienced sex partner may intimidate the passive male. The female who shows her revulsion for the sex act or has the desire to "get it over in a hurry" can render the male impotent. The psychophysiology of erection and ejaculation have been described.[4, 8]

TREATMENT

Such drugs as testosterone to increase the libido, anesthetic ointments to abolish sensitivity of the glans penis, and prostatic massage have only a placebo effect. Premature ejaculation is often refractory to all types of psychotherapy. Misconceptions and faulty attitudes toward sexual matters must be corrected by re-education. The male who is sometimes impotent requires only superficial psychotherapy.

Strong reassurance under hypnosis often establishes confidence for the prematurist. Von Schrenck-Notzing[8] reported many forms of impotence that were treated by suggestion and directive hypnotherapy. The first step is to demonstrate that the patient is capable of an erection. Recovery is initiated once self-confidence is strengthened and reinforced. The constant preoccupation with the symptom can be reduced if an indifferent attitude over failure is suggested. Forcing the sex act is harmful.

Von Schrenck-Notzing cured 10 out of 18 patients by direct symptom-removal. Six of these were somnambules. The number of sessions varied from 1 to 56. Many cases demanded considerable patience and time. The reader is referred to his book for a thorough description of his hypnotherapeutic approach.

More recently, technics have been developed utilizing revivification of previous satisfactory sex contacts under autohypnosis. This effectively conditions the prematurist to perform adequately. In others, especially in those who have never had a satisfactory sex act, the premature ejaculation can be treated by reversing the fear of too rapid ejaculation. The following posthypnotic suggestion is illustrative: "You might consider the possibility of being very concerned over *not* being able to ejaculate, regardless of how hard you try. The more you try, the more difficult it will be to lose your erection."

Time distortion can be employed to prevent premature ejaculation in a good subject by making him think that he has maintained an erection for a relatively long time. During deep hypnosis it is suggested, "Thirty seconds of subjective or experiential time *will seem* like 2 minutes of world, clock or chronologic time." Thus, if the prematurist maintains an erection for only 30 seconds, he will think that he had it for 2 minutes. This positive hallucination by which time is "expanded" can be reinforced through further posthypnotic suggestions; it rapidly helps to restore confidence in the patient's staying ability. The wife should be apprised of the situation and told to praise her husband's ability. Naturally, the husband is not made aware of this.

The above hypnotic technics are incorporated with supportive psychotherapy. If the patient feels accepted, he will wittingly or unwittingly reveal the basis for his fears and anxieties that are associated with his sexual inadequacy. Guidance directed toward breaking up the harmful reflex patterns enables the individual to react to his problem in a healthier manner. Extensive probing and attempting to exhume the past is fruitless, especially for the impotent male, who has never been erectively and ejaculatively potent. What should be emphasized is that the spiritual relationship between the partners influences the performance of the sex act.

Sensory-imagery conditioning under autohypnosis is especially effective for refractory cases, as the following illustrates:

S. M., aged 26, married 2 years, had never achieved penetration, due to premature ejaculation. Whenever his fully erect penis touched his wife's body, he ejaculated. After preliminary training in hypnosis and autohypnosis, it was suggested that 1 minute of subjective time would seem like 10 minutes of actual time— that everytime his penis touched any portion of his wife's body, it would seem like minutes. During autohypnosis, he would "see" himself lying alongside his wife and "feel" the vigorous erection being successfully maintained. This type of sensory-imagery conditioning was performed about 5 or 6 times daily. Within 7 weeks, he reported that he retained a good erection until he attempted penetration.

Inasmuch as he had never experienced genital-to-genital contact, considerable descriptive imagery was required to enable him to feel what it was like to insert and maintain friction of the penis in the vagina. Several sessions were required for this phase of the sex act. His wife was instructed in methods to re-duce his excitement and promote relaxation. It was further suggested that it was not too important if he had a rapid emission, and that he was to think more of his wife's admirable qualities and the need to give satisfaction to her on the basis of real love than of his own satisfaction.

Following several unsuccessful attempts, he was able to have an insertion with friction that lasted for over 2 minutes. Further posthypnotic suggestions, making use of time distortion and directing his fears toward the possibility that he would *not be able to ejaculate at all*, ultimately enabled him to have satisfactory sex relations. Several relapses occurred. Almost 1 year of painstaking training in the technics just described, together with supportive psychotherapy, was required to achieve good results.

The most disheartening cases are of those unfortunate individuals who contend that they are unable to develop an erection during the sex act. The author sees many of them. The majority of these, too, are psychogenic in origin. It has been demonstrated recently that the midline and the anterior thalamic nuclei via the limbic system cortically control sexual functioning. A modification of autogenic training is helpful.

The following case is typical:

A 42-year-old male who had not had an erection for 12 years was seen by the author. While he was in the Army, he had been stationed in India, where he had been informed that the intense heat often produced impotency in foreigners. After being discharged, he returned home to find that his wife was in love with another man. He divorced his wife and never went out with another woman, stating, "They were all just no good."

When first seen, he was depressed and suicidal. After a preliminary discussion, he was trained in hypnosis and autohypnosis. It was suggested that he would first imagine his legs getting warm. He was told, "Imagine you are slowly putting your legs into your bathtub, which is full of warm water." At first this hallucination was difficult to produce, but within several weeks he was able to induce a feeling of warmth in the extremities. In similar fashion, he was asked to hallucinate coldness in his arms by imagining that his hands were immersed in a bucket of ice-cold water. Further suggestions to imagine that his extremities were getting longer, shorter, thicker and thinner were given in successive sessions.

After 4 months, through autohypnosis, he

was able to develop various sensory alterations in the limbs. Posthypnotic suggestions were now directed toward reducing his resentment toward all women. Oblique remarks about the need to go out with girls, dance and "pet" with them were continually made in a casual manner. He reported that he had met an attractive widow at a church social and that he was able to develop an erection just by thinking about her. Age-regression was utilized for recalling the pleasant memories of sexual acts prior to his arrival in India. Several sessions were required to establish the necessary confidence for satisfactory coitus. This was not too difficult as he already had an indelible imprint of such experiences.

His deep-seated resentments toward women were worked through and, within 2 years of the time he started treatment, he had met another girl and married her. He has been happy in his marriage.

No attempt was made to probe deeply or to understand the underlying responsible "dynamics." It was felt that symptom-removal in itself was a triumph, and since the patient had accomplished this under autohypnosis there was little need to worry about the possible occurrence of symptom equivalents. Over 60 per cent of such individuals can be helped by conditioning under autohypnosis. The results are relatively permanent, but the work is tedious and often heartbreaking for therapist and patient.

CYSTOSCOPY AND SURGICAL PROCEDURES

There are several reports on the use of hypnoanesthesia for cystoscopy,[1] with or without pyelography and other urologic procedures such as urethral dilatation and catheterization. Posthypnotic suggestions of relaxation can prevent postinstrumental spasms.

Many different types of minor surgical procedures have been performed under hypnoanesthesia, such as amputation of the penis, circumcision, meatotomy, vas ligation and fulguration of venereal warts. Many huge scrotal tumors, weighing up to 80 pounds, were removed by Esdaile[2] under hypnosis per se. He also performed circumcisions, removed testes, injected hydroceles, and did other similar surgery—*all without anesthesia* and all before 1850!

Today there is no need to eliminate anesthesia, but hypnosis can reduce preoperative anxiety and tension, as well as neurogenic shock in seriously ill patients.

VASECTOMY

Pseudo-orientation in time or hallucinated age-progression can be employed to ascertain possible contraindications for vasectomy. The author vividly recollects the following case:

A patient ardently requested this procedure, hoping it would save his unhappy marriage. His wife, who had 2 children, had an inordinate fear of pregnancy and was frigid. She stated, "I no longer love my husband; he is too selfish and immature." Under deep hypnosis and amnesia it was suggested to the husband, "It is now 1965 (it was 1959). You had your vas ligated 6 years ago. How do you feel now about being sterilized?" The resultant violent acting out characterized by remorse, self-recrimination and hostility toward the wife indicated that problems other than his wife's fear of pregnancy were involved. It was also apparent that the sterilization was contraindicated. After dehypnotization, it was suggested that he and his wife undergo therapy for their marital difficulties, rather than resort to a procedure that might lead only to frustration and disappointment. He refused therapy, and several months later his wife instituted divorce proceedings.

Since posthypnotic amnesia is always necessary, this procedure can be used only in good hypnotic subjects. Pseudo-orientation in time and abreaction under hypnosis do not necessarily prove that a vasectomy may produce serious psychological repercussions. However, it is better to err on the side of safety when highly charged material evoked without the subject's knowledge points toward a personality difficulty which might be aggravated years after the sterilization. Therefore, the motivation for vasectomy must always be evaluated carefully in terms of its psychological significance.

MALE INFERTILITY

The male is responsible for over 50 per cent of the barren marriages. Little is known about the relationship of disturbed emotions to semen quality and motility. These, rather than the total sperm count, are often important factors in the ease of conception. There is a growing awareness that emotional conflicts can alter the sperm's fertilizing capacity. It is well known that fatigue, shock, worry and tension often produce infertility in both animals and humans.[5] This is due to overproduction of endogenous norepinephrine, secondary to specific or nonspecific stress. Hypnosis has not been able to increase the sperm count or influence sperm motility. However, adverse enzymatic changes can be produced in the sperm, secondary to autonomic imbalance, and thus inactivate the sperm's ability to penetrate the ovum even though the sperm appears morphologically normal and adequate in quantity.

FEMALE INFERTILITY

Posthypnotic suggestions directed toward relaxation, tranquility and freedom from anxiety may be helpful for certain cases of infertility in the female that defy all types of therapy. Though the author has no adequately controlled data to present in this important and neglected entity, it offers a fruitful area for further research.

REFERENCES

1. Brown, T. B.: Hypnosis in genitourinary diseases, Am. J. Clin. Hypnosis *1*:165-168, 1959.
2. Esdaile, J.: Hypnosis in Medicine and Surgery, New York, Julian, 1957.
3. Fleming, A. R.: The use of Urecholine in the prevention of postpartum urinary retention, Am. J. Obst. & Gynec. 74:569-571, 1959.
4. Kroger, W. S.: Psychosomatic aspects of frigidity and impotency, Internat. Rec. Med. *171*:469-478, 1958.
5. ——: An Integrated Approach to Infertility. (In press.)
6. Nourse, M. H.: Management of the patient who fails to void after operation, J.A.M.A. *171*:84-86, 1959.
7. Owen-Flood, A.: *in* Hypnosis in Modern Medicine, Springfield, Ill., Thomas 1959.
8. von Schrenck-Notzing, A.: The Use of Hypnosis in Psychopathia Sexualis, New York, Julian, 1956.
9. Williams, G. E., and Johnson, A. M.: Recurrent urinary retention due to emotional factors, Psychosom. Med. *18*:77-80, 1956.

SUPPLEMENTARY READING

Cucinotta, S.: Acute urinary retention successfully treated with hypnosis, Am. J. Clin. Hypnosis 3:201-202, 1961.
Doberneck, R. C., and McFee, A. S.: The prevention of postoperative urinary retention by hypnosis, Am. J. Clin. Hypnosis 3:235-238, 1961.
Kroger, W. S.: Hypnotic pseudo-orientation in time for determining psychologic effects of vasectomy and sterilization in the female. Paper read at the meeting of the Pacific Coast Fertility Society, Oct. 6, 1962.
Solovey, G., and Milechnin, A.: Concerning the treatment of enuresis, Am. J. Clin. Hypnosis 2:22-31, 1959.

39

Hypnosis in Oncology

EFFECT OF EMOTIONS

Undoubtedly, no single factor is responsible for cancer. Recently, however, psychological factors have been considered in the causation, pathogenesis and prognosis of neoplasms.[7, 13, 14, 16, 17, 26, 28] Some investigators believe that there is a typical personality profile.[3, 12, 22, 23, 27, 29] Psychometric evaluation of patients that are known to have cancer have been reviewed by numerous authors.[1, 2, 5, 6, 11, 18, 20, 25] It has been observed that rapport is an important factor; that patients treated by one physician tended to have a smoother course than those treated by another; and that patients seem to do better if informed of the nature of their condition. In a presidential address to the American Cancer Society in 1959, Pendergass stated, "There is a distinct possibility that within one's mind is a power capable of exerting forces which can either enhance or inhibit the progress of this disease."

Cortical-hypothalamic and neurohumoral pathways exist for stimulating the endocrine glands, which are basically end organs of the central nervous system. Any derangement in the cortical dynamics alters emotional equilibrium, which results in excessive or diminished hormonal output. This mechanism has been implicated in the growth or arrest of certain tumors such as those involving the breast and the prostate. These, in part, are dependent on the degree of hormonal activity.

PERSONALITY FACTORS AND EMOTIONAL REACTIONS

There is an extensive literature on the effect of personality patterns on cancer growth. Unfortunately, the investigations and the findings are subject to rather generalized interpretations. For instance, the studies of withdrawn schizophrenics show that the death rate for carcinoma is half that for the population at large. Yet, for paranoid schizophrenics with overt hostility, it is 4 times the normal rate.[1] The personality patterns responsible for the development of cancer vary from grief over deprivation,[13] inhibited rage, sexuality, and masochism,[3] inability to tolerate emotional stress, constitutional inadequacy,[23] marital status (higher rate amongst widowed),[16] to overcompliance, sincerity and dependability.[28]

The investigative procedures used were anecdotal, by interview, by sociologic and demographic analysis, and by psychological testing. In spite of faulty design, inadequate controls and statistical evaluation, there is a general consistency in the surveys,[20] i.e., cancer patients are immature, depressed, fearful, full of self-recrimination, have suffered a loss of some type, are sexually maladjusted and are incapable of expressing anger. Patients with rapidly growing tumors appear to be more defensive, anxious and inhibited than those with slow-growing malignancies. Of course, the above emotional reactions are similar to those noted in psychoneurotics and are not specific for cancer. However, it may be that specific personality factors became operative in the presence of other variables—the correct combination resulting in carcinoma.

PSYCHOPHYSIOLOGIC AND BIOCHEMICAL FACTORS

Emotional factors, in essence, consist of sensory information coming in through various input channels which are transmitted to the integrating centers by codified nerve impulses. Since every cell in the organism is part of a huge intercommunication system, the transmission of this information is governed by the "feedback principle." This concept, as discussed in Chapter 30, is central to the automatic regulation of all neurophysiologic processes.

Feedback regulates the biochemical processes that go along with the morphologic differentiation and regeneration of cells. As one substance is converted into another, the substance produced at the end of a chain reaction acts as an automatic control mechanism to inhibit the production of unnecessary chemicals. When the cellular machinery is upset due to "noise" in the transmission of incorrect signals or instruction for the function and growth of cells, the resultant positive feedback causes unnecessary substances to be produced endlessly.

Work along these lines has been initiated by physical chemists, geneticists and physicists. They are using information theory in an attempt to understand the processes responsible for the correct molecular arrangement of the protein molecules necessary for maintaining the proper functioning of the cell. Interference with this arrangement by antagonistic agents denies information to chemical feedback systems regulating the rate of cell division. According to Potter,[21] the key role may be played by the enzyme-forming systems controlled by the desoxyribose nucleic acid (DNA) pattern and molecules in a metabolic pool. He states:

> The successive mutations that produce cancer cells may be due to inherent errors in nucleic acid replication, to errors induced by carcinogens, or to loss by segregation of enzyme-forming systems that fail to replicate fast enough during cell division.

This theory hypothesizes that "certain viruses might substitute for endogenously altered nucleoproteins." More specifically, the DNA of the viruses may replace the mechanisms controlling the enzyme-forming systems, while the ribonucleic acid (RNA) of viruses would substitute for the enzyme-forming systems themselves. Certain protein molecules are remarkable—they can reproduce like living things. It is hoped that in this fascinating area the baffling problem of cancer ultimately will be solved.

SPONTANEOUS REMISSION AND THE ADAPTIVE RESPONSES

As pertinent as the changes in the cell is the kind of person who has the cancer. Host resistance appears to be affected, in part, by emotional factors. Individuals who have the "will to live" often survive longer than others with similar degrees of cancer involvement. The phenomenon of "voodoo death" is illustrative. Stress and poor immunologic mechanisms also have been held responsible for rapid metastases and recurrences of cancer after surgery.

Spontaneous remission of neoplasms has been reported.[10] Though rare, and inexplicable, the possibility of spontaneous regression of cancer may be of some psychotherapeutic value in offering hope to sufferers and relatives of patients with "incurable" cancer. Often, indeed, the mere thought that regression might possibly take place changes their attitude from complete despair to hopeful toleration.

It has long been recognized that wart tumors, even though on a viral basis, respond in astonishing fashion to suggestion and/or hypnosis (see Chapter 35). Here almost any type of suggestion, irrespective of "psychodynamics" or personality patterns, affects tissue pathology. This noteworthy example is pertinent to our discussion.

HYPNOTHERAPEUTIC MANAGEMENT OF CANCER PATIENT

There are several reports[8, 9, 15, 19] indicating that hypnosis assists in the relief of pain, anxiety and depression, and in the reduction of drugs.[8] Another report[9] emphasizes that hypnosis lessens the ill effects of x-rays. Together with empathy, it decreases the shock resulting from the disclosure that they have cancer. Increased motivation, improved mental attitudes and relaxation in cancer patients have been attributed to hypnosis.[19] It is of interest that successful management of pain and suffering does not depend as much on hypnotic depth as on rapport.[15]

The author has used hypnosis as an adjunct for the management of intractable pain in terminal cancer patients. Many were considering lobotomy, posterior rhizotomy or chordotomy for pain relief. All were on high doses of opiates. After these patients learned how to induce glove anesthesia under autohypnosis, the dosage of narcotics was drastically decreased in over 60 per cent of them.

Hypnosis apparently blocked the perception of pain—it was a sort of "psychological" lobotomy. When it is used individually for direct symptom relief, the procedure is tedious and the results are often disappointing. Another investigator[15] has had indifferent success with direct hypnosis. Group hypnosis (1 hour per week) is preferable, as faith, hope and confidence are mobilized more readily; susceptibility to posthypnotic suggestions is increased when the readiness to respond to painful stimuli is minimized by misdirection of attention.[4]

There are some striking instances of the "will to live."

For instance, a 44-year-old male had a large fungating lesion removed from the splenic flexure of the colon. The surgeon palpated glands along the aorta and nodules on the liver. He performed an end-to-end anastomosis of the colon and did not give the patient more than 6 months at best. Following surgery, the patient was apprised of his prognosis. He thought hypnosis might help his discomfort. Posthypnotic suggestions were directed toward the development of glove anesthesia, decreasing his awareness of physical sensations in the abdominal region and bolstering his morale. The patient also became deeply religious, praying every morning and evening. To the author's surprise, he began to gain weight and was free of all symptoms. Two years later, he developed a bowel obstruction, and a laparotomy revealed an adhesion instead of the expected recurrence of the tumor. There was no sign of cancer. Today, after 6 years, the patient is in good health.

It is difficult to account for this patient's recovery except on the basis of faith.

Other cancer victims are not so fortunate. However, if the therapist himself conducts the group sessions and uses a positive approach, hypnosis can be most helpful in mitigating the discomfort and the suffering produced by cancer.

REFERENCES

1. Abrams, R. D.: Social casework with cancer patients, Social Casework *32*:425, 1951.
2. Abrams, R. D., and Finesinger, J. E.: Guilt reactions in patients with cancer, Cancer *6*:474, 1953.
3. Bacon, C. L., Renneker, R., and Cutler, M.: A psychosomatic survey of cancer of the breast, Psychosom. Med. *14*:453, 1952.
4. Barber, T. X.: Toward a theory of pain: relief of pain by prefrontal leucotomy, opiates, placebos and hypnosis, Psychol. Bull. *56*:430-460, 1959.
5. Bard, M.: Psychological impact of cancer, Ill. Med. J. *22*:155-160, 1960.
6. Bard, M., and Dyk, R. B.: The psychodynamic significance of beliefs regarding the cause of serious illness, Psychoanalyt. Rev. *43*:146, 1956.
7. Blumberg, E. T., West, P. M., and Ellis, F. W.: A possible relationship between psychological factors and human cancer, Psychosom. Med. *16*:277, 1954.
8. Butler, B.: The use of hypnosis in the care of the cancer patient, Cancer *7*:1, 1954.
9. Cangello, V. W.: Medical News, July 8, 1959.
10. Everson, T. C., and Cole, W. H.: Spontaneous regression of malignant disease, J.A.M.A. *169*:142-143, 1959.
11. Finesinger, J. R., Shands, H. C., and Abrams, R. D.: Managing the emotional problems of the cancer patient *in* Clinical Problems in Cancer Research, p. 106, Sloan-Kettering Institute Seminar, 1948-49.
12. Fisher, S., and Cleveland, S. E.: Relationship of body image to site of cancer, Psychosom. Med. *18*:304, 1956.
13. Greene, W. A., Jr.: Psychological factors and reticuloendothelial disease: I. Preliminary observations on a group of males with lymphomas and leukemias, Psychosom. Med. *16*:220, 1954.
14. Kowal, S. J.: Emotions as a cause of cancer, Psychoanalyt. Rev. *42*:217, 1955.
15. Lea, P. A., *et al.*: The hypnotic control of intractable pain, Am. J. Clin. Hypnosis *3*: 3-8, 1960.
16. LeShan, L., and Worthington, R. E.: Some psychologic correlates of neoplastic disease: a preliminary report, J. Clin. & Exper. Psychopath. *16*:281, 1955.
17. Meerloo, J. A. M.: Psychological implications of malignant growth: a survey of

hypotheses, Brit. J. M. Psychol. 27:210, 1954.

18. Miles, H. H. W., Cobb, S., and Shands, H. C.: (eds.): Case Histories in Psychosomatic Medicine, New York, Norton, 1952.

19. Morphis, O. L.: Paper read at 10th meeting Soc. Clin. & Exper. Hypnosis, Chicago, Oct. 7, 1959.

20. Perrin, G. M., and Pierce, I. R.: Psychosomatic aspects of cancer, Psychosom. Med. 21:397, 1959.

21. Potter, V. R.: Address to Federation of Am. Soc. Exper. Biology, Philadelphia, Apr. 29, 1958.

22. Renneker, R., and Cutler, M.: Psychological problems of adjustment to cancer of the breast, J.A.M.A. 148:833, 1952.

23. Reznikoff, M.: Psychological factors in breast cancer: a preliminary study of some personality trends in patients with cancer of the breast, Psychosom. Med. 17:96, 1955.

24. Rosen, H.: The hypnotic and hypnotherapeutic control of severe pain, Am. J. Psychiat. 107:919, 1951.

25. Shands, H. C., Finesinger, J. E., Cobb, S., and Abrams, R. D.: Psychological mechanisms in patients with cancer, Cancer 4:1159, 1951.

26. Stephenson, J. H., and Grace, W. J.: Life stress and cancer of the cervix, Psychosom. Med. 16:287, 1954.

27. Tarlau, M., and Smalheiser, I.: Personality patterns in patients with malignant tumors

of the breast and cervix; exploratory study, Psychosom. Med. 13:117, 1951.

28. Trunnell, J. B.: Second Report on Institutional Research Grants of the American Cancer Society, p. 181, New York, American Cancer Society, Inc., 1952.

29. Wheeler, J. P., and Caldwell, B. McD.: Psychological evaluation of women with cancer of the breast and of the cervix, Psychosom. Med. 17:256, 1955.

SUPPLEMENTARY READING

Cangello, V. W.: Hypnosis for the patient with cancer, Am. J. Clin. Hypnosis 4:215-227, 1962.

Erickson, M. H.: Hypnosis in painful terminal illnesses, Am. J. Clin. Hypnosis 2:117-122, 1959.

Le Shan, L.: A basic psychological orientation apparently associated with malignant disease, Psychiat. Quart., April, 1961, 1-18.

——: Some methodological problems in the study of the psychosomatic aspects of cancer, J. Gen. Psychol. 63:309-317, 1960.

——: Psychological states as factors in the development of malignant disease: a critical review, J. Nat. Cancer Inst. 22:1-19, 1959.

Le Shan, L., and Gassmann, M. L.: Some observations on psychotherapy with patients suffering from neoplastic disease, Am. J. Psychotherapy 12:723-734, 1958.

Schon, R. C.: Addendum to "hypnosis in painful terminal illness," Am. J. Clin. Hypnosis 3:61-63, 1960.

40

Hypnosis in Pediatrics

Hypnotherapy is an effective and flexible tool for selective cases of enuresis, nail-biting, stammering, asthma, psychomotor epilepsy, tics and behavior problems associated with chronic tensions, stress and environmental difficulties. Hypnotherapy is also useful for attacking the psychogenic components of organic disorders such as heart disease, diabetes, physical defects, mental retardation, neuromuscular involvements and chronic debilitating ailments requiring prolonged bed rest. In both instances, it accelerates therapy and conserves the energy of the therapist. Hypnoanesthesia can be used for children as well as for adults to minimize fear reactions prior to surgery.

Children over 5 are easily hypnotized; their blind trust and vivid imaginations make them very susceptible to suggestions. Children have a short attention span and the best induction procedures are those which continually involve them in fantasy experiences such as those described under Picture Visualization Technics, page 57.

Dentists who hypnotize children draw "Mickey Mouse" on their thumbnails and maintain interest by relating a series of humorous incidents built around him. Games appeal to children, and they are easily shifted from reality to unreality by such measures, often being dissociated without their knowledge. Thus, fear reactions are minimal because criticalness is reduced.

Because of children's autistic tendencies, a light to medium stage is usually sufficient for hypnotherapy. Picture or scene visualization is employed to "see" himself as a character on an imaginary television screen —this reinforces the artificial dissociation.

Further imagery manipulation is oriented around the child's rapidly developing emotional responses by utilizing his greater flexibility, overtness and curiosity, his intense desire to learn and his eagerness to participate. However, since he has only a limited ability to understand the meaning of a suggestion, communication must be at his level. One should never use "baby talk," "speak over his head" or "talk down to him," as this angers the child.

If he is told what actions to expect rather than be taken by surprise, rapport is enhanced. Startle reactions usually terminate the hypnosis and produce resistances. Asking the child to imagine himself relaxing in his bed or on a comfortable couch deepens hypnosis. The escalator technic is helpful for further deepening. The child, at all times, must be flattered and given the impression that the suggested ideas originated from his own feelings, thinking and experience.

A reward for his efforts, such as a medal, a prize or a treat, strengthens the interpersonal relationship, shows the therapist's appreciation and increases motivation. If new ideas are presented in such a manner as to apprise him fully that therapy is a collaborative venture, co-operation is increased. An authoritative approach rarely succeeds with children. They require patience and understanding; it is easier to agree that a symptom is annoying than to argue a child out of it. This helps to establish further rapport. Children seldom respond to logical ideas but readily comprehend those dealing with their own experiences, especially those affording them the most satisfaction and achievement.

Thus, with an enuretic child, it is useless to suggest that "Only babies wet the bed." It is better to ask, "How do your playmates feel about this? How many of them do this?" If the answers indicate a desire for help, therapy can be instituted. If not, further interrogation should be made. Assuming a desire for treatment, the next statement is, "With your help, I think we can lick this problem together. Wouldn't you like to do this? If you really want to, I'll show you how it can be a 'do-it-yourself' treatment." Such statements invite the child's participation in helping to remove an undesirable habit pattern which he recognizes as his problem. They also build up self-esteem. All psychotherapy must be directed toward helping the child cope with the emotional significance of his difficulties. Recently, the coping mechanisms of children have received considerable attention.[32]

The use of hypnosis in child therapy has been discussed,[6, 8, 15, 23, 33] varying from supportive treatment directed toward release of tension, reassurance and re-education to acting out and other complex hypnotherapeutic procedures. Unfortunately, space limitations preclude their detailed description. The reader is referred to an excellent bibliography on these aspects prepared by Weitzenhoffer.[20] Several of the commonest conditions that are amenable to hypnosis will now be discussed.

NOCTURNAL ENURESIS

ETIOLOGY

Bed-wetting is a difficult symptom to treat. The causes can be divided into 2 broad classifications: physical and psychogenic. Physical causes comprise spina bifida, congenital and mechanical factors,[31] a small bladder capacity,[11] neurogenic factors, cystitis, hypospadias and other involvements. [7a, 10a, 14b] Psychogenic factors[4] such as sibling rivalry, loss of a mother or a nurse, faulty attitudes toward masturbation, improper development of urinary control due to frequent micturition, inadequate toilet-training, poor hygiene, deep sleep, and emotional immaturity due to overprotection must be considered.

Often the symptom is a manifestation of a passive rebellious interplay between child and parents. Once the child realizes, following his initial bed-wetting, that he now possesses a weapon against the parents, he may maintain a conditioned pattern long after the original cause for his hostility is forgotten. When this reflex becomes firmly entrenched, the harder he tries *not* to wet the bed on a volitional level, the more likely he will be to lose control during sleep.

Even though it is used as an aggressive act, the child is ashamed of the bed-wetting. However, he is loath to give up the secondary gain value that the symptom of enuresis affords. The mother, unable to cope with the problem, resorts to nagging, which, in turn, makes the child more frustrated. She also becomes insecure, intolerant and harsh, and displaces her own hostilities and tensions upon him, not realizing that he desperately needs sympathy and support. This further increases the child's tensions and insecurities so that he is unable to adjust to more mature levels of development. The chronic bed-wetter has never developed beyond the diaper stage! In dealing with the situation thus created, the parents (usually the mother) must be treated concurrently with the child.

TREATMENT

Before instituting therapy, the presence of physical problems such as kidney infections, bladder involvements and diseases of the nervous system must be eliminated. Treatment is not simple, and various combinations of therapy such as re-education and psychotherapy must be used together. Parents must not humiliate, punish or use the child for the displacement of their own tensions. Hypnotherapy has been used successfully by numerous investigators.[7, 10, 14, 18, 19] The following illustrates the author's approach:

The child usually is brought in for the initial visit against his will. Therefore, a friendly relationship must be established immediately. The following ruse is often effective: In mock anger, the mother is asked, "Why did you bring Johnny in on such a beautiful day?" Without waiting for her reply, I remark, "Isn't that right, Johnny?" Wide-eyed, he now sees in me a new-found friend. (The mother has been apprised of these tactics prior to the first appointment.)

Then he is told, "Johnny, you have a perfect right to wet the bed as often as you please, and it is also your privilege to stop wetting the bed whenever you feel like it." After listening carefully to his views, one can ask him, "How would you like to play a little game where you can relax and imagine seeing your favorite television program?" Invariably, Johnny will agree, because of the good rapport that has been established. Visual-imagery technics are used to induce hypnosis.

After hypnosis is achieved, the child is asked, "Do you enjoy wetting the bed?" If a negative response is elicited, the following questions are asked: "How many of your classmates wet their bed?" (By indirection, this makes him feel unusual and helps to establish the motivation for a change.) "If you slept overnight at a friend's house who did not wet his bed, and had an accident, how would you feel?" If he agrees that this would be embarrassing, he is asked, "Would you like to be helped to avoid this situation in the future?"

These questions focus his attention on the fact that he has a problem, and yet he has not been made to feel guilty. They also reveal his personality structure and, hence, the most appropriate therapeutic route. With an aggressive child, a permissive approach is used in order not to identify the therapist with the parents. The therapist can also point out, providing the child is mature enough, that he is harming himself more than his parents. If the child is passive and dependent, he can be encouraged to assert himself the way others of his age group do, by allowing him to vent his resentments on the therapist, and later, channel his aggression into more constructive outlets.

The usual posthypnotic suggestions for symptom-removal are presented briefly as follows: "Would you try holding your water (urine) as long as possible during the day?" (This increases the bladder capacity.) "Also, perhaps you might be interested to see how well *you can start and stop* the passing of your water." (This invites his participation.) "Maybe you will gain better control than your friends. If you concentrate on what it *feels* like to pass your water during the day, you will have little or no trouble *feeling*

this identical sensation even when you are sound asleep. And after you have gone to the toilet, you will return to your bed and immediately fall deep asleep." The child should be given positive suggestions that, when he gets out of bed to urinate during the night, the time intervals between trips to the toilet will be increased until he can sleep through the night without urinating.

Under hypnosis, he is taught how to contract the diaphragm and simultaneously relax the pubococcygeus muscles; the downward push on the vesical neck stimulates contraction of the detrusors and opens the internal sphincter, which leads to urination. Rehearsal of the act of urination should be repeated several times during each session. Under autohypnosis he can "rehearse" or have a "dry run" of all the accompanying sensations of micturition, and thus speed up bladder control.

The next step is to reverse the child's fears about the bed-wetting. The youngster is asked, while under hypnosis, "Would you be interested in how much of your bed can remain dry?" This shifts his attention from himself to the bed. It can be suggested that since *he* controls his own bladder functioning, he can have a *dry* bed if he wants it badly enough. The word "wet" is never used! The mother also is instructed always to speak in terms of a "dry bed." She can remark, "My goodness, your bed was three quarters dry!" or "Last night it was all dry!" If this positive approach is used over a period of time, the idea of a "dry bed" will be indelibly imprinted on the child's mind. Convincing the child that a dry bed is a sign of maturity is in itself often therapeutic.

Therapy is facilitated, in some instances, by establishing a time limit for when the bed will be dry. Most effective are posthypnotic suggestions such as, "Johnny, you can set a time when you will be able to have full bladder control." If he names a date, this goal can be strengthened by saying, "You can be very proud if you reach your goal beforehand." This, of course, implies that bladder control will be developed (extraverbal suggestion). A child can be hypnotically conditioned to derive pride in the achievement of establishing bladder control. These suggestions may be repeated as necessary to effect a conditioned response. Any reason for failure should be analyzed.

The urine also can be measured every morning, a larger amount indicating increased bladder capacity. It is very helpful, too, to give a reward for achieving a goal within a certain period. A calendar used to mark off the nights on which the bed was dry helps to add to the sense of achievement. Drugs to reduce the depth of sleep, tranquilizers, atropine, and such procedures as fluid restriction have only a placebo effect. However, if parents and child are convinced of their utility, they may be employed. Interrupting sleep is of little help and only increases tension. Devices which sound alarms when the bed is wet are seldom helpful.

The parents are instructed not to scold or chastise the child over a wet bed. Humiliation and ridicule only serve to compound the problem. The entire family should look upon the child's progress in overcoming his difficulty as an important event, and he should be praised for each small victory. He should likewise be encouraged to overcome a sense of defeat if the bed is wet on occasions. Often the problem is intensified if the child cannot communicate effectively with his parents. The insecurity, the inadequacy and the tensions present in the mother, therefore, must be corrected. She can be advised to read a bedtime story in a soft and soothing manner and to emphasize her love for the child. Other members of the family who need help for their own tensions often must be treated as part of the total therapy. The following case illustrates the author's approach:

Simon B., a 12-year-old boy, was a chronic bed-wetter. In addition to poor grades in school, he had poor relationships with playmates, superiors and relatives. The bed-wetting began soon after the adoption of a sister for him when he was four.

He was hypnotized readily in the first session. During the second session, he was taught autohypnosis. It was also suggested that he practice inducing self-hypnosis frequently; that the more he practiced, the more proficient he would become. On the third visit, a week later, he readily induced self-hypnosis, and related how his mother continually "rode" him, that he was unwilling to accept any of his mother's suggestions because she favored his adopted sister. During subsequent sessions, he stated that he was looking for ways to get even with his parents and that perhaps the bed-wetting pattern was being maintained for this purpose.

At this time, Simon's mother was interviewed. She said that Simon had always wanted a baby sister; he knew that she was adopted. She thought that perhaps because of her own perfectionistic attitudes and demands she had pushed Simon too rapidly. In addition, she was not getting along too well with her husband and wondered if she might not be displacing her tensions to Simon. Simon and his sister were constantly fighting, and this, too, made her nervous. For some reason, she always protected the little girl. One day, in a fit of anger, Simon remarked, "Pretty smart girl we've got here." After this, she noted that Simon was becoming increasingly argumentative and sulky. During the next few sessions, other ambivalent attitudes toward his mother were brought out. He angrily remarked, "The tone of my mother's voice annoys me. She never even lets me finish what I have to say."

Other areas of insecurity were explored. During the next 3 sessions, at weekly intervals, he was given posthypnotic suggestions to maintain a full bladder until the last possible moment; to remember the sensations accompanying a full bladder, and to re-experience these sensations even during the deepest sleep. It was emphasized that all sensations accompanying a full bladder would be "telephoned" to his brain and would wake him up; that if he wished, he would then awaken and go to the toilet, empty his bladder and promptly return to his bed and fall asleep.

Simon reported at the next session that during sleep his bladder "felt like a big balloon," and that he awakened, was able to pass his water and again immediately fall asleep. It was now suggested that under no circumstances would the symptom be given up until he was willing to yield it, and that this would occur through autohypnosis and in full accordance with his wishes. When autohypnosis is employed, here is little possibility that other symptoms equivalents will be produced.

The mother was also instructed never to mention the word "wet" but always to speak in terms of a "dry bed." She was advised particularly to watch the tone of her voice when speaking to Simon. In several sessions, at nonhypnotic levels, it was made evident to her that she should love the boy for himself rather than for his intellectual accomplishments. She was advised not to vent her ire on him; this would curb his rebellious attitudes. Through the combined use of hypnosis, directed toward symptom-removal, and psychotherapy for the mother, Simon overcame his bed-wetting pattern within 3 months from the time he began therapy.

Another interesting case was that of a 10-year-old boy who presented a problem of generalized irritability and enuresis. All efforts to cure the bed-wetting had been unsuccessful. Although outwardly diffident and hesitant, the boy was an alert and co-operative patient who was easily hypnotized by a visual-imagery technic. Intellectually, he manifested a sophistication and an awareness of adult values beyond his years.

The history revealed a feeling of guilt over masturbation, and that his behavioral problems originated in the home, primarily from the father who, the boy stated, "never spends any time with me." He, too, readily admitted that he wet his bed to get even with his parent, saying, "What other way is there to get even with my dad?"

Hypnotherapy was directed at both the symptom and the characterological level. The same posthypnotic suggestions were employed as in Simon's case. During subsequent sessions, it was pointed out that he had a continual need to assert himself but was inhibited by his inadequate concept of himself. He also felt compelled to adhere to the high standards set up by his strict father. He viewed his parent's concern and attention as a burden, yet he feared his father's authority and loss of support. Additionally, he showed increasing concern, guilt and anxiety over masturbation, which was allayed by re-education and reassurance that "it was not a wicked act."

The enuresis improved after the father began to spend more time with him, and when the boy was made aware that the enuresis served as an outlet for his growing aggression toward his parent and increased sense of shame. As a result, his confidence and self-esteem were increased, and a complete cure was established after the parent relaxed his ambitions and high standards for the boy. Sixteen sessions were required to effect these results.

NAIL-BITING

Nail-biting is generally indicative of insecurity and anxiety. Therefore, therapy must be directed to the causes of the child's tensions, which usually involve the parents. The latter must be cautioned against evincing displeasure over the habit, as this only mobilizes more guilt and frustration and serves to perpetuate the vicious cycle.

TREATMENT

Hypnotherapy can be employed for direct symptom-removal; at least, the conditioned pattern can be interrupted until the emotional needs are elicited, as the following case illustrates:

A child of 9, who had an older and a younger sister, began to bite her nails following the birth of the younger one. Utilizing the permissive technics described above, posthypnotic suggestions were employed as follows: "Would you like to stop biting your nails by your own efforts? Then, perhaps, you might be willing to bite *one nail* on each hand as often as you wish. Which one would *you* like to choose?" If the forefinger on each hand is chosen, one can remark, "Let's make the nail-biting more interesting. Maybe you would like to start biting the nail on the left side of your mouth first, using one bite from each tooth in succession across the mouth, and then doubling back to the side where you started. You will find it fun to repeat this at least 3 times. If you still think you are not satisfied, turn the nail upside down and repeat the same procedure." This makes the nail-biting so complicated that it becomes a chore.

As soon as the other nails began to grow, the child was praised for following instructions: "Aren't you really proud that the other 4 nails on each hand are as good looking as your girl friends'? Haven't any of your schoolmates noticed the other nice-looking nails?" Under hypnosis, it was suggested, "You can increase or decrease biting the nail you selected to the degree that you think necessary." Such a suggestion is designed to make the nail-biting a routine and boring task against which the patient will rebel just as she did against parental admonitions not to bite the nails. This reaction follows the law of reversed effect.

Four more sessions were required to "wean" the child from biting the one nail. During this period, the procedure was continually made more complex until the child's natural resistance to regimentation made the nail-biting nonrewarding in terms of her oral satisfactions. At this point, she described her jealousy of her parents' attention to her baby sister.

Therapy was now directed toward the emotional needs for the nail-biting. She was asked whether it was her desire to stop the habit or whether it was the wish of her parents that she do so. In order to determine how much of the habit the patient needs to maintain equilibrium, it is necessary to evaluate the strength of the desire to stop as opposed to the degree of oral satisfaction obtained. At a subsequent session, the child was asked to see herself as a little baby, and it was pointed out that it was perfectly natural for her at this earlier age to put a rattle or a thumb in her mouth. She readily agreed to this and stated, "I guess I was trying to be a little baby all the time, wasn't I?"

The parents were instructed to pay equal attention to all the children, to ignore the nail-biting and not to punish the girl if the habit returned. Further psychotherapy directed toward the parents, and permissive technics employed for reinforcement, enabled the patient to break the habit in several months.

Often, excessively dominating parents, or those who delegate the care of their youngsters to servants, need psychotherapy more than the child who is made insecure by such factors. Children who are unresponsive to permissive technics can be conditioned by a more direct approach: "Whenever you bite your nails, you will get a very bitter taste in your mouth; you will feel sick to your stomach." Weekly reinforcements under hypnosis are necessary to break the habit. In general, however, a permissive approach is more successful.

TICS OR HABIT SPASMS

Tics or habit spasms may involve all sorts of facial or bodily movements. They occur usually in hyperkinetic, sensitive and nervous children. Other extenuating factors, such as familial traits and mannerisms, quarreling parents, an insecure mother who continually screams at the child, or physical defects, contribute to the child's unhappiness and tensions. Anxiety over poor grades, lack of interests, fright, and identification with children who display similar involvements are other causes. It is also believed that some tics are suggested, as in the following case:

A 7-year-old child had developed an incessant twisting of the lips inwardly, accompanied by raising her eyebrows and pushing her chin

downward. She had been a bed-wetter and a thumb-sucker, and was the most insecure of 4 small children. The father was overly concerned with the position of the girl's teeth and constantly admonished her that she would have "buck teeth" if she sucked her thumb. Involuntarily, the child began to pull the upper lip over and under the upper teeth in a futile attempt to push them back. Under a medium stage of hypnosis, it was suggested, "Your teeth are fine; the next set of teeth will grow in right. Don't worry about them." Even a light or hypnoidal stage is often very efficacious. In this case, reassurance under hypnosis and reduction of the father's undue concern were sufficient to allay the child's tensions. As a result, the tic disappeared without further probing.

A 13-year-old boy who was failing in school had had a blinking tic of the eyelids for 3 years. The constant blinking was accompanied by a severe conjunctivitis. He had been treated unsuccessfully by psychotherapy. His father was a physician and wanted the boy to follow in his footsteps. However, the boy was more interested in mechanical hobbies such as radio and electronic devices. It was apparent that the frustrated father was attempting to live out his life in the son.

Under hypnosis it was suggested, "Would you mind twitching the forefinger of your right hand several times a minute? This will take the tension off your lids." Four sessions were required for reinforcement of this suggestion under autohypnosis before the blinking tic of the lids was transferred to a finger-twitch. During the next 6 sessions, the finger-twitch was reduced in frequency until it, too, subsided. The father's faulty attitudes were discussed, and he decided not to push the boy.

Symptom-transformation is usually successful because it is much easier to remove a recently acquired conditioned reflex than a long-standing one. When the new reflex is manifested, one can be fairly certain of a successful outcome. If psychological guidance is combined with conditioning under autohypnosis and proper posthypnotic suggestions, better results can be obtained. For refractory cases, the specialized technics discussed in Chapter 47 are indicated.

STUTTERING

Stuttering in young children, adolescents or adults is often a very difficult problem. There are some interesting references to the use of hypnosis in speech therapy and clinical audiology.[6, 17, 22, 24, 29, 34]

TREATMENT

Stuttering is an enormously resistant symptom which cannot be removed by simple posthypnotic suggestions. Some cases, especially those of mild stutterers, do respond to this approach. However, a moderate or a severe stutterer ordinarily requires an intensive evaluation of what is taking place between himself and his hearers. Ordinarily, there is a great deal of repressed hostility, the expression of which is masked. The stutterer feels insecure around other persons, and is unable to express his feelings since he is always on guard. Stuttering is a compromise between the simultaneous desire to express an idea and to inhibit it.

In children, the anticipation of stuttering brings it about by setting up a conditioned pattern. The attempt to defeat this anticipation and to control it, and the resulting heightened tension, lead to further hesitation and disruption of speech. Thus, the stutterer believes that he is going to stutter, and that he must not stutter. He is controlled by these 2 conflict-ridden thoughts, which have become entrenched through repeated enforcement in speech situations, often since he first started to talk. He now finds it impossible to eliminate them by will alone.

Most stutterers are, of course, very reluctant to deal with the symptom itself. The stutterer is so ashamed and overwrought about the symptom that he is unable to cope with it directly. Because stuttering is not a uniform phenomenon, its severity is more or less dependent upon the environmental situation.

Therefore, one must elicit situations that the individual fears or emotional expressions in relation to other people that he finds it impossible to make freely. Under hypnosis, the symptom is much more amenable to a direct attack as he can rehearse speech situations particularly dreaded by him, especially in relation to those who upset him.

Hypnosis is an excellent method for investigating the particular situations and stimulus patterns that produced the stuttering. It enables the patient to understand the need for the avoidance reaction, to rehearse it and to work it through so as to help to release the specific tensions which arise in his oral musculature during the act of speaking. Exploration through hypnotic age-regression in good subjects often helps to pinpoint specific episodes which brought about these inhibitory patterns.

The stutterer often develops auxiliary symptoms which are a misguided effort to overcome his speech defect. He blinks his eyes, stamps his foot or pounds his fists in order to overcome the blocking. He develops these reactions to avoid becoming aware of certain words and sounds. He then substitutes other words or sounds in a vain attempt to hide his stuttering. These attempts invariably lead to more symptoms. The individual who starts out by stuttering and finds that, initially at least, he stutters less when he lifts his head, will begin to lift his head more and more until he develops a real spasm. And this spasm can often become more disabling than the initial stuttering symptom which he is trying to overcome by this mechanism.

Successful hypnotherapy must be directed to all the accompanying symptoms. The subject is shown that in the hypnotic state he can speak in a manner that is more satisfactory both to himself and to his listeners. Stutterers are surprised that they can speak without the involuntary head motions, the foot stamping, the finger snapping or whatever other muscular manifestation they employ.

The tape recorder can be used to good advantage with hypnotherapy. Stutterers are almost always free of symptoms when their ears are plugged, when they are reading from a prepared text, when they are speaking in unison with someone else, or when alone. It is helpful to have the individual speak into the tape recorder while he is by himself. Then he listens to himself while under hypnorelaxation, and reads the same passage in unison with his tape-recorded verbalization. The resulting good, fluent speech encourages him to identify with a person who obviously is able to speak normally.

This procedure is accomplished best by a permissive approach, judiciously utilizing posthypnotic suggestions. Suggesting that the subject is never going to stutter again is seldom effective, as this works for only a short time. As a result, the patient becomes disheartened and loses confidence not only in the therapist but also in hypnotherapy.

Posthypnotic suggestions and autohypnosis can be limited to specific situations; for example, comfort and ease can be induced in the child who dreads speaking in class by remarking, "Under self-hypnosis you will imagine that you feel relaxed and more comfortable in class, and if you can see yourself talking without difficulty in your imagination, you will find it easier to talk." If each situation is approached through sensory-imagery conditioning, there is a good chance that, to a degree, the vicious fear-reaction cycle in which the child has become enmeshed can ultimately be reversed. The following selected case is illustrative of the author's technic:

A 12-year-old child was taught hypnosis and autohypnosis in one 50-minute session. He was a hissing stutterer who took about half a minute to say one word. Yet, under hypnosis, he said, "Around the rugged rock the ragged rascal ran" and other tongue twisters, all in one breath, without any hesitation whatsoever. This indicated that a psychological approach would be helpful.

Since his speech difficulty began at age 2, it was patently impossible to elicit traumatic episodes that might have occurred prior to this age. He also had received intensive psychotherapy. It was decided that the best course was to break up the reflex at one level or another.

During the next session, he spoke under hypnosis into a tape recorder without difficulty. It was suggested: "If, under autohypnosis, you listen enough to yourself, you will become accustomed to the sound of your own voice speaking normally. After all, when we hear a tune played over and over again, do we not hum the tune exactly the way we heard it?" Such measures establish a healthy pattern, so that the stutterer has a firm foundation upon which to build a more natural and normal type of speech. At first, if he wishes, he can hum a tune, then sing words, and later speak short sentences. The first tapes can be compared with later ones; the resultant improvement instills confidence.

During the third hypnotic session, it was suggested that perhaps the blocking of the muscles involved in speaking might be transferred to another portion of the body. It was pointed out that the subject had no control over the gestures and the spasms that usually accompanied his stuttering; that Nature's first line of defense could be employed in a constructive manner by giving him something that he could control. A twitching of one of the fingers of either the right or the left hand was suggested. Under hypnosis, he was asked, "Which finger would you like to twitch; would it be the little finger on the left hand, or perhaps the little finger on the right hand, or even the thumb on the left hand?" The fact that he was given a choice led him to believe that he was acting under his own volition. A posthypnotic suggestion was given that "Each time you feel that you are going to stutter, you can control it by twitching your finger. And you can, if you feel embarrassed, do this with your hand closed. In this way no one will see it."

The transfer of the blocking from the muscles of the speech to the muscles of the finger is a "trading down" or an attempt to siphon off the energy with which the original symptom is invested. Furthermore, the finger-twitch takes the place of stuttering in fulfilling the need for a symptom. Symptom-transformation of this type does not remove the symptom all at once but, rather, substitutes a weak conditioned-response for a noxious or well-entrenched one. In this case, the child made progressively more use of the finger twitch for several weeks. At this point, the twitch could be either increased or decreased. If it can be increased, obviously it can be decreased. The child was eventually weaned from the finger-twitch by posthypnotic suggestions directed toward increasing and diminishing it. During this period, considerable improvement in his speech difficulty was manifested.

Under hypnosis, he was next taught "loose contact." Most stutterers have difficulty only with the first letter or two of any word on which they block. Therefore, it is advisable to reverse the emphasis by suggesting, "You are going to worry about the last syllables. For example, if you have trouble saying the word 'democratic' and you find yourself saying 'de-, de-, de-,' become more interested in the 'mocra-tic' portion, and you will notice that if you direct your attention to the bulk of the word, you will easily slide over the first two or three letters."

In the case just described, the child had considerable resentment toward the father, who was too busy to spend an appreciable amount of time with him. In another case, that of the son of a physician, a similar mechanism was elicited. In both instances the parents were interviewed and these problems were discussed. Both boys were completely cured of their stuttering after attending the author's group hypnosis speech-training program. In many instances, such patients must be prepared for a relapse. Rather than regarding this as a failure, they should be asked to describe the factors that produced the relapse. Patients are urged to return at monthly or bi-monthly intervals for reinforcement suggestions.

Other posthypnotic suggestions are commonly employed, such as, "If possible, try looking at the face of the person to whom you are speaking." Most stutterers look down or away in shame. It is emphasized that they should maintain a steady gaze at all times; that, just as they need not be ashamed of speaking rapidly, they likewise should not feel embarrassed if they speak slowly. Reading backward and forward again and again helps to slow rapid speech, and also favorably conditions the auditory centers to adopt normal speech patterns. Other posthypnotic suggestions are directed toward improvement in vocalization and articulation.

Another feasible approach, as described above, is via the use of sensory-imagery conditioning under autohypnosis. In this technic, the individual imagines that he is speaking normally. Just as we have a "mind's eye," we have a "mind's ear." In the hypnotic state, the subject is asked to "listen" to his own voice, and to "hear" himself talking on a wide variety of subjects, without hesitation, blocking, or difficulty of any type. After he begins to think that he can "speak" normally, he finds it much easier to speak at nonhypnotic levels.

It is easier to recognize the basic speech patterns than to direct treatment primarily to the cause of the speech disorder. As fluency improves, the stuttering will diminish, particularly if training is directed to sensory functions rather than to motor ones. The thinking processes involved in speech are more important than the talking process. Thus, as the ear-training establishes a good mental pattern of speech, talking becomes "thinking out loud." As a result, the autonomic portion of the brain transmits impulses to the mouth; the words "say themselves." Sensory-imagery conditioning was most efficacious in the case of a 16-year-old boy with hysterical aphonia who had not spoken for 2 years because of profound guilt over masturbation.

Another valuable approach is to suggest that the stutterer speak out loud as often as necessary when he is alone. A 15-minute session daily is suggested. Through posthypnotic suggestions, the duration can be decreased by one minute daily, and then one minute every other day, every third day, etc., until he is weaned off the symptom. It is surprising that, when a stutterer deliberately tries to stutter, he is unable to do so. By reversing his fears, one can break up the reflex; through hearing his own voice speaking normally, the stutterer gains confidence in his ability.

Group hypnotherapy is ideal for the stutterer. The same group dynamics outlined in the chapter on obstetrics (Chap. 33) operate with beneficial effects when stammering is being treated by hypnosis. Most stutterers feel that they are "all in the same boat" and do not hesitate to speak before other members of the group. It is surprising how quickly they pick up another individual's mistakes and make constructive suggestions for improved speech. This, of course, increases the stutterer's self-esteem and confidence and motivates him toward further therapy.

Faulty parental attitudes can arouse tensions in a child and lead to stuttering. Many parents are worriers and perfectionists.[12] They react to their child's nonfluent speech with concern or impatience. By correcting him, they make the child conscious that his speech is unacceptable. He responds by talking less and less, with the growing fear of failure—until he is speaking with the fear and stress of a stutterer. Hence, parents should allow the child to develop at his own pace, and his speech should not be judged by adult standards.

L. D., a 15-year-old boy, had a history of stuttering since the age of 2 or 3. He felt inadequate socially and in school, even though he was of superior intelligence. His parents were always correcting him; they were perfectionists who made excessive demands on him. He was expected to act like a man and yet was treated like a child.

The therapeutic goals were directed toward symptom-removal and toward helping him to solve some of his adolescent problems, which consisted of withdrawal tendencies and anxiety over suppressed rage toward his parents. They were advised of their faulty attitudes. Posthypnotic suggestions were employed also to redirect his aggressive needs along healthy outlets such as taking a paper route, using the money to go out with girls and thus improving his self-esteem. Eighteen sessions at weekly intervals were required. Such brief hypnotherapy effected a healthier personality integration.

Since stuttering often begins early, there is no use exhuming a great deal of memorial data, nor is it helpful to search for early traumata by questioning about events before the age of 4 or 5. Attempting this generally yields diminishing returns. Johnson[13] states: "Considerable research to date provides no appreciable support for the hypothesis that stuttering is characteristically associated with or symptomatic of severe emotional disturbance or neuroses in a clinically significant sense." In this regard, he states that speech training often does more harm than good, as it emphasizes the use of the will rather than the imagination. The stutterer becomes more conscious of his speech difficulty, and it thus becomes intensified.

According to Johnson, the symptom developed because the stutterer had too critical a listener during a crucial period of speech learning. It begins the day that a listener, usually the mother, begins to worry that perhaps her pre-school-age youngster is unduly repeating himself or hesitating in his speech. Once this notion enters her head, the stage is set for the child to become a stutterer.

If the mother would pay no attention to his hesitancy and repetitiveness—which is a natural part of speech development in a 3- to 4-year-old—there would be no stutterers in the world. Unfortunately, however, too many mothers judge a child's speech by adult standards. They make the child conscious of their own unfounded fears. They attempt to correct the child's speech, and the child, if he is desirous of pleasing the parents, will develop doubt and fear of his ability to express himself and stuttering begins.

If a child gets past the age of 3 or 4 years without being classified as a stutterer, the chances are that he will never stutter unless he runs into the same problem with listeners when he enters school. There are approximately two and one-half times as many male stutterers as female. One possible explanation of this is that mothers are less likely to be critical of the speech of girls than of boys.

Marchesi[14a] cured 75 to 80 per cent of 98 cases of stammering by hypnotherapy directed toward symptom-removal even though antecedent emotional tensions and traumas apparently were causative factors. Stammering developed as an imitative reflex; removal from the person who caused it is all that is necessary. The condition also may be due to an accident, with personal involvement or as a witness.

The specific treatment begins with a study of the vital capacity of the lungs, as breathing exercises are employed with hypnotherapy. The breathing is chosen as the starting-point because the arrhythmic respiration, upon which the stammering is based, is restored to a more normal rhythm. More important, as a result of the rhythmic breathing, the emotional aspect of the stammering is now separated from the association with the abnormal breathing. Hypnotherapy is continuously maintained—on the average, two sessions weekly for about one month. The breathing exercises are prescribed in the office for use during hypnorelaxation there as well as at home. Concentration is directed to the character of the breathing as well as to subjective thoughts. However, the patient is informed that he should not try to concentrate too hard, as failure is inevitable. At the beginning, he is apprised that progress will not be upward; that relapses can be expected.

Marchesi stresses a nondirective hypnotic approach which leads to very deep hypnotization because criticalness is not developed. This provides considerable self-satisfaction because the patient gets the impression that the operator needs his help. Objectivity and the self-realization that hypnosis produces psychophysiologic alterations enhances the expectancy level of the patient. By the second week, the patient is able to develop numbness and lightness of the extremities, and is able to breathe so that the rhythm is undisturbed by any type of noise. After this the breathing becomes smooth in type.

The stammering is attacked by asking the patient to spell out words which caused difficulty in the past. Success in doing this leads to a more positive attitude. The patient who does not respond is asked to speak under those emotional conditions which formerly caused the stammering. Attention is directed to spasmodic contractions of the diaphragm, the glottis and the character of the breathing. Errors are pointed out and under hypnosis he is asked to breathe as taught, to spell words without any hesitation and note the differences in speech when these functions are correctly performed. This, too, adds to his confidence.

In the failure group, 15 per cent did not respond due to insufficient attention by the therapist. About 5 per cent did not have the necessary intelligence to participate in the program.

MENTAL RETARDATION

McCord[26, 28] finds that mentally retarded children are readily hypnotized; good intelligence is not an important requisite for hypnotizability.[28] Rather, these children are "uneducated" and really have never been taught how to learn; I.Q. tests are not indicative of their learning capacity; and many generalizations about "intelligence" do not apply to the mentally retarded child.

Hypnosis, by increasing motivation, convinces the child that he can learn more than was anticipated; thus, the child's self-concept is altered and healthier attitudes are developed. The author noted similar findings when he was working with spastic children, as described in Chapter 36; their learning capacity was improved after teaching them how to "tap their forgotten assets."

A mentally retarded boy of 12, with an I.Q. of 62, showed improvement in learning after instruction in autohypnosis. After reading a page, he induced self-hypnosis to "see" an after-image of what he had read. This enabled him to develop a "photographic mind," and with repeated posthypnotic suggestions his learning subsequently improved.

A 14-year-old boy with an I.Q. of 92 was trained to utilize time distortion for speeding up his learning ability. This resulted in an observable increase in learning. Here, too, autohypnosis was employed. His mother had divorced her husband when the child was 6, and she continually berated him so that the boy had really never been encouraged to study. The psychometric evaluation indicated a lack of confidence in himself rather than a marked learning deficit.

McCord[27] recently reported on a series of "mongoloid-type" subjects with I.Q.'s under 40. In addition to bringing about an increased motivation to learn, vocational motivation and a lengthening of the attention span, hypnosis was believed to be of possible help in controlling perseverative excitement, including relaxation and relief of insomnia.[25]

Uhr's[35] excellent review of the effects of hypnosis on learning indicates that the results are inconclusive. However, the clinical observations overwhelmingly show definite and possibly striking improvements in learning. Other experiments indicated an improvement in learning from 2 to 40 per cent when time distortion, specifically time condensation, was employed.

The consensus of opinion from Uhr's studies indicates that "suggestion" or "motivation" or "attention" may well prove to be the crucial variable, the *hypnosis merely potentiating these factors.* This view is in keeping with what is known about hypnosis.

THUMB-SUCKING

Most infants suck the thumb, but the maneuver becomes more marked when a baby is weaned too soon. This results in an inner need for more sucking activities and, unless he gets more food, he may suck his thumb or even his whole hand. Not all children are alike, and the process of weaning cannot be governed by a timetable. Thumb-sucking at this early stage of development is not harmful even though it is done vigorously. The baby teeth may be distorted, but the effects are temporary, provided that the youngster discontinues the habit before the permanent set erupts.

Interference only intensifies the symptom and makes the child rebellious. Thumb-sucking usually is gradually stopped by the age of 4. Some children return to it as a consolation when bored, tired, sleepy or hungry. Others revert when lonely, tense or upset because a younger brother or sister is getting more attention. If the youngster is made to feel important, loved and secure, the habit disappears completely.

But something must be done if the child persists in sucking the thumb after the fourth birthday. Elbow-splints, mitts, rings and horrible-tasting concoctions are valueless. Little is accomplished through nagging, shaming, bribing, teasing or punishing an already unhappy child. Parents should make it a point to fuss over the child, and it will help if other children in the family, relatives and friends will do the same, or at least make *no* mention of the habit. Adequate rest and play outlets should be encouraged.

Eventually most children give up the habit, as by age 5 they are capable of self-discipline and can be taught to help themselves. But if the problem has been mishandled, the youngster may switch to nail-biting. Hypnotherapy can be very helpful in thumb-sucking and is employed in a fashion similar to that used for nail-biting (see p. 253).

BEHAVIOR DISORDERS

The behavior pattern of the child is laid down from the first few weeks of life. Recently it was shown that, if newborn monkeys were taken away from their mothers and nursed on a wire surrogate "monkey," these monkeys, deprived of warmth, became asocial, detached, quarrelsome, nervous and, in short, psychoneurotic adults. When a control group was nursed on a soft, cuddly Teddy bear "monkey," they grew up to be warm, gregarious, mature adults, normal in every respect. It was also found that leaving the monkeys on the wire "mother" for only a week and then transferring them to the Teddy bear monkey did not reverse the harmful patterns that were laid down. This ingenious experiment indicates that personality is molded early in life.

The developing personality, in order to mature into a healthy one, as pointed out by Freud, must pass through the early emotional mileposts of infantile sexuality. If an individual is unable to adapt himself to a mature orientation, he will do one of two things: He will either retreat to a previous stage of development or remain at the latest one. This is analogous to the soldier who finds that the pillbox which he is attempting to attack is too heavily fortified, and so he retreats back to his slit trench where he once knew safety. Immature, frustrated individuals who are insecure hate to leave the "slit trench of childhood" and remain fixated at early levels of development.

To encourage growth of the personality, parents, particularly the mother, of necessity, have to "walk a tightrope"; they must give the child an equal amount of love and of discipline. However, children must not be reared as if they were mass-produced; each child needs to have his own particular needs, wishes and feelings satisfied in his own particular manner. Therefore, mothers especially must make their children feel that they are loved for themselves and not for their accomplishments. If he is given a considerable amount of love, the child will be willing to abandon his hostility and reciprocate with compliance and the giving up of earlier patterns of behavior. "Smother love" is not "mother love," and mothers must be careful not to be oversolicitous toward the child. This will only make him more dependent and less likely to mature in a healthy fashion.

Parents should also remember that unruly behavior, rebellion and delinquency of any type are often used as attention-getting devices—the child uses these mechanisms to invite interest on the part of the parents. This type of behavior is often seen in the chronically ill child, who uses complaints as a means of gaining sympathy and attention.

It is important to ascertain whether or not parents are taking out their own frustrations on a child as a means of acting out their own neurotic needs. Other parents live out their own thwarted ambitions through the child—the stage mother is a typical example. And still others make unreasonable demands that the child is unable to fulfill, and, as a result, he retreats to earlier levels of behavior and develops many of the sequelae described in this book.

A big problem in evaluating the emotional behavior of a child is that the same symptom may signify different levels of disturbance in different children. There are criteria for evaluating the seriousness of a child's behavioral difficulty that can be helpful in determining whether or not a child needs hypnotic treatment. Whether the conflicts are internalized or external is an important criterion. Problems created by the environment are much easier to deal with than internal conflicts.

Another criterion is whether the disturbance is limited or affects most aspects of the child's development. Does the child have difficulty getting along with his mother only, or does he have difficulty in other interpersonal relationships? Most normal adolescents are in a state of turmoil. In fact, the adolescent who is not struggling to conquer his impulses and to achieve independence is the one who may eventually need psychological care. However, the particular type of emotional disturbance which develops depends on the parental behavior, the degree of the child's exposure, and the response of the parents and others to his psychological disorder. The length of time that the disturbance has been present also is important. One present for a month will clear up more readily than a symptom present for years.

School phobia can be treated in the incipient stage by posthypnotic suggestions directed to increasing the child's interest in his studies. If this approach is not successful, arrangements can be made for the mother to sit in class with the child for gradually diminishing periods of time. If the classroom, schoolmates or teachers are disturbing factors, these should be discussed at either hypnotic or nonhypnotic levels.

Eating problems, appearing early in life, usually represent hostility toward parents.

When eating becomes a means of expressing pleasure or displeasure, hunger ceases to dictate the amount of the food intake; a vicious cycle is established, the origin of which is eventually forgotten. In this situation, the mother needs greater confidence in her ability as a parent. She must recognize that the child's own physiology will ensure an adequate dietary intake as long as she does not fuss about his eating habits.

Dawdling is probably normal in preschool children and it, too, denotes resentment of the "nagging" parent. Fear of punishment or loss of love causes the child to choose this pattern rather than one of overt rebellion. Therapy should be directed against parental overreaction but, the longer dawdling has existed, the more time and support will be required to help parents guide their child through this phase of adjustment.

Rebellious behavior suggests that the child is angry and has such a poor relationship with his parents that he fears neither punishment nor loss of love. At other times, rebellion occurs when the child feels omnipotent as a result of lacking parental control. Thus, the parents require guidance regarding the need for parental unity in providing realistic, consistent demands on the child, combined with continuing love and acceptance.

Sadistic and destructive behavior gives pleasure to most 2- or 3-year-old youngsters, as they seek and even enjoy punishment for their misdeeds. Parents should recognize this as an attention-getting device, and increase approval, and decrease rejection and punishment. If the syndrome is noted too late, psychotherapy will be required when the child is older.

Ambrose[2] employed hypnotherapy in a child guidance clinic and reported cures or improvement in phobias, nightmares, chronic anxiety states, and other psychosomatic disorders. Symptomatic cure was established in over 60 per cent of the cases. In investigations,[1, 5] he demonstrated how hypnosis could speed up psychotherapy, as compared with more time-consuming methods. Hypnotherapy was utilized primarily to relieve tension, and positive suggestions were stressed along with re-education and supportive therapy for both parents and children. Symptom-removal by direct authoritative suggestion is seldom effective.[16]

JUVENILE DELINQUENCY

Hypnotherapy has been employed effectively in juvenile delinquency.[3,9] Relaxation alone, under hypnosis, relieved the significant tensions.[9] Behavioral problems such as stealing, truancy, sex offences and lying were helped in patients who were followed for 1 to 6 years.

Ambrose and Newbold[6] have an excellent chapter devoted exclusively to the use of hypnotherapy in delinquency. They point out that many anxious children have a need to provoke their parents into punishing them for their wrong-doings. The causes may be an overly strict upbringing, too high standards, parental hostility or rejection. Hypnosis was used to allow children to vent their fears and, together with re-education, helped a high percentage of delinquents. Parents were also treated to correct aggravating factors. When they saw the improvement in their children through hypnosis, the parents became even more co-operative. In some cases, abreaction, regression and revivification were used to relieve actual traumatic episodes. The protective value of hypnosis as well as its corrective features is emphasized.

Mellor[30] recently cured 13 of 14 hardened juvenile delinquents, who had resisted all types of therapy, in an average of 6 sessions. He made use of communication with the "unconscious" by technics involving finger- or hand-levitation to produce answers establishing the authenticity of traumatic or emotional causative factors. This technic (finger signalling) rapidly eliminated emotional blocks and avoided anger and defiance.

In several cases the benefits occurred during the first session. It is likely that the finger signalling here acts as a "magical gesture," fitting in with the subject's inordinate need for security, attention and love. This, together with a permissive and noncritical approach, could be of distinct value in the juvenile delinquent.

Weitzenhoffer[21] recently questioned the validity of eliciting the so-called "wisdom" of the "unconscious" by ideomotor finger signalling. He believes that there is little justification for assuming that some sort of psychic entity, "the unconscious," has been communicated with or is responsible for the observed phenomena. Nevertheless, Mellor's brief pilot study indicates that the method established good motivation for self-improvement. Regression, revivification and cathartic recall aided recognition and understanding of the underlying reasons for the tensions. Mellor thinks that, during hypnosis, subjects overcome their difficulties by developing insight and learning better ways of responding to their tensions.

The following interesting behavior problem was helped in 5 sessions of hypnotherapy:

G. I., a 13-year-old, had run away from school, was continually at odds with his parents, and was always making inordinate demands on his family for a motorcycle, a "hot-rod" auto, etc. He had been suspended from 2 schools because of obscene language, insubordination and poor grades.

Through hypnosis, a good rapport was readily established and was used to express some of his hostile attitudes toward his parents. He and his younger sister were adopted. He realized that he needed his parents' support, yet he felt a considerable amount of hostile dependence toward them. This attitude was projected to teachers and other surrogate figures.

His parents, who had adamantly refused to let him go out with girls, were advised to let him "go steady" with a girl of his own age. Posthypnotic suggestions were utilized to improve his concentration, especially for spelling and reading. His grades improved. The nature of his rebellious attitudes and attempts to retaliate for excessively strict supervision was also worked through by re-education, enabling him to make a satisfactory adjustment. Hypnosis here speeded up the psychotherapeutic process.

ASTHMA

Diamond[36] recently reported the complete cure of 40 cases of asthma by eliciting the "causative" factors, emotional or environmental. He stresses that hypnosis is never to be used for symptom-suppression. Others[6] agree with this tenet.

HYSTERICAL SYMPTOMS

Ambrose and Newbold[6] have classified under hysterical reactions a group of bodily symptoms which had "purposive" aspects and symbolic significance. Here, hypnotherapy with re-education was helpful.

The author treated an interesting case of a 16-year-old boy who had a fetish for masturbating whenever he was able to obtain female undergarments. Re-education and a permissive hypnotic approach over 5 months (14 sessions) cured this boy of his fetish. Although his identification was purely masculine, he was very dependent on his widowed mother. She was cold and austere, and the boy's lack of affection from her drove him to such satisfying outlets, not only for his sexuality but for a deep-seated need to get even with his mother; the fetish undoubtedly was a way by which he could vent his aggression in a symbolic manner.

MISCELLANEOUS CONDITIONS

Many of the other psychosomatic disorders described in the chapter on hypnotherapy in internal medicine have been treated effectively by hypnotherapeutically oriented pediatricians. Other conditions reputedly treated by hypnosuggestive procedures are the hyperkinesis of infectious chorea, hyperkinetic syndromes associated with encephalitis and other neurologic conditions. The hypnosis was employed as a symptomatic auxiliary method to other forms of medical therapy.

REFERENCES

1. Ambrose, G.: The value of hypnotic suggestion in the anxiety reactions of children, Brit. J. M. Hypnosis 2:20, 1951.
2. ——: Psychological treatment in a child guidance clinic with special reference to hypnotherapy, Brit. J. M. Hypnosis 3:24, 1951.
3. ——: Hypnotherapy in the treatment of the delinquent child: I. The intelligent delinquent, Brit. J. M. Hypnosis 3:56, 1952.
4. ——: in Schneck, J. M. (ed): Hypnosis in Modern Medicine, pp. 195-7, Springfield, Ill., Thomas, 1959.
5. ——: Positive hypnotherapy versus negative psychotherapy in child psychiatry, Brit. J. M. Hypnosis 4:26, 1953.
6. Ambrose, G., and Newbold, G.: Handbook of Clinical Hypnosis, London, Baillière, Tindall & Cox, 1956.
7. Braithwaite, J. V. C.: Enuresis in childhood, Practitioner 165:273, 1950.
7a. Brajevic, C., et al.: Paper read at First European Congress on Orthopsychiatry, Sept., 1960.
7b. Epstein, P.: Quoted by Platonov, K. I., in The Word as a Physiological and Therapeutic Factor, Morcan, Foreign Language Publishing House, 1955.
8. Erickson, M. H.: Pediatric hypnotherapy, Am. J. Clin. Hypnosis 1:25-31, 1958.
9. Gilbert, S. F.: Hypnotherapy in children, Brit. J. M. Hypnosis 6:36, 1954.
10. ——: Juvenile enuresis: hypnotherapy in children, Brit. J. M. Hypnosis 8:43, 1957.
10a. Holman, P. G., and Anderson, E. G.: Paper read at First European Congress on Orthopsychiatry, Sept., 1960.
11. Higham, A. R. C.: An approach to the problem of simple enuresis, Proc. Roy. Soc. Med. 46:889, 1953.
12. Johnson, W.: The Onset of Stuttering, Minneapolis, Univ. Minnesota Press, 1959.
13. ——: Problems of impaired speech and language, J.A.M.A. 170:148-150, 1959.
14. Koster, S.: Hypnosis in children as a method of curing enuresis and related conditions, Brit. J. M. Hypnosis 5:32, 1954.
14a. Marchesi, C.: Hypnotic Treatment of Stammering. Paper read at Pan-American Medical Assn. Meeting, May 5, 1960.
14b. Muellner, S. R.: Systematic training to enlarge the bladder capacity: a new concept of cause and therapy, J. of Urol. 84:714-716, 1960.
15. Schneck, J. M.: Hypnosis in Modern Medicine, pp. 329-332, Springfield, Ill., Thomas, 1959.
16. Solovey, G., and Milechnin, A.: Conduct problems in children and hypnosis, Dis. Nerv. System 16:249, 1955.
17. ——: Concerning the nature and treatment of stuttering, Brit. J. M. Hypnosis 10:2-9, 1959.
18. ——: Concerning the treatment of enuresis, Am. J. Clin. Hypnosis 2:22-30, 1959.
19. Van Pelt, S. J.: Hypnotism and the Power Within, London, Skeffington, 1950.
20. Weitzenhoffer, A.: A Bibliography of Hypnotism in Pediatrics, Am. J. Clin. Hypnosis 2:92-96, 1959.
21. ——: Reflections upon certain specific and current "uses of the unconscious" in clinical hypnosis, Internat. J.C.E.H. 8:165-177, 1960.
22. Wolberg, L.: Medical Hypnosis, New York, Grune & Stratton, 1948.
23. Wright, M. E.: Hypnosis and child ther-

apy, Am. J. Clin. Hypnosis 2:197-205, 1960.
24. McCord, H.: Hypnotherapy and stuttering, J.C.E.H. 3:40-48, 1955.
25. ——: Some unusual uses for hypnosis in a therapeutic school for mentally retarded children, Brit. J. M. Hypnosis 7:37, 1955-56.
26. ——: Hypnosis as an aid to the teaching of a severely mentally retarded teen-age boy, J.C.E.H. 4:21, 1956.
27. ——: The hypnotizability of the mongoloid-type child, J.C.E.H. 4:19, 1956.
28. ——: Hypnotizing the mentally retarded child, Brit. J. M. Hypnosis 8:17, 1956-57.
29. Madison, L. R.: The use of hypnosis in the differential diagnosis of a speech disorder, J.C.E.H. 2:140, 1954.
30. Mellor, N. H.: Hypnosis in Juvenile Delinquency. Read before 35th Pan-American Med. Assn. Meeting, May 4, 1960.
31. Moodie, W.: Survey of Child Psychiatry, p. 103, Med. Pub. London, Oxford, 1939.
32. Murphy, L. B.: The child's way of coping: a longitudinal study of normal children, Bull. Menninger Clin. vol. 24, May, 1960.
33. Ray, J. A.: Hypnosis in children, Brit. J. M. Hypnosis 2:11-17, 1960.
34. Rosen, H.: Hypnotherapy in Clinical Psychiatry, New York, Julian, 1953.
35. Uhr, L.: Learning under hypnosis: What do we know? What should we know? J.C.E.H. 6:121-135, 1958.
36. Diamond, H. H.: Hypnosis in children: asthma, Am. J. Clin. Hyp. 1:124-129, 1959.

Supplementary Reading

Traphagen, V.: A survey of attitudes toward hypnotherapy with children, Am. J. Clin. Hypnosis 2:138-143, 1960.
London, P.: Hypnosis in children: an experimental approach, Internat. J. Clin. Exper. Hypnosis 10:79-93, 1962.

41

Hypnosis in Orthopedics

Hypnosis can be an adjunct to psychotherapy for certain types of spasmodic torticollis, hysterical contractures, backache due to "vertebral neuroses," pain relief in traumatic emergencies and the setting of fractures where analgesia or anesthesia are unavailable. It also can help to reduce neurogenic shock in debilitated or elderly individuals requiring extensive surgical procedures such as the nailing of hip fractures and spinal fusion. Rheumatism, fibrositis and certain types of arthritis which have a psychogenic component are amenable to a combination of hypnotherapy and medical procedures.

TORTICOLLIS

Spasmodic torticollis or wry neck is due to a hysterical conversion reaction; the torsion often symbolizes deep-seated anxieties which are too difficult to face. This condition is extremely resistant to physical therapy and often requires resection of muscles and nerves. Hypnosis has proven effective in numerous cases of recent origin.

Kraines[5] described a woman who "avoided looking at her work" when she felt inadequate to assume the responsibility of a new job. He cured the patient in a few sessions by hypnosis and psychotherapy. The following verbalization was used:

"Now relax your neck; relax it still more. Your head feels so very good, and all the tension is gone. It relaxes still more and still more. Now the head begins to straighten itself out. It turns to the midline—and your head tips to the opposite side. Good. Now your chin is down and your head is in normal position. It will continue to be normal. It feels so good now. Your head will remain normal." (After these specific suggestions, the emotional bases behind the symptom should be dealt with.) "Your aver-

sion to your employer will disappear, and you'll regard him as an old and disagreeable person, but you will not be affected by his manners. You will not be disturbed by your husband's irritability but will just let his anger fall off you—like water off a duck's back. That's why you will face everything straightforwardly. Your head is straight now and will stay that way. Next time you come here you will go to sleep more easily and quickly, and until then your head will remain in midline. Now gradually wake up, and you feel very well. Wake up completely."

Kirkner[4] reported 3 cases in which one case was completely cured, another partially, and one resulted in failure. Often hypnosis dramatically removes the torticollis in a single session, but invariably it returns; this indicates its functional significance. If the condition is of long duration and accompanied by muscle hypertrophy and scoliosis, the prognosis is well-nigh hopeless. Where no anatomic involvement exists there is a better response to hypnosis.

A 33-year-old male was seen with a torticollis of 14 months' duration. No gross anatomic changes were observable. Eight months before the onset of the torticollis, he had fainted while receiving an injection. Two months later he saw his mother fatally burned. Following this latter episode, he developed dizzy spells, and always "needed more air." One month later his wife suffered a nervous collapse which required shock therapy. Soon after, his neck started turning to the left. However, the torsion was relieved whenever he held a pencil in the right side of his mouth or whenever he touched the top of his head. Posthypnotic suggestions were directed toward increasing utilization of these two mechanisms, which inhibited the turning of the head. Through sensory-imagery conditioning, he imagined these acts to be associated with a normal alignment of his head and neck. The more he actually put the pencil in his mouth and touched the top of his head, the longer the torticollis disappeared, often for several hours. Posthypnotic suggestions were given that he could, if he wished, increase the intensity of the torsion. It was further explained that whenever one could increase the severity of a symptom, one could deliberately *decrease* it! An uncovering type of psychotherapy revealed considerable resentment over his wife's sexual coldness. He related that he had had considerable hostility toward his mother, "who was always cold and distant." After his wife had a "nervous breakdown," he was unable to look directly at the customers of his small-town drugstore because of his strong guilt feelings. Alleviation of his anxiety and feeling of guilt, together with hypnotic manipulation of the symptom, as described above, and a cathartic type of psychotherapy altered his attitudes toward his wife's sexual problems. These, together with the sensory-imagery conditioning, ultimately resulted in dissolution of the spasm and tic.

In another case, a 44-year-old woman developed a spasmodic torticollis, more marked when she had to talk before groups. Particularly significant in her history was her husband's demand for intercourse *almost every night* of their 25 years of marriage. She acquiesced in the act merely as a wifely duty. After having a mechanical-like coitus, her husband would fall asleep promptly. An interview with the husband revealed strong fears of impotence. Since the patient was Catholic, she was referred to her priest for consultation on the moral aspects of the intolerable situation. He advised psychotherapy for the husband, which was refused. Autohypnosis and the use of sensory-imagery conditioning directed toward imagining she was public speaking without anxiety afforded some relief of the torticollis. However, she generally relapsed within several days. Posthypnotic suggestions to twitch the forefinger of the right hand helped to decrease the intensity of the spasm. She was advised to face and discuss the sexual situation with her husband, who finally agreed to decrease his inordinate demands. Soon after, the spasmodic tic of the neck cleared up. However, on a follow-up 6 months after the author had left the area, it was discovered that she had relapsed. Further psychotherapy for the husband, who eventually reverted to his former demands for intercourse, was strongly recommended.

HYSTERICAL CONTRACTURES

Recent hysterical contractures can be relieved in a few sessions by hypnosis. If active participation of the patient is enlisted by autohypnosis, the results are more permanent than when direct symptom-removal is used. The hypnotherapeutic approach is similar to that described for the torticollis cases. When chronic joint fixation or fibrosynovitis are marked, the outlook is poor.

VERTEBRAL NEUROSES

Spasm of the neck and back muscles, and their etiology, differential diagnosis and psychotherapeutic approach have been reviewed in detail by Kroger and Freed.[6] Backache may be a conversion reaction to the commonly observed physiologic expression of emotional tensions. They state:

It seems clear to us that "low back pain" in the neurotic personality may very well be a conversion reaction to (1) emotional insecurity, as an excessive need for attention and sympathy; (2) strong dependency attitudes, as inability to make decisions and pronounced inclination to lean on others; (3) antisocial feelings, resulting from a marked reaction to poverty or an intense opposition to existing social or moral codes; (4) deep-seated guilt, as "pangs of conscience" because of expressed or unexpressed hostility which was unacceptable to the patient.

When situations arise that are demanding, the physical complaints are aggravated, especially when the patients feel threatened by feelings of deep humiliation and worthlessness. The following case history is illustrative:

Mrs. M. O. complained of low back pain for several years. Orthopedic evaluation was negative. She was extremely ambivalent toward a very dominant mother who continually berated and criticized her so that she felt utterly helpless without her. Unable to express her hostility toward her mother, she developed a façade of solicitude for her mother's needs. The mother died unexpectedly, and soon afterward Mrs. O. developed a severe, incapacitating low backache. Glove anesthesia transferred to the back area resulted in only temporary relief. Her symptoms disappeared only after hypnotically working through the rationale for her guilt feelings toward her mother and the need for the back pain. She became aware that the suffering was used to atone for the "sin" of hating her mother.

PSYCHOGENIC RHEUMATISM

Most cases of psychogenic rheumatism are conversion symptoms, usually hysterical in nature, in which the emotional conflict symbolically expresses itself in musculoskeletal disorders.[3] Functional camptocormia, in which the patient assumes a position of extreme kyphosis after trauma, falls into this category. These patients are not malingerers but, rather, are exploiting the symptom for secondary gain purposes. Establishing the need for the symptom can be accomplished by hypnosis. This enables such individuals to face their life situations more realistically. Autohypnosis, glove anesthesia and sensory-imagery conditioning can be utilized to implement psychotherapy.

In infectious arthritis, traumatic synovitis, gout and rheumatoid arthritis, hypnosis potentiates medical and physical therapy. The clinical applications have been discussed in Chapter 31.

MISCELLANEOUS APPLICATIONS

Hypnosis helps to reduce the excruciating pain of traumatic emergency cases encountered in military and civilian settings. Although it is usually difficult to induce, hypnosis can relax an injured person and ease the discomfort when drugs are unavailable. Before attempting induction in such situations, the therapist must develop a rapid rapport. He can remark, "I know that you are in great discomfort, but if you wish to relax and have *less* discomfort, then follow my instructions." A direct authoritative approach is more effective in such instances.

Hypnoanesthesia minimizes neurogenic shock in amputations, in the setting of fractures, and in cases requiring extensive major surgery, such as spinal fusion and hip-pinning in elderly individuals. Hypnosis is particularly indicated for the setting of fractures and orthopedic surgery in children, as psychic trauma is minimized. Children from 3 to 8 years of age respond to nursery tales, cartoons and popular TV shows and to suggestions such as "You are very tired," accompanied by prodigious yawns on the part of the anesthesiologist. As has been mentioned, television provides almost inexhaustible material for hallucinatory or sensory-imagery conditioning in the 8- to 14-year-old group. These youngsters will even recite commercials along with the story plot when they imagine that they are watching their favorite show. Orthodox eye-fixation technics can be used on those over 14 years of age.

Bachet and Weiss[1] used group hypnosis for pain relief in a series of patients who had undergone amputation of limbs. They cured more than 80 per cent. Opiates and sedatives were drastically reduced. Phantom limb pain, spasm and clonus were alleviated in many instances by hypnotic inhibition.

The author is frequently called in consultation for many bizarre types of pain syndromes associated with orthopedic conditions.

Several years ago he was asked to see a ballet dancer who was suffering from a classic internal derangement of the left ankle joint, which apparently had responded to surgical removal of the offending piece of cartilage. Her postoperative recovery was good until 2 years later, at which time she complained of pain in the left ankle, the etiology of which could not be confirmed by physical and roentgenographic findings. The diagnosis was functional disturbance of the ankle joint. She was hypnotized during the first session and given posthypnotic suggestions that "You will see yourself dancing without difficulty, and also feel that your ankle has never bothered you." She was taught autohypnosis on the second visit, and it was suggested that, through sensory-imagery conditioning, she could remove all discomfort. Two sessions were sufficient to effect complete recovery from the obstinate pain and the disability. Her referring physician, a prominent orthopedic specialist, informed me that he recently had heard from her. She had stated, "I am dancing with a ballet group. The hypnotherapy completely relieved me of all my symptoms, and I am very happy."

HICCOUGHS

Persistent hiccoughs are included in this section because the orthopedic specialist is often called in to resect the neck muscles and the nerves. Hiccoughs are due to involuntary spasms, which are caused by reflex action, and are usually unilateral. They occur with a wide variety of physiologic and functional disorders. The entire subject has been reviewed.[2] The usual therapy consists of interrupting the reflex action by pharmacologic measures and surgical intervention. From 1 to 10 hypnotic treatments were required to relieve 14 of 18 patients who had not responded to other therapeutic procedures.[2] Hypnosis induced complete relaxation and relieved the spasm.

My experiences are similar to those reported by Dorcus and Kirkner[2]—about 75 per cent of the patients can be helped by a permissive hypnotic approach.

An elderly male, who had been hiccoughing for 56 days and was almost *in extremis*, was relieved in several visits. He had been extremely hostile toward an older sister for whom he worked as a tailor. Prior to the onset of the hiccoughing, she had promoted a fellow worker to a higher position than the one he occupied. The symptom began immediately after this incident. No attempt was made to work through these factors. Rather, the necessity for producing cessation of the intractable hiccoughing was considered more important. Six sessions of hypnotherapy stopped the symptom.

Often a single session dramatically and permanently alleviates the most intractable cases. Psychological probing is seldom indicated because of the time factor. It is also of considerable interest that direct symptom-suppression does not result in other symptom-equivalents taking the place of the hiccoughs.

In another case, an aftermath of a gallbladder removal, the author succeeded in stopping distressing hiccoughs that occurred every 2 or 3 minutes and had not been helped by a multiplicity of procedures such as the administration of drugs and carbon dioxide inhalations.

REFERENCES

1. Bachet, M., and Weiss, C.: Treatment of disorders of amputated subjects by hypnotic inhibitions, Brit. J. M. Hypnotism 4:15-20, 1952.
2. Dorcus, R. M., and Kirkner, F. J.: The control of hiccoughs by hypnotic treatment, J.C.E.H. 3:104-108, 1955.
3. Dunbar, F.: Psychosomatic Diagnosis and Treatment, St. Louis, Mosby, 1948.
4. Kirkner, F. J.: in Dorcus, R. M.: Hypnosis and Its Therapeutic Applications, New York, McGraw-Hill, 1956.
5. Kraines, S. H.: The Therapy of the Neuroses and Psychoses, pp. 232-233, Philadelphia, Lea & Febiger, 1943.
6. Kroger, W. S., and Freed, S. C.: Psychosomatic Gynecology Including Problems of Obstetrical Care, Chicago, Free Press, 1956.

42

Hypnosis in the Removal of Habit Patterns

ALCOHOLISM

Chronic alcoholism is a symptom of a deep-seated personality disorder usually selected to avoid intolerable life situations. There is no typical personality profile, but hostility, insecurity and feelings of inadequacy are usually present. Alcoholics have a low frustration tolerance, increased sensitivity and feelings of omnipotence characterized by the belief that "nothing can happen to me." Outwardly they present a diffident appearance, which is usually a façade for their deep-seated dependency needs.

Some have little or no concern about the trouble caused by the habit. For instance, a binge, with its days of misery and sickness, often results in a lost job, a ruined career and a broken marriage. The alcoholic is an "injustice collector" for whom the overt self-punishment fulfills a pleasurable need, as well as a rationalization for the inability to face reality. Seldom is he aware of his masochistic needs to suffer.

Such individuals do not have the courage to commit suicide and are, in reality, slowly destroying themselves by the noxious habit. To allay their tensions they retreat to a child-like behavior pattern, with a need for attention, pity and love. By becoming inebriated, the alcoholic develops a greater capacity to give and receive attention from others. This temporarily increases his self-esteem and well-being.

Many alcoholics have never emerged from adolescence—the undifferentiated period of their psychosexual development which is characterized by homosexual tendencies. The *esprit de corps* noted among gregarious drinkers at any bar illustrates the desire to be a "part of the gang" spirit. The homosexual manifestations are seldom overt, but merely represent a strong identification with an individual of the same sex. The alcoholism serves the purpose of fending off unrecognized homosexual drives (panic). Often, however, the drunkenness removes the inhibitions and allows these tendencies to emerge.

In the typical history of the alcoholic there is a compulsive pattern represented by repeated incidents involving self-debasement, various types of sexual involvements, and defiance of authoritarian and other surrogate figures. When the demands for sympathy and attention are not met, more frequent "binges" are usually necessary to provide a respite from the mounting tensions. Exhortations aimed either at shaming the individual into sobriety or pointing out the harmful medical sequelae are useless. Since the alcoholic seldom realizes the needs for his habit, he cannot control his drinking. Successful therapy requires that these needs must become self-evident to him. Intellectualizing or moralizing on the dire mental and physical dangers are utterly futile in the chronic alcoholic.

TREATMENT

The purpose of therapy is first to motivate the individual to stop drinking, then teach him how to adapt to his difficult problems rather than using regressive behavior patterns at the first sign of stress. Here a sympathetic, noncondemnatory attitude will make the patient feel that he is being treated like an adult and this helps establish healthy motivation. Chronic drinkers are seldom motivated if their immaturity and strong dependency preclude admitting that they have a drinking problem.

Since most alcoholics are generally passive and dependent, the hypnotic relationship initially helps the patient in therapy at a time when he is most resistant. Later this dependency is dissolved and the needs for it and other reasons are worked through. Because of greater rapport with the therapist, the patient now is willing to trade his self-destructive tendencies and immature attitudes for healthier goals.

The chronic alcoholic who does not wish to be helped, or who is literally brought in by friends or relatives against his will, cannot be helped by any psychotherapeutic approach unless he is institutionalized for long-term psychotherapy. The prognosis is usually poor, as each recovery is only a "flight into health." His ardent protests that he is cured and his vows that he will never drink again are only rationalizations for the breakng off of therapy. Overcompliance merely follows the old adage, "If you can't fight them, join them." Follow-up studies indicate that severe cases are difficult to help, irrespective of the therapy employed.

Conditioned Reflex Treatment by Hypnosis

Conditioned reflex treatment[3] has been successful for some patients. In this approach the individual is given a drink and an emetic is administered. An association between vomiting and drinking is produced by this method, but it is not helpful unless the patient is highly motivated or is seen immediately after a "hangover." Relatively permanent recovery in carefully selected patients is obtained by reinforcing this technic through posthypnotic suggestions to vomit at the sight, taste or smell of liquor.[2] Under sensory-imagery conditioning, the patient recalls repeatedly the horrible nausea and the disgusting sensations produced by the emetic. Thus, the unpleasant memory is seldom forgotten, and the constant revivification of a repugnant experience dissuades him from drinking.

If a healthy relationship exists between therapist and the patient, the recovery forces will be mobilized. The desire to abstain is reinforced by appropriate posthypnotic suggestions. Motivation is increased by such other posthypnotic suggestions as the setting of a deadline for the daily or the weekly decrease in the quantity consumed, and the stressing of the health factor, and, above all,

by the effect of the patient's self-esteem that has been enhanced by the permissiveness of the therapeutic regimen.

The key points in the conditioned reflex treatment under hypnosis, outlined by Kroger,[2] Wolberg,[6] Miller[4] and others, are based on repeatedly emphasizing, under hypnosis, the deleterious effects of alcohol, the conditioned repugnance for alcoholic beverages and the patient's ability to control his own behavior, and finally establishing the emotional needs for the symptom. The self-destructive drives should be channeled into healthy outlets such as hobbies, sports, social activities and other constructive endeavors.

Aversion Treatment

After hypnosis and autohypnosis have been instituted, strong suggestions are given, such as, "Each time that you even think of drinking, you will develop a horrible disgust and taste for the liquor by associating it with the most horrible, repugnant smell and taste that you have ever experienced. After you have said this to yourself again and again, you will *really* begin to believe that a drink will smell and taste awful." Such autosuggestions are repeated continuously for reinforcement purposes. After sobriety has been maintained, these can be made at longer intervals.

Wolberg[6] has described a very interesting technic in which symptom-substitution is utilized. He informs the patient that "Every time you crave a drink you will reach for a malted milk tablet and this will give you a sense of pleasure and relaxation."

Another effective method is to open a bottle of whiskey while the patient is hypnotized and to assure him that the bottle has not been tampered with or opened. He is offered a drink, and requested to hold it in his mouth for several minutes to get the full taste. Naturally, a burning sensation on his tongue is created. After the patient has finally swallowed the drink, he is asked how he liked it. His usual reply is, "It tasted fine," whereupon the therapist informs the subject that he has been deceived. "You have not been given whiskey but a mixture of lemon juice and ammonia." If hypnotized, the subject will exhibit marked revulsion and disgust.

If this is unsuccessful, the procedure is

repeated and the chances are that the next time he will react in the expected manner. Before concluding the hypnotic session, the patient should be given a posthypnotic suggestion that any time he is offered a drink these reactions will certainly occur. Even the thought or the smell of a drink will induce profound distaste.

A substitute habit should be suggested to take the place of the drinking. For instance, drinking nonalcoholic beverages satisfies the oral cravings. Whenever a deeply ingrained habit pattern is changed, it should be replaced by a more innocuous substitute habit. Tranquilizers or amphetamines can be employed during the "weaning-off" period.

Before terminating every session, suggestions should be made that the patient will feel very relaxed. Immediately after dehypnotization, he can be offered a drink to see how much disgust is immediately produced. In selected subjects, this approach often produces a 60 to 70 per cent total abstinence. Social drinking is discouraged. Suggestions to bolster self-confidence and overcome feelings of inadequacy can be given during hypnosis.

Group Therapy

The success of Alcoholics Anonymous (A.A.) depends upon the same factors described in Chapter 33. The powerful group identification factor, which makes the sufferer feel accepted, and his intense desire to please the leader of the group or the person assigned to him (his sponsor) are additional factors. The group situation mobilizes the inherent competitiveness present in every individual and, through the strong support given by other members, his weak personality structure is bolstered. Finally, as a result of healthy motivation established by the emotional contagion, and alliance with a power greater than himself, the recovery forces of the individual are unleashed. Faith in a beneficent power means the difference between success and failure. The alcoholic has little or no reason to take issue with this new parental figure or to challenge his omnipotence. Through further friendly exhortations from former alcoholics, he often renounces his drinking habit. The author has a high regard for A.A.

Individual Hypnotherapy

Most problem drinkers are looking for a magical gesture and, because of their strong dependency strivings, attempt to "crawl into the lap" of the therapist. From the initial visit, they must be informed that this is a "do-it-yourself" program, that results are in direct proportion to the desire for recovery and the willingness to perfect their sensory-imagery conditioning technics. By using such measures the therapist cannot get "out on a limb," nor "lose face" with the patient.

It also is stressed that if the symptom returns, it can be controlled by autohypnosis; resistances are diminished whenever suggestions are self-originated. The therapist must not be too authoritative.

To avoid criticalness, the author states, "You will stop drinking as soon as you desire to, will you not? And it will be because you really want to do so down deep inside. I am only a friend who wishes to guide you as long as you need me." This obviates the therapist's being placed in the role of a dominating parental figure.

Group Hypnotherapy

The author of this book has found that the results in small groups are often better than with individual hypnotherapy. In addition to hypnosis, the technics include free discussion and expression of feelings, re-education, reassurance, strong emotional support and thorough explanations of the commonly encountered problems.

There are many rationalizations that alcoholics use to explain their drinking. They must recognize that dishonesty with themselves and with others, omnipotence, impulsiveness, guilt, shame and the inability to establish durable relationships are related to the drinking. The manner in which tensions are displaced, self-abuse, the striving for perfection and the need to manipulate others also should be pointed out.

When a permissive approach is employed that is directed toward these needs, guilt, anxiety, insecurity and fear can be resolved, especially if the individual identifies with strong members of the group. The stronger the identification, the more will the alcoholic emulate those whom he admires. The important factor in group as well as in individual psychotherapy is giving the patient the feeling that the therapist really understands the patient's problems and is willing and able to help him. The greater ability to concentrate speeds up any type of psychotherapy. When group hypnotherapy is combined with decreasing doses of Antabuse medication, maximal improvement occurs. Wallerstein[5] obtained 53 per cent improvement with Antabuse, 36 per cent with group hypnotherapy, 26 per cent with milieu therapy, and 24 per cent with conditioned-reflex treatment.

Two-hour weekly sessions are held. Each one begins with a general discussion of alcoholism. Questions and answers pertaining to all aspects of drinking are conducted the first half hour. Then several former patients, who have been helped and who have returned to visit the group, cured, relate their experiences. They usually state that initially they could not believe that this kind of an approach would help them. Then, after observing improvement in other members, they were more motivated to obtain similar results. One or more grateful patients describe how they were taught hypnosis, autohypnosis and how through sensory-imagery conditioning they finally developed a profound disgust for alcohol (the technics outlined in the section below were used). Having a sufferer sincerely relate his feelings to the group, a considerable amount of hope rapidly develops, especially for the neophyte or the unsophisticated or the disbeliever.

Those volunteers who are successfully hypnotized are given the appropriate suggestions for producing disgust and a strong aversion for drinking. Since a specific disgust to taste and smell will vary from patient to patient, it is wise to let each one pick these. In successive sessions, the technics of autohypnosis and sensory-imagery are inculcated into each person. The incidence of success is much higher where autohypnosis is employed. With this approach, the patient realizes that he must achieve the results through his own efforts. This is highly motivating and contributes to his self-esteem.

The medical management of the chronic alcoholic is not within the scope of this presentation. It involves a knowledge of the effects of long-term consumption of alcoholic beverages, including metabolic factors. The rehabilitation of the chronic alcoholic is tedious and requires painstaking attention, patience and a mixture of empathy and firmness. At all costs, the therapist must not become too involved and must maintain a prestige position at all times.

Importance of Autohypnosis

It is not difficult for the alcoholic to practice autohypnosis. Frequently, however, he may procrastinate, saying, "I just can't find the time," or "I don't feel up to it." Here a careful step-by-step explanation should be given, stressing that the autosuggestions so necessary for his recovery should be under his control. This factor is of the utmost importance for establishing healthy motivation. Under autohypnosis, the patient can suggest when he thinks he will be able to substitute a soft beverage for the liquor. Through use of these measures, direct symptom-removal is not employed. Instead, recovery is obtained by a weaning-off process in which the patient decides *how* and *when* to cut down on the number of drinks taken per day. It is also helpful to allow a choice of the type of beverage substitute that is to replace the liquor.

Importance of Posthypnotic Suggestions

Irrational fears of the patient that he will not be able to stop drinking can be reversed through posthypnotic suggestions directed to the possibility *that maybe he will stop too abruptly.* Other posthypnotic suggestions can be given to pick a date in the not-too-distant future when he will have reduced his drinks to one or two a day. It is suggested that he will be extremely worried as to whether he is going to be taking one drink a day or three drinks a day by the chosen date. Such extraverbal suggestions produce overreaction, with resultant improvement.

As in the treatment of obesity, posthypnotic suggestions are given that, if the patient is in doubt about taking a drink, he will see me in fantasy, shaking my head in disapproval. When all these technics are employed with supportive psychotherapy consisting of rapport, ventilation of problems and skilful guidance, excellent results can be obtained in a high percentage of patients.

If a patient, who apparently is doing well, relapses or "falls off the wagon," he is never censured or criticized. However, the question can be raised with him as to *what* the particular situation was for doing this and *why* he had to take 10 drinks—perhaps he could have gotten by with 4 drinks, or 2 drinks, or perhaps one drink. Also, what was he thinking about before he began drinking? These and other problems are fully discussed. It is important to emphasize that, with most chronic alcoholics, the ultimate therapeutic goal is directed toward total abstinence.

With greater maturation and growth of the personality, the alcoholic thinks more like an adult and eventually realizes that he no longer has the need to utilize harmful tension-allaying mechanisms to meet his life problems. Even after the problems responsible for the need to drink are made self-revealing to the patient, they are frequently of such magnitude that he feels there is no solution. Here it is imperative that one of two things be done: either the individual must be given the knowledge to make the proper decision as to what course he will adopt (and it should be emphasized that the decision must come from him and him alone), or, if he is unable to make a decision, he should walk away from the problem and stop using it for self-punishment.

The following verbalization is typical for the aversion treatment of alcoholism: "John, you are deeply relaxed. Listen to all my suggestions, as each one will be indelibly imprinted in your mind. You will not remember all these suggestions today, but eventually you *will* remember all of them. Each and every suggestion will be remembered over the coming weeks and months.

"If you really wish to stop drinking, think of the most disgusting, nauseating taste that you have ever had. Maybe a drink will taste like onions, rutabagas, parsnips, or whatever other food you dislike. That's right. You are beginning to taste something awful, are you not?" ("Yes.") "Did you say it's turnips; is that what you said?" ("Yes.") "Now, each time you even think of taking a drink, you are going to experience this taste of turnips . . . this vile, horrible taste of the turnips during the next few weeks and months. Each

and every time you take a drink, you will associate it with the disgusting taste of turnips. Right now, this awful taste is getting more and more marked, is it not?" ("Yes.")

"Now, think of the most putrid smell that you've experienced. Take your time and try to think of the most horrible stench that you've ever smelled. . . . Rotten eggs? Well, that's a good one. All right, now each and every time you hold a drink in your hand and smell it, you will think of rotten eggs . . . the horrible, violent, disgusting smell of rotten eggs. And each and every time you even think of taking a drink now, you are not only going to get the terrible taste of turnips but also the smell of rotten eggs. This may not make itself apparent until you have said this to yourself over and over again, perhaps 50 or 100 times, under autohypnosis. Eventually you will associate this smell with the odor of liquor until you are sure that you really hate the sight, taste and smell of a drink (sensory-imagery conditioning).

"John, the next thing I'd like to have you do is to recollect how horrible you felt after you had a lot of drinks last Saturday night, just as if you were doing it all over again (age-regression). Remember the terrible feeling that you had in your stomach, and how you had to vomit? Recollect, if you will, that sickening feeling you had and how you trembled and shook all over and how weak you were, and the headache and the dizziness and all the other symptoms associated with your hang-over. Recall all the details of that hang-over and, if you really think about it, you will really become disgusted with drinking. Each and every time you even think of taking a drink, all of these positively awful tastes and smells will be etched in your mind. You can re-experience all of these sensations in a few minutes even though the hang-over lasted for several hours.

"I'm going to show you how this can be done by condensing (distorting) time. You know how when you're waiting for a cab on a cold, wet, rainy day and the cab is due in 2 minutes . . . it seems like 20 minutes. Or, conversely, when you're chatting with an old friend and a cab is due in 20 minutes, it seems like 2 minutes. And so, during the next 2 minutes, you are going to be able to experience all of the unpleasant, disgusting sensations associated with a half hour of the hangover that you had last Sunday morning. Fifteen minutes of actual time will *seem* like 1 minute of time. So, therefore, in 2 minutes by the clock, you will be able to relive all of the disgusting feelings that you experienced in approximately one half hour." (Two minutes elapse, during which the individual screws up his mouth, begins to get sick and has a tendency to vomit.) "Your time is now up. Wasn't that a horrible sensation? Now, each time when you have the desire to take a drink, you will re-experience the horrible sensations of that last hang-over.

"Remember, this is your problem. If you wish to drink, it is your privilege. After all, as I mentioned, this is your mind and your body, and it's up to you to direct your own treatment. Over the next few weeks, you might raise the question as to exactly how much you have the *need* to drink. Do you need to drink 80 per cent of the time, or 50 per cent, or 10 per cent? Maybe 5 or 10 per cent will fulfill your needs. I'm sure that once you realize the need to drink, you should be able to recognize the deep-seated feelings responsible for the habit. Don't press or try to think of these reasons, but just rest assured that some of the reasons will become apparent to you in the near future.

"Now, John, perhaps you can step out of yourself, much as you would in a dream (depersonalization). Look at yourself standing at a bar, uncertain, wobbling, making a fool of yourself. Take another good look at yourself. Are you not disgusted with the terrible smell of liquor on your breath? Observe the sloppiness of your clothes. When you are sober, you are always very neat. Are you not disappointed with what you see?" (depersonalization often can be very effective in creating a disgusting self-image).

"Picture yourself at one of the drunken brawls where everybody is making fools of themselves. Is it not disgusting to see someone you respect sink lower and lower into utter insensibility and helplessness? I am interested in all your problems, and I want you to remember that any time you feel you need my help, regardless of where you are, I want you to please call me. If this is not possible, and if you are in doubt as to

whether or not you should take that second or third drink, you will really see me standing beside you, shaking my head in disapproval (introjection of therapist).

"And now you can come out of this very nice state of relaxation, which is not sleep or unconsciousness and is not a trance. You can slowly open your eyes in the following manner: Number 1, say to yourself, 'I will go deeper next time.' Number 2, 'I will follow all the suggestions that I am giving to *myself* to the best of my ability.' Note that I said, '*I am giving to myself*,' rather than 'those given by Dr. Kroger.' Three, 'I will open my eyes. I will feel supremely confident that I can lick my problems.'

"You will feel, John, that you were the one who did it. Remember that. You were the one who was able to *control your need to drink*. Remember, the degree of success you achieve will be in direct proportion to the amount of effort you put forth. Practice makes perfect! Think of a foul-smelling, evil-tasting sensation every time you crave a drink. If you do this again and again, *you will be able to break up this vicious habit*.

"You need not feel guilty if you 'fall off' at any particular time. Progress is never in a straight line. It is characterized by a series of ups and downs. However, the long-term trend will ever be upward.

"You have a very powerful tool that is only as good as you use it. Use it well, sharpen it and it will cut to the core of your problem. The manner in which you use it can be very helpful in this regard. A tape of this discussion with you is being recorded. It would be a good idea if you played it on your tape-recorder every night. Then these suggestions will be deeply implanted again and again into your mind until they achieve a conditioned response. Whenever we hear a suggestion again and again, we eventually carry out the suggested act. You do have a great deal of confidence in yourself and you know that you can lick this problem in your own particular fashion."

EXCESSIVE SMOKING

Excessive smoking is one of the commonest symptoms the hypnotherapist is asked to treat. Almost every chain smoker has at one time or another attempted to break the habit.

He seldom realizes that this cannot be accomplished by will power, nor is he aware that it can be broken more readily through the use of his own imagination.

The following is a sample verbalization of the posthypnotic suggestions that the author has used successfully on many smokers: "Use your imagination to curb your desire rather than your will. Therefore, each time you even think of smoking a cigarette, associate the pleasurable aroma and taste of a cigarette with the most horrible and awful smell and taste that you have ever experienced. Under autohypnosis and sensory-imagery conditioning you can convert your craving for a cigarette into an aversion. This will not happen immediately but, after you have given yourself a sufficient number of autosuggestions in this regard, you will notice that slowly and surely you will have less and less desire for cigarettes.

"Next, if you really wish to stop smoking, every time you puff on a cigarette, associate the taste and aroma of a cigarette with the most repugnant taste and odor that you have ever experienced. The craving will be converted into an aversion with continuous practice.

"You will agree that the best results are obtained if one has a goal. Hence, suggest smoking half as much during the next 2 weeks. Then cut down half as much again for the following 2 weeks until you are able to wean yourself off the habit. You can set the goal and arbitrary number of cigarettes to be smoked daily according to your needs and at your own pace.

"Since you are right-handed, would you mind *holding the cigarette in the left hand* and, instead of placing the cigarette in the right side of your mouth, which is customary for you, would you mind using the left hand for putting the cigarette in the left side of your mouth? You will, I am sure, find that if you follow these suggestions, smoking will be a chore.

"Would you mind holding the cigarette first between your thumb and little finger, then your thumb and ring finger, middle finger, or other fingers. By utilizing different combinations you will soon find that smoking becomes rather inconvenient.

"If you really are interested in giving up this habit, allow several cigarette butts to remain in the ash tray until they develop a very stale odor. Then sniff this odoriferous ash tray at least once every hour. If you do this, you will easily develop a distaste for cigarettes. May I suggest that another ash tray with stale butts be placed on your night stand beside your bed just before retiring. When you no longer can bear the obnoxious smell, place the ash tray out in the hall, but do not empty the ash tray, as you should repeat this procedure the next night until every fresh cigarette reminds you of a stale one.

"After your smoking is reduced, you might consider the possibility of trading down to a more innocuous habit. How about substituting a peppermint Lifesaver for each cigarette that you do not smoke? You will find that, whenever the tip of your tongue is put into the hole of the Lifesaver, the same satisfaction will be obtained as if you had smoked a cigarette. If this is not feasible, you can use chewing gum or a dummy cigarette instead. You can hold the latter between your lips and imagine it's real."

In addition to the above suggestions, one can stress the health and other beneficial factors related to abstinence. If the individual is a heavy smoker he usually has his nails discolored by nicotine. One can, with tongue in cheek, point out that this discoloration occurs in the bronchial tubes, too; that the inside of the bronchial tubes actually "stinks" like the stale cigarettes. It is emphasized that all these suggestions, if given by the patient to himself, afford a distinct possibility that the habit can be broken because of his own efforts. Furthermore, it should be emphasized that all credit for breaking the habit belongs to him, since he really did it through his imagination. The posthypnotic suggestions are useful for symptom-removal. About 40 per cent of the patients relapse. Therefore, it is advisable to reinforce the suggestions at least every week.

When the excessive chain smoking is a symptom of the underlying tension, the needs for the nervous tension must be eliminated. When hypnosis was used for symptom-removal, the author has never seen the slightest harm. What is the difference between cessation of smoking through hypnosis and spontaneous remission? This author is not in accord with those who are continually pointing out the dangers of symptom-removal. If these dangers are real, then proprietary products sold to stop smoking are also dangerous!

An ingenious method for smoking control has been described which uses a complicated ritualistic 21-day approach.* The "will" is not utilized, but rather an appeal on physical, cosmetic, personal and financial grounds. Medications, as antihistamines and barbitals, are used to control "withdrawal" symptoms.

INSOMNIA

Hypnosis effects improvement in acute cases of insomnia. Often a single session is effective in restoring the sleep cycle, particularly if autohypnosis has been taught on the initial visit. It can be suggested that the autohypnosis will merge with real sleep. The following posthypnotic suggestions are efficacious: "After you have established a deep state of autohypnosis, with each breath you will find yourself going deeper and deeper relaxed. And as your breathing gets slower, deeper and more regular, you will find yourself going into a deeper and deeper state of relaxation. And as you relax deeper, you will find that you will become drowsier and drowsier until you get sleepier and sleepier."

Chronic insomnia, however, is more difficult to treat. Many patients have deep-seated problems and the symptom cannot be alleviated unless the patient is able to recognize and deal objectively with these problems. When the tensions are decreased, the insomnia can be controlled. Here, too, the imagination plays an important role. Patients are instructed that the harder they try to fall asleep, the less chance they will have of doing so; that lack of sleep seldom produces harm but that worry wreaks more havoc than lack of sleep. Following the law of reverse effect, the posthypnotic suggestions must be directed *toward the need to keep awake!* The harder they try to remain awake, the more they will fall asleep. Adjunctive procedures such as regular hours for going to sleep, mild exercise to induce fatigue, hot drinks and warm baths are help-

* King, A. (See Additional References.)

ful for promoting relaxation. Barbiturates and other drugs should not be removed at once but reduced gradually. Environmental factors such as noise must also be eradicated.

More specifically, hypnosis can be directed to symptom-removal as follows: "At first you might consider the possibility of deliberately trying to keep awake; that is, do *not* try to fall asleep but, rather, imagine that you must stay awake as long as possible. Thus, you can imagine that you are an airplane spotter; that it is necessary to screen all unusual sounds you hear. You will notice that it will become increasingly difficult to deliberately stay awake, and that sleep will gradually come over you.

"Next, sleep can be facilitated by 'stepping out of yourself.' In a dream you can see yourself performing all sorts of tasks, can you not? Thus, during hypnosis you can also stand alongside the bed and see yourself there with your eyes closed. As you look at yourself you can notice your breathing getting slower, deeper, and more regular, the rhythmic rise and fall of your chest, and the relaxed expression on your face. And as you keep looking at this image of yourself, you will become very, very relaxed. Very, very relaxed. As long as you keep your arms and legs in a nice, comfortable position you will find that every muscle is relaxing more and more, and with every breath you will get very drowsy. And as you get very, very drowsy you will find that even though your eyes remain tightly closed you will get sleepier and sleepier."

In general, one must minimize the importance of sleep and reverse the patient's fears by suggesting that he remain *awake*, that the harder he tries to keep awake, the deeper he will get. Also, one can use strong suggestions that the hypnotic relaxation will merge with true sleep. Where hypnosis is not successful, intensive psychotherapy is indicated.

NARCOTIC ADDICTION

Drug addiction involves many of the psychological factors that account for chronic alcoholism and obesity. In general, there are three types. In the first, the addict attempts to meet stressful situations with more equanimity through the use of drugs. In the second, individuals use drugs to give them a "lift." In the third, the addict requires drugs to help to overcome depressive reactions due to characterologic disorders.

It is contended that an uncontrollable craving occurs in predisposed individuals even after a single exposure to a narcotic drug. Regardless of the method of addiction, drugs are utilized to provide the equivalent of sexual gratification, security and self-esteem. The fact that the emotional needs are more important than the physiologic factors is noted in the response of the addict after withdrawal symptoms have ceased. Usually he will return to the use of whatever drug satisfied his emotional needs.

Addicts are usually immature, impulsive individuals who have a low frustration tolerance. They are irresponsible, with a limited ability to face reality and a distorted idea of social values. Many feel inadequate and inferior even though they present a façade of arrogance and confidence. They also manifest strong dependency strivings but, instead of looking for assistance from healthy individuals, they seek other equally maladjusted persons.

Therapy should be directed toward restoration of their self-confidence, elimination of despondency, induction of a sense of well-being or elation and, in some instances, simply toward maintenance of normal equilibrium. All methods of psychiatric rehabilitation yield poor results, since addicts seldom can relinquish a method that affords them prompt gratification of their fantasies. Most addicts find greater satisfaction in the immediate attainment of self-confidence by drugs and cannot tolerate the time-consuming work-and-reward process of secure individuals.

The results with hypnosis in narcotic addiction, on the whole, have been poor. Some addicts do better for a while, but ultimately relapse. Many have conditioned pain-pattern syndromes that are well established, and it is difficult for such persons to give up the drug even temporarily. In my opinion, group hypnotherapy is more likely to achieve results, especially if it is employed in an institution where withdrawal symptoms can be handled and where the addict can be kept under strict supervision. Other adjuvant medical therapy, such as drugs for withdrawal symptoms, vitamins, occupational therapy, sedation and a nutritious diet can be helpful.

Autohypnosis is especially helpful for withstanding the disagreeable subjective sensations produced by withdrawal. Posthypnotic suggestions and deep relaxation help to reduce the intensity of the suffering, particularly the nervousness and the insomnia. Other posthypnotic suggestions, similar to those given to the alcoholic, help to reduce the craving for the drug. It has been reported that hypersuggestibility tends to decrease with the withdrawal of drugs.[7] This factor, together with a weak personality structure, accounts for the poor results.

In several refractory cases, the author has suggested that the addict use sensory-imagery conditioning to imagine that he is giving himself an injection or taking a drug by mouth while under autohypnosis. Where individuals can actually revivify the pleasurable effects afforded by the drug, withdrawal is accomplished more readily. In general, particular attention must be paid to the individual who has the addiction problem rather than to the symptom! Treatment by any method cannot be considered successful until craving has been abolished permanently. The methods for handling narcotic addicts by group psychotherapy under hypnosis have been described.[1]

Hamblin,[1a] in an excellent review of the literature, recently described a case of Percodan addiction cured by posthypnotic suggestions directed toward relief of headache, backache and other psychosomatic symptoms. In all, 66 sessions were required; hypnosis was used in the greater part of 45 periods. An underlying schizophrenic reaction was responsible for the symptom.

REFERENCES

1. Fox, J.: The systematic use of hypnosis in individual and group psychotherapy, I.J.C.E.H. 8:109-114,1960.
1a. Hamblin, M.: Hypnotherapy in overcoming narcotic addiction, I.J.C.E.H., in press.
2. Kroger, W. S.: The conditioned reflex treatment of alcoholism, J.A.M.A. *120*:714, 1942.

3. Lemere, F.: Psychotherapy of alcoholism, J.A.M.A. *171*:106-107, 1959.
4. Miller, M. M.: Treatment of chronic alcoholism by hypnotic aversion, J.A.M.A. *171*: 164-167, 1959.
5. Wallerstein, R. S.: Hospital Treatment of Alcoholism, New York, Basic, 1958.
6. Wolberg, L.: Medical Hypnosis, vol. 1, New York, Grune & Stratton, 1948.
7. Vogel, V. H.: Suggestibility in Narcotic Addicts, Pub. Health Rep. Suppl. 132, 1937.

ADDITIONAL REFERENCES

Bjorkhem, J.: Alcoholism and hypnotic therapy, Brit. J. M. Hypnotism 7:23, 1956.

King, A.: The Cigarette Habit, New York, Doubleday, 1959.
Paley, A.: Hypnotherapy in the treatment of alcoholism, Bull. Menninger Clin. *16*:14, 1952.
Paul, J.: Research design in evaluation of hypnotherapy, J.C.E.H. *6*:70-82, 1958.

SUPPLEMENTARY READING

Livshitz, L. S.: A study of higher nervous activity in man under hypnosis and its significance in developing a treatment for alcoholism, Zh. vyssh. nervn. deiatel'. 9:838-844, 1959.
Mann, H.: Hypnotherapy in habit disorders, Am. J. Clin. Hypnosis 3:123-127, 1961.

43

Hypnodontics: Hypnosis in Dentistry

Aaron A. Moss, d.d.s., f.s.c.e.h.

As mentioned in this volume, the hypnosis movement faded into oblivion for the third time as a result of Freud's abandonment of it. Two generations later, it was again "rediscovered," thus giving rise to the current resurgence, which is the fourth turn in the hypnosis cycle. At this time the United States is the world's geographic center of activity in hypnosis. The impetus for the current resurgence is due to a few dentists, of whom the writer is one, who banded together to teach the "gospel" of hypnosis at the end of World War II. Initially, only dentists were interested; later on, physicians and psychologists "joined the movement." This combination now outweighs the number of dentists. *However, credit is due the dentists for initiating the current widespread interest in hypnosis.*

The writer coined the term Hypnodontics in 1948, to signify the use of hypnosis in dentistry. This was to overcome the irrational prejudices of the lay public as well as in the dental and allied professions. The role dentists played in bringing hypnosis to the fore is as much a tribute to American dentistry as what they did in introducing general anesthesia one hundred years earlier, when Drs. Morton and Wells, both dentists, gave the first clinical demonstrations in general anesthesia. The latter, oddly enough, was introduced to nitrous oxide, or "laughing gas," during an exhibition of hypnosis in 1844 by Colton, an itinerant chemist and hypnotist.*

* Colton's claim to fame is that he was undoubtedly the world's first professional anesthetist. A little-known letter set forth clearly how hypnosis led to the development of anesthesia:

DENTAL APPLICATIONS OF HYPNOSIS

What are the uses of hypnosis in dentistry? Although hypnosis can be a very dramatic way of producing anesthesia, that is not its primary or most prevalent use. If there were no other application, hypnodontics would be nothing more than a spectacular phenomenon, quite impractical for general dental application, since only a small percentage of people are susceptible to complete hypnoanesthesia. Actually, there are several other areas in dentistry in which hypnosis can be applied. Space limitations permit the presentation of only a few of these applications. The uses of hypnodontics fall into two categories:

1. Therapeutic
   A. Patient relaxation
   B. Elimination of patient's tensions and anxieties, and fears of pain and discomfort
   C. Removal of objections to necessary orthodontic or prosthetic appliances after the patient had agreed to accept them
   D. Maintenance of patient's comfort

"Dr. I. C. Green   Colton Dental Association
Dear Sir: 19 Cooper Institute
                        New York, Feb. 2, 1891

"The only claim I have to the discovery of anesthesia is that I was the accessory of the discovery; and that I administered the nitrous oxide gas to Dr. Horace Wells of Hartford, Conn. on the 11th of December, 1844 for the first tooth that was ever extracted without pain. This was honor enough for me. The discovery was made at my exhibition (to facilitate hypnosis) of the gas the evening previous.

Yours very truly,
G. Q. Colton"

during long, arduous periods of dental work

E. Accustoming the patient to orthodontic or prosthetic appliances

F. Modification of certain noxious dental habits

2. Operative

A. Reduction of anesthesia or analgesia

B. Amnesia for unpleasant work

C. Substitution for and/or in combination with premedication in general anesthesia

D. Prevention of gagging and nausea

E. Control of salivary flow

F. Control of bleeding

G. Postoperative anesthesia

H. Reduction of postoperative shock.

TYPES OF SUGGESTION

Hypnodontics is that branch of dental science which deals with the application of controlled suggestion and/or hypnosis to the practice of dentistry.[6] Hypnodontics does not necessarily eliminate analgesia or anesthesia; rather, it is used as an adjunct to chemoanesthesia. Thus, there is no danger of overemphasizing the use of hypnoanesthesia in hypnodontics.

Although the term hypnosis has been defined, the meaning of controlled suggestion needs some elaboration. The deliberate and careful feeding of a suggestion into the brain in order to accomplish a given effect is known as controlled suggestion.[2] If the desired effect is accomplished, the suggestion is said to be realized. When a suggestion is realized, it effects the following changes.[3]

1. *Sensory change:* the hand (or any other part of the body) may feel colder or warmer, or have a tingling sensation

2. *Motor change:* the arm may rise or float into the air; the leg may become rigid

3. *Emotional change:* feelings of guilt, fear or anger may be aroused

4. *Change in ideas or beliefs:* confidence may be lost or enhanced (in the latter case, the patient develops a good rapport with his dentist)

Suggestion can be divided arbitrarily into 2 types: direct and indirect. A direct suggestion is one received during full awareness. It is used in the process of hypnotic induction. An indirect suggestion is one which by-passes awareness and, as a result, affects the perceptual processes subliminally; the subject is seldom aware of being exposed to the suggestion. Therefore, his responses are generally spontaneous. Since he is not aware of its origin, his defenses and resistance are not mobilized.

TESTS

Tests for hypnotic susceptibility, such as the falling back test or the handclasp test are good examples of direct suggestion. The contagious effect of yawning after one has observed someone else doing it is an example of indirect suggestion. The individual concerned may be completely oblivious of his behavioral response to the suggestion.

HYPNODONTIC INDICATIONS AND APPLICATIONS

Does the hypnodontist apply his technics to every patient? Yes and no. This answer is contradictory, and requires further explanation. For instance, hypnotic states are induced rarely and only when all other methods of dealing with the patient's problems have failed. They are used when drugs have failed to produce the desired anesthesia necessary for patient control and co-operation.

Normally, the routine patient that comes to a hypnodontist's office is handled in only a slightly different manner from the one who goes into some other dentist's office. This slight difference consists of the routine application of hypnotic technics. The 4 levels or areas in which hypnodontics may be applied are: controlled suggestion and light, deep, and waking hypnotic suggestion.

CONTROLLED SUGGESTION

In the dentist's office, controlled suggestion is applied constantly in both direct and indirect forms. In attempting to win a patient's confidence, the office personnel's choice of words is of the utmost importance. Mannerisms and the general office atmosphere constitute suggestions of prime significance.

The dentist's personality and appearance are also of tremendous importance in establishing the patient's confidence. For instance, the patient would doubt the dentist's ability to remove the decay from a tooth or the infection from a socket if he had dirty fingernails or soiled gown. Negative conditioning on the part of the dentist initiate powerful negative suggestions in the patient, making him mistrust the dentist. More often than not, the patient is not even aware of the fact that such indirect suggestions are affecting him. Thus, he may reject the dentist's recommendations by rationalizing that the fees are too high.

Other less obvious but equally negative suggestions are: not washing one's hands after answering the telephone, handling a soiled handkerchief, coughing into it or picking an object off the floor; being late for appointments; not properly organizing office routine; fumbling for instruments, charts, etc.

The application of hypnodontics to an office routine implies the administration of as many positive indirect suggestions as possible, such as instruction in proper toothbrushing technics and giving the patient a mirror to verify that all the decay has been removed from his tooth. These steps indicate to the patient that the dentist is interesed in and concerned about his welfare.

Thus, by carefully controlled, positive indirect suggestion, confidence can be established and good rapport developed between dentist and patient. Persons interested in practice management and business administration can learn much from this phase of hypnodontics.

LIGHT HYPNOSIS

Another application of hypnodontics is the use of direct suggestion in producing light hypnosis to facilitate relaxation. In this state, the patient is amenable to suggestions directed to the lessening of tensions and the building of confidence. It takes only 5 or 10 minutes to achieve relaxation by means of direct suggestion. Since this type of hypnosis is not intended to produce anesthesia, conventional analgesic drugs may be used if necessary. This phase of hypnosis is used the most frequently.

There are several advantages to hypnorelaxation: it consumes relatively little time, it is successful in over 80 per cent of the cases, and the patient retains full awareness. Controlled relaxation, attained by the application of hypnotic technics, effectively influences the frightened dental patient whose pain threshold has been lowered as the result of negative emotions.

DEEP HYPNOSIS

Deep hypnosis is used when medication is contraindicated or when drugs alone or drugs in combination with light hypnosis are ineffectual. Generally the time element involved in producing a deep hypnotic state and the fact that less than 20 per cent of patients are susceptible make it impractical for use as a routine procedure. However, once somnambulism has been induced, it takes but a few minutes to re-establish it at the next appointment. Most dentists have the misconception that those who use hypnosis apply the deep state to every patient that comes to their offices.

Hypnotic or direct suggestion is used by some dentists to correct certain objectionable dental habits such as nail-biting, thumbsucking and bruxism (grinding of teeth). This involves psychotherapy and *should therefore be practiced only in conjunction with a psychotherapist or a physician.* Hypnodontics may also be used to condition patients to wear dentures that fit well but which cause gagging for psychological reasons. These cases are not very common, yet there are instances in which a light state is generally effective.

CONTRAINDICATIONS FOR HYPNODONTICS

The author would like to sound a strong warning to dentists using hypnosis: *Hypnodontics should not be abused by the dental profession.* The dentist using hypnosis has the means at his disposal of probing into the emotional problems of an individual. Even with limited experience, he can produce such characteristic phenomena of hypnosis as age-regression, revivification, negative and positive sensory hallucinations, catalepsy and automatic writing. These phenomena *lie in the highly specialized fields of either psychotherapy or experimental psychology*, and the training, the experience and the background of a dentist *do not qualify* him for this work! This does not mean that the dentist should hesitate to use hypnosis in his work. Hypnosis can be a very valuable instrument in his hands as can a lancet, but having the legal and moral right to use it does not entitle him to remove an appendix with it. The dentist, as well as the physician, has an ethical and moral obligation to his patients to borrow knowledge from all fields of science to alleviate pain, suffering and discomfort, and to improve the general welfare of mankind. Because of this, the dentist should avail himself of hypnosis and apply it to his dental practice. Therefore, he should make judicious use of the lancet and the hypnotic technic, which, like anesthesia and drugs, are instruments that belong to the dentist's as well as to the physician's armamentarium.

LIMITATIONS OF HYPNODONTICS

The dentist should understand enough basic psychology or psychiatry to realize the fact that he is dealing with a complex tool if he exceeds his competence in using hypnosis for medical or nondental purposes. For instance, he should not attempt to cure the smoking habit, which may be a manifestation of tension and serve as an outlet for the release of nervous energy. He must know that smoking, like thumb-sucking, constipation, headache or inferiority feelings, is often the resultant of many hidden, powerful emotional forces. The removal of a habit, even by the trained psychotherapist, without "trading down" to a less noxious symptom may throw the entire psyche of a deeply disturbed person into confusion and imbalance.

The untrained therapist may be satisfied with the dramatic and forceful removal of a symptom, but the sophisticated one knows that a permissive approach, preferably by autohypnosis, will prevent the appearance of other symptoms which sometimes can constitute a powerful threat to the entire personality structure. Symptom-removal by such measures does not have a traumatic effect and is in sharp contradistinction to the authoritative "bull in a china shop" hypnotic approach.

Psychodental therapy, however, is strictly within the province of dentistry. The elimination of fear and anxiety associated with drilling and surgery has been a constant problem for dentists. When necessary, the dentist has resorted to drugs such as sedatives, and to premedication. Hypnosis is an extremely useful substitute for these.

The elimination of fear and apprehension is difficult owing to the deeply ingrained conviction that these are the concomitants of dental work. It is hard to convince a person that he will not have pain when all his life's experience tells him otherwise. Because the oral cavity is a very important erotogenic zone and all parts of it have great psychic importance, it may be that exposing these areas to the manipulation of another individual could have a highly disturbing emotional significance to many individuals. It is from these roots that fear and anxiety may spring. The extraction of teeth, for instance, may be associated with punishment, masochism or even castration. The patient is not aware of this; however, the hypnodontist should be.

Because of these facts, one cannot possibly remove or even reduce fear in all patients, but it is possible to remove all fear in some people, and some fear in most people. More than one session may be required to accomplish this. Before dental work is started, perhaps 2 or 3 sessions should be devoted to hypnosis for the removal of fear. Severely emotionally disturbed individuals, particularly, require extra time and effort. As to the time factor, once fear and anxiety have been eliminated via hypnosis, or hypnoanesthesia has been produced, a hypnotic state can be induced almost instantaneously in all subsequent sessions.

HYPNODONTIC PROCEDURES

For didactic purposes, the hypnodontic procedure is divided into 7 steps:

1. Mind-set (indoctrination)
2. Testing
3. Induction
4. Deepening
5. Utilization (operation)
6. Posthypnotic suggestions
7. Dehypnotization (termination)

1. *Mind-set.* Mind-set is the procedure used to accomplish a state of receptivity or co-operation on the part of the patient. This is done in several ways, as described in

Chapter 11, but primarily via a preliminary conversation before the use of any hypnotic procedures. The object of this step is to correct the subject's previous misconceptions or inaccurate ideas about the hypnotic state. Only in this way can good co-operation and proper motivation be obtained.

2. *Testing.* Certain tests, already described in detail, are utilized to determine the patient's susceptibility to hypnosis. Frequently, these may constitute the first stage of induction into hypnosis. There are many who consider it unwise to make tests for susceptibility in actual clinical practice. It is the author's opinion that all patients should be considered susceptible unless actual experience proves otherwise.

3. *Induction.* There are many procedures used to induce hypnosis. Hypnotic mechanical aids may be employed although, as a rule, verbal suggestions can accomplish the same results. Certain rotating spirals on a dental engine can be used as a hypnotic aid. The Brain Wave Synchronizer is another aid. For a dentist, the ordinary pen light on the dental unit is as effective an aid as any, when used in conjunction with the *eye-fixation* technic.

Induction may be *direct* or *indirect.* The direct method is used when the subject is aware that hypnosis is being employed. The indirect method implies the use of subterfuge; that is, the subject is prevented from becoming aware that hypnosis is being used. It is also known as a *hidden approach* in contrast with the *open approach*, in which direct hypnosis is used with the subject's awareness.

4. *Deepening.* Although it may take only a few minutes to induce a light hypnotic state, it may require several sessions to deepen it to the level at which it is compatible with the purpose for which hypnosis is being used. One of the commonest reasons for lack of success is failure to deepen the hypnotic state to one consistent with the requirements for Step 5. Step 4 requires training, patience, perseverance and experienced judgment.

5. *Utilization.* The purposes for which hypnosis is to be used may vary widely. For example, the purpose for which the obstetrician uses it may be entirely different from that of the psychotherapist. The purposes of hypnosis in dentistry were outlined earlier under the headings Therapeutic and Operative (see pp. 279 and 280).

6. *Posthypnotic Suggestions.* Posthypnotic suggestions, in addition to making it easier and quicker to induce hypnosis at subsequent sittings, are used also for therapeutic dental purposes, as previously mentioned. At the final hypnotic session, the operator always gives the posthypnotic suggestion to the patient that in the future no one but a physician, a dentist or a qualified psychologist will be able to place him in a hypnotic state. This procedure, called *locking the "unconscious,"* is a precaution against the patient's being exploited by a parlor or vaudeville hypnotist for entertainment. The author is aware that some feel that this is not successful for the purpose intended; he takes issue with these objecting individuals.

7. *Dehypnotization.* It is important that no patient be permitted to leave the office unless he is completely and fully co-ordinated. More about this will be said later in this chapter.

HYPNODONTIC TECHNICS

The following technic lends itself very adequately to producing relaxation prior to a dental operation. It is not dependent on somnambulism and, therefore, it has a wide range of success. It may be presented to the patient in such a manner that the words hypnosis, trance and sleep are never mentioned.

The patient is seated comfortably, with eyes fixed on a given spot slightly forward and upward. There should be no strain on any part of the body; the hands are unclasped, resting comfortably in the lap. Instruct the patient to close his eyes when he feels like it and to keep them closed. The exact verbalization for *patient relaxation via hypnotic induction* is (Step 1, *mind-set*, and Step 2, *testing*, are omitted.):

I will teach you to relax. You will relax not only your body, but your mind as well. . . . When I pick up your right (or left) hand, let it fall limp. (Pick up one hand.) No, you've helped. Let your hand fall limp as though it were without any power or life, like the hand of a rag doll. Do not help or anticipate. (Try again and again until the hand and the arm are completely relaxed. This may take from 3 to 5 minutes, but it is absolutely necessary to accomplish complete relaxation before proceeding. Be patient and persevering. Then continue.) Breathe in deeply and relax your diaphragm. . . . Again. (This must be done 5 or 6 times in unison with the patient's breathing. Hyperventilation of the lungs will tend to relax mind and body.) Now, relax your feet and legs the same way as you did your hands. Make them very, very heavy. You'll probably find a very pleasant, tingling, relaxed feeling in your toes. It will travel through the soles of your feet, up your legs, to your abdomen and chest. (Pause.) Take another deep breath and relax your diaphragm still more. . . . Again. . . . Now relax your lower jaw . . . more . . . relax your cheeks. (By this time, the eyes are usually closed. If they are not, continue as follows.) Now your eyes are very tired and heavy. They are closing, closing, closing. (The eyes will then close.) Remove the wrinkles from your forehead and relax more. Let only my voice reach you. Drift pleasantly into a pleasing state of relaxation as you hear my voice. (Now give 3 suggestions, repeating each several times.)

1. You will remain relaxed as you are with eyes closed for 2 minutes. I'll inform you when the time is up.

2. When you open your eyes, you will be fully alert but completely relaxed and full of confidence for your dental appointment.

3. Each time, when you come back for your dental appointment, you will relax quickly and deeply with this method.

(After about 1½ minutes, dehypnotize the patient, using the following words) When I count 3, you will open your eyes and be completely relaxed, feeling fine. One . . . 2 . . . 3. (If the patient does not open his eyes immediately, do not become alarmed, but repeat the above suggestions about 3 minutes later. Never show alarm or anxiety at slow dehypnotization.)

The above technic may be used routinely on all tense patients, provided, of course, that they will co-operate. It has some degree of success in over 80 per cent of cases. The technic is not spectacular, yet one will hear the following comment from the patient: "I feel very relaxed, but I was not hypnotized." The answer should be: "It was not the intent to hypnotize you but only to relax you." This should always be done prior to the operation, and the patient should be completely out of hypnosis before any dental work is attempted, the technic being intended for use as a substitution for or in conjunction with premedication.

HYPNODONTICS IN ADAPTATION TO PROSTHETIC DEVICES

Another use of dental hypnotherapy is in the conditioning of a patient to wear a prosthetic or orthodontic appliance. This is accomplished by giving him, while in hypnosis, positive, firm, posthypnotic suggestions that he will have no difficulty in becoming accustomed to the appliance. In this connection, there are times when it may be necessary to question the patient under hypnosis to get at the root of the problem. This is not recommended for the dentist, as he should realize that certain dental symptoms may ramify into the field of psychotherapy and he should evaluate the advisability of using hypnosis accordingly. If direct suggestions are applied in several sessions, good results can frequently be obtained. But if the patient stubbornly persists in retaining his symptom, the case should be referred to a qualified psychotherapist.

HYPNODONTICS IN ANESTHESIA

The use of hypnosis in conjunction with or as a substitute for premedication prior to general anesthesia is quite a common practice today among medical anesthesiologists. Raginsky[7] mentions that fear of anesthesia may be due to fear of loss of consciousness, or mutilation, of loss of life, or of the unknown. He states that it results in change in blood pressure, heart rate, capillary permeability, urinary output, coronary flow, rate and depth of respiration and carbon dioxide content of the blood. He writes:

He (the anesthesiologist) must learn the structure or normal personality, and see how and to what degree the patient to be anesthetized deviates from that of the normal. With this knowledge (hypnosis) he can quiet the patient more effectively, use much less of the anesthetic agent and have a smoother induction.

When this was written in 1948, the thought of offering hypnosis as part of the training and background of the anesthesiologist was far-fetched and remote. Today, this training has become routine for many anesthesiologists. If possible, the dentist, like the anesthesiologist, should see his patient several days before the scheduled operative procedure and begin the initial induction so that, by the time the patient reaches the office on the day of the operation, he may receive the full benefits of previous hypnotic conditioning. This brings about lessening of fear and anxiety, which results in less and easier anesthetic induction if it should be necessary. The element of safety is thus an outstanding feature in the use of hypnosis in conjunction with general anesthesia.

ELIMINATION OF GAG REFLEX

An important application of hypnosis is in eliminating the gag reflex which is so frequently a nuisance to the dentist. It is not necessary to place the patient under hypnosis for this purpose, because the elimination of gagging can be accomplished exceptionally well by *waking hypnotic suggestion*. The author and other dentists to whom he has taught this technic have had most gratifying results. The following technic is used for eliminating gagging reflex via waking hypnotic suggestion, for taking x-rays or impressions:

Stand in front of the patient and direct him to keep his gaze fixed continuously on your eyes during the entire procedure. Should his gaze wander, call this to his attention and start again from the beginning. Fix your own gaze on the bridge of the subject's nose. *Do not stare into his eyes.* Say:

1. "I am going to eliminate your gag reflex by instructing you in breathing exercises. You must keep your gaze fixed on my eyes at all times."
2. "Take a deep breath and hold it while I count to 5. 1, 2, 3, 4, 5. Now relax."
3. Repeat Step 2, never allowing the patient's gaze to wander.
4. "Now I have eliminated your gag reflex." Say firmly, with conviction, "You will not be able to gag. You may try as hard as you can *but you will not be able to gag.*" The patient's gaze must not be allowed to wander until the entire suggestion in Step 4 is completed.
5. "You may now relax, and *you will not gag* while I take your impressions (x-rays)."
6. The previous 5 steps should be repeated, after saying, "To make sure that you will not gag, I shall repeat the entire procedure once more." Continue Steps 1 through 5 and proceed to take the impressions (x-rays).

The success of the above procedure is largely dependent on the strength of the operator's conviction. If it is weak and without firmness, the incidence of success diminishes.

This technic will be found quite adequate for taking roentgenograms or impressions; it will not be effective in eliminating gagging or nausea due to the wearing of dentures. The latter requires a more intensive approach. First and foremost, it must be ascertained that the dentures are well constructed and properly fitted. After this is ascertained, posthypnotic suggestions should be given which are aimed at helping the patient to use the dentures for twice the period that he was able to use them heretofore before gagging or nausea took place. For example, if the patient reported in his original interview that he could wear the denture for only 10 minutes, then the posthypnotic instruction should be, "You will find that upon coming out of hypnosis you will have no difficulty in keeping your denture comfortably in position for 20 minutes. You will repeat this on the hour daily, and report to me in 3 days." After the patient returns and is again hypnotized, the time is increased to 30 minutes, or perhaps 35. He is to repeat this every hour and a half, etc. It will be found that, with this technic, at least 50 per cent of all denture gaggers either can be entirely improved or at least helped. It is important to take a very thorough history before using hypnosis.

It is inadvisable for the dentist who made the denture to treat the gagger. It is better to refer him to another "neutral" or disinterested dentist. When it is known that the patient is a gagger, dentures should not be constructed or even impressions made until after several therapeutic hypnotic sessions. These can save considerable time and trouble. In preventive hypnosis, however, it is acceptable for the dentist doing the prosthetic work also to perform the hypnosis. When failure to eliminate gagging via hypnosis occurs, it is advisable to refer the patient to a psychotherapist for further treatment. The symptom may be related to a deep-seated neurosis.

If the dentist uses hypnosis in this fashion for the treatment of gagging or of any other noxious habit, he is well within the limits of his field. Dangers are insignificant if the dentist does not resort to probing of the "unconscious." A clinical follow-up of failures referred to a psychotherapist showed that half of the cases have successful outcomes. In other words, it may safely be said that with proper management, 3 out of every 4 patients can be safely cured of denture gagging or nausea (50% by the dentist and 25% by the psychotherapist).

CONTROL OF SALIVATION

Control of the flow of saliva can be achieved by hypnotic means, since the autonomic nervous system is subject to volitional control. It is possible, in the experimental laboratory, to bring about (through hypnotic suggestion) vasoconstriction or vasodilation of peripheral blood vessels and to produce blushing or even blanching of a hand or a face. It is therefore not surprising that the flow of saliva can be affected in the same way. The advantages for the dentist are obvious. Fortunately, a patient need not be in a very deep hypnosis to obtain this control. The salivary flow not only can be influenced during hypnosis but for a reasonable time thereafter by means of posthypnotic suggestion.

PREINDUCTION PROCEDURES

Because of the existing prejudices among the public, the method of suggesting hypnosis to the patient is of paramount importance. If the nature of the hypnotic phenomenon is not properly presented, the patient may refuse to undergo induction. Sometimes prejudices are so deeply rooted that, even with the proper approach, consent to hypnosis cannot be obtained. There are two ways of handling such resistance:

1. The direct technic
2. The indirect (disguised) technic

DIRECT TECHNIC

With the direct technic, the patient is told, either by the dentist himself or by his assistant, of the many advantages of hypnodontics. It may be helpful for him to observe another patient being operated on while in a hypnotic state. The role of the dental assistant is of great importance and, in many instances, by a careful approach, she can induce the patient to request hypnosis from the dentist even without the dentist having suggested it. Pamphlets or brochures on hypnosis may be placed carefully in the reception room. A patient should never be forced to accept hypnosis.

INDIRECT TECHNIC

In the disguised approach, nothing is told to the patient which would make him aware that he is about to be hypnotized. He is told simply that he is being taught to relax; that he should make himself comfortable and let his arms and legs become loose and heavy. It is explained that in a relaxed state the threshold of pain is markedly raised, and also that fear and apprehension can be lessened if he remains completely relaxed physically and mentally. Through these means, using the technic previously described for waking relaxation, he is gradually brought into hypnosis. The patient is then unaware that he has been hypnotized. While such a method is usually successful, it must be understood that a patient might realize what is transpiring and become resentful. This can result in a bad relationship.

AUDIO-ANALGESIA TECHNIC

In discussing the disguised or indirect technic of hypnosis induction, it behooves the author to include two additional "nonhypnotic" technics of producing anesthesia and relaxation in dentistry. Reference has already been made to the first, namely, the use of nitrous oxide. Currently, another technic known as *audio-analgesia* is also in vogue. Although most advocates of the latter technic may be unaware of the underlying principle, namely, the state of hypnosis or suggestion, as the reason for its success, it is the opinion of the author that both these technics lean heavily on the disguised technic of hypnosis. This is not written with the intent of denying the strong analgesic or anesthetic action of the nitrous oxide gas. Rather, it is intended to point out that in many instances the anesthesia which might be attributed to the gas is due partly or solely to the effect of hypnosis or suggestion.

At a recent meeting of the American Analgesic Society in New York City, attended by about 100 dentists, the author, who was the clinician for the evening, asked for a show of hands of all those who had, at one time or another, obtained all the effects of nitrous oxide analgesia without actually administering the gas, either because of an oversight or deliberately. At least a third of those present raised their hands, indicating that they had obtained positive analgesic effects when the patient thought he was getting the nitrous oxide while in reality he was inhaling only atmospheric air. The conclusions are quite obvious. The author has no doubt that the sounds coming through to the patient by means of the audio-analgesia set-up have the same psychological effects in producing anesthesia and relaxation in dental patients.

There is no question as to the efficaciousness of both nitrous oxide and audio-analgesia as hypnotic agents. In an article written by Cherry and Pollin in 1948,[1] a technic is described in which music is fed to the patient while nitrous oxide is being administered. The authors describe an elaborate set-up of earphones, connected to a phonograph with a microphone tie-in, and attached to the patient's ears, allowing the anesthetist to speak directly to the patient. Selected music, such as *Clair de Lune, Moonlight Sonata, Evening Star,* etc., were used. The authors conclude that, ". . . in this method designed to reduce reflex irritability without resorting to depressing premedication, the "nitrous oxide" oxygen mixtures were maintained with a minimum of 24 per cent oxygen. Nausea, retching, excitement, jactitation, soft tissue obstruction, aspiration and swallowing have been *conspicuously absent.*"

Handling Resistant Patients

Even though these technics are presented by the author as hypnotic aids or placebos, there are instances in which they are indicated in preference to outright hypnosis. For example, one encounters patients whose prejudices compel them to reject hypnosis. There are still other patients whose deep-seated resistance to hypnosis makes them refractory to its use. But with the aid of nitrous oxide or audio-analgesia, the resistances, both conscious and unconscious, are not mobilized. Thus, the patient can "let go" without having his self-esteem threatened.

"SEALING" THE PATIENT AGAINST HYPNOSIS

The hypnodontist should give the patient posthypnotic suggestions which will serve as a protection against the experimenting amateur or vaudeville hypnotist. The wording of these suggestions might be: "In the future, no one will be able to hypnotize you except a dentist, a physician, or some other qualified person such as a psychologist. Unless you expressly desire to be hypnotized, no one can hypnotize you." It is important not to close out all future susceptibility, as the patient might later be a subject for therapeutic purposes.

DEHYPNOTIZATION

Before dismissing any patient who has been in a hypnotic state, it is imperative to observe two rules:

1. Remove any hypnotic suggestion that might continue to operate in the posthypnotic period.

2. Make certain that the patient is alert.

Any suggestions which might have been given, perhaps as tests, such as "paralysis" of a limb, should be removed. If a countersuggestion is not made, there is a remote possibility that such a "paralysis" may continue to operate in the posthypnotic period. It is important to set a time limit to any analgesia or anesthesia in the posthypnotic period. If a negative or a positive sensory hallucination has been produced during hypnosis, it is important to remove it before dehypnotization. These are important considerations, whether the operator be a dentist, a psychologist, a psychiatrist or an amateur hypnotist.

The hypnodontist, as well as the psychotherapist, is legally and morally responsible for a patient's condition and welfare at the time he leaves the office and after he has been in hypnosis. This is just as true for hypnosis as it is for general anesthesia. If a patient should meet with an auto accident because of a partially depressed state owing to incomplete dehypnotization, the practitioner might be involved in legal complications. This is also the case with an ambulatory patient after the administration of a general anesthetic. It is wise to observe every patient for a short time and to converse with him before dismissing him to ascertain his complete recovery from the hypnotic state. This precaution is necessary only when a patient has been in a very deep state.

OPERATIVE HYPNODONTICS

The management of the operative dental technics after a patient is in a hypnotic state is known as *operative hypnodontics*. Through trial, error and experimentation, a method of managing the patient has been established.

The following is the procedure which the author has developed and applied to hundreds of cases over the past several years:

Maintenance of Hypnotic Level: After inducting the patient and testing for depth, always end by assuring him that he will not awaken from the hypnotic state until you dehypnotize him. This will require several strong hypnotic suggestions such as, "You will remain deeply relaxed until I 'awaken' you. Nothing, absolutely nothing, will awaken you until I do!" This is the first step before attempting any work in the mouth.

Approach to Treatment in the Mouth: Sometimes, despite the above precaution, when the patient is asked to open his mouth, he may come out of hypnosis. Therefore, this second step is always applied with the following verbalization: "With eyes closed and without 'awakening,' open your mouth . . . wider!" Then massage the jaw muscles lightly on the outside of the face and continue, "Your jaw is becoming stiff, like a vise. It is now so stiff that you cannot close your mouth. You may try, *but you will find it impossible*. Stop trying! Deep, deep asleep. Your mouth will remain open until I tell you otherwise."

This step, known as muscle catalepsy, is taken not only to ensure an open mouth throughout the entire operation but also to act as a test in determining the depth of hypnosis; and, finally, to deepen the hypnotic state. Whenever a test in the technics of hypnotic induction is made successfully, the suggestion of deep, deep "asleep" tends to deepen the hypnosis.

Production of Anesthesia: One should never assume that anesthesia is present, even though a patient may be in deep hypnosis. Always include this step to produce anesthesia first; then test before operating. The procedure is to take hold of the tooth to be treated between the index finger and the thumb, rocking it and at the same time depressing it in the socket, gently at first but gradually more firmly. While doing this, say: "As I press down on this tooth, you will find that it is getting numb and losing all its feeling. It is beginning to feel as though you've had an injection. You feel a tingling sensation . . . cold and numb . . . etc." Then test for anesthesia.

Test for Anesthesia: Take a sharp explorer and gently press into the gingival area around the tooth, saying, "I am pricking your gum with this point, but, you see, you feel absolutely no discomfort." Stop, and say, "I shall do the same to the other side of your mouth, but you will feel a sharp pain there." Then prick the gingival tissues on the normal side very lightly. Almost always, the patient will react with a sudden start. Now go back to the first side and indicate the difference to the patient. If there is any doubt in the operator's mind, either the hypnosis should be deepened and the above words repeated, or the patient should be given procaine and further tests should be made.

Operative Procedure: The author always applies the following rules:

1. Never operate without an assistant.

2. Never attempt too much during the first visit.

3. Advise the patient to keep his eyes closed throughout the entire operation.

4. Keep the patient passive and do not disturb him by requesting that he spit or bend over. This can be avoided by the constant use of an aspirator by the assistant. The patient should be treated as though he were in a state of general anesthesia.

5. Never overheat the tooth. Work slowly and have a constant stream of water running on the tooth from any of the special water-cooling attachments on the market.

6. Complete the entire operation, including restoration, while the patient is in hypnosis. This is important because, in this way, it is possible to produce complete amnesia

for the operative procedure and to avoid focusing of the normal waking attention on the operation in the posthypnotic period. Thus, it is necessary to place the matrix band, the wedges, and the restoration, and to remove the excess and carve the restoration while the patient is still in a hypnotic state.

Termination of Hypnosis: When terminating the hypnosis, always give the following posthypnotic suggestions:

1. There will be no recollection of any pain or discomfort.

2. If the patient is in a somnambulistic state, complete amnesia for the entire period of hypnosis may be suggested successfully. There are some who feel that amnesia is not desirable. The author often finds it useful.

3. The patient will feel normal, cheerful and happy when he is dehypnotized.

4. He will enter hypnosis quickly and deeply each time in the future that it is suggested to him, providing, of course, that it is in accord with his wishes to be induced.

5. He will have no fear or anxiety about dental treatment at subsequent visits. Any other therapeutic suggestions might be given at this time.

After dehypnotization of a patient, never question him about discomfort. Always assume that it was diminished. Do not press a patient to exceed his threshold of response. Inform him of what you have done as though he knows nothing about it. Assure him that the procedure was entirely successful, as planned, and that he will do even better next time.

The author would like to emphasize that the above is a sketchy outline of the technic used. Certain factors had to be omitted, such as the importance of the attitude of the dentist as a determinant of success or failure; the practice of running a continuous commentary throughout the operative procedure to maintain a constant hypnotic depth and to prevent the patient from coming out of it; and the occasional need to stop treatment to deepen the hypnosis if signs of spontaneous dehypnotization appear. These and many other details must be excluded because of the necessary brevity of this chapter, but they are discussed elsewhere in this book.

PEDIADONTICS

Hypnosis is particularly indicated in the control and the management of emotionally disturbed children who require dental work. The author, who specializes in dentistry for the emotionally disturbed and handicapped, has various means of coping with this class of patients. Among the technics in his armamentarium are all forms of drugs, such as local and general anesthetics, sedatives, tranquilizers, analgesics, etc. But hypnosis is always used as an attempt to eliminate or lessen the amounts used. In some instances, it is possible to avoid the use of general anesthesia in cases which had been scheduled for it.

DISADVANTAGES OF HYPNODONTICS

From the foregoing, it would appear that there is only good associated with the use of hypnosis in dentistry. Unfortunately, this is not the case. A disadvantage in using hypnosis is the time consumed in conditioning a patient. However, this can be obviated by group training (see Chapter 33). Busy dentists may find it impractical and undesirable to spend the required time on individual patients, in view of the uncertainty involved. Many practitioners also feel that the training and experience required for a high percentage of success is an obstacle. Insofar as time is concerned, it must be pointed out that reinduction of hypnosis is only a matter of a few seconds or a few minutes, when proper posthypnotic suggestions to this effect have been given. There are times when a psychologist trained in hypnosis or a hypnodontic specialist may be called upon to condition a patient, either at his own office or at that of the dentist. Rapport can then be transferred to the dentist. There are more skilled psychologists capable of such work today than at any time in the past, owing to the growing use of and interest in hypnosis in fields other than dentistry.

ADVANTAGES OF HYPNODONTICS

Against the above disadvantages, there are a number of advantages which have been discussed throughout the text. Hypnosis is extremely useful in the relaxation of nervous and excitable patients, eliminating fear and tension, making long, arduous sittings more tolerable. The well-conditioned patient approaches the dental appointments with pleasant anticipation instead of dread and anxiety. There is a definite enhancement in the prestige of the hypnodontist because of his added interest, skill and ability. It is the usual experience of hypnodontists that new patients seek appointments and request hypnosis when word-of-mouth information is spread by patients who have experienced hypnotic treatment. Many dentists, including the author, have found that with some patients it becomes unnecessary to continue the use of hypnosis after the initial sessions have overcome the fear and anxiety.

Although less than 10 years ago a dentist had to be a courageous pioneer in using hypnosis, this is not the case today. The company in which he travels, of those using hypnosis in disciplines other than dentistry, is quite dignified and substantial. The Boards in Hypnosis consist of 3 separate entities, of which the American Board of Dental Hypnosis is one. The others are in Medicine and Psychology. The fact that hypnosis is taught in at least a dozen dental colleges speaks for itself. It is hoped that those reading this chapter will view sympathetically the possibilities and the potentials of the use and the application of hypnodontics.

CONCLUSIONS

1. The average dentist is capable of learning the technics of hypnodontics.

2. It is completely harmless in every way and from every point of view *when used by a dentist for dental purposes.*

3. There is no possibility of emotional or psychological trauma if no experimentation in psychiatric therapy is attempted. Stay within the limitations of dentistry. Do not attempt to practice psychiatry!

4. Susceptibility to hypnosis is not related to intelligence or to strong- or weak-mindedness.

5. It is a practice-builder, as it enhances the prestige of the dentist.

6. At present, it is relatively widely accepted by the medical, the dental and the psychiatric professions, as compared with only 10 or 15 years ago.

7. There is a deep personal satisfaction in being able to render such a useful service to the patient.

8. Failures cannot be avoided, but practical experience, together with adequate postgraduate instruction, will minimize the incidence of failures.

REFERENCES

1. Cherry, H., and Pollin, I. M.: Music as a supplement in dental anesthesia, Dental Digest *10*:455, 1948.
2. Conklin, Edmond S.: Principles of Abnormal Psychology, New York, Holt, 1936.
3. Furneaux, W. D.: Experimental Hypnosis, New York, Macmillan, 1952.
4. Mintz, V. W.: The use of suggestive aids in denture gaggers, Dent. Survey *27*:653, 1952.
5. Moss, A. A.: Elimination of gagging by waking hypnotic suggestion, Dent. Survey *26*:1958.
6. ——: Hypnodontics, or Hypnosis in Dentistry, Brooklyn, N. Y., Dental Items of Interest Publishing Co., 1952.
7. Raginsky, B. B.: Mental suggestion as an aid to anesthesia, J. Anesthesiology, p. 467, Sept., 1948.

SUPPLEMENTARY READING

Horland, L. R., and Epstein, S.: Psychological evaluation of hypnosis in dentistry, J. Am. Dent. Ass. 62:54-65, 1961.
Secter, I. I.: The psychologically oriented dentist, Am. J. Clin. Hypnosis 2:1-3, 1959.
Shaw, S. I.: Failures in the use of hypnosis applied to dentistry, Internat. J. Clin. Exper. Hypnosis 10:43-59, 1962.
——: Survey of the management of children in hypnodontia, Am. J. Clin. Hypnosis 1:155-163, 1959.
Staples, L. M.: A psychological approach through hypnosis to certain psychosomatic problems in dentistry and medicine, Am. J. Clin. Hypnosis 2:116-122, 1960.
Stolzenberg, J.: Psychosomatics and Suggestion Therapy in Dentistry, New York Philosophical Library, 1950.

44

Miscellaneous Indications for Hypnosis

HYPNOSIS IN ELECTROCONVULSIVE AND NONCONVULSIVE THERAPY

Posthypnotic suggestions have been used to decrease apprehension in patients undergoing nonconvulsive[26] and electroconvulsive shock therapy (E.C.T.).[15] However, most psychotics are difficult to hypnotize, especially if in a manic phase. There is also a report of a disturbed patient treated successfully by simulated or "as-if" electroshock therapy under hypnosis.[19]

Hypnosis reputedly has helped to recover the loss of memory commonly noted after E.C.T. The few cases, however, in which the author of this book attempted restoration of important memory gaps were not benefited by hypnotic age-regression or revivification. Apparently, damage of the association pathways is irreversible. Bowers and Beckowitz[2] contend, however, that if hypnosis was administered preceding E.C.T. some of its disturbing effects could be mitigated.

IMPROVEMENT IN LEARNING AND PERCEPTION

Recent data indicate that both hypnotic and posthypnotic suggestions[11] improve various task performances, whereas, by comparison, waking suggestion is unsatisfactory.[18, 27] Time distortion often facilitates recall in highly motivated persons.[5, 6] Those investigators[10, 24] who disagree with these findings, unfortunately, did not use time distortion, and *studied only the permanence of learning* —not its immediate effects. Another report[23] indicated that learning was increased in a group of students given special remedial learning sessions under hypnosis. All had tried the more conventional methods without success.

Posthypnotic suggestions directed to more favorable attitudes and moods facilitated problem-solving behavior.[7, 9] Thus, favorable results can be expected when there is good motivation, hypnotic rapport and time distortion. The degree of meaningfulness of the learned material is an important variable.[29]

These methods have been particularly suitable for actors and actresses, musicians and students, as the following case reports show:

Two medical students with C averages were trained to concentrate better through hypnosis. Both were in danger of "flunking." Within 6 months, each was a B-average student. The depth of hypnosis could not be correlated with the increment in learning.

A male voice student, aged 35, was treated by hypnosis to facilitate the learning process because he was beginning his singing studies at a relatively advanced age. Within 6 months, his voice coach reported that he had learned what ordinarily would have taken 2 years. Autohypnosis, sensory-imagery conditioning and time distortion were employed. Also, tape recordings, made by the author, were used in the pre-sleep period to reinforce the posthypnotic suggestions. At present, he is completing his career abroad. The author has made several other tape recordings from time to time, which were necessitated by the subject's advanced studies.

A famous singer always developed "mike fright" and usually required from 6 to 10 retakes when she recorded an album. Using the same technics described above, she sang beautifully *without a single mistake* on her first attempt. According to her severest critics, she performed better than at any other time in her entire career. Posthypnotic suggestions to really "live the song" and allay nervousness were important factors. Also, she was cued to enter hypnosis over the telephone. Several months later, she was hypnotized over the long distance telephone to allay her opening night nervousness, and gave a very successful performance. This has been done for other prominent performers.

A well-known stage and screen star, who was an alcoholic and very undependable, always had trouble remembering his "lines." Concurrently, while being treated for his alcoholism, he memorized an *entire script after it was read to him while he was in a somnambulistic state in a single 3-hour session.* Once, when he was regressed to the age of 5, he spoke in a foreign language. Upon dehypnotization, he emphatically stated that he had forgotten his native tongue as he had emigrated to America when he was 6 years old. Although he never overcame his drinking, he gave many sterling film and stage performances and never again had trouble remembering his roles.

An actress had to learn a difficult role in 3 days. She was the star of a stage play and carried the bulk of the dialogue. She, too, was trained in autohypnosis, time distortion and sensory-imagery conditioning. Suggestions were given that one hour of action dialogue, as measured by the clock, would be condensed into 5 minutes of subjective time. In other words, one hour of the play would be "seen" and "heard" in her mind's "eye" and "ear," respectively, in one twelfth of the actual time. In this way, she could have 12 "dry runs" or rehearsals for every hour that she spent rehearsing under hypnosis. According to the reviews, she gave one of the most magnificent performances ever seen on the American stage, and she received worldwide acclaim not only for her marvelous performance but also for the means through which it was accomplished!

The author has a large clientele of motion-picture, television and other performers. He has utilized the technics described above for concert violinists, pianists and even writers who just "went stale." Rachmaninoff, who had been unproductive for several years, reportedly composed one of his famous concertos following posthypnotic suggestion.

Recently, the author saw one of his former students and his wife at a medical meeting. The wife had always been unable to speak in public, and the author was asked to hypnotize her for her handicap. As the result of *one session,* she became an excellent speaker and today is president of the women's auxiliary of her husband's state medical association.

These are only a few of many interesting cases. It is the author's impression that this increase in performance occurs not only because of attitudinal changes but also because the inhibitory factors are reduced. The reader must not infer that all subjects respond as well as those just described; failures do occur. It may be that the confidence and enthusiasm of the operator and the creation of a proper mental-set were the responsible factors. Nevertheless, from an objective viewpoint, most patients were pleased with their increased self-confidence and greater ability to concentrate and learn.

PERCEPTION DURING ANESTHESIA

Cheek[4] contends that much of what is said during surgery can later be recalled by age-regression technics. Ideomotor signaling was employed under hypnosis to give "yes" or "no" answers as to the validity of the supposedly "heard" conversation. He admits that recollection of the operating-room experiences may have been colored by what one imagines goes on during surgery, or that the productions may have been an attempt to please the formulations of the investigator. However, the material obtained under hypnosis, when compared with the data obtained by a tape recorder set up in the operating room, showed some startling similarities.

Cheek's experiments were not rigidly controlled as to the depth of anesthesia and the evocation of irrelevant conversation. It is only natural to assume that "meaningful" data pertinent to the type of surgery readily could be fabricated by intelligent patients. "Talking to the subconscious," developed on the basis of ideomotor responses, is also open to question.[30]

Another one of Cheek's findings that should be explored is the distinct possibility of engrafting constructive posthypnotic suggestions on surgical and obstetrical patients who are coming out of anesthesia. During a light plane of anesthesia the sensory input channels are open and, where criticalness is reduced, constructive "programming" can be achieved. If Cheek's contentions are validated, all personnel must be careful about what is said and done in the operating room.

Another interesting speculation adduced by Cheek is that confidence can be instilled during anesthesia to improve the outlook for hopeless cancer patients. Suggestions inspiring faith and confidence are certainly helpful at all levels of awareness. However, in attributing all sorts of benefits to hypnosis, we must not, as serious-minded scientists, allow our enthusiasm to claim that hypnosis is going to solve all the ills and tribulations of mankind. However, the modern physician, with emphasis on pharmacologic therapies, laboratory investigations and physical modalities, has grossly underestimated the "power of the mind." Figuratively, "faith can move mountains" and should not be neglected!

HYPNOSIS IN RADIOLOGY*

Radiologists report that hypnotic relaxation in selected patients facilitates diagnostic procedures. In gastrointestinal work-ups on tense, anxiety-ridden patients, pathology often may be observed by bowel spasm, flatus, extreme alterations in motility, delayed or rapid emptying time, forceful evacuation of the barium enema, eructations and vomiting of the barium meal, esophageal spasm and aerophagia.

During fluoroscopy, reassuring suggestions improve patient co-operation. The following suggestions are even more effective when given under hypnosis: "Let your arms drop limply to your sides. Lean forward. Allow your chin to touch the front of your chest. Relax your abdomen and stick it out as far as you can. Now take a deep breath. Loosen up all over." Some apprehensive patients undergoing fluoroscopy are frightened by the darkness, the awesome sounds and the lights; therefore, any degree of physical and mental relaxation is worthwhile. All such patients should be hypnotized beforehand as it is virtually impossible to do it during the examination, especially if they are uncomfortable from the barium or have the desire to expel it. Hence, to ensure optimal relaxation, hypnotic conditioning must be established before fluoroscopy is performed.

Edel states:

During the initial interview, even if I am familiar with the symptoms, I have him discuss

* I am indebted to Dr. J. W. Edel, Baltimore, Md., for most of the material in this section.

his present complaints and past history for the psychotherapeutic value. By evincing further interest, better rapport is established. I try to evaluate his present emotional status. If he appears tense, I ask if he is apprehensive about the examination. I always stress the importance of relaxation during the examination and ascertain if he would like to learn hypnorelaxation. If "yes," I then proceed with hypnotic induction and conditioning, stressing the advantages of relaxation. If induction fails, an antispasmodic and sedative are prescribed just before the next examination. This relaxes the patient so that hypnosis is readily induced just prior to the examination.

The technic for the initial induction depends on a number of factors; it should be informal, and one that effectively employs a posthypnotic suggestion for rapid reinduction. The shoulder cue is readily reproducible and easily remembered. Technics which involve sensory-imagery conditioning are the best for controlling involuntary functioning of the viscera. In accordance with the law of dominant effect, one must have the subject revivify a relaxing episode that actually happened. Therefore, specific suggestions for gastrointestinal relaxation will not work unless previous associational reflexes have been reactivated. Relaxation through autohypnosis is even more effective. Well-trained patients can enter a very satisfactory state of autohypnosis in a matter of seconds during the roentgenographic examination.

Edel states:

The use of more complex hypnotic technics as revivification and age-regression depends on the discretion and training of the radiologist. This also depends on the evaluation of the personality and the relationship. If one feels insecure in the use of hypnosis and if one constantly seems to accentuate and amplify its dangers rather than its potentialities, it would be wise to resolve this insecurity before one proceeds further.

Those who continually bleat about the dangers of hypnosis might heed these wise words.

In properly conditioned patients, the characteristic patterns of gastrointestinal functioning can be observed during fluoroscopy. If the diagnosis is evident, no further procedures are necessary. When in doubt, the cue for hypnotic induction can be given, and, in the vast majority of cases, immediate relaxation of bowel spasm and diminution of intestinal peristalsis occurs. During deep hypnosis, there is almost complete cessation of peristaltic activity, and all manifestations of spasm disappear. The gastrointestinal relaxation permits the examination to be made in half the time, and with less chance that hidden lesions might be overlooked. Hazards due to repeated examinations are obviated and there is no loss of prestige. During a barium enema examination, a patient who formerly squirmed, groaned and evacuated on the table, experiences minimal discomfort when hypnotized. The patient should be dehypnotized slowly after the examination, and given the usual suggestions of well-being.

Other conditions in which the roentgenographic diagnosis can be facilitated by hypnotic relaxation are:

Respiratory
1. Bronchography, whether by bronchoscopy, tracheal catheterization or drip method
2. Diagnostic pneumothorax
3. Antral puncture and oil contrast studies

Cardiovascular
1. Arteriography
2. Cardiac catheterization
3. Angiocardiography
4. Retrograde thoracic aortography

Gastrointestinal
1. G. I. series
2. Esophagus, stomach and duodenum
3. Barium enema

Genitourinary
1. Retrograde urography
2. Intravenous urography
3. Rubin's test and other patency tests
4. Hysterogram and pneumoperitoneum

Neurologic
1. Pneumoencephalography
2. Ventriculography
3. Cerebral angiography
4. Myelography
5. Diskography

In these specialized examinations, hypnosis is used for anesthesia, analgesia, and relief of tension, anxiety and fear. Psychogenic and allergic reactions secondary to injections can be controlled by hypnosis and drugs. During intravenous urography, the hypnotized patient is much more at ease and does not

mind being strapped to the table with a pressure bag for from 1 to 2 hours. There is a better concentration of dye, less gas to obscure film detail and, when hypnotic induction precedes injection, the reactions are minimal.

Heyer[12] investigated digestive disturbances in women by means of hypnosis. He observed gastrointestinal functioning at hypnotic and nonhypnotic levels. He remarks: "Most impressive were the disturbances in passage of the meal in patients who had in addition to their psychogenic disturbances organic complications such as adhesions."

Kroger and Freed[14] noted that irritability of the reproductive tract is a manifestation of autonomic disharmony and is the commonest cause for the erroneous diagnosis of tubal occlusion made by the radiologist. However, spasm at the uterotubal or the isthmotubal portion of the fallopian tubes, which often is not relieved by sedation, can be relaxed during tubal insufflation in tense and anxious individuals by hypnosis; this can obviate mistaken diagnoses.

Hypnosis reduces the side-reactions associated with radiation sickness, and can decrease the pain of carcinoma in selected patients. Radiologists trained in hypnosis can prepare such patients in groups. As more radiologists employ hypnosis for diagnostic procedures and report their results, it is certain that Edel's and Heyer's observations will be confirmed.

HYPNOSIS IN GERIATRICS

Posthypnotic suggestions, in responsive persons, can effectively raise the aged patient's confidence and help direct thoughts from himself to external events; this can minimize depressive reactions and hypochondriasis. The suggestions also can help establish closer interpersonal relationships; many are quarrelsome, hostile over their infirmities and envious of younger and more agile persons.

Definitive suggestions potentiated by hypnosis can be directed to: (1) taking an interest in the plans of younger persons (in this way the tragedy associated with the loss of friends or a mate is reduced); (2) developing avocational interests concerned with creativity, the acquisition of special motor skills, cultural activities; (3) exercise, as walking, as much as possible; (4) watching the diet and the weight; (5) correcting elimination; (6) overcoming insomnia; and (7) physical involvements, as cardiac congestion, arthritis and neuromuscular involvements.

HYPNOSIS IN SPORTS

The commonest artificial method for increasing athletic performance is using the amphetamines; side-effects often contraindicate their use. All methods of evoking an athlete's highest potential have been under fire, and even hypnosis has now been considered dangerous and unsportsmanlike.

Hypnosis and suggestion, in one form or another, have been used to motivate athletes for many years, and there is not a shred of adequately controlled evidence to indicate that they ever did any harm. The author once heard Knute Rockne, the great Notre Dame coach, "hypnotize" his team between halves when they were behind. The powerful effect of his exhortations and personal magnetism were such that the team literally swarmed over its opponents to win. It was an excellent example of group hypnosis similar to the type used by spell-binders and evangelists.

The author has used hypnosis for improving the ability of a considerable number of athletes competing in baseball, football, pugilism and golf, without deleterious effects. The results ranged from good to spectacular.

One patient was a professional baseball player who had been severely "beaned." He became "plate shy" and changed his batting stance so that he always had "one foot in the bucket" in order to back away more quickly. He was given a posthypnotic suggestion that the possibility that such an event would happen again was exceedingly remote. Through sensory-imagery conditioning, he was to re-imagine the extreme confidence with which he formerly strode to the plate. As soon as this "subconscious feel" was impressed strongly in his mind, his batting average quickly returned to normal.

A leading professional golfer was referred to the author for hypnorelaxation to improve his putting, especially during tournament play, when large crowds around the green caused him to become so nervous that his booming long drives and approaches were nullified by his miserable putting. He was taught self-hypnosis and sensory-imagery conditioning and within 4 sessions was able readily to enter a somnambulistic state. It was suggested that he could become completely oblivious to spectators any time he wished, and that, furthermore, he would "see" a dotted line between his ball and the cup. As further insurance of success, he was to suggest that the cup would appear from 2 to 3 times its normal size. He was also given suggestions that his self-confidence would not be shaken when he made a bad shot. Rather, he would imagine every stroke successful before it was played! To do this, he would "feel" the impact of the club and "see" the flight of the ball as if he had actually hit it.*

Although this golfer normally hit a long ball, it was suggested that he would have unusual driving power. Through this conditioning, both his putting and his driving improved greatly. A short time later he tied the course record in the National Open and missed winning only because of one bad hole when his ball hit a spectator and caromed into a trap. Several months later, he won a coveted championship. He attributed a good measure of his success to the hypnotic conditioning.

The daily press contains examples of basketball players who have scored a phenomenal number of points after hypnotic conditioning, boxers who have become veritable champions, and trackmen who have far surpassed their best previous records. The fact recently has been proved again by Ikai, who conclusively demonstrated that there is no danger of an athlete's going beyond his physiologic limit, and that all improved performances are a result of removing inhibitions (disinhibition) which psychologically limit performances. The built-in or involuntary reflexes protect the individual against danger at all levels of awareness.

Yogis have been performing prodigious feats for centuries, and their psychological attitudes are conditioned by years of concentration. Hypnosis under any other name is still hypnosis.

One of the author's close personal friends is a former track star who, in college, participated unknowingly in experiments conducted by the

* Two recent popular books, *How You Can Play Better Golf Using Self-Hypnosis* and *How You Can Bowl Better Using Self-Hypnosis*, by Jack Heise, Wilshire Book Co., Los Angeles, describe other excellent technics.

psychology department of the University of Illinois. As a quarter miler, he customarily ran just slightly faster than a teammate who was given a placebo pill and told that he would beat my friend that day. Beat him he did, and my friend recalls that he was really beaten from the time that his teammate took the pill. The following week my friend was given a pill and broke the Big Ten record, while the man who had beaten him the week before, minus his pill, finished exhausted and sick.

Suggestion? Hypnosis? Just one thing is certain: The cause of victory was the elimination of inhibiting psychological factors. There was nothing physiologic in the process.

In conclusion, it should be stated that, always deferring to further research, there is no reason why a competent hypnotherapist should not use his skill in helping an athlete to eliminate detracting psychological factors which prevent him from operating at his highest efficiency. There are no indications that he will drop dead in the stretch, at least not from the effects of hypnosis.

HYPNOSIS IN SPACE TRAVEL

Physicians and psychologists are being called upon to utilize their knowledge in the rapidly expanding experimentation to make safe man's flight into space. Hypnosis is a neglected (so far as is known) but potentially useful tool for learning more about man's ability to survive and function efficiently in space. For instance, in the interest of realism, hypnosis may be used to convince the space candidate that he is undergoing an actual, rather than a simulated, test.

Hypnotic relaxation can be utilized to reduce the metabolic rate and the oxygen consumption. Hypnosis would be of inestimable value in helping spacemen to maintain uncomfortable positions for long intervals. These conditions might be intolerable under normal circumstances. Hindu fakirs who allow themselves to be buried in a sealed coffin for several hours actually do so under autohypnosis. Since the number of cubic feet of air in the casket is known, the slowing down of respiration to 5 or 10 per minute enables the individual to remain underground for what seems to be an incredible period of time. Thus, suggestions of calmness and drowsiness slow down metabolic and oxygen requirements as well as digestive processes. The maintenance of "unbearable" positions under hypnosis was described in the section on plastic surgery. Also, it is known that hypnotic subjects can submit to tremendous amounts of physical stress without apparent reactions.

The nonspecific and the specific stress induced by weightlessness, cramped quarters, unnatural living conditions, and other psychophysiologic factors encountered by the first space travelers can be reduced. At least, their adaptive responses can be raised through conditioning under hypnosis.

Another potent tool to overcome boredom is the use of time condensation to speed up time. Although drugs can be employed for nearly all the above-mentioned purposes, subjects under their influence cannot awaken completely and respond or perform as effectively as they can under hypnosis. Well-trained subjects can be conditioned to enter into relaxed states for any desired period upon a designated signal. They also could be rapidly dehypnotized with a different signal.

These are only a few of the uses of hypnosis which can aid in testing space survival. The illusions of reality, the alteration of physiologic functioning, and other phenomena associated with hypnosis may play an important role in interplanetary travel. This author has acted in the capacity of consultant for these and other matters pertaining to utilization of hypnosis for space medicine. Halleck McCord, in a personal communication, has indicated his interest in the research possibilities of hypnosis in these areas.

HOMOSEXUALITY

Homosexuality is a neurosis that begins early in life. This subject has been reviewed by Dr. Bergler and myself.[1a] The hypnotic treatment of female homosexuality has been described by the author and Dr. Freed.[14] It is important to determine whether or not a feeling of guilt is present and if the patient really desires therapy. The homosexual has never emerged from the undifferentiated period of adolescence. It is surprising how few homosexuals desire to change. There are two main types—the passive-feminine and the active-aggressive. Also, there are mixed types, as well as borderline cases who are bisexual. Every individual has latent homosexual tendencies which are more or less repressed and can be activated under conducive circumstances.

There are many reports on the use of hypnosis in the treatment of homosexuality. Gilbert[8] noted that the active-aggressive (male partner) was resistant to therapy. The degree of success depends not only on the motivation but also on the type of technic employed. An authoritarian approach is apt to be more successful with the passive-feminine type of homosexual, while a permissive approach is more effective with the active-aggressive type. Therefore, before instituting hypnotherapy or any other reconstructive therapy, the physician must ascertain the type and the degree of homosexual involvement. Some authors[20, 21] contend that latent homosexuality decreases susceptibility to hypnosis. This has also been the author's experience. It may be that those who have only a dim awareness of their homosexual tendencies will deny or resist recognizing the need for correcting these elements of their personalities.

Unfortunately, those who evince a strong desire to change usually have deep-seated needs which prevent them from making heterosexual adjustments. Even though this type is readily hypnotizable, few permanently recover. Some make a temporary adjustment but quickly relapse.

Since homosexuality is a manifestation of a deep-seated conflict, it should not be treated except by a psychiatrically oriented therapist. Homosexuals who are able to function adequately in their life situations without symptoms often are better off if they are not treated. For those malcontents who are continually involving themselves with the law, psychotherapy is indicated, rather than punishment.

The author has used a permissive hypnotherapeutic approach on selected homosexuals. However, rapid results are not obtained, as a considerable amount of time is necessary for psychobiologic reorganization of the personality. Usually a minimum of one year is required for any type of therapy. As the patient begins to show improvement, the sessions are further apart so that he can test

his ability to face his problems and decide whether he really wishes to adjust. The goal of all psychotherapy in homosexuality is to establish maturation of the personality and enable successful adjustment to the opposite sex to take place. Posthypnotic suggestions to have intercourse with females are never successful.

The results depend on the therapist's ability to relieve guilt, anxiety and tensions and to guide the patient toward a mature orientation. The strong dependency created by the hypnotic relationship is advantageous and is deliberately fostered in order to keep the patient in therapy during the initial phases when resistances to change are marked. Later, the utilization of autohypnosis and sensory-imagery conditioning enables the patient to develop fantasies which ultimately will attract him to the opposite sex. By the time he makes the transition to the opposite sex, he is ready to be "weaned off" the therapist. The reasons for the dependency are made clear to him. Often it is the desire to please the therapist that enhances the motivation of the patient. One must continually bear in mind that a "flight into health" can and does occur with this approach; the homosexual has a flurry of heterosexual affairs but ultimately reverts to his previous patterns. Reinforcement hypnotic suggestions should be given at monthly intervals after the patient has been discharged from regular hypnotherapy.

MULTIPLE PERSONALITY

Dual and multiple personalities have been described from the earliest recorded history until modern times. They undoubtedly occur more frequently than is commonly supposed. Multiple personality must be distinguished from dissociation due to hypnosis, schizophrenia, hysteria, mediumistic trances and simulation by spiritualists. Often multiple personalities are spontaneously or deliberately brought out by hypnosis.[22] The induced personality then functions as the representative of the repressed facets of the individual's primary personality.

In true multiple personality, the other personalities usually have no knowledge of each other's existence: they are repressed from awareness. However, during hypnosis one or more of the personalities may have a complete or a fragmentary knowledge of the memories of the others, and the primary personality may interact with the repressed ones.

The production of multiple personalities by hypnosis has been discussed.[28] Studies indicate that the induced personality takes on many of the characteristics of the subject's overt personality, as well as the ones hidden from awareness. Recently a case of multiple personality which appeared to be bound up by a severely obsessive-compulsive defense, so that the "conscious personality" was constricted, rigid and cold, was reported.[3] The Rorschach responses revealed that one of the personalities was schizophrenic. It was felt that studies of this type might be helpful in understanding psychotic development.

TREATMENT

Often, trauma may be an etiologic factor, as in Prince's famous case of Miss Beauchamp, who had 5 personalities.[17] Therapy should ascertain the reasons for the dissociation. Integrating the various personalities into one is the goal of all successful therapy. Hypnosis speeds up this reintegration, and the secondary personality or personalities usually can readily be "directed" toward this end. Fortunately, most individuals with multiple personalities are good hypnotic subjects, but the therapy can be difficult in the absence of good rapport with all the hidden personalities.

Odencrants[16] noted that one of the first indications is lapses of consciousness, which often cause confusion and concern to those around them. After hypnotherapy is initiated, the various personalities, be they one or more, must be identified. They may reveal themselves automatically, voluntarily, through automatic writing and by posthypnotic suggestion. The record is held by a patient who displayed, at one time or another, 23 different personalities.[17]

Through hypnotic amnesia, the relationship of the various personalities to each other can be understood readily. The hypnotherapist should maintain an interested and sympathetic attitude with the various personalities at all times, or he may lose contact with them. Furthermore, he must not be impatient or surprised, as often the personalities which emerge may be wholly contrary to the patient's primary personality; petulance, immaturity and sadistic tendencies make their unexpected appearance.

Through hypnosis, any one of the personalities which the therapist wishes to study can be summoned, and invariably the personality will reveal its name. From then on, it is really remarkable how quickly the various personalities can be made to appear and disappear. A recent book, *Three Faces of Eve*,[25] described how very dramatic situations arose as the patient switched from one personality to another. At times, one personality will be amazingly well developed mentally, and at other times, childlike. Each of the personalities should be evaluated for simulation; chronologic time orientation may show considerable disparity. The therapist must be able to recognize the religious fanatics; they usually represent some departed soul and might be categorized as pseudo multiple personalities.

HYPNOSIS IN CRIMINOLOGY

Hypnosis has been used extensively in the solving of crimes and in criminology.[1] It can help eye-witnesses recall details of a crime. For instance, after a staged "crime," the men recalled few details, but they gave fuller accounts after being hypnotized. When hypnotized again, they were able to write detailed reports as to the "killer's" weapon, hair style and clothes.

The author of this book recently was asked to help solve a crime wherein a policeman was shot by burglars who escaped after being apprehended. As they sped away in their car, the policeman caught a glimpse of the license number but promptly forgot it because he was in shock. Several months later he was hypnotized and, through revivification, he was able to recall all the numbers on the license and to give an accurate description of the men. Although the automobile was found, the men are still at large. However, the authorities have an excellent description of them.

Confessions can be obtained under hypnosis, but few courts have recognized these as evidence. It must be remembered, however, that an individual can lie just as glibly under hypnosis as he would under ordinary circumstances. Estabrooks[7b] has also written on the use of hypnotism in the detection of crime, particularly in stimulating recall of long since forgotten information. An interesting possibility is building up an informer service among trained subjects who have been criminals or who are willing to act as stool pigeons. If the subject were a somnambulist, he would have no knowledge that he had been given a posthypnotic suggestion to "keep his ear to the ground." Authorities could plant such individuals in strategic places.

Hypnotic technics might be useful in the detection of crime, and interrogators might add these methods to the ones already in use.[11a] It is interesting that another authority specifically points out that hypnosis could not be an important factor in the production of crime.[11a]

Orne,[16a] in an exhaustive treatise on the utility of hypnosis in interrogation procedures, believes that it is doubtful if hypnosis can be induced in resistant subjects. He, too, questions the accuracy of information obtained during hypnosis as the subject can easily distort ideas, despite hypnotic suggestions to the contrary. He found that hypnosis was not a useful defense against interrogation. Rather, appropriate instructions and autogenic training might be helpful.

He makes the distinction between hypnosis per se, and the hypnotic situation. The latter could be used, as mentioned, quite effectively for interrogation purposes. The common belief that an individual in hypnosis is not responsible for his actions, though probably incorrect, could be exploited. The hypnotic situation, by relieving the subject of responsibility for his actions, alleviates guilt and thus allows the prisoner to divulge information which he might not otherwise yield.

Methods by which such a situation could be exploited, according to Orne, are the use of drugs, the use of a "magic room" (filled with instruments to detect lying), and various psychological measures such as a reward. Other investigators are using remote sensing devices capable of noting subtle changes in psychological functioning. By such measures they can tell whether or not a subject is telling the truth.

HYPNOSIS IN MILITARY MEDICAL PRACTICE

Hypnosis has been found to be of considerable value in the military setting. Its use in the treatment of acute traumatic neuroses in World Wars I and II has been well documented. Todorovic[26a] has reviewed some of the indications in military medical practice. Some of these are the treatment of burns, injuries, mass hysteria and other problems associated with nuclear warfare. He points out that hypnosis might be life-saving and could decrease suffering where there was an unavailability of medical supplies. It could be used, in those who are amenable, as an analgesic or anesthetic agent, as an adjunct to facilitate the healing of severe burns and, finally, in the treatment of shell shock and combat fatigue. With reference to group hypnotherapy, hypnosis could be used to make up for an acute shortage of psychiatrists.

Hypnosis is assuming an ever-increasing role in the psychological aspects of warfare. For instance, a good subject can be hypnotized to deliver secret information. The memory of this message could be covered by an artificially induced amnesia. In the event that he should be captured, he naturally could not remember that he had ever been given the message. He would not remember the message. However, since he had been given a posthypnotic suggestion, the message would be subject to recall through a specific cue, this having been given to him in the form of a posthypnotic suggestion.

Hypnosis has also been used to extract information from prisoners. The best way is to talk to the subject while he is asleep and, when the conversation is carried out so that the subject will not be awakened by the talking, a great deal of important data can be revealed. Individuals who are lightly asleep can be readily hypnotized. Posthypnotic suggestions can be engrafted to steal faked military plans. The individuals are then allowed to escape. Consequences are obvious as the enemy acts upon this information.

Estabrooks[7a] has an excellent chapter on other areas, such as the interrogation of prisoners, espionage and counterespionage, sabotage and brain washing. The reader interested in this latter area is referred to Sargent's[18a] excellent book, *Battle For the Mind*.

"PORT-OF-LAST-CALL" PATIENT

Hippocrates once stated, ". . . it is impossible to make all the sick well." This maxim applies to many chronic emotionally ill persons. Many of these miserable "traveling case histories" have made the rounds of clinics, physicians and quasi-medical healers—without success—the "port-of-last-call" patient. They constitute a high percentage of this author's practice.

All are desperate for aid and hopeful that the omniscient hypnotherapist can cure them by a "magical gesture." At the risk of raising false hopes, I must state that some respond surprisingly to hypnotherapy. It is admitted that we do not always know how the recovery forces are unleashed. Not infrequently, the dedicated therapist can provide the vital spark necessary to transform an apparently hopeless situation into one of renewed health. Years of suffering, hopeless resignation and even suicide have been forestalled in the "port-of-last-call" patient. Often compassion constitutes competence; wisdom and interest are as effective as drugs.

The "will to get well" and the physician's utilizing his art to his fullest capacity are decisive factors in the alleviation of much misery due to illness. It is here that the hypnotherapist-physician rises to his greatest heights. Because of space limitations, several illustrative cases will only be mentioned; nearly all the pertinent details will have to be omitted.

Several "needle-shy patients," who had a phobia of injections were cured by sensory-imagery conditioning; they imagined the "injections." One had refused surgery for an early carcinoma of the cervix; the hypnotic removal of the symptom was indirectly a life-saving procedure.

Several female patients with restless leg syndrome (Ekbom's syndrome) accompanied by severe insomnia were relieved by symptom-substitution and symptom-transformation. Several males with severe and generalized muscle spasms of unknown origin were helped by glove anesthesia.

Many cases of hysterical blindness, aphonia, amnesias, tics and other conversion reactions responded dramatically to symptom-removal by hypnosis. Some obsessive compulsives, of all types, although more difficult to treat, responded to sensory-imagery conditioning and autohypnosis when conventional therapy had failed.

A 44-year-old Negro male with suicidal tendencies due to incapacitating migraine headaches was cured by autohypnosis, glove anesthesia, ventilation of repressed feelings and an empathic approach. He had consulted over 28 physicians. Follow-up 2 years later revealed that he now was able to function adequately.

A 57-year-old female, potentially psychotic, complained of intractable insomnia. She recovered through depersonalization technics and sensory-imagery conditioning. A normal sleep pattern was established after 4 months of therapy. She, too, was suicidal.

An impotent male recovered through time distortion to give him self-confidence. Posthypnotic suggestions, autohypnosis and sensory-imagery were utilized. A weak personality structure that had been resistant to other psychotherapeutic methods was effectively "shored up."

A potentially suicidal 26-year-old female with severe dyspareunia due to vaginismus was able to save her marriage by autohypnosis, hypnorelaxation and sensory-imagery conditioning. Supportive therapy under hypnosis forestalled a psychotic break.

A 45-year-old female with Raynaud's disease developed sensory changes of warmth in the limbs with hypnotic conditioning and was able to control the symptom.

A 40-year-old female alcoholic who had recently attempted suicide was helped by creating posthypnotic amnesia and engrafting a painful stiffness of her upper lip to determine if she really wished to die. When she complained bitterly of this discomfort at the next session, posthypnotic suggestions that she would be free of the symptom *for at least 10 years* was tantamount to telling her she was going to live for at least that length of time. After many of her problems were worked through by hypnoanalysis, she was able to cope with her difficult life situation.

A 38-year-old paraplegic with bowel and bladder incontinence was improved through sensory-imagery conditioning.

A most unusual case was a 72-year-old blind woman who complained of hundreds of "faceless monsters always coming at me," rather than her loss of eyesight. Posthypnotic suggestions to "allow them to come closer," and at other times "to go further and further away," were given. By manipulating the symptom, she eventually controlled it. As a result, life became more bearable.

These are only a few of the very disturbed individuals helped by "patient-centered hypnotherapy" directed primarily toward symptom-removal. Nearly all can be treated within the framework of any type of supportive psychotherapy.

REFERENCES

1. Barmann, G. J.: Solving crime by hypnosis, Popular Mechanics, April, 1960.
1a. Bergler, E., and Kroger, W. S.: Kinsey's Myth of Female Sexuality, New York, Grune & Stratton, 1953.
2. Bowers, M. K., and Beckowitz, B.: Clinical observations on the effects of electroconvulsive therapy in the hypnotic state, J. Nerv. & Ment. Dis. *118*:355, 1953.
3. Bowers, M., and Brecher, S.: The emergence of multiple personalities in the course of hypnotic investigation, J.C.E.H. *3*:188-199, 1955.
4. Cheek, D. B.: Unconscious perception of meaningful sounds during surgical anesthesia as revealed under hypnosis, Am. J. Clin. Hypnosis *1*:101-113, 1959.
5. Cooper, L. F., and Rodgin, D. W.: Time distortion in hypnosis and non-motor learning, Science *115*:500-502, 1952.
6. Cooper, L. F., and Tuthill, C. H.: Time Distortion in Hypnosis and Motor Learning, J. Psychol. *34*:67-76, 1952.
7. Dickson, J. T.: Effects of hypnotically-induced emotional states, difficulty of task and anxiety on psychomotor behavior, Dissertation Abstracts *15*:149-150, 1955.
7a. Estabrooks, G. H.: Hypnotism, New York, E. P. Dutton & Co., Inc., 1943.
7b. ——: Hypnotism, New York, E. P. Dutton & Co., Inc., 1957.
8. Gilbert, S. F.: Homosexuality and hypnotherapy, Brit. J. M. Hypnotism *5*:2-7, 1954.
9. Glasner, S.: Two experiments in the modification of attitude by the use of hypnotic and waking suggestion, J.C.E.H. *1*:71-75, 1953.
10. Gray, W. H.: The effects of hypnosis on learning to spell, J. Educ. Psychol. *25*: 471-473, 1934.
11. Hammer, E. F.: Post-hypnotic Suggestion and Test Performance, J.C.E.H. *2*:178-185, 1954.
11a. Heron, W. T.: Hypnosis as a factor in the production and detection of crime, Brit. J. M. Hypnotism, vol. 3, No. 3, Spring, 1952.
12. Heyer, G. R.: Psychogene Funktionsstörungen des Verdauungstraktes. *in*: Schwarz, O.: Psychogenese und Psychotherapie körperlicher Symptome, pp. 229-257; bibliography, pp. 464-466, Wien, Springer, 1925.
13. Kirsner, J. B.: The treatment of the "untreatable" patient, Ill. Med. J., pp. 385-400, June, 1960.
14. Kroger, W. S., and Freed, S. C.: Psychosomatic Gynecology Including Problems of Obstetrical Care, p. 284, Chicago, Free Press, 1956; reprinted, Los Angeles, Wilshire Book Co., 1962.
15. Maholick, L. T., and Warkenton, J.: Hypnosis in electric shock treatment, Am. J. Psychiat. *105*:623, 1949.
16. Odencrants, G.: *in* LeCron: Experimental Hypnosis, New York, Macmillan, 1954.
16a. Orne, M. T.: The potential uses of hypnosis in interrogation.
17. Prince, M.: The Dissociation of a Personality, New York, Longmans, 1925.
18. Salzberg, H. C.: The effects of hypnotic, post-hypnotic and waking suggestion on performance using tasks varied in complexity, Internat. J.C.E.H., October, 1960.
18a. Sargent, W.: Battle for the Mind, New York, Doubleday & Co., Inc., 1957.
19. Schafer, D. W.: As-if electroshock therapy by hypnosis, Am. J. Clin. Hypnosis *2*: 225-226, 1960.
20. Schneck, J. M.: Notes on the homosexual component of the hypnotic transference, Brit. J. M. Hypnotism *1*:24, 1950.
21. ——: Some aspects of homosexuality in relation to hypnosis, Psychoanalyt. Rev. *37*: 351, 1950.
22. ——: Hypnosis in Modern Medicine, Springfield, Ill., Thomas, 1959.
23. Sears, A. B.: A comparison of hypnotic and waking learning of the International Morse Code, J.C.E.H. *3*:215-221, 1955.
24. Strickler, C. B.: A quantitative study of posthypnotic amnesia, J. Abnorm. & Social Psychol. *24*:108-119, 1929.
25. Thigpen, C. H., and Cleckley, H.: Three Faces of Eve, McGraw-Hill, N. Y., 1957.

26. Thoheld, F. H: Nonconvulsive electro-stimulation under narcotic hypnosis, J.C.E.H. 2:175-177, 1954.

26a. Todorovic, D. D.: Hypnosis in military medical practice, Military Medicine, August, 1958.

27. Uhr, L.: Learning under hypnosis: What do we know? What should we know? J.C.E.H. 6:121-135, 1958.

28. Weitzenhoffer, A. M.: Hypnotism, New York, Wiley, 1953.

29. ——: The influence of hypnosis on the learning processes, J.C.E.H. 3:148-164, 1955.

30. ——: Unconscious or co-conscious? Reflections upon certain trends in medical hypnosis, Am. J. Clin. Hypnosis 2:177-196, 1960.

SUPPLEMENTARY READING

Das, J. P.: Learning under conditions of hypnotically induced anxiety and non-anxiety, Internat. J. Clin. Exper. Hypnosis 9:163-169, 1962.

Eitelberg, R.: Practical applications of hypnosis in space flight, Brit. J. Med. Hypnotism 13:22-31, 1962.

Fowler, W.: Hypnosis and learning, Internat. J. Clin. Exper. Hypnosis 9:223-233, 1961.

Kroger, W. S.: Psychotherapy of "port-of-last-call" patient. Paper delivered at meeting of Academy of Psychosomatic Medicine, Minneapolis, Nov. 1, 1962.

McCord, H., and Sherrill, C. I., III: A note on increased ability to do calculus post-hypnotically, Am. J. Clin. Hypnosis 4:124-125, 1961.

45

Practical Hints in Hypnodiagnosis

Although time exigencies because of patient overload make adequate history-taking more and more difficult, this unfortunate lack should be avoided at all costs in hypnotherapy. With physical diseases ruled out, preferably by a psychosomatically oriented internist, the alert hypnotherapist should first understand the methods by which patients deal with their anxiety-provoking tensions. He must realize, however, that his patients are only vaguely, if at all, aware of their emotional problems. Rather, physical discomfort and general anxiety are their chief concerns, and they seldom relate their symptoms to specific needs such as those described below.

Most individuals with these needs develop certain defensive behavior patterns in an attempt to allay their tensions. It is by such measures that they make a partial adjustment to difficult life situations. Some of the emotional manifestations of these disturbances, as hypochondriacal, addictive, hysterical, paranoid, depressive, obsessive-compulsive and phobic reactions do not always fall into clear-cut nosologic classifications. However, any of these reactions alone or in combination, through experiential conditioning, can symbolically be represented by physiologic complaints referable to the cardiovascular, respiratory, genitourinary and gastrointestinal systems. These complaints are restlessness, diarrhea, palpitation, globus, vomiting, vague pains and discomforts, anorexia, headaches, lassitude, fatigability, profuse sweating, and even paralysis.

Nearly all such patients believe they are suffering from a physical malady and, when the therapist attempts to talk them out of this idea, he is apt to have a hostile ex-patient. Unfortunately, too, our public educational program, which has attempted to make emotional illness as socially acceptable as physical involvements, has not been wholly effective. Therefore, most emotionally disturbed persons feel stigmatized and rationalize the diagnosis of "mental" illness until there is no other way to turn.

Mentioning that few persons in our culture escape being upset at one time or another is helpful in enabling them to face their real difficulties. One should discuss as simply as possible the "mind-body" inter-relationships concerned with the bodily expression of emotional tensions by a simple explanation of how "nervous feelings," fears and depression can interfere with the working of internal organs. He may cite the more commonly observed symptoms such as rapid heart action in response to excitement, "slowed" heart action caused by intense fear, and loss of appetite during periods of depression. The explanation should not involve the use of terms that imply mental disturbance, such as "psychoneurotic" or "psychotic," nor should terminology be employed that could give the patient the impression that his complaints are considered the result of an overactive imagination. To make light of the patient's suffering is a grave mistake, and may damage the doctor-patient relationship irreparably. He must let the patient know that he is aware that discomfort of psychological origin is always *real* to the person who feels it.

Actually, however, there is always a reciprocal and dynamic interaction between psychological and physical factors. Every emotion consists of a sequence of physical reverberations in the central nervous system. This aspect has been stressed throughout this book. Clinically, however, our knowledge is far from complete as to how and why specific organs are chosen for displacement of repressed emotional tensions. It cannot be said that any emotion can disturb the function of any organ, but, rather, that there is an intimate affinity between certain emotional states and certain vegetative functions; that emotional and physical factors in the production of symptoms vary in relative significance from individual to individual; and that typical emotional patterns in certain physical diseases also exist in persons with no physical symptoms.

CLINICAL MANIFESTATIONS OF ANXIETY

Anxiety is a universal human response due to hidden tension. It becomes pathologic when, without provocation or awareness, fears are experienced. When these fears cannot be handled, then even minor stresses lead to emotional disturbances. These will be discussed further in this book. These are chiefly insecurity, lack of self-esteem, inadequacy, inability to relate to others or to express pent-up feelings, and inordinate demands for attention. A typical example of an acute anxiety reaction is a person thrown into panic when some friend has suffered a heart attack or a nervous breakdown, or has developed cancer. Such symptoms can be corrected by adequate reassurance, wise counseling and strong countersuggestions.

Repressed anxiety, on the other hand, is usually due to a painful emotion which cannot be expressed directly. Instead, the associations with the original conflict are blocked from awareness by a secondary or defensive symptom, which generally prevents further personality decompensation. These defensive symptoms constitute the bulk of the symptomatology.

There are roughly 3 types of anxiety reactions that are based on *indirect* expression. These can be classified as follows: *Physiologic conversions* which are characterized by changes in smooth muscle, organ and glandular functions leading to psychophysiologic or psychosomatic illnesses, fatigue states and debilitated conditions. These disorders have a logical evolution, their history can be recalled, and they are subject to educational correction by psychotherapy including hypnosis.

The second type includes *hysterical re-actions* such as the functional paralysis of a limb. The disorder has a logical development and an onset which can be recalled but cannot be corrected by re-education per se. This symptom requires not only re-education but reversal of the negative sensory spiral of belief which led to its development.

In hysterical conversions, the fright leads to expectation of anxiety in similar situations. The condition can be relieved only *after it is deconditioned or re-experienced without anxiety.* That is why the driver, following an automobile accident, should immediately get behind the wheel to prevent mobilization of fear and chronic anxiety; the lack of fear leads to the rebuilding of self-confidence. Hypnosis is almost specific in these disorders.

The third type is *psychological conversions,* in which the effects of anxiety are converted through many devious pathways into psychological symptoms and reactions. These include phobias, dissociation reactions, depressions, hypochondriasis, obsessions and compulsions and certain character and personality disorders, as well as the regressive behavior and symptoms associated with the psychoses.

These last-named disorders might be termed "logic-proof"; their genesis cannot be recalled, their history is rationalized and the symptoms cannot be educated away. They are relieved, but with difficulty, by reevaluation of the patient's needs and by positive conditioning. The second and the third types, to some degree, parallel the effects of posthypnotic suggestions. There are many combinations of these disorders. It is useless to elaborate on the specific characteristics of each one, as was stated, because of the overlapping mechanisms common to all.

DIFFERENTIAL DIAGNOSIS

Psychosomatic illness is one of the most insidious of all human afflictions and the end-product of an emotional illness which evolved so imperceptibly that no one, least of all the patient, recognizes it. To assume that the symptoms are functional without first being able to recognize and understand positive signs of the psychogenic disorder beclouds the issue, dulls the therapist's acumen, and exposes him to the dangers of committing serious clinical errors. Even the most severe psychoses which appear with dramatic suddenness have a long history of gradual development. The hypnotherapist will be better equipped to diagnose the manifestations of long-standing emotional difficulties if he has had training in the fundamental principles of psychiatry. Therefore, it cannot be emphasized too strongly again that *it is always necessary to rule out a physical basis* as follows: After a thorough physical examination, the need for certain laboratory tests can be suggested tactfully. The resultant discussion may reveal the fears, such as of heart trouble, cancer and tuberculosis. Negative tests are of distinct psychotherapeutic value. The physical and the laboratory examinations thus help to establish rapport, as the patient now feels that he is a collaborator. If all the findings are negative, the patient can be informed that there is no sign of physical disease and that his presenting complaints are on a psychological basis.

The unsophisticated hypnotherapist, unfamiliar with psychiatric concepts and technics of history-taking, is quite likely to experience difficulty in obtaining the anamnesis necessary to understand the functioning of the personality. Patients who consult a hypnotherapist seldom recognize the inordinate need for their symptoms. Some of the commonest of these are the need to inadvertently exaggerate the severity of their complaints as a means of getting more attention; for avoiding the responsibilities of marriage or parenthood; for dominating their home environment in a neurotic manner to compensate for their complete inability to deal with their problems in a realistic and mature manner; and, finally, using symptoms as a means of self-punishment for guilty fears.

Many such patients, even if aware of their needs, are unable to face their emotional problems. They resist psychological probing with puzzled silence or offer only vague replies when questioned. For such difficult cues, the skillful hypnotherapist may wish to devote several multi-evaluation sessions for formal history-taking. These diagnostic sessions will be more productive if he proceeds in a casual manner to gather his data. If he is

a generalist, he can start with the physical examination. It is here, during unguarded moments, that much valuable information can be gathered. After this, he can discuss the present illness, the pertinent facts that led up to it, and, more important, the patient's attitude toward these facts.

One need not follow a schematic outline. If the therapist knows what he is looking for, there is no need to be overly formal in his approach. Rather, he should let the information come freely and without pressure. He can gently guide the patient to tell his story if there is too much digression. The discussion of sexual and intimate information will be discussed below.

In the following section the material is presented in the first person singular to secure the greatest possible immediacy in description. I usually state, "Your organs are perfect, but you are emotionally upset. Please do not infer that I think you are mentally ill; rather, you seem to be deeply involved in your emotional problems. I think I can help you to help yourself."

Differentiation of the types of emotional disorders can be accomplished at either hypnotic or nonhypnotic levels as follows: Are the symptoms connected with, or aggravated by, emotional upsets? Is there any evidence of a previous personality disturbance? What was the patient's reaction to other environmental difficulties? How have acute or chronic illnesses interfered with sexual and social adjustments? Are the complaints compatible with the physical findings? Finally— and this is most important in females—does the woman really accept herself as a woman? A high percentage of the females seen by the generalist do not have "female trouble" but have "trouble being females"!

DIAGNOSIS FROM HISTORY-TAKING

When you are seeking answers to the above questions, control your intonation and choice of words so that you do not bias the patient's replies during the history-taking. Look for unintentional "slips of the tongue" or accidental remarks. Also, watch for frequent sighing, inordinate laughing or crying. Are significant symptoms such as restlessness, insomnia, anorexia and palpitation minimized? Conversely, are fleeting abdominal pains and headaches exaggerated? Look for flushing or blanching of the face, flickering or lowering of the eyes, tensing of the jaws or the fists and, most important, assess the quality of the patient's speech, particularly where blocking or silence occurs. If the patient stammers, it usually indicates that highly charged emotional material has been touched.

When a patient blocks or is silent for any length of time, I usually say, "Just take your time. Don't talk until you can do so without effort. You can act just as you actually feel, so keep your thoughts to yourself until you are ready to talk about them. After all, you are the one who controls things—not me." The anxiety-ridden patient is grateful for being helped, and usually the brief period of silence is followed by spontaneous expressions involving present needs and aspirations. As soon as the patient realizes that he has the freedom to choose when and what to say and to whom, he feels more secure in my presence, and then usually begins to reveal meaningful material.

I avoid rapid-fire questions, as this only invites glib answers. Remember also that two questions, asked simultaneously, enable the patient to dodge *one* question by focusing *entirely* on the other. *I never ask routine questions, because routine questions deserve only routine answers.* If I wish to understand the personality structure, I always take the history myself.

In interrogating disturbed patients, the following points are important:

1. The emotionally upset individual is extremely susceptible to chance remarks. Therefore, I seldom ask intimate questions or probe very deeply until good rapport is obtained. In general, the anxious patient should be handled with tact and consideration.

2. I find it helpful to be warm, sympathetic and reassuring because as soon as the patient senses that I am interested in solving his troubles he develops more confidence in me. Then he is likely to "open up" and tell me what is "really bothering him," especially if he is relaxed and certain that the room is soundproof and free from interruptions. If I can give the patient the feeling that I am going to try to understand what his frustrations, hopes and suffering mean to him, then greater faith and optimism for his recovery will be inspired.

3. It is a good idea, when taking the history, to make the patient feel accepted and, above all, to avoid a dictatorial or "know-it-all" attitude.

4. It is not good to make premature pronouncements such as, "You are going to be all right," especially if the diagnosis has not been made as yet.

5. It is prudent to keep within your psychotherapeutic limitations, and probing for deeply repressed material should be avoided unless you know what to do with it when it appears.

6. I always avoid such platitudinous remarks as, "A lot of people are worse off than you," or "Go home and forget about it." These are fighting words to the emotionally disturbed patient because now he *really* has to prove the validity of his complaints. He will also feel that I am giving him a "brush-off," and then he is apt to visit another physician and exaggerate his suffering in order to impress him with the gravity of his condition.

7. Before obtaining sexual information, be sure that you can discuss any type of sexual behavior objectively, *without* any overt signs of disgust and without social or moral evaluation. The skilled therapist will ask all questions relative to sex without hesitation or apology. Naturally, if patients sense that you are embarrassed over sexual matters you can usually expect incorrect or dishonest answers. Also, many are evasive about their sex life because of shame or have unformulated reasons for exaggerating or minimizing the facts. Likewise, many are confused or rationalize the *real* reasons for their complaints. Many who complain of pain and fatigue are using the symptoms as a façade for psychosexual difficulties.

8. If additional information is needed, it is very helpful to interview other members of the family. Referral to a clinical psychologist for the Rorschach or ink-blot test and other psychometric evaluations is a tremendous timesaver and affords a rapid survey of the personality. When patients question the rationale for these tests, I explain, "Just as laboratory tests and x-rays are useful for physical diagnosis, so are psychological tests valuable for uncovering the hidden personality factors responsible for many psychosomatic ailments."

It should be remembered that negative examinations should not contribute to the common error of diagnosing neurosis by exclusion. Here it should be re-emphasized that it is just as important to obtain *positive evidence* in the diagnosis of neurosis as it is in any other pathologic condition; a valid diagnosis of neurosis is not made by exclusion of organic factors, but by positive signs that an emotional conflict exists, which the physician must recognize or learn to recognize. It is the emotionally disturbed patient who is not too sick who often presents the real diagnostic problem.

When taking the history, comparison of the adult personality with childhood behavior and reaction patterns is an excellent idea. It is also a good rule to accept nothing that seems significant at its face value. Patients are often confused about the nature of their illnesses, both past and present, and tend to exaggerate their importance or unnecessarily minimize them. Careful inquiry will usually reveal the reasons behind such attitudes. It should also be pointed out that the prominent personality features have their opposites in sharp contrast, such as amiability and hostility, dependence and independence, submissiveness and aggressiveness. Obviously these traits are contradictory, but the hypnotherapist should not be unduly surprised to find them coexisting. He must help the patient to understand these contradictions in his personality before he can help him to achieve an inner harmony.

After obtaining sufficient information, the physician may want to discuss the history material with a psychiatrist in order to better understand its significance and to plan whatever therapy is indicated. Even the psychiatrically trained physician will at times seek this consultation, and certainly the physician-hypnotist who has not had psychiatric training will save himself much time and trouble if he recognizes the need for and accepts this type of help.

46

Practical Hints in Hypnotheraby

It is difficult to separate diagnosis from therapy as the latter begins the moment the patient enters the office, if not before. In this section, the practical "how-to-do-it" approach for eliciting the emotional *needs and intentions* that many emotionally disturbed persons have for maintaining the chronicity of their symptoms will be discussed. Naturally, the following suggestions for understanding most behavior disorders do not have to be followed literally. Rather, the therapeutic procedure needs to be varied from patient to patient and may even have to be changed as therapy progresses.

Highly complex hypnoanalytic procedures should be attempted only by the well-trained hypnotherapist. However, the mature physician, who has already proven his competence by successfully handling psychoneurotics in his practice, can use hypnotherapy as outlined below. The applications depend on the extent of his training and his ability to adequately understand the needs and values of symptoms.

Brief hypnotherapy for symptom-removal, as distinguished from hypnoanalysis, can achieve relatively permanent results in psychosomatic disorders. Throughout this book it has been demonstrated that hypnosis is more than mere suggestion; it is a powerful vehicle for the communication of new ideas and understandings. Whenever a person relaxes, he can more effectively concentrate upon another's communications, and, as a result, he becomes more receptive, self-objective and, therefore, more capable of examining his needs. This leads to a better understanding of his difficulties and also establishes greater co-operation.

The following maxims should be re-emphasized: that a patient is *not* treated by hypnosis, but in hypnosis; that hypnosis merely intensifies the rapport between therapist and patient; and, therefore, it merely extracts the patient's potentialities.

Hypnotic technics can be incorporated into any school of psychotherapy. The choice depends upon the nature and duration of the therapy and the experience of the therapist. Raginsky[3] wisely states: "There is little scientific justification and limited value for a concept of hypnosis which remains isolated from the mainstream of psychological thinking and research."

Assuming that the therapist finds out how and under what extenuating factors the symptoms occurred, and how they operate, he should then ask himself if he thinks he can modify and control these factors by hypnosis. There are no absolute rules for conducting hypnotherapy. What is necessary are common sense, clinical judgment and intuition, and a good knowledge of human behavior. All physicians, whatever their specialties, should be able to carry out hypnotherapy as skillfully as any other medical maneuver. Since psychosomatic problems constitute a large percentage of medical practice, it is inexcusable for any physician *not* to be able to use hypnotherapy, within the usual restrictions, as an adjunct to psychotherapy.

To be a successful hypnotherapist, one does not have to have a powerful personality. He does not have to sit behind the patient, or look for "complexes," or necessarily have to probe the "unconscious" in order to give "insight" into "causative" factors. Most patients accept logical and meaningful communications, especially if these help allay their tensions. The most successful communications include anything and everything that is part of a person—his hopes, his fears, his motivations, his attitudes toward right and wrong and even his religious concepts and beliefs.

Modern-day hypnotherapy emphasizes the value of the present—the here and the now. Explaining human relatedness in terms of instinctual energies or libidinous drives, though helpful for understanding how a particular symptom developed, is not always necessary for attacking and removing symptoms. It is necessary, however, that emotional needs, satisfactions and goals be understood rather than irrelevant minutiae of the entire life span. Hypnosis is more effective if the total life situation is viewed more in terms of current opportunities, successes and reasons for past failures. It should never be forced on the patient.

The goal of hypnotherapy is to establish a willingness to accept those ideas that can enhance the patient's understandings. By such measures, the subject can recognize the need for symptoms used for secondary gain purposes. Through positive and constructive suggestions, he can neutralize harmful symptoms produced by destructive thoughts, feelings and memories.

Under autohypnosis, one often can more readily explore the needs for a symptom. At least, the "how" and the "why" of a symptom are ordinarily more readily understood in a contemplative state of self-absorption. The unique receptivity or self-reflection which characterizes the autohypnotic state usually is conducive to greater understanding.

Many times a symptom which is maintaining a neurosis can be "kept on leash" by posthypnotic amnesia. By such measures, the therapist can be on the alert for possible symptom-substitution. When trading down is successful, the patient can describe how he feels now that he no longer has to contend with the symptom.

Most disturbed patients suffer more from their inability to deal with their current problems than they do from hidden traumas. Therefore, they should be encouraged to express their feelings as to how they react to these and what they propose doing about them. This is of the utmost importance. This is more valuable than merely telling a patient that he should "give love and affection" to replace hostility and aggression.

These are, at best, ineffective intellectualizations. It is much better to teach him how to recognize and adjust to the everyday situations that affect his functioning.

Successful hypnotherapy, too, is in reality a collaborative and reciprocal effort between therapist and patient—each learning from the other. Thus, it is not the type of therapy but the strength of the interpersonal relationship that is responsible for recovery.[2]

In some instances, an understanding of the role that the symptom-complex plays in the patient's emotional economy is important. It is for such patients that hypnotherapy must be modified into an uncovering technic and adapted to a specific patient's needs. In this way, access to those aspects of the personality not accessible to psychotherapeutic technics at a nonhypnotic level can be gained. For such therapy to be effective, the therapist must give the patient an opportunity to gratify certain *basic needs* which are present in varying degrees in all psychosomatic processes.[3]

THE EMOTIONAL NEEDS

1. **The Need To Talk.** *Talking is the best method for alleviation of tensions.* The patient discharges pent-up feelings. A permissive attitude provides him with a sympathetic listener. Since the patient depends on the physician for understanding and guidance, therapy begins with the initial interview. Listening to what the patient states is really an art. The good clinician must pay particular attention to *everything* that is being heard. To the trained listener, the body "language" is as clear as a symphonic arrangement. There are no fixed rules which can be used for this phase of hypnotherapy. The following general principles, however, will be of assistance:

A. It is wise to *let the patient talk*, especially during deep hypnosis since it is here that important facts are often revealed.

B. *Listen patiently* to what the patient is saying. Then he will feel that you are really interested in him and his problems.

C. Never interrupt when inconsequential material is being discussed. Keep in mind the old adage: "If one opens his mouth enough times, he will stick his foot into it." In a patient-physician interview *the patient is expressing his feelings as well as talking about what he thinks are the facts.*

D. Always put yourself in the patient's position. Understand not only what he is saying but *how* he is saying it, and *why* he says what he does at this particular moment. Does he need sympathy? Is he misinformed? Does he feel guilty and is he therefore seeking reassurance? Is he angry, afraid and/or evasive as he talks about highly charged topics?

E. *Show empathy and personal warmth.* Ask for richer details, more complete examples or amplifications of what he has stated. Ask, "Then what happened?" "So?" "And then?" Or, more pointedly, "Why?"

F. *Avoid criticism, argumentation and condemnation.* Remember that emotionally disturbed individuals can accept only a part of what they know to be the whole truth. *Psychoneurotics deceive themselves over a long period of time*; seldom are they able to see themselves as objectively as others see them. *Therefore, never tell the patient that he is "seeking sympathy."*

Always encourage the patient to talk about himself, and his attitudes toward work, marriage, recreation and politics. Religious views should be brought into the conversation. Many deeply religious individuals misinterpret religious tenets and feel guilty.

A certain amount of time (30 to 50 minutes) should be allotted to each interview. The time interval can be *in keeping with the needs of the individual patient.* At times 2 to 4 hours may be necessary for psychiatric emergency patients. Some patients need to talk of their childhood, their handling by parents, their attitudes toward school and work and sexual experiences. The discussion should permit ventilation of the patient's true feelings and this will indicate how faulty attitudes and sentiments have developed. Such questions as, "How did you *feel* when that happened?" or "What did you *feel like doing* when your father (or your husband or your mother-in-law) did or said that?" help to spur the patient to relate other significant experiences.

A detailed account of pertinent life situations which decreased or increased the patient's self-esteem, as well as those in which he experienced a sense of frustration and failure, is meaningful. Specific incidents at home, at work and at play throw light on the *pattern of the personality*, with particular attention to faulty behavior or *attitudes.* These attitudes are brought to the fore by asking, "Why did you act in this particular way." "What purpose did it serve?" These questions may bring out that the patient's needs to be independent and successful at all costs; that he feels resentful toward those whom he tries to please; or that he has a need for perfectionism to avoid criticism. Here hypnosis can be used in a supportive role, as it more readily permits the release of ideas and feelings which in themselves exaggerate conflictual situations associated with the presenting symptoms.

2. **The Need To Be Told What To Do.** The patient comes to the doctor in need of support and guidance. He wants someone who can alleviate his sufferings. The value of an authoritarian approach may be attributed in part to being told what to do by a therapist who plays "God." The immature and emotionally disturbed individual *wants to be told what to do just as a child does.* Patients who look upon the therapist as an omnipotent father-confessor, and who expect a relatively paternal authoritative attitude in him, respond best to hypnotherapists who use such an approach. On the other hand, those who anticipate the most effective help from a therapist who is permissive do better with those who assume this role. A therapist must be flexible and, if critical attitudes are mobilized by an authoritative approach, he should be able to adapt his technic to the patient.

3. **The Need To Be Accepted.** The patient with psychosomatic complaints usually is tense, worried and anxious. Often guilt is present because of hostile attitudes, depressed feelings or the self-depreciation that makes him believe that he is "no good" or "a failure." Such a patient needs reassurance. (However, many an emotionally disturbed person is looking for *personal* reassurance rather than a "clean bill of health," that is, assurance that he is a *worthwhile* person.) The physician who makes a diagnosis of "no emotional disease," often will not help the emotionally inadequate person; he will be chagrined when such patients are not

"cheered up" or pleased. Not infrequently, they may even feel worse—to the dismay of the well-meaning doctor.

However, if the physician shows that he is pleased with a co-operative patient's progress, he has given the patient what he really needs. When patients are told that they are co-operative ("You have done your best to help me") or are directly complimented ("That was an intelligent account of the development of your symptoms"), most of them begin to feel a sense of increased self-esteem. They generally respond with a desire to please the doctor who is so "understanding"! This is shown by an increased willingness to discuss personal topics and a readiness to accept the fact that they are immature, dependent and inadequate; this is in contradistinction to previous patterns of blaming others for their troubles. With this approach, patients will feel complimented by your personal interest in their illnesses and encouraged to go on to discuss personal problems. I do not hesitate to prescribe medication that I deem is indicated.

4. The Need To Be One's Real Self. Therapy which allows ventilation relieves pent-up feelings; this often leads to emotional security. Thus, patients are able to accept the responsibility for their behavior. In most discussions, patients reveal their dependence on the opinions of others and they relate how they have avoided every opportunity to get away from the domination of their parents, or what they believed to be the demands of an employer or a husband or a wife. Patients will now be encouraged to do what they *really want to do*. When a patient reports an incident of behavior, he is asked, "What did you *really* want to do? Why didn't you do it?" The patient, who already has accepted the doctor as an equal and a collaborator, begins to practice what he has been taught. He brings in reports showing how he has asserted himself in a life situation and is complimented on his progress. Gradually, he learns to speak up for himself and to please himself as well as others. He literally learns to think of himself and for himself for the first time; heretofore he had been apprehensive about the possibility of offending everyone with whom he came into contact. The patient becomes his true self and, with this change in behavior, there comes a sense of freedom of action and a feeling of well-being which he has not experienced for many years.

5. The Need To Emancipate Himself From the Influence of the Hypnotherapist. Finally, there is the need the patient has to break off his dependency on the doctor. Any type of suggestion in the form of advice fosters dependency. I usually eliminate dependency through utilization of autohypnosis. Likewise, dependency is eradicated if I tell the patient, "You hypnotized yourself. I didn't. You were the one who developed the symptom, were you not? The same mechanisms by which you became anxiety-ridden can be used for dissolution of your problems if you yourself do it through autohypnosis." This takes hypnotherapy out of the realm of magic.

As hypnotherapy progresses, usually less regular interviews are necessary. Visits should be reduced and then discontinued as the reasons for the needs for the symptoms are clarified and recovery takes place. Patients who do not understand their problems should not be discharged, as not infrequently such patients will keep their neurotic symptoms. These will limit their activities and keep them semi-invalids, who become wholly dependent on the physician. This breaking up of the patient-physician relationship is of the utmost importance. It should be emphasized that the patient is not improved until he has completely dismissed his therapist, put aside his drugs and other routines, and progressed to the point where he feels free to act as a healthy, emotionally secure individual, in keeping with his own personal needs and interests.

REFERENCES

1. Conn, J. H.: Psychologic Treatment of Psychosomatic Disorders, read before The Academy of Psychosomatic Medicine annual meeting, October, 1957.
2. Kroger, W. S.: And psychotherapy is indicated, West. J. Surg. *68*:138-140, 1960, and *68*:196-198, 1960.
3. Raginsky, B. B.: The use of hypnosis in internal medicine, Internat. J.C.E.H. October, 1960.

47

Specialized Hypnotic Technics ·

There are specialized technics which the physician trained in hypnosis can employ in selected patients. Some of these can be used within the framework of other types of psychotherapy. These technics potentiate the patient's capacities to learn, react and respond with supramaximal functioning to recognize the needs for an emotional disorder. It is this understanding which brings about recovery.

Depending on the patient's difficulties, there are some hypnotic technics which are better than others for tapping the "forgotten assets" of an individual and facilitating adjustment to reality situations. This often can be accomplished without tracing symptoms to their root causes. As mentioned in Chapter 49, casual relationships, established through "insight," can be based wholly upon the therapist's interpretations, which, in turn, often are in accordance with his insight.

The patient's self-esteem, self-assurance and self-confidence should be raised by all available measures such a wise counseling, encouragement of self-expression, and, most important where necessary, full acceptance of his acting-out behavior patterns; the latter usually obviates resistant maneuvers.

Many of the cases described in this chapter were treated successfully by brief hypnotherapy, consisting of symptom-substitution, symptom-transformation, symptom-amelioration and symptom-utilization. These technics are far different from symptom-removal by an authoritarian approach. Since minimal resistances are created, there is greater therapeutic leverage.

Erickson[7a] notes such an approach results "in increased receptivity, objectivity in viewing the self, and meeting neurotic needs ordinarily difficult to obtain by more formalized methods. This receptivity, unique to hypnosis, is characterized by an exact reception of ideas without an elaboration of them in terms of implied or associated meanings." In this process of presenting ideas, understanding is accelerated and gives the patient the "capacity to examine ideas for their inherent values, rather than in terms of prejudgments, opinions, mistaken beliefs, or faulty attitudes."

Some of these highly specialized hypnotic technics borrow heavily from more ancient methods. For instance, the value of systematic training in self-objectivity during states of deep meditation was stressed centuries ago by the Tantrik philosopher-psychologists of India who espoused pure Yoga. This kind of Tantrik training, according to Huxley,[12] is simply being aware of the events going on inside or outside the organism. He points out that, long ago, neuroses were not treated by dredging up traumatic experiences from the unconscious, but by "training the patient to live here and now in the world of reality experiences instead of in the world of emotionally charged symbols relevant only to events that took place long ago." How different is this from the currently popular Existentialist approach?

BRIEF HYPNOTHERAPY BY SYMPTOM-REMOVAL

Brief hypnotherapy for symptom control, consisting of from 2 to 30 or more sessions, is particularly applicable to individuals who have been frustrated by deep psychotherapy and those who ordinarily would terminate therapy prematurely. The latter often respond because deeper anxieties are not evoked by minimal probing. However, there are certain patients who are not amenable to this approach. These should be referred for other types of psychotherapy.

Brief hypnotherapy reaches its greatest potential and is indicated if desensitization or deconditioning is to be employed, especially the relaxation technics involving reciprocal inhibition psychotherapy, as proposed by Wolpe.[38] It makes full use of motivation, guidance and suggestion by indirection. Frank[8a] notes that suggestion and persuasion constitute some of the universal factors operative in mental healing.

If a patient can remember what it's like to experience relief from a specific symptom during hypnosis, then such improvement can be re-experienced after dehypnotization. Through appropriate sensory-imagery conditioning, autohypnosis and sufficient reinforcement sessions, the results can be gratifying. Direct symptom-removal technics, however, are justified for sufferers from emphysema, bronchiectasis, tuberculosis or peripheral vascular diseases because of the emergency nature of their conditions. Likewise, cardiacs and hypertensives endangered by overweight are legitimate candidates for this type of hypnotherapy. It can be lifesaving in status asthmaticus,[13] intractable hiccoughing or continual sneezing; for these conditions there is little time to analyze personality functioning. Here, even temporary cessation of the symptom acts as an incentive to enhance the potentialities for recovery.

The following are typical examples of direct symptom-removal combined with brief hypnotherapy:

A 56-year-old attorney had severe wheezing and coughing spells preventing his working. During each of 6 sessions, the pulmonary spasm was alleviated by hypnotic relaxation. The coughing and wheezing were controlled for varying periods by sensory-imagery conditioning involving pleasant memories. He was instructed under hypnosis that he would have 5 or 10 minutes more relief each day. Concurrently, posthypnotic suggestions were directed toward developing a profound disgust toward cigarettes. The prompt and dramatic improvement in his breathing stimulated him to practice diligently the development of an aversion toward smoking. Within 8 weeks he could talk for long intervals without coughing. He also stopped smoking. He maintained improvement and soon resumed his legal occupation. A follow-up 6 months later showed that he still was able to function with a minimal need for medications.

An 18-year-old male somnambule with severe status asthmaticus was relieved in almost a similar fashion through the combined use of time-distortion, autohypnosis and sensory-imagery conditioning. He was trained to abort an attack as soon as he felt one coming on by "contracting" time (making 30 minutes seem like 1 minute). As a result, he could "telescope" an attack into 1 minute. The attacks became less frequent and finally disappeared.

Recently the author saw a 42-year-old male who had been hiccoughing for several weeks following a prostatectomy. In 2 sessions, the symptom was controlled by suggesting that *it would occur only when he voluntarily held his breath*. The author left town for an extended visit and referred him to a colleague for further care. When he returned, he was surprised to discover that his colleague's attention had not been needed. This patient had never realized that all he had to do was to breathe normally.

HELPFUL HINTS IN BRIEF HYPNOTHERAPY

There is no rule of thumb for the use of brief hypnotherapy. Each case requires an individual approach, and this depends upon the sagacity and the skill of the therapist. As was mentioned, the therapist must restructure the patient's beliefs and then he behaves differently because he thinks differently. The patient is not overwhelmed or coerced into yielding the symptom. Rather, its dissolution occurs in accordance with his wishes and needs. A permissive approach sets the terms for each new and constructive change. Patients are not in a "one-down position" or subservient to the therapist at any time; they are not prodded, forced or ordered to give up their symptoms. Thus, the possibility that another symptom-equivalent will take the place of the removed one is highly unlikely when such technics are utilized.

What the patient may expect from brief hypnotherapy should be discussed in a detailed and confident manner. Apprehensive patients often ask, "Doctor, do you think that I can respond to hypnosis?" Though the following is a gross oversimplification, the therapist can remark, "It is not a question of whether or not you can respond, but whether or not you wish to 'unhypnotize' yourself out of a symptom that you have actually hypnotized yourself into. After all, this is your mind, your body and your problem; you are the one who developed the symptom and, therefore, you are the only one who can remove it. Would you believe it—not a single person has been cured by hypnosis, *but hundreds of individuals have learned how to help themselves* through hypnosis, especially when they *really* wanted to use it to better work through their problems.[11]

One also can raise the question of the need, and how much of his symptom the patient really wishes to keep. These contradictory suggestions, at one and the same time, suggest that the symptom can be removed and yet can be kept if it is still utilitarian in the patient's emotional economy. Such suggestions, as well as more general ones, are not a direct order to change and hence do not mobilize critical attitudes. The *sine qua non* of brief hypnotherapy always is to get the patient to realize that recovery is wholly dependent upon *his* efforts rather than upon those of the therapist. Most patients also feel that because of the need to practice autohypnosis and sensory-imagery conditioning, they now have "something to sink their teeth into," and that they can contribute to their recovery. Actually, "patients are helped to help themselves."

HANDLING RESISTANT PATIENTS BY BRIEF HYPNOTHERAPY

In the presence of hostility, the reasons should be discussed immediately to prevent further resistances. Some resistant patients undermine the therapist by following the old adage, "If you can't fight them, join them."

Illustrative was an alcoholic who had defeated innumerable therapists by his disarming mannerisms. He attempted to "seduce" the author by gifts, invitations to his home and other blandishments. It was pointed out that behind his ardent wish to stop drinking was his stronger wish to cling to his pleasurable neurosis. This was evidenced by his ingratiating gestures—all designed to defeat the therapist.

When successful, such persons boast that "No one can help me." They seldom realize that they maneuvered their defeat. Other resistant patients continually flatter the therapist. Here, too, "Beware of the smiling patient" is a wise aphorism to heed.

A noncondemnatory manner and being impervious to irritating remarks are conducive to the establishment of good motivation. Personal bias, blaming the patient for failure to recover, or discussions of wholly irrelevant matters arouse critical attitudes. Other resistances arise when the patient expects hypnotherapy to be an inordinately rapid method. The explanation that hypnotherapy is not the sole therapeutic agent, but that it merely facilitates recovery in the same way that an anesthetic agent expedites surgery, is helpful.

If the therapist pays strict attention to what the patient is saying, this minimizes the resistances. The grateful patient, because he realizes that the therapist is giving of himself, reacts in a healthier manner; each small victory paves the way for further therapeutic gains.

Some resistant persons, such as alcoholics, especially if seen after a "hang-over," should be hypnotized on the very first visit. At this time they are more highly motivated than later. If hypnosis is not induced, some feel rejected and will not return. However, the usual course with most patients is to take a good history and make a careful appraisal, remarking, "I do not use hypnosis until I have found out what your case is all about; then I can make plans as to how I shall treat you." Highly resistant and disturbed individuals are reassured by such remarks.

Haley[9] recently reviewed the brilliant methods of handling resistances described by Erickson, the leading protagonist of the brief hypnotherapeutic approach. The current functions of the symptom are explored, rather than childhood experiences. From the beginning, the patient's behavior is controlled by emphasizing, directly or indirectly, that he can either talk or be silent; this permissiveness usually enables him to ventilate his feelings readily. What he says and what he does not say are noted and, through specific instructions, he is asked to continue to do something that he is doing already, but to do it under the therapist's direction.

Rather than interpreting a woman's inability to speak as resistance, Haley describes how Erickson complimented her on being able to communicate, at least, by nodding and shaking her head. He asked her if she could write and, after she had nodded her head in the affirmative, he placed a pencil in her left hand. Since she was right-handed, he asked her, "How do you feel about that?" In this structured situation, since she could not write, she had to speak.

In Erickson's other cases, resistances are reduced and co-operation is obtained by always emphasizing the positive aspects of the patient's behavior. For instance, if a patient thinks that he is a failure, Erickson compliments him on whatever determination he shows; the passive person's ability to endure is stressed; the agility of the short person; the solidity and strength of the large individual. The patient cannot combat such obvious reasoning. Thus, the positive aspects of the patient's behavior are accepted and utilized so that a change can be produced. Symptomatic behavior is encouraged, but always under direction of the therapist. For instance, a highly resistant, obese patient was instructed to *overeat* enough to maintain a weight of 260 pounds instead of her current 270 pounds. Thus, her needs to overeat, to lose weight and to rebel were satisfied at the same time.

Another resistant obese woman was deliberately instructed to *gain* from 15 to 25 pounds. While gaining, she was asked to speculate on how she would go about losing the weight. Despite her reluctance to gain more weight, he insisted that she gain 20 pounds. Then she was "permitted" to stop gaining weight, which subsequently led to a permanent loss. The acceptance of the need to gain weight is encouraged, and, as a result, the patient looks to the therapist for further direction. In general, the method involves the self-respect, the needs and the desire of the patient to give up the symptom by committing him to "some activity which he does not like (but preferably feels he should accomplish) and persuading him to go through with the activity as directed."[11]

Often resistance can be circumvented by hypnotically directing attention to other activities rather than to the symptom itself. Erickson instructed an enuretic to walk when he wet the bed. This served a 2-fold purpose: the enuresis indirectly came under the control of the therapist; the walking was self-punishment. An insomniac was told to stay awake deliberately, but to polish the floor all night for self-punishment reasons. A migraine sufferer was told to remember what her headache felt like in order to alter it within a month. The hidden meaning implied is, "You might consider the possibility of skipping your headache for 3 weeks or a month."[10] Patients who are controlled without knowing it are usually unable to resist the directives (extraverbal suggestions). For instance, a casual comment arouses a patient's interest in a topic, and the later mentioning of another apparently unrelated topic "unconsciously" connects the two in his mind.

BRIEF HYPNOTHERAPY BY SYMPTOM-SUBSTITUTION, TRANSFORMATION, AMELIORATION AND UTILIZATION

Symptom-Substitution

Erickson[5, 8] intentionally manipulates neurotic symptomatology in those who are inaccessible to a total psychotherapeutic approach. In these persons, direct symptom-removal by hypnosis fails and usually results in resistance to further therapy; the neurotic manifestations are maintained continuously until satisfactory adjustments and needs are achieved.

Illustrative is a patient who desperately needed to keep his neurotic disability. Since the underlying maladjustments were impossible to correct, Erickson substituted another neurotic disability that was similar to the existing one, but nonincapacitating in character. Shifting attention from anxiety-provoking symptoms to less urgent problems makes the patient less preoccupied with his present difficulties. The substitutive symptom also satisfies the personality needs and, as a result, a healthy adjustment to reality occurs. Erickson[6] concludes: "Regardless of how farcical, the above technic met his symptomatic needs."

Symptom-substitution should be used to "trade down" to a less handicapping symptom; the new substitute symptom is more readily removed. The poorly motivated individual, the "psychiatric veteran," or the geriatric patient responds well to symptom-substitution; fortunately, deep hypnosis is seldom required.

Symptom-substitution can be used with superficial therapy, as in the following case:

An extremely depressed and suicidal 60-year-old male complained bitterly of a pain in his left foot. He continually "cracked" the bones in one foot to relieve the pain. His trouble had been called "psychosomatic" by consultants; one physician told him that the cuboid bone in his foot was "slipping out of place." However, orthopedic evaluation was negative. He was told that the pain in his foot was real but was brought on by gout (he had a high uric acid level). Agreement that he had real pain established prompt rapport. Through posthypnotic suggestions, he was instructed to "crack" the knuckles of his left hand. The pain in his foot cleared up as soon as his attention was shifted to his hand. Further discussion revealed that he was envious of a younger and more successful brother on whom he depended for a livelihood. Multi-evaluation sessions of his problems made him realize that the incapacitating symptom not only accounted for his dependency but also served as a useful alibi for his deep, underlying sense of inadequacy. He made a partial recovery but never returned to work, since he was unwilling to face his difficult life situation.

This method took into consideration the patient's needs for independence and self-help. By "trading down," he made it much easier to give up the symptom. Though the underlying maladjustment was not corrected, the patient developed more self-esteem. He did not realize that he had received directive therapy which undoubtedly had prevented a possible psychotic break or suicide.

Autohypnosis and sensory-imagery conditioning can be combined with symptom-substitution. A more effective response to suggestions occurs during autohypnosis, and this in turn depends upon the effort that the patient puts forth and how often and how well he practices. However, the therapist must never get himself "out on a limb" by raising the patient's hopes too high. Active participation in meditation, self-reflection, self-absorption or whatever term one wishes to use when thoughts are subjectively turned inward, must be encouraged in all patients, especially in those who dislike being helped by another person. This approach works well

in the patient who has an inordinate need for attention-getting symptoms.

The author was called in consultation to see a 57-year-old male who developed a paralysis of both arms following a "whiplash injury" incurred in a minor auto collision. He had a bilateral hysterical paralysis of the legs sustained 28 years earlier, which had been diagnosed as astasia abasia, and which necessitated the use of crutches and braces on both legs. In the presence of the referring neuropsychiatrist, a pseudo-erudite discussion of a placebo diagnosis was conducted (while the patient was under hypnosis) as follows: "This is a typical case of a partial compression of the cervical vertebrae; several nerves are pinched, and this accounts for the paralysis of both arms. They usually *run a typical course* and clear up in 6 weeks. However, for some unknown reason, the little finger on each hand does not recover full motion. But, it, too, eventually clears up." It was suggested that the patient work on one arm first, and that, he imagine under autohypnosis that he was able to move it up slowly—about an inch or two each day. He practiced faithfully, and at the end of almost 6 weeks he regained full function of both arms. He complained bitterly of the involvement of the little finger on each hand for some time. When it was suggested that he might be able to eventually walk without his crutches and braces, he stated, "I want to rest for a while before undergoing more therapy." Since the personality needs were met sufficiently to achieve a satisfying, constructive, personal success, it was decided to abide by his decision. As yet he has not returned for further therapy.

This patient had been in the limelight for many years as a well-known actor. When he no longer was noticed, he developed the "paralysis." It would have been useless to confront him with this or use logical persuasion. My discussion with his physicians concealed suggestions which were really directed toward him. Inasmuch as he was not aware that he was being influenced, his criticalness was decreased, and he was thus made much more receptive to the suggestions. The placebo diagnosis fitted in with his needs, and the emphasis on "run a typical course" placed the recovery *within him.* Most important, the "rug was not pulled from under his feet"; he was left with a temporary paralysis of the little finger. However, during therapy he was "allowed" to remove this symptom—but, of course, not too rapidly. Orienting the therapy around the patient's accomplishing the results and taking full credit for these is the key to a successful outcome.

Symptom-Removal by Symptom-Transformation

It is generally the author's policy to teach the patient how to control specific ideomotor and ideosensory activities, such as thermal changes, alterations in size and shape of the limbs, arm-levitation and breathing. When assured that he can produce these changes readily, the patient realizes that he can either remove or develop other somatization reactions through autohypnosis.

A middle-aged woman, because of an intense hostility toward her mother-in-law, developed a hysterical tic. She was treated by symptom-transformation. She was instructed, under hypnosis, to transfer the twitching of the face to the little finger of her left hand; all her symptomatology could be "condensed" into the finger. She could, if she wished, choose the time of day that this would occur. After this occurred, permission was given to allow the twitching of the little finger to increase or decrease. In the meantime, the facial tic disappeared. She was then given a powerful but concealed posthypnotic suggestion: "You will gradually lose the twitching of your little finger. Perhaps it will be next week, next month or within the year. I am sure that when I see you, at any time during the next 5 or 10 months, you will be free from all involuntary movements."

In other words, there was no question that she would be relieved within a year, or sooner. When such individuals realize that they can transfer their difficulties to other areas, they realize that self-mastery over their symptom is now possible. A specific time limit is not set. Symptom-transformation should never be attempted until the patient can follow posthypnotic suggestions readily and develop a posthypnotic amnesia. Attainment of these are "proof positive" that he will comply with suggested alterations in either sensory or motor areas.

Although this approach is seemingly similar to symptom-substitution, the neurotic behavior is utilized by transformation of the symptom to a less noxious one *without changing the character of the symptom itself.* Erickson[5] describes the following case:

An adult enuretic who was about to be drafted was cured by transferring a bed-wetting anxiety to a lesser anxiety situation. Amnesia was engrafted for a complicated series of posthypnotic suggestions designed to transform his fears over the enuresis into anxieties about a forthcoming visit with relatives. After this was accomplished, his only anxiety was over his mother's adjustment to his being drafted into the service.

Recovery was accomplished by systematically utilizing the patient's anxiety through a process of redirecting and transforming it. He was deliberately confused and distracted by the complexity of the posthypnotic suggestions. Then his anxiety about his wet bed and home relationships was transformed into anxiety about relatives. The final transformation became that of his mother's anxiety about his military service. Thus, some degree of anxiety was continually utilized and ultimately transformed (traded down) into a normal emotion which permitted a normal adjustment.

Symptom-Amelioration

This approach is indicated when the patient is inaccessible to most types of intensive psychotherapy.

A 15-year-old boy, who had been in therapy with several excellent psychiatrists, was referred with a hysterical reaction which involved the continual plucking of his eyelashes. Although he recognized that it was a masturbatory-equivalent symptom, it had gotten worse. Under hypnosis, it was suggested that he alternately increase and decrease the plucking. His symptom was ameliorated on the basis that whatever can be increased can be decreased.

However, not all cases respond as dramatically. Good rapport, motivation and a warm sympathetic approach are particularly indispensable in this approach.

Symptom-Utilization

Symptom-utilization consists in encouraging, accepting and redefining behavior in order to control it. Typical was the un-co-operative patient who continually paced the floor during the therapeutic sessions described below. By having his acting-out behavior shifted into more co-operative activity, the patient eventually follows other directions. These technics utilize the subject's own attitudes, thoughts, feelings and behavior in a manner similar to that in which an induction procedure makes full use of the patient's own ideomotor and ideosensory responses. This differs from the more commonly used hypnotic technics for symptom-removal. These are particularly applicable for stressful situations or for those not amenable to direct hypnotic symptom-removal. The reader is referred to Erickson's excellent and extensive writings for a more detailed description of his technics.[5-8]

Recently, an agitated, suicidally depressed patient, was seen in psychiatric consultation. As he walked up and down the office, gesticulating wildly, he stated, "No doctor can take care of me. My condition is hopeless." I asked him why he felt this way. He stated, "I must keep walking all the time, can't sit still, and I make every therapist nervous. They all gave me up as a bad job." I softly remarked, "You know, your walking is most refreshing to me. After all, *every* other patient either sits or lies down, and at least you are different." Taken aback, he said, "Do you really mean that?" I stated, "Of course I do. But there is one thing I must ask of you. Notice my pictures on the wall. They are all in line and not askew. Now you can walk as much as you wish, but please walk in a perfect square." Needless to say, he was readily hypnotized and eventually recovered.

Also, an experience that happened to the therapist or to another person can be related, and a definitive idea to change can be included, which the patient recognizes as applicable to himself and defends himself against. However, while he is defending himself against the idea, other suggestions can encourage change by misdirection. There is seldom a need to work with resistances, as control of a symptom can be achieved by requesting that it be manifested at a different time than usual, or in a different context or purpose. When a relapse is inevitable, the conditions for its occurrence can be suggested so that it becomes part of a co-operative endeavor rather than resistance by the patient. Symptoms are encouraged to remain until there is no need for their utilization. If a resistant patient states that he is getting worse, Erickson negates this idea and accepts it by remarking, "Since you are worse, might it not be time for a change?"

Insight, transference interpretations or connections between past and present are not employed. Erickson's fundamental purpose is to "bring about a change in the patient, not to focus on his mental or emotional structure." His ingenious structuring of the therapeutic situation is most rewarding.

Corrective Emotional Responses Obtained by Ideomotor Signaling

Time and effort are saved and unrecognized needs for acting-out behavior can be understood when repressed material is brought into awareness by hypnotic self-exploration. Deeply hypnotized patients are instructed to review material long since forgotten, and, after the material is verbalized, its significance is revealed to the patient. It has been observed that the ease with which understanding occurs is most impressive; often an apparently hopeless situation turns into an understandable, logical and ready accomplishment.

In this technic, it is carefully impressed upon the subject that his "unconscious mind" will reveal information pertinent to his problem that was heretofore inaccessible. However, the information revealed is seldom in an immediately recognized form. To understand it, ideomotor signaling (finger responses that are involuntarily given to indicate "yes" or "no") is resorted to so that the "unconscious" can meaningfully answer questions that it cannot answer at the so-called conscious level. The author of this book has never been particularly impressed with this approach. The reasons for seldom using it are discussed on page 292.

Discussion of Rationale of Brief Hypnotherapeutic Methods

Direct suggestions to elicit physiologic responses are generally ineffective. Scene or picture visualization should be used. For instance, in treating the insomniac, posthypnotic suggestions should be that he "see" himself in a deep state of repose, that he "see" his chest moving up and down rhythmically, and, finally, that he "picture" himself deep asleep. This is more effective than the direct posthypnotic command, "You will get drowsy and fall asleep as soon as you lie down on your pillow."

When there is no apparent progress, the therapist should make full use of extraverbal suggestion irrespective of the degree of improvement. As an example, a patient can be asked to report when he slept one minute longer. When the patient concedes this, the groundwork is laid for further recovery by pointing out that, at least, he has taken a "turn for the better."

During symptom-removal by brief hypnotherapy, continual reinforcement at monthly intervals is necessary for most cases. These sessions also can be used to follow the patient's progress and provide the necessary adjustments to changing conditions.

When therapist-centered hypnosis is used, the patient gives up the symptom to please him; it will disappear only as long as the patient has faith in the all-powerful therapist. Relapse occurs because the enforced dependency fosters ambivalence (the co-existence of love and hate) toward the therapist. As soon as the resentment gains the upper hand, the symptom returns. Therefore, all patients are informed as soon as they are taught autohypnosis, "You are now on your own, and each day you will have less dependency on me."

Janet, Freud and many of the older hypnotists contended that, even though a temporary cessation could be achieved dramatically by hypnosis, symptom-removal was not lasting. This was true because *of the way in which they used hypnosis.* They seldom made full use of autohypnosis, sensory-imagery conditioning and other sophisticated refinements. Had they been oriented in the technics of brief hypnotherapy described in this chapter, symptom-removal would have been more permanent. Irrespective of the therapeutic goals, symptom-removal by brief hypnotherapy provides many despondent patients with faith and hope.

PSYCHOBIOLOGY HYPNOTHERAPY

Throughout this volume the author has espoused the dictum that "Anything and everything that helps the patient should be employed." In the psychobiologic approach, such medications as sedatives, tranquilizers and other drugs can be used with hypnotization to induce a psychobiologic reorganization of the personality. Wolberg[37] has described how healthy relationships based on guidance, reassurance, persuasion, re-education and reconditioning under hypnosis can raise the threshold to anxiety-provoking stimuli. In an excellent presentation, Wolberg classified these as follows:

Guidance: The therapist assumes the role of a surrogate figure, and suggestions are in line with the psychological principles involved in guidance.

Reassurance: When suggestions are given by an omniscient authority they are more convincing.

Persuasion: Hypnosis reinforces persuasive arguments, and certain directions are followed more readily.

Re-education: When individuals hold themselves "out at arm's length for inspection," they become aware of their faulty behavior patterns, and a change occurs when the "sting" is taken out of these—densensitization.

Reconditioning: Conditioned reflexes are more readily engrafted when intensification of emotional stimuli occurs.

RECIPROCAL INHIBITION PSYCHOTHERAPY

Wolpe,[38] has developed effective hypnotherapeutic technics which yield results of almost 90 per cent "apparently cured" and "much improved." He contends that a habit can be eradicated by forming a new and antagonistic one toward the same stimulus situation. By deliberately opposing responses antagonistic to anxiety responses, neurotic anxiety response habits can be overcome— this is the reciprocal inhibition principle.

This principle was developed from the observations that only 3 kinds of processes can produce lasting changes in an organism's habit of response to a given stimulus situation. These are growth, lesions and learning. Since neurotic behavior originates in learning, it can be eliminated only by "unlearning." Such other responses as relaxation and assertive sexual ones are capable of inhibiting anxiety. Breathing, conditioned-motor and conditioned-avoidance responses are employed in special situations. These conditions are always arranged in such a way that neurotic anxiety will be maximally inhibited by the antagonistic response selected.

Reciprocal inhibition therapy makes full use of progressive relaxation and hypnosis to counter the effects of anxiety-evoking stimuli. An "anxiety hierarchy" list is constructed, consisting of those stimuli to which the patient reacts with unadapted anxiety. The hypnotized patient is told to imagine the weakest item or the smallest "dose" of phobic stimulation on the list. If the relaxed state is not disturbed by this, a slightly stronger "dose" is presented at the next session from the next item on the list. The "dosage" is gradually increased from session to session, until at last the phobic stimulus can be presented at maximal intensity without impairing the depth of relaxation. This eventually prevents the patient from reacting with his previous anxiety to those situations that are associated with even the most intense phobic stimuli.

This systematic desensitization technic is applicable to most neuroses, as they are basically unadaptive conditioned-anxiety reactions. According to Wolpe, all psychotherapy is based on the reciprocal inhibition principle: emotional responses are evoked which have the capacity to inhibit anxiety. He recognizes that a nonspecific placebo effect (about 50%) is operative in all psychotherapeutic methods, ranging from traditional counseling to psychoanalysis. Thus, 50 per cent of his patients profit from this effect, but other factors must be considered, since his "cure" rate is almost 90 per cent.

SYSTEMATIC DESENSITIZATION

The patient first gets a "homework" task, wherein he is asked to make up a list of everything that frightens, disturbs or embarrasses him. Systematic desensitization to increasing amounts of these anxiety-evoking stimuli is initiated under hypnosis. The basic assumption underlying this procedure is that the response to the imagined situation resembles that to the real situation. Experience bears out that individuals become anxious when they imagine stimuli that are fearful in reality. These will be used for desensitizing the patient.

In the first desensitization session, scene visualization is suggested by hypnosis. The least disturbing items from the bottom of the list are first presented at 2- or 3-second intervals. When tension is exhibited, the hand is raised as a signal and the ongoing scene is immediately "blacked out." After dehypnotization, the patient is asked if the scenes were clear and which ones were disturbing.

During the second desensitization session, those items that produced no disturbance are omitted and the next higher items are presented. If anxiety is manifested after the presentation of a weak scene, a weaker item must be substituted. Stimuli with a high anxiety-evoking potential must not be presented prematurely. If a major setback occurs, several hypnotic sessions should be devoted to deep relaxation without scene visualization. At subsequent sessions, subject matter far down the list from the items that produced the setback are introduced cautiously. Weaker reactions usually ensue when the same scene is presented several times during the session. When this occurs, therapy is accelerated.

With proper handling, most patients will report a progressive decrease of sensitivity in from 10 to 25 sessions. Progress also varies with hypnotic depth. Nonhypnotizable patients, however, ultimately do as well but are slower. A failure of about 50 per cent occurs in those who cannot imagine the suggested scenes. Progress is impeded when the disturbed reaction to the imagined scene is not experienced as reality. Here, the relevant emotions can be aroused by having the patients *verbalize* the scenes; they then progress the same as the other patients do. Some patients, particularly those with hysterical conversion-reactions, are treated by the repeated presentation of meaningful experiences under hypnosis. The reader is referred to Wolpe's excellent presentation describing desensitization sessions conducted during hypnosis. Illustrative case histories indicate that the method is useful regardless of the character of the neurotic responses; they disappear when the power of the stimuli to evoke anxiety is removed. He reports cures in ulcer, impotency, insomnia, migraine, paranoid obsessions, phobic reactions and a wide variety of other psychosomatic conditions.

MISCELLANEOUS SPECIALIZED TECHNICS OF HYPNOTHERAPY

Yoga or Y-State of Hypnosis

According to Meares,[22] the Yoga or Y-state of hypnosis is characterized by profound abstraction that is produced and maintained by an *active* effort of the will concentrated on a single idea. It differs from sleep and ordinary hypnosis in that the cerebration is active and controlled and concerned primarily with subjective ideation. It is also particularly helpful for those who are unsuitable for hypnoanalysis and for certain types of introverts whose greater subjectivity facilitates the Y-state. Also, those who readily enter meditative, prayer or reverie states appear to do better in the Y-state. Meares uses routine hypnosis for therapeutic suggestions and relaxation; here the patient remains utterly *passive*. The Y-state, on the other hand, is more suitable for autohypnotherapeutic technics.

Religious Hypnotherapy

Rodriquez[25] makes full use of a religious approach in conjunction with hypnotherapy. Emotional balance is established whenever the patient's "rationalizations are organized into a new system which helps him solve his immediate problems as well as to regulate his emotions in a more efficient manner in the future." A constructive interpersonal relationship facilitates acceptance of the rationalizations.

Today, many clergymen, especially those who are also psychologists and psychiatrists, are employing hypnotherapy with astonishing success. Since they are already a sort of father-confessor to many of their parishioners, they are in an enviable position to help them because of well-established faith. Pastoral counseling has made rapid strides recently, and it is only a matter of time until there will be more clergymen making use of hypnotherapy. This author has taught hypnotherapy to several clergymen who also were psychiatrists or psychologists. They report gratifying results when hypnosis is utilized within a religious framework.

Suggestive "Sleep"

Platonov,[23] in a psychophysiologic treatise on psychotherapy and hypnosis, describes how he has used suggestive "sleep" for the past 50 years for achieving positive therapeutic effects in thousands of patients. His beliefs are in line with Pavlov's, namely, that hypnosis affords curative protective inhibition (regenerative self-healing) of neurons disturbed by excitatory processes.

Platonov's hypnotherapy utilizes direct symptom-eliminating suggestions, as follows:

"What you have suffered belongs already to the past and does not trouble you any more. You have forgotten all your suffering, and when you remember it, it does not distress you." In treating a patient who has a fear of thunderstorms, he made the following suggestion, "You are no longer afraid of thunderstorms, and they do not disturb you."

According to orthodox pavlovian doctrine, when the suggestion, "Your suffering belongs to the past and does not trouble you any more," is repeated several times, an "inhibition of the point of concentrated excitation" is brought about. The words, "What you have suffered belongs to the past," represent an inhibitory conditioned reflex directed toward the suppression of the excitatory "trigger zone" in the cortex. In other words, the deranged regulatory activity of the cortex rather than the symptom is treated, and this is accomplished by the use of appropriate word stimuli.

Platonov's hypnosuggestive methods are combined with an eclectic psychotherapeutic approach. Therapy is begun with a series of interviews to ascertain how the symptom developed. Thus, a careful history becomes an integral part of the psychotherapeutic approach to the patient as it establishes good rapport, especially in neurotics. Explanation and persuasion are used first, and this is followed by suggestion under hypnosis for the purpose of consolidating what has been said to the patient before the induction of hypnosis.

It is interesting that Platonov and his associates, who have hypnotized many thousands of persons in the Soviet Union for over half a century, remark:[24]

We have never observed any harmful influence on the patient which could be ascribed to the method of hypnosuggestive therapy, presumably leading to the development of an "unstable personality," "slavish subordination," "weakening of the will," or an "increase or pathological urge for hypnosis."

It is also of considerable interest that he describes the important work done in 15 "hypnotariums" organized by the Leningrad City Board of Health over 20 years ago. The Russians, sparked by Pavlov's pioneering research in hypnosis, have made some remarkable contributions.

ACTIVE COMPLEX PSYCHOTHERAPY

Another hypnotherapeutic approach based on the pavlovian model is Volgylsi's[31] active complex psychotherapy. Hypnosis is directed toward influencing higher cortical activities (psychic functions) as well as subcortical mechanisms (affective) by a psychoprophylactic method involving conditioned reflexology under hypnosis and a psychosomatic approach. In his recent book,[32] he describes how he treated over 56,500 patients by a combination of group psychotherapy, hypnosis and supportive technics. His work rejects mystic, superstitious, dogmatic or one-sided psychologizing "which is not based on scientific neurophysiologic data."

HYPNOSYNTHESIS

Conn[2] refers to his method as hypnosynthesis. He utilizes hypnotherapy without extensive probing. The patient uses it as he sees fit, without being given any symptom-eliminating suggestions or being forced to remember unpleasant events, or being given preconceived interpretations or directions. With this method, in which no importance is attached to the depth of the hypnosis, Conn has obtained very satisfactory results in a wide variety of cases. In studying the psychodynamics of recovery under hypnosis, he remarks that "Much of the current interest in hypnotherapy is a rebellion against Freud's dictum that a patient can only get well at the price of sweat and tears and by an expenditure of much time and money."[4] His experience substantiates our contentions, namely, that the hypnotist only "sets the stage"; it is

the patient who induces the "trance" by doing what is expected of him.[3]

Solovey and Milechnin[29] base their hypnotherapeutic approach on Conn's principles but, in addition, they incorporate extraverbal suggestions intended to increase the well-being of the patient. They, too, find that light hypnosis usually is adequate for giving rationalizations that may act as stimuli for what they term "emotional stabilization."

HYPNOANALYSIS

Watkins[35] contends that the hypnotic concept of "trance" and the psychoanalytic concept of "transference" are essentially identical. Even though many subjects are in a deep state of hypnosis, this does not necessarily imply that they are in a static state, but, rather, as emphasized in this book, they fluctuate up and down the broad continuum of what is referred to as consciousness (the sleep-wakefulness cycle). This will vary from second to second. Thus, when such hypnoanalytic technics as automatic writing, projective technics and crystal-gazing are employed, and the patient is required to talk, the patient inevitably shifts from deeper stages to lighter ones. For those hypnotherapists who wish to follow psychoanalytic technics, there is an extensive bibliography on the subject.[1, 14, 15, 26, 28, 36]

When hypnosis is used with psychoanalytic procedures, the entire process can be speeded up, and there is no such undue dependency as compliance. Also, significant emotional participation occurs when deeply hidden material is released and, with appropriate technics, the meaningfulness of this data can be integrated into full awareness. If one wishes to work with resistances, these can be analyzed as in an orthodox analysis. Hypnoanalysis thus derives from hypnosis "a penetrative technical instrument that obviates many of the time-consuming elements which often render ordinary psychoanalysis objectionable and in some cases impossible."[16]

APPLICATIONS OF, CONTRAINDICATIONS AND INDICATIONS FOR HYPNOANALYSIS

APPLICABILITY

Anyone who can be hypnotized can be hypnoanalyzed to a degree. Individuals who can attain deeper stages of hypnosis are the best subjects for hypnoanalysis. This limits the method to less than 20 per cent of the population.

CONTRAINDICATIONS

Those who can enter a sufficiently deep state and who are able to bring forth highly charged emotions require a competent and well-trained psychotherapist to deal with the material. Therefore, cases must be selected. The manic-depressive, with wide mood swings, is seldom a good candidate for hypnoanalysis, as his disorganized mental state results in inadequate concentration. It is virtually impossible to treat detached schizophrenics, who are not in contact with reality, by this method. The lack of reality perception is a prime contraindication to hypnoanalysis.

The fearful individual, with weak and inadequate characterologic defenses, who is likely to be overwhelmed by the intensity of the therapy, and those who are too preoccupied with their negative fantasies, or those who fear an attack on their homosexual strivings, should not be treated by this approach.

INDICATIONS FOR HYPNOANALYSIS

Hypnoanalysis is particularly indicated for psychoneurotics who do not respond to brief hypnotherapeutic procedures, or for those who already have had some type of unsuccessful psychotherapy. It is particularly suited for the poorly motivated patient such as the psychopath. Here utilization of posthypnotic suggestions to "bind" the patient in therapy is a distinct advantage until a healthy rapport is established. Though an extreme degree of dependency is fostered deliberately, it can be worked through and dissolved during later sessions.

Hypnoanalysis is both an investigative and a therapeutic technic in the refractory obese individual, the narcotic addict and the alcoholic. This approach can lend support to the healthy aspects of the personality until the need for the symptom is worked through and controlled. Hypnoanalysis also has shown considerable promise in the treatment of phobias and compulsions.

Appropriate safeguards, such as enabling the patient to remove his own maladaptive responses through sensory-imagery conditioning and other technics, as a rule, prevent recurrence of the phobic or compulsive reaction. Rosen[27] has described how age-regression was hypnotherapeutically induced in several patients as an emergency measure to prevent suicide.

METHODOLOGY OF HYPNOANALYSIS

Patients are first trained in hypnosis, autohypnosis and other phenomena of the deep state. This may require 20 sessions or more. The number varies with the type of emotional involvement, the motivation of the patient, his inherent ability to achieve a deep state, and the effort he puts forth. At the end of the preliminary training period, the following criteria should be met: (1) The patient must be capable of entering a hypnotic state upon a given posthypnotic signal or through autohypnosis. (2) He should be able to follow posthypnotic suggestions readily, especially those which produce amnesia and age-regression. (3) Through revivification he must be able to re-experience events long since forgotten.

Stillerman[30] emphasizes that steps must be taken in the first few sessions to understand the patient's reaction to the therapeutic situation, that is, his anxieties, his reactions to the hypnotherapist, and why and how he is defending himself and thus resisting change and progress. Before attempting induction, he questions the patient regarding his reactions either to observing or to experiencing hypnosis and how he feels about being hypnotized. Next, the subject's reactions to either physical or mental activities are closely observed, and he is immediately asked what he is thinking about. After the initial induction, the various emotional reactions experienced while entering hypnosis, being in it, or coming out of it are elicited. In subsequent sessions, dreams as well as verbal and nonverbal productions are included.

Following the training period, the analytic phase may be instituted. The resistances and the defenses are clarified by development of the transference neurosis. This phase of hypnoanalysis closely parallels the standard psychoanalytic procedure. The process utilizes free associations, dreams, analyses and recollections, all of which are interpreted by the hypnoanalyst.

HANDLING RESISTANCES

Whenever marked resistances are encountered, the patient can be deeply hypnotized and the resistances in question undercut. The efficacy of hypnoanalysis, according to Lindner,[15] is not reduced by undercutting resistances, nor is this merely superficial therapy. All the resistances are not dispelled through hypnosis. As mentioned in the preceding chapter, the blocks are handled through discussion, interpretation and evocation of the reasons for the various defensive mechanisms employed by the patient. This includes the more serious resistances which relate to the character structure, and the symptomatology of the patient, such as loss of memory for traumatic events and defense mechanisms, character malformation and distortion through symptom-formation.

HANDLING SYMPTOM-FORMATION

Many hypnoanalysts believe that, for lasting therapeutic benefits, a protective amnesia for each hypnotic session must be induced in order to guarantee that the entire personality will participate in the therapeutic process. Lindner,[17] the chief protagonist of this approach, has described how the imposition of posthypnotic amnesia is used in the recovery of lost, repressed or rejected memories or in the disintegration of resistances. He terms this the "interim phenomenon." Briefly, once repressed material has been divulged during hypnosis, the patient is slowly prepared to receive this information at nonhypnotic levels. Lindner states:

In other words, in the interim between the disclosure of significant but repressed memories or other resistance-forming material and waking free association, the ego is readied for the reception of what it had formerly rejected, for any one or a combination of possible reasons.[18]

Actually, this obviates the lengthy and controversial "analysis of resistances" which plagues so many psychoanalytic sessions. The saving in time is considerable, and the patient is prepared to accept what he formerly defended himself against.

A spontaneous flow of the material for which the amnesia was imposed filters up into awareness either after the termination of the hypnotic session or during a subsequent visit. Therefore, nothing of importance to therapy is lost and, more important, the patient participates with full awareness in the therapeutic processes. Finally, through posthypnotic suggestions, the patient can be instructed that some of the material which was too traumatic for him to face during the session can be the basis for a dream between now and the next visit. Thus, if there is a symbolic correlation between the revealed data and the dream, the validity of the exhumed material can be cross-checked via this approach.

Posthypnotic suggestions, used for reinforcement, help bolster the changes in the personality organization. Hence, adaptation to new and difficult situations becomes less painful and time-consuming. Hypnosis may also contribute to the dissolution of the transference relationship which is managed as in a routine analysis. The energies that were formerly of pathogenic significance and monopolized by the symptom can be redistributed along the line dictated by the entire course of the therapy.

Since the accord between patient and analyst is closer and more intense than in other forms of psychotherapy, the tools for therapy are sharper, more incisive. This undoubtedly accounts for the rapidity with which exploration of deeply repressed material can take place in hypnoanalysis. It is unfortunate that hypnoanalysis is too often ignored, as it is a valid therapy even though limited to those patients capable of entering deep hypnosis.

OTHER UNCOVERING HYPNOANALYTIC TECHNICS

HORIZONTAL EXPLORATION

Horizontal exploration of the personality structure can be utilized at various levels through hypermnesia.[33] Here, the therapist identifies himself as a friend of the parents, or acts as one of the parents. The patient can be asked, "How did things go with you today?" Or, "What seems to be bothering you?" Or, after engrafting an amnesia for his own identity, the skillful therapist assumes the role of a sibling, a friend, a teacher, an employer, a lover or a mate. In this situation, the patient's verbalization and behavior will reveal the way he felt toward significant persons in his life at different age levels.

Vertical Exploration

Vertical exploration can also be used to trace the origin and the development of specific attitudes. Interweaving of the chronologic past with the present rapidly assesses earlier attitudes. This seems to be a function of the interpretative cortex, in which past events timelessly blend with current realities. Regression is attained by stating, "You are looking at a large calendar on the wall. Instead of numbers for each day and month, you will see numbers of the years. Whenever you wish, you may tear off each page. The first one is 1961. Now 1960, 1959," etc. (until the desired age is attained). The statements must be in the present tense, as, "It is now 1941. Do you know that today is your birthday? You are 8 years old *now*, are you not? What are you thinking of doing this afternoon?"

Other attitudes such as love, hate, fear and sexual ones can be traced by *age-progression*. For instance, if a patient who has regressed to age 7 mentions that at age 5 he was extremely bitter toward his mother, he can be told, "You are no longer 5. With each breath you take, you are growing older. Five, 6, 7. Now you are 15 years old. How does it feel to be in high school?" If the answer is in the present tense and the person appears to talk and act in accordance with the suggested age, the age-regression is valid. He is now asked, "Do you love your mother?" If the answer is affirmative, the hostility in all probability is deeply repressed and it will require other and more complex methods such as projective technics to uncover the genesis of emotion. If the answer is negative, considerable light on the origin and the development of the hostility can be obtained.

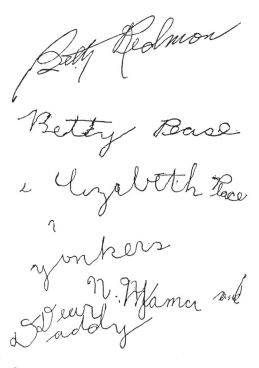

(*Top*) Normal handwriting at age 44. (*Center*) Sample of handwriting while regressed at age 8. (*Bottom*) Part of letter written to parents.

Dissociated or Automatic Handwriting

This technic can be used to ascertain the reasons for a conflict. After the arm and the

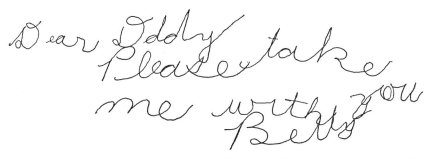

Age 10: angry with her father because he never took her with him when he went away. (Compare with the following samples.)

hand are dissociated, the patient, upon direct questioning, may give one answer while his hand is writing something else. This is because the dissociated hand is released from cortical control. The written material can be a clue for the cause of the patient's anxiety.

Illustrative is the case of a frigid 44-year-old woman who had an intense hostility toward her husband, who symbolized a father-figure whom she hated. The onset of this attitude was evinced by the following material, obtained under automatic writing.

When asked to explain the writing, after dehypnotization, she stated that she was very angry toward her father when she was 8 years old because he sent her to boarding school. The automatic writing reactivated a long-forgotten incident, and also revealed the cause of her hostile attitude toward her husband. She remarked, "My husband is just like Dad. He is always so bossy and opinionated. I just can't stand him."

Each patient should be "restored" to his present chronologic age and the hand "returned" to normal before dehypnotization. While still under hypnosis, the patient should be instructed to remember everything that was written. Protective amnesia can be instituted if the material is too traumatic to be faced at this time. An explanation of the written material, intelligible only to the patient, can be facilitated by posthypnotic

suggestion, provided he really wants to explain it.

PROJECTIVE HYPNOANALYSIS

Such psychometric tests as the Rorschach, or other stimulating situations, are presented in the form of what seems to be nonsense material. Here, while not on guard, patients project significant conflicts. Variations such as the theater technic, crystal-gazing, or scene-visualization obtained by gazing at a blank card, often reveal inner feelings which can be discussed after dehypnotization. However, as Watkins has mentioned, the more the situation is structured, the less significant will be the material which emerges.

Another useful technic is the Thematic Apperception Test (T.A.T.), which consists of the presentation of various pictures about which the hypnotized patient is asked to imagine a story or a theme suggested by them. In the Jung Association Test, the patient is requested to give the association evoked by the next stimulus word. Each response becomes the stimulus for the next. Regression can also be used. In an unreported series with Helen Sargent, the author has validated Watkins' contentions.

HYPNODRAMA

The methods introduced by those interested in psychodrama also can be employed

(*Top*) Age 16: son is born. (*Center*) Age 30: sample handwriting. (*Bottom*) Age 47: Written in answer to the question "What is bothering you?" (Son's wife had divorced him; mother is worried about son.)

while the patient is under hypnosis. The whole conflict situation can be dramatized, and the therapist or a professional actor can play one of the roles. While the patient is under hypnosis, a posthypnotic suggestion is given that he play the part of a specific character. The two then dramatize a situation in which the inner conflicts of the imaginary character with whom the patient has identified are portrayed.

The personality structure also can be split or dissociated for separate study: the patient can act out both roles. Naturally, the dissociation should be along the lines of the inferred conflict. In this way the patient actually re-enacts his own inner conflicts. Regression, dissociated handwriting and any of the projective technics can be used in conjunction with hypnodrama.

ABREACTION

An emotional reliving or re-enacting of traumatic experiences, with a resultant release of energy, can be obtained in good hypnotic subjects. This approach is valuable for anxiety and hysterical reactions of recent origin, particularly those associated with war neuroses. The nature of repressed impulses can be studied to determine their purpose. Following release of the inhibited guilt, rage or fear impulses, intellectual as well as emotional reintegration can be accomplished.

Experience with these methods in a military setting indicates that, through enactment of the conflict, the original frustrating situations are brought to a more satisfactory and realistic solution. It is believed that:

An emotionally corrective experience is undergone which "completes" the unfinished strivings, which are the repetitive core of the neurosis and relieves the need to continue its symptomatic manifestations.[34]

THE AFFECT-BRIDGE OR IN-AND-OUT METHOD

Watkins[33] makes use of yet another interesting technic wherein a hypnotically well-trained patient is given a revealing statement while hypnotized. After the patient is dehypnotized, the material is discussed and then he is rehypnotized for further discussion and questioning to ascertain whether or not his understanding is complete. The entire session may develop into an in-and-out interview for uncovering new material or understanding old points. Weaving between hypnotic and nonhypnotic levels of awareness helps the patient to reintegrate concepts at both levels. In other words, bridging of the "unconscious to conscious" achieves a more lasting change in the personality structure.

INDUCTION OF DREAMS

Meares,[20] in an excellent presentation, describes special procedures to facilitate hypnoanalysis. He makes use of analysis of dreams produced through direct or indirect posthypnotic suggestions. This is a useful technic for cases in which regression and abreaction cannot be induced.

INDUCED HALLUCINATIONS

In a fashion similar to that in the technics described by Watkins, hallucinations are suggested without suggesting their nature. Conflicts ordinarily inaccessible to hypnoanalysis are revealed by this technic. The induced hallucinations are produced by suggesting that the subject visualize himself on a theater screen, or in a house in which he has been at one time, or that he "see" images which will appear in a crystal ball (crystal-gazing). The analysis of the content of the induced hallucination often throws considerable light on the repressed conflicts.

UNSTRUCTURED HALLUCINATIONS

Unstructured hallucinations are induced without structuring the therapeutic situation. Merely by asking the subject, while he is in deep hypnosis, to relate what is happening, significant material may be revealed, and spontaneous regression and abreaction often occur.

PRODUCTION OF EXPERIMENTAL CONFLICTS

An artificial situation which resembles the patient's conflict situation often can afford sufficient insight as to how and why he reacts to his own conflict. The patient is led to experience the appropriate emotion and he reacts to it with his own particular neurotic behavior. Posthypnotic suggestions are directed for recall of those experiences and feelings which the patient had while hypnotized. Thus, while observing the reaction to an imaginary conflict, insight is gained into the nature of his conflict situation. This approach should be used only by experienced hypnotherapists.

Narcohypnoanalysis or Narcosynthesis

Skillful hypnotherapists seldom use drugs. However, occasionally a refractory patient may be given a small amount of Pentothal Sodium; this often allows the patient to talk more freely. The patient who benefits most by this approach is the one who states, "I doubt if I can be hypnotized." Other individuals, who associate hypnotizability with gullibility, respond well to various drugs such as scopolamine. Such patients are merely looking for some excuse to respond to the suggestions of the therapist; they do not feel stigmatized by drug-induced "hypnosis."

Hypnography

Meares uses a form of graphic expression which has a much wider application than automatic writing in hypnoanalysis. Hypnography is integrated with verbal hypnoanalysis and waking psychotherapy. He has described hypnography as a "technique in hypnoanalysis in which the hypnotized patient projects psychic material in black and white painting." While under hypnosis, the patient associates to the painting. Meares feels that it is useful for patients who do not talk readily in hypnosis. He believes that graphic expression of conflicts has a greater therapeutic effect than verbal expressions of the same conflicts, as it speeds up hypnoanalysis. Suppressed and repressed material is disclosed more readily, and there is greater emotional participation of the patient in the treatment. The patient is less apt to defend himself from his emotions, and greater emotional participation usually leads to spontaneous regression and abreaction. This approach is particularly indicated for those who cannot adjust to current reality conflicts. The reason for this is that, when the patient is actually confronted with the problem which he expresses in hypnography, he develops a greater tolerance of the conflict. As a result, he is not so disturbed by it and makes a better adjustment to reality.

Often, however, when the elicited material is presented to the patient at nonhypnotic levels, it leads to anxiety manifestations. With somatic improvement, the patient slowly gains insight through the ventilation of traumatic material by hypnography. Often without any "waking psychotherapy," further symptomatic improvement results, which manifests itself by a change of the paintings. Partial amnesia often occurs after the sessions. Since conflicts are being expressed graphically and verbally by associations, hypnography facilitates hypnoanalysis. For a more complete account of hypnography, the reader is referred to Meares's excellent monograph on this subject.[19]

The dangers here are that the sudden and permanent recognition of the significance of the repressed material may result in an attack of acute anxiety. This necessitates a deeper stage of hypnosis. Meares points out that an unconscious misinterpretation of the therapist's behavior can result in the patient's not being able to be dehypnotized—a sort of defense reaction which calls for an elastic ("psychodynamic") handling of the hypnosis.

Hypnoplasty

This technic in hypnoanalysis resembles hypnography. The hypnotized patient uses clay to model whatever he wishes to make. The patient's conflicts find expression in plastic rather than graphic form. He is asked to associate to the model, and the disclosed material is used in his psychotherapeutic handling.

When the patient talks about the shapes which he has made, the specific meanings and the nature of the conflict which has motivated the making of a particular model are brought to light. Meares believes that this is an excellent approach for the resistant patient, and that hypnoplasty has a real place in hypnoanalysis. For a more complete account of hypnoplasty, the reader is referred to another fine monograph.[21]

REFERENCES

1. Brenman, M., and Gill, M. M.: Hypnotherapy, New York, Internat. Univ. Press, pp. 121-134, 1947.

2. Conn, J. H.: Hypnosynthesis; hypnosis as a unifying interpersonal experience, J. Nerv. & Ment. Dis. *109*:9-24, 1949.

3. ——: Cultural and clinical hypnosis, placebos and aspects of suggestibility, Int. J. Clin. & Exper. Hypnosis 7:175-186, 1959.

4. ——: Psychodynamics of recovery under hypnosis, J. Clin. & Exper. Hypnosis 8:3-16, 1960.

5. Erickson, M. H.: Special techniques of brief hypnotherapy, J. Clin. & Exper. Hypnosis 2:109-129, 1954.

6. *Ibid.*, p. 111.

7. ——: Self-exploration in the hypnotic state, J. Clin. & Exper. Hypnosis 3:49-57, 1955.

7a. ——: Certain Principles in Medical Hypnosis. Paper read at Pan American Med. Assn., May 5, 1960.

8. ——: Further clinical techniques of hypnosis: utilization techniques, Am. J. Clin. Hypnosis 2:3-21, 1959.

8a. Frank, J. D.: Persuasion and Healing: A Comparative Study of Psychotherapy, Baltimore, Johns Hopkins Press, 1961.

9. Haley, J.: Control in brief psychotherapy, A.M.A. Arch. Gen. Psychiat. *4*:139-154, 1961.

10. *Ibid.*, p. 143.

11. *Ibid.*, p. 146.

12. Huxley, A.: Human potentialities, Menn. Clin. Bull. 25:53-68, 1961.

13. Kaufman, M. R.: Hypnosis in psychotherapy, Arch. Gen. Psychiat. *4*:30-39, 1961.

14. Kline, M.: Dynamic Psychology, New York, Julian Press, 1955.

15. Lindner, R. M.: Hypnoanalysis as psychotherapy, Brit. J. Medical Hypnotism *4*:34, 1952.

16. *Ibid.*, p. 35.

17. ——: Hypnoanalysis as a Psychotherapeutic Technique *in* Specialized Techniques in Psychotherapy, New York, Basic Books, Inc., 1953.

18. *Ibid.*, p. 34.

19. Meares, A.: Hypnography, Springfield, Ill., Thomas, 1957.

20. ——: A System of Medical Hypnosis, Philadelphia, Saunders, 1960.

21. ——: Shapes of Sanity, Springfield, Ill., Thomas, 1960.

22. ——: The Y-State: An Hypnotic Variant, J. Clin. & Exper. Hypnosis 8:237-242, 1960.

23. Platonov, K.: The Word as a Physiological and Therapeutic Factor, Moscow, Foreign Languages Publishing House, 1959.

24. *Ibid.*, p. 424.

25. Rodriguez, R.: Quoted in Ref. 29.

26. Rosen, H.: Hypnosis in Psychiatry, New York, Julian Press, 1953.

27. Rosen, H.: Regression hypnotherapeutically induced as an emergency measure in a suicidally depressed patient, J. Clin. & Exper. Hypnosis 3:58-70, 1955.

28. Schneck, J.: Hypnosis and Modern Medicine, Springfield, Ill., Thomas, 1953.

29. Solovey, G., and Milechnin, A.: Hypnosis as the substratum of many different psychotherapies, Am. J. Clin. Hypnosis 3:9, 1960.

30. Stillerman, B.: The management in analytic hypnotherapy of the psychodynamic reaction to the induction of hypnosis, J. Clin. & Exper. Hypnosis 5:3-11, 1957.

31. Volgyesi, F. A.: On the Psycho-therapeutic Importance of Hypnotic Sleep and Sleep Protective Inhibition, Brit. J. Med. Hypnotism 3:2, 1951.

32. ——: Ueber Aktiv-Komplexe Psychotherapie und die Blivegung "Schule der Kranken," Berlin, Verlag Volk & Gesundheit, 1959-60.

33. Watkins, J.: Hypnotherapy of War Neuroses, New York, Ronald, 1949.

34. *Ibid.*, p. 105.

35. ——: Trance and transference, J. Clin. & Exper. Hypnosis 2:284, 1954.

36. Wolberg, L.: Hypnoanalysis, New York, Grune & Stratton, 1945.

37. ——: Medical Hypnosis, New York, Grune & Stratton, 1945.

38. Wolpe, J.: Psychotherapy by Reciprocal Inhibition, Stanford, Calif., Stanford Univ. Press, 1958.

SUPPLEMENTARY READING

Estabrooks, G. H.: Hypnosis: Current Problems, New York, Harper, 1962.

Haley, J.: The control of fear with hypnosis, Am. J. Clin. Hypnosis 2:109-116, 1960.

McCartney, J. L.: Hypnoanalysis: combined use of hypnosis and analytic psychotherapy, Brit. J. Med. Hypnotism *13*:27-33, 1962.

Meares, A.: Shapes of Sanity, Springfield, Ill., Thomas, 1960.

Schneck, J. M.: Hypnoanalysis, Internat. J. Clin. Exper. Hypnosis *10*:1-13, 1962.

Watts, A. W.: Psychotherapy East and West, New York, Pantheon, 1961.

48

Evaluation of Valid and Invalid Criticisms of Hypnotherapy

Criticism of hypnotherapy will exist as long as its many proponents do not recognize its limitations. However, even though their numbers are decreasing, some psychotherapists seldom content themselves with this valid rebuke. Even though many are unfamiliar with modern hypnosis, they dismiss it with a blanket indictment.

Fortunately, neo-Freudian psychoanalysts and eclectic psychiatrists are changing their outmoded views toward hypnosis, but there is still a powerful segment whose sweeping generalizations must be combated. Therefore, the purpose of the author is not only to discuss the *valid* criticisms and limitations of hypnosis, but also to clarify unwarranted objections. This necessitates a critical evaluation of the criticisms given by those who oppose hypnosis. The author has no intent to malign other systems of therapy, but sincerely hopes that the best feature of all recognized therapeutic methods will be synthesized and absorbed into the mainstream of American psychiatry.

DO WE KNOW HOW HYPNOSIS WORKS?

One common criticism is, "No one knows why it works."[30] This is not a valid objection. No one knows the exact modus operandi of electroshock therapy, yet we use it. Two leading investigators,[16] in a recent treatise on hypnotherapy, explain hypnosis on the basis of traditional psychoanalytical tenets, but it is the substratum of many therapies. We know that the process of hypnosis is based on a strong *interpersonal* relationship between therapist and patient, and that the response is a meaningful *intrapersonal* experience for the patient, particularly con-

ducive to the establishment of specific convictions. Older investigators, because of their omnipotent approach, overlooked this dynamism. Mesmer, for instance, failed to realize that an expectant attitude catalyzed the imaginative processes to unleash the inherent recovery forces. No wonder he was unable to explain the curative effects of his "magnetic principle." Might not many Freudians as well as some analytically minded hypnotherapists have fallen into the same trap for similar reasons?

Freud,[12] with his characteristic zeal and scientific relentlessness, indicated that psychoanalytic theory needed more validation. Yet, because of his apparent lack of understanding of hypnosis as a subjective phenomenologic experience, he failed to consider it as even partial validation of his concepts. In his search for the truth, he considered suggestion "as a nucleus of hypnosis and the key to its understanding. . . ."[11] Thus, like the other healers, he denied that his therapeutic results were due to suggestion, and instead resorted to complex formulations to explain them. Because he erroneously thought of hypnosis as a therapist-directed modality, he avoided it for reasons described below.

It is of more than passing interest that the wheel now has made a complete turn from mesmerism and/or hypnosis to psychoanalysis and back to a more sophisticated hypnosis. Had Freud been acquainted with these very advanced technics instead of authoritatively removing symptoms under somnambulism, he surely would have understood its rationale and recognized the value of its therapeutic potency. This undoubtedly would have enhanced his other brilliant concepts which laid the foundation for the psychological sciences.

HYPNOTHERAPY IS NOT A PANACEA

It was not until mesmerism divorced itself from thought transference and clairvoyance that it made the transition into Braid's hypnotism. Thus, if hypnosis is to receive further acceptance as a psychological tool, it must divorce itself completely from the unwarranted and sensational claims made by some of its ardent proponents. These have done it more harm than its uninformed opponents have. The latter, however, are as much in error, because, while they deny its therapeutic efficacy, they impute great harm to even a single posthypnotic suggestion. Without more accurately controlled follow-up data, it cannot be claimed that hypnotherapy is more curative than other psychotherapies. However, it is a relatively rapid method when compared with the more orthodox psychotherapies, and can reach certain types of disorders ordinarily refractory to conventional psychotherapy, as chronic conversion reactions, phobias and compulsive disorders.

It is unfortunate that most lay individuals and some uninformed therapists look upon hypnotherapy as a "magical gesture." Desperately ill persons "clutch at straws," and, when disillusionment sets in, they are apt to become more depressed. Although some degree of "magic" is necessary to establish conviction phenomena, hypnotherapy should not be oversold; otherwise it will soon be another nostrum.

DOES STRONG DEPENDENCY ON THE THERAPIST EXIST?

One criticism repeatedly stressed is that extreme dependency on the therapist is fostered because the hypnotic interpersonal relationship is "like that of parent and child."[10] Where dependency occurs, it may be due to the *manner in which the hypnotic interpersonal relationship was utilized!* The therapist, as an omniscient and authoritative figure, will foster dependency irrespective of the therapeutic approach. Why then should hypnotherapy be singled out for censure? Dependency is produced by both the emotional needs of the therapist and the degree of neurotic involvement of the patient.

One can conclude that dependency is not brought to the fore because of the hypnotic situation but rather *due to the nature of the interactional processes between therapist and patient.* What patient is not strongly dependent upon his physician? In psychoanalysis, this dependency is analyzed as part of the therapeutic process. This also can be done when it occurs during hypnotherapy.

Kubie[22] remarks that he would have difficulty demonstrating the constancy of archaic relationships indicative of regressive trends in either the process of induction or the final state of hypnosis. He also has noted dependency in many experiments, both with and without the use of drugs as adjuvants, and with or without the presence of a living hypnotist. Wolberg[40] states that, in hundreds of patients and volunteers who have been hypnotized a great many times, not a single patient has been made unduly dependent or has become "addicted" to hypnotherapy. Thus, here are two experienced psychoanalysts, leaders of their schools, dispelling the myth of hypnotic dependency. Permissive procedures, autohypnosis and sensory-imagery conditioning cannot produce any more than the usual dependency noted in any doctor-patient relationship.

DOES HYPNOTHERAPY SEXUALIZE THE DOCTOR-PATIENT RELATIONSHIP?

One continually hears that, in hypnotherapy, the patient "falls in love" with the therapist, and that the relationship has an erotic root in that trance and transference are similar.[36] Since sexual attraction between patient and therapist occurs in other therapeutic relationships, this is not limited to hypnotherapy. Merely being hypnotized cannot be equated with sexual submission. During deep hypnosis, most subjects can resist the operator's suggestions and actions if these violate their moral codes. Nor is there a real danger that a person will act out his sexual fantasies in a properly conducted hypnotic session.

Most patients intuitively sense what the therapist wishes to hear. No therapist in our culture can be an asexual, value-free figure. In the Western world, sexual attraction and "falling in love with the doctor" are universal phenomena; neither is particularly intensified by the hypnotic relationship. The myth of sexual submission associated with hypnosis should have been exploded long ago. Sexual submission is a highly selective process and, where it occurs, it is definitely due to factors other than hypnosis. Experiments on waking suggestibility substantiate this.[9]

With reference to a hypnosis-homosexual identification, this, too, is no greater than when other therapies are employed. Frequently, in overt homosexuals, passive submissiveness is equated with hypnosis prior to therapy. In such cases, the only contraindication to hypnotherapy would be if the therapist were a homosexual, incapable of restraining his own sexual drives. If this happened, it would not be an indictment of hypnosis, but of the interpersonal relationship.

Kline[21] states:

The hypnotic relationship is, of necessity, an incorporation of previously experienced relationships and *ideas* about relationships. It is possible to form a variety of different kinds of relationships even with the same subject and the same hypnotist and certainly a different kind of relationship hypnotically will be experienced by the same subject with a different hypnotist.

IS ANALYSIS OF THE TRANSFERENCE NECESSARY IN HYPNOTHERAPY?

The old concept of transference has undergone many changes. It is no longer considered a blind repetition of childhood relationships. This changed concept of transference has been evaluated and reviewed recently by Brandt.[3a]

According to the old concept, transference is the displacement from the patient to the analyst of those reactions and attitudes which he had toward important figures in his life. It is contended that, if the therapist can remain a shadowy and unknown figure, the patient will see how and why he reacted in the past toward surrogate figures. The basis for transference

also is to unmask and neutralize in the superego (conscience) the irrational forces first established in the child's mind by parental prohibitions. It is further contended that, if irrational anxieties and guilty fears brought about by the conscience are eased, and if the repressive forces are abolished to reveal the "cause" of the neurosis, then the instinctual drives no longer would be manifested as neurotic symptoms. This theory cannot account for the innumerable anxieties and guilt reactions of a lifetime that remain repressed or "encapsulated" without ever producing symptoms. Nor can it explain spontaneous cures.

Freud took hypnotic rapport and called it transference. His remark that there was "something positively seductive in working with hypnosis,"[27] indicated that he felt threatened by the closeness of the hypnotic interpersonal relationship. It has not been clarified whether or not Freud observed or knew of clear-cut erotic transference manifestations in hypnosis, unless one considers the incident described in his autobiography in which a woman, coming out of hypnosis, embraced and seriously embarrassed him. It is possible that his over-concern with erotic elements in the therapeutic relationship was due to his own repressed sexual feelings (counter-transference).

One is justified in asking, "Does the application of the transference concept lead to a higher recovery rate than do other therapies?" There is no data to substantiate this. Transference may be another instance of misdirection obscuring the nonspecific placebo effects of psychoanalytic therapies.

Watkins[38] observes that the patient during analytic sessions is often in hypnosis without the analyst's being aware of it, and that during hypnosis the hypnotherapist's own attitudes are to a degree displaced to the patient without the former's recognizing it.

The analytic setting is most conducive to enhancing suggestibility and even hypnosis in susceptible persons. Since it appears that increased suggestibility is characteristic of hypnotic rapport and analytic transference, the latter is understood better in this sense than it is by assuming it to be a manifestation of child-parent relationships.

Freud denied the use of suggestion in his

therapeutic approach. Despite this denial or lack of awareness, he stated:[11a]

In psychoanalysis we work upon the transference itself, dissipate whatever stands in the way of it and manipulate the instrument which is to do the work. Thus, it becomes possible for us to derive entirely new benefits from the *power of suggestion; we are able to control it*; the patient alone no longer manages his suggestibility according to his own liking, but insofar as he is amenable to its influence at all, *we guide his suggestibility.**

Freud also insisted that the therapist maintain a detached and unemotional attitude. However, by this maneuver he *eliminated the very basis for all psychological healing—the empathy of the interpersonal relationship*—all because of an assumption that, by the therapist's trying to remain neutral, the patient could better work through his difficulties by means of the development of the so-called "transference neurosis."

"Transference" for Freud became a wider concept than faith, and psychoanalysis made full use of reparation to obviate pain, anxiety, shame and guilt.[3] As in spiritual-religious healing, full use was made of expiation, atonement and sacrifice, as well as of faith in both the method and the analyst. Perhaps it was his avowed atheism that caused him to overlook the importance of faith and thus to deny the effects of hypnosis. It is not surprising that Masserman[25] recently remarked: "Freud built myths into systems, and systems into myths, and psychotherapy is nearer to an art and religion than it is to science."

Actually, it is difficult to see how *an unemotional attitude* in the therapist, if this is possible, *could ever hope to alleviate an emotional condition*.[32] Is it any wonder that so many patients complain bitterly about the cold, passive approach of many orthodox analysts? An impersonal approach, silence and passivity, and sitting behind the patient to uncover repressed material are assuming less significance in psychoanalysis. Rather, transference is now being viewed as a growth process involving the total personality. It is learning in the broadest sense,

* The italics are mine.

enabling a disturbed person to reach a healthier balance between his rational and irrational needs.

ARE FREE ASSOCIATIONS NECESSARY?

Freud modified the hypnotic technic of applying pressure to the forehead and urged the patient to repeat everything that came to his mind. This was taught to him by Liébeault and Bernheim. Later he discarded the "pressure method" and utilized the "free association" method. He used "the flight of ideas" to recapture significant experiences and overcome resistances (often created by his direct suggestive approach).

Borrowing from Galton's ideas on free association, Freud found that highly charged and meaningful material came up with greater frequency than unimportant matters. Schmideberg[31] asks:

Are free associations sufficiently standardized to permit comparable observations on different days and with different patients? Will a minimum of interference necessarily insure relatively unweighted samples of what is going on in the brain which receives hundreds of memories an hour? More important, can such observations make predictions possible?

Freud equated hypnosis with unconsciousness and erroneously stated that free association was associated with consciousness, and could not be used with hypnosis. This is not consistent with general agreement that hypnosis is a state of *hyperawareness*.

The most oversimplified aspects of his theory were that free associations would help to understand the patient's distorted thoughts and ultimately trace the origin of his symptoms. If free associations and their interpretations resulted in a higher recovery rate than that of standard psychotherapy, it would have been a significant contribution. However, deliberate and faulty interpretations of associations often lead to betterment.

DOES HYPNOTHERAPY OVERCOME RESISTANCES?

Freud thought hypnosis concealed the resistances.[14] The skillful hypnotherapist is well aware that resistances are less apt to occur if extraverbal suggestions combined with an intimate knowledge and understanding of the patient's needs are utilized. Haley[18] points out that there is often no need even to allow the resistances to develop during hypnotherapy: "A resistant maneuver is dissipated by having it accepted and redefined as co-operation." He believes that "this type of interaction is central to winning control of a relationship; maneuvers to define the relationship are not opposed but 'taken over.'"

As Freud himself suggested, it was his own relative inability to induce deep hypnosis and obtain enduring benefits from posthypnotic suggestions that led him to abandon it reluctantly and create psychoanalysis. His primitive and very authoritative hypnotic method may have created resistances. Is it any wonder that he referred to hypnosis as the "tyranny of suggestion"?[15] Especially since he also found hypnosis tedious and laborious? The hypnotic relationship produces an intensive awareness in the patient of the therapist's own feelings. Because of his own insecurity and doubts about its efficacy, he felt uncomfortable with it. As a result, he dismissed hypnosis as uncertain and unpredictable. Being a dedicated scientist, however, he was puzzled about hypnosis, and repeatedly tried to fit "the riddle of suggestion" into his theoretic formulations. Unfortunately, he accepted the emotionally conditioned "findings" of others in regard to hypnosis rather than his own observations.

Kline[21] points out that Freud *avoided* rather than *rejected* hypnosis. He was by no means an authority in hypnosis. Thus, it is difficult to understand how one can deny the value of hypnosis merely because of Freud's well-meaning, but erroneous, beliefs. In the light of these questions, perhaps "we need a psychoanalysis of current psychoanalytical resistance to the use of hypnosis."[24]

Classic psychoanalytic technics may be improved and shortened by the newer technics developed by hypnoanalysis.[23] Hypnoanalysis allows greater flexibility if the therapist wishes to work with dissolution of the resistances.

WHAT IS THE ROLE OF PSYCHODYNAMICS IN PSYCHOTHERAPY?

Psychodynamics has been defined as the motivational basis for human behavior. This implies that almost every act and thought is meaningful. The first matter for consideration is the term "psychodynamics." According to Bailey:[1]

There is no generally accepted definition of psychodynamics, but those addicted to this form of explanation believe psychic events have power to create behavior, or, better, that psychic events have access to, or are controlled by, a special source of power, variously spoken of as the Soul or ego.

He further states:[2]

The psychodynamicists must cease to teach their neophytes in terms of mythological pseudoscientific entities—that the system of explanation used by psychodynamics is really too simple to satisfy other than immature minds. It amounts to no more than a set of elaborate fictions.

In a scathing denunciation of the loose thinking which characterizes the psychodynamicists, he remarks "Psychodynamics in attempting to hold on to both faith and reason is in a fair way to become a sophisticated Christian Science."[2]

Unfortunately, there are still some psychiatrists who should know better, but who, in order to justify their approach, would restrict the general practitioner in the use of hypnotherapy because "He does not understand the underlying psychodynamics." They ignore the fact that suggestion and/or hypnosis has been the basis for psychological healing methods for centuries, and with as good or better results than psychodynamic psychotherapy. Let us consider why faith in psychodynamics can be challenged, and if, as Dreikurs[8] asks, "Are all psychological schools of thought outdated?"

Schmideberg[31] observes:

. . . that specific factors etiogenic for neuroses are found in normal individuals . . . that psychoanalysts are not always aware as to what causes recovery . . . that emphasis on character analysis after symptom-removal was abandoned did not yield more satisfactory results . . . and finally that present-day psychoanalysis *is no more effective* than that of 30 years ago, in spite of better patient selection and more extensive training of analysts.

Freud,[12] shortly before his death, spoke very resignedly about the poor results of psychoanalysis in an article seldom mentioned by his loyal followers. Rado[28] states: "Digging into the past yields diminishing returns." Others question the value of recapturing early fantasies and memories.

Heilbrunn[19] notes:

So often are simple mechanisms forced into weird double and triple twists to create seemingly new editions of familiar biological situations, full of interpretative sound and psychodynamic fury, signifying either nothing or at best the author's compounded fantasies.

It is more obvious that all present theories of psychodynamics "have low predictive value; their inner logic is hazy; their terms are at best vague indications of some shared experience."[29]

This is not to imply that many of Freud's observations in human behavior will not be of enduring value. Contemporary technics in hypnoanalysis could not have developed had it not been for his penetrating insights into the *needs* or *drives* for pleasure. The powerful influences of libidinal stages as first described by him on the development of the personality cannot be denied. However, an understanding of these is more prophylactic than therapeutic.

According to physical scientists, not only must a theory be confirmed—it also must be capable of being *negated*. Can anyone prove that a child did *not* have an Oedipus complex? No one has answered this question satisfactorily.[20] If the cornerstone of psychoanalytic theory cannot be proven false, then obviously there is no way to prove that it is true.

In this country, the physical scientists are attempting to explain the many facets of behavior in terms of systems that can be evaluated statistically. This may provide a better understanding of behavior, particularly higher nervous activities. In this regard, the open systems theory of von Bertalanffy,[37a] the information-communication theory of Shannon and Weaver,[24] and the cybernetics of Wiener[39] should prove helpful (see Chapter 31). It is becoming more apparent that psychotherapeutic mechanisms will never be explained by the current hypotheses of the psychodynamicists. Electroencephalography and toposcopic examination of the dynamic activities of the cortex are beginning to supply evidence substantiating the theories of Pavlov, whose contributions to hypnotic conditioning loom even larger today.

ARE INTERPRETATIONS VALID?

Although denied by psychodynamicists, the interpretations are powerful extraverbal suggestions. Patients' productions are often made to please the therapist, and are, therefore, usually completely unreliable. "To explain symptom causality and its dissolution on this basis convinces only two people—the patient and the therapist."[1] This is because each has faith in the other. Furthermore, any system using its own data to prove itself can only encounter a paradox (Gödel's theorem).

When the therapist offers interpretations, is it not largely *what he thinks is going on,* and is not the patient being controlled without realizing it?[34] Irrespective of recovery, there is no reliably controlled evidence that the interpretations are responsible for the results. Before such contentions can be validated, there must be a control group in which the postulated cause produces similar symptoms. It is more than likely that it is not the validity of the interpretations, but the mobilization of faith in the therapist's methods, which leads to cure. A knowledge of psychodynamics is not necessary.

For many years the author utilized various forms of psychodynamic psychotherapy for female disorders. He "cured" by making the facts fit his theories. Analysis of his successes and failures necessitated shifting away from extensive probing and interpretation. Guidance was provided rather than "insight." He now realizes that those who recovered did so chiefly because of the empathic approach, rapport and strong motivation.

The hypnotherapy enabled the interpersonal relationship to operate with more incisiveness when it was used. It also was structured in a highly individual way for each patient. It has been emphasized that the hypnotic interpersonal relationships are determined, in part, by the therapist's personality, his security with the method and his own value systems, as well as by the patient's expectations and beliefs.[4] *The latter are more important than uncovering repressed material.*[5]

This does not imply that all patients will be "cured" in a few hypnotic sessions. Rather, recovery ensues from an "affective emotional reconstruction process coming from within and not from without."[37] Exhortations to change based on logic and common sense are often valueless.

IS SYMPTOM-REMOVAL DANGEROUS?

The current dictum, "Never remove the symptom unless the cause is understood," is continually emphasized by the critics of hypnotherapy. It seems that, when hypnosis is incorporated in a psychoanalytic approach, there is no criticism, but when it is used for symptom-removal, the objections are numerous. The validity of this criticism is open to serious question. The bulk of medical therapeutics is directed to symptom-removal. Why cannot hypnotherapy be "prescribed" in selected cases for symptomatic relief in the same manner as pharmacologic agents? The tranquilizers are used without criticism in mental illnesses for symptomatic relief without attacking the "cause of a symptom." Physicians employ pharmacologic therapy for headaches, asthma, colitis and other psychogenically based disorders without worrying about the so-called dangers of symptom-removal. To Freud's everlasting credit, he noted that hypnosis had no deleterious effects, and that it was not a dangerous tool.[14]

Most psychotherapists know that spontaneous remission of symptoms occurs in schizophrenics, yet they tend to ignore them when neurotics are considered. Denker[6] showed that 72 per cent of 500 cases left untreated recovered within 2 years and 90 per cent within 5 years! Even hospitalization without psychotherapy yields more than a 60 per cent recovery rate.[26] Dorcus[7] hypnotically treated various syndromes such as pain, blindness, deafness, convulsions, headaches, paralyses, tics, tachycardias, nausea, ulcers, dermatoses, impotence and many other symptoms by symptom-removal. He states that:

Dealing with symptoms and present problems does not necessarily produce other symptoms and recurrence of old symptoms, since one could expect the percentage of patients who have recovered or improved to markedly diminish as time progresses.

According to pavlovians,[41] the removal of psychological symptoms by hypnotherapy is more lasting. Symptom-removal by hypnosis, "prevents the reinforcement of the inappropriate responses and new appropriate ways of handling the conflicts. As a result, the appropriate responses are reinforced."[7] On the basis of the evidence, it can be concluded that no one has proved that symptom-removal is dangerous and that other symptom-equivalents take the place of the removed one. The criticism that symptom-removal is dangerous, like other errors in medicine, is due to the error of the observer. It is apparent that the psychodynamicists' contentions apply to only a limited number of patients at best, and that the manner in which other symptoms originate is open to a number of interpretations.

IS INSIGHT REALLY NECESSARY?

In stuttering, globus hystericus, torticollis, nail-biting, phobias, obsessional neuroses and conversion-reactions cured by hypnotherapy, no untoward symptoms developed during several years of observation by the author, even though no insight therapy was used. Dorcus and other reputable investigators have made similar observations. Hypnotherapy *without insight* is equally as effective in dealing with symptomatic behavior as those therapies which provide insight. Furthermore, the recovery persists as long as do the "cures" of those treated by "insight therapy." Obviously, whenever two therapists disagree as to whether or not a patient recovers because of "real" insight, one of them must have thought that suggestive procedures without insight produced recovery. If insight is necessary, then how do the various schools of psychotherapy explain the success of those groups that do not require insight?

Freud[13] obtained recoveries in short analyses without realizing that they were carved out of the faith that he disowned. Recently, brief psychotherapy, consisting of a few visits, yielded good results. Was insight obtained and, if so, how and why so quickly? Insight and recovery are not dependent on each other. Yet an almost magical omniscience is attributed to making the "unconscious" conscious and the undoing of repression.[34] If the cause of a conflict is repressed, perhaps reinforcing it would be as effective as dissipating it. Pathology is often cured by lymphocytic infiltration's sealing off an infection. Most deep-seated conflicts are forgotten with the passing of time, and insight is never achieved.

An ulcer is due to psychosomatic factors. The sufferer is not taught the emotional significance of the abnormal histologic findings and malfunctioning of his intestines—this might upset him. Therefore, why should insight have any therapeutic value in other psychosomatic disorders? Often "insight" is not the patient's insight, but the therapist's preconceived notion of what "insight" the patient should have. In many instances, the patient merely takes over the value systems, the faith and the confidence of the therapist —this is actually what makes emotionally disturbed individuals better!

DO DEFENSES HAVE TO BE ANALYZED?

It is difficult to understand what is meant by "analyzing the defenses."[33] Should they systematically be broken down, modified or increased? Systematic breaking-down of defenses is more likely to push "borderline cases" into psychoses than are reassurance and guidance.[23a] The present disillusionment with psychoanalytic "mystique" is due partly to vague theories about the very nature of defenses. Modern hypnotherapy uses the defenses by establishing newer ones; the more recent defenses are easier to remove than those of long standing. This is why symptom-substitution or "trading down" to a less well-established conditioned process is more valuable than "analyzing the defenses."

IS AUTOHYPNOSIS DANGEROUS?

The question of the dangers of autohypnosis—whether it should be employed only after multisessions of psychiatric evaluation —and the objection to its use in sports already have been answered fully in this book. Autohypnosis, in one ritualistic form or another, is employed in Zen Buddhist meditation, the Samadhic state of Yoga, the Jewish cabbalistic state of Kavannah, and other religious rites. The hypnotic relationship and autohypnosis, even though it is denied, are also responsible for the recoveries obtained by Christian Science, Science of Mind, Theosophy, the Emmanuel Movement, and many other spiritualistic religious-healing modalities. Therefore, it is difficult to see how autohypnosis can be dangerous when the very essence of prayer is based on the fundamental principles of autohypnosis.

SUMMARY

In conclusion, nearly all the criticisms applied to contemporary hypnotherapy are untenable. Also, they are directed toward a type of hypnotherapy that was practiced in the last century. The objections are due largely to inadequate knowledge of the subject on the part of its critics.

There is no proof of the superiority of any psychotherapeutic approach, as it is virtually impossible to eliminate the importance of the interpersonal relationship[17] and suggestion in any 2-way communication process. Well-trained psychotherapists, with considerable experience, cannot show a higher recovery rate than gifted neophytes with lesser training. It has been aptly stated that psychiatrists are born and not made! These remarks must not be construed to mean that a good knowledge of human behavior and a common sense approach are not fundamental to any system of psychotherapy.

However, there are limitations to hypnotherapy, and these are the same as those found in any other type of psychotherapy. The reason for this is that all forms of psychotherapy *originated from hypnosis.*

Current research in hypnosis does not substantiate a single reason for Freud's avoidance of hypnosis. The reader is referred to an excellent monograph on the subject, *Freud and Hypnosis*,[21] for a detailed description of Freud's reasons for avoiding hypnosis.

Had Freud realized that hypnosis had an unusual ability to elicit the patient's hidden potentials for recovery, and if he had not considered it to be an "abnormal mental state," he would have attached more significance to hypnotherapy. Had he been aware of the specialized hypnotic technics described in Chapter 47, the concept of symptom-replacement might never have evolved. Likewise, if he had been oriented in the permissive approach, there would have been no need for his "discovery" of the technic of free association and the interpretations to unmask resistances. Finally, he mistakenly assumed that deep hypnosis was always necessary. Today, there are many successful psychotherapists who do not require deep hypnosis to obtain results.

Since scientific hypnosis was in its infancy at that time, one can hardly blame Freud for his naïveté. However, there is no valid reason why his successors should continue to use this embryonic period in the historical development of hypnosis to criticize contemporary hypnotherapy, as used today. Freud, because of his relative inexperience with hypnosis, could hardly be classified as an authority. Yet his views are still used to refute modern hypnotherapy. Would there have been a need for his other concepts if he had recognized that hypnosis is essentially a meaningful interpersonal relationship in which the patient is not stupefied or under anybody's control except his own?

Actually, he merely "used hypnosis in slow motion," and through misdirection substituted his technics for commonly known hypnotic ones of this era. Speaking about these he wrote prophetically:

It is very probable too, that the application of our therapy to numbers will compel us to alloy the pure gold of analysis with the copper of direct suggestion; and even hypnotic influence might find a place in it again as it has in the treatment of war neuroses.[15a]

Psychodynamicists should at least become conversant with recently developed hypnotic technics, much as progressive physicians do with new drugs.

REFERENCES

1. Bailey, P.: Modern attitudes toward the relationship of the brain to behavior, A.M.A. Arch. Psychiat. 2:25-42, 1960.
2. *Ibid.*
3. Bergman, P.: The role of faith in psychotherapy, Bull. Menn. Clin. 22:104-109, 1958.
3a. Brandt, R.: The dynamics of transference, Philosophical Rec. 25:199-223, 1956.
4. Conn, J. H.: Psychodynamics of recovery under hypnosis, Int. J. Clin. & Exper. Hypnosis 8:3-17, 1960.
5. ——: Cultural and clinical aspects of hypnosis, placebos and suggestibility, Int. J. Clin. & Exper. Hypnosis 7:175-187, 1959.
6. Denker: Quoted by Eysenck, N. J.: The effects of psychotherapy: an evaluation, J. Consult. Psychology 16:319-322, 1952.
7. Dorcus, R. M.: The Treatment of Symptoms with Special Reference to Removal by Hypnosis. In press.
8. Dreikurs, R.: Are psychological schools of thought outdated? J. Individual Psychology 16:3-10, 1960.
9. Eysenck, H. J.: Suggestibility and hysteria, J. Neurol. and Psychiat. 6:22-31, 1943.
10. Ferenczi, S.: Introjection and transference (1909), *in* Sex in Psychoanalysis, Translated by E. Jones, Richard G. Bedger, Boston, The Gorham Press, 1916.
11. Freud, S.: Standard Edition of (His) Complete Psychological Works, translated by James Strachey, vol. 5, p. 11, London, Hogarth Press, 1955.
11a. ——: A General Introduction to Psychoanalysis, (ed.) Riviere, J.: p. 459, New York, Perma Books, 1957.
12. ——: Analyses terminable and interminable, Int. J. of Psychoanalysis, vol. 18, 1937.
13. ——: The History of an Infantile Neurosis, Coll. Papers III, London, Hogarth Press, 1949.
14. ——: The Psychotherapy of Hysteria *in* Collected Papers, vol. 5, translated by J. Strachey, p. 262, London, Hogarth Press, Ltd., 1950.
15. ——: Group Psychology and the Analysis of the Ego, 1921, Strachey, London, Hogarth Press, Ltd., 1948.
15a. ——: Turnings in the ways of psychoanalysis *in* Collected Papers, vol. 2, p. 392, New York, Hogarth, 1948.
16. Gill, M. and Brenman, M.: Hypnosis and Related States, New York, Int. Univ. Press, 1960.
17. Grinker, R. R: A philosophical appraisal of

psychoanalysis in science and psycho-analysis, Academy of Psychoanalysis *1*: Integrative Studies; ed. J. H Masserman, *126*:143, 1950.

18. Haley, J.: Control in psychoanalytical therapy, Progress in Psychotherapy, *4*:55, 1959.

19. Heilbrum, G.: Psychoanalysis of yesterday, today and tomorrow, Arch. Gen. Psych. *4*:32, 1961.

20. Hook, Sidney (ed.): Psychoanalysis, Scientific Method and Philosophy, New York, University Press.

21. Kline, M.: Freud & Hypnosis, New York, Julian Press, 1958.

22. Kubie, L. S.: Hypnotism: a focus for psychophysiological and psychoanalytic investigations, Arch. Gen. Psychiat. *1*:77, 1961.

23. Lindner, R.: Hypnoanalysis as a psychotherapeutic technique, Brit. J. Med. Hypnotism *7*:2-15, 1956.

23a. Mac Alpine, L.: The development of the transference, Psychoanalytic Quart. *19*: 501-537, 1950.

24. Marcuse, F. L.: Hypnosis, Fact & Fiction, Penguin Books, 1959.

25. Masserman, J. H: Paper delivered at meeting of American Psychiatric Assoc., May 9-13, 1960.

26. Masserman, J. H., and Carmichael, H. J.: Diagnosis and prognosis in psychiatry, J. Ment. Science *84*:893, 1938.

27. Puner, H. W.: Freud, His Life and Mind, New York, Grosset and Dunlap, 1947.

28. Rado, S.: Recent advances of psychoanalytical therapy in psychiatric treatment, Proc. Assoc. for Research in Nervous and Mental Disease *31*:57, 1953.

29. Rapoport, A.: *In* Locke, N.: Semantic psychotherapy: an exchange of views, E.T.C.: A Review of General Semantics *15*:37, 1957.

30. Rosen, H.: Hypnosis, the cure that can be dynamite, This Week Magazine, July 17, 1960.

31. Schmideberg, M.: Goals and values in psychoanalysis, Psychiat. Quart. *32*:233-265, 1958.

32. *Ibid.*, p. 251.

33. *Ibid.*, p. 250.

34. *Ibid.*, p. 248.

35. Shannon, C. E., and Weaver, W.: The Mathematical Theory of Communication, Urbana, Ill., U. of Ill. Press, 1949.

36. Spiegel, H.: Hypnosis and transference, A.M.A. Arch. Psychiat. *1*:96-101, 1959.

37. Strupp, H. H.: Future of research in psychotherapy, Behavioral Science *4*:66, 1959.

37a. von Bertalanffy, L.: An Evaluation of Modern Biological Thought, New York, John Wiley & Sons, Inc., 1952.

38. Watkins, J.: Trance and Transference, J.S.C.E.H., *II*, 284-290, 1954.

39. Wiener, N.: Cybernetics, or, Control and Communication in the Animal and the Machine, Cambridge, Mass., Technology Press, 1948.

40. Wolberg, L. R.: Medical Hypnosis, vol. I, New York, Grune & Stratton, 1948.

41. Wolpe, J.: Psychotherapy by Reciprocal Inhibition, Palo Alto, Calif., Stanford Univ. Press, 1958.

SUPPLEMENTARY READING

Eysenck, H. J.: Behaviour Therapy and the Neuroses, London, Pergamon, 1960.

Glover, E.: The therapeutic effect of inexact interpretation, *in* The Technique of Psychoanalysis, New York, Internat. Univ. Press, 1955.

——: Therapeutic criteria of psychoanalysis, *in* The Technique of Psychoanalysis, New York, Internat. Univ. Press, 1955.

Kroger, W. S.: Analysis of valid and invalid objections to hypnotherapy, Paper read at meeting of the American Society of Clinical Hypnosis, Chicago, Oct. 19, 1962.

Mann, H.: Hypnosis: an analysis of unfounded criticisms, Am. J. Clin. Hypnosis *4*:98-102, 1961.

Thigpen, C. H., and Cleckley, H. M.: Freudian psychodynamics—science or mirage? The New Physician *10*:97-101, 1961.

49

Failures in Hypnotherapy

In this book, many cases that have recovered following hypnotherapy have been described for illustrative purposes. However, just as there are dramatic successes, there are equally dramatic failures. These can be divided into problems during induction and problems during hypnotherapy.

FAILURES DURING INDUCTION

Fortunately, in the hands of a sophisticated hypnotherapist, failure to attain some degree of hypnosis is rare. This is especially true if the onus and the responsibility for going into hypnosis are carefully explained to the patient beforehand. Nearly all individuals can be hypnotized to some degree if the permissive and motivational technics described in this book are utilized. In the rare cases of those who cannot be hypnotized, one should be sure that certain misconceptions have been clarified. Some of these are described below.

FEAR OF SUBMISSION

The egocentric type of individual who fears being subordinated by the hypnotherapist's suggestions can be difficult to hypnotize. In spite of careful explanations to the contrary, many apparently willing individuals harbor this fear. Within this group are persons who have dominant personalities or who have a need to maintain a "one-up" position. To obviate this fear, which is a common cause for failure, the operator can casually remark during the initial phases of the induction, *"You need follow only those suggestions which are fully in accord with your needs and wishes."* It is really surprising how conducive to greater hypnotizability this statement is, if it is unobtrusively inserted during the verbalization technic. For example:

A very successful insurance company executive, a chronic alcoholic, could not be hypnotized by several physician-therapists or by 2 lay hypnotists. During the author's initial discussion with him, it was obvious not only that he feared being relegated to a subservient role but that he was poorly motivated to relinquish the symptom. Because of his repeated failure to be hypnotized, he was emphatically assured before induction, "You will hypnotize yourself; I will only act as teacher. If you follow my instructions, and I cannot *force* you to follow these, you will develop a deep state of relaxation *at your own pace and in your own particular fashion.* You have actually hypnotized yourself to the point where, try as hard as you might, you cannot stop drinking. You are the one who developed the symptom, and you are the only one who can remove it." He agreed that all these assertions were logical and that he would do his best to follow all suggestions.

Five inductions were attempted over a period of 2 weeks. At no time did he appear to enter hypnosis, regardless of the technic employed. Following each session he triumphantly stated, "Doctor, I didn't feel a thing. I did everything you said. Guess I'm a hopeless case. You sure tried your best." Although it is easy to blame the patient, without doubt this individual was wholly unable to submit to another person's directions because of his inordinate need to maintain control. Furthermore, he was looking forward to defeating every therapist, and by such maneuvers he had a perfect alibi for maintaining the chronicity of his symptom.

LACK OF MOTIVATION

Those who have little or no desire to get well are poor subjects for hypnosis. It is almost impossible to induce hypnosis unless the patient is sufficiently motivated. Many patients, such as alcoholics, smokers and overeaters, do not wish to yield their symptoms because they have a "pleasurable neurosis." The following is a typical example:

An extremely obese female, who had seen numerous physicians, stated that she would like to try hypnosis for weight-reduction, and that she would follow a diet, take her medication and faithfully follow all directions. During her first visit she was informed, "Of course you mean every word you say, but behind your ardent protestations that you wish to lose weight are deeply unrecognized desires to cling to your symptom. We shall see how well you do." Hypnosis was attempted by a wide variety of technics during several intensive sessions. In all instances she stated, "I hear everything you say and I do follow all of your suggestions, but I just can't relax." She decided to break off therapy. Perhaps it would have been better if the nature of her resistances had been discussed and worked through before attempting hypnotic induction.

The hypnotherapist must recognize that, even though such failures will be encountered, there are other patients who, even though poorly motivated, can be helped by the establishment of healthy objectives. In cases such as the one just described, for instance, emphasizing the value of hypnosis as a powerful therapeutic adjunct in relationship to the cosmetic and health factors is highly motivating. The therapist must mobilize the patient's faith that he will be helped.

During the actual induction, many reluctant and poorly motivated individuals, especially those with habit patterns, can be induced by such suggestions as, "If you really wish to control your bodily functions (such as your appetite) and co-ordinate your thinking with your bodily processes, all you have to do is to slowly raise your arm about an inch at a time. With each inch that you raise your arm, tell yourself, 'I am going deeper and deeper with each movement of my arm upward. I will indeed go deeper and deeper relaxed. In this way I will obtain greater mastery over such functions as my appetite.'" These suggestions are given just before arm-levitation is suggested, and they can be repeated several times while the subject's arm is slowly being lifted to the perpendicular position.

To avoid failure, motivating the subject each step of the way usually ensures success, especially if the individual's attention is focused on one suggestion after another.

If the suggestions are not clear to the patient, failure in induction can be expected. The commonest one is during eye-closure or arm-levitation. The patient will remark, "I thought my eyes (or arm) would close (or be raised) by itself."

RESISTANCES TO INDUCTION

The handling of resistances to induction has been discussed elsewhere in this book. (Chap. 13). In general, those manifested during the induction procedure are utilized to defy the hypnotherapist. Many patients equate hypnotizability with imbecility; others are too analytic or know too much about the "misdirection of attention" that is involved in hypnotic induction. Still others, like the one just described, have an "I'll-bet-you-can't-hypnotize-me" attitude. Such individuals fear someone who they think is omnipotent. The explanation that no one hypnotizes another individual can eliminate this resistance. One can remark, "You are the only one who can hypnotize yourself; I really have very little to do with it. If you follow the simple suggestions, and I have no way of knowing whether or not you follow these, then you will follow the more complicated suggestions. However, if you break one link in the chain, then the entire sequence of suggestions will be interrupted. For instance, if I suggest that you count to yourself and you do not, since I have no way of knowing this, I cannot do very much about that, can I?" Such measures enlist the active co-operation and participation of the patient.

Other patients panic when they feel themselves entering into a hypnotic state.

Recently a very well-known screen actor consulted me for his homosexuality. As he felt himself sinking deeper and deeper into the hypnotic state, he began to shake, perspire and show other symptoms of inner turmoil. When asked why he was acting in this fashion, he stated that he had a mutual masturbatory fantasy which involved me. By such measures the patient was attempting to seduce me and yet at the same time he was attempting to comply. Since he had ambivalent feelings with reference to the acceptance or the rejection of my suggestions, he experienced panic when he felt that he was about to be hypnotized. Naturally, these feelings were worked through before further induction was attempted.

Other patients' resistances can be handled by asking them to discuss their feelings. It is generally a good idea to interrupt the hypnotic induction if the patient is not following the suggestions. For example, if the patient does not raise his arm when it is suggested, one can remark, "If you wish to continue, it's up to you. Your arm will *not* move up by itself. If you want to go into a deep, deep relaxed state, you will raise your arm at your own pace, and in your own particular fashion. Remember, you are in charge." If the arm does not rise, the hypnotic induction should be terminated. The therapist must not evince the slightest show of anger or blame the patient. Rather, it is much better to state, "Perhaps I did not make myself entirely clear in our preliminary discussion. You did very well, and next time I am certain that you will do much better."

Often, arrogant and skeptical patients cannot be hypnotized by the conventional approach. A disguised technic or giving a placebo under the guise of its facilitating hypnosis often increases the susceptibility of refractory subjects.

FEAR OF LOSING THE DEFENSES

In some instances, the fear of being stripped of his defenses can produce a panic-reaction in a patient during the induction. To illustrate:

A psychoanalyst referred an attractive young woman for hypnosis. She was affect-blocked and suffered from severe bruxism, grinding her teeth at night. He was unfamiliar with hypnotic technics and hoped that hypnosis would break through her repressions. An induction procedure was initiated in his presence, and the patient immediately began to shake violently. She began to sob convulsively, crying, "Why must I love him so much? I'll never be able to have him; he is already married. What a fool I am!" The hypnotic induction was immediately terminated. The patient was told that she would be handled without condemnation or moral evaluation, just as by her therapist. This reassurance, together with the emphasis on the fact that all interpretations would be made by her analyst, enabled a successful induction to be accomplished readily. This case illustrates how lack of rapport can account for failure.

FAILURES DURING HYPNOTHERAPY

Disraeli once stated that there are 3 types of lies: little lies, big lies and statistics. There are no accurate data available, comprising long-term follow-up studies, to evaluate the failure rate in selective cases treated by hypnosis. These probably do not exceed those treated by other psychotherapeutic methods. However, most of the cases of failure, as herein described, are in the therapy of symptoms of a bizarre nature which have exhausted other therapeutic approaches. Therefore, it is not surprising that a relatively high incidence of failure will occur during hypnotherapy.

These failures are due to (1) difficulties in the patient; (2) difficulties in the hypnotherapeutic management; and (3) difficulties in the therapist management. All these, singly or in combination, are usually responsible for failures in patients, even if they readily can be hypnotized. One should, therefore, continually bear in mind the dictum, "One is not treated by hypnosis, but rather, in hypnosis."

DIFFICULTIES IN THE PATIENT

To avoid such failures in this group, patients should be carefully screened and selected.

Recently, a 42-year-old male was referred for hypnotherapy because he had a profound dislike for his facial appearance. Since childhood, he had been called "Hawky" because of his sharp, aquiline features, particularly his nose. In reality, he was a nice-looking, well-groomed individual of excellent body build. He had had 3 marriages, the first to a prostitute, the second to a burlesque dancer, and the third to a woman who had become pregnant by another man before he married her. His third wife, because of his ugliness, insisted that she had the right to have sexual relations with another man. Otherwise, she threatened to divorce him. He never had been able to relate to women and had poor social relationships. He had no understanding of his deep-seated masochistic needs, evidenced by his neurotic attachments (all 3 of his wives browbeat him and were below his social and intellectual status). He stated that he had been in "therapy" for several years. Now he asked, "Can't you just hypnotize me into thinking that I am good-looking?"

It was obvious that he attributed all his

troubles with women to his appearance, never realizing that he had a deep-seated personality problem. He was informed that it would be impossible to produce an amnesia by hypnosis for the feelings associated with his facial features. He mentioned that he was going to have plastic surgery for correction of his narrow nose. It was emphasized that this should be postponed until he understood the real *needs* for his emotional difficulties. Despite this advice, he insisted on being hypnotized. Naturally, this was refused. He went to another hypnotist-physician, who failed to help him for the obvious reasons given above. Fortunately, also, he could not get a plastic surgeon to operate on him.

If hypnotherapy is utilized as an adjunct in the framework of a psychotherapeutic approach based upon a good doctor-patient relationship, failures will be less frequent.

When hypnosis is indiscriminately employed, without careful patient-selection, it is only logical to assume that a high incidence of failures will occur. Therefore, the therapist, on the basis of his judgment and clinical acumen, should understand the motivations behind the desire for hypnotherapy when it is requested. It is these motivations that can be the determining factor as to whether or not failure will ensue. All too often, patients are looking for the magical removal of symptoms and expect to be cured "in the third act." Failures are inevitable if patients are unwilling to recognize their unrealistic demands. Also, the patient who is trying to "climb into the therapist's lap" is destined to be a failure.

A 44-year-old woman alcoholic requested that hypnosis be tried for the alleviation of drinking. She revealed that she was frigid with her husband but sexually responsive to another man with whom she had many clandestine meetings. She evinced considerable guilt over her extramarital relationships as therapy progressed, but refused to recognize the deep-seated need to suffer and atone evidenced by her continual need to degrade herself in drunken debauches.

Though readily hypnotizable, she made little progress—she wished to maintain her relationship with her lover but could not face the realities of divorce. She had hoped that hypnosis would effectively suppress her drinking. It was pointed out that she could not have her cake and eat it, too; that if she wished to continue in therapy, she would have to decide whether or not she could make an adjustment to her husband, leave him, or "beat her head against a stone wall" by remaining in her present situation. She broke off therapy soon after, but returned at a later date—sadder but wiser—and at present is making an attempt to adjust to her husband.

DIFFICULTIES DUE TO HYPNOTHERAPY

Many individuals expect the impossible from hypnosis. Often they have had years of psychotherapy and yet, when they consult the hypnotherapist, they expect to be cured in several sessions. By far the commonest cause of failure with hypnotherapy is the termination of treatment because the progress is not as rapid as the patient had assumed it would be. It is also surprising how many physicians think that hypnosis is a rapid method. Although many cases involving severe disorders can be improved even in a few visits, the bulk of chronically disturbed patients require many visits, and intensive therapy. Even so, this is more rapid than some of the more orthodox approaches.

The most difficult patient is the one who adopts a hopeless resignation about eventual recovery. It is here that the physician must give the subject greater self-confidence and inculcate a more optimistic outlook. Patients who do not develop the necessary mental-set which is a prerequisite for the acceptance of posthypnotic suggestions are destined to fail. Their prejudices, biases and other negativistic attitudes militate against the full acceptance of hypnotherapy. Additional difficulties during hypnotherapy are due to the communication problem. Some therapists "talk down" to their patients; others may "talk over their heads." Still others show their indifference at nonverbal levels—they lack empathy and do not establish an effective rapport.

Many failures occur in hypnotherapy because the *needs* for the symptom are not made clear to the patient; this is a potent cause for failure. Psychoneurotics cling to their symptoms, as this provides them with a value system which often may act as a defense. It is obvious, also, that not all individuals can recover, as the very nature of their illness precludes recovery.

Many failures result when hypnosis is utilized indiscriminately, without definitive goals. The author remembers a writer who came in with a prepared list of suggestions, all of which involved concentration, creativity, enhancement of his ability and following through on assignments. This patient expected hypnosis to remove his poor motivations. He had consulted several lay hypnotists without success. Such cases only point up the need to understand the nature of the complaints as they relate to the total character structure.

The following case of failure in hypnosis was tragic:

An exceptionally obese 48-year-old man was referred for weight loss. He had recently suffered a coronary attack. This individual was a successful, hard-driving business man who was always looking for "angles." When the author stated his fee, the patient made a counterproposal that he would pay $10 for each pound that was lost. The patient thought that he was going to get the best of the bargain, but, much to his surprise, he lost 40 pounds in 2 months; thus, he owed much more than he would have if he had come in at the regular fee. As a result, he broke off treatment and died several months later of another heart attack. A thorough evaluation of this man's incorporative needs was suggested during treatment but was refused. The characterologic difficulties should have been worked through before any type of therapy was instituted.

Another female alcoholic made "a flight into health." She, too, had been in analysis and had been referred by her psychoanalyst for hypnotherapy. After 4 sessions she stopped drinking for 3 months, but then considered herself cured and refused to return either to the analyst or to myself. It was obvious that she used the referral as a means of escaping from the analysis, and the temporary improvement to avoid further therapy.

Naturally, as expected, she resumed her drinking and she became very hostile for a slight pretext, namely, that I didn't talk to her long enough on the telephone when she called at 4 A.M. to announce that she had started drinking again. Her drinking was a defense against her intense anger toward an impotent, weak and passive-feminine husband, who had her "caught in a trap." The defensive nature of her actions was pointed out.

To obviate difficulties due to hypnotherapy, it is important to outline therapeutic goals. Hypnosis can be directed either to a symptomatic approach or to a characterologic rehabilitation. Individuals who can be treated by symptom-removal are those who have poor emotional resources, inadequate time and poor motivation. For instance, hypnosis can be used for symptomatic relief of smoking in the patient who has a carcinoma of the lungs, or in the one who has a bronchiectasis, without working through the need for the symptom. On the other hand, relief of the symptoms of insomnia or alcoholism may be successful from one standpoint but still may be considered a failure because the individual is wholly unable to adjust to his life situations for other reasons.

In order to avoid these difficulties, it is best to enable the individual to function without the need for frustrations and tensions. Hypnotherapy can also be directed toward facing life problems, rather than retreating into childlike or regressive behavior. Such an approach facilitates a good work and relaxation record, unimpaired sexuality and ability to adapt to life stresses. Some patients have to be taught how to accept a subordinate role without "boiling up inside." Others must understand that they can assume leadership, and still others must realize their limitations. In general, hypnotherapy will eliminate difficulties, if encountered, if the therapy is directed toward the establishment of confidence, self-assertiveness and greater tolerance.

The use of autohypnosis usually enables the patient to use self-exploration to work out his problems more effectively. However, autohypnosis is seldom successful if the patient is not motivated to participate in the working-through processes.

Difficulties in hypnotherapy are noted in the individual whose emotional resources are inadequate to cope with his problems. Often it is permissible for the therapist to assume the role of a paternal figure and deliberately foster dependency. This is especially helpful for those who have had a recent bereavement. In others, who wish to cling to their symptoms, one can utilize symptom-substitution, as described in other situations, to avoid therapeutic failure. In the case of the stutterer, for instance, anxiety was averted by teaching him to transfer his blocking to the twitching of one of his fingers. There are other individuals who never can completely recover. For these, partial improvement based on limited goals is not a failure. In the case of the passive dependent alcoholic, who can be controlled for short periods and who makes only a partial adjustment, some modicum of success is achieved.

Other individuals rationalize their reasons for seeking hypnotherapy, and this results in failure. In one instance, a psychopathic male prostitute attempted to save his unhappy marriage through being hypnotized. At first he presented himself with symptoms of insomnia and nervousness. During the anamnesis the real reasons for seeking hypnosis were revealed. He was advised to seek marital counseling.

Another individual wished to learn autohypnosis, ostensibly to be able to concentrate on his work as a physicist. In reality, he felt wholly inadequate around women, and he had hoped that hypnosis would give him more self-reliance. He stated that he had been in psychotherapy for several years, but had heard that autohypnosis enabled individuals to overcome all sorts of psychological problems. A thorough personality evaluation was advised, together with a discussion of his various difficulties. It is important for the therapist to recognize that overcoming inadequacies and lack of confidence requires learning how to handle the reasons derived in therapy. This takes a considerable amount of time.

Difficulties occur when passive individuals such as certain types of homosexuals submit to hypnotherapy only to derive masochistic gratification from the all-powerful figure of the therapist. Unless these neurotic motivations are understood, improvement will be retarded. A case in point is a homosexual male school teacher who was unable to carry out his sexual needs for fear of apprehension. As the result of his frustration, he utilized the hypnotic situation to yield to and to fight against authority at one and the same time. Failure was averted when it was pointed out how he was fulfilling his passive needs and also re-enacting the same conflict he had had with other surrogate figures. He ultimately made a satisfactory recovery.

To summarize, lack of motivation and inability to face life's problems are the commonest reasons for difficulties in hypnotherapy. Those who have no desire to make an adequate adjustment to their situations, because they develop anxiety reactions, fall into this group. Those who have poor inner resources and are unable to tolerate frustration and anxiety usually do not have sufficient strength to receive help from any type of hypnotherapy. Another common difficulty is the secondary gain value of the symptom to the psychoneurotic individual. All these difficulties have been discussed in this book.

DIFFICULTIES IN THE THERAPIST

In general, hypnotherapy should utilize the individual's own capacities to work out his problems. If the therapist assumes an authoritarian role, the patient will never become completely free from authority, nor will his character structure be changed. Therefore, throughout this volume, the use of autohypnosis and sensory-imagery conditioning has been stressed repeatedly. Every patient is informed that it is his problem, that he has "sales-talked himself into it, and, likewise, he can just as readily sales-talk himself out of his complaints." It is really remarkable how such a gross oversimplification can be highly motivating to the skeptical and resistant patient.

Often the therapist may set standards that are too high for the patient to fulfill; this only causes further depression and anxiety. By such an approach the therapist does not give the patient enough motivation to seek further assistance; this only mobilizes hostility and usually results in discontinuance of the therapy. Also, such a parental or authoritative approach never allows the individual to grow up and develop an acceptance of himself. He will remain dependent upon the therapist, requiring repeated reinforcement and support. If all these mechanisms are not understood, strong dependency always will be maintained.

It is surprising how minor factors may produce difficulties due to the therapist. The author recollects an interesting patient who had complained of menopausal symptoms of several years' duration. It is his custom after the third or fourth visit to call his patients by their first names. When this was done in her case, the patient broke off therapy, even though she was making good progress.

The commonest difficulty stemming from the therapist is his own countertransference feelings or the *way he feels about the patient and hypnotherapy*. If he feels some personal antagonism to the patient, he should not treat him. Or if he feels insecure with the method, he will, on the basis of subliminal cues, transmit his own insecurities to the patient. Such therapists will, as a result, see nothing but dangers, because hypnotherapy is, in reality, *dangerous for them!* Therefore, those therapists who think that hypnotherapy is fraught with dangers are undoubtedly transmitting their personal convictions.

In this chapter, the author has attempted to present briefly some of the reasons for failures with hypnotherapy. Usually, successful cases are stressed for teaching purposes. The hesitancy to present failures or unsuccessful cases is understandable, but these are equally valuable for instruction. Admission of failure is a sign of intellectual and emotional maturity. The author conducts a weekly class for postgraduate students which might well be called "My mistakes of the week clinic."

Hypnotherapy, while an ancient science, is still struggling against great handicaps because of irrational prejudice. This author has his share of failures and relapses following hypnotherapy. However, he generally attempts to analyze the reasons for them. He also is well aware that the placebo effect of any type of psychotherapy is over 60 per cent, and that many get better irrespective of the therapy. There are also spontaneous remissions. It is the author's hope that this chapter will contribute to a better understanding of the role that hypnosis plays in psychotherapy. Also, it should be pointed out that one can overemphasize failures with hypnotherapy as well as sensationalize cures; neither should be told to patients. An increasing knowledge of its successful applications and the reasons for its failures eventually will accord this modality a secure position in medical practice and therapy.

In conclusion, it can be stated that the same measures may be utilized to avoid failures in hypnotherapy as in any other psychotherapeutic procedure. First the nature of the patient's values as well as his motivation for recovery should be explored; next, the need for his symptoms in terms of their secondary gain value. Such information can usually be obtained in the one or more evaluation sessions before hypnotherapy is instituted or even attempted. To avoid failures, hypnosis should be used, in most instances, with re-education, supportive and persuasive psychotherapy, group therapy and other eclectic procedures, including drugs.

Index

Abortion, spontaneous, emotional, hypnotherapy, 202-203
  case report, 202-203
Abreaction as hypnoanalytic technic, 327
Abulafia, 112
Aertnys-Damen, 108
Affect-bridge or in-and-out method, 327
Age, "progression," 16-17
  regression, 15-16
Alcoholics Anonymous, 271
Alcoholism, chronic, 269-274
  hypnotherapy, autohypnosis, importance of, 272
    aversion, 270-271
    conditioned reflex, 270
    group, 271-272
    individual, 271
    purpose of treatment, 269
    suggestions, posthypnotic, importance of, 272-274
Allergy, hypnotherapy, 179-180
  case report, 179-180
Amblyopia, hypnotherapy, 233
Ambrose, G., 234, 261-263
Amenorrhea, hypnotherapy, 206-207
  case report, 207
American Medical Association, Council on Mental Health, Committee on Hypnosis, medical training for hypnosis, 104
  quoted, use of hypnotherapy, 96-97
  recommendations concerning instruction in hypnosis, 4-5
American Psychiatric Association, report on hypnosis, 96
American Society for Clinical Hypnosis, 5
Amnesia, hypnotic, 13-14
  with somnambulism, 18
Amphetamines as appetite depressants, 174
Amputation of both legs, use of prosthesis, hypnotherapy, case report, 228
  reduction of pain after, hypnotherapy, 228
Amygdaloid complex of limbic system, 127-128
Analgesia, hypnotic. See Hypnoanalgesia
Andreev, B. V., 165
Anesthesia, "glove," for hunger control, 176
  for dermatologic problems, 220

Anesthesia, "glove"—(Continued)
  development, as indication of depth of hypnosis, 47
  nausea and vomiting in pregnancy, 202
  in obstetrics, 196-197
    postpartum period, 199
    verbalization for, 197
  for pain control in arthritis and rheumatism, 171
  hypnodontics, 284-285
  hypnotic, 17
  hysterical, 17
  progressive of Watkins, as technic in hypnosis, 65-66
Animal hypnosis, 10
Animals, preservation by catalepsy or tonic immobilization, 22
Ankylosis of knee, postoperative, hypnotherapy, case report, 228
Anokhin, P. K., 153
Anorexia nervosa, hypnotherapy, 177
Antisocial aspects of hypnosis, 93-97
  dangers from stage hypnosis, 94-95
Anxiety, clinical manifestations of, 304-307
  diagnosis, differential, 304-305
    from history-taking, 305-307
  as hindrance to induction of hypnosis, 49
  hysterical reactions to, 304
  repressed, 304
  as response to hidden tension, 304
  types of reactions, 304
Aphonia, hysterical, hypnotherapy, 237
  case reports, 237
Approval and growing use of hypnosis, 4
Aquinas, Thomas, 108
A.R.A.S. (ascending reticular activating system), 153-154
Aristotle, quoted, 6
Arm-levitation technic in hypnosis, 64-65
  handling resistance, 66-67
  modified, 65
  sensory image with, 67-69
Arnold, M. B., 130
  quoted, 135-136
Arrhythmias, hypnotherapy, 162-163

Arthritis, hypnotherapy, 171-172
    case report, 171-172
Asthma, bronchial, hypnotherapy, 177-179, 262
    case reports, 178
Atavistic hypothesis of hypnosis, 22-23, 152
Attention, concentrated, law of, 41
    misdirection by suggestion, 8
Autogenic training in hypnosis, 87-88
Autohypnosis, 10, 80-86
    contraindications to, 85
    dangers in, 85
    deepening technics, 83-84
    definition, 80, 85
    dehypnotization, 84
    dynamics, 80-81
    glove anesthesia, in obstetrics, 196-197
    importance of, in treatment of chronic alco-
        holism, 272
    instructions, to patient, 82-83
        to physician, 81-82
    methodology, 80
    recognition of, 84
    for relaxation and mobility of joints in ar-
        thritis and rheumatism, 171
    resistance, handling of, 84-85
    self-control in, 80

Bachet, M., 267
Baer, R. F., 226-227
Bagnone, Francisco, 1
Bailey, P., quoted, 334
de Barbarin, Chevalier, 2, 113
Barber, T. X., 26-27
Barron, R. R., 185
Bates's system of eye training under hypnosis
    for myopia, 233
Bateson, G., 141
Bechterew, W. V., hypothesis of hypnosis, 26
Beckowitz, B., 291
Beecher, H. K., quoted, 184
Behavior disorders, as attention-getting devices,
    260
    frustrations of parents as contributing factor,
        260-261
    hypnotherapy, 260-262
        dawdling, 261
        eating problems, 261
        rebellion, 261
        sadism and destruction, 261
        school phobia, 261
Belief, relation to hypnotic phenomena, 135-
    137
Bergler, E., 296
Bernheim, Hippolyte, 2-3, 333
    De la Suggestion, 3
von Bertalanffy, L., 335
Bertrand, A., 2
Bible, allusions to hypnoticlike procedures, 1

Biochemical factors in hypnotherapy in oncol-
    ogy, 245-246
Blackboard technic in visual imagery, 69
Bladder, irritability, chronic, hypnotherapy,
    240-241
Bleeding, uterine, dysfunctional, hypnotherapy,
    208
        case report, 208
Blepharospasm, hypnotherapy, 234
    case report, 234
Blindness, hysterical, hypnotherapy, 233
    case reports, 233
"Blood-pressure" method in hypnosis, 73
Bowers, M. K., 112, 113, 291
Braid, James, 2, 116
Brain, neuroanatomy, 9
Brain-washing, 9
Bramwell, J. M., 102
Brandt, R., 332
Breathing, character of, as indication of depth
    of hypnosis, 46
Breuer, J., 3
Bridgman, P. W., 108
British Medical Association, approval of limited
    use of hypnotherapy and hypnoanesthesia, 4
    quoted, on exaggeration of dangers of hypno-
        tism, 96
Buddhism, comparison with hypnotic phenom-
    ena, 109-110

Cancer patient, hypnotherapeutic management,
    246-247
    case report, 247
Cannon, W. B., 136
Capacity to be hypnotized, 9
Carbon dioxide, use in hypnosis, 75
Carlson, E. R., 223
Carotid sinus method in hypnosis, 74
Catalepsis as technic in hypnosis, 71-72
Catalepsy, 11
    arm, as indication of depth of hypnosis, 47
    discovered by Petètin, 2
    eyelids, as indication of depth of hypnosis,
        46-47
Cerebral palsy, hypnotherapy, 226-227
    case reports, 227
Charcot, J. M., theories of hypnosis, 3
Cheek, D. B., 292
    quoted, 97
Chevreul's pendulum test, 12, 36-37
    in autohypnosis, 85
Child, hypnosis, instructions at his intellectual
    level, 75
Childbirth, "natural," comparison with hyp-
    nosis and psychoprophylactic relaxation,
    193
        personality factors in suggestive anesthesia
            methods, 192-193

Christian Science, attitude toward hypnosis, 118
  autohypnosis in, 337
  rise of, 117-118
Christian Scientists as objectors to hypnosis, 108
Clairvoyance, 12
Cloquet, J., use of mesmerism in performing a breast amputation, 2
Cohen, M. H., 234
Coin technic in hypnosis, with eyes closed, 61-62
  with eyes open, 60-61
  handling resistance, 62
Colitis, hypnotherapy, 165-166
  case report, 166
  ulcerative, hypnotherapy, 166-167
  case report, 167
Collins, Vincent, 189
Colton, Gardner Q., 4, 279
Communication, role in psychotherapy, 140-141
  as control mechanism, 141-142
  helpful hints, 142-143
Computer(s), analogy(ies), brain function, 151
  theoretic evaluation of hypnotic responses and controlled adaptive behavior, 151-153
  and brain function, 151
  general purpose (G.P.C.), 151
  special purpose (S.P.C.), 151-152
Concentration, as aid to induction of hypnosis, 50
  lack of, as problem in hypnosis, 39
Conditioning, positive, use in induction of hypnosis, 51
  sensory-image, for control of pain in arthritis and rheumatism, 171
Confidence, as aid to induction of hypnosis, 50
  of operator, importance, in deepening hypnosis, 78-79
Conflicts, experimental, production of, as hypnoanalytic technic, 327-328
Confusion technic in hypnosis, 72
Conn, J. H., quoted, 99, 121
Consciousness, definition, 134
  loss of, as misconception about hypnosis, 30
Constipation, hypnotherapy, 168
Contact lenses, adjustment to, hypnotherapy, 233-234
Contractures, hysterical, hypnotherapy, 266
Contraindications to hypnotism, 99
Conversions, physiologic, in anxiety, 304
  psychological, in anxiety, 304
Conviction, as aid to healing, 8
  relation to hypnotic phenomena, 135-137
  depth of hypnosis, 137

Cooper, L. F., 19
Coronary disease, hypnotherapy, 163
Cortex, cerebral, interpretive, role in mediation of emotions at nonhypnotic levels, 126-127
  role in mediation of emotions at nonhypnotic levels, 126
Coué, E., 80
Crasilneck, H. B., 185
Criminology, hypnosis in, 298-299
  case report, 298
Criticisms of hypnotherapy, evaluation, 330-338
  dangers of autohypnosis, 337
  defences, necessity of analysis, 337
  dependency on therapist, 331
  effectiveness, 330
  free associations, necessity of, 333
  insight, necessity of, 336-337
  interpretations, validity of, 335-336
  not a panacea, 331
  psychodynamics in psychotherapy, role of, 334-335
  resistances, overcoming, 333-334
  sexualization of doctor-patient relationship, 331-332
  symptom-removal, danger of, 336
  transference, necessity of analysis, 332
Cybernetics, analogy between computer and brain function, 151
  applications to psychotherapy and hypnosis, 146-147
  comments on adaptive control systems as they may relate to psychotherapy, 154-155
  definition, 146
  importance of psychocybernetics to therapy, 157-158
  models of learning, 147-154
  feedback, 147
  games theory, 149-151
  information theory, 147-149
  relation of neurophysiology to psychic processes and hypnosis, 153-154
  theoretic evaluation of hypnotic responses and controlled adaptive behavior based on computer analogies, 151-153
Cystoscopy, hypnoanesthesia for, 243

Dangers from hypnosis, 96-98
Danini-Aschner phenomenon, 162
Davis, H., 108
Davis, L. W., susceptibility scoring system, 43
Dawdling by children, treatment, 261
Deafness, hysterical, hypnotherapy, 236
"Death-feint" theory, 22
Deepening technics, 76-79
  escalator, 77-78
  hand rotation, 77

Deepening technics—(*Continued*)
  helpful hints, 78
  importance of confidence on part of operator, 78-79
  maintaining depth, 79
  Vogt's fractionation, 77
  Weitzenhoffer's, 77
  See also Depths of hypnosis
Definition of hypnosis, 22-23
Dehypnotization, 137-138
  in autohypnosis, 84
  fear of inability to terminate state as misconception of hypnosis, 31
  in hypnodontics, 283, 287-288
  postoperative, verbalization for, 188
  precautions in, 101-103
    difficult patient, 102-103
    for somnambulist, 101-102
    suggestions to patient for reinduction, 101
DeLee, J. B., quoted, 192
DeLee, S. T., 189-190
Delinquency, juvenile, hypnotherapy, 262
  case report, 262
Delorme, T. L., muscle-strengthening technic for poliomyelitis, 225
Denker, R., 336
Dentistry, hypnosis in. *See* Hypnodontics
Depersonalization, 14
Depths of hypnosis, clinical observations and management, 45-48
  catalepsy, arm, 47
    eyelids, 46-47
  character of breathing, 46
  development of glove anesthesia, 47
  eye changes, 45-46
  following positive and negative hallucinations, 47
  following posthypnotic suggestions, 47
  limpness of limbs, 46
  movements of head, 46
  somnambulism, 47-48
  recognition of, 43-44
  See also Deepening technics
Dermatology, hypnosis in, 217-221
  contraindications to symptom-removal, 219
  emotions, effect on skin, 217
  technics, 218-221
    authoritarian, verbalizations, 218
    glove anesthesia, 220
    permissive, for symptom-removal, 219
    sensory-imagery conditioning, 219-220
      case report, 219
    specialized, 220-221
      case reports, 221
    symptom substitution, 220
Desensitization, systemic, in reciprocal inhibition psychotherapy, 320-321

Deslon, C., quoted, 119
Destruction by children, treatment, 261
Diabetes mellitus, hypnotherapy, 172
Diamond, H. H., 262
Diarrhea, emotional, hypnotherapy, 167
  case report, 167
Dieckmann, W. J., 204
Discomfort, physical, as hindrance to induction of hypnosis, 49, 50
Disguised technic in hypnosis, 72
Disraeli, Benjamin, 342
Dissociation, 14, 24
Doberneck, R. C., 185
Dorcus, R. M., 99, 167, 185, 228, 268
  quoted, 336
Doshay, L. J., 225
Dreams, induction of, as hypnoanalytic technic, 327
Dreikurs, R., 334
Drug hypnosis, 74-75
Drugs, and placebo effect, 121-122
  as therapy, obesity, 174
  "wonder," 121
Dubois method of persuasion, 116
Dunbar, H. F., 164
  quoted, 206
Dupotet, M., 2
Dupuytren, B. G., quoted, 183
Du Sommeil, of Liébeault of Nancy, 2
Dyskinesia, biliary, hypnotherapy, 168
Dysmenorrhea, functional, hypnotherapy, 208-209
Dysphonia, hysterical, hypnotherapy, 237
  case reports, 237

Eating problems, treatment, 261
Eclampsia, hypnotherapy, 203-204
E.C.T., hypnosis in, 291
Eddy, Mary Baker, 113, 117-118
Edel, J. W., 237-238, 294
  quoted, 293
Edward the Confessor, 1
Edwards, G., 179
Effect, dominant, law of, 42
  reversed, law of, 41
Effort syndrome, hypnotherapy, 162-163
Ego-psychological theory of hypnosis, 27
Egyptian soothsayers, use of hypnoticlike procedures, 1
Eisenberg, B. C., 178
Electroconvulsive shock therapy, hypnosis in, 291
Elliotson, John, as advocate of mesmerism, 2
Emerson, Ralph Waldo, 116
Emmanuel Church, 116
Emmanuel Movement, autohypnosis in, 337
Emotions, effect of, in oncology, 245
  maladjustments, relation to colitis, 165-166

Emotions—(*Continued*)
  needs of patients, 309-311
    emancipation from influence of hypnotherapist, 311
    to be accepted, 310-311
    to be one's self, 311
    to be told what to do, 310
    to talk, 309-310
  reactions in hypnotherapy in oncology, 245
  role in gastrointestinal disorders, 164
  skin affected by, 217
  status of subject as hindrance to induction of hypnosis, 49
Entropy, definition, 148
Enuresis, nocturnal, etiology, 250
  hypnotherapy, 250-253
    case reports, 252-253
Epilepsy, hypnotherapy, 229
  case report, 229
Epistaxis, hypnotherapy, 237-238
  case report, 237-238
Erickson, M. H., 19, 93, 312, 314-315, 317, 318
Escalator technic for deepening hypnosis, 77-78
Esdaile, James, 2, 183, 243
  quoted, 24-25
Estrabrooks, G. H., 299
Ether, use in hypnosis, 75
Ethical aspects of hypnosis, 106-107
Evangelistic appeals, 9
Evans, W. F., 113
  quoted, 117
Evil spirits, exorcism of, 1
Examination, pelvic, hypnosis in, 214
  roentgenologic, barium enema, hypnosis in, 294
Expectation of success as aid to induction of hypnosis, 50
Experimentalists, 2
Exploration, horizontal, as hypnoanalytic technic, 324-325
  vertical, as hypnoanalytic technic, 325
Eyeball-set test of suggestibility, 34-35
Eye(s), changes, as indication of depth of hypnosis, 45-46
  closure and after-image technic in hypnosis, 70
  fixation technic, with sleep suggestions, 57-58
    without sleep suggestions, 58-59
  opening-and-closing technic in hypnosis, 70
  surgery, hypnosis in, 234

Failures in hypnotherapy, 340-346
  difficulties, due to hypnotherapy, 343-345
    case report, 344
  difficulties, in patient, 342-343
    in therapist, 345-346

Failures in hypnotherapy—(*Continued*)
  during induction, 340-342
    case report, 341-342
    fear, of losing defences, 342
      case report, 342
    of submission, 340
      case report, 340
    lack of motivation, 340-341
      case report, 341
    resistances to, 341
Faith, as aid to healing, 8
  in religion and hypnosis, 119-120
Faith-healing, 119-120
  spiritual, 115-116
    development from hypnosis, 116
    rise of various movements, 116-117
Faria, Abbe, 2
Fear, of losing defenses, failure of hypnotherapy from, 342
    case report, 342
  of not being dehypnotized, as misconception about hypnosis, 31
Flexibilitas cerea, 11
Fluidism theory of Paracelsus and Mesmer, 2
Fluoroscopy, hypnosis in, 293-294
Fogelman, M. J., 185
Francis I, of France, 1
Frank, J. D., 313
Freed, S. C., 22, 202-204, 266, 294, 296
Freud, Sigmund, 3, 260, 279, 330, 332-338
  quoted, 333, 338
Freud and Hypnosis, 3
Friedman, A. P., 170
Frigidity, hypnotherapy, 210-211
  case report, 211
  types of love, 210-211
Frustration, relief from, oral methods, 173

Gag reflex, elimination, hypnotherapy, 285-286
Gagging, hypnotherapy, 237
Gall, Franz, 116
Galton, 333
Gassner, Johann, 1
Gastrointestinal disorders, psychosomatic, hypnotherapy, 164-168
Genitourinary conditions, hypnotherapy, 240-244
  cystoscopy and surgical procedures, 243
  ejaculation, premature, 241-243
    case reports, 242-243
  impotence, 241-243
    case reports, 242-243
  irritability of bladder, chronic, 240-241
  retention of urine, postoperative, 240
  vasectomy, 243
  infertility, female, 244
    male, 243-244
  vasectomy, case report, 243

Geriatrics, hypnosis in, 294-295
Gilbert, S. F., 297
Gindes, B. C., 26
Glaser, G. H., quoted, 127, 150
Glasner, S., 112
Glaucoma, hypnotherapy, 232
Glick, S., 226
Globus hystericus, hypnotherapy, 236-237
    case report, 236-237
Godel's theorem, 335
Goll, H., 203
Goodwin, P., 167
Gray, J. D., 202
Greatrakes, Valentine, 1
Greek oracles, use of hypnoticlike procedures, 1
Grimes, Stanley, 116
Grinker, Julius, quoted, on so-called dangers from hypnotism, 97
Group hypnosis, 89-92
    preliminary discussion, 89-91
    technic, 91
    verbalization, 91-92
Gullibility, confusion with hypnotizability, 31
Guze, H., 153
Gynecology, hypnosis in, 206-215
    amenorrhea, 206-207
    bleeding, uterine, dysfunctional, 208
        case report, 208
    dysmenorrhea, functional, 208-209
        case report, 209
    examination, pelvic, 214
    frigidity, 210-211
        case report, 211
        types of love, 210-211
    hysterosalpingography, 214
    infertility, 209-210
    intersexuality, case report, 213-214
    menopause, 213
    pain, pelvic, 212
        case report, 212
        low back, of psychosomatic origin, 211-212
            case report, 212
    pseudocyesis, 207-208
        case report, 207-208
    psychogynecic conditions, miscellaneous, 214
        case reports, 214
    psychosomatic factors, 206
    sterilization, 215
    surgery, gynecologic, minor, 214
    tension, premenstrual, 212-213

Habit patterns, removal, hypnotherapy, 269-277
    alcoholism, 269-274
        treatment, autohypnosis, importance of, 272

Habit patterns, removal, hypnotherapy, alcoholism, treatment—(*Continued*)
    aversion, 270-271
    conditioned reflex, 270
    group, 271-272
    individual, 271
    purpose, 269
    suggestions, posthypnotic, importance of, 272-274
    insomnia, 276
    narcotic addiction, 276-277
    smoking, excessive, 274-276
Habit spasms (tics), hypnotherapy, 254
    case reports, 254
Haley, J., 314, 334
    quoted, 141, 142
Hallucinations, induced, as hypnoanalytic technic, 327
    positive and negative, as indication of depth of hypnosis, 47
    posthypnotic, 18
    unstructured, as hypnoanalytic technic, 327
Hamblin, M., 277
Handclasp, technic in hypnosis, 59
    test of suggestibility, 33
    use in progressive-relaxation technic, 70-71
Hand-drop test of suggestibility, 35-36
Hand-levitation test of suggestibility, 35
    modified, 35
Hand-rotation technic for deepening hypnosis, 77
Handwriting, changes in hypnotic subject, 16
    dissociated or automatic, as hypnoanalytic technic, 325-326
        case report, 326
Head, movements, as indication of depth of hypnosis, 46
Headache, migraine, etiology, 170
    treatment, hypnotherapy, 170-171
        case report, 170-171
Heartburn in pregnancy, hypnotherapy, 203
Heath, R. G., 128
Heilbrunn, G., quoted, 335
Hell, Maximillian, of Vienna, magnetic cures, 1
Hemiplegia, cerebrovascular, hypnotherapy, 227-228
    case report, 228
Herrick, C. J., 128
Heyer, G. R., 203, 294
    quoted, 206
Hiccoughs, hypnotherapy, 267-268
    case report, 268
Hindrances to hypnotic induction, 49
Hindu fakirs, use of hypnoticlike procedures, 1
Hippocampus, 128
Hippocrates, quoted, 300
History of hypnosis, 1-5
Holmes, Oliver Wendell, quoted, 121

Homosexuality, hypnotherapy, 296-297
Hudgins, C. V., 140
Hull, Clark, 4
Husband, R. W., susceptibility scoring system, 43
Huxley, A., 312
Hyden, H., 156
Hyperesthesia, 17-18
Hyperkinesis, of chorea, infectious, hypnotherapy, 263
  with encephalitis, hypnotherapy, 263
Hypermnesia, 14-15
Hypersuggestibility theory of hypnosis, 25-26
Hypertension, essential, hypnotherapy, 161-162
    case report, 161-162
Hyperthyroidism, hypnotherapy, 177
Hyperventilation technic in hypnosis, 71
Hypnoanalgesia, 17
Hypnoanalysis, 322
  applicability, 322-323
  contraindications, 323
  indications, 323
  projective, 326
  technics, 323-328
    affect-bridge or in-and-out method, 327
    conflicts, experimental, production of, 327-328
    dreams, induction of, 327
    exploration, horizontal, 324-325
      vertical, 325
    hallucinations, induced, 327
      unstructured, 327
    handwriting, dissociated or automatic, 325-326
      case report, 326
    hypnography, 328
    hypnoplasty, 328
    narcohypnoanalysis or narcosynthesis, 328
    resistances, handling of, 324
    symptom-formation, handling of, 324
Hypnoanesthesia, first recorded uses, 2
  historical considerations, 4
  mechanism, 186
  in obstetrics. *See* Obstetrics, hypnosis in
  technics for surgery, 186-187
    maintenance, 187-188
    rehearsal, 187
Hypnodiagnosis, practical hints, 303-307
    anxiety, clinical manifestations of, 304-307
      diagnosis, differential, 304-305
        from history-taking, 305-307
      repressed, 304
      types, 304
Hypnodontics, 279-290
  adaptation to prosthetic devices, 284
  advantages, 289-290
  in anesthesia, 284-285
  applications, 280-281

Hypnodontics—(*Continued*)
  contraindications, 281-282
  deep hypnosis, 281
  dehypnotization, 283, 287-288
  disadvantages, 289
  elimination of gag reflex, 285-286
  handling resistant patients, 287
  indications, 280-281
  light hypnosis, 281
  limitations, 282
  management of emotionally disturbed children, 289
  operative, 288-289
  procedures, 282-283
    preinduction, 286
  salivation control, 286
  "sealing" patient against hypnosis, 287
  suggestion, controlled, 280-281
    types, 280
  susceptibility for hypnosis, tests, 280
  technics, 283-285
    audio-analgesia, 286-287
Hypnodrama, 326-327
Hypnography as hypnoanalytic technic, 328
Hypnonarcosis, for dermatoses, itching, chronic, 218
Hypnoplasty as hypnoanalytic technic, 328
Hypnosemantics, role in therapy, 139-140
Hypothalamus, anterior, transmission of emotional influences to gastrointestinal tract, 164
  posterior, transmission of emotional influences to gastrointestinal tract, 164
  role in mediation of emotions at nonhypnotic levels, 129
Hypnosis, aspects, everyday, 8-9
  different from sleep, 2
  for entertainment, condemnation, 5, 106, 107
    dangers, 94-95
  early uses, 4
  mass, 9
  term coined by James Braid, 2
Hypnosynthesis, 322
Hypnotherapy, medical, theoretic dangers, 97-98
  modern type, 3-4
  practical hints, 308-311
    emotional needs, 309-311
  war neuroses, 4
Hypnotism, modern, James Braid as "father" of, 2
  term coined by James Braid, 2
Hypnotizability, confused with gullibility, 31
Hysteria, as anxiety reaction, 304
  hypnosis as state of, 23
Hysterical symptoms, hypnotherapy, 263
    case report, 263
Hysterosalpingography, hypnosis in, 214

Ideomotor activities, 11-12, 24
Ideosensory activities, 11
Imagery, sensory, with arm-levitation technic, 67-69
  visual, technics, blackboard, 69
    television, 69
    use in deepening autohypnosis, 83-84
Imagination, role, in digestive upsets, 164
  in production of psychological symptoms, 8
Immobilization theory of hypnosis, 22-23
Induction of hypnosis, hindrances, 49
  practical hints, 50-52
Infertility, female, hypnotherapy, 244
  hypnotherapy, 209-210
  male, hypnotherapy, 243-244
Inhibition theory of hypnosis, 24
Insomnia, hypnotherapy, 276
Insurance aspects, physicians using hypnosis, 105-106
Internal medicine, hypnosis in, 160-180
  allergy, 179-180
    case report, 179-180
  anorexia nervosa, 177
  bronchial asthma, 177-179
    case reports, 178
    treatment, 178-179
  hyperthyroidism, 177
  metabolic diseases, diabetes mellitus, 172
  obesity, 173-177
    psychological factors, 173-177
  psychogenic cardiac disorders, 162-164
    arrhythmias, 162-163
    congestive heart failure, 164
    coronary disease, 163
    effort syndrome, 162-163
    palpitation, 162-163
    postcoronary syndrome, 163-164
  psychosomatic disorders, arthritis, 171-172
    case report, 171-172
    cardiovascular, 161-164
      essential hypertension, 161-162
        case report, 161-162
    gastrointestinal, 164-168
      biliary dyskinesia, 168
      colitis, 165-166
        case report, 166
        ulcerative, 166-167
          case report, 167
      constipation, 168
      emotional diarrhea, 167
        case report, 167
      peptic ulcer, 165
      postgastrectomy syndrome, 167-168
      summary, 169
    migraine headache, etiology, 170
      treatment, 170-171
    rheumatism, 171-172

Internal medicine, hypnosis in, psychosomatic disorders—(*Continued*)
    tuberculosis, 169-170
    reasons for use, 160-161
International Society of Clinical and Experimental Hypnosis, 5
Intersexuality, hypnotherapy, case report, 213-214
Ivy, A. C., 168

Jacobson, Edmund, 88
James, L. S., quoted, 194
James, William, 116-117
Janet, Pierre, 3, 116
  quoted, 4, 97
Johnson, W., quoted, 258
Jone, H., 108
Judaism, comparison of kavanah with autohypnosis, 111-112
Jung Association Test, 326
Juvenile delinquency, hypnotherapy, 262
  case report, 262

Kavanah, Jewish cabbalistic state of, autohypnosis in, 337
  comparison with autohypnosis, 111-112
Kelsey, J. H., 185
Kenny, Sister, 224
Kirkner, F. J., 185, 265, 268
Kline, M. V., 67, 143, 157, 219, 226, 234
  Freud and Hypnosis, 338
  quoted, 24, 135, 144, 224, 236, 332
Klüver, H., 128
Koestler, Arthur, *The Lotus and the Robot*, 111
Kohnstamm, phenomenon of, 36
  "test" of suggestibility, 36
Kraines, S. H., 265
Kroger, W. S., 22, 202, 266, 270, 294
Krout, R. M., 227
Kubie, L. S., 331

Labor, management, hypnosis, 197-198
  helpful suggestions, 198-199
  induction, 199-200
Lactation, hypnosis as stimulating technic, 203
La Fontaine, C., use of magnetism, 2
Laryngology, hypnotherapy, 236-237
  aphonia, hysterical, 237
  dysphonia, hysterical, 237
    case reports, 237
  euphonia, hysterical, case reports, 237
  gagging, 237
  globus hystericus, 236-237
    case report, 236-237
Lashley, K. S., 156
Laws of suggestion, 41-42
Learning, improvement in, hypnotic and posthypnotic suggestions, 291-292
  case reports, 291-292

Learning—(*Continued*)
  role in hypnosis, 144
LeCron-Bordeaux scoring system for indicating depth of hypnosis, 44
Legal aspects of hypnosis, 105
Liébeault, A. A., of Nancy, 2, 3, 116, 203, 333
  Du Somneil, 2
Limbic system, amygdaloid complex, 127-128
  direction of repressed emotional forces to skin, 217
  hippocampus, 128
  role in mediation of emotions at nonhypnotic levels, 127-129
Limbs, limpness, as indication of depth of hypnosis, 46
Lindner, R. M., 324
  quoted, 324
Livingston, R. B., 128
Long, Crawford, 2
Lourdes, miraculous cures at, 120
Love, types, 210-211
Lowell, F. C., quoted, 179

McCord, H., 259
McCulloch, W., 144
McDowell, M., 219
McKay, D. M., 149
MacLaren, W. R., 178
Magic, role in healing, 115
Magnetism, animal, 1
Magnetization, as practiced by Phineas Quimby, 117
Magoun, H. W., 129, 154
Maimonides and kavanah, 112
Malpractice, accusations and suits, precautions by physician, 99-100
  aspects of hypnosis, 105
Mangan, J. T., 108-109
Marchesi, C., 258-259
Marmer, M. J., 185, 188
Maxwell, Wm., 1
Meares, A., 22, 37, 63, 153, 321, 327, 328
Mechanical technics in hypnosis, 73-74
Medical training in hypnosis, 104-105
Medicine men, tribal, use of hypnoticlike procedures, 1
Mellor, N. H., 262
Memory, mechanisms, 126
  neurophysiologic theories, 155-157
  recall, 14-15
Menopause, hypnotherapy, 213
Meprobamate preparations, use in hypnosis, 74
Mesmer, Franz, 1-2, 116, 118
Mesmerism, for pain relief during surgery, 2
  spread of, 2
Metabolic diseases, hypnotherapy, 172
Misconceptions about hypnosis, 30-32
  removal, as aid to induction of hypnosis, 50

Mihalyka, E. F., 235
Milechnin, A., 322
Military medical practice, hypnosis in, 299-300
Miller, G. A., 131
Miller, M. M., 270
Miloslavsky, M. Y., 202
Mishra, R. S., description of Yoga and its technics, 110-111
Mitchell, S. Weir, 116
Mitty, W., 189
Mohr, Fritz, 203
Moody, H., 165
Morton, W. T. G., 279
Moss, A. A., 237
Motivation, good, as aid to induction of hypnosis, 50
  lack of, failure of hypnotherapy from, 340-341
    case report, 341
Moya, F., quoted, 194
Muftic, M. K., 131
Multiple sclerosis, hypnotherapy, 226
  case reports, 226
Music therapy, neuromuscular disorders, 223-224
Myopia, hypnotherapy, 233

Nail-biting, case report, 253-254
  hypnotherapy, 253-254
Narcohypnoanalysis, 328
Narcosynthesis, 328
Narcotic addiction, hypnotherapy, 276-277
Nature of hypnosis, 7-8
Nausea and vomiting in pregnancy, hypnotic management, 200-202
  case report, 200-201
  technic, 201-202
Nervous system, autonomic, role in cutaneous physiopathology, 217
Von Neumann, J., 149
Neuromuscular disorders, music therapy, 223-224
  physical rehabilitation of, discussion, 229-230
    epilepsy, 229
      case report, 229
    hypnotherapy, 224-228
      amputation, of both legs, use of prosthesis, case report, 228
        reduction of pain after, 228
      ankylosis of knee, postoperative, case report, 228
      cerebral palsy, 226-227
        case reports, 227
      hemiplegia, cerebrovascular, 227-228
      multiple sclerosis, 226
        case report, 226
      pain, low back, case report, 228
      parkinsonism, 225-226

Neuromuscular disorders, physical rehabilitation of, hypnotherapy, parkinsonism—(*Continued*)
  case report, 225
  poliomyelitis, 225
    case report, 225
  placebo therapy, 223
  psychosomatic factors, 224
Neurophysiologic mechanisms in mediation of emotions, during hypnosis, 130-132
  at nonhypnotic levels, 125-132
    cortex, interpretative, role of, 126-127
    role of, 126
    hypothalamus, role of, 129
    limbic system, role of, 127-129
    reticular activating system, role of, 129-130
Neurophysiology, relation to psychic process and hypnosis, 153-154
Neuroses, vertebral, hypnotherapy, 266
  case reports, 266
Neurotics, susceptibility to hypnosis, 39
Newbold, G., 262, 263
Nitrous oxide, use in hypnosis, 75
Noises as hindrance to induction of hypnosis, 49, 50
Noizet, S., 2
Nonconvulsive shock therapy, hypnosis in, 291

Obesity, etiology, psychological factors, 173-177
  hypnotherapy, 173-177
    group, 177
Obstetrics, hypnosis in, 192-205
  abortion, emotional spontaneous, 202-203
    case report, 202-203
  advantages, 193-194
  disadvantages and contraindications, 194-195
  discussion, 204-205
  eclampsia, 203-204
  heartburn in pregnancy, 203
  labor, helpful suggestions, 198-199
    induction, 199-200
  lactation, 203
  nausea and vomiting, management, 200-202
    case report, 200-201
    technic, 201-202
  personality factors in suggestive anesthesia methods, 192-193
  postpartum period, helpful suggestions, 199
  pre-eclampsia, 203-204
  preparation of patient, 195-197
    determining responsiveness, 195
    group training, 200
    training, 196-197

Obstetrics, hypnosis in—(*Continued*)
  reasons for choice, 196
  susceptibility of subject, 192
  toxemias of pregnancy, 203-204
Odencrants, G., 298
Oil-witching, 12
Olfactory test of suggestibility, 36
Oncology, hypnosis in, 245-247
  cancer patient, 246-247
  emotions, effect of, 245
  personality factors and emotional reactions, 245
  psychophysiologic and biochemical factors, 245-246
  spontaneous remission and adaptive responses, 246
Ophthalmology, hypnotherapy, 232-234
  adjustment to contact lenses, 233-234
  blepharospasm, 234
  blindness, hysterical, 233
    case report, 233
  glaucoma, 232
  orthoptics, 233
  surgery of eye, 234
Orne, M. T., 93-94, 299
Orthopedics, hypnosis in, 265-268
  contractures, hysterical, 266
  hiccoughs, 267-268
    case report, 268
  miscellaneous applications, 267
    case report, 267
  neuroses, vertebral, 266
    case reports, 266
  rheumatism, psychogenic, 267
  torticollis, 265-266
    case reports, 265-266
Orthoptics, hypnotherapy, 233
Osler, William, 121, 169
Ostfield, A. M., 171
Otology, hypnotherapy, 234-236
  deafness, hysterical, 236
  tic douloureux, 235-236
  tinnitus, 234-235
    case reports, 235
Ouija board, 12
Overeating, psychological factors, 173-177
  rationalizations, 174

Pain, low back, of psychosomatic origin, hypnotherapy, 211-212
    case report, 212
  pelvic, hypnotherapy, 212
    case report, 212
Palpitation, hypnotherapy, 162-163
Papez action circuit, 127
Papez, J. W., 128
Paracelsus, P. A., 1

Parkinsonism, hypnotherapy, 225-226
  case report, 225
Pastoral psychiatry, 120
Pastoral psychology, 116
Pavlov, I. P., 4, 22, 154, 162, 224, 321, 322
  quoted, 140
  protective "sleep" inhibition therapy, 128
Pediadontics, 289
Pediatrics, hypnosis in, 249-263
  asthma, 262
  behavior disorders, 260-262
    as attention-getting devices, 260
    dawdling, 261
    eating problems, 261
    frustrations of parents as etiologic factor, 260-261
    rebellion, 261
    sadism and destruction, 261
    school phobia, 261
  enuresis, nocturnal, 250-253
    etiology, 250
    treatment, 250-253
      case reports, 252-253
  hyperkinesis, with encephalitis, 263
    of infectious chorea, 263
  hysterical symptoms, 263
  juvenile delinquency, 262
    case report, 262
  mental retardation, 259
    case report, 259
  nail-biting, 243-254
    case report, 253-254
  stuttering, 254-259
    treatment, 255-259
      case reports, 256, 258
      correction of faulty parental attitudes, 257-258
      group, 257
      sensory-imagery conditioning under autohypnosis, 257
      speaking aloud when alone, 257
      tape recorder, 255
  thumb-sucking, 259-260
  tics or habit spasms, 254
    case reports, 254
Pendulum test of suggestibility, of Chevreul, 36-37
  in autohypnosis, 85
Penfield, W., 126
Pentobarbital sodium, use in hypnosis, 74-75
Pentothal Sodium, use in narcohypnoanalysis or narcosynthesis, 328
Peptic ulcer, hypnotherapy, 165
Perception, during anesthesia, 292-293
  extrasensory, 12
  improvement in, hypnotic and posthypnotic suggestions, 291-292
  psychophysiology of, 144

Perception—(*Continued*)
  role in hypnosis, 143-144
Persian magi, use of hypnoticlike procedures, 1
Personality, dominant, required by hypnotist, as misconception, 31
  factors in hypnotherapy in oncology, 245
  multiple, hypnotherapy, 297-298
Persuasion, definition, 6
Peters, J. J., 227
Petètin, discoverer of catalepsy, 2
Phenobarbital, use in hypnosis, 74
Phenothiazine derivatives, use in hypnosis, 74
Phobia, school, hypnotherapy, 261
Phrenomagnetism, 116
Physician, instructions to, for autohypnosis, 81-82
  precautions in use of hypnosis, 99-100
Pitts, W. S., 144
Pituitary-adrenal axis, transmission of emotional influences to gastrointestinal tract, 164
Pius XII, Pope, statements about hypnosis, 109
Placebo effect, concept, 120-121
  and drugs, 121-122
  and hypnosis, 122
  in psychotherapy, 122
    neuromuscular disorders, 223
Plastic surgery, hypnotherapy, 185
Platonov, K., 200, 202, 237, 321
  quoted, 97, 321-322
Pleune, F. G., quoted, 219
Poliomyelitis, Delorme technic of muscle-strengthening, 225
  hypnotherapy, 225
    case report, 225
Pommerenke, W. T., 204
Pond, D. A., 229
"Port-of-last-call" patient, hypnotherapy, 300-301
  case reports, 300-301
Postcoronary syndrome, hypnotherapy, 163-164
Postgastrectomy syndrome, hypnotherapy, 167-168
Postural-sway test of suggestibility, 33-34
Posture, as hindrance to induction of hypnosis, 49
  swaying technic of Watkins, 59-60
  use in progressive-relaxation technic, 70-71
Potter, V. R., quoted, 246
Poyen, Charles, 117
Prayer, autohypnosis in, 337
  similarities to hypnotic induction, 112
Precautions in use of hypnosis, 99-100
  dangers, to method, 100
    to operator, 99-100
    of symptom-removal, 99
Pre-eclampsia, hypnotherapy, 203-204

Pregnancy, heartburn in, hypnotherapy, 203
  nausea and vomiting. *See* Nausea and vomiting in pregnancy
  phantom, hypnotherapy, 207-208
    case report, 207-208
  toxemias, hypnotherapy, 203-204
Preinduction talk, 53-54
Prejudice against hypnosis, 4
Pressure on "nerve centers" as technic in hypnosis, 73
Prince, Morton, 3, 116, 298
Pringle, J. W. S., 156
"Progression, age," 16-17
Projection, subliminal, 9
Propaganda, 9
Prostheses, dental, adaptation to, hypnotherapy, 284
Pruritus ani and vulvae, psychosomatic aspects, 217-218
Pseudocyesis, hypnotherapy, 207-208
  case report, 207-208
Psychobiology hypnotherapy, 319
Psychocybernetics, importance to therapy, 157, 158
Psychogynecic conditions, miscellaneous, hypnotherapy, 214-215
  case reports, 214
Psychophysiologic factors in hypnotherapy in oncology, 245-246
Psychophysiologic mechanisms, 134-138
  belief and conviction, 135-137
    relation to depth of hypnosis, 137
  dehypnotization, 137-138
  reality and perceptual awareness, 134-135
  three stages of hypnosis, 137
Psychosomatic theories of hypnosis, 27
Psychotherapy, active complex, 322
  group, pioneer work of Mesmer, 2
  reciprocal inhibition, 319-321
de Puységur, Marquis, first description of artificial somnambulism, 2

Quimby, Phineas, 113, 117
  quoted, 117

Rachmaninoff, Serge, 292
Radiology, barium enema examination, hypnosis in, 294
  fluoroscopy, hypnosis in, 293-294
  hypnosis in, 293-294
Raginsky, B. B., 157, 163, 284
  quoted, 171
Rapport in hypnosis, 10-11
  good, as aid to induction of hypnosis, 50
R.A.S. (reticular activating system), 153
Ravitz, L. J., 131-132
Read, G. D., 193

Rebellion, in children, treatment, 261
Recamier, pioneer use of hypnoanesthesia, 2
Regression, age, 15-16
  hypnotic, for arrhythmias due to rheumatic fever in childhood, 162
  hypothesis as explanation for hypnotic behavior, 152
  to infancy theory of hypnosis, 25
Relaxation, progressive, motivational technic in achieving, 55-57
  utilizing handclasp and postural sway, 70-71
  psychoprophylactic, comparison with hypnosis and "natural childbirth," 193
Religion, approach in hypnotherapy, 321
Religious attitudes toward hypnosis, 108-113
  comparative evaluation of religions and hypnotic phenomena, Buddhism, 109-110
    Judaism, 111-113
    Yoga, 110-111
    Roman Catholic Church, 108-109
  unconscious use of hypnosis in various forms, 112-113
Religious leaders, use of hypnoticlike procedures, 1
Remission, spontaneous, in hypnotherapy in oncology, 246
Repetition technic for handling resistant patients, 63
Research in hypnosis, 5
Resistance(s), handling, in autohypnosis, 84-85
  to induction of hypnotherapy, 341-342
    case report, 341-342
Responses, adaptive, in hypnotherapy in oncology, 246
Retardation, mental, hypnotherapy, 259
  case report, 259
Reticular activating system (R.A.S.), 153
  ascending (A.R.A.S.), 153-154
  role in mediation of emotions at nonhypnotic levels, 129-130
Revivification, 15-16
Rheumatism, hypnotherapy, 171-172
  psychogenic, hypnotherapy, 267
Rhinencephalon, 127, 128
Rhinitis, hypnotherapy, 238
Rhinology, hypnotherapy, 237-238
  epistaxis, 237-238
    case report, 237-238
  rhinitis, 238
Roberts, D. R., 26
  quoted, 130-131
Rodriquez, R., 321
Role-playing theory of hypnosis, 24-25
Roman Catholic Church, attitude toward hypnosis, 108-109
Rorschach test, 326
"Royal touch," healing by kings and princes, 1

Ruesch, J., 141
Rund, J., 112

Sadism in children, treatment, 261
Salivation, control, hypnodontics, 286
Sargent, Helen, 326
Sargent, W., *Battle For the Mind*, 300
Schmideberg, M., quoted, 334-335
Scholem, G. G., 112
Von Schrenck-Notzing, A., 241
Schultz, J. H., 184
  Autogenic Training, 87-88
Science of Mind, autohypnosis in, 337
Sciences, physical and behavioral, relation to
    psychotherapy and hypnosis, 146-158
  cybernetic applications. *See* Cyber-
    netics
Scopolamine, use in hypnosis, 75
  use in narcohypnoanalysis or narcosynthesis,
    328
Secrets, revelation of, as misconception about
    hypnosis, 31
Seizures, hippocampal, 128
Self-hypnosis. *See* Autohypnosis
Sensory-imagery conditioning for symptom-
    removal in dermatologic problems, 219-
    220
  case report, 219
Seventh-day Adventists, as objectors to hypno-
    sis, 108
Sex as factor in incidence, stuttering, 258
Shannon, C. E., 148, 335
Shapiro, A. K., 122, 226
  quoted, 120
Shires, E. B., 227
Shock technic in hypnosis, 74
Shrine-healing, 112-113
Shurrager, P. S., 228
Sidis, B., 3, 116
Siryananda, C., quoted, 109
Sleep, hypnosis as conditioned process leading
    to, 23-24
  hypnosis different from, 2
  "partial," in hypnosis, Pavlov's theory, 23
  relation to hypnosis, 23-24
  suggestions, eye-fixation with and without,
    57-59
  stare technic with and without, 62-63
"Sleep" inhibition therapy, protective, of Pav-
    lov, 128
  suggestive, 321-322
Smoking, excessive, hypnotherapy, 274-276
Society for Clinical and Experimental Hyp-
    nosis, adoption of ethical code, 106-107
Sodium Amytal, use in hypnosis, 74-75
Solovey, G., 322
Somnambulism, 14, 18-19, 137
  amnesia with, 18

Somnambulism—(*Continued*)
  artificial, first description of, 2
  as indication of depth of hypnosis, 47-48
Sparer, P. J., *Personality, Stress and Tubercu-
    losis*, 169
Spiritualism, 116
Spiritualists, 2
Sports, hypnosis in, 294-295
  case reports, 295-296
Spurzheim, J. C., 116
Stare technic in hypnosis, with and without
  sleep suggestions, 62-63
"State," hypnoidal, 9-10
Sterilization, emotional disorders connected
  with, hypnotherapy, 215
Stillerman, B., 323
Stress, allergic reactions with, 179
Stuttering, hypnotherapy, 254-259
  case reports, 256, 258
  faulty attitudes of parents, 257-258
  group, 257
  sensory-imagery conditioning under auto-
    hypnosis, 257
  speaking aloud when alone, 257
  tape recorder used with, 255
  incidence, sex as factor, 258
Submission, fear of, during induction of hypnotherapy, 340
Suggestibility, nature of, in hypnosis, 6-7
  similarity to hypnosis, 9
  tests, 33-38
    disguised, 37
    eyeball-set, 34-35
    handclasp, 33
    hand-drop, 35-36
    hand-levitation, 35
      modified, 35
    Kohnstamm, 36
    olfactory, 36
    pendulum, of Chevreul, 36-37
    postural-sway, 33-34
      forward, 34
    thermal, 36
Suggestion(s), aspects, everyday, 8-9
  controlled, in hypnodontics, 280-281
  definition, 6
  doctrine of, of James Braid, 2
  in hypnodontics, types, 280
  introduction of concept, 3
  laws, 41-42
  mass, 9
  of operator, changing to a different technic
      for minimizing resistance to induction
      of hypnosis, 50
    clarity and simplicity as aid to induction
      of hypnosis, 50, 51
  posthypnotic, and conditioning, 12-13
    as indication of depth of hypnosis, 47

Suggestion(s), posthypnotic—(*Continued*)
  technic for, 57
  as therapy, for arthritis, 171
  founded by Liébeault of Nancy, 2
  types, 6
  use in faith-healing, 120
Sulzberger, M. B., 218
Surgery, and anesthesiology, hypnosis in, 183-191
  advantages and disadvantages, 184
  case reports, 189-190
  dehypnosis, postoperative verbalization, 188
  historical considerations, 183
  indications, 185-186
  mechanism, 186
  postoperative, 184
  recent developments, 183-184
  review of literature, 185-186
  technics, 186-187
    disguised, 188-189
    maintenance, 187-188
    rehearsal, 187
  gynecologic, minor, hypnosis in, 214
Susceptibility to hypnosis, aids to operator, 39-40
  factors influencing, 39-40
  scoring system, of Davis and Husband, 43
    LeCron-Bordeaux, 44
  stages, divisions, 43
Swedenborg, Emanuel, 113
Symptoms, removal of, dangers of, 99

Talmud, allusions to hypnoticlike procedures, 1
  on kavanah, 112
Tantrik philosopher-psychologists of India, 312
Technics of hypnosis, direct or authoritarian, 55-63
  coin method, 60-62
  eye-fixation, with sleep suggestions, 57-58
    without sleep suggestions, 58-59
  handclasp, 59
  motivational, utilizing progressive relaxation, 55-57
  posthypnotic suggestions, 57
  postural sway, of Watkins, 59-60
  repetition for handling resistant patient, 63
  stare, with sleep suggestions, 62
    without sleep suggestions, 62-63
  indirect or permissive, 64-75
    arm-levitation, 64-65
      handling resistance, 66-67
      modified, 65
      sensory-imagery with, 67-69
    "blood-pressure" method, 73
    carotid sinus method, 74
    catalepsis, 71-72
    combinations of methods, 67

Technics of hypnosis, indirect or permissive—(*Continued*)
    confusion, 72
    disguised methods, 72
    drugs, 74-75
    eye-closure and after-image, 70
    eye-opening-and-closing, 70
    hyperventilation, 71
    mechanical methods, 73-74
    pressure on "nerve centers," 73
    progressive relaxation, utilizing handclasp and postural sway, 70-71
    shock, 74
    tension and relaxation, 71
    visual imagery, blackboard, 69
      television, 69
  specialized, 312-328
    brief hypnotherapy, handling resistant patients, 314-319
      case report, 314
      corrective emotional responses obtained by ideomotor signaling, 318
      rationale of methods, 318-319
      symptom-amelioration, 317
        case report, 317
      symptom-removal by symptom-transformation, 317
        case reports, 317
      by symptom-substitution, 315-317
        case reports, 316
      symptom-utilization, 317-318
        case report, 318
      by symptom-removal, 312-314
        case reports, 313
        helpful hints, 313-314
    psychobiology, 319
    reciprocal inhibition, 319-321
      systemic desensitization, 320-321
    religious approach, 321
    Yoga or Y-state, 321
  Watkins' progressive anesthesia, 65-66
  See also under individual disorders
Television technic in visual imagery, 69
Tension, premenstrual, hypnotherapy, 212-213
  profound, as hindrance to induction of hypnosis, 49
  relief, overeating, 173
Tension-and-relaxation technic in hypnosis, 71
Test(s), Jung Association, 326
  pendulum, of Chevreul, 12, 85
  Rorschach, 326
  for susceptibility, hypnotic, 280
  suggestibility. *See* Suggestibility, tests
  thermal, of suggestibility, 36
Test-operate-test-exit (TOTE) concept, 131
Theories of hypnosis, 22-28
  atavistic hypothesis, 22-23
  based on changes in cerebral physiology, 23

Theories of hypnosis—(*Continued*)
 as conditioned process leading to sleep, 23-24
 dissociation, 24
 hypersuggestibility, 25-26
 ideomotor activity and inhibition, 24
 immobilization, 22-23
 miscellaneous, 26-27
 psychosomatic, 27-28
 regression, 25
 role-playing, 24-25
 state of hysteria, 23
Theosophy, autohypnosis in, 337
Thermal test of suggestibility, 36
Thumb-sucking, hypnotherapy, 259-260
Tic douloureux, hypnotherapy, 235-236
Tics (habit spasms), hypnotherapy, 254
 case reports, 254
Time distortion, 19-20
Tinnitus, etiology, 234
 hypnotherapy, 234-235
 case reports, 235
Todorovic, D. D., 299
Tom, K. S., 192
Torticollis, hypnotherapy, 265-266
 case reports, 265-266
TOTE unit (test-operate-test-exit) concept, 131
Toxemias of pregnancy, hypnotherapy, 203-204
Tranquilizers, placebo effect of, 123
Travel, space, hypnosis in, 296
Trilene, use in hypnosis, 75
Trousseau, quoted, 121
Tuberculosis, hypnotherapy, 169-170

Uhr, L., 259
Ullman, M., 218
Urine, retention, postoperative, hypnotherapy, 240

Vagus nerves, transmission of emotional influences to gastrointestinal tract, 164
Vasectomy, hypnotherapy, 243
 case report, 243
Vaughn, V., 186
Vigdorovich, 200
Vogt, O., 87
 fractionation technic for deepening hypnosis, 77

Voltaire, F., quoted, 121, 183
Vomiting in pregnancy. *See* Nausea and vomiting in pregnancy

"Waking hypnosis," 9
Warts, hypnotherapy, 218
Water-witching, 12
Watkins, J., 59-60, 65-66, 322, 326, 327, 332
Weakmindedness as misconception about hypnosis, 31
Weaver, W., 148, 335
Weiss, C., 267
Weitzenhoffer, A., 77, 250, 262
Wells, Horace, 4, 279
Wennerstrand, G. O., 165
Werbel, F. W., 185
West, L. J., 131, 154
 quoted, 26, 135
Whanger, A. D., 235
Wheeler, P., use of mesmerism in nasal polypectomy, 2
Wiener, N., 335
Will, surrender of, as misconception about hypnosis, 30-31
William III, 1
Williams, G. W., 102
Willingness to co-operate and use imagination as aid to induction of hypnosis, 50, 51
Witch doctors, use of hypnoticlike procedures, 1
Wolberg, L. R., 96, 233, 270, 331
 quoted, 27, 97
Wolf, J., 218
Wolpe, J., 313, 319, 320
Worcester, Elwood, 116
Writing, automatic, 19

Yoga (or Y-state), 312, 321
 comparison with hypnotism, 110-111
 Samadhic state of, autohypnosis in, 337
 Tantra, autogenic training, 88
Yogi, Indian, use of hypnoticlike procedures, 1

Zen Buddhist meditation, autohypnosis in, 337
 comparison with hypnotism, 110
Zoist, reports of mesmeric phenomena, 2

Sid Kimel